Managing Customer Relationships

....

A Strategic Framework

Don Peppers

Martha Rogers

WILEY

John Wiley & Sons, Inc.

Published by John Wiley & Sons, Inc., Hoboken, New Jersey

Published simultaneously in Canada

For general information on our other products and services, or technical support, please contact our Customer Care Department within the United States at 800-762-2974, outside the United States at 317-572-3993 or fax 317-572-4002.

Wiley also publishes its books in a variety of electronic formats. Some content that appears in print may not be available in electronic books.

For more information about Wiley products, visit our Web site at *www.wiley.com.*

Library of Congress Cataloging-in-Publication Data:

Peppers, Don.
  Managing customer relationships : a strategic framework / Don Peppers, Martha Rogers.
    p. cm.
Includes index.
  ISBN 0-471-48590-X (cloth)
    1. Customer relations—Management.   2. Consumers' preferences.   3. Relationship marketing.
  4. Marketing information systems.   5. Information storage and retrieval systems—Marketing.
  I. Rogers, Martha, Ph.D.   II. Title.
HF5415.5 .P458 2004
658.8'12—dc22

2003020608

Printed in the United States of America

10   9   8

Contents

Preface

Our goal with this book is to provide a methodical overview of the background, the methodology, and the particulars of managing customer relationships for competitive advantage. We begin with background and history, move through an overview of relationship theory, outline the *Identify-Differentiate-Interact-Customize* (IDIC) framework, and then address metrics, data management, customer management and company organization, channel issues, and the store of the future. We end the book with an appendix called "Where Do We Go from Here?," which contains some very basic tools needed by individuals embarking on a new career in managing customer relationships or—even more difficult—learning to help an existing company make the transition to using customer value as the basis for executive decisions.

Since January 1990, when we met and within five minutes had decided to write a book together, we began to question what would happen to marketing as a result of the fractionalization of communication. It didn't take us long to realize that the real question that needed to be answered was bigger: What are the implications, for business, of information, interaction, and mass-customization technologies?

The ongoing quest to answer that question, or at least to explore the next logical question, and the next, led us to write our first book, *The One to One Future: Building Relationships One Customer at a Time* (Currency/Doubleday, 1993). In it, we hypothesized how technology might change the dimensions of competitive strategy. We thought about the quest for share of customer rather than just market share, and the idea of managing customers, not just products and brands. Before long, we had the opportunity to work with some bright pioneers in industry, who were wrestling through one-to-one and customer management. Based on four years of field experience, we wrote our second book, *Enterprise One to One: Tools for Competing in the Interactive Age* (Currency/Doubleday, 1997).

Since then we have had the chance to speak at several colleges and universities, where more and more coursework and curricula are addressing electronic media, database marketing, and more importantly, customer relationship management, data analytics, and a host of related topics that serve to prepare business, management, marketing, information technology (IT), and statistics students for careers in the growing field of competitive advantage through understanding individual customers better, getting the most valuable ones for an enterprise, keeping them longer, and growing them bigger. We have also taught countless seminars and workshops and have worked in depth with consultants in the dozen worldwide offices of Peppers and Rogers Group, for clients who themselves have taught us a lot about what it takes to build customer equity. Our third book, *The One to One Fieldbook: The Complete Toolkit for*

Implementing a One to One Marketing Program (Currency/Doubleday, 1999), coauthored with Bob Dorf, was a compendium of what we had learned about how to help people understand the basic principles. Our goal was to provide a framework for learning that was based on a methodology that we had tested and proven in a variety of client companies in a variety of industries around the world. That was the beginning of the IDIC approach.

Meanwhile, professors and classrooms across the United States and around the world were beginning to teach one-to-one and customer relationship management (CRM). They sometimes used one of our early books as readings, along with other excellent work that was being published by a group of other early explorers on this and related topics. But the field was too new, and the academic market too small, to justify the work (yet) on an academic textbook or desk reference *per se*.

In 2000, NCR Teradata donated the funding for the Teradata CRM Center at Fuqua School of Business at Duke University, where Martha is an adjunct professor and codirects the center. The center's mission is threefold: to help support rigorous academic research, to provide top-level teaching and curriculum materials, and to bring together academicians and practitioners for mutual learning. One of the first activities of the center was to support the background research and project management of a textbook on managing customer relationships, which we agreed to write. (You can reach the Center, and take advantage of the help it offers professor and students for classroom learning as well as research, at *www.teradataduke.org*. You can reach us about this book at *MCRtext@fuqua .duke.edu* .)

However, even though we welcomed the chance to codify and synthesize the learning and thinking about managing customer relationships, we also thought this book should not reflect just our views. Obviously, we know more about our own work (some might say obsession) than about anyone else's, and this book predictably draws heavily on our own experience from the past 10 years. But we had also been reading excellent work done by others, and so invited many of them to share their views, to include their voices. Nearly everyone generously agreed, and we found that the challenge of coordinating such a large chorus was offset by the benefit of gathering together many of the thoughtful leaders in this emerging field. We thank all of the contributors, as well as the nine anonymous reviewers who pushed us to make the text better in many ways, as well as James Barnes, Mary Jo Bitner, Anthony Davidson, Julie Edell, Susan Geibs, Rashi Glazer, Neil Lichtman, Janis McFaul, Marion Moore, Ralph Oliva, Phil Pfeiffer, and Jag Sheth, who also shared suggestions and support.

At the time of this writing, we believe this is the first book to appear that is designed to help the pedagogy of managing customer relationships, with an emphasis on customer strategies and building customer value. We hope it will be useful to professors and students, and hope that all of you who see this first edition will help improve the textbook in its second edition. Please send your suggestions and comments, as well as citation to your work if we haven't yet included it, to *MCRtext@Fuqua.duke.edu*. While we hope this work will teach our readers, we also implore our readers to teach us. Our goal is to build the most useful learning tool available on the subject of managing customer relationships to build competitive advantage.

HOW TO USE THIS BOOK

The table of contents provides not only a guide to the chapter topics, but also a listing of the contributions and contributors who have shared their insights, findings, and ideas.

Each chapter begins with an overview, and closes with a Summary (which is really more about how the chapter ties into the next chapter), Food for Thought (a series of discussion questions), and a Glossary. In addition, chapters include the following elements:

- Glossary terms are printed in **boldface** the first time they appear in a chapter, and their definitions are located at the end of that chapter. All of the glossary terms are included in the index, for a broader reference of usage in the book.
- Sidebars provide supplemental discussions and real-world examples of chapter concepts and ideas.
- Contributed material is indicated by a shaded background, with contributor names and affiliations appearing at the beginning of each section.

We anticipate that this book will be used in one of two ways: Some readers will start at the beginning and read it through to the end. Others will keep it on hand and use it as a reference book. For both readers, we have tried to make sure the index is useful for search by names of people and companies, as well as topics.

If you have suggestions about how readers can use this book, please share those at *MCRtext@fuqua.duke.edu*.

ACKNOWLEDGMENTS

We started the research and planning for this book in 2001. Our goal was to provide a handbook/textbook for students of the movement to focus companies on customers, and to build the value of an enterprise by building the value of the customer base. We have made many friends along the way, and had some interesting debates. We can only begin to scratch the surface of all those who have touched this book, and helped to shape it into a tool we hope our readers will find useful.

Thanks to Dr. Julie Edell, who has team-taught the Managing Customer Value course at Duke with Martha for over four years. Special thanks to:

- Peter Heffring and Rick Staelin, the original co-directors with Martha at the Teradata CRM Center at Duke[1], who approved funding support for the early stages of research and background work
- Josh Rose, who managed the Center when this project began and proved helpful to this very large project
- Katie Lay and others at the Center, who assisted with background work and graphics.

We are honored to be contributing all royalties and proceeds from the sale of this book to the Center.

This book wouldn't be what it is without the voices of the many contributors who have shared their viewpoints throughout this book—you'll see their names listed in the table of Contents. We thank each of you for taking the time to participate in this project.

The book has been greatly strengthened by the critiques from some of the most knowledgeable minds in this field, who took the time to review the book and share their insights and suggestions with us. This is an enormous undertaking and a huge professional favor, and we owe great thanks to Jim Barnes at Memorial University of Newfoundland; Mary Jo Bitner and James Ward at Arizona State; Ray Burke at Indiana; Anthony Davidson at NYU; Susan Geib at MSUM; Rashi Glazer at U.C. Berkeley; Jim Karrh at University of Arkansas; Neil Lichtman at NYU; Charlotte Mason at UNC; Janis McFaul at Lawrence Tech; Ralph Oliva at Penn State; Phil Pfeiffer and Marian Moore at U.VA; David Reibstein at Wharton; and Jag Sheth at Emory. Thanks to John Deighton, Jon Anton, Devavrat Purohit, and Preyas Desai for additional contributions, and we also appreciate the support and input from Mary Gros and Corinna Gilbert at Teradata. Thanks to half a dozen anonymous reviewers whose comments also helped to improve the manuscript. And thanks to Maureen Morrin and Eric Greenberg at Rutgers, who has contributed to the Web site supporting this book.

Much of this work has been based on the experiences and learning we have gleaned from our clients and the audiences we have been privileged to encounter in our work with Peppers and Rogers Group. Dozens and dozens of the talented folks who have been PRGers over the past three years have contributed to our thinking—many more than the ones whose bylines appear on some of the contributions you will see in the book. Special additional thanks to Elizabeth Stewart, Tom Shimko, Tom Niehaus, Abby Wheeler, Lisa Hayford-Goodmaster, Lisa Regelman, Marji Chimes, and many others. In the past year, we couldn't have finished the many details necessary for a book like this without help from Jenny Smith, Judy White, and Jennifer Makris, and we owe special, huge thanks to

---

[1]The Teradata Center for Customer Relationship Management at Duke University (the Center) advances the field of Customer Relationship management (CRM) through research and learning. This multi-million dollar global think tank, based at Duke's Fuqua School of Business, was established in January 2001 through a grant from Teradata, a division of NCR. Through this dynamic partnership between the University and Teradata, the Center leverages the intellectual resources of a leading academic institution and corporation to merge theory and practical business experience, thereby creating a world-class center in CRM research and curriculum design.

Holly Daniels, who has patiently and capably assisted in winding us through the morass of minutiae generated by a project of this scope.

Our editor at John Wiley & Sons, Inc., Sheck Cho, has been an enthusiastic supporter of and guide for the project since Day One. We owe much to his talented production and marketing teams, especially Jennifer Hanley. As always, thanks to our literary agent, Rafe Sagalyn, for his insight and patience.

We thank the many professors and instructors who are teaching the first "Customer Strategy" or "CRM" course at their schools, and who have shared the syllabi for their courses with the Teradata CRM Center at Duke University and thereby helped us shape what we hope will be a useful book for them, their students, and all our readers who need a ready reference as we all continue the journey toward building stronger, more profitable, and more successful organizations by focusing on growing the value of every customer.

DON PEPPERS AND MARTHA ROGERS, PhD
2004

Principles of Managing Customer Relationships

The *Learning Relationship* works like this: If you're my customer and I get you to talk to me, and I remember what you tell me, then I get smarter and smarter about you. I know something about you my competitors don't know. So I can do things for you my competitors can't do, because they don't know you as well as I do. Before long, you can get something from me you can't get anywhere else, for any price. At the very least, you'd have to start all over somewhere else, but starting over is more costly than staying with me.

Evolution of Relationships with Customers

1
Chapter

We have only two sources of competitive advantage:

1. The ability to learn more about our customers faster than the competition.
2. The ability to turn that learning into action faster than the competition.

—Jack Welch, former CEO, General Electric[1]

The goal of this book is not just to acquaint the reader with the techniques of **customer relationship management (CRM)**. *The more ambitious goal of this book is to help the reader understand the essence of customer strategy as a necessary and important element of managing every successful enterprise in the twenty-first century. A firm's most valuable asset is its customers, and given our new and unfolding technological capabilities to recognize, measure, and manage relationships with each of those customers in order to thrive, a firm must focus on deliberately increasing the value of the customer base. Customer strategy is not a fleeting assignment for the marketing department; rather it is an ongoing business imperative that requires the involvement of the entire enterprise. Organizations need to manage their customer relationships effectively to remain competitive in the* **interactive era**. *Technological advancements have served as the catalyst for managing customer relationships more efficiently.*

The dynamics of the customer-enterprise relationship have changed dramatically over time. Customers have always been at the heart of an enterprise's long-term growth strategies, marketing and sales efforts, product development, labor and resource allocation, and overall profitability directives. Historically, enterprises have encouraged the active participation of a sampling of customers in the research and development of their products and services. But until

---

[1]Bloomberg News Service, 2000.

recently, enterprises have been structured and managed around the products and services they create and sell. Driven by assembly-line technology, mass media, and mass distribution, which appeared at the beginning of the twentieth century, the Industrial Age was dominated by businesses that sought to mass-produce products and to gain a competitive advantage by manufacturing a product that was perceived by most customers as better than its closest competitor. Product innovation, therefore, was the important key to business success. To increase its overall market share, the twentieth-century enterprise would use mass marketing and mass advertising to reach the greatest number of potential customers.

As a result, most twentieth-century products and services eventually became highly *commoditized*. Branding emerged to offset this perception of being like all the competitors; in fact, branding from its beginning was, in a way, an expensive substitute for relationships companies could not have with their newly blossomed masses of customers. Facilitated by lots and lots of mass-media advertising, brands have helped add value through familiarity, image, and trust. Historically, brands have played a critical role in helping customers distinguish what they deem to be the best products and services. A primary enterprise goal has been to improve *brand awareness* of products and services, and to increase *brand preference* and *brand loyalty* among consumers. For many consumers, a brand name testifies to the trustworthiness or quality of a product or service. But brand reputation has become less important among shoppers.[2] Indeed, consumers are often content as long as they can buy one brand of a consumer-packaged good that they know and respect. Whether shopping in a store, online, or from a catalog, consumers are just as satisfied whether a retailer carries a trusted store brand or a trusted manufacturer's brand.[3]

> For many years, enterprises depended on gaining the competitive advantage from the best *brands*. Brands have been untouchable, immutable, and inflexible parts of the twentieth-century mass-marketing era. But in the interactive era of the twenty-first century, enterprises are instead strategizing how to gain sustainable competitive advantage from the *information* they gather about customers.

For many years, enterprises depended on gaining the competitive advantage from the best *brands*. Brands have been untouchable, immutable, and inflexible parts of the twentieth-century mass-marketing era. But in the interactive era of the twenty-first century, enterprises are instead strategizing how to gain sustainable competitive advantage from the *information* they gather about customers. As a result, enterprises are creating a *two-way brand*, one that thrives on customer information and interaction. The two-way brand, or *branded relationship*, transforms itself based on the ongoing dialogue between the enterprise and the customer. The branded relationship is "aware" of the customer (giving new meaning to the term *brand awareness*) and constantly changes to suit the needs of that particular individual.

[2]Peppers and Rogers Group, and Institute for the Future, "Forecasting the Consumer Direct Channel: Business Models for Success" (2000), p. 48.

[3]Ibid., p. 50.

ROOTS OF CUSTOMER RELATIONSHIP MANAGEMENT

The goal of every enterprise, once you strip away all the activities that keep everybody busy every day, is simply to get, keep, and grow customers. Whether a business focuses its efforts on product innovation, operational efficiency and low price, or customer intimacy,[4] that firm must have customers or the enterprise isn't a business—it's a hobby. This is true for nonprofits (where the "customers" may be donors or volunteers) as well as for-profits, for firms large and small, for public as well as private enterprise. What does it mean for an enterprise to focus on its customers as the key to competitive advantage? Obviously, it does *not* mean giving up the product edge, or the operational efficiencies, that have been successful in the past. It does mean using new strategies, nearly always requiring new technologies, to focus on growing the value of the company by deliberately and strategically growing the value of the customer base.

To some executives, customer relationship management (CRM) is a technology or software solution that helps track data and information about customers to enable better customer service. Others think of CRM, or one-to-one, as an elaborate marketing or customer service discipline. We even recently heard CRM described as "personalized email."

This book is about much more than setting up a business Web site or redirecting some of the mass-media budget into the call center database. It's about increasing the value of the company through specific customer strategies (see Exhibit 1.1).

Enterprises determined to build successful and profitable customer relationships understand that the process of becoming an enterprise focused on building

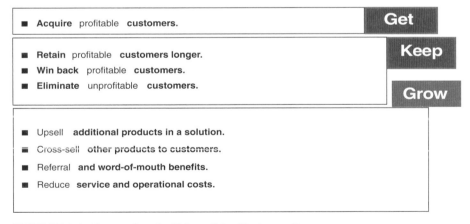

EXHIBIT 1.1   Increasing the Value of the Customer Base

[4]Michael Treacy and Fred Wiersema, *The Discipline of Market Leaders* (New York; Addison-Wesley, 1995).

Enterprises determined to build successful and profitable customer relationships understand that the process of becoming an enterprise focused on building its value by building customer value doesn't begin with installing technology, but instead begins with:

• A strategy or an ongoing process that helps transform the enterprise from a focus on traditional selling or manufacturing to a customer focus, while increasing revenues and profits
• The leadership and commitment necessary to cascade the thinking and decision-making capability throughout the organization that puts customer value and relationships first

An enterprisewide business strategy for achieving customer-specific objectives by taking customer-specific actions.

its value by building customer value doesn't begin with installing technology, but instead begins with:

• A strategy or an ongoing process that helps transform the enterprise from a focus on traditional selling or manufacturing to a customer focus, while increasing revenues and profits
• The leadership and commitment necessary to cascade the thinking and decision-making capability throughout the organization that puts customer value and relationships first

The reality is that becoming a customer-strategy enterprise is about using information to gain a competitive advantage and deliver growth and profit. In its most generalized form, CRM can be thought of as a set of business practices designed, simply, to put an enterprise into closer and closer touch with its customers, in order to learn more about each one and to deliver greater and greater value to each one, with the overall goal of making each one more valuable to the firm. It is an enterprisewide approach to understanding and influencing customer behavior through meaningful communications to improve customer acquisition, customer retention, and customer profitability.[5]

Defined more precisely, and what makes CRM into a truly different model for doing business and competing in the marketplace, is this: It is an enterprisewide business strategy for achieving customer-specific objectives by taking customer-specific actions. It is enterprisewide because it can't be assigned to marketing if it is to have any hope of success. Its objectives are customer-specific because the goal is to increase the value of each customer. Therefore, the firm will take customer-specific actions for each customer, made possible by new technologies.

In essence, CRM involves *treating different customers differently*. Today, there is a CRM revolution underway among businesses. It represents an inevitable—literally, irresistible—movement. All businesses will be embracing CRM sooner or later, with varying degrees of enthusiasm and success, for two primary reasons: First, CRM represents the way customers, in all walks of life, in all industries, all over the world, want to be served. Second, it is simply a more efficient way of doing business. We find examples of customer-specific behavior, and business initiatives driven by customer-specific insights, all around us today:

---

[5]George S. Day, *Market-Driven Strategy: Processes for Creating Value* (New York: Free Press, 1999); Frederick Newell, *The New Rules of Marketing* (New York: McGraw-Hill Professional Book Group, 1997); Don Peppers and Martha Rogers, PhD, *The One to One Future* (New York: Doubleday Books, 1993); Ronald S. Swift, *Accelerating Customer Relationships: Using CRM and Relationship Technologies* (Upper Saddle River, NJ: Prentice Hall, 2001); Fred Reichheld, *The Loyalty Effect* (Boston, MA: Harvard Business School Press, 1996).

- A car-rental customer rents a car without having to complete another reservation profile.
- An online customer buys a product without having to reenter his credit card number and address.
- A company saves money by eliminating duplicate mailings.
- A firm's product-development people turn their attention to a new service or product based on customer feedback captured by the sales force.
- An insurance company not only handles a claim for property damage, but also connects the insured party with a contractor in his area who can bypass the purchasing department and do the repairs directly.
- A supervisor orders more computer components by going to a Web page that displays his firm's contract terms, his own spending to date, and his departmental authorizations.

Taking customer-specific action, treating different customers differently, building relationships with customers that go on through time to get better and deeper: That's what this book is about. In the chapters that follow, we will look at lots of examples. The overall business goal of this strategy is to make the enterprise as profitable as possible over time by taking steps to increase the value of the customer base. The enterprise makes itself, its products, and/or its services so satisfying, convenient, or valuable to the customer that he becomes more willing to devote his time and money to this enterprise than to any competitor. Building the value of customers increases the value of the **demand chain**, the stream of business that flows from the customer up through the retailer all the way to the manufacturer. A customer-strategy enterprise interacts directly with an individual customer. The customer tells the enterprise about how he would like to be served. Based on this interaction, the enterprise, in turn, modifies its behavior with respect to this particular customer. In essence, the concept implies a specific, one-customer-to-one-enterprise relationship, as is the case when the customer's input drives the enterprise's output for that particular customer.[6]

CRM has become a buzzword of late, and like all new initiatives, suffers when it is poorly understood, improperly applied, and incorrectly measured and managed. But by any name, strategies designed to build the value of the customer base by building relationships with one customer at a time are by no means ephemeral trends or fads, any more than computers or interactivity are.

A good example of a business offering that benefits from individual customer relationships can be seen in today's popular PC banking services, in which a consumer spends several hours, usually spread over several sessions, setting up an online account and inputting payee addresses and account numbers, in order to be able to pay his bills electronically each month. If a competitor opens a branch in town offering lower checking fees or higher savings rates, this consumer is unlikely to switch banks. He has invested time and energy in a relationship with

[6]Don Peppers and Martha Rogers, PhD, *One to One B2B* (New York: Doubleday Broadway Books, 2001).

the first bank, and it is simply more convenient to remain loyal to the first bank than to teach the second bank how to serve him in the same way. In this example, it should also be noted that the bank now has increased the value of the customer to the bank, and has simultaneously reduced the cost of serving the customer, as it costs the bank less to serve a customer online than at the teller window or by phone.

The term CRM is also known by other labels, coined by various experts in their respective fields, such as *integrated marketing communications* (Don Schultz), *one-to-one relationship management* (Don Peppers and Martha Rogers), *real-time marketing* (Regis McKenna), *customer intimacy* (Michael Treacy and Fred Wiersema), and a variety of other terms. Clearly, CRM involves much more than marketing, and it cannot deliver optimum return on investment without integrating individual customer information into every corporate function, from customer service, to production, logistics, and channel management. A formal change in the organizational structure is usually necessary to become an enterprise focused on growing customer value. As this book will show, CRM is both an operational and an analytical process. **Operational CRM** focuses on the software installations and the changes in process affecting the day-to-day operations of a firm. **Analytical CRM** focuses on the strategic planning needed to build customer value, as well as the cultural, measurement, and organizational changes required to implement that strategy successfully. [7]

FOCUSING ON CUSTOMERS IS NEW TO BUSINESS STRATEGY

The move to a customer-strategy business model has come of age at a critical juncture in business history, when managers are deeply concerned about declining customer loyalty as competitors lure away their customers through lower prices and purchasing incentives. As customer loyalty decreases, profit margins decline, too, because the most frequently used customer acquisition tactic is price-cutting. Enterprises are facing a radically different competitive landscape as the information about their customers is becoming more plentiful and as the customers themselves are demanding more interactions with companies. Thus, a coordinated effort to get, keep, and grow valuable customers has taken on a greater and far more relevant role in forging a successful long-term, profitable business strategy.

If the last quarter of the twentieth century heralded the dawn of a new competitive arena, in which commoditized products and services have become less reliable for business profitability and success, it is the new computer technologies and applications that have arisen that assist companies in managing their interactions

---

[7]META Group defines these terms as follows: **Operational CRM** is the automation of horizontally integrated business processes involving front-office customer touch points across sales, marketing, and customer service via multiple, interconnected delivery channels; **Analytical CRM** is the analysis of data created on the operational side of CRM and through other relevant operational data sources for the purposes of business performance management and customer-specific analysis.

with customers. These technologies have spawned enterprisewide information systems that help to harness information about customers, analyze the information, and use the data to serve customers better. Technologies such as **enterprise resource planning (ERP)** systems, supply chain management software (SCM), enterprise application integration software (EAI), **data warehousing**, **sales force automation (SFA)**, and other enterprise software are helping companies to mass-customize their products and services, literally delivering individually configured products or services to unique customers, in response to their individual feedback and specifications.

The accessibility of the new technologies is motivating enterprises to reconsider how they develop and manage customer relationships. CEOs of leading enterprises have made the shift to a customer-strategy business model a top business priority for the twenty-first century.[8] Technology is making it possible for enterprises to conduct business at an intimate, individual customer level. Indeed, technology is driving the shift. Computers can enable enterprises to remember individual customer needs and estimate the future potential revenue the customer will bring to the enterprise.

SIDEBAR 1.1
Traditional Marketing Redux

Historically, traditional marketing efforts have centered on the "four Ps"—product, price, promotional activity, and place—popularized by marketing expert E. Jerome McCarthy[a] and Philip Kotler. To be fair, these have been enhanced by our greater (and deeper) understanding of consumer behavior, organizational behavior, market research, segmentation, and targeting. In other words, using traditional sampling and aggregate data, a broad understanding of the market has preceded the application of the four Ps, which enterprises have deployed in their marketing strategy to bring uniform products and services to the mass market for decades.[b] In essence, the four Ps are all about the "get" part of "get, keep, and grow customers." These terms have been the focal point for building market share and driving sales of products and services to consumers. The customer needed to believe that the enterprise's offerings would be superior in delivering the "four Cs": customer value, lower costs, better convenience, and better communication.[c] Marketing strategies have revolved around targeting broadly defined market segments through heavy doses of advertising and promotion.

This approach first began to take shape in the 1950s. Fast-growing living standards and equally fast-rising consumer demand made organizations aware of the effectiveness of a supply-driven marketing strategy. By approaching the market on the strength of the organization's specific abilities, and creating a product supply in accordance with those abilities, it was possible to control and guide the sales process. Central to the strategic choices taken in the area of marketing were the—now traditional—marketing instruments of product, price, place, and promotion—the same instruments that served as the foundation for Philip Kotler's theory and the

---

[8]"CEO Global Business Study" (A.T. Kearney, 1999).

SIDEBAR 1.1 *(continued)*
....

same instruments that still assume an important role in marketing and customer relations today.

The four Ps all, of course, relate to the *aggregate market* rather than to individual customers. The market being considered could be a large, mass market, or a smaller, niche market, but the four Ps have helped define how an enterprise should behave toward all the customers within the aggregate market:

- *Product* is defined in terms of the average customer—what *most* members of the aggregate market want or need. This is the product brought to market, and it is delivered the same way for every customer in the market. The definition of *product* extends to standard variations in size, color, style, and units of sale, as well as customer service and aftermarket service capabilities.

- *Place* is a distribution system or sales channel. How and where is the product sold? Is it sold in stores? By dealers? Through franchisees? At a single location or through widely dispersed outlets, like fast food and ATMs? Can it be delivered directly to the purchaser?

- *Price* refers not only to the ultimate retail price a product brings, but also to intermediate prices, beginning with wholesale; and it takes account of the availability of credit to a customer and the prevailing interest rate. The price is set at a level designed to "clear the market," assuming that everyone will pay the *same* price—which is only fair, because everyone will get the same product. And even though different customers within a market actually have different levels of desire for the same product, the market price will be the same for everybody.

- *Promotion* has also worked in a fundamentally nonaddressable, noninteractive way. The various customers in a market are all passive recipients of the promotional message, whether it is delivered through mass media or interpersonally, through salespeople. Marketers have traditionally recognized the trade-off between the cost of delivering a message and the benefit of personalizing it to a recipient. A sales call can cost $300 or even more, but at least it allows for the personalization of the promotion process. The cost per thousand (CPM) to reach an audience through mass media is far lower, but requires that the same message be sent to everyone. Ultimately, the way a product is promoted is designed to differentiate it from all the other, competitive products. Except for different messages aimed at different segments of the market, promotion doesn't change by *customer*, but by *product*.

[a]E. Jerome McCarthy, *Basic Marketing: A Managerial Approach,* 1st ed. (Homewood, IL: Irwin, 1958).

[b]Philip Kotler, *Marketing Management: Analysis, Planning, Implementation, and Control,* 9th ed. (Upper Saddle River, NJ: Prentice Hall, 1997), pp. 92-93.

[c]Philip Kotler, *Kotler on Marketing* (New York: Free Press, 1999), pp. 116–120.

Dr. Philip Kotler, who, with Jerome McCarthy, is responsible for our understanding and practice of traditional marketing, shares his views of the transition to the customer strategies mandated by new technologies.

THE VIEW FROM HERE

Philip Kotler
S. C. Johnson Distinguished Professor of International Marketing,
Kellogg School of Management, Northwestern University

When I first started writing about marketing 36 years ago, the Industrial Age was in its prime. Manufacturers churned out products on massive assembly lines, stored them in huge warehouses where they patiently waited for retailers to order and shelve so that customers could buy them. Market leaders enjoyed great market shares from their carefully crafted mass-production, mass-distribution, and mass-advertising campaigns.

What the Industrial Age taught us is that if an enterprise wanted to make money it needed to be efficient at large-scale manufacturing and distribution. The enterprise needed to manufacture millions of standard products and distribute them in the same way to all of their customers. Mass producers relied on numerous intermediaries to finance, distribute, stock, and sell the goods to ever expanding geographical markets. But in the process, producers grew increasingly removed from any direct contact with end users.

Producers tried to make up for what they didn't know about end users by using a barrage of marketing research methods, primarily customer panels, focus groups, and large scale customer surveys. The aim was not to learn about individual customers but about large customer segments such as women ages 30 to 55. The exception occurred in business-to-business marketing where each salesperson knew each customer and prospect as individuals. Well-trained salespeople were cognizant of each customer's buying habits, preferences, and peculiarities. Even here, however, much of this information was never codified. When a salesperson retired or quit, the company lost a great deal of specific customer information. Only more recently, with sales automation software and loyalty building programs, are business-to-business enterprises capturing detailed information about each customer on the company's mainframe computer.

As for the consumer market, interest in knowing consumers as individuals lagged behind the B to B marketplace. The exception occurred with direct mailers and catalog marketers who collected and analyzed data on individual customers. Direct marketers purchased mailing lists and kept records of their transactions with individual customers. The individual customer's stream of transactions provided clues as to other items that might interest that customer. And in the case of consumer appliances, the company could at least know when a customer might be ready to replace an older appliance with a new one if the price was right.

GETTING BETTER AT CONSUMER MARKETING

With the passage of time, direct marketers became increasingly sophisticated. They supplemented mail contact with the adroit use of the telephone and telemarketing. The growing use of credit cards and customers' willingness to give their credit card numbers to merchants greatly stimulated direct marketing. The emergence of fax machines further facilitated the exchange of information and the placing of orders. Today, the Internet and e-mail provide the ultimate facilitation of direct marketing. Customers can view products visually and verbally order them easily, receive confirmation, and know when the goods will arrive.

But whether a company was ready for *customer relationship management (CRM)* depended on more than conducting numerous transactions with individual customers. Companies needed to build comprehensive *customer databases*. Companies had been maintaining product databases, salesforce databases, and dealer databases. Now they needed to build, maintain, mine, and manage a customer database that could be used by company personnel in sales, marketing, credit, accounting, and other company functions.

As customer database marketing grew, several different names came to describe it, including individualized marketing, customer intimacy, technology-enabled marketing, dialogue marketing, interactive marketing, permission marketing, and one-to-one marketing.

Modern technology makes it possible for enterprises to learn more about individual customers, remember those needs, and shape the company's offerings, services, messages and interactions to each valued customer. The new technologies make mass-customization (otherwise an oxymoron) possible.

At the same time, technology is only a partial factor in helping companies do genuine one-to-one marketing. The following quotes about customer relationship management (CRM) make this point vividly:

- "CRM is not a software package. It's not a database. It's not a call center or a Web site. It's not a loyalty program, a customer service program, a customer acquisition program or a win-back program. CRM is an entire philosophy." (Steve Silver)
- "A CRM program is typically 45 percent dependent on the right executive leadership, 40 percent on project management implementation and 15 percent on technology." (Edmund Thompson, Gartner Group)

Where in the Industrial Age, companies focused on winning market share and new customers, more of today's companies are focusing on customer share, namely increasing their business with each existing customer. These companies are focusing on customer retention, customer loyalty, and customer satisfaction as the key management objectives.

CRM is more than just an outgrowth of direct marketing and the advent of new technology. It requires new skills, systems, processes, and employee mindsets. As the Interactive Age progresses, mass marketing must give way to new principles for targeting, attracting, winning, serving, and satisfying markets. As advertising costs have risen and mass media has lost some effectiveness, mass-marketing is now more costly and more wasteful. Companies are better prepared to identify meaningful segments and niches and address the individual customers within the targeted groups. They are becoming aware, however, that many customers are uncomfortable about their loss of privacy and the increase in solicitations by mail, phone, and e-mail. Ultimately, companies will have to move from an "invasive" approach to prospects and customers to a "permissions" approach.

The full potential of CRM is only beginning to be realized. The goal now is not just to offer excellent products and services but to get, keep, and grow the best customers. The objective is to focus more on customer retention and growth rather than pursue all types of customers at great expense only to lose them.

MANAGING CUSTOMER RELATIONSHIPS IS A DIFFERENT TYPE OF COMPETITION

A lot can be understood about how traditional, market-driven competition is different from today's customer-driven competition by examining Exhibit 1.2. The direction of success for a traditional aggregate-market enterprise (i.e., a traditional company that sees its customers in markets of aggregate groups) is to acquire more customers (widen the horizontal bar), whereas the direction of success for the customer-driven enterprise is to keep customers longer and grow them bigger (lengthen the vertical bar). The width of the horizontal bar can be thought of as an enterprise's market share—the proportion of customers who have their needs satisfied by the enterprise, or the percentage of total products in

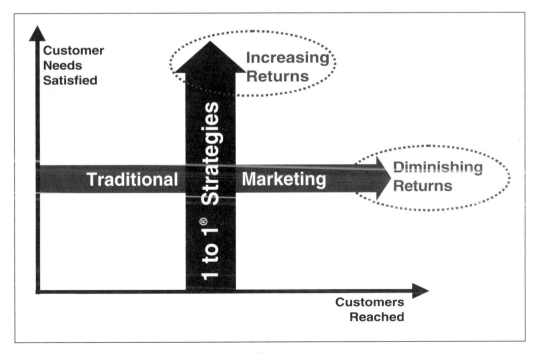

EXHIBIT 1.2   **Market Share versus Share of Customer**

an industry sold by this particular firm. But the customer-value enterprise focuses on **share of customer**—the percentage of this customer's business that a particular firm gets—represented by the height of the vertical bar. Think of it this way: Kellogg's can either sell as many boxes of cornflakes as possible to whomever will buy them, even though sometimes cornflakes will cannibalize raisin bran sales, *or* Kellogg's can concentrate on making sure its products are on Mrs. Smith's breakfast table every day for the rest of her life, and thus represent a steady or growing percentage of that breakfast table's offerings. Ford can try to sell as many Tauruses as possible, for any price, to anyone who will buy; or it can, by knowing Mrs. Smith better, make sure all the cars in Mrs. Smith's garage are Ford brands, including the used car she buys for her teenaged son, and that Mrs. Smith uses Ford financing and credit cards, and gets her service, maintenance and repairs at Ford dealerships—throughout her driving lifetime.

Although the tasks for growing market share are different from those for building share of customer, the two strategies are not antithetical. A company can simultaneously focus on getting new customers as well as growing the value of and keeping the customers it already has.[9]

Customer-strategy enterprises are required to interact with a customer and use that customer's feedback from this interaction to deliver a customized product or service. Market-driven efforts can be strategically effective and even more efficient at meeting individual customer needs when a customer-specific philosophy is conducted on top of it. The customer-driven process is time-dependent and evolutionary, as the product or service is continuously fine-tuned and the customer is increasingly differentiated from other customers. The aggregate-market enterprise competes by differentiating products, whereas the customer-driven enterprise competes by differentiating customers. The traditional, aggregate-market enterprise attempts to establish an actual product differentiation (by launching new products or modifying or extending established product lines) or a perceived one (with advertising and PR). The customer-driven enterprise caters to one customer at a time and relies on differentiating each customer from all the others.

The principles of a customer-focused business model differ in many ways from mass marketing. For one thing, the traditional marketing company, no matter how friendly, ultimately sees customers as adversaries, and vice versa. The company and the customer play a zero-sum game: If the customer gets a discount, the company loses profit margin. Their interests have traditionally been at odds: The customer wants to buy as much product as possible for the lowest price, while the company wants to sell the least product possible for the highest price. If an enterprise and a customer have no relationship prior to a purchase, and they have no relationship following it, then their entire interaction is centered on a single, solitary transaction and the profitability of that transaction. Thus, in a transaction-based, product-centric business model, buyer and seller are adversaries, no matter how much the seller may try not to

---

[9]See George S. Day, *Market-Driven Strategy: Processes for Creating Value* (New York: Free Press, 1999), for a useful discussion of the difference between "market-driven" and "market-driving" strategies.

act the part. In this business model, practically the only assurance a customer has that he can trust the product and service being sold to him is the general reputation of the brand itself.[10]

By contrast, the customer-based enterprise aligns customer collaboration with profitability. Compare the behaviors that result from both sides if each transaction occurs in the context of a longer-term relationship. For starters, a one-to-one enterprise would likely be willing to fix a problem raised by a single transaction at a loss if the relationship with the customer was profitable long term (see Exhibit 1.3).

> The central purpose of managing customer relationships is for the enterprise to focus on increasing the overall value of its customer base–and customer retention is critical to its success.

The central purpose of managing customer relationships is for the enterprise to focus on increasing the overall value of its customer base—and customer retention is critical to its success. Increasing the value of the customer base, whether through *cross-selling* (getting customers to buy other products and services), *upselling* (getting customers to buy more expensive offerings), or customer referrals, will lead to a more profitable enterprise. The enterprise also reduces the cost of serving its customers by making it more convenient for them to buy from the enterprise.

TECHNOLOGY ACCELERATES—IT IS NOT THE SAME AS—BUILDING CUSTOMER VALUE

The interactive era has accelerated the adoption and facilitation of this highly interactive collaboration between the customer and the company. In addition, technological advancements have contributed to an enterprise's capability to capture the feedback of its customer, then customize some aspect of its products

MARKET- SHARE STRATEGY	SHARE-OF-CUSTOMER STRATEGY
Product (or brand) managers sell one product at a time to as many customers as possible.	Customer manager sells as many products as possible to one customer at a time.
Differentiate products from competitors.	Differentiate customers from each other.
Sell *to* customers.	Collaborate *with* customers.
Find a constant stream of new customers.	Find a constant stream of new business from established customers.
Use mass media to build brand and announce products.	Use interactive communication to determine individual needs and communicate with each individual.

EXHIBIT 1.3 **A Comparison of Market-Share and Share-of-Customer Strategies**

[10]Don Peppers and Martha Rogers, PhD, *The One to One Manager* (New York: Doubleday, 1999).

or services to suit the customer's individual needs. Enterprises require a highly sophisticated level of integrated activity to enable this customization and personalized customer interaction to occur. To effectuate customer-focused business relationships, an enterprise must integrate the disparate information systems, databases, businesses units, customer touch points, and many other facets of its business to ensure that all employees who interact with customers have real-time access to current customer information. The objective is to optimize each customer interaction and ensure that the dialogue is seamless—that each conversation picks up from where the last one ended.

Many software companies have developed enterprise point solutions and suites of software applications that, when deployed, elevate an enterprise's capabilities to transform itself to a customer-driven model. (You'll find more about technology in Chapter 8.) And while one-to-one customer relationships are enabled by technology, executives at firms with strong customer relationships and burgeoning **customer equity** believe that the enabling technology should be viewed as the means to an end, not the end itself. Managing customer relationships is an ongoing business process, not merely a technology. But technology has provided the catalyst for customer relationship management to manifest itself within the enterprise. Computer databases help companies remember and keep track of individual interactions with their customers. Within seconds, customer service representatives can retrieve entire histories of customer transactions and make adjustments to customer records. Technology has made possible the mass customization of products and services, enabling businesses to treat different customers differently, in a cost-efficient way. (You'll find more about mass customization in Chapter 10.) Technology empowers enterprises and their customer contact personnel, marketing and sales functions, and managers by equipping them with substantially more intelligence about their customers.

> Within seconds, customer service representatives can retrieve entire histories of customer transactions and make adjustments to customer records.

Implementing an effective customer strategy can be challenging and costly because of the sophisticated technology and skill set needed by relationship managers to execute the customer-driven business model. A business model focused on building customer value often requires the coordinated delivery of products and services aligned with enterprise financial objectives that meet customer value requirements. While enterprises are experimenting with a wide array of technology and software solutions from different vendors to satisfy their customer-driven needs, they are learning that they cannot depend on technology alone to do the job. Before it can be implemented successfully, managing customer relationships individually requires committed leadership from the upper management of the enterprise and wholehearted participation throughout the enterprise. Roger Siboni reiterates that in the next contribution, which reminds us that while customer strategies are driven by new technological

> The foundation for an enterprise focused on building its value by building the value of the customer base is unique: Establish relationships with customers on an individual basis, then use the information gathered to treat different customers differently, and increase the value of each one to the firm.

capabilities, the technology alone does not make a company customer-centric. While the payoff can be great, the need to build the strategy to get, keep, and grow customers is even more important than the technology required to implement that strategy.

The foundation for an enterprise focused on building its value by building the value of the customer base is unique: Establish relationships with customers on an individual basis, then use the information gathered to treat different customers differently, and increase the value of each one to the firm. The overarching theme of such an enterprise is that the customer is the most valuable asset the company has, and that's why the primary goals are to get, keep, and grow profitable customers.

GET, KEEP, AND GROW CUSTOMERS IN THE TWENTY-FIRST CENTURY

Roger Siboni
Chairman of the Board, E.piphany

Let's start by assuming that every enterprise in the Fortune 500 has in place an ERP system to manage its back office, and some front-office software to manage its customer-facing processes. How do those systems help an enterprise increase its capability to get, keep, and grow its best customers? The short answer is, they do not. ERP and traditional CRM systems only manage the processes, they do not focus on the customer. But why is it so important to begin focusing on the customer now? If you look at the potential return from focusing on these areas, the answer is obvious.

Getting customers is all about making the sales and marketing process not only more efficient, but also more effective. The Fortune 500 spends approximately $700 billion every year on sales and marketing, yet most of these companies do not have a single view of who those customers are, individually. Achieving even a 10 percent increase in sales and marketing effectiveness by focusing on the right customer at the right time would generate a return of $70 billion.

Keeping customers addresses the biggest challenge in business today: managing customer attrition. Some people believe this is simply a question of increasing loyalty in order to decrease turnover rates. But the challenge is far greater than that. Keeping customers is also about knowing which are the right customers to keep, because some customers are best when they're someone else's problem. Fundamentally, this is a question of profitability. If an airline customer flies 100,000 miles a year, mostly in business class, he is probably a very profitable customer for the airline and should receive royal treatment every time he calls on the phone, shows up at the airport, clicks on the Web site, or gets on the plane. The cost of that customer taking half of his business to a competitive airline is probably 10 times the cost of a leisure traveler shopping elsewhere. At the same time, a low-fee credit card customer who shops very modestly and carries a zero balance most of the year is costing the credit card company money every time he gets a bill or contacts the call center. When that customer calls to complain about a late charge, it might be the most profitable business tactic just to let the customer walk away. But how can you tell which customers are profitable and which ones might be converted into profitable customers? The Fortune 500 generates more than $2 trillion in annual profits. If answering the customer profitability question could generate a mere 5 percent increase in corporate profits, this would amount to more than $100 billion a year.[11]

Finally, *growing customers* is about increasing every customer's lifetime value to a company. The two ways to grow customers are to increase their lifetime, and increase the amount of revenue generated from every customer interaction during that lifetime. The first part is straightforward—understanding a customer and effectively anticipating and responding to that customer's needs is the fastest way to increase loyalty and make sure that customer is around for a long time. The second part—increasing the sales yield per every contact—involves predicting a customer's needs and reacting in real time to his actions with personalized, relevant offers. Every customer interaction is an opportunity to build on that relationship and grow that customer's value. It has been estimated that a customer who phones into a call center with a general service or support question and has a favorable experience is three times more likely to purchase additional products or services at that moment than someone who randomly walks into a store or visits a Web site. The Fortune 500 generates more than $6 trillion of revenue every year. Achieving just a 5 percent increase in corporate revenues would add some $300 billion of incremental revenue every year.

No matter how you analyze the numbers, it's clear that the potential benefits of CRM are to be measured in the hundreds of billions of dollars. It is an incredibly leveraged business strategy with enormous potential for generating business revenue and profit. The technology of modern CRM is finally being delivered to fulfill its promise. Gone are the days when enterprises were willing to spend money on the traditional CRM solutions that plagued the market in the past.

At its inception, CRM focused on automating processes and trying to drive efficiencies into the call center or the sales force with a heavy client/server and inflexible architecture. These solutions are costly to deploy, costly to maintain, and have a low rate of adoption.

Modern CRM software has challenged the early CRM software vendors by redefining the space around a differentiated CRM solution that is based on an intelligent, open architecture that operates across **multiple channels** in real time. Modern CRM software provides the flexibility to meet the needs of the organization's business processes at the department or individual level. Modern CRM software is driven by an embedded **recognition** of the customer, followed by immediate, real-time action to meet the needs of the customer. Modern CRM software embraces a pure Web architecture that leverages existing investments,

---

[11]Frederick F. Reichheld, *The Loyalty Effect: The Hidden Force behind Growth, Profits, and Lasting Value* (Boston: Harvard Business School, Inc., 1996).

delivers rapid return on investment (ROI), a low total cost of ownership, and a higher adoption rate.

The benefits that modern CRM software delivers over early CRM software are clear to any business user or CIO.

The leading enterprises will move quickly to implement modern CRM technologies and customer strategies to lock in customer value; then they will retain those customers through understanding their preferences and being relevant to their lives.

WHAT IS A RELATIONSHIP?

What does it mean for an enterprise and a customer to have a *relationship* with each other? Do customers have relationships with enterprises that do not know them? Can the enterprise be said to have a relationship with a customer it does not know? Is it possible for a customer to have a relationship with a brand? Perhaps what is thought to be a customer's relationship with a brand is more accurately described as the customer's attitude or predisposition toward the brand. Experts have studied the nature of relationships in business for many years, and there are many different perspectives on the fundamental purpose of relationships in business strategies. (You'll find two in-depth discussions on the nature of relationship in the next chapter.)

This book is about managing customer relationships more effectively in the new era of interactivity, which is governed by a more individualized approach. The critical business objective can no longer be limited to acquiring the most customers and gaining the greatest market share for a product or service. Instead, to be successful in the era of interactivity, when it is possible to deal individually with separate customers, the business objective must include establishing meaningful and profitable relationships at least with the most valuable customers, and making the overall customer base more valuable. Technological advances during the last quarter of the twentieth century have mandated this shift in philosophy.

In short, the enterprise strives to get a customer, keep that customer for a lifetime, and grow the value of the customer to the enterprise. Relationships are the crux of the **customer-strategy enterprise**. Relationships between customers and enterprises provide the framework for everything else connected to the customer-value business model. The exchange between a customer and the enterprise becomes mutually beneficial, as customers give information in return for personalized service that meets their individual needs. This interaction forms the basis of the *Learning Relationship*, an intimate, collaborative dialogue between the enterprise and the customer that grows smarter and smarter with each successive interaction.[12]

---

[12]B. Joseph Pine II, Don Peppers, and Martha Rogers, PhD, "Do You Want to Keep Your Customers Forever?" *Harvard Business Review* (March–April 1995).

SIDEBAR 1.2

Who Is the Customer?

....

Throughout this book, we refer to *customers* in a generic way. To some, the term will conjure up the mental image of shoppers. To others, those shoppers are *end users* or *consumers*, and the customers are downstream businesses in the distribution chain— the companies that buy from producers and either sell directly to end users or manufacture their own product. In this book, *customer* refers to the constituents of an organization, whether it's a business-to-business (B2B) customer (which could mean the purchasing agent or user at the customer company, or the entire customer company) or an end-user consumer—or, for that matter, a hotel patron, a hospital patient, a charitable contributor, a voter, a university student or alum, a blood donor, a theme park guest, and so on. That means the *competition* is anything a customer might choose that would preclude choosing the organization that is trying to build a relationship with that customer.

LEARNING RELATIONSHIPS: THE CRUX OF MANAGING CUSTOMER RELATIONSHIPS

The basic strategy behind Learning Relationships is that the enterprise give a customer the opportunity to teach the company what he wants, remember it, give it back to him, and keep his business. The more the customer teaches the company, the better the company can provide exactly what the customer wants and the more the customer has invested in the relationship. Ergo, the customer will more likely choose to continue dealing with the enterprise rather than spend the extra time and effort required to establish a similar relationship elsewhere.[13]

The Learning Relationship works like this: If you're my customer and I get you to talk to me, I remember what you tell me, and I get smarter and smarter about you. I know something about you that my competitors don't know. So I can do things for you my competitors can't do, because they don't know you as well as I do. Before long, you can get something from me you can't get anywhere else, for any price. At the very least, you'd have to start all over somewhere else, but starting over is more costly than staying with me.

Even if a competitor were to establish exactly the same capabilities, a customer already involved in a Learning Relationship with an enterprise would have to spend time and energy—sometimes a lot of time and energy—teaching the competitor what the current enterprise already knows. This creates a significant **switching cost** for the customer, as the value of what the enterprise is providing continues to increase, partly as the result of the customer's own time and effort. The result is that the customer becomes more loyal to the enterprise, because it is simply in the customer's own interest to do so. It is more worthwhile for the customer to remain loyal than to switch. As the relationship progresses, the customer's convenience increases, and the enterprise becomes more

---

[13]Ibid.

valuable to the customer, allowing the enterprise to protect its profit margin with the customer, often while reducing the cost of serving that customer.

Learning Relationships provide the basis for a completely new arena of competition, separate and distinct from traditional, product-based competition. An enterprise cannot prevent its competitor from offering a product or service that is perceived to be as good as its own offering. Once a competitor offers a similar product or service, the enterprise's own offering is reduced to commodity status. But enterprises that engage in collaborative Learning Relationships with individual customers gain a distinct competitive advantage, because they know something about one customer that a competitor does not know. In a Learning Relationship, the enterprise learns about an individual customer through his transactions and interactions during the process of doing business. The customer, in turn, learns about the enterprise through his successive purchase experiences and other interactions. Thus, in addition to an increase in customer loyalty, two other benefits come from Learning Relationships:

1. *The customer learns more about his own preferences from each experience and from the firm's feedback,* and is therefore able to shop, purchase, and handle some aspect of his life more efficiently and effectively than was possible prior to this relationship.
2. *The enterprise learns more about its own strengths and weaknesses from each interaction and from the customer's feedback,* and is therefore able to market, communicate, and handle some aspect of its own tactics or strategy more efficiently and effectively than was possible prior to the relationship.[14]

> Customers, whether they are consumers or other enterprises, do not want more choices. Customers simply prefer getting exactly what they want–when, where, and how they want it.

Cultivating Learning Relationships depends on an enterprise's capability to elicit and manage useful information about customers. Customers, whether they are consumers or other enterprises, do not want more choices. Customers simply prefer getting exactly what they want— when, where, and how they want it. Technology now makes it possible for companies to give it to them. Interactive and database technology permits enterprises to collect large amounts of data on individual customer's needs and to use that data to customize products and services for each customer.[15]

When it comes to customers, businesses are shifting their focus from product sales transactions to **relationship equity**. Most soon recognize that they simply do not know the full extent of their profitability by customer.[16] Not all customers are equal. Some are not worth the time or financial investment of establishing

---

[14]Katherine Lemon, Don Peppers, and Martha Rogers, PhD, "Managing the Customer Lifetime Value: The Role of Learning Relationships," working paper.

[15]B. Joseph Pine II, Don Peppers, and Martha Rogers, PhD, "Do You Want to Keep Your Customers Forever?" *Harvard Business Review* (March–April 1995), pp. 103–114.

[16]Ian Gordon, *Relationship Marketing* (New York: John Wiley & Sons, Inc., 1998).

Learning Relationships, nor are all customers willing to devote the effort required to sustain such a relationship. Enterprises need to decide early on which customers they want to have relationships with, which they do not, and what type of relationships to nurture. (See Chapter 5 on customer value differentiation.) But the advantages to the enterprise of growing Learning Relationships with valuable and potentially valuable customers are immense. Because much of what is sold to the customer may be customized to his precise needs, the enterprise can potentially charge a premium (as the customer may be less price-sensitive to customized products and services) and increase its profit margin. [17] The product or service is worth more to the customer because he has helped shape and mold it to his own specifications. The product or service, in essence, has become *decommoditized*, and is now uniquely valuable to this particular customer.

Managing customer relationships effectively is a practice not limited to product and services. When establishing interactive Learning Relationships with valuable customers, customer-strategy enterprises remember a customer's specific needs for the basic product, but also the goods, services, and communications that surround the product, such as how the customer would prefer to be invoiced or how the product should be packaged. Even an enterprise that sells a commodity-like product or service can think of it as a bundle of ancillary services, delivery times, invoicing schedules, personalized reminders and updates, and other features that are rarely commodities. The key is for the enterprise to focus on customizing to each individual customer's needs.

When a customer teaches an enterprise what he wants or how he wants it, the customer and the enterprise are, in essence, *collaborating* on the sale of the product. The more the customer teaches the enterprise, the less likely the customer will want to leave. The key is to design products, services, and communications that customers *value*, and on which a customer and a marketer will have to collaborate for the customer to receive the product, service, or benefit.

> Enterprises that build Learning Relationships clear a wider path to customer profitability than companies that focus on price–driven transactions.

Enterprises that build Learning Relationships clear a wider path to customer profitability than companies that focus on price-driven transactions. They move from a "make to forecast" business model to a "make to order" model, as Dell Computer did when it created a company that reduced inventory levels by creating each computer *after* it was paid for. By focusing on gathering information about individual customers and using that information to customize communications, products, and services, enterprises can more accurately predict inventory and production levels. Fewer orders may be lost because mass customization can build the products on demand, and thus make products that cannot be stocked ad infinitum available to a given customer. (We will discuss customization further in Chapter 10.) Inventoryless distribution from a build-to-order business model can

---

[17]B. Joseph Pine II, Don Peppers, and Martha Rogers, PhD, "Do You Want to Keep Your Customers Forever?" in James H. Gilmore, and B. Joseph Pine II, eds., *Markets of One: Creating Customer-Unique Value through Mass Customization* (New York: Harvard Business School Publishing, 2000).

prevent shortages caused in distribution channels, as well as reduce inventory carrying costs. The result is fewer "opportunity" losses. Furthermore, efficient mass customization operations can ship built-to-order custom products faster than competitors that have to customize products.[18]

Learning Relationships have less to do with creating a fondness on the part of a customer for a particular product or brand, and more to do with a company's capability to remember and deliver based on prior interactions with a customer. An enterprise that engages in a Learning Relationship creates a *bond of value* for the customer, a reason for an individual customer to want never to deal with a competitor again, provided that the enterprise continues to deliver a product and service quality at a fair price and to remember and act on the customer's preferences and tastes.[19] Learning Relationships may also be based on an inherent trust between a customer and an enterprise. For example, a customer might divulge his credit card number to an organization, which records it and remembers it for future transactions. The customer trusts that the enterprise will keep his credit card number confidential. The enterprise makes it easier and faster for him to buy from it because he no longer has to repeat his credit card number each time he makes a purchase. (In the next chapter, we'll learn more about the link between attitude and behavior in relationships.)

> Learning Relationships have less to do with creating a fondness on the part of a customer for a particular product or brand, and more to do with a company's capability to remember and deliver based on prior interactions with a customer.

THE TECHNOLOGY REVOLUTION AND THE CUSTOMER REVOLUTION

During the last century, as enterprises sought to acquire as many customers as they possibly could, the local proprietor's influence over customer purchases decreased. Store owners or managers became little more than order takers, stocking their shelves with the goods that consumers would see advertised in the local newspaper or on television and radio. Mass-media advertising became a more effective way to publicize a product and generate transactions for a wide audience. But, now, technology has made it possible, and therefore competitively necessary, for enterprises to behave, once again, like small-town proprietors, and deal with their customers individually, one customer at a time.

CUSTOMERS HAVE CHANGED, TOO

The technological revolution has spawned another revolution, one led by the customers themselves, who now demand products just the way they want them,

---

[18]David M. Anderson, *Agile Product Development for Mass Customization* (New York: McGraw Hill Professional Book Group, 1997).

[19]B. Joseph Pine II, Don Peppers, and Martha Rogers, PhD, "Do You Want to Keep Your Customers Forever?" *Harvard Business Review* (March–April 1995), pp. 103–114.

SIDEBAR 1.3

Initial Assessment: Where Is a Firm on the Customer Strategy Map?

Recognizing that two families of technology have mandated the competitive approach of building customer value by building customer relationships, we can map any organization—large or small, public or private, profit or nonprofit—by the level of its capabilities in the arenas of *interacting* with customers and *tailoring* for them. A company would be rated high on the interactivity dimension if it knows the names of its individual customers, if it can send different messages to different customers, and can remember the feedback from each one. A low rating would go to a company that doesn't know its customers' identities, or does but continues to send the same message the same way to everybody. On the tailoring dimension, a firm would rate highly if it mass-customizes in lot sizes of one; it would rate low if it sells the same thing pretty much the same way to everybody. Based on its rating in these two dimensions, a company can be pinpointed on the Enterprise Strategy Map (see Exhibit A)

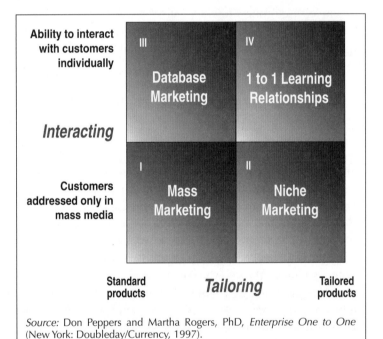

Source: Don Peppers and Martha Rogers, PhD, *Enterprise One to One* (New York: Doubleday/Currency, 1997).

EXHIBIT A **Enterprise Strategy Map**

Quadrant I: Traditional Mass Marketing. Companies that compete primarily on cost efficiencies based on economies of scale and low price. Companies in this quadrant are doomed to commoditization and price competition.

Quadrant II: Niche Marketing. Companies that focus on target markets, or niches, and produce goods and services designed for those defined customer groups. This more strategic and targeted method of mass marketing still offers the same thing the same way to everyone, but in a small, relatively homogeneous group.

SIDEBAR 1.3 *(continued)*

....

Quadrant III: Database Marketing. Companies utilize database management to get better, more efficient use of their mailing lists and other customer information. Generally focused primarily on continuation of traditional strategies, but at lower costs to serve.

Quadrant IV: One-to-one Learning Relationships. Companies use data about customers to predict what each one needs next, and then is able to *treat different customers differently,* and increase mutual value with the customer.

In Quadrants I through III, the focus is still primarily on the product to be sold, with an eye to finding customers for that product. In Quadrant IV, the *direction* of the strategy changes; the Quadrant IV company will focus on a customer and find products for that customer. To realize the highest possible return on the customer base, the goal of an enterprise will be to move *up* and *to the right* on the Enterprise Strategy Map.

- To move *up* on the Enterprise Strategy Map, an enterprise has to be able to recognize individual customers' names and addresses, to be able to send different messages to different customers, and to remember the responses of each.

- To move to the *right* on the Enterprise Strategy Map, an enterprise has to be able to increase its production and logistics flexibility. The most flexible production would entail customizing and delivering individual products for individual customers. The least flexible would be mass-producing a standardized product or service for a large market. (We'll talk more about customization in Chapter 10.)

---

and flawless customer service. Enterprises are realizing that they really know little or nothing about their individual customers and so are mobilizing to capture a clearer understanding of each customer's needs. Customers, meanwhile, want to be treated less like numbers and more like the individuals they are, with distinct, individual requirements and preferences. They are actively communicating these demands back to the enterprise. Where they would once bargain with a business, they now tell managers of brand retail chains what they are prepared to pay, and specify how they want products designed, styled, assembled, delivered, and maintained. When it comes to ordering, consumers want to be treated with respect. The capability of an enterprise to remember customers and their logistical information not only makes ordering easier for the customers, but also lets them know that they are important. Computer applications that enable options such as "one-click," or express, ordering on the Web are creating the expectation that good online providers take the time to get to know customers as individuals so they can provide this higher level of service.[20]

The customer revolution is part of the reason enterprises are committing themselves to keep and grow their most valuable customers. Today's consumers and businesses have become more sophisticated about shopping for their needs across multiple channels. The online channel, in particular, enables shoppers to

---

[20]Peppers and Rogers Group, and Institute for the Future, "Shopping Behavior in the Age of Interactivity," Focus Group Summary (Spring 2000), pp. 12–13, available at: *www.1to1.com.*

locate the goods and services they desire quickly and at a price they are willing to pay, which forces enterprises to compete on value propositions other than lowest price. Chapter 15, " Store of the Future and the Evolution of Retailing," discusses how enterprises are selling goods and services directly to customers and establishing more effective Learning Relationships in the process.

CUSTOMER RETENTION AND ENTERPRISE PROFITABILITY

Enterprises strive to increase profitability without losing high-margin customers, by increasing their customer retention rates or the percentage of customers who have met a specified number of repurchases over a finite period of time. A retained customer, however, is not necessarily a loyal customer. The customer may give business to a competing enterprise for many different reasons.

SIDEBAR 1.4
Royal Bank of Canada's 9 Million Loyal Customers

Organizations have accelerated their customer-focused strategies during the last few years, but managing customer relationships has been a business discipline for many years. Before the Industrial Revolution, and before mass production was born, merchants established their businesses around *keeping* customers. Small towns typically had a general store, a local bank, and a barbershop. Each proprietor met and knew each one of his customers individually. The bank teller, for example, knew that Mr. Johnson cashed his paycheck each Friday afternoon. When Mr. Johnson came into the bank, the bank teller already had his cash ready for him in twenties and tens, just as he liked it. If Mr. Johnson unexpectedly stopped cashing his paycheck at the bank, the teller would wonder what had happened to him. In short, the bank depended on the relationship with the individual customer and how much the people who worked for the bank knew about that customer. The teller's memory in this example is akin to today's data warehouses, which can store millions of data points, transaction histories, and characteristics about customers. Personal memory enabled the teller to fulfill each customer's individual banking needs and, ultimately, to build a profitable relationship with each one. The more the teller knew about a customer, the more convenient he could make banking for that customer—and the more likely the customer would continue to use the bank.

But here's the important question a hundred years later: Can an international financial services enterprise with 9 million customers ever hope to deliver the same intimate customer service as a small-town bank? Absolutely, says Shauneen Bruder, senior vice president of marketing and planning at Royal Bank of Canada (RBC).

RBC developed superior computing and database power, along with sophisticated statistical programs, to analyze customer information and test specific actions it should take with specific customers. Only then could the bank's front-line personnel be able to deliver more effective personal contact and attention to individual customers.

To learn the most about its customers, RBC has undertaken an intense, ongoing statistical analysis of them. It is developing and refining the prototype for an algorithm to model the long-term lifetime values of its individual customers. Part of this

> **SIDEBAR 1.4 *(continued)***
>
> effort includes a "client potential" model that measures how "growable" certain kinds of customers are to the bank. The bank also analyzes a customer's vulnerability to attrition and tries to flag the most vulnerable before they defect, in order to take preventive action in a focused, effective way.
>
> To expand share of customer, Royal Bank also tries to predict statistically which additional services a customer might want to buy, and when. Royal Bank not only makes different offers to different customers, it also equips its sales and service people with detailed customer profiles. Thus, rather than providing a one-size-fits-all service, the bank's customer-contact people spend their time and energy making on-the-spot decisions based on each customer's individual situation and value. Note that this type of business practice not only benefits from individual customer interactions, it *requires* individual interactions to achieve the greatest success. In fact, Bruder says the bank discovered it "could lift contributions and penetration rates by up to 10 percent by virtue of the contact alone."[a]
>
> [a]Martha Rogers, PhD, "Royal Bank's 9 Million Loyal Customers," *Inside 1to1* (September 1999). Available at: *www.1to1.com*.

In 1990, Fred Reichheld and W. Earl Sasser analyzed the profit per customer in different service areas, categorized by the number of years that a customer had been with a particular enterprise.[21] They discovered that the longer a customer remains with an enterprise the more profitable he becomes. Average profits from a first-year customer for the credit card industry was $30; for industrial laundry, $144; for industrial distribution, $45; and for automobile servicing, $25.

Four factors contributed to the underlying profit growth:

1. *Profit derived from increased purchases.* Customers grow larger over time and need to purchase in greater quantities.
2. *Profit from reduced operating costs.* As customers become more experienced, they make fewer demands on the supplier and fewer mistakes when involved in the operational processes, thus contributing to greater productivity for the seller and for themselves.
3. *Profit from referrals to other customers.* Less needs to be spent on advertising and promotion due to word-of-mouth recommendations from satisfied customers.
4. *Profit from price premium.* New customers can benefit from introductory promotional discounts, while long-term customers are more likely to pay regular prices.

No matter what the industry, the longer an enterprise keeps a customer, the more money it can make. Reichheld and Sasser found that for one auto service company, the expected profit from a fourth-year customer is more than triple the

---

[21]Frederick F. Reichheld and W. Earl Sasser, Jr., "Zero Defections: Quality Comes to Services," *Harvard Business Review* 73 (September–October 1990), pp. 59–75.

INDUSTRY	YEAR 1	YEAR 2	YEAR 3	YEAR 4	YEAR 5
Credit Card	$30	$42	$44	$49	$55
Industrial Laundry	$144	$166	$192	$222	$256
Industrial Distribution	$45	$99	$123	$144	$168
Auto Servicing	$25	$35	$70	$88	$88

Source: Frederick F. Reichheld and W. Earl Sasser, Jr., "Zero Defections: Quality Comes to Services," *Harvard Business Review* (September–October 1990).

EXHIBIT 1.4   Profit One Customer Generates over Time

profit that same customer generates in the first year. Other industries studied showed similar positive results (see Exhibit 1.4).

> No matter what the industry, the longer an enterprise keeps a customer, the more money it can make.

Enterprises that build stronger individual customer relationships enhance customer loyalty, as they are providing each customer with what he needs.[22] Loyalty building requires the enterprise to emphasize the value of its products or services and to show that it is interested in building a relationship with the customer.[23] The enterprise realizes that it must build a stable customer base rather than concentrate on single sales.[24]

A customer-strategy firm will want to reduce customer defections because they result in the loss of investments the firm has made in creating and developing customer relationships. Customers are the lifeblood of any business. Loyal customers are more profitable because they buy more over time if they are satisfied. It costs less for the enterprise to serve the retained customer over time because transactions with the repeat customer become more routine. Loyal customers tend to refer other new customers to the enterprise, thereby creating new sources of revenue.[25] It stands to reason that if the central goal of a customer-strategy company is to increase the overall value of its customer base, then continuing its relationships with its most profitable customers will be high on the list of priorities.

On average, U.S. corporations tend to lose half their customers in five years, half their employees in four, and half their investors in less than one.[26] Fred

---

[22]Authors' note: Garbarino and Johnson disagree. See Ellen Garbarino and Mark Johnson, "The Different Roles of Satisfaction, Trust, and Commitment in Customer Relationships," *Journal of Marketing* 63 (April 1999), pp. 70–87.

[23]Jill Griffin, *Customer Loyalty: How to Earn It, How to Keep It* (San Francisco: Jossey-Bass, 1997).

[24]See Werner Reinartz and V. Kumar, "The Mismanagement of Customer Loyalty," *Harvard Business Review* (July 2002), pp. 86–94, for a different view of the value of loyalty. Reinartz and Kumar's work shows that more loyal customers are not necessarily more profitable as a class, especially using their methodology of one moment in time; but we should also point out that in the case of an individual customer, the more loyalty and the greater share of customer achieved from one customer *over time*, the more valuable by definition that individual customer will become.

[25]Phillip Kotler, *Kotler on Marketing* (New York: Free Press, 1999).

[26]Fred Reichheld, "Learning from Customer Defections," *Harvard Business Review* (March–April 1996), pp. 87–88.

Reichheld describes a possible future in which the only business relationships will be one-time, opportunistic transactions between virtual strangers.[27] However, he found that disloyalty could stunt corporate performance by 25 to 50 percent, sometimes more. In contrast, enterprises that concentrate on finding

---

SIDEBAR 1.5

CRM ROI in Financial Services

Managing individual customer relationships has a profound effect on enhancing long-term customer loyalty, thereby increasing the enterprise's long-term profitability. Relationship strategies, for example, have a substantial effect on customer retention in the financial services sector. A study conducted in 2000 by Peppers and Rogers Group (with Roper Starch Worldwide) found that only 1 percent of consumers who rate their financial services provider high on relationship management say they are likely to switch away products. One-fourth of consumers (26 percent) who rate their primary financial services provider as low on relationship management attributes say they are likely to switch away one or more products during the next 12 months. The financial implications of these findings are staggering (see Exhibit A). Using a conservative average annual profitability per household for U.S. retail banks of $100, a reduction in attrition of 9 percent represents over $700 million in incremental profits for all U.S. households with accounts. If an individual financial institution with 20,000 customers can reduce attrition by 9 percentage points by providing excellent customer relationship management (e.g., recognizing returning customers, anticipating their needs, etc.), that institution can increase profits by $180,000. For a similar-sized financial institution with an average household profitability of $500, the increase in profitability climbs to $900,000.

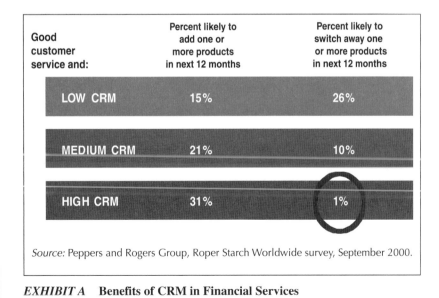

Good customer service and:	Percent likely to add one or more products in next 12 months	Percent likely to switch away one or more products in next 12 months
LOW CRM	15%	26%
MEDIUM CRM	21%	10%
HIGH CRM	31%	1%

Source: Peppers and Rogers Group, Roper Starch Worldwide survey, September 2000.

EXHIBIT A **Benefits of CRM in Financial Services**

---

[27]Fred Reichheld, *The Loyalty Effect* (Boston, MA: Harvard Business School Press, 1996).

and keeping good customers, productive employees, and supportive investors continue to generate superior results. For this reason, the primary responsibility for customer retention or defection lies in the CEO's office. (See Fred Reichheld's section on managing for loyalty, "Loyalty-Based Management," in Chapter 13.)

Customer loyalty is closely associated with customer relationships and may, in certain cases, be directly related to the level of each customer's satisfaction, over time. According to James Barnes, satisfaction is tied to what the customer gets from dealing with a company as compared with what he has to commit to those dealings or interactions.[28] You'll read more about Dr. Barnes's views on satisfaction and relationships in the next chapter. For now, it's enough to know that the customer satisfaction issue is controversial—maybe even problematic. There are issues of relativity (Are laptop users just harder to satisfy than desktop users, or are they really less satisfied?) and skew (Is the satisfaction score the result of a bunch of people who are more or less satisfied, or a bimodal group whose members either love or hate the product?). Barnes believes that by increasing the value that the customer perceives in each interaction with the company, enterprises are more likely to increase customer satisfaction levels, leading to higher customer retention rates. When customers are retained because they enjoy the service they are receiving, they are more likely to become loyal customers. This loyalty leads to repeat buying and increased share of customer. (We will discuss more about the differences between attitudinal loyalty and behavioral loyalty, as well as ways to measure loyalty and retention, in the next chapter.)

Retaining customers is more beneficial to the enterprise for another reason: Acquiring new customers is costly. Many Internet start-up companies, without any brand-name recognition, faced an early demise largely because they could not recoup the costs associated with acquiring new customers. The typical Internet "pure-play" spent an average of $82 to acquire one customer in 1999, a 95 percent increase over the $42 spent on average in 1998.[29] Much of that increase can be attributed to the dot-com companies' struggle to build brand awareness during 1999, which caused Web-based firms to increase offline advertising spending by an astounding 518 percent. Based on marketing costs related to their online business, in 1999 offline-based companies spent an average of $12 to acquire a new customer, down from $22 the previous year. Online firms spent an unsustainable 119 percent of their revenues on marketing in 1999. Even with the advantages of established brands, offline companies spent a still-high 36 percent.

The problem is simple arithmetic. Given the high cost of customer acquisition, a company can never realize any potential profit from most customers, especially if a customer leaves the franchise (see Exhibit 1.5). High levels of

---

[28]James G. Barnes, *Secrets of Customer Relationship Management* (New York: McGraw-Hill, 2001).

[29]Boston Consulting Group and Shop.org, "The State of Online Retailing" (April 2000), available at: *www.shop.org*.

	MCKINSEY & CO.	BOSTON CONSULTING GROUP
Internet-only retailers	$95	$82
All online retailers		$32
Store-based		$31
Catalog-based		$11
Multichannel	$15 to $30	

Sources: McKinsey & Co., 2000; Boston Consulting Group, "The State of Online Retailing," 2000.

EXHIBIT 1.5 **Customer Acquisition Costs (2000)**

customer churn trouble all types of enterprises, not just those in the online and wireless industries. The problem partly results from the way companies reward sales representatives: with scalable commissions and bonuses for acquiring the most number of customers. (We'll talk more about salaries and compensation in Chapters 11, 12, and 13.) Fact is, many reps have little, if any, incentive for keeping and growing an established customer. In some cases, if a customer leaves, the sales representative can even be rewarded for bringing the customer back again! Although it's always somebody's designated mission to get new customers, at most companies, nobody has responsibility for making sure this or that particular customer sticks around or becomes profitable. Often, a service company with high levels of churn needs to rethink not only how its reps engage in customer relationships but how they are rewarded (or not) for nurturing those relationships, and for increasing the long-term value to the enterprise of particular customers.

> The problem is simple arithmetic. Given the high cost of customer acquisition, a company can never realize any potential profit from most customers, especially if a customer leaves the franchise.

Throughout this book, we will see that becoming a customer-value enterprise is difficult. It is a strategy that can never be handled by one particular department within the enterprise. Managing customer relationships is an ongoing process, one that requires the support and involvement of every functional area in the organization, from the upper echelons of management through production and finance to each sales representative or contact center operator.

Indeed, customer-driven competition requires enterprises to integrate five principal business functions into their overall customer strategy:

1. *Financial custodianship of the customer base.* The customer-strategy enterprise treats the customer base as its primary *asset* and carefully manages the investment it makes in this asset.
2. *Production, logistics, and service delivery.* Enterprises must be capable of customizing their offerings to the needs and preferences of each individual customer. The Learning Relationship with a customer is useful only to the extent that interaction from the customer is actually incorporated in the way the enterprise behaves toward the customer.

3. *Marketing communications, customer service, and interaction.* Marketing communications and all forms of customer interaction need to be combined into a unified function to ensure seamless individual customer dialogue.

4. *Sales distribution and channel management.* A difficult challenge is to transform a distribution system that was created to disseminate standardized products at uniform prices into one that delivers customized products at individualized prices. Disintermediation of the distribution network is sometimes one solution to selling to individual customers.

5. *Organizational management strategy.* Enterprises must organize themselves internally by placing managers in charge of customers and customer relationships, rather than just products and programs.[30]

A customer-strategy enterprise seeks to create one centralized view of each customer across all business units. Every employee who interacts with a customer has to have real-time access to current information about that individual customer so that it is possible to pick up each conversation from where the last one left off. The goal is instant interactivity with the customer. This process can be achieved only through the complete and seamless integration of every enterprise business unit and process.

SUMMARY

A customer-strategy enterprise seeks to identify what creates value for each customer and then to deliver that value to him. As other chapters in this book will demonstrate, a customer-value business strategy is a highly measurable process that can increase enterprise profitability. We'll also show that the foundation for growing a profitable customer-strategy enterprise lies in establishing stronger relationships with individual customers. Enterprises that foster relationships with individual customers pave a path to profitability. The challenge is to understand how to establish these critical relationships and how to optimize them for profits. Learning Relationships provide the framework for understanding how to build customer value.

Increasing the value of the customer base by focusing on customers individually and treating different customers differently will benefit the enterprise in many ways. But before we can delve into the intricacies of the business strategies behind this objective, and before we can review the CRM analytical tools and techniques required to carry out this strategy, we need to establish a foundation of knowledge with respect to how enterprises have developed relationships with customers over the years. That is our goal for the next chapter.

---

[30]Don Peppers and Martha Rogers, PhD, *Enterprise One to One* (New York: Doubleday Broadway Books, 1997).

FOOD FOR THOUGHT

1. Understanding customers is not a new idea. Mass marketers have done it for years. But because they see everyone in a market as being alike—or at least everyone in a niche or a segment as being alike—they "understand" Customer A by asking 1,200 (or so) total strangers in a sample group from A's segment a few questions, then extrapolating the average results to the rest of the segment, including A. This is logical if all customers in a group are viewed as homogeneous. What will a company likely do differently in terms of understanding customers if it is able to see one customer at a time, remember what each tells it, and treat different customers differently?

2. If retention is so much more profitable than acquisition, why have companies persisted for so long in spending more on getting new customers than keeping the ones they have?

3. How can we account for the upheaval in orientation from focusing on product profitability to focusing on customer profitability? If it's such a good idea, why didn't companies operate from the perspective of building customer value 50 years ago?

4. In the age of information (and interactivity), what will happen to the four Ps, traditional advertising, and branding?

5. "The new interactive technologies are not enough to cement a relationship, because companies need to change their *behavior* toward a customer and not just their *communication*." Explain what this statement means. Do you agree or disagree?

GLOSSARY

Analytical CRM   What a firm has to know about a customer to make him more valuable.

Customer equity   *See* relationship equity.

Customer relationship management (CRM)   Making managerial decisions with the end goal of increasing the value of the customer base through better relationships with customers, usually on an individual basis.

Customer-strategy enterprise   An organization that builds its business model around increasing the value of the customer base. This applies to companies that may be either product-oriented, operations-focused, or customer-intimate.

Demand chain   As contrasted with the supply chain, refers to the demand from customers.

Enterprise data warehousing   A process that captures, stores, and analyzes a single view of enterprise data to gain business insight for improved decision making.

Enterprise resource planning (ERP)   The automation of a company's back-office management.

Interactive era   The current period in business and technological history, characterized by a dominance of interactive media, rather than the one-way mass media more typical from 1910 to 1995. Also refers to a growing trend for businesses to encourage feedback from individual customers, rather than relying solely on one-way messages directed at customers.

Multiple channel   An organization that sells through more than one distribution channel (e.g., the Web, a toll-free number, mail-order catalogue). Can also refer to firms that interact with customers through more than one channel of communication (e.g., the Web, e-mail, fax, direct mail, phone).

Operational CRM   What a firm has to do to make customers more valuable.

Recognition   The ability to recognize an individual customer *as that customer* through any shopping or buying channel, within any product purchase category, across locations or geographies, and over time. These individual data points are linked for a universally recognized, or *identified*, customer.

Relationship equity   The value to the firm of building a relationship with a customer, or the sum of the value of all current and future relationships with current and potential customers.

Sales force automation (SFA)   Connecting the sales force to headquarters and to each other through computer portability, contact management, ordering software, and other mechanisms.

Share of customer (SOC)   Each customer buys a certain amount of goods or services in various categories. If you are a vendor in one of those categories— say, cars—then the share of customer you have with any one customer is the percentage of that customer's business you get in that category. If a family owns four cars, and two of them are your brands, then you have a 50 percent share-of-garage for cars. But you may also be interested in your SOC for service and repairs, and your share-of-wallet for your automotive credit card.

Switching cost   The cost, in time, effort, or money, to a business customer or end-user consumer of switching to a firm's competitor.

The Thinking behind
Customer Relationships

2

Chapter

So far, our discussion of CRM has shown how businesses are undergoing a vast cultural shift—transforming from the mass-marketing, product-siloed thinking of the Industrial Age to the customer-based culture of the Information Age, where the primary goal is building relationships with individual customers who become measurably more valuable to the enterprise. In this new business era, managing individual customer relationships means an organization will use the knowledge gained from these relationships to improve the quality of the overall customer experience. Consequently, it is incumbent on the enterprise to understand what constitutes a relationship, how relationships are formed, and how they can be strengthened or weakened. Many different perspectives have been developed about what comprises customer relationships and how businesses can profit from them. So before we can move forward with our discussion of becoming a customer-focused enterprise, we need to explore a couple of views besides our own about relationships.

What exactly *is* a relationship, anyway? Webster's defines the term, among other things, as "a state of affairs existing between those having relations or dealings."[1] And dictionary.com defines it as "a state involving mutual dealings between people or parties."

WHAT CHARACTERIZES A RELATIONSHIP?

Because we are talking about relationships between businesses and their customers, it is important that we agree on a few of the elements that make up a genuine relationship. And while dictionary definitions are not bad as starting points, the most important issue for us to consider is how well our own definition of *relationship* helps companies succeed in the "customer dimension" of

[1]*Merriam Webster's Collegiate Dictionary*, Tenth Edition, 1997.

competition. So, rather than settle for a few words from a dictionary, let's list some of the distinct qualities that should characterize a relationship between an enterprise and a customer.

First, a relationship implies **mutuality**. In order for any "state of affairs" to be considered a relationship, both parties have to participate in and be aware of the existence of the relationship. This means that relationships must inherently be two-way in nature. This might seem like common sense. You can't have a relationship with another person if she doesn't have a relationship with you, right? But it's a very important distinction for parsing out what does and doesn't constitute relationship-building activities with customers. Can a person have a genuine relationship with a brand? Yes, but it doesn't happen just because the customer herself likes the brand and buys it repeatedly. A customer can have a great deal of *affection* for a brand all by herself but, by our definition, a *relationship* between the customer and the brand can only be said to exist if the brand (i.e., the enterprise behind the brand) is also aware of the individual customer's existence, creating a neodefinition of an interesting new twist for the term *brand awareness*.

SIDEBAR 2.1

Continuing Roles for Mass Media and Branding

....

- Communicate to nonusers who have not yet raised their hands.
- Build image and brand identity.
- Establish a brand position with nonusers to help users make a statement about their own image.

Second, relationships are driven by *interaction*. When two parties interact, they exchange information, and this information exchange is a central engine for building on the relationship. This, of course, also implies mutuality. But interactions don't have to take place by phone or in person or on the Web. An interaction takes place when a customer buys a product from the company that sells it. Every interaction adds to the total information content possible in the relationship.

This leads to the third characteristic of a relationship: It is **iterative** in nature. That is, since both parties are interacting mutually, the interactions themselves build up a history, over time—a context. This context gives a relationship's future interactions greater and greater efficiency, because every successive interaction represents an iteration on all the previous ones that have gone before it. The more you communicate with any one person, the less you need to say the next time around to get your point across. One practical implication of the iterative nature of a customer relationship is that it generates a convenience benefit to the customer for continuing the relationship. Amazon.com remembers your book preferences, your address, and your credit card number, based on your previous interactions with it. To purchase your next book from Amazon.com, you need only find the book and click on it. If you've bought enough books already at Amazon.com, you might not even need to find the next one—it can do a pretty good job of finding it for you. The richer the context of any customer relationship, the more difficult it will be for the customer to re-create it elsewhere, and so the more loyal the customer is likely to be.

Another characteristic of a customer relationship is that it will be driven by an *ongoing benefit* to both parties. The customer's convenience is one type of benefit, for the customer, but not the only one. Participating in a relationship will involve a cost in money, time, or effort, and no customer will engage for long in any relationship if there is not enough continuing benefit to offset this cost. However, precisely because of the context of the relationship and its continuing benefit to both parties, each party in a relationship has an incentive to recover from mistakes. This is because the future value that each party expects from the continued relationship can easily outweigh the current cost of remedying an error or problem.

Relationships also require a *change in behavior* on the part of both parties— the enterprise as well as the customer—in order to continue. After all, what drives the ongoing benefit of a relationship is not only its context—its history of interactions, developed over time—but also the fact that each party's current and future actions appropriately reflect that historical context. This is an important characteristic to note separately, because companies sometimes mistakenly believe that interactions with a customer need only involve routine, outbound communications, delivered the same way to every customer. But unless the enterprise's actions toward a particular customer are somehow tailored to reflect the customer's own input, there will be no ongoing benefit for the customer, and as a result the customer might not elect to continue the relationship.

Yet another characteristic of a relationship, so obvious it might not seem worth mentioning, is *uniqueness*. Every relationship is different. Relationships are constituted with individuals, not with populations. As a result, an enterprise that seeks to engage its customers in relationships must be prepared to participate in different interactions, remember different histories, and engage in different behaviors toward different customers.

Finally, the ultimate requirement and product of a successful, continuing relationship is *trust*. Trust is a quality worth a book all by itself, but fundamentally what we are talking about is the common-sense proposition that if a customer develops a relationship with an enterprise, the customer tends more and more to trust the enterprise to act in the customer's own interest. Trust and affection and satisfaction are all related feelings on the part of a customer toward a company with which she has a relationship. They constitute the more emotional elements of a relationship; but for an enterprise to acknowledge and use these elements profitably, it must be able to reconcile its own culture and behavior with the requirement of generating and sustaining the trust of a customer. (More on this issue in Chapters 3 and 9.)

Over a decade ago, Jag Sheth and Atul Parvatiyar predicted that companies are "likely to undertake efforts to institutionalize the relationship with consumers—that is, to create a corporate bonding instead of a bonding between a front-line salesperson and consumer alone.[2]

In the next section, Julie Edell and Josh Rose offer a perspective on relationship that provides an outline of the way relationship theorists have addressed the issue.

THINKING ABOUT RELATIONSHIP THEORY

Julie Edell Britton
Associate professor, Fuqua School of Business, Duke University

Josh Rose
Director of Marketing, TriVirix

Personal and business relationships have many similarities. In a marriage, for example, the two individuals agree to exchange only with one another as long as the balance of trade is favorable to both and greater than what can be derived from the greater market.[3] The benefits of a successful marriage include companionship, intimacy, personal growth, shared finances, and shared household responsibilities, and must be perceived to provide value to both relationship members if it is to continue. Buyer-seller relationships, whether between an enterprise and an individual consumer (B2C) or between enterprises (B2B), are made up of similar components and follow a similar development process. In this section we will review these relationship components in more detail and provide a way of thinking about relationships that will help us explore the ways businesses build relationships with customers.

The process of relationship formation between individuals provides a fitting analogy to the formation process of business relationships between buyers (customers) and sellers (enterprises). Relationships between individuals are typically formed through a systematic, multistage process. While the process might vary, the main building blocks are the same: identification, establishing rapport, information gathering, initial interaction, and intensification of interaction through commitment. For the relationship to succeed, certain elements or guidelines must be followed. For example, proper identification requires a basic understanding of the type of individual one is seeking to meet. Establishing rapport requires adaptation to the other party's interaction style. Information gathering has to be relevant and provide insight into the likes and needs of the other member.

[2]Jagdish N. Sheth and Atul Parvatiyar, "Relationship Marketing in Consumer Markets: Antecedents and Consequences," *Journal of the Academy of Marketing Science* 23, no. 4, p. 265. See also Atul Parvatiyar and Jagdish N. Sheth, eds., *Handbook of Relationship Marketing* (Thousand Oaks, CA: Sage Publications, 1999).

[3]N. Kumar, L. Scheer, and J. Steenkamp, "The Effects of Perceived Interdependence on Dealer Attitudes," *Journal of Marketing Research* (1995).

TYPES OF BUYER-SELLER EXCHANGES

Not all buyer-seller exchanges can be characterized as relationships. Some are merely **transactional**. Many enterprises have only just begun to think about their customers as parties with whom they might want to have a sustained relationship (and vice versa). In organizations focused on the sales of products, each transaction is thought of as a discrete transaction with no correlation to any prior or future transactions. Thus, exchanges can be viewed as existing on a continuum between discrete transactions on one end, and **relational**, or collaborative, exchanges on the other.

The concept of a discrete exchange involves money on the one side, an easily measured commodity on the other, and the complete absence of any relational element. It is characterized by very limited communication and narrow content. In its abstracted form, it is an instantaneous exchange between anonymous parties that will very likely never interact in the future. Economically, the transaction is a zero-sum game. (See the discussion about mass marketers in the previous chapter.) The more one party receives, the less remains for the other party. As an example of a discrete transaction, imagine an out-of-town consumer passing through a town stopping to purchase five gallons of unbranded gasoline for $6.00 paid in cash to an independent station. This transaction is discrete. There have been no previous transactions, no way to know who made this one, and no future ones are anticipated.[4] As the exchange moves to the right in the continuum (see Exhibit 2.1), it has the potential to become more relational. Perhaps a customer traveling across the country repeatedly purchases the same brand of gasoline. To the customer then, these transactions are related. When she buys this brand, she expects that it will provide the same level of performance as the last tank of gasoline provided, even though the price, service, location, and other factors may vary. Whether these transactions are seen as discrete to the gasoline seller or as having a connection depends on whether that seller can relate the transactions over time to this particular customer. If the customer pays for each of these transactions with her gasoline company credit card, then the company has the potential to recognize the connection between the transactions and determine whether she is someone with whom it would like to build a relationship. At this point, the customer is visible as a *customer*, not just a series of discrete, independent transactions.

Relational exchanges transpire over time with each transaction acting as a link in a chain having a history and an anticipated future. In contrast to the situation where there is no relational content in the discrete exchange, participants

Discrete (transactional) ←--------------------------------→ Relational (collaborative)

EXHIBIT 2.1 **Transaction/Relationship Continuum**

[4]F. R. Dwyer, P. Schurr, and Sejo Oh, "Developing Buyer-Seller Relationship," *Journal of Marketing* (April 1987).

in relational exchanges share information and hope to improve on the quality of the exchange for both the customer and the enterprise. This often means that the nature of the deliverable becomes less obvious, necessitating deeper discussion, preplanning, and, most importantly, trust. Especially in uncertain environments, cooperation is required to meet the needs of both parties.

The significance of the difference between the characteristics of exchanges on either end of the continuum lies in the extent to which relational exchanges contribute to product or service differentiation that create incentives to remain in the relationship, thus creating a competitive advantage. As a relationship deepens, it becomes increasingly difficult for either party to see how other parties could provide the same degree of benefit as received by the existing relationship.

An alternative mapping of the realm of buyer-seller relationships is represented by the matrix in Exhibit 2.2. Here, each party's interest in developing the relationship forms a dimension. Some relationships are not symmetric; the two parties view the relationship differently. If a seller has a great deal of interest in developing a relationship, but the buyer does not, we might see repeated attempts by the seller to extract information from the consumer, but the consumer failing to respond. Conversely, when the buyer has a great interest in developing a relationship with the supplier, she might contact the enterprise and provide it feedback about how it could better meet her needs, but the enterprise is uninterested in using that information to customize its offerings to her. Note that the continuum described in Exhibit 2.1 exists along the main diagonal of the Exhibit 2.2 matrix. Purely discrete exchanges exist when neither the buyer nor seller is interested in developing a relationship, while strong relational exchanges exist only when both parties have a great deal of interest.

RELATIONSHIP DEVELOPMENT PROCESS

An understanding of how relationships develop provides insight into how to improve and to maximize the benefits from the relationship. F. R. Dwyer,

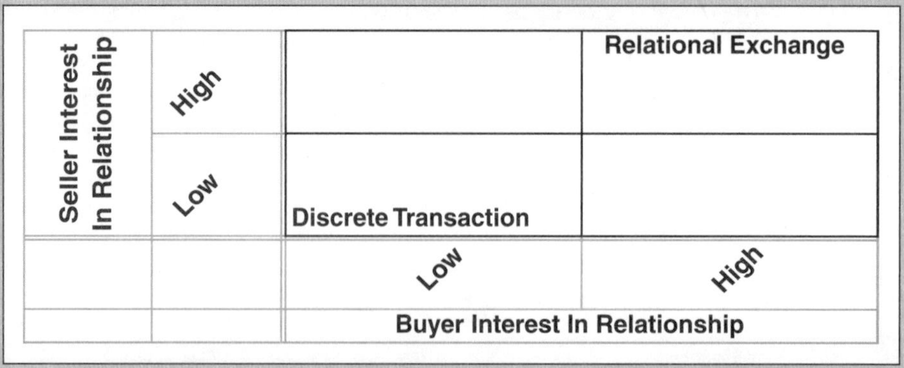

EXHIBIT 2.2   **Relationship Development Process**

P. Shurr and Sejo Oh[5] suggest that business-to-business (B2B) relationships evolve through five general phases:

1. *Awareness.* In this preexchange or transition phase, the parties recognize each other as viable relationship partners. While the parties work to demonstrate their attractiveness via signaling or self-promotion, there is no interaction in this phase.
2. *Exploration.* This phase is a testing period for the relationship. Potential relationship members engage in search-and-trial activities in an effort to determine goal compatibility, integrity, and performance capabilities of the other. Communication takes place and is used to convey wants, issues and priorities. Initial negotiations could signal the willingness of the potential relationship members to be flexible and work toward mutual value creation. The lack of perceived willingness to negotiate could lead to termination of the relationship development process. In similar fashion, participant fairness is also evaluated. Demonstrating commitment to achieving joint goals and fair exercise of power will provide momentum to advance the relationship. It is important to point out that while this phase is an important one, it is also a very fragile one. Minimal commitments or investments by the parties have been made, allowing for easy termination of the building process.
3. *Expansion.* Positive outcomes of the exploratory phase provide evidence of the other relationship member's worthiness, thus the impetus to advance to the expansion phase. This phase is characterized by an increase in the derived relationship benefits and by an increase in interdependence and risk taking. At the same time, participants are testing and reaffirming perceptions developed during the exploration phase.
4. *Commitment.* In this phase, relationship members have achieved a level of value and satisfaction that enables them to comfortably make a commitment to the relationship and, by doing so, significantly lower their focus on alternative relationships. Three measurable criteria denote commitments[6]:
   1. *Inputs.* Both parties provide high level of inputs to the relationship.
   2. *Consistency.* Inputs quality is reliable and allows accurate prediction of future relationship outcomes.
   3. *Durability.* Exchange benefits are identifiable and can be expected to continue in future exchanges.
5. *Dissolution.* Dissolution that leads to relationship disengagement can occur at any stage in the development process. In contrast to relationship development, which requires painstaking bilateral effort, dissolution is easy and can be initiated unilaterally. Dissolution occurs when a participant evaluates the value of the relationship and determines that the cost of continuation outweighs the benefits.

[5]Ibid.

[6]Ibid.

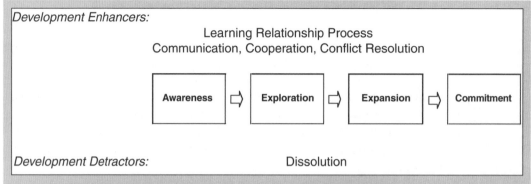

EXHIBIT 2.3   **Learning Relationship Process**

Throughout the relationship development process, there are certain elements that act as enhancing agents. *Communication*, defined as formal or informal sharing of information through two-way interchange, positively acts to strengthen the relationship. Although not specifically required, especially given recent advancements in personalized electronic communication, personal contact can lead to increased commitment and to development of customer trust[7] (the role of trust in buyer-seller relationships is significant and will be described further later in the chapter). *Cooperation*, defined as coordinated actions taken by both relationship members to achieve mutually desirable outcomes, enhances the development process by increasing the communication component, prolonging the exchange, and providing a sense of future reciprocity. While conflicts can have negative impacts on the relationship, effective *conflict resolution* can have a positive influence. Reaching mutually agreeable compromises without the use of formal procedures increases the sense of trust and commitment of the relationship members.

Finally, the Learning Relationship process,[8] in which enterprises and customers engage in a series of interactions that serve as continuous feedback loop, allows each party to learn about the other (needs, preferences, responsiveness) while at the same time learning about themselves. The Learning Relationship process can be employed at every phase of the development process just outlined. Viewing each phase as an opportunity for learning via a feedback loop enables the relationship to develop faster and to a deeper level. Exhibit 2.3 provides a conceptual representation of the ideas put forth in this section.

RELATIONSHIP BUILDING BLOCKS

The previous section provided an overview of the relationship development process. This section provides a more granular perspective by analyzing the six

[7]K. De Ruyter, L. Moorman, and J. Lemmink, "Antecedents of Commitment and Trust in Customer-Supplier Relationships in Technology Markets," *Industrial Marketing Management* 30, no. 3 (2001), pp. 271–286.

[8]Katherine Lemon, Don Peppers, and Martha Rogers, PhD, "Managing the Customer Lifetime: The Role of Learning Relationships," working paper.

most important building blocks, or key mediating variables, that are required for relationships to form. Relational building blocks are not to be confused with relational contingencies (i.e., reasons why relationships form), such as necessity, efficiency, and stability.[9] Rather, the building blocks uniformly influence the resulting nature of the relationship, irrespective of the originating motive.

Exhibit 2.4 provides a representation of the building blocks as they influence relationships. The position of the individual building blocks on the discrete/relational continuum is representative of its relative importance to relationship formation. For example, *trust* is located closest to the relational side since it is more important to the relationship forming process than *symmetry*, which is located closest to the discrete side. The box with the curved bottom side preceding each building block contains the antecedents, or conditions, for the block. The rectangle that follows each block shows the aspects of the relationship it impacts.

Trust

Trust is defined as one party's confidence in the other relationship member's reliability, durability, and integrity, and the belief that its actions are in the best interest of and will produce positive outcomes for the trusting party. As evidenced by the abundance of literature on the importance of trust in the formation of relationships, the presence of trust is central to successful relationships.[10] As an illustration, consider the situation where a consumer pays for a one-year subscription to a magazine. The magazine has not yet been produced, and its content and quality are subjective and unknown at the time of payment. Trust that the service provider will live up to its obligation is what allows the exchange to proceed. (We will discuss more about trust in the Learning Relationship process in Chapter 3). The benefits of a relationship based on trust are significant and are described next:

- *Cooperation.* Trust acts to mitigate feelings of uncertainty and risk, thus acting to engender increased cooperation between relationship members.[11] By increasing the level of cooperation, members learn that joint efforts lead to outcomes that exceed those achieved individually.
- *Commitment.* Also a relationship building block, commitment entails vulnerability, hence will be formed only with trustworthy parties.[12]
- *Relationship duration.* Trust encourages relationship members to work to preserve the relationship and to resist the temptation to take short-term gains and/or act opportunistically. Trust of a seller firm is positively related

[9]C. Oliver, "Determinants of Interorganizational Relationships: Integration and Future Direction," *Academy of Management Review* (1990).

[10]Moorman, Rohit, and Zaltman, "Factors Affecting Trust in Market Research Relations," *Journal of Marketing* (1993), pp. 70.

[11]Morgan and Hunt, "The Commitment Trust Theory of Relationship Marketing," *Journal of Marketing* (1994).

[12]Ibid.

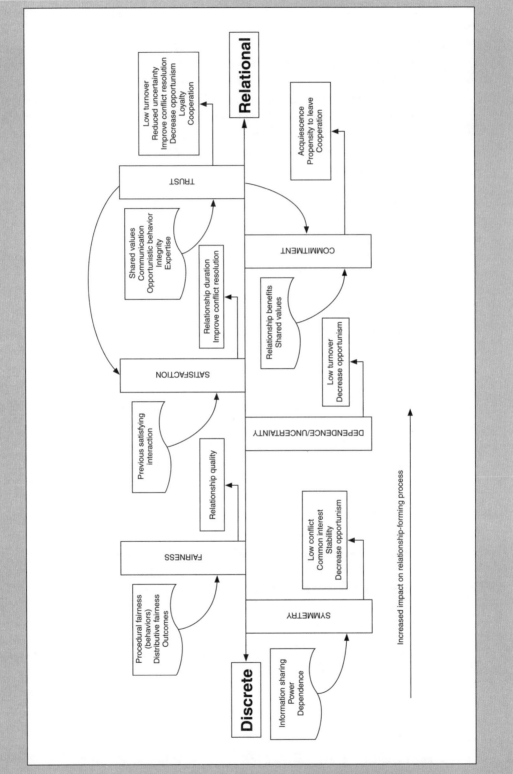

EXHIBIT 2.4   **Relationship-Forming Building Blocks**

to the likelihood that the buyer will engage in future business, therefore contributing to increasing the duration of the relationship.[13]

- *Quality.* Trusting parties are more inclined to receive and use information from a trusted partner, and in turn to derive greater benefit from the information.[14] Finally, the existence of trust allows disputes or conflicts to be resolved in an efficient and amicable way. In the absence of trust, disputes are perceived as signals of future difficulties and usually bring about relationship termination.

Trust is clearly very beneficial and important to those seeking to establish a relationship. However, becoming a trusted party is not easy and requires concerted effort. The following factors are the main contributors to formation of trust:

- *Shared values.* Values are fundamental to the development of trust. The extent to which parties in a relationship share beliefs regarding appropriate behaviors, goals, and policies will influence the ability to develop trust in one another. After all, it would be difficult to trust a party whose ideas about what is important and appropriate are inconsistent with one's own.
- *Interdependence.* Dependence on another party implies vulnerability. To reduce the associated risk, parties will seek out relationships with others who can be trusted.
- *Quality communication.* Open and frequent communication, whether formal or informal, serves to align expectations, resolve disputes, and alleviate uncertainty associated with exchanges. For communication to result in formation of trust, it must be frequent and of high quality; or, in other words, it must be relevant, timely, and reliable. While past positive communication leads to trust, trust—in turn—leads to better communication.
- *Nonopportunistic behavior.* Behaving opportunistically is fundamental to discrete exchanges. After all, there is only one shot at maximizing benefits. However, long-term relationships based on trust require that participating parties are not solely self-serving and that they act to increase shared long-term benefits. This is related to a relationship member's credibility and integrity, which are imperative for trust to evolve.

Commitment

A second building block in the relationship formation process is commitment. Commitment is the belief that the importance of a relationship with another is so significant as to warrant maximum effort at maintaining it. Like trust, commitment is viewed as extremely important in the formation of customer relationships. Morgan and Hunt stated that, "The presence of relationship commitment

[13]Doney and Cannon, "An Examination of the Nature of Trust in Buyer-Seller Relationships," *Journal of Marketing* (1997).

[14]Moorman, Rohit, and Zaltman, "Factors Affecting Trust in Market Research Relations, *Journal of Marketing* (1993).

and relationship trust is central to successful relationship marketing . . . Commitment and trust lead directly to cooperative behaviors that are conductive to relationship marketing success."[15]

Generally, there are two different types of commitment: *calculative* and *affective. Calculative commitment* results from an economic analysis of the costs and benefits of making a commitment. For example, the decision to commit resources to an enterprise to develop a new technology might result from the lack of other potential relationship members in the market, or from the inability to obtain the necessary services/products at a lower price outside the relationship. Calculative commitment is related negatively to trust and is based on calculated cost and benefits. It is thus not conducive to a long-term successful relationship. In contrast, *affective commitment* is based on continuing the relationship not just because of its short-term economic benefits, but because each of the parties feels an emotional or psychological attachment toward the other relationship member. Affective commitment is positively related to trust and thus supports relationship benefits much longer in duration, decreased opportunism, and the willingness to resolve conflicts in a way that is amicable to both parties.

Because commitment entails vulnerability, parties seek relationships with those who are trustworthy. Hence, trust is a strong contributor to commitment. Along similar lines, communication and open exchange of information can be used to create a positive attitude toward relationship members and can be used to reinforce the benefits of the relationship. Relationship members who demonstrate the ability to deliver superior benefits will be highly valued by others who will gladly commit to a relationship. Finally, relationship members who are in a position of power and who don't revert to coercive tactics, even when they can, will be perceived positively, thus increasing the likelihood of long-term commitment to a relationship.

Satisfaction

The third relationship building block is satisfaction. The overall role that customer satisfaction plays in the formation of relationships is intuitive: A dissatisfied customer will generally seek to replace the supplier with an alternative, if it is available. The converse is also intuitive: Satisfied customers are generally more inclined to remain in the relationship. While it is accepted that there exists a positive relationship between customer satisfaction and customer loyalty, the relationship between customer satisfaction and the duration of the relationship is more complex.

As enterprises seek effective ways to have relationships with customers, many have turned to the traditional tool of customer satisfaction monitoring. While customer satisfaction tools have long been used to understand customer perceptions of products and services, they are also now being used to monitor customer

[15]Morgan and Hunt, "The Commitment Trust Theory of Relationship Marketing," *Journal of Marketing* (1994).

relationships. By contacting customers directly by telephone, enterprises can demonstrate to their customers that they are interested in them as customers and value their input. Enterprises strive to uncover the reasons for customer dissatisfaction without alienating or losing customers entirely. Automobile repair services companies, in fact, which call their customers for a customer satisfaction survey, have experienced an increase in repeat business as a result.[16] Many enterprises measure their customer satisfaction index (CSI), surveying customers and asking them to rate the product or service to indicate whether they are "very satisfied" or "very dissatisfied." (Chapters 6 and 11 discuss the differences and similarities between a satisfied customer and a loyal customer.)

The duration of buyer-seller relationship depends on the customer's subjective assessment of the value of a relationship that is continuously updated based on perceptions of previous experiences.[17] Customers tend to weigh prior satisfying experiences more heavily than they do new experiences. While this is consistent with the relationship benefits of trust and commitment identified in the previous section, it has some interesting managerial implications. It suggests that new customers are far more vulnerable to relationship mishaps than customers with longer satisfying relationships. Companies must focus more closely on customer satisfaction during the early stages of the relationship. Mishaps early in the relationship have a higher probability of resulting in a defection than if the same problems occurred after a satisfying relationship had been more firmly established. We might think of this as the basic principle of first impressions.

Customers also weigh negative experiences or losses more heavily than they weigh positive experiences, or gains. Companies attempt to entice customers to stay longer by attempting to improve existing satisfaction levels. This is known as the *satisfaction trap*,[18] in which companies become preoccupied with satisfaction ratings scores at the expense of attention to relationship duration. Focusing on improving the customer experience (i.e., more gains) should not come at the expense of assuring the lack of customer mishaps. In fact, customers with longer satisfying relationships tend to evaluate recent negative encounters against previous levels of satisfaction. Thus, for longer-duration customers, emphasis should be placed on preventing negative encounters.

Uncertainty and Dependence

Two related variables that influence the relationship formation process are the degree of uncertainty in the environment and the degree to which relationship members are dependent upon each other. Dependence as a contingency for

[16]Charles E. Gengler and Peter T.L. Poplowski Leszczyc, "Using Customer Satisfaction Research for Relationship Marketing: A Direct Marketing Approach," *Journal of Direct Marketing* (Winter 1997), pp. 23–29.

[17]Ibid.

[18]Frederick F. Reichheld, *The Loyalty Effect: The Hidden Force Behind Growth, Profit, and Lasting Value* (Boston: Harvard Business School Press, 1996).

Relationships based on uncertainty and/or dependence tend to be less stable as they focus on present existing conditions. Changes in external conditions, availability of resources, and environmental uncertainty could modify the original parameters that once justified the formation of the relationship, such that the resulting relationship no longer provides mutual benefits. In addition, as dependence is not a strategically desirable situation, relationship members will constantly seek relationships that provide them with more favorable positioning. Thus, while dependence plays a role in long–term relationship development, it is not sufficient to maintain the relationship. An element of trust is also required for a dependence–based relationship to have a long–term orientation.

relationship formation is rooted in the scarcity of resources (product, services etc.). Relationships are formed when each relationship member has access to resources essential to the other.[19] By working together, relationship members secure better access to essential resources than working independently. Uncertainty impacts the availability of resources, thus creating the dependence. By forging relationships, parties are better able to gain control over their environment, thereby reducing uncertainty. In B2B relationships, "resources" takes on a broader meaning to include access to markets, creating market entry barriers, and strategic positioning.

Relationships based on uncertainty and/or dependence tend to be less stable as they focus on present existing conditions. Changes in external conditions, availability of resources, and environmental uncertainty could modify the original parameters that once justified the formation of the relationship, such that the resulting relationship no longer provides mutual benefits. In addition, as dependence is not a strategically desirable situation, relationship members will constantly seek relationships that provide them with more favorable positioning. Thus, while dependence plays a role in long–term relationship development, it is not sufficient to maintain the relationship. An element of trust is also required for a dependence-based relationship to have a long-term orientation.[20]

Fairness

The fifth relationship building block is fairness. While relationship quality is a somewhat subjective term, it is plausible to measure relationship quality based on the levels of trust, commitment, and ability to resolve conflicts effectively. The higher the levels of these contributors, the greater the quality of the relationship. High-quality relationships result in lower levels of conflict, greater expected continuity, greater willingness of relationship members to invest in the relationship, and thus lead to more successful long-term relationships. Research has shown that the perception of relationship fairness also enhances relationship quality.[21]

There are two distinct types of relationship fairness: *distributive* and *procedural*. **Distributive fairness** is based on the perception of relationship rewards

---

[19]W. Keep, S. Hollander, and R. Dickinson, "Forces Impinging on Long-Term Business-to-Business Relationships in the United States: An Historical Perspective," *Journal of Marketing* (1998).

[20]S. Ganesan, "Determinants in Long-Term Orientation in Buyer-Seller Relationships," *Journal of Marketing* (1994).

[21]N. Kumar, L. Scheer, and J. Steenkamp, "The Effects of Supplier Fairness on Vulnerable Resellers," *Journal of Marketing Research* (1995).

versus relationship burdens or obligations, and is therefore more focused on relationship outcomes. **Procedural fairness** is based on the perception that procedures and processes used are fair, and is therefore more focused on behaviors, independent of the outcome. Viewed in the context of a relationship, distributive fairness is influenced by a combination of elements that may or may not be under the control of the relationship members. It is entirely possible that a relationship fails, not because of the actions of either the buyer or seller, but rather because of an act of nature, like the birth of a baby, or a job transfer that necessitates a move. In contrast, procedural fairness is influenced largely by elements under the control of the relationship members, such as notifying the buyer if she is on the wrong subscription plan rather than allowing her to continue to pay a higher price than necessary.

Of the two types, procedural fairness has a much stronger effect on the development of trust and commitment and is therefore a stronger contributor to the development of an effective long-term relationship. Focused more on outcomes, distributive fairness tends to be more unstable, as outcomes change. Procedurally fair exchange systems have a more enduring quality and are more likely to constitute the basis for a sustainable relationship. It is especially important that the stronger relationship member develop processes and procedure that other relationship members judge to be fair, in order to sustain the relationship in times of disagreements.

Symmetry

The final relationship building block is symmetry. Relationship symmetry refers to the degree of equality between relationship members. It is a function of many relationship elements, including information sharing, dependence, and power. Symmetric relationships are more stable than asymmetric ones, because asymmetry undermines the balance of power and creates motivation for the stronger party to take advantage of the weaker party, especially in difficult economic conditions.[22] Commonality of interests is strongest when the relationship is symmetric. Symmetry discourages the development and expression of conflict because the relationship members have equivalent stakes in the relationship. In contrast, parties in **asymmetric relationships** are more likely to have diverging interests and greater motivation to engage in conflict, thus are more dysfunctional and less stable.[23]

Asymmetric dependence is a specific type of symmetry. Dependence describes the (lack of) options that one may have to replace the relationship member, or a measure of one party's need to maintain the relationship in order to achieve its goals. Symmetric interdependence exists when the relationship members are equally dependent on each other. As the difference between the relative dependence between the members increases, the relationship becomes

---

[22]E. Anderson and B. Weitx, "Determinants of Continuity in Conventional Industrial Channel Dyads," *Marketing Science* (1989).

[23]Ibid.

more asymmetric and less stable. From the perspective of the less dependent, or stronger member, structural impediments preventing opportunistic behavior are reduced. The more dependent member may feel vulnerable, seek to better her relationship position, and be constantly looking for a more favorable relationship.

To increase relationship quality, relationship members should seek to lower the level of asymmetry and increase the degree of interdependence. Achieving perfect symmetry in a relationship is extremely difficulty and fairly rare. Reducing the degree of asymmetry or modifying the relative dependence of relationship members is a more achievable goal. The more vulnerable member can reduce dependence by developing additional relationships with others. Alternatively, the more vulnerable member can increase dependence by increasing her value to the relationship. Of the two approaches, the more dependent member should seek the latter. Striving for autonomy by seeking alternatives may reduce the level of asymmetry, but it will come at the expense of relationship benefits.[24]

Finally, it should be noted that trust and commitment can develop in asymmetric relationships, if the vulnerable party is treated fairly and with respect.[25] While the more powerful relationship member might be tempted to act unfairly by imposing self-serving procedures, avoiding these behaviors can lead to a more lasting relationship that provides greater benefits.

CRM is powerful in theory but, some say, troubled in practice. Customer satisfaction rates in the United States have fallen over the last few years while complaints, boycotts, and other consumer discontent has risen. Some say there has been a decline in the fundamentals of relationship building among enterprise executives who are more concerned with building quarterly profits than establishing closer ties to profitable customers. Every aspect of CRM is affected by the firm's understanding of relationships. Enterprises must examine and fully comprehend the basic foundations of relationships, in general, and the basic principles of the Learning Relationship, before embarking on a CRM initiative.

Views on relationships and their role in business vary, but all provide a relevant perspective to building a framework for CRM. Jim Barnes says that relationships between enterprises and their customers can exist at four different levels:[26]

1. *Intimate* relationships are characterized as personal and friendly and generally involve the disclosure of personal information. This relationship may involve physical touching, such as the relationship between a doctor and her patient or a hairstylist and her client.

[24]N. Kumar, L. Scheer, and J. Steenkamp, "The Effects of Perceived Interdependence on Dealer Attitudes," *Journal of Marketing Research* (1995).

[25]Ibid.

[26]James G. Barnes, *Secrets of Customer Relationship Management* (New York: McGraw-Hill, 2001).

2. *Face-to-face* customer relationships may or may not require the customer to reveal personal information. Such relationships occur in a retail store.
3. *Distant* relationships involve less frequent interactions and might occur over the telephone, online, or through videoconferencing.
4. *No-contact* relationships rarely or never require a customer to interact with an enterprise directly. Customers typically interact with a distributor or agent, as in the case of buying a favorite brand of soda at a supermarket.

So far, we have discussed the foundation of relationship theory and the benefits of getting, keeping, and growing customers. The discussion has included concepts that foster an often-emotional involvement between the customer and the enterprise. The Learning Relationship is a highly personal experience for the customer. A Learning Relationship ensures that it is always in the customer's self-interest to remain with the enterprise with which she first developed the relationship. We believe this may go beyond emotional attachment and beyond a customer's favoritism for any enterprise. It may or may not be derived from some sense of obligation or duty. Instead, by establishing a Learning Relationship, the customer-focused enterprise increases customer retention by making loyalty more beneficial for the customer than nonloyalty.

Here we present a different view of customer relationships: Jim Barnes believes relationships work only when the customer acknowledges that we are having one.

CRM: THE CUSTOMER'S VIEW

James G. Barnes
Professor of marketing, Memorial University of Newfoundland

To understand customer relationship management, we must first understand its three components; customers, relationships, and their management. I have always believed that a relationship is special. After all, if you were to ask a friend or even a stranger to tell you about her *relationships*, it is most likely that the conversation would center on relationships with family, friends, neighbors, workmates, and team members. Few, I would suspect, would begin by talking about Marriott Hotels, United Airlines, Coke, or Wal-Mart. Relationships are intensely personal concepts. In fact, some people have great difficulty associating the term *relationship* with the commercial interaction between a company and its customers.

If we insist on using the word *relationship* in our modern approach to business building, and in the context of long-term customer loyalty, then I suggest it is critical that enterprises understand what relationships are all about. One of the best perspectives I have encountered of what I believe to be the correct view of customer relationships is that of John Czepiel who wrote that a marketplace-based relationship is "the mutual recognition of some special status between exchange partners."[27] Such a perspective reflects that a relationship can exist between customers and enterprises, customers and brands, and that the customer has to *feel* the existence of the "special status."

When it comes to understanding customers, many managers simply do not. They make the mistake of viewing their company's interaction with its customers through their own eyes rather than the customers' eyes. They believe that certain things are likely to drive satisfaction among customers, when in fact those customers are interested in quite different things. One of the most important lessons that marketers and other managers can learn is that having a great product at a great price is not nearly enough to guarantee customer satisfaction and repeat buying. In fact, I have come to the conclusion, based on 30 years of research with customers, that a large portion of what contributes to long-term satisfaction and loyalty has absolutely nothing to do with products or prices. It has a great deal more to do with how the customer is treated, what she goes through, and ultimately how she feels about dealing with an enterprise.

This is where "understanding the customer" meets "relationships." Most customers are quite receptive to the idea of building relationships with enterprises and brands. If there was any doubt that customers develop relationships with brands, that notion has been put to rest through the work of Susan Fournier, who describes in vivid detail the emotional connection between customers and the brands that they use regularly.[28] Customers do not deliberately set out to create such relationships; the relationships simply evolve. Relationships take time to develop and must be nurtured, but once they develop, customers feel a genuine, long-lasting sense of loyalty to the enterprise or brand. Most customers want to deal with enterprises and use brands they feel they can trust and rely upon— organizations with which they feel comfortable, those that treat them fairly and honestly. Unless enterprises understand how customers develop such relationships and what customers get from them, those firms will not begin to understand how to build them.

Instead, they are likely to fall into the trap of believing that an enterprise can simply decide to have a relationship with a customer, *whether or not that customer wants one*. The result is the mistaken belief that customer relationships can be built or even *imposed* through the creation of customer databases or frequent shopper programs. Or, enterprises think they have a relationship with a customer because they have succeeded in locking the customer into a five-year service contract or a ten-year home mortgage. A European banker recently told me that the objective of his company's customer relationship management program is to "create high levels of customer entanglement."

---

[27]John Czepiel, "Service Encounters and Service Relationships: Implications for Research," *Journal of Business Research* 20 (1990), pp. 13–21.

[28]Susan Fournier, "Consumers and Their Brands: Developing Relationships Theory in Consumer Research," *Journal of Consumer Research* 24 (March 1998), pp. 343–373. [Authors' note: to qualify as such, a *relationship* must be two-way instead of one-way. Therefore, a true relationship with a brand, which doesn't—can't—respond to a customer it is not aware of, is not strictly a relationship, per se. This is really a preference or proclivity, no matter what we call it.]

Such associations between enterprises and their customers are not relationships in the customers' eyes. Do they offer benefits and rewards for the customer, and might they evolve into more genuine relationships over time? Absolutely! But the existence of such programs in and of themselves does not constitute a relationship.

SOCIAL PSYCHOLOGY ROOTS OF RELATIONSHIP THEORY

To understand customer relationships, we should go back to the basics—back to the social psychology origins of interpersonal relationships.[29] There is much to be learned from the research that has been conducted by leading thinkers in social psychology over the past 60 or 70 years. Their conclusions about what contributes to the development and strength of interpersonal relationships are just as valid in allowing us to better understand what customers want in their dealings with businesses and other organizations.

If we are to overcome the simplistic view of relationship building as something that can be imposed on customers, it is essential that managers appreciate that a relationship is an emotional concept. A relationship in its simplest form, and as understood by customers, is based on feelings and emotions. It is not behavioral, although there are behavioral effects of customers developing solid relationships with enterprises. Customers go back there again and again, they spend more money there, and they refer their friends and associates. But the behavior is the outcome of the relationship, not the relationship itself. The behavior results from the creation of the relationship.

There is a tendency within some businesses to mistake behavior for loyalty. Just because customers buy a large percentage of their category purchases from a particular company, or visit or purchase on a regular basis, does not mean that they are loyal or that a relationship exists. It is possible to have a high level of "behavioral loyalty," without having any **emotional loyalty**. Many customers, for example, will buy a large percentage of their groceries from a supermarket that is close to their homes. They shop there every week and may have been doing so for years. When asked why they are "loyal," customers will point to factors such as convenience of location, 24-hour access, large parking lot, short lines at the checkouts, one-stop shopping, and so on. All of these reasons relate to more functional factors that drive repeat buying. These customers are exhibiting **functional loyalty**.

With the functionally loyal, there is a noticeable absence of any sense of attachment to the enterprise; there is no *emotional* connection. If they were to move across town or to a new city, the customers would likely seek out an equally convenient supermarket for the bulk of their grocery shopping. Their

[29]James G. Barnes and Daphne A. Sheaves, "The Fundamentals of Relationships," in Teresa A. Swartz, David E. Bowen, and Stephen W. Brown (eds.), *Advances in Services Marketing and Management,* Vol. 5 (Greenwich, CT: JAI Press, Inc., 1986).

form of loyalty is very vulnerable; there is no relationship from the customers' perspective.

Contrast this with other customers who shop regularly at a particular supermarket, often driving past three or more competing supermarkets to get there. When asked why they shop where they do, they will say it is because they are known there, they feel comfortable shopping there, they have come to know the cashiers, or they go there with friends for coffee. Theirs is an emotional loyalty, a connection between the customers and the enterprise, a lasting bond that is grounded not in functional factors, but in genuine emotions. When these customers move to a new location, they seek out a branch of *their* supermarket. Their loyalty is much less vulnerable.

RELATIONSHIP MANAGEMENT

Which brings us to the notion of relationship "management," the very idea of which many find abhorrent. Successful relationships are bidirectional—both parties win. Relationships that are put in place principally for the benefit of one of the parties are doomed to fail simply because the relationship partner who is the object of the affection will not remain in the relationship unless clear and obvious benefits are seen and felt.

Yet much of what is labeled *customer relationship management* in the modern business world is decidedly one-sided. Enterprises build databases and use CRM analytical techniques to better target mail campaigns so as to optimize the probability of making a sale. Others encourage customers to engage in repeat buying by rewarding them with "points" that are redeemable for "free" merchandise or flights or hotel nights. But what does this really have to do with relationships when a large percentage of customers do not want to receive the direct mail material and when the motivation for being a member of the frequent-shopper program is the accumulation of points so that rewards may be claimed? It is no wonder that some authors have expressed concern that such practices, carried out as they are in the name of relationship building, are actually giving CRM a bad name.

Do database marketing programs succeed in increasing sales? Of course, some of them do. Do frequent-shopper clubs lead to increased share of wallet and repeat buying? Yes, in many cases they do. Do integrated CRM software solutions create a more efficient customer environment that leads to increased customer satisfaction? Again, the answer is often yes. In all of these cases, however, the focus is on the creation of customer relationships as seen from the perspective of the company and as defined by management, not by the customer.

The principal conclusion is that customer interaction does not constitute a genuine relationship unless the customer *acknowledges* that it does. So-called customer relationships that are based upon incentives or rewards or that result from the collection in a database of a great deal of information about the characteristics of customers and their purchasing patterns are not relationships from the customer viewpoint. They are merely attempts to encourage repeat buying

Where a genuine cus-
tomer relationship
exists, there is more than a
functional connection; it is
highly emotional. It is characterized by dimensions
such as trust, reliability,
shared history and values,
mutual respect, caring,
empathy, warmth, social
support, and effective two-
way communications.

behavior and to sell larger volumes[30] of products and services. Customers know when they have relationships with
enterprises. Genuine relationships exist when customers go
back to enterprises again and again because they *want* to, not
because there is an incentive to do so or because they will
receive a price discount. In fact, where genuine customer
relationships exist, customers often knowingly and willingly
pay *higher* prices for the satisfaction that comes from the
relationship.

Relationships cannot be imposed upon customers. They
have to be nurtured and even earned by businesses and
brands. The customer knows when a relationship is in place—as defined by her.
If it is not, then they will not sanction the use of the word in the context of business dealings. When asked to comment on their relationships with certain businesses, customers (some of whom may give those businesses 100 percent of
their purchases) will say, "That's not a relationship; I never hear from them." Or
they will say, "That's not a relationship; I don't know anyone there."

Where a genuine customer relationship exists, there is more than a functional
connection; it is highly emotional. It is characterized by dimensions such as
trust, reliability, shared history and values, mutual respect, caring, empathy,
warmth, social support, and effective two-way communications. Where high
levels of such characteristics are present, something approaching a genuine customer relationship may be said to exist.

And such relationships exist in many situations. Despite observations made
by some marketing practitioners that "loyalty is dead," there is ample evidence
that many customers develop and maintain close relationships with enterprises
and brands. Such relationships, as is the case with human relationships in general, serve a useful purpose in the lives of individuals. As with most similar phe-
nomena, relationships may be said to exist on a continuum, anchored by very
functional relationships at one end and by very emotional relationships at the
other. The more emotional relationships are the more solid and lasting. They
serve as anchors in what has become for most people a very challenging and
chaotic world. Being able to rely on certain firms and brands, and knowing that
they will provide consistency of service and an emotional connection, helps to
provide stability and to reduce risk and vulnerability.

REWARDS OF CUSTOMER RELATIONSHIPS

What is the evidence that companies will benefit by creating solid, genuine relationships with their customers, by creating a high level of emotional, instead of
functional, loyalty? By measuring customers' relationships with enterprises and

---

[30]Susan Fournier, Susan Dobscha, and David Glen Mick, "Preventing the Premature Death of Relationship Marketing," *Harvard Business Review* 76, no.1 (January–February 1998), pp. 42–51.

brands, I have demonstrable evidence that the creation of emotion-based, genuine relationships with customers pays back handsomely for enterprises. The identification of the emotional content of the interaction with customers allows us to determine where the relationship is weak and where it is strong. Where the relationship is emotionally strong, and where customers have a genuine attachment to an enterprise or brand, we find extraordinary results. A customer is much more likely to remain a customer for many years. The customer gives the enterprise or brand a significantly larger share of her category spending; she spends more with the enterprise and she is significantly less price-conscious. Moreover, the customer is significantly more likely to recommend the company to friends and associates.

The evidence in favor of establishing more emotional content in the customer relationship is considerable. The payback to the enterprises that achieve that is enormous. The issue then becomes one of how to accomplish it. The enterprises that are most successful are those that have adopted a *relationship focus*. They realize that satisfying customers in the short term is not enough to guarantee long-term patronage and support. The customers who develop genuine loyalty are those who feel closeness and an attachment to the enterprise or brand; it has taken on *meaning* in their lives. Reaching this focus requires, in many enterprises, a change in corporate culture, driven usually by a CEO who understands the long-term payback to be realized[31] (see Chapter 13 for a discussion on organizational change). It requires that all aspects of the enterprise and how it interfaces with its customers must be coordinated and integrated so as to create the highest possible levels of long-term customer satisfaction. In enterprises such as these, the emphasis is not so much on meeting monthly sales quotas or making the quarterly earnings projections as it is on making the customer feel good about doing business with us.

THE NATURE OF LOYALTY

The whole point of a relationship is to keep and grow a customer. Isn't that fundamentally the same as building loyalty? We have seen that admiration is not the same as loyalty.

So what is customer loyalty? Those who've tried to answer that question have approached it from two different directions: attitudinal (what Barnes calls "emotional") and behavioral (what Barnes calls "functional"). Although each of these two definitions of loyalty is valid, they have different implications and lead to very different prescriptions for businesses.

The attitudinal definition of loyalty implies that loyalty is a state of mind. Customers are loyal to a brand or a company if they have a positive, preferential

---

[31]James G. Barnes, "CRM Demands Leadership from the Top," Customer Intermarketing Newsletter, crm-forum.com (October 2, 2001), available at *www.crm-forum.com/cgi-bin/item.cgi?id=59369&d=101&h=&dateformat=%0%20%B%20%Y.*

attitude toward it. They *like* the company, its products, or its brands, and they therefore *prefer* to buy from it, rather than from the company's competitors. In purely commercial terms, the attitudinal definition of customer loyalty would mean that someone who is willing to pay a premium for Brand A over Brand B, even when the products they represent are virtually equivalent, is loyal to Brand A. But the emphasis is on *willingness*, rather than on actual behavior, per se. In terms of attitudes, then, increasing a customer's loyalty is virtually equivalent to increasing the customer's preference for the brand. It is closely tied to product quality and customer satisfaction. Any company wanting to increase loyalty, in attitudinal terms, will concentrate on improving its product, its image, or other elements of the customer experience, relative to its competitors.

The behavioral definition of loyalty would mean that someone is willing to pay a premium for Brand A over Brand B, even without respect to the attitudes or preferences that underlie that conduct. By this definition, customers are loyal to a company if they buy from it and then continue to buy from it. Loyalty is concerned with repurchase activity, regardless of any internally held attitudes or preferences. In the behavioral definition, loyalty is not the *cause*, but the *result* of brand preference. A company wanting to increase customer loyalty will focus on whatever tactics will in fact increase the amount of repurchase behavior—tactics that can easily include, without being limited to, raising consumers' general preference for the brand or their level of satisfaction with it.

For a variety of reasons, we prefer using the behavioral definition of customer loyalty, rather than the attitudinal one, although we respect both. For our purposes, defining loyalty as a behavior, rather than as an attitude, is simply more useful and practical. So when we say a customer is loyal, we are talking about the fact that she is a repeat purchaser, plain and simple.

In terms of addressing the issues that companies face on a day-to-day basis in their competition for customers, defining loyalty as an attitude rather than a behavior creates some problems. One analytical issue, for instance, is that attitudinal loyalty and brand preference are redundant concepts. The attitudinal definition of loyalty sheds no additional light on what any company should do. If there is no real difference between customer loyalty and brand preference, then why have a separate term at all?

But second, if loyalty is a purely attitudinal preference, then it does not necessarily have to spring from any *continuing* relationship, and this simply flies in the face of the common English definition of the word. By the attitudinal definition, if Customer A and Customer B have an equally strong preference for a particular product, then they must have an equal amount of loyalty to that product. But what if Customer A has never consumed that product before, while Customer B has consumed it regularly in the past? It is a far more useful concept to consider that both customers have a *preference* today for the product, but that Customer B is *loyal* to it, because of her current and past *behavior*.

And, third, the concept of customer loyalty should have as direct a connection as possible to a company's financial and operational results. That is, we ought to be able to "connect the dots" between whatever strategies and tactics a company employs to increase its customers' loyalty and the actual economic outcomes of those actions. An enterprise should be able to see a clear and direct economic benefit of some kind, as the result of a customer's loyalty. But if loyalty is an attitude, then it has no immediate economic result. Internally held attitudes have no intrinsic value to a firm, because there is no financial result to measure until and unless these attitudes are somehow manifested into actions. A company could have a thousand highly loyal customers, but no financial benefit at all, if none of the customers has any money or if the company has run out of product to sell.

The distinction between attitude and behavior, as a basis for defining loyalty, is more than a conflict over proper terminology. It has very real implications for how we think about and tackle the problems that companies face in a competitive situation. In addition to the fact that customers can be attitudinally loyal without actually exhibiting loyal behavior, there is also the fact that customers who are not at all attitudinally loyal may engage in loyal behavior, making repurchases and continuing to patronize a business. The world is full of examples of this. A retail bank's customer may be highly dissatisfied with bank, but remain a customer nevertheless, because it is simply too much trouble to switch banks, or because the customer's expectation is that the service at most competitive banks would be just as bad.

For all these reasons, defining customer loyalty in terms of attitudes, preferences, allegiances, or desires is simply not as useful as defining it as a type of activity, conduct, or behavior. But what type of behavior, *exactly*?

In our own consulting practice and methodology, we make an explicit assumption that a customer can be made more loyal by, in effect, making it more convenient for the customer to repurchase than to switch to a competitor. We usually recommend accomplishing this by trying to tailor or customize some aspect of the enterprise's behavior to an individual customer's own unique specifications. For the customer to get the same level of service from a competitor, even one who offers the same type of customization, the customer would first have to teach the competitor what she has already taught the original enterprise. The implication is that a customer experiencing such a benefit will be more likely to remain loyal to the original firm, because it is more convenient (i.e., less costly, in terms of time, effort and money) for her to do so.

As a straight yes-or-no proposition, the concept of customer loyalty, as a behavior, is relatively easy. A magazine subscriber who elects to renew her subscription at the end of the first year is engaging in loyal behavior. Unfortunately, however, the real world is rarely described adequately in strict yes-or-no terms. If the magazine subscriber renews her subscription again in the third year, and perhaps again in the fourth, fifth, and sixth years, doesn't her behavior exhibit a *greater and greater degree* of loyalty?

And what about a new car buyer? The owner of a Brand A car who buys another Brand A when she retires the first one would be said to be loyal, of course, but what about using her dealer's service area or getting her car financed from Brand A's financial services division? Or what if she owns two cars, but only one of them is Brand A?

The loyalty concept is equally difficult to deal with in other categories. If a breakfast cereal consumer buys one box per month of Brand B for her family, and then begins buying two boxes a month, does this mean she is twice as loyal as before? What if she also goes from buying one box a month of Brand C to buying three boxes a month?

The fact is, a much more useful concept than *loyalty*, when thinking about desirable customer behaviors, is *lifetime value*. The net present value of the expected stream of future profits from a customer is a much more rigorous and useful variable. In its ideal state (a state that can never actually be achieved, of course), lifetime value would capture all the various behaviors and activities of a customer that have any bearing at all on the enterprise's profit from that customer.

SUMMARY

Our goal for this chapter has been to give the reader enough of an overview to provide a grounded perspective of how Learning Relationships enable enterprises to develop more personalized and collaborative interactions with individual customers. Our next step is to begin to understand "the business sense" of building a customer-strategy enterprise. Learning Relationships, after all, result in many pragmatic and financial benefits, not only for the customer but also for the enterprise that engages in them. The objective of increasing the overall value of the customer base by getting, keeping, and growing a customer is achieved through these highly interactive relationships.

The enterprise determined to increase the value of the customer base will start with a commitment to increase customer value, and then move to implement the strategic levels of the Learning Relationship. The tasks needed to make this happen are: identifying their customers individually, ranking them by their value to the company, differentiating them by their needs, interacting with each of them, and customizing some aspect of the business for each. From the enterprise's perspective, these tasks are by no means chronological or finite. We will examine each of them more carefully in the next chapters.

FOOD FOR THOUGHT

1. Based on what we now know about the essence of relationships, is it possible for a customer to have a relationship with a commercial (or other) firm? Is it possible for a customer to have a relationship with a brand? Is it possible for a firm to have a relationship with a customer—especially a customer who is one of millions of customers? If you said no to any of these, what conditions would have to be met before a relationship *would* be possible?

2. Barnes says an important ingredient to a good relationship is an emotional connection, but customer relationships have elsewhere been

referred to as a "bond of value" or a "bond of convenience." What do you think? Do customers have to love a product or company in order to have a relationship with that enterprise? Or is a perceived benefit—especially one that grows from a vested interest—enough? How would you approach a debate on this controversy?

3. Consider the relationship enhancers and building blocks mentioned by Edell and Rose. For each one, think of a for-profit or a nonprofit enterprise that serves as an example.

4. Assume that there exists asymmetrical dependence between a buyer and a seller. Answer the following questions two ways: First, assume the buyer is more dependent; next, assume the seller is more dependent.[32]
   a. How do you reduce uncertainty if you are a buyer? A seller?
   b. Will there always be some transactional purchases?
   c. How is the relationship with your buyers/sellers different from the way it would be with symmetrical interdependence?

GLOSSARY

Asymmetric relationship   The two parties view the relationship differently; it is more important or salient, perhaps, to one party than the other. Asymmetric dependence refers to a situation where one party has few alternatives but to remain in the relationship, whereas symmetric interdependence exists when the relationship members are equally dependent on each other.

Distributive fairness   Based on the perception of relationship rewards versus relationship burdens or obligations and, therefore, focused on relationship outcomes.

Emotional loyalty   Attitudinal loyalty, or a preference for, one brand over another. Customers with attitudinal loyalty may buy another brand or shop elsewhere for practical reasons (accepting a Pepsi instead of the preferred Coke on an airplane, for example, because the Coke is not available).

Functional loyalty   Behavioral loyalty, or, basically, buying the same thing over and over, or repeatedly from a particular vendor.

Iterative   Builds on itself—a relationship is iterative because it gets smarter and smarter over time. It can pick up where it left off; it doesn't need to start all over at the beginning with each contact.

Mutuality   Refers to the two-way nature of a relationship.

Procedural fairness   Based on the perception that procedures and processes are fair, and focused on behaviors, regardless of outcome.

Relational versus transactional   Relational strategies take into account the lifetime costs and payoffs of the total of all projectable interactions and

---

[32]Suggestion from an anonymous reviewer.

transactions, whereas transactional approaches concentrate on the value of the current transaction. This is important because, for example, a company that focuses on a relationship and the long-term value of a customer would be willing to resolve that customer's complaint about a single transaction by taking a loss on the transaction, whereas the company that focuses just on the value of transactions insists on making a profit on each transaction.

Transactional versus relational   *See* relational versus transactional.

PART Two

IDIC Implementation Process: A Model for Managing Customer Relationships

In order for a firm to build customer value through managed relationships, the company must *identify* customers, *differentiate* them, *interact* with them, and *customize*.

Customer Relationships: Basic Building Blocks of IDIC and Trust

3
Chapter

In order for a firm to build customer value through managed relationships, the company must engage in a four-step process we call IDIC, an acronym for identifying customers, differentiating them, interacting with them, and customizing for them. These steps represent the mechanics of any genuine relationship, which by definition will involve mutuality and customer-specific action. But while the IDIC process represents the mechanics *of a relationship, generating a customer's trust is the* objective *of that process. Relationships simply cannot happen except in the context of customer trust, as we will learn from Charles Green later in this chapter. In succeeding chapters, we'll take a more detailed look at each of the IDIC tasks, but for now, what's important is to get an overview of both the mechanics and the objective of relationship building.*

We've seen that the customer relationship idea has many nuances. For instance, there likely will be an emotional component to most successful customer relationships (at least in consumer marketing), but it's important to recognize that the obverse of this statement is not necessarily true: Because you have an emotional attachment to a company does not mean you have a relationship with that company.

We can't afford to dismiss entirely the notion that nonemotional relationships between an enterprise and its customer do, in fact, exist. For instance, you probably have no actual emotional connection with one or more banks whose credit cards you carry in your wallet. But does that mean you have no *relationship* with such a company, even though it communicates with you monthly, tracks your purchases, and (at least in the best cases) proactively offers you a new card configuration based on your own personal usage pattern? Yes, there might be an element of emotion involved in this relationship, but must that always be the case?

Conversely, you might have a highly emotional attachment to an enterprise, but if the enterprise itself isn't even "aware" that you exist, does this constitute anything we can call a relationship? The simple truth is that, in most cases, your relationship with a brand is analogous to your relationship with a movie star. You might love his pictures, you might follow his activities avidly in the magazines, but will he even know who you are? It can only be said to be a relationship if the movie star somehow also acknowledges it. This is because, as we said in Chapter 2, the most basic, core feature of any *relationship* is mutuality. Mutual awareness of another party is a prerequisite to establishing a relationship between two parties, whether we are talking about movie star and fan, or enterprise and customer. People who are emotionally involved with a brand, not unlike the most avid fans of a rock music group, are usually engaged in one-way affection. There's nothing wrong with this at all. One-way affection for a brand has sold a lot of merchandise. But this kind of affection will be only part of a relationship if the brand is mutually involved; and in the overwhelming majority of cases, it is not.

So let's return to the basic, definitional characteristics of a relationship, as outlined at the beginning of the last chapter, and try to derive from this list of characteristics a set of actions that an enterprise ought to take if it wants to establish relationships with its customers. A relationship is mutual, interactive, and iterative in nature, developing its own richer and richer context over time. A relationship must provide an ongoing benefit to each party; it must change each party's behavior toward the other party; and it will therefore be uniquely different, from one set of relationship participants to the next. Finally, a successful relationship will lead each party to trust the other. In fact, the more effective and successful the relationship is, from a business-building standpoint, the more it will be characterized by a high level of trust.

TRUST AND RELATIONSHIPS HAPPEN IN TANDEM

The first few relationship characteristics we've seen are simply analytic descriptions of the nature of a relationship, while the last characteristic—trust—is a much richer term that could serve as a proxy for all the affection and favorable emotion that most of us associate with a successful relationship. In any case, what should be apparent from the outset is that we are talking about an enterprise engaging in customer-specific behaviors. That is, because relationships involve mutuality and uniqueness, an enterprise can easily have a wonderful relationship with one customer but no relationship at all with another. It can have a deep, very profitable relationship with one customer but a troubled, highly unprofitable relationship with another. An enterprise cannot have the same relationship with both Mary and Shirley anymore than Mary could have the same relationship with both her bank and her golf instructor.

A business strategy based on managing customer relationships, then, necessarily involves treating different customers differently. A firm must be able to **identify** and recognize different, individual customers, and it must know what makes one customer different from another. It must be able to **interact** individually with any customer on the other end of a relationship, and it must somehow change its behavior to meet the specific needs of that customer, as it discovers those needs. And to build trust, it must act in the customer's best interest, as well as its own.

In short, in order for an enterprise to engage in the practice of treating different customers differently, it must integrate the customer into the company and adapt its products and services to the customer's own, individual needs. But as a company begins to understand the customer, interact with him, learn from him, and provide feedback based on that learning, the customer's view of what he is buying from the company will probably also begin to change. For instance, a person may shop from L.L. Bean initially to buy a sweater. But over time, he may browse the L.L. Bean Web site or flip through the catalog to match other clothes to the sweater, or look for Christmas gift ideas, or research camping equipment. Now L.L. Bean has become more than just a place to buy sweaters; it is a source of valuable information about future purchases. Ultimately, this is likely to increase the importance of trust, as an element in the relationship. So will the no-questions-asked return policy, as well as the fast, reasonably priced shipping. The more the customer trusts L.L.Bean, the more likely he will be to accept its offers and recommendations.[1]

It is customer information that gives an enterprise the capability to **differentiate** its customers one from another. Customer information is an economic asset, just like a piece of equipment, a factory, or a patent. It has the capability to improve an enterprise's productivity and reduce its unit costs. Individual customer information, if used properly, can yield a return for many years. And because customer information is based on an individual, not a group, it is more useful for its scope, rather than its scale. When two enterprises are competing for the same individual customer's business, the company with the greatest scope of information about that customer will probably be the more effective competitor. And, because technology now makes it possible for businesses of nearly any size to keep track of individual relationships with individual customers, the scale of a company's operations may become less important as a competitive advantage. Cultivating a profitable customer relationship will depend primarily on having information about a specific customer and using it wisely. It will not matter as much who has the most customers.

Once a company begins to take a customer-specific view of its business, it will begin to think of its customers as assets that must be managed carefully, in the same way any other corporate asset should be managed. From a strictly financial perspective, this kind of strategy will tend to focus more corporate resources on satisfying the needs of those customers offering higher long-term value to the firm, while limiting or reducing the resources allocated to lower-value customers. But, operationally, increasing the long-term value of a particular customer will necessitate addressing that customer's own individual needs, even to the point of tailoring—or at least mass-customizing—individual products and services for individual customers.

The technologies that allow a company to track individual customers and treat them differently have made it possible to create what is, in effect, an individual *feedback loop* for each customer. This loop ensures that a successful

---

[1]See Ellen Garbarino and Mark Johnson, "The Different Roles of Satisfaction, Trust, and Commitment in Customer Relationships," *Journal of Marketing* 63 (April 1999), pp. 70–87.

relationship continues to get better and better, one customer at a time. When such a relationship exists between a customer and an enterprise, many traditional marketing principles, formerly held sacred, will simply be irrelevant, at least insofar as that particular customer is concerned. No longer must the enterprise rely on surveys of current or potential customers to determine which action is appropriate for this customer, nor is it necessary to plot the reach and frequency with which its advertising message is getting out, in order to determine its effectiveness with this customer. Instead, the customer and the enterprise are mutually engaged in a continuously improving relationship: "I know you. You tell me what makes this work for you. I do it. You tell me if I did it right. I remember that, and I do it even better for you next time."

The secret to keeping and growing a single customer forever is this feedback loop. Creating it requires the customer's own participation and effort, along with his trust in the company that's getting his information. It is the effort on the part of the customer that results in a better product or service than the customer can get anywhere else from anyone who is not so far up his learning curve. The successive interactions that characterize such a Learning Relationship ultimately result in the enterprise's capability to make its products and services highly valuable to an individual customer—indeed, the Learning Relationship, because it is unique to that customer, and because it has been formed in large part from the customer's own participation, can become *irreplaceably* valuable to that customer, ensuring the customer's long-term loyalty and value to the enterprise.

IDIC: FOUR IMPLEMENTATION TASKS FOR CREATING AND MANAGING CUSTOMER RELATIONSHIPS

Setting up and managing individual customer relationships can be broken up into four interrelated implementation tasks. These implementation tasks are based on the unique, customer-specific and iterative character of such relationships. We list them roughly in the sequence in which they will likely be accomplished, although as we'll see later in this book, there is a great deal of overlap among these implementation tasks (e.g., an enterprise might use its Web presence primarily to attract the most valuable customers and identify them individually, rather than as a customer interaction platform), and there may be good reason for accomplishing them out of order:

1. *Identify customers*. Relationships are only possible with individuals, not with markets, segments, or populations. Therefore, the first task in setting up a relationship is to identify, individually, the party at the other end of the relationship. Many companies don't really know the identities of many of their customers, so for them this first step is absolutely crucial. But for all companies, what the identify task also entails is organizing the enterprise's various information resources so that the company can take a customer-specific view of its business. It means ensuring that the company has a

> An enterprise must be able to *recognize* a customer when he comes back, in person, by phone, online, or wherever.

mechanism for tagging individual customers, not just with a product code that identifies what's been sold, but also with a customer code that identifies the party that the enterprise is doing business with—the party at the other end of the mutual relationship. An enterprise must be able to *recognize* a customer when he comes back, in person, by phone, online, or wherever. Moreover, enterprises need to "know" each customer in as much detail as possible—including the habits, preferences, and other characteristics that make each customer unique. When you call the toll-free number at Speigel, the rep knows about your last catalog order.

2. *Differentiate customers.* Knowing how customers are different allows a company (1) to focus its resources on those customers who will bring in the most value for the enterprise, and (2) to devise and implement customer-specific strategies designed to satisfy individually different customer needs. Customers represent different levels of value to the enterprise and they have different needs from the enterprise. Although not a new concept, customer grouping—the process by which customers are clustered into categories based on a specified variable—is a critical step in understanding and profitably serving customers. The customer differentiation task will involve an enterprise in categorizing its customers by both their value to the firm and by what needs they have. Some call centers constantly change the order-to-serve of the customers on hold based on the different values of the waiting customers. Although it would be ideal to answer every call on the second ring, when that's not possible, it would be better to vault the customers keeping you in business ahead of the customers of dubious value. In many call centers, this reshuffling is not at all apparent to customers.

> Customers represent different levels of value to the enterprise and they have different needs from the enterprise.

3. *Interact with customers.* Enterprises must improve the effectiveness of their interactions with customers. Each successive interaction with a customer should take place in the context of all previous interactions with that customer. A bank may ask one question in each month's electronic statement, and next month's question may depend on last month's answer. A conversation with a customer should pick up where the last one left off. Effective customer interactions provide better insight into a customer's needs.

> A conversation with a customer should pick up where the last one left off.

4. *Customize treatment.* The enterprise should adapt some aspect of its behavior toward a customer, based on that individual's needs and value. To engage a customer in an ongoing Learning Relationship, an enterprise needs to adapt its behavior to satisfy the customer's expressed needs. This might entail mass-customizing a product or tailoring some aspect of its service.[2] This customization could involve the way an invoice is rendered or how a product is packaged.

[2]Don Peppers, Martha Rogers, PhD, and Bob Dorf. *The One to One Fieldbook: The Complete Toolkit for Implementing a 1to1 Marketing Program* (New York: Doubleday, 1999).

> The enterprise should adapt some aspect of its behavior toward a customer, based on that individual's needs and value.

This IDIC process implementation model can also be broken into two broad categories of activities: *analysis* and *action* (see Exhibit 3.1). The enterprise conducts the first two tasks, identify and differentiate, behind the scenes and out of the customer's sight; they constitute *analysis*. The latter two tasks, interact and customize, are customer-facing steps that require participation on the part of the individual customer. Visible to the customer, they constitute *action*. You'll recall from Chapter 1 that "interacting" and "customizing" are the two capabilities an enterprise must have to engage customers in relationships, and that the degree to which a firm uses each of these capabilities is an easy way to categorize the type of customer strategy it is doing—mass, niche, database, or one-to-one Learning Relationship. We can also think of the identify and differentiate steps as the tasks that make up analytical CRM, while interact and customize are the tasks involved in operational CRM.

Throughout the rest of this book, we will refer back to this set of four implementation tasks as the *IDIC methodology*. As a model for relationship management processes, this methodology can be applied in any number of situations. For instance, it could help a company understand the steps it must take to make

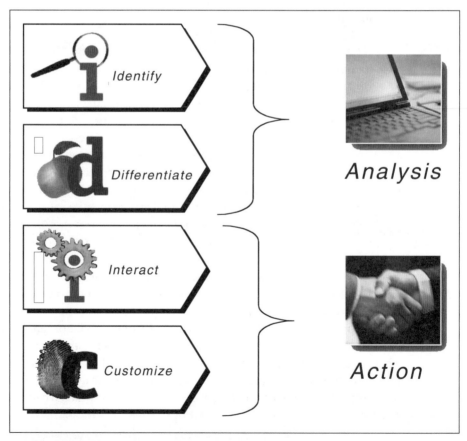

EXHIBIT 3.1   **IDIC: Analysis and Action**

better use of its call center for initiating and strengthening customer relationships. Applied to a sales force, it could be used to understand the strengths and weaknesses of a new contact management application, or to improve a sales compensation policy. We will devote specific chapters in the book to examining all the activities and processes, as well as the pitfalls and problems, associated with each of these four tasks.

HOW DOES TRUST CHARACTERIZE A LEARNING RELATIONSHIP?

But before we begin this journey, we ought to spend the rest of this chapter discussing in greater detail just what it means to say that trust is a quality that will characterize a good customer relationship. In an enterprise focused on customer-specific activities, any single customer's purchase transactions will take place within the context of that customer's previous transactions, as well as future ones. The buyer and seller collaborate, with the buyer interacting to specify the product and the seller responding with some change in behavior appropriate for *that* buyer. In other words, the buyer and seller, in a relationship, must be willing to trust each other far beyond the general reputation of the brand. By extension, we can easily see that the more "relationshiplike" any series of purchase transactions is, the more that trust will become a central element in it.

A relationship of trust is one in which both parties feel "comfortable" continuing to interact and deal with each other, whether during a purchase, an interaction, or a service transaction. Trust rarely happens instantaneously. Even if the trusted source has been recommended by another, a customer must "feel" the trust from within before he will begin to divulge personal information about himself.

The element of trust is an indispensable component of a healthy, growing relationship between a company and its customer, but it is not an absolute requirement for *any* relationship. A customer may remain in a relationship with a company either because he desires the relationship or simply because he perceives no suitable alternative. It should be obvious, however, which relationship will be the stronger, from the standpoint of increasing the customer's long-term value to the enterprise. The customer's own level of commitment to his relationship with a company will depend on the extent to which the relationship derives from dedication, rather than from constraint. Trust-based relationships foster dedication.[3]

Enterprises create trust-based customer relationships through the actions of their employees and partners, and through company strategies and policies. There are sound ways to think about the trust-building process and the policies necessary to generate trust. In the next section, Charles Green shares his views on trust between customer and supplier by discussing what he calls the "myths" of trust.

[3]Leonard L. Berry, *Discovering the Soul of Service* (New York: Free Press, 1999).

THE TRUST EQUATION: GENERATING CUSTOMER TRUST

Charles H. Green
President, Trusted Advisor Associates

CRM is a powerful tool to identify high-loyalty-potential customers as well as to fine-tune products and services to elicit loyalty. And the literature of retention economics is well documented, as well as intimately bound up with CRM. That customer loyalty is immensely profitable is not in dispute by anybody not living under a rock for the past 10 years.[4]

> The presence or absence of trust is a significant driver of economic profit.

But the role of trust in the economic equation is rarely noticed. For one thing, research generally suggests that high levels of customer satisfaction are only mildly correlated with high levels of loyalty. Other data show that while satisfaction might not lead to loyalty, dissatisfaction clearly leads to disloyalty. It is only when high levels of customer satisfaction are encountered that we find a major upswing in customer loyalty, hence in customer profitability. And there are some data to suggest that extremely high levels of customer satisfaction and loyalty are also examples of extremely high trust.[5] What all this suggests, in actuality, is that the presence or absence of trust is a significant driver of economic profit.

Also, the business literature is now full of books and articles linking customer loyalty directly to profit, and describing the issue more or less purely in business-process terms. High profits are said to derive from high customer retention rates because of efficiencies such as increased familiarity with buying processes and customer-enterprise-shared processes, or from price insensitivity and referrals. But viewed from just a slightly different angle, these same process improvements arise directly from the greater sense of trust that particular customers have with the enterprise they're dealing with.

There can be trust-based relationships without a one-to-one business model. And, there may be companies operating customer-specific businesses that are not very successful at creating trusted relationships (think about the companies that still call you at the dinner hour.) Clearly, however, for an enterprise to generate the kind of long-term, profitable, ongoing relationship with a customer that is the subject of this book, the customer must have some level of trust in the enterprise.

But trust is not always so easily understood, and the steps required to generate a customer's trust aren't necessarily simple. In fact, with all the emphasis on process, a number of businesses have focused more on the activities required, rather than the desired outcome. As a result, several myths about trust ought to be exposed at the outset:

---

[4]Despite a few detracters, the literature and research findings overwhelmingly support the correlation between longevity and profits.

[5]See Heiman Miller, *Strategic Selling* (Warner Books, 1998); Travesano Brooks, *You're Working Too Hard to Make the Sale* (New York: McGraw-Hill, 1995).

Myth 1. Intimate customer relationships require time and proximity.

Fact: Intimacy is the one trust factor that can be instantaneous; it can be conveyed by a tone of voice, by attentive listening, or by a sense of being understood. It is also not dependent on proximity; consider Internet chat rooms; consider conversations between seatmates on transcontinental plane flights.

Myth 2. Trust takes time.

Fact: Trust requires the repetition of experiences, not time per se. Experiences let customers form assessments of credibility, reliability, and **self-orientation**. The accumulation of repeated experiences *used to* take time; now, they can be accumulated rapidly.

Myth 3. More **customized** contact is better.

Fact: If I am passed from one customer service agent to another, and the second agent knows my name and transaction history, I am pleased. If a cold-call direct marketer knows my name and transaction history, I am not pleased. Context and intent are everything.

Myth 4. People trust companies.

Fact: Reliability is the only trust component that people associate with enterprises. Credibility, and especially intimacy and self-orientation, are traits associated almost entirely with individual persons, not organizations. The movie *The Godfather* had it wrong: It *is* business, and it *is* personal.

Myth 5. People like to be asked their opinion.

Fact: People like to be *listened to,* which is not the same thing as being asked. When was the last time you filled out an in-room hotel service questionnaire?

Trust is a genuine buzzword; nearly everyone uses it and assumes that what they mean is what everyone else means when they use it. In fact, it has many different meanings, hence many opportunities for misinterpretation if it is not clearly and mutually defined.

The bulk of those meanings, however, can be captured in a simple model I call the trust equation.

$$\text{Trust} = (C + R + I)/S$$

where:

C = *credibility.* Credibility has to do with words; "I can trust what he says about. . . ." Other related terms include *believability* and *truthfulness.*

R = *reliability.* Reliability has to do with actions; "I can trust that he'll do. . . ." Other related terms include *predictability* and *familiarity.*

I = *intimacy.* Intimacy has to do with perceived safety; "I can trust talking with him about. . . ." *Security* and *integrity* are related to intimacy.

S = *self-orientation.* Self-orientation has to do with focus; "I can trust that he's focused on me. . . ." A low level of self-orientation on the part of the enterprise enhances the customer's trust, while a high level of self-orientation destroys trust. Self-orientation appears in many guises—selfishness, self-consciousness, and self-preoccupation.

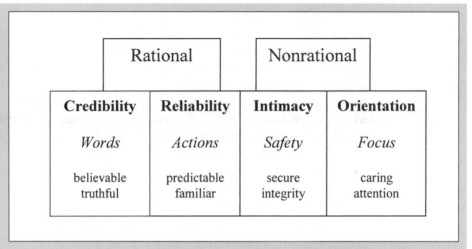

	Rational		Nonrational	
Credibility	**Reliability**	**Intimacy**	**Orientation**
Words	*Actions*	*Safety*	*Focus*
believable truthful	predictable familiar	secure integrity	caring attention

EXHIBIT 3.2   **Components of Trustworthiness**

These components are shown graphically in Exhibit 3.2. The first two components—credibility and reliability—operate mainly in the rational realm. The second two—intimacy and self-orientation—are largely nonrational (*not* the same as irrational).[6]

The power of the fourth component—self-orientation—is greater than the other three, as evidenced by its solo position in the denominator. A customer who perceives lack of credibility may sense empty words. If the customer senses low levels of reliability, he may say the offer is "flaky." If the customer senses low levels of intimacy, he may view the enterprise as technical, or full of technicians. All these are destructive of trust, of course. But none so much as being perceived as having high levels of self-orientation, for that goes to motive—high self-orientation is equated with insincerity, a lack of caring, and deviousness.

The trust equation allows us to see more clearly the trust-destroying nature of many of the activities enterprises engage in when they install CRM technologies without adopting an appropriately customer-oriented business philosophy. Companies might have the best of intentions; but few technology implementations are perfect, and when little attention is paid to the enterprise's own philosophy of business, the results can often be counterproductive. A few examples are:

- *False accuracy*. Errors in detailed information, like street names, reduce credibility.
- *Presumed intimacy*. Using precise information as a lever, as in "now that you bought green house paint, you'll probably be wanting XYZ" can make

[6][Authors' note: Charles Green's use of the terms "rational" and "nonrational" closely parallel the more widely accepted terms "cognitive," which refers to "thinking," and "affective," which refers to "feeling." These terms may also be seen as reflecting the current controversy about rational versus "emotional" processes.]

a customer feel as though Big Brother is watching, which not only reduces intimacy but greatly increases perceived self-orientation.

- *Inconsistent application of CRM.* If an automated answering system asks a customer to key in an ID, don't ask him to repeat it verbally later in the call—it reduces perceived reliability.
- *Unintegrated application of CRM.* If you're a bank offering overdraft protection on checks written by key customers, make sure the online banking side of the house offers the same service for online checks written; otherwise, you lower credibility and perceived reliability.
- *Giving customized answers before being asked.* A computer company's CRM system may give a sales rep 98 percent confidence that a particular product is right for a given customer, but if the rep tries to "sell" the solution before the customer feels listened to, then he will not buy, even if buying would be the "rational" thing to do. Jumping to conclusions before the customer feels listened to combines the two major process trust violations.

High trust leads to higher sales. Yet many selling models do not actually foster the development of high levels of trust. Some models view trust as entirely rational—a subset of rational decision making, in fact. But trust includes some critical, nonrational components. Some selling models view trust-based relationships as one-dimensional, moving from impersonal and distant to intimate and close. Trust is more complex than that.

To generate trust, the enterprise must address all four components of it in the customer's mind—credibility, reliability, intimacy, and self-orientation (i.e., the self-orientation of the seller).

CREDIBILITY ENHANCERS

For example, online information is an excellent vehicle for increasing a customer's sense of credibility of the seller. This is partly because the buyer can browse at his own pace and depth. But it is also because the online buyer is free to assess credibility without any of the social interactions necessary to judge intimacy or self-orientation. You don't have to be polite when reading a Web site; nor does the Web site (usually) tell you to hurry up or slow down.

CRM can help tremendously in such credibility enhancement; Amazon's programs for customization by past purchases offer deep customization in a way that is seen as value-adding by customers.

RELIABILITY ENHANCERS

Reliability can be enhanced in several ways. The most obvious is to be religious about delivering on promises made—don't ask the customer to input an ID number if you're going to ask them to repeat it later in the call; don't mislead customers regarding availability; and so forth. Another is to create a number of implied promises and then deliver on them. Such promises might include a call back within x minutes, a successful handoff on a service call, or a revision made to a database. Yet another is to improve familiarity; customers perceive as reliable someone who can adapt their ways to the customer's own habits, be it mildly customized Web sites, adoption of personal terms on a phone call, or matching the formality of language to the other.

CRM can be helpful in this regard as well; anytime that the enterprise can act vis à vis a customer, given full awareness of all previous interactions, perceived reliability is increased.

INTIMACY ENHANCERS

CRM offers numerous chances to either increase or destroy intimacy. Intimacy is all about security, comfort, integrity, confidentiality, and a sense of safety. Someone with detailed information about me can make me feel very good or very bad, depending entirely on how he handles that information. If he hides his knowledge of me, or pretends it doesn't exist, then he runs the risk of appearing like Big Brother. If, on the other hand, the information is openly acknowledged, then it can become a useful tool. Similarly, if a company flaunts customer-specific data with no apparent purpose in mind, it will appear cavalier and untrustworthy. But if it brings specific information to bear on the problem at hand ("Do you want to use the same MasterCard number you used last time?") then it becomes highly useful.

To understand this difference, consider two different ways a CSR might use customer-specific information in an interaction with the customer:

Version A:

> Customer: "I'm calling because my computer Start button won't engage; it's ticket number LFX897A."
>
> CSR: "Okay, this is your fourth call on the 'won't start' problem. Are you sure you did what we suggested last time?"

Version B:

> Customer: "I'm calling because my computer Start button won't engage; it's ticket number LFX897A."
>
> CSR: "Hmm, my records say this is your fourth call on that ticket number; is that right? You must be getting a little frustrated by now; tell me about the problem."

Both CSRs have access to tremendously powerful CRM data, but the CSR in version A turns data into a negative by using basic trust-destroying language (stating the CRM data as definitive, rather than asking for confirmation; starting with solutions before going through problem definition; failing to listen or express empathy). By contrast, the CSR in version B is able to turn real-time CRM data into a true asset, simply by utilizing it in a trust-sensitive context.

What this goes to show is that it isn't just having the right technologies or information available that creates trust. Instead, an enterprise hoping to build and preserve its customers' trust must be concerned about how customer-specific information is actually deployed, how proficiently the customer-contact people operate with it, and, above all, whether the business is prepared to acknowledge that meeting genuine customer needs is the most important overall goal.

ORIENTATION ENHANCERS

CRM can help increase trust; it can also serve to decrease trust. Trust itself is a major factor in customer satisfaction, customer loyalty, and firm profitability. But there is a catch-22: You can't become trustworthy by focusing very narrowly on your own bottom line.

Self-orientation carries more weight in the trust equation than the other three factors. And the approach that the enterprise takes to CRM will speak volumes to a customer about the enterprise's level of self-orientation. If anything, the application of CRM raises the already-high stakes on the self-orientation part of the trust equation.

CRM starts with customer focus. But there are two kinds of customer focus: One is focus on the customer for the sake of the enterprise; the other is focus directly on the customer's interests, with the belief that if those needs are addressed, the enterprise will also be well served.[7] Customers easily and quickly detect the difference in these two approaches. If the research implications are right—that trusted relationships are profitable relationships—then the fastest way to kill trust is to demonstrate that you are only in it for the money, for yourself. If your customers trust you, you'll be very profitable; but if you try to become profitable by using trust as a self-serving tactic, it won't work. Enterprises actually have to care; customers can tell the difference.

There is nothing wrong, of course, with strategic customer management and customer profitability studies, and CRM is extremely helpful in doing such analysis. But an enterprise's focus is critical to establishing relationships of trust with its customers. People do not tend to trust enterprises that act clearly, consistently, and only in their own self-interests. The question is not whether CRM should be used as a profit management tool—of course it should. The larger question is whether profit is best maximized by acting directly on profit levers, or by achieving profit through focus on identifying and meeting customer needs. An enterprise that embarks upon CRM with purely mercenary aims such as "increase share of wallet" (an inherently zero-sum concept), or "eliminate unprofitable customers," has a mind-set that is fundamentally self-oriented at the outset. The implementation runs the risk of never getting to the larger, win-win implications of CRM—to find out what customers truly need, and then to make informed decisions on the basis of that knowledge—including customer focus, deselection and so forth.

> People do not tend to trust enterprises that act clearly, consistently, and only in their own self-interests.

---

[7]We might say that a vulture is highly customer-centric and customer-focused. It's just that the *purpose* of the focus has nothing to do with the "customer," and everything to do with the vulture itself.

Green's outline here of the types of policies and practices necessary to create a trust-building environment for customers is very helpful. One of the most important aspects of his essay is the concept he introduces regarding an enterprise's self orientation. It is closely akin to what we call the **trusted agent**[8] concept.

BECOMING THE CUSTOMER'S TRUSTED AGENT

Green's formula places the enterprise's perceived level of self-interest in the denominator of the trust equation because his thought is that the degree to which a customer is likely to trust any company is inversely proportional to the amount of "me-first" attitude shown by the company. The more it appears to a customer that the enterprise is acting in its own interest, the less willing the customer will be to trust the enterprise's suggestions and recommendations. And we know that the more a customer does trust an enterprise, the more the customer is likely to want to continue in a relationship with it.

It follows that the most secure, most influential, most profitable type of relationship between an enterprise and a customer is one in which the customer actually trusts the enterprise to act in his own interest. In such a relationship, the customer perceives the enterprise to be his trusted agent, making recommendations and giving advice that furthers the customer's interest, even when it occasionally conflicts with the enterprise's self-interest, at least in the short term.

> Trust is the currency of all commerce.

Earning the customer's trust is one of the earliest goals in any enterprise's effort to build a long-term relationship. Only in a relationship of trust can information pass back and forth freely between buyer and seller. Moreover, in a world of increasingly commoditylike products and services, a relationship founded on trust can provide a genuinely sustainable competitive edge. Trust is the currency of all commerce.

Many professional relationships are based on the concept of the trusted agent. Doctors, lawyers, psychologists, and financial planners must learn a lot about a customer before they can make their individualized recommendations; and their sense of professionalism compels them to make these recommendations in the best interests of their customer. This is, in fact, one of the hallmarks of any profession—that the client's interest will be paramount. The truth is, it's in a doctor's interest to keep his patients ill, so he can continue billing them. But true professionals don't act in their own self-interest; they act in the client's interest, as trusted agents.

Becoming a trusted agent involves more than simple policy decisions on a company's part, no matter how revolutionary those policies might be. A deep, cultural change in attitude at most firms will also be required.

---

[8]Don Peppers and Martha Rogers, PhD, *The One to One Manager* (New York: Doubleday, 1999).

SIDEBAR 3.1

Corporate Heresy[a]

....

As a corporate policy, [being a trusted agent] is a heretical undertaking at most companies, and flies directly in the face of product-centered principles of marketing and competition. If you and I have no relationship prior to the purchase, and we have no relationship following it, then our entire interaction is centered on a single, solitary transaction. And our interests are diametrically opposed. I want to buy the most product at the lowest price from you, and you want to sell me the least product at the highest price.

In a transaction-based, product-centric business model, buyer and seller are adversaries, no matter how much the seller may try not to act the part. In this kind of business model, nearly the only assurance a customer has that he can trust the product and service being sold to him is the general reputation of the brand itself.

But in a one-to-one marketing model, the purchase transaction exists within the context of previous transactions and more that will follow it. Moreover, the buyer and seller collaborate, with the buyer interacting to specify the product, and the seller responding with some change in behavior appropriate for *that* buyer. In the CRM business model, in other words, the buyer and seller must be willing to trust each other far beyond the general reputation of the brand itself.

[a]Excerpted from Don Peppers and Martha Rogers, PhD, *The One to One Manager* (New York: Doubleday,1999).

When General Robert McDermott took the helm at the USAA insurance company in 1968 (see Chapter 8, Sidebar 8.3), he turned this stodgy, bureaucratic company into what was to become a virtual icon of great customer service. To do so he instituted a large amount of reorganization, retraining, computer technology, and reengineering. In addition, he implemented a single, overriding company policy with respect to customer service, which he called his "Golden Rule of Customer Service." McDermott's policy, to be adhered to by all USAA employees, was: "Treat the customer the way you would want to be treated if you were the customer." And, today, the trusted agent mentality at USAA has earned it one of the most loyal and valuable customer bases in the financial services industry.

Conditions exist today that make it even more competitively important for enterprises to take on a role as trusted agent for their customers. In particular:

- *Commoditization.* Traditional marketers have always viewed customers through the lens of "which product are we trying to sell?" Accordingly, in the old economy, a key driver of value was the "rent" producers of products could extract—derived from restricted information flows, brand "uniqueness," and other high-friction elements. Today, the Internet and computer technology have dramatically reduced the friction that used to characterize the exchange of information, with the result that products are becoming more and more like interchangeable commodities, thereby putting the squeeze on rents.

- *Needs, not products.* More relevant—more rent-producing than specific products—are the surrounding services. Customers are not looking for products as much as they are searching for solutions to problems. Consequently, value propositions are shifting. Value will increasingly be produced based on what companies know about "that customer" and what they do to provide customized product/service bundles to meet that customer's needs, or to solve that customer's problem.

To foster a trusted relationship, a customer-based enterprise ensures that it always has a customer's interest in mind. It would not hesitate, for instance, to sell a customer a competitor's product rather than send the customer away empty-handed to look for help at the competitor's door. The focus of every twentieth-century business was its product and inventory. In the twenty-first century, a company's products may be important, but a company can still exist without any products at all. Now, the company must have *customers* to thrive. A trusted agent is one that can be relied upon to make the customer's interest paramount, to speak on the customer's behalf in all its dealings.

A trusted agent's role is to improve the customer's ability to make choices, to manage his life or business. If that means using the agent's own products or services, so much the better. But in any given situation, it might well mean not using the agent's products. An online bookstore, for example, might warn a customer that the book he just ordered does not fit his Web profile, and that other people who have read and enjoyed books similar to the ones he has bought from the bookstore in the past have not liked this particular book. As of this writing, Amazon.com has a policy somewhat (but not exactly) like this in place. Click on a book, and using a one-to-five-star system, Amazon will predict your rating of it, based on your previous purchases and ratings of other books, and incorporating all the other book buyers who have tastes and preferences somewhat similar to yours. While the company displays higher ratings prominently, it doesn't show any ratings on some books—apparently the ones you might not score so highly.

> The focus of every twentieth-century business was its product and inventory. In the twenty-first century, a company's products may be important, but a company can still exist without any products at all. Now, the company must have *customers* to thrive.

The trusted agent is confident that, in the long term, its knowledge of a customer's individual needs and preferences can be *monetized* at a higher value and with greater dependability than can a product or service differentiation. The trusted agent is betting that customer relationships will give it a refuge from the assault of product and service commoditization. Instead of focusing on the profitability of a single transaction, the trusted agent focuses on the profitability of the long-term relationship with the customer. Wall Street calls it "loyalty equity," a concept that is virtually synonymous with "customer equity" and "relationship equity" (see Chapters 1, 5, 11, and 13).

How, exactly, can a trusted agent actually go about monetizing a relationship if it doesn't push its own products in a preferential manner? Many possible trusted agent business models exist. The easiest to imagine is the financial counselor who recommends a variety of products and services to a customer, even though some of these might be offered by competitors. The counselor will likely get a disproportionate share of the customer's business simply because the customer trusts his judgment. Trusted agency is almost certainly the future of relationship management. A trusted agent will recommend product-service combinations based on a customer's individual needs, irrespective of the level of profit that will be made on any particular transaction, and nearly irrespective of the companies that might participate in the product-service delivery. Trusted agency is a compelling, perhaps irresistible response to the increasing commoditization of products and services.

Relationships, to be effective, must be built on trust, but the problem is that most enterprises view their businesses and their enabling technologies through the "wrong end of the telescope." If an enterprise starts by asking how it can use interactivity, databases, and personalization to sell its customers more products, then failure is almost inevitable. This view of the issue is highly self-oriented and simply cannot build a significant level of customer trust. Without trust, customer relationships will not take root, and the company, in the end, will find it impossible to achieve its business goals. The right question to ask, instead, is how can the enterprise use interactivity, databases, and personalization technologies to add value for its customers, by saving them time or money, or creating a better fitting or more appropriate product?

> The right question to ask, instead, is how can the enterprise use interactivity, databases, and personalization technologies to add value for its customers, by saving them time or money, or creating a better fitting or more appropriate product?

RELATIONSHIPS REQUIRE INFORMATION, BUT INFORMATION COMES ONLY WITH TRUST

Customers will ultimately have to decide how much information they are willing to share about themselves with an enterprise. Those who are freer with their information will receive more customized and personal service, but will sacrifice a level of privacy. The future of a customer-strategy business world depends on gaining the customer's trust; relationships don't exist without it. Without trust, customers will not give an enterprise the information it needs in order to serve that customer better. Lose customer trust and everything is lost. If a customer wasn't sure that his insurance company was not sharing his vital information with other companies, would he even think about filling out all those forms? If a customer does not trust his bank, would he give it every single iota of financial information about his business to qualify for a loan? (Businesses give their patronage to more than one bank so they won't be unduly dependent on any single institution, but some consumers give their business to more than one bank so that no single financial institution will have complete knowledge of their finances.)

Fred Newell wrote that as marketers develop more and more information about the lives and lifestyles of customers, the privacy issue heats up around the world. "Privacy issues will have to be examined from fresh perspectives if we are to continue the delicate balance between the marketer's need for information and the consumer's desire to control that information. The marketing community, so anxious for a continuing flow of customer information, must work to keep the balance by sharing more positive stories of customer benefits, to balance the media focus on Big-Brotherism, and the legislators' zeal to 'protect us' from ourselves."[9]

Once customers feel assured that their data are safe with the company, the next logical step is to make it comfortable for them to share more and more information. It is better to build a customer relationship gradually, one piece at a time, than to flood the relationship with massive doses of data. (Think of this kind of information exchange as *drip irrigation*, a concept we'll discuss in Chapter 7). At every step of the collaboration, enterprises need to concentrate on gathering the information useful to them. To build the necessary trust for customers to do that, enterprises often need to offer their customers something of value in return for the information. Many offer direct, cash-oriented benefits such as discounts, coupons, or promotions.

> Privacy issues will have to be examined from fresh perspectives if we are to continue the delicate balance between the marketer's need for information and the consumer's desire to control that information.

Not surprisingly, some of the most successful companies working on this kind of "information exchange" take steps to individualize the offer so that it has greater value to a particular customer.

Customers are also becoming comfortable using automatic personalization tools on the Web. While these tools are fine for customizing Web sites, they often fall short for nurturing enterprise/customer relationships. The enterprise must work harder to truly get to know the customer. A customer is more likely to stay loyal if he has taken the time to personalize a Web site himself, and the enterprise acts on the information given. One of the primary goals of the enterprise focused on building customer value is to use the information it gathers about a customer to customize some aspect of its product or service to suit the customer's needs. The enterprise should begin to offer the customer things relevant to him, things that the customer could never find anywhere else, not from any generic offering that doesn't have information to use about him to meet his needs better. As a result, the customer will trust the company more.

Once the flow of information begins between the customer and the enterprise, it is imperative for the enterprise to enable the customer to feel he controls his information. The enterprise should enable the customer to use the information to save him time and money and deliver value. All of this will fulfill the customer's expectations of trust and earn his lifetime loyalty. Using a customer's information to his advantage might involve reminding him when he is going to run out of a product he uses regularly or developing a related product or service he could use.

---

[9]Frederick Newell, *The New Rules of Marketing* (New York: McGraw-Hill Professional Book Group, 1997).

The irony of the ongoing privacy debate is that, provided the customer is doing business with a legitimate enterprise committed to responsible privacy protection, the ultimate loser will be the consumer himself, if the information flow to the enterprise is severed. Precise product targeting can dramatically lower marketing costs and subsequently product prices. While some consumers have said that they want customized offerings and the advantages enterprises can give them by tracking their personal data, it is essential to guarantee that the customized benefits provided will not jeopardize their privacy. Customers need to know that the company will use that data in a limited way for services agreed on in advance. Without such trust, customization is not a benefit.

SUMMARY

Trust is the currency of all commerce. The single most powerful position in any customer's mind is a position of trust. For that reason, earning the customer's trust almost always becomes one of the earliest goals in any effort to build a long-term relationship with a customer. Tom Peters points out that, "In our world gone mad, trust is, paradoxically, more important than ever."[10] Let's face it: In a world of increasingly commodity-like products and services, a relationship founded on trust is the only genuinely sustainable competitive edge. Without trust, you're back to square one: *price competition*. The alternative is Learning Relationships, and the way to a Learning Relationship is IDIC.

> Trust is the currency of all commerce.

In the next chapter, we'll talk in more detail about the first implementation task in the IDIC methodology: identifying customers.

SIDEBAR 3.2

CRM Scenario: Governments Develop Learning Relationships with "Citizen-Customers"

The "citizen as customer" is an innovative concept that is becoming more of a reality in the interactive era. Governments are becoming more "citizen-centric." State motor vehicle departments are streamlining and customizing the task of renewing a driver's license. Municipalities now allow residents to pay parking tickets and municipal bills online. Municipalities that develop Learning Relationships with their individual citizens can benefit primarily by being able to spend the taxpayer's money more productively and fairly. Suppose the parks department of a small city were to distribute bar-coded cards that could be swiped each time a citizen uses a parks service, permitting easy identification, record-keeping, and tracking of individual interactions. By identifying who is using the city's swimming pools, playing fields, summer camps,

---

[10]Tom Peters, at *www.tompeters.com.*

or senior citizens' programs, the agency could see which services are in higher demand on the part of particular citizens, or types of citizens. It might then be able to save money by customizing the seasonal fliers and catalogs it mails. For those citizens who have shown an interest in park concerts, e-mail messages could notify them of upcoming events. Perhaps even the department's services could be tailored to reflect the more specific needs of the town's most interested and active citizens.

One thing that is very clear is that building a Learning Relationship between a citizen and a government will require just as much trust as does building a commercial relationship. But can a government really build this kind of trust? And would the answer to this question be different in different countries? If a government were indeed capable of providing a great deal more convenience to you, would you trust it with the information required to do so?

E-ZPass, an automated toll-collection technology designed to reduce traffic volume at New York City's bridge and tunnel tollbooths, has provided a tool for the government to use individual information to improve itself and the efficiency of its public service—the roads, bridges, and tunnels. The electronic pass automatically identifies the vehicle as it passes through the tollbooth and automatically charges the toll to the owner's credit or debit card. This both permits faster movement through the tolls and enables database tracking of an individual's whereabouts (and presumably the speed with which the car gets from one checkpoint to the next!). The New York Transit Authority has maintained that the owner's information will be protected. Becoming a genuine, citizen-focused government agency, therefore, requires much more thought and effort than a few programs such as E-ZPass. As businesses everywhere are discovering, what really ensures a customer's goodwill and loyalty is not just putting up a Web site, but creating Learning Relationships with her.

Suppose a city began to monitor traffic intersections with video surveillance to nab vehicles that run through red lights. Would you object if the city sent you a traffic ticket because it had videotaped evidence of your car involved in such a misdemeanor? What if the city decided to keep track of your vehicle's location as it passed video cameras around town? Or what if it kept records of photos of you and your passengers without your knowledge?

In the context of a government developing individual relationships with its citizen-customers, there is a give-and-take scenario that emerges with respect to the right to privacy and the demand for personalization (see Chapter 9 for a detailed discussion on privacy). In this scenario, the citizen-customers would want a government that could personalize their experience of living and working in the city; at the same time they would want to be able to trust the government enough to protect and respect any personal information that it gathered about them. The government, in contrast, would want to collect as much information as possible about each citizen-customer to create a more personalized living experience.

It must be noted, however, that, with respect to privacy, there is a big difference between a government and an enterprise. An enterprise that collects personal information about a customer would hold it in confidence from other enterprises because its proprietary nature provides a competitive advantage. The more it knows about an individual customer that its competitor does *not* know, the better an enterprise can personalize its relationship with that customer and grow its share of that customer's business. The customer would be less likely to defect to a competitor. A government, however,

> **SIDEBAR 3.2** *(continued)*
>
> ....
>
> would like to know all it could about its citizens, and might find advantages in sharing information with other government agencies. One government agency, for example, might like the capability to cross-check a criminal's driver's license number with his Social Security number and all of his prior aliases. While this would make it harder to commit a crime under such a jurisdiction, many citizen-customers would likely object to such an invasion of privacy. Indeed, a number of influential citizens objected to allowing intelligence agencies and criminal investigation agencies to share information about specific suspects in an effort to prevent future terrorist attacks—a government activity that was made legal by the post-September 11, 2001, Patriot Act.

FOOD FOR THOUGHT

1. Think about the companies you do business with as a customer. Name an example of a company that identified and recognized you, one that differentiated you by need or value, one that has made interaction easy and fun, and one that has changed something about the way it does business with you now, based on what it knows about you.

2. Do you agree or disagree that a relationship must always be characterized by some level of emotional involvement?

3. Now that you've read Green's essay on trust, can you think of examples of companies that have little or no self-orientation? What are the signs that a company has too much self-orientation?

4. Within the last few years we have seen many examples of the breakdown between company governance and stakeholder interests. Do you think these corporate scandals might have played out differently if the corporations involved had built their businesses on the basis of becoming trusted agents for their customers? Is it really possible for companies to be trusted?

GLOSSARY

Customize   Become relevant by doing something for a customer that no competition can do who doesn't have all the information about that customer that you do.

Differentiate   Prioritize by value; understand different needs.

Identify   Recognize, link, remember.

Interact   Generate and record feedback.

Self-orientation   Self-interest. A company that focuses on building customer value is obviously interested in its own bottom line, but believes the bottom line is best served by focusing on the needs of customers.

Trusted agent   A person or organization that makes recommendations and gives advice to a customer that furthers the customer's own interest, even when it occasionally conflicts with the enterprise's own self-interest, at least in the short term.

Identifying Customers

4

Chapter

Before any relationship can start, both parties to it have to know each other's identities. The goal of identifying customers refers not so much to figuring out which customers we want (that comes later) but to recognizing *each customer* as that customer *each time we come in contact with her, and then linking those different data points to develop a full picture of each particular customer. This chapter addresses the issues of "identify" for consumers as well as business customers, and defines the different elements of the identify task. We also address* frequency marketing *in the context of customer identification. Contributions help round out the discussion. Stewart Alsop's classic article about Amazon.com, written before the company became profitable, helps to clarify the role the Internet played in enabling companies to create a profitable business model based on identifying individual customers. The result? No less than a customer data revolution. Rashi Glazer adds to our understanding with his insights into the role of so-called smart markets in managing relationships with customers.*

All enterprises use information about their customers to make smarter decisions. But for most traditional marketing decisions and actions, information is really only needed at the aggregate, or market, level. That is, any marketer needs to know the *average* demand for a particular product feature within a population of prospective customers, or the range of prices that this market population will find attractive. The enterprise then uses this information to plan its production and distribution, as well as its marketing and sales activities.

But building relationships with individual customers necessarily involves making decisions and taking actions at the level of the *individual* customer, using customer-specific information in addition to information about the aggregate characteristics of the market population. So the competitor trying to win with superior customer strategies needs first to know the individual *identities* of the customers who make up the traditional marketer's aggregate market population. Then the enterprise will make different marketing, sales, distribution, and production decisions, and take different actions, with respect to different customers, even within the same market or niche population.

INDIVIDUAL INFORMATION REQUIRES CUSTOMER RECOGNITION

The essence of managing customer relationships is treating different customers differently; therefore, the first requirement for any enterprise to engage in this type of competition is simply to "know" one customer from another. However, identifying individual customers is not an easy process, and usually not a perfect one. Not many years ago, a British utility launched a December promotion to recognize its very best customers by mailing each of them a holiday greeting card, and to the astonishment of its management, nearly 25 percent of these cards were returned to the company unopened in January. Apparently, many of the firm's "most valuable customers" were actually lampposts. Until that time, this company's management had equated electric meters with customers, comfortable in the knowledge that because they tracked meters, they also tracked customers. But lampposts don't read mail.

Most enterprises will find it difficult simply to compile a complete and accurate list of all the uniquely individual customers they serve, though some businesses and industries are more naturally able to identify their customers than others. Consider the differences among these businesses:

- *Long-distance phone companies* generally sell directly to the consumers who buy their "Dial 1" service. After all, to bill a customer for her calls in any given sales period, a long-distance phone company's computers must track that customer's calling activities—numbers connected to, time spent in each connection, day of week, and time of day. But in many areas of the United States, the long-distance company's billing is simply included in the local exchange carrier's monthly bill to the customer, so that the long-distance carrier has no mechanism to interact with the customer, or even to identify her. The long-distance carrier will know the phone number and all its various transactions, but in such a case only the local exchange carrier will know the customer's actual identity.

- *Retail banks* must know individual customer identities to keep track of each customer's banking activities and balances. But the credit card offered to customers by the same bank is processed in the credit card division, rather than the branch banking division, and information about whether a branch banking customer is also a credit card customer is often not readily available to either separate division. Similarly, a home equity loan may come from yet another, separate division. And the retail consumer who is also a business owner will most likely be thought of as two separate customers by the same bank.

- *Consumer packaged goods* companies sell their grocery and personal care products in supermarkets, drug stores, and other retail outlets. Although their true end customers are those who walk into the stores and buy these products, there is no technically simple way for the packaged goods companies to find out who these retail consumers are.

- *Insurance companies* can nearly always tell you how many policies they have written, but many cannot tell you how many customers they have, or even how many households or businesses they serve.
- *A computer equipment company* selling systems to other companies in a business-to-business environment may be able to identify the businesses it is selling to, but it is much more difficult for the firm to identify the individual *players* who actually participate in each organization's decision to buy. Yet within any business customer it is these players—decision makers, influencers, specifiers, approvers, contract authorities, purchasing agents, reviewers, end users—with whom the selling company should be developing relationships.
- *Carmakers,* as well as state and local governments, have for decades recorded the current owner of each registered automobile by the vehicle identification number (VIN), visible through the front window of any car. However, even though the owner of each car can be determined, the cars belonging to each owner cannot. More recently, carmakers have begun relying on customer identification numbers, in order to tell whether two VINs are concurrently or sequentially owned by the same customer.

Identifying customers, therefore, is not usually very easy, and the degree of difficulty any company faces in identifying its own customers is largely a function of its business model and its channel structure. In her book, *Customers.com*, business consultant Patricia Seybold speculates that Microsoft probably has more than 100 million customers who have purchased its products through indirect channels (i.e., buying the software bundled on a computer, ordering it through a catalog, or picking it up at a store). And yet, for many years, the only end customers Microsoft knew about were the 90 enterprise accounts it maintained and the 25 million people who had sent in warranty registration cards. Then, in the late 1990s, as customers flocked to Microsoft's Web site and interacted with the company, Microsoft began identifying much greater numbers of its customers, and collecting specific information about them individually, including e-mail addresses and product preferences.[1]

To engage any of its customers in relationships, an enterprise needs to know these customers' identities. Thus, it must first understand the limitations, make choices, and set priorities with respect to its need to identify individual customers. How many end-customer identities are actually known to the enterprise today? How accurate are these identities? How much duplication and overlap is there in the data? What proportion of all customer identities are known? Are there ways the enterprise could uncover a larger number of customer identities? If so, which customer identities does the enterprise want to access first?

---

[1]Patricia B. Seybold, *Customers.com: How to Create a Profitable Business Strategy for the Internet and Beyond* (New York: Random House, 1998).

STEP 1: HOW MUCH CUSTOMER IDENTIFICATION DOES A COMPANY ALREADY HAVE?

To assess more accurately how much customer-identifying information it already has, an enterprise should:

1. *Take an inventory of all of the customer data already available in any kind of electronic format.* Customer identification information might be stored in several electronic places, such as on the Web server or in the call center database.
2. *Find customer-identifying information that is "on file" but not electronically compiled.* Data about customers that has been written down but not electronically recorded should be transferred to a computer database, if it is valuable, so that it will be accessible internally and protected from loss or unnecessary duplication.

Only after it assesses its current inventory of customer-identifying information should a company launch its own programs for gathering more. Programs designed to collect customer-identifying information might include, for instance, the purchase of the data, if it is available, from various third-party database companies; or the scheduling of an event to be attended by customers; or a contest, a frequency marketing program, or some other promotion that encourages customers to "raise their hands."

SIDEBAR 4.1

Real Objective of Frequency Marketing Programs

Frequency marketing is a tactic by which an enterprise rewards its customers with points, discounts, merchandise, or other incentives, in return for the customer patronizing the enterprise on a repeated basis. When a frequency marketing program is run in connection with an automated information-gathering and database system, the program itself can provide an indispensable tool, enabling a company to identify and track its customers, one customer at a time, across different operating units or divisions, through different channels, and over long periods of time. By providing the customer with an incentive for purchasing that is linked to the customer's previous purchases, the enterprise ensures that she has an interest in (1) identifying herself to the company, and (2) "raising her hand" whenever she deals with the company. The customer wants the incentive, and in order to get it, she must engage in activity that allows the enterprise to identify her and track her transactions, over time.

It is not absolutely necessary for a frequency marketing program to be linked to a customer ID system. Top Value (TV) stamps and S&H Green Stamps programs were very popular in the 1950s and 1960s. As a consumer, you might choose to shop at grocery stores or gas stations that gave away green stamps. You'd pay your bill and get a receipt and your stamps in exchange. Then you would go home and paste the stamps into the right places on the pages of the little paperback books you had been given. Six books would get you a toaster; 4,300 books would buy a fishing boat.

SIDEBAR 4.1 *(continued)*

··

These giveaways were not used to identify customers, however. Clearly customers had an incentive to patronize those establishments giving out the stamps, but the stamps themselves constituted the program's currency; no customer information was generated for any of the participating companies. There was no central customer database maintaining any records of the purchase transactions. When a customer brought in her books of stamps to redeem them for merchandise, there was no mechanism to track this customer back to her specific transactions. She could collect stamps for her cash purchase at a gas station without her transaction being tracked at all. Nevertheless, we would still classify such a program as a frequency marketing program, because customers are indeed rewarded for the frequency and volume of their purchases, but such "unlinked" programs are practically useless when it comes to aiding a company in its effort to build customer relationships.

So from our standpoint, when we discuss frequency marketing, we will be talking about the type of program that is backed by some form of database of transactions that supports the reward decisions. The primary objective of frequency marketing programs of this type should be to accumulate customer information by encouraging purchasers to identify themselves. For some companies—particularly those firms that find it difficult to identify and track customers who nevertheless engage in frequent or repeated transactions—frequency marketing programs can perform a vital part of the identify task, allowing a firm to link the interactions and transactions of a single customer from one event to the next. Grocery frequent shopper programs are excellent examples of this kind of frequency marketing.

This has an important implication about the "cost" of such a program. If, essentially, goods and services are discounted with stamps or points, and that's the entire program, then it is a *parity strategy;* and after competitors match the points or the miles, the only thing the sponsoring company will end up with are reduced profit margins. But if, say, the points are given in exchange for shopping basket data or other information about a customer that can be used to deepen the relationship, then the information derived is an investment that can be returned as the company builds a more loyal relationship with a customer.

As a matter of practice, many companies implement such programs with the sole intention of rewarding customers for giving them more of their patronage. The risk to the enterprise of doing this is that if the frequency program is a success, competitors will eventually offer customers the same or similar rewards structures for buying from them. Over time, the program will be reduced to nothing more than a sophisticated form of price competition, as in fact happened to the S&H Green Stamps program.

To a customer, the incentive itself (e.g., free miles, free goods, and discounts) will almost certainly be the immediate motive for participating. Then it is up to the enterprise to use the information to treat the customer differently. It is the information about an individual customer's purchases and needs that enables the enterprise to tailor its behavior or customize its product or service for that particular customer. Such information is critical to building an ongoing Learning Relationship. The greater the level of customization, the more loyal customers can become.

It is not always so easy to figure out how to treat different customers differently, however, even when they can be individually identified and tracked. A grocery store's frequency marketing program can return a rich detail of information about the individual shopping habits of the store's customers, but what should the store then do with this information? From a practical standpoint, the store cannot customize

---

SIDEBAR 4.1 *(continued)*

....

itself to meet the needs of individual customers. The store is destined to be the same for every customer who enters it, because it would be totally impractical to rearrange the merchandise to meet the needs of any particular customer. Nevertheless, it should be possible to use the information about the mix of products consumed by a single customer in such a way as to make highly customized offers to that customer.

Tesco, for instance, with 670 stores, is the largest supermarket chain in the United Kingdom, and has a highly successful frequency marketing program that illustrates exactly what it means to make different offers to different customers. Tesco's Clubcard program boasted more than 10 million members in 2001, when we first started writing this book, and its members' purchases accounted for about 80 percent of all Tesco's in-store transactions.

Since implementing Clubcard, in-store product turnover increased more than 51 percent behind a mere 15 percent increase in floor space. The company credits its success with the fact that it is engaged in "rifle-shot" marketing to its customer base, rather than the more traditional scatter-shot approach of the mass merchant. The Clubcard program allows Tesco to link product information with each individual customer's past purchases. So, for example, based on its individual customer data, Tesco can send a Clubcard member a personalized letter with coupons aimed squarely at that particular customer's own shopping needs. This program generates an astonishing *high* redemption rate of some 90 percent!

Tesco has differentiated more than 5,000 different "needs segments" among its customers, and uses this insight to send out highly customized offers. All members also receive a remarkably mass-customized quarterly magazine. Tesco has defined eight primary "life state" customer groups, with each edition's editorial content specifically written for its target group. Counting the multiplicity of third-party advertisements, Tesco's magazines are printed and distributed in literally hundreds of thousands of combinations. (See Patty Seybold's section on Tesco in Chapter 15.)

Some enterprises charge customers a membership fee to belong to a frequency marketing program. Car rental companies, for example, have in the past had programs that charge customers a separate membership fee to guarantee preferential treatment at airports; these programs tracked the customer's individual transactions as well. Customers who are willing to invest money in a continuing Learning Relationship with an enterprise become committed to the collaborative solution of a problem. And any enterprise that collaborates with its customers is more likely to be able to ask the types of questions needed to achieve a higher share of a customer's business. It is easier for the enterprise to ask questions of a customer who has agreed to enter a relationship with the enterprise.

STEP 2: GET CUSTOMERS TO IDENTIFY THEMSELVES

Sales contests and sponsored events are often designed for the specific purpose of gathering potential and established customer names and addresses. But to engage a customer in a genuine relationship, a company must also be able to link the customer to her own specific purchase and service transaction behavior. Analyzing past behavior is probably the single most useful method for modeling a customer's future value, as we'll see in Chapter 5, on customer differentiation, and Chapter 12, on analytics. So although a one-time contest or promotion might help a company identify customers it did not previously "know," linking the customer's identity to her actual transactions is also important.

Frequency marketing programs suit both purposes, providing not only a mechanism to identify customers, but also a means to link customers, over time, with the specific transactions they undertake. These so-called loyalty programs, such as the frequent shopper plans offered by many retail grocery chains, have been used for years to strengthen relationships with individual customers. It is important to recognize, however, that a frequency marketing program is a tactic, not a strategy. It is an important enabling step for a broader relationship strategy, because a frequency marketing program provides a company with a mechanism for identifying and tracking customers, individually; but this will only lead to a genuine relationship-management strategy when the company actually uses the information it gets in this way to design different treatments for different customers. (See Sidebar 4.1.)

WHAT DOES "IDENTIFY" MEAN?

Given that the purpose of identifying individual customers is to facilitate the development of relationships with them individually, we are using the word *identify* in its broadest possible form. What we are really saying is that an enterprise must undertake all of these identification activities:

IDENTIFICATION ACTIVITIES

- *Define.* Decide what information will comprise the actual customer's identity: Is it name and address? Home phone number? Account number? Householding information?
- *Collect.* Arrange to collect these customer identities. Collection mechanisms could include frequent shopper bar codes, credit card data, paper applications, Web-based interactions, radio frequency identification (RFID) microchips (such as E-ZPass and ExxonMobil's Speedpass), or any number of other vehicles.
- *Link.* Once a customer's identity is fixed, it must be linked to all transactions and interactions with that customer, at all points of contact, and within all the enterprise's different operating units and divisions. It is one thing, for instance, to identify the consumer who goes into a grocery store, but a frequent shopper program is usually the primary mechanism to link that shopper's activities together, so that the enterprise knows it is the same shopper, every time she comes into the store. If a customer shops online for a product but then contacts the company's call center to order it, the relationship-oriented enterprise wants to be able to link that customer's online interactions with her call-in order.
- *Integrate.* The customer's identity must not only be linked to all interactions and transactions, it must also be integrated into the information systems the

enterprise uses to run its business. Frequent-flier identities need to be integrated into the flight reservations data system. Household banking identities need to be integrated into the small business records maintained by the bank.

- *Recognize.* The customer who returns to a different part of the organization needs to be recognized as the same customer, not a different one. In other words, the customer who visits the Web site today, goes in to the store tomorrow, and calls the toll-free number next week needs to be recognized as the same customer, not three separate events or visitors.
- *Store.* Identifying information about individual customers must be stored and maintained in one or several electronic databases.
- *Update.* All customer data, including customer identifying data, is subject to change and must be regularly verified, updated, improved, or revised.
- *Analyze.* Customer identities must serve as the key inputs for analyzing individual customer differences (see Chapter 12).
- *Make available.* The data on customer identities maintained in an enterprise's databases must be made available to the people and functions within the enterprise that need access to it. Especially in a service organization, making individual customer-identifying information available to front-line service personnel is important. Computers help enterprises codify, aggregate, filter, and sort customer information for their own and their customers' benefit. Storing customer identification information in an accessible format is critical to the success of a customer-centered enterprise.
- *Secure.* Because individual customer identities are both competitively sensitive and threatening to individual customer privacy, it is critical to secure this information to prevent its unauthorized use.

Technology is enabling enterprises to identify customers in ways never before imagined. Some enterprises still might use the old Rolodex card-file system, but computer databases and sophisticated customer information data warehouses are quickly supplanting these handwritten cards for the same reason that public libraries have abandoned their card catalog systems: because card catalog systems cost much more than their electronic counterparts, and are only available for search in the physical library building. Sophisticated electronic data systems allow library patrons to search a library's holdings from anywhere, and help the library cut its own costs at the same time.

Data warehouses not only help reduce costs. More importantly, they also help identify patterns that aren't possible when the data is in silos. The more the company integrates data from all corners of the enterprise, even including the extended enterprise, the more rich in value the customer information becomes in planning and executing customer-focused strategies.

The end customer of an enterprise is the one who consumes the product or service it provides. That said, sometimes it is more of an indirect relationship, which makes it more difficult to tag the customer and link information to her. The product or service might be purchased by one customer but used by another member of a household, or by the recipient of a gift.

CUSTOMER IDENTIFICATION IN A B2B SETTING

A business-to-business (B2B) enterprise must still identify customers, and many of the issues are the same; but there are some important differences that merit additional consideration. For instance, when selling to business customers, the B2B enterprise must consider who will be on the other side of the relationship. Will it be the purchasing manager or the executive who signs the purchase order? Will it be the financial vice president who approved the contract? Or will it be the production supervisor who actually uses the product? The correct way for an enterprise to approach a B2B scenario is to think of each of these individuals as a part of the customer base. Each is important in her own way, and each one should be identified and tracked. The greatest challenge for many businesses that sell to other businesses is identifying the product's end users. Discovering who, within the corporate customer's organization, puts a product to work (who depends on the product to do her job) is often quite difficult. Some methods for identifying end users include: [2]

- If the product consumes any replenishable supplies (e.g., inks, drill bits, recording paper, chemicals), providing a convenient method for reordering these supplies is an obvious service for end users.
- If the product is complicated to use, requiring a detailed instruction manual or perhaps different sets of application notes, or even training, one way to secure end-user identities is to offer such complicated instructions in a simplified, individually tailored format.
- If the product needs periodic maintenance or calibration or regular service for any reason, the enterprise can use these occasions to identify end users.

B2B firms use many strategies to get to know the various role players within the corporations they are selling to, from end users to CFOs—setting up personal meetings, participating at trade shows, swapping business cards, sponsoring seminars and other events, inviting people to work-related entertainment occasions, and so forth. But the single most important method for identifying the "relationships within relationships" at an enterprise customer is to provide a service or a benefit for the customer that can only really be fully realized when the players themselves reveal their identities and participate actively in the relationship. An excellent example of this type of program is Dell Computer's Premier Pages program (see Chapter 10). Thus, even though relationship marketing has always been a standard tool in the B2B space, today's new technologies are making it possible more than ever before to manage the actual mechanics of these individual relationships, from the enterprise level. In so doing, the enterprise ensures that the relationship itself adheres to the enterprise, not just to the sales representative or other employee conducting the activity.

[2]Don Peppers, Martha Rogers, PhD, and Bob Dorf, *The One to One Fieldbook: The Complete Toolkit for Implementing a 1to1 Marketing Program* (New York: Doubleday, 1999).

CUSTOMER IDENTIFICATION IN A B2C SETTING

Can we identify—and recognize again—*millions* of customers? In the B2C space, the technology-driven CRM movement has only recently made it possible even to conceive of the possibility of managing individual consumer relationships. But while managing relationships within the B2C space might be a relatively new idea, mass marketers have always understood that customer information is critical and that the possible ways of identifying customers are nearly limitless. Identifying information includes their characteristics, geographic locations, and channel position. Professor George Day, in his book *Market-Driven Strategy: Processes for Creating Value,* wrote that identifiers are the relatively enduring and generic descriptions of customers that can be used to reach them with a marketing strategy.[3] These descriptions are usually based on demographics or aspects of the customer's lifestyle or decision-making process.

New technologies have made it possible to identify customers without their active involvement. ExxonMobil, the gasoline retailer, dispenses RFID microchips that can be carried around on the keychain of a customer who participates in its Speedpass campaign. When the customer drives up to a gas pump, the car-mounted device automatically activates the pump and charges the customer's credit card for the transaction. The customer is rewarded with a speedier exit from the gas pump, although she still must pump her own gas. The company, in turn, can identify each customer every time she buys gas at any ExxonMobil station and link that identification with every transaction.

Of course, few would deny that the Internet is what has given the biggest push to the customer-relationship movement in the B2C arena. The last five years of the twentieth century saw an expanding wave of new, consumer-oriented Internet sites, sponsored both by existing businesses and by entirely new, Internet-only companies. This boom generated a stampede of new capital investors, with the result that there were a number of not-so-well-thought-out business ideas getting funded at extraordinarily high valuations, some with very large amounts of cash. The ready funding of poorly developed new ideas created the financial "bubble" that burst at the turn of the new century.

But lost in the finger-pointing that followed this boom-and-bust turmoil were some genuinely new ideas that, for the most part, turned on the area of using the Internet as an individually interactive tool to manage individual customer relationships at the consumer level. Stewart Alsop had it pegged in 2001.

[3]George Day, *Market-Driven Strategy: Processes for Creating Value* (New York: The Free Press, 1999). See also Jag Sheth, Rajendra Sisodia, and Arun Sharma, "The Antecedents and Consequences of Customer-Centric Marketing," *Journal of the Academy of Marketing Science* 28, no. 1 (Winter 2000), pp. 55–66; Hugh Watson, Thilini Ariyachandra, and Robert J. Matyska, Jr., "Data Warehousing Stages of Growth," *Information Management* (Summer 2001), pp. 42–50.

THE INTERNET'S ROLE IN CUSTOMER IDENTIFICATION: BETTING ON AMAZON[4]

Stewart Alsop
General partner, New Enterprise Associates
Columnist, *Fortune*

I believe the Internet represents a fundamental change in the way business gets done. eBay is amazing: profitable, unique, with a great culture and attitude. But other Internet companies have also made remarkable contributions. Amazon.com is one.

Most people think of Amazon.com as an e-tailer, and value it for how it sells products and distributes them. Those people make the fundamental mistake of comparing Amazon.com with other retailers and direct-marketing companies.

I think of Amazon.com as a technology company. It may be the only company to have mastered the use of technology in serving individual customers. No other outfit comes close to tracking what its customers do and using that information to make its customers happy. The result: As time goes by, I find myself buying more and more stuff from Amazon.com and feeling good about it. I actually look forward to getting e-mail messages from Amazon.com promoting stuff that I can buy. They are the only commercial e-mails that don't irritate me —the only ones.

During February and March 2001, I got 16 e-mails from Amazon. Six showed me new products in my favorite categories: books, movies, music, and consumer electronics. The other 10 promoted special offers or specific products tailored to me. For instance, on March 20, I got an e-mail that started out, "As somebody who has purchased movies directed by David Lean, you might like to know that *Lawrence of Arabia* will be released April 3 on DVD. For the next few days, you can preorder your copy at a savings of 30 percent by following the link below." So I clicked on the link and preordered the DVD. And while I was shopping, Amazon also recommended *Ben-Hur* and *Cleopatra*. So I bought those, too.

Amazon.com has created a successful system of one-to-one marketing. It's the first company to really take advantage of something the Internet makes possible. In the old days, only small outfits could keep track of customers: your local tailor, the local barber, the butcher at the grocery store. As retailing and customer services have consolidated, we've bemoaned the loss of that personal touch. The Internet can bring it back.

At most companies, internal conflicts make that very difficult. The sales department at a Fortune 500 company, for instance, rarely works well—if at all—with the customer service folks. But Amazon.com is a company founded by a visionary who understood that the real opportunity was in using the technology to build long-term relationships. Jeff Bezos focused early on building a

[4]Adapted with permission from "I'm Betting on Amazon," a column in *Fortune* magazine about the way companies are managing customer relationships (April 30, 2001).

technology platform: He hired the best IT managers and engineers, he set rules that favored the customer, and he relentlessly built a customer-oriented culture. A couple of years ago I asked Bezos what I thought the killer question was: "Jeff," I asked, "when are you going to know that Amazon needs to make a profit, rather than putting growth first?" He replied, "Customers come first. If you focus on what customers want and build a relationship, they will allow you to make money." That creates a long-term sustainable advantage, one that tends not to be subject to the quantitative analysis performed by most Wall Street analysts. It's the one that results in the 17 orders I made one year, totaling $774.19 in revenue for Amazon.com.

What Amazon.com has done is invent and implement a model for interacting with millions of customers, one at a time. Old-line companies can't do that—I like Nordstrom, Eddie Bauer, Starbucks, and Shell, but they have to reach out to me with mass advertising and marketing. Amazon's technology gives me exactly what I want, in an extraordinarily responsive way. The underlying technology, in fact, is revolutionizing the way companies do business on the Web.

CUSTOMER DATA REVOLUTION

Clearly, in the interactive era, an enterprise can reach and communicate with individual customers one at a time; and it can follow strategies for its customer interactions that are based on relevant, customer-specific information stored in a customer database. The computer can now store millions of customer records—not just names and addresses, but age, gender, marital status and family configuration, buying habits, and history, and demographic and psychographic profiles. Individuals can be selected from this database by one, two, three, or more of their identifying characteristics.[5] CRM expert Stan Rapp has said that the computer has brought about "three awesome powers": the power to *record*, the power to *find*, and the power to *compare*.

> The computer has brought about "three awesome powers": the power to *record*, the power to *find*, and the power to *compare*.

- *The computer's power to record.* In the precomputer days, there would have been no point in recording by typewriter dozens of bits of information about each customer or prospect on thousands of index cards. Without the computer, there would have been no practical way to make use of such information. As computer data storage rapidly became more economical, however, it became possible and desirable to build up and use a prospect or customer record with great detail.
- *The computer's power to find.* Selections can be made from the prospect or customer file by any field definitions or combination of field definitions.

[5]Stan Rapp, *The Great Marketing Turnaround* (Upper Saddle River, NJ: Prentice Hall, 1990).

- *The computer's power to compare.* Information on customers with one set of characteristics can be compared to customer information using a different set of characteristics. For instance, the computer can compare a list of *older people* and a list of *golfers.*

For all its power, however, the truth is that when it comes to customer-oriented activities, the computer is an underutilized technology at most businesses—not because companies don't want to use it, but because most customer data are simply not fit for use in an analytical database. Seventy to 80 percent of the cost of operating a data warehouse is in extracting and transforming operational data for decision-making use.[6] The development of a database of customer information requires a *data model*—the tool required to bring data complexities under control. The data model defines the structure of the database and lays a map for how information about customers will be organized and deployed.

At present, most customer data is often duplicated in multiple-operational databases. Multiple instances of data usually create data quality issues (think of how many times you've gotten mail from your bank with your name misspelled or the wrong address) that need to be addressed head-on in order to be successful. This raises issues of data ownership and accountability, and can become a politically-charged issue in the organization. But those companies that try to implement customer relationship management without addressing this critical issue usually fail. It has to start with a single view of each customer.

WHAT DATA DO WE NEED WHEN WE IDENTIFY A CUSTOMER?

After it has mined its existing customer databases and developed a plan to gather new customer information, the enterprise then decides how to tag its customers' individual identities. Names are not always a sufficient customer identifier. More than one customer might have the same name, or a customer might use several different varieties of the same name—middle initial, nickname, maiden name, and so forth. To use a customer database effectively, therefore, it is usually necessary to assign unique and reliable customer numbers or identifiers to each individual customer record. It could be the customer's phone number, a "user name" selected by the customer, or an internally generated identifier.

In addition to transaction details, other types of data generated from internal operations can make significant contributions. Information relating to billing and account status, customer service interactions, back orders, product shipment, product returns, claims history, and internal operating costs all can significantly affect an enterprise's understanding of its customers. Directly supplied data consists of data obtained directly from customers, prospects, or suspects. It

[6]Frederick Newell, *Loyalty.com* (New York: McGraw-Hill, 2000).

is generally captured from lead-generation questionnaires, customer surveys, warranty registration cards, customer service interactions, Web site responses, interviews, focus groups, or other direct interactions with individuals.

Directly supplied data consists of three obvious types:

1. *Behavioral* data, such as purchase and buying habits, clickstream data, interactions with the company, communication channels chosen, language used, product consumption, and company share of wallet.
2. *Attitudinal* data, reflecting attitudes about products, such as satisfaction levels, perceived competitive positioning, desired features, and unmet needs, as well as lifestyles, brand preferences, social and personal values, opinions, and the like.
3. *Demographic* (i.e., "descriptive") data, such as age, income, education level, marital status, household composition, gender, home ownership, and so on.[7]

In categorizing data contained in a customer database, it's important to recognize that some data—*stable data*, such as birth date or gender—will only need to be gathered one time. Once verified, this data can survive in a database over long periods and many programs. Updates of stable data should be undertaken to correct errors but, except for errors, stable data won't need much alteration. In contrast, there are other data—*adaptive data*, such as a person's intended purchases or even her feelings about a particular political candidate—that will need constant updating. This is not a binary classification, of course. In reality, some data are *relatively* more stable or adaptive than other data.

WHY IS IDENTIFICATION IMPORTANT?

Ultimately, of course, the central purpose of collecting customer information is to enable the development of closer, more profitable relationships with individual customers. In many cases, these relationships will be facilitated by the availability to the enterprise of information that will make the customer's next transaction simpler, faster, or cheaper. Remembering a customer's logistical information, for instance, will make reordering easier for her, and therefore more likely. Remembering this type of information will also lead the customer to believe she is important to the company, that her patronage is valued.

In order to make any of this work, however, it is essential for the enterprise to establish a trusting relationship with the customer, so she feels free to share information. There is a vocal privacy-protection movement—perhaps more active in Europe than in North America—that has been energized by the increasing role that individual information plays in ordinary commerce, and the per-

---

[7]David Shepard, *The New Direct Marketing* (New York: McGraw-Hill Professional Book Group, 1999).

ceived threat to individual privacy that this poses. However, both practical experience as well as a number of academic studies have shown that the vast majority of consumers are not at all reluctant to share their individual information whenever there is a clear value proposition for doing so. Therefore, if a company can demonstrate to the customer that individual information will be used to deliver tangible benefits (and provided the customer trusts the enterprise to hold the information reasonably confidential beyond that), then the customer is usually more than willing to allow the use of the information. Trusting relationships or not, protecting customer privacy and ensuring the safety and security of customer-specific information are critical issues in the implementation of customer strategies, and will be discussed in greater detail in Chapters 7 and 9.

INTEGRATING DATA TO IDENTIFY CUSTOMERS

The process of identifying customers in order to engage them in relationships requires that customer-identifying information be integrated into many different aspects of an enterprise's business activities. It used to be that customer data could be collected over a period of time, and then the customer database would be updated with revised profile and analytic information in batches. On weekends, perhaps, or late at night, information collected since the last update would be used to update the customer database. Increasingly, however, companies rely on Web sites and call centers to interact with customers, and this places a much greater emphasis on ensuring real-time access to customer identifying information.

Enterprises must be able to capture customer information and organize it, aggregate it, integrate it, and disseminate it to any individual or group, throughout the enterprise, in real time. Technology is enabling enterprises to accelerate the flow of customer information at the most strategically timed moment. Enterprises strive for **zero latency**, or no lag time required for the flow of information from customer to database to decision maker (or to a rules-based decision-making "engine"). The computer-driven processes of data mining, collaborative filtering, and predictive modeling will increasingly alter the process of forecasting how consumers behave and what they want.[8]

Seamless interaction with customers is a function of company size, with larger companies significantly more likely than smaller firms to force customers to deal with different departments and divisions that have no knowledge of past interactions. According to a Peppers and Rogers Group/Roper Starch survey,[9] for example, while just 40 percent of consumer financial institutions report being able to present a "single face" to their customers, a quarter of those that do are relatively small companies.

[8]Chuck Martin, *Net Future* (New York: McGraw-Hill Professional Book Group, 1999).

[9]Peppers and Rogers Group and Roper Starch Worldwide, "Customer Relationship Management in Financial Services: A National Perspective," Research Report, September 2000.

Moreover, in any service context, it is critical that an enterprise's customer-facing people have ready access to customer-identifying data, as well as to the records attached to particular customer identities. Swissair maintains a data warehouse where all customer information is stored. The airline has developed a simple form, called the **Customer Loyalty Information Program (CLIP)**, that identifies its club members and their preferences, using the information from the customer data warehouse. During preflight briefings, attendants review customer data and carry the CLIP form with them. Attendants now know in advance, for instance, that the passenger in seat 3B received a complimentary bottle of champagne recently to make up for what may have been a less-than-stellar performance during a previous flight, and that the passenger in 18F filled out the customer survey form on a flight a month ago and rated the crew "excellent." Any good customer database will contain information such as this, but for Swissair, CLIP makes this valuable customer information available to the customer-facing employees who need it most: the front-line staff. The CLIP forms are used by flight attendants not only to help provide enhanced customer services, such as booking a rental car or hotel room, or making alternate plans in the event of a flight cancellation, but also to permit flight attendants to better "know" their individual passengers individually, based on the information that Swissair already has about them.[10]

As of early 2000, Swissair had planned to install a server onboard one aircraft so staff could view and add information on the airline's customer database. Flight attendants would be able to check who is in seat 1A and how her last few flights went. If her luggage was lost, they could apologize to the customer face to face. It is part of an overall effort to make a database of customer information available to Swissair employees at every point of customer contact.[11]

Borders Group is assembling a one-terabyte data warehouse to give managers a consolidated view of its customers, including those from Borders Books, Borders Music, Waldenbooks stores, and the Borders.com Web site. The move is an attempt to integrate customer information scattered across multiple databases more quickly and clearly. Now Borders can discern whether customers who purchased books in its retail stores are the same ones who bought online. Borders is using data-integration technology to build the system, and software to analyze the data and manage customer relationship campaigns based on the findings.[12]

Many enterprises underestimate the cost and difficulty of creating an integrated view of customer identification information. According to John McKean, author of *Information Masters*, testing an enterprise's competency for using

---

[10]Don Peppers, "Customer Service at a CLIP," *Inside 1to1* (June 10, 1999), available at: *www.1to1.com.*

[11]Cheryl Rosen, "Swissair Takes Customer Data Airborne," *Information Week* (November 20, 2000), p. 119.

[12]Rick Whiting, "Borders Wants to Read Its Customers Like a Book," *Information Week* (August 21, 2000), p. 34.

customer data requires that every aspect of the enterprise's information environment affecting the efficiency of information flow be taken into account. This includes what McKean considers important, customer-facing functional areas, including direct marketing, customer service, and sales.[13] McKean divides enterprises into three distinct categories based on their customer information competency: mass market, transitional, and information mastery:

- *Mass-market customer information competency.* Essentially, a firm devoting a majority of its resources to processing transactional-oriented information. This task is viewed as an obligatory encumbrance to finish transactional tasks within the firm; for example, sending out bills, invoices, accounting practices, and customer notices.
- *Transitional customer information competency.* Still similar in many respects to the mass-market category, yet this firm has had pockets of success in increasing the level of information sophistication.
- *The customer information master, or an "information-based competitor."* A firm that believes customer information is truly its most valuable asset and provides its only sustainable, distinct operational competency.

Rashi Glazer clarifies the implications of an enterprisewide view of the customer—what several authorities have called "one view of the truth."

ROLE OF SMART MARKETS IN MANAGING RELATIONSHIPS WITH CUSTOMERS

Rashi Glazer
University of California at Berkeley, Walter A. Haas School of Business

Perhaps the most important implication of the information age for business is the emergence of information-intensive or *smart markets*—that is, markets defined by frequent turnovers in the general stock of knowledge or information embodied in products and services and possessed by firms and consumers. In contrast to traditional "dumb" markets—which are static, fixed, and basically information-poor—smart markets are dynamic, turbulent, and information-rich.

Smart markets are based on smart products, those product and service offerings that have intelligence or computational capability built into them and therefore can adapt or respond to changes in the environment as they interact with customers. Smart markets are also characterized by smart consumers, consumers who, from the standpoint of the firm, are continually "speaking" (i.e.,

---

[13]John McKean, *Information Masters* (New York: John Wiley & Sons, Inc., 1999).

they are not mute, or "dumb"); and, in so doing, educate or teach the firm about who they are and what they want. In such an environment, competition is less about who has the best products and more about which firm can spend the most time interacting with—and therefore learning from—its customers.

A major implication of information-intensive, or smart markets, is the widespread breaking down of boundaries where there once were well-defined roles or discrete categories:

- Boundaries between products are breaking down (in particular, the boundary between products and services).
- Within the firm, boundaries between departments are breaking down, as no department or area has all the information necessary (and the flow of information between departments is not fast enough) to respond to customer requests before the competition does.
- Most significantly, the boundaries between the firm and the external world are breaking down, between the firm and its competitors, as firms realize they need to partner in order to put in place the infrastructure issues necessary for the sale of their own products; and, of course, between the firm and its customers, as customers participate or collaborate in the design and delivery of their own products, and as communications become more interactive and two-way.

INFORMATION-INTENSIVE/SMART STRATEGIES

The evolutionary response of leading firms to the emergence of smart markets is the development and execution of what may be termed *information-intensive* or *smart strategies*. By observing the activities of firms across a variety of industries, it is now becoming possible to identify a set of "generic" information-intensive strategies (notable because of the degree to which they have been repeated across a variety of situations) and to develop a preliminary "taxonomy," or categorization, scheme that can be used to compare and contrast them. The goal is to place these individual strategies within an overall conceptual framework that parallels the models that have been developed for more traditional strategic alternatives.

The organizing "tool," or asset, on which the full range of information-intensive strategies is based is the Customer Information File (CIF), a single virtual database that captures all relevant information about a firm's customers. The database is described as "virtual" because, while operating as though it were an integrated single source housed in one location, it may in reality comprise several isolated databases stored in separate places throughout an organization.

Although the concept of the CIF as the core corporate asset should be comfortable to marketers, it is nevertheless one that is at odds with the conventional view. Many firms may pay lip service to the notion that "our customers are our most important resource," but the typical firm's real assets are still seen to be its products or services and the facilities and operations used to support them. This is reflected in the product (or brand) management organizational structure—that is, where profit and loss responsibility is defined with respect to a set of products—that still predominates in most firms (even those leading the way in information-intensive strategies).

Within the newer framework being developed here, the firm sets as its overall objective maximizing the returns to the CIF (as the key corporate asset) and then chooses any one or several information-intensive strategies to accomplish this objective. Before discussing the various strategic alternatives that are available, we first describe the composition of the CIF (see Exhibit 4.1). The rows (or records) are individual customers—both actual as well as potential—not segments. The columns are data that have been collected about customers. At least conceptually, these can be organized into three categories:

1. *C: Customer characteristics.* Typically (though not exclusively) composed of demographic data, this is information about customers (who they are) that is independent of the firm's relationship with the customer.
2. *R: Response to firm decisions.* Perception and preference (e.g., product attribute importance weights) and other marketing-mix response data (price sensitivity, sources of information, channel shopping behavior), this is information about customers (when, where, how, and why they buy) that is based on some (perhaps limited) level of interaction between the firm and its customers.
3. *P: Purchase history.* Data on which products customers have purchased, as well as the revenues, costs, and, thus, profits associated with these purchases, this is information that is based on the firm's actual transactions with its customers.

Low------TRANSACTION-DEPENDENT------High		
CUSTOMER CHARACTERISTICS	RESPONSE TO FIRM DECISIONS	PURCHASE HISTORY
C_{11} C_{12} C_{13}. . . .	R_{11} R_{12} R_{13}. . . .	P_{11} P_{12} P_{13}. . . . $P_{1t}*$
C_{21} C_{22} C_{23}. . . .	R_{21} R_{22} R_{23}. . . .	P_{21} P_{22} P_{23}. . . . $P_{2t}*$
C_{31} C_{32} C_{33}. . . .	R_{31} R_{32} R_{33}. . . .	P_{31} P_{32} P_{33}. . . . $P_{3t}*$
	What	
	When	
Who They Are	*Where } They Buy*	
	How	
	Why	
C_{i1} C_{i2} C_{i3}. . . .	R_{i1} R_{i2} R_{i3}. . . .	P_{i1} P_{i2} P_{i3}. . . . $P_{it}*$
		$\sum P_{it}*$

EXHIBIT 4.1   Customer Information File

Note in the exhibit that the categories of data—C, R, and P—are arranged in order of the degree to which they are dependent on actual transactions and/or contact between the firm and its customers. This is not necessarily the same as the degree of difficulty in collecting the respective data. Thus, both P, purchase history, and C, customer characteristics, are typically much easier to collect than R, marketing-mix response data. (P, for potential, but not current, customers is, of course, empty.)

As shown in Exhibit 4.1, there is one additional column of information in the CIF (at the far right), labeled as P^*. If P_{it} is the actual profit realized from customer i in period t, then P^*_{it} is the potential profit that could have been realized from customer i had the firm made the optimum use of its information assets. P^*–P thus represents foregone or unrealized profits. The purpose of executing a set of information-intensive strategies is to minimize (P^*-P) across all customers in all periods; or to maximize $\sum P_{it}$—the overall value of the Customer Information File. (If one is serious about the CIF's role as the key corporate asset, then this may also be a measure of the value of the firm.)

A range of information-intensive strategies that have been observed in practice can now be discussed in light of this overall framework. In general, the goal of any particular strategy is to use information collected about customers and their previous dealings with the firm to increase the revenues and/or decrease the costs associated with future transactions. As is true in typical marketing research, in implementing a given strategy, the key questions are: To what extent can C, customer characteristics, be used to understand and influence R, marketing-mix response; and to what extent can R be used to understand and influence P, purchase history?

> The goal of any particular strategy is to use information collected about customers and their previous dealings with the firm to increase the revenues and/or decrease the costs associated with future transactions.

Three classes of generic strategies can be conceptualized: *Row, Column,* and *Whole-File*; and, within this general framework, six specific strategies have been identified:

1. Mass Customization (Column)
2. Yield Management (Column)
3. Capture the Customer (Row)
4. Event-Oriented Prospecting (Row)
5. Extended Organization (Whole File)
6. Manage by Wire (Whole File)

Column Strategies

Column strategies are rooted in the fact that, for a given firm decision, customers are different and have different responses (tastes, preferences, etc.) to the decision as undertaken by the firm. Column strategies represent an extension of the traditional marketing concept (find out what consumers want and give it to them), but taken to the individual customer level in a way that was not possible before the adoption of information technology.

Mass Customization.   Perhaps the most prevalent of column strategies is *mass customization.*[14] Mass customization takes advantage of developments in flexible manufacturing and/or operations that enable firms to tailor or customize individual offerings at little additional marginal cost. Typically, this involves a significant up-front investment in fixed costs that effectively replaces hardware-intensive processes with software-intensive ones (the factory as a computer). Thus, customers of National Bicycle Industrial Co., Ltd., in Japan (the Panasonic brand in the United States), sit on a "smart bike" at the dealer's showroom that takes their vital statistics (height, weight, length of legs, etc.) and relays the data to the factory where a customized offering is manufactured (in three minutes!) from more than 1 million templates (based on data collected from customers). Levi's has introduced a similar system for women's jeans, and Dell and Gateway are doing this in computers, as are many financial services organizations. The printer R.R. Donnelley & Sons was, at one time, reported to be publishing as many as 8,000 different editions of the monthly *Farm Journal,* each one focusing on a narrow subset of the overall readership.

While mass customization usually is associated with flexible manufacturing and operations, it can also refer to strategies based on flexible marketing methods—customizing the nonproduct elements of the marketing mix. The mail-order catalog company Fingerhut customizes personal messages and promotions on different products for individual customers. Indeed, Fingerhut engages in "flexible pricing" by offering specialized credit terms on an individual basis to different customers (many of whom have low household incomes, but are deemed to be creditworthy). In all these instances, it is the data in the CIF, and the knowledge about both individual and aggregate customer preferences and marketing-mix sensitivities, that guide both the degree and kind of customization that the firm is willing to undertake. (Chapter 10 is devoted to mass customization and customization in general).

Yield Management.   The second major information-intensive column strategy is *yield management* (sometimes referred to as *revenue management*). Yield management builds on flexible or discriminatory pricing to take advantage of customers' heterogeneous price sensitivity with respect to time (as well as the technical and legal ability to price discriminate) in order to maximize the total return to a fixed asset, particularly where the marginal cost of providing an additional unit is low and the product in question cannot be inventoried. Typically observed in service businesses, it has been practiced in its most sophisticated form by the airlines (though the actual pioneers have been utilities, with their peak-load pricing strategies). American Airlines has used the data collected from its reservations records and frequent fliers to predict temporal ticket purchase patterns and thus selectively discount seats on a given flight. If, for example, a competitor initiates an advanced-purchase-required across-the-board price cut on a flight, American might choose to match on only 70 percent of its

[14]B. Joseph Pine II, *Mass Customization: The New Frontier in Business Competition* (Cambridge, MA: Harvard Business School Press, 1992).

seats, knowing that the remaining 30 percent are likely to be purchased (at the last minute) by price-insensitive business customers. Information-intensive retailers have also used flexible pricing to move inventory quickly ("Attention Kmart shoppers") and manage the store's overall yield.

While yield management to date has been observed primarily in service businesses, there is an important if underappreciated relation between this strategy and mass customization that suggests its applicability to manufacturing and the evolution of information-intensive strategies in general. As suggested, the conditions under which yield management is appropriate are: a high fixed-cost asset, where the marginal cost of providing an additional unit is low, and the product cannot be inventoried. Increasingly, these are the conditions underlying the implementation of mass customization. Thus, although technically National Bicycle or Dell can inventory their products (whereas American Airlines cannot), much of the impetus for mass customization is just-in-time manufacturing and the elimination of inventory. Indeed, for both National and Dell (as for American) the real cost is downtime on the system—that is, moments when the expensive fixed asset (whether a plane or a factory) is not being used to capacity. At these times, any revenue at all will be contributions to fixed costs (since marginal costs are so low); and, to the extent that customers can be separated based on their price sensitivity with respect to time, the mass-customizing manufacturer (just as the service provider) has the incentive to practice yield management.

Row Strategies

As their name implies, information-intensive row strategies work by attending to particular rows of the CIF, that is, by maximizing both the quality and quantity of the interactions/transactions with individual customers. Given a customer, the goal is to learn as much as possible about that customer and then offer the widest possible set of responses to the firm's decisions/offerings. Indeed, central to truly successful row strategies is a focus on the lifetime value of the customer.

Capture the Customer.   Also known (perhaps more benignly) as *customer intimacy, affinity marketing,* or *relationship management,*[15] the capture-the-customer strategy has as its ultimate objective to realize as high a share as possible of a customer's total (lifetime) purchases in a given (often expanding) set of product categories. Stated another way, the strategy has as its objective to increase the value of the customer to the enterprise by increasing the value of the enterprise to the customer. The capture-the-customer approach relies heavily on interactive communications (telemarketing and, increasingly, the Internet or other online media) and capitalizes on the firm's capability to use the information collected and processed from previous encounters with a customer to influence subsequent encounters and transactions. Critical to this strategy is the fact

---

[15]Robert C. Blattberg and John Deighton, 1991; Peppers and Rogers, 1993.

that the marketing expenses (particularly communications) associated with any one customer are seen as an essentially fixed cost that the firm would like to amortize over as many different transactions (products/services) as possible. This may be contrasted with column strategies such as mass customization that revolve around an initial investment in fixed manufacturing costs, which the firm hopes to spread over many different product variants (targeted at different customers).

There are several ways in which capture-the-customer strategies have been implemented. Oracle software's telemarketing sales effort is driven by a sophisticated relational database, from which an Oracle representative interacting with a prospect can call up all relevant information on the product in question, competitors' offerings, as well as all previous interactions with the caller (including other people at the customer's firm who have interacted with Oracle). The system has documented yields, or "hit rates," of over 90 percent—referring to the proportion of prospects who, after a single call, have either purchased some product/service or have been converted into highly qualified leads. American Express (AE) has implemented a "relationship billing" program with its commercial customers (e.g., restaurants), in which AE first provides a given establishment with a demographic analysis of its customers and then uses this information to sell the establishment advertising space in specialized publications (e.g., restaurant guides) targeted at the same demographic groups. More generally, capture-the-customer strategies have been used to cross-sell an increasingly wide range of products to the same customer by firms as diverse as Fidelity and Charles Schwab in financial services to Pioneer (now part of Du Pont) in seeds and agricultural commodities.

Event-Oriented Prospecting. A particular and increasingly important version of the more general capture-the-customer strategy is the event-oriented prospecting (EOP) approach. EOP is based around the firm's capability to store and process life-cycle-related and other situational information about its customers that might trigger a purchase incident. The goal is to anticipate the customer's life cycle or other situational needs and to time the interaction in such a way that the firm appears with a solution just when the problem arises—creating the appearance of literally reading the customer's mind. A leader in using this strategy is USAA Insurance, where the information system will, for example, automatically direct that information about driver education (as well as automobile insurance) be sent to a client whose teenage son is approaching legal driving age.

Whole File Strategies

These strategies typically rely for their successful implementation on treating the entire CIF as an integrated file, rather than focusing on particular sets of rows or columns.

Extended Organization. Also known as the *virtual company*, extended organization strategies go beyond the more traditional Electronic Data Interchange

(EDI) processes and involve the use of the CIF by one firm to manage a set of activities of another firm in its value chain, in effect, dissolving the functional boundaries between the two (technically distinct) organizations. Thus, Federal Express has built upon its original COSMOS customer service system, which tracks every movement of every package in the network (through hand-held computers carried by all employees who handle packages), and now provides customers with terminals and/or software (or encourages customers to use its Web site) so that they can tie into the system directly. In effect, this allows Federal Express to manage its own shipping department and, in the process, create high customer switching costs. McKesson, the pharmaceutical wholesaler, whose pioneering ECONOMOST system (placing terminals in drugstores tied in to McKesson's central computer) was originally designed to expedite order processing and control inventory, rejuvenated the wholesale drug distribution industry (not, coincidentally, resulting in the elimination of dozens of competitors) and is now effectively managing retail drugstores for many of its clients by selling back to them summaries of information collected daily. Inland Steel differentiated itself in a mature "commodity" product category by helping customers to manage their own operations after installing and operating an interactive computer network. It began as an attempt to keep customers informed as to the status of their orders and now provides a wide range of value-added services, from billing and funds transfer to consulting on technical product specifications.

Manage by Wire. By analogy to the "fly-by-wire" methodology in aviation (in which computer systems are used to supplement a pilot's manual adjustments to dynamic environmental changes), the Manage by Wire concept (Haeckel and Nolan 1993) is based on the ability to manage a business essentially by understanding its "informational representation." Drawing on the CIF and other databases, as well as a set of appropriate "expert systems" and other decision tools, the goal is to model the enterprise and "commit to code" as much as possible the procedures that form the basis of managerial decision making. The objective is not to replace, but to augment, the managerial function; under the assumption that the complexity associated with information-intensive environments demands a "sense and respond" (as opposed to "command and control") orientation that can only be achieved by combining the decision-making and data-processing capabilities, respectively, of human beings and machines. No companies to date have fully achieved the potential inherent in Manage by Wire, but several have undertaken pioneering efforts in limited domains. Thus, Mrs. Fields Cookies has been able to run a worldwide network of more than 800 stores (company-owned and -franchised) with a small corporate staff from rural Utah based on its capability to capture in software (to "clone") the way Debbie Fields managed her first store in Palo Alto, California. Brooklyn Union Gas of New York has codified a major portion of its customer service operations (meter reading, bill collection, etc.), allowing the company to respond quickly and cost-effectively to the individualized service needs of its large customer base. Aetna Insurance has embarked upon a similar program in the financial services area, with the goal of facilitating its account executives to be able to respond to customer requests for new products and services in rapidly changing and increasingly competitive markets.

A NEW SET OF PERFORMANCE MEASURES

When a firm sets as its overall performance objective the task of maximizing returns to the CIF, then notions such as profitability per sales period or market share per product are replaced with concepts such as profitability per customer (increasingly referred to as *lifetime value of customer* (LTV)) and *share of customer* (the total share of a customer's purchases in a broadly defined product category, such as VISA's "share of wallet" or "share of personal consumption expenditures"). To the degree that LTV or share-of-customer measures are inherently difficult to operationalize, intermediate metrics such as *customer satisfaction* are emerging as important surrogates and/or leading indicators, with mixed success.

Perhaps one of the most challenging tasks facing the information-intensive service firm—and proof of the extent to which it is serious about the required transformation in perspective—is the integration of these new measures of performance into the organization's traditional accounting system. At one level, for example, few organizations actually know the costs associated with having sold a service to an individual customer and thus are unable in practice to identify the respective profits. More generally, because the typical firm's real assets are still seen to be its products or services and the facilities and operations used to support them, this is reflected in the product (or brand) management organizational structure, that is, where profit and loss responsibility is defined with respect to a set of products.

SUMMARY

The first task to accomplish in building relationships with a customer is to recognize each one at every point of contact, across all products purchased or locations contacted, through every communication channel, over time. This requires knowing the identity of each customer at every contact point in the organization.

FOOD FOR THOUGHT

1. Describe and name two companies you have done business with as a customer. One of them treats you as though you are a new customer every time you show up, or at least any time you show up anywhere you haven't done business with the company before. At the other company, you are

recognized as *you* every time you have any dealings with the company. What's the effect on you of these disparate approaches? How would you guess each company manages its data, given their different approaches to customers?

2. How can a company identify customers when those customers don't talk to its representatives very often, if at all—at least not individually? (Consider a pet food manufacturer that sells to retailers, not directly to consumers. Or a convenience store that operates on a cash basis. Or a fast-food chain. Or a business-to-business company that doesn't have a human sales force.)

3. What will encourage customers to "raise their hands" and agree to be identified and recognized?

GLOSSARY

Customer Loyalty Information Program (CLIP) Swissair's program that identifies its club members and their preferences, using the information from the customer data warehouse.

Zero latency No lag time required for the flow of information from customer to database to decision maker (or to a rules-based decision-making "engine").

Differentiating Customers: Some Customers Are Worth More Than Others

5

Chapter

Fact: A company's most valuable customers are frequently the ones responsible for keeping the firm in business. So, really, it makes no sense to spend the same resources on all customers, as if they were all worth the same. In this chapter, we explore the most fundamental ideas about the actual and potential value of individual customers, and the ways a firm can rank-order its customers by these kinds of values and make better decisions about resource allocation and treating different customers differently. A contribution by Jill Collins gives us an overview of customer valuation and shares the details of a real-world example.

Identifying each customer individually and linking the information about that customer to various business functions prepares the customer-strategy enterprise to engage each customer in a mutual collaboration that will grow stronger over time. The first step is to identify and recognize each customer at every touchpoint. The linking of that information allows a company to see each customer completely, as one customer throughout the organization, and enables the company to compare customers—to *differentiate* them, one from another. By understanding that one customer is different from another, the enterprise reaches an important step in the development of an interactive, customer-centric Learning Relationship with each customer.

To an enterprise, the two most important and useful differences among customers are that they *need different things* from the enterprise and that they *have different values* to the enterprise. All other types of customer descriptions, such as demographics, satisfaction level, psychographics, geographic origin, or marital status, are just data points designed to help an enterprise get a better picture of what it is a customer needs or what value the customer might represent. But a customer's needs and value are the most fundamental qualities that differ from customer to customer.

Knowing which customers are more valuable to the enterprise than others will enable the enterprise to prioritize its competitive efforts, allocating

> The inability to see cus-
> tomers as being different
> does not necessarily mean
> the customers are the same
> in need or value, only that
> the firm sees them that way.

relatively more time, effort, and resources to those customers likely to yield higher returns. Knowing what an individual customer needs from it makes it possible for the enterprise to cater to that particular customer's needs, and by doing so lock in the customer's loyalty, increasing his value to the enterprise.

The inability to see customers as being different does not necessarily mean the customers are the same in need or value, only that the firm sees them that way. Understanding, analyzing, and profiting from individual customer differences are tasks that go to the very heart of what it means to be a customer-strategy enterprise—an enterprise that engages in customer-specific behaviors, in order to increase the overall value of its customer base. In this chapter we will discuss the concept of customer *valuation*, including various ways a company might rank its customers by their individual values to the enterprise. In Chapter 6, we will address the issue of customer *needs*. Importantly, we'll be returning again and again throughout the book to these two issues: individual customer valuations and needs. For instance, we will return to the customer valuation discussion in Chapter 11 on metrics and measurements. And we'll come back to the issue of differentiating customers by their needs during our discussion on customization and mass customization in Chapter 12.

CUSTOMER VALUE IS A FUTURE-ORIENTED VARIABLE

Mail-order firms, credit card companies, telecommunications firms, and other marketers with direct connections to their consumer customers often try to understand their marketing universe by doing a simple form of prioritization called *decile analysis*—ranking their customers in order of their value to the company, and then dividing this top-to-bottom list of customers into 10 equal portions, or deciles, with each decile comprising 10 percent of the customers. In this way, the marketer can begin to analyze the differences between those customers who populate the most valuable one or two deciles and those who populate the less valuable deciles. A credit card company may find, for instance, that 65 percent of top-decile customers are married and have two cards on the same account, while only 30 percent of other, less valuable customers have these characteristics. Or a catalog company may find that a majority of customers in the bottom three or four deciles have never before bought anything by direct mail, compared to only 15 percent of those in the top two deciles.

It would not be unusual for a decile analysis to reveal that 50 percent, or even 95 percent, of a company's profit comes from the top one or two deciles of customers. While mail-order houses and other direct marketers are more likely to have used decile analysis in the past, largely as a means for evaluating the productivity of their mailing campaigns, this kind of customer ranking analysis will become increasingly important as more companies begin to adopt a customer focus.[1]

But just how does a company rank-order its customers by their value in the first place? What data would the credit card company use to analyze its customers individually and then array them from top to bottom in terms of their value? And what variables would go into the mail-order firm's customer rankings? What do we mean when we talk about the **value** of a customer, anyway?

For our purposes, the value a customer represents to an enterprise should be thought of as the same type of value any other financial asset would represent. To say that some customers have more value for the enterprise than others is merely to acknowledge that some customers are more valuable, as assets, than others are. The primary objective of a customer-strategy enterprise should be to increase the value of its customer base; that is, it should strive to increase the sum total of all the individual financial assets known as customers.

But this is not as simple as it might sound, because in the same way any other financial asset should be valued, a customer's value to the enterprise is a function of the profit the customer will generate *in the future* for the enterprise.

Let's take a specific example. Suppose a company has two business customers. Customer A generated $1,000 per month in profit for the enterprise over the last two years, while Customer B generated $500 in monthly profit during the same period. Which customer is worth more to the enterprise?

Knowing only what we've been told so far, we can say it's *probable* that Customer A is worth more than Customer B, but this is not a certainty. If Customer A were to generate $1,000 in profit per month in all future months, while Customer B were to generate $500 per month in all future months, then certainly A is worth twice as much to the enterprise as B. But what if we know that Customer A plans to merge its operations into another firm in three months and switch to a different supplier altogether, while Customer B plans to continue doing its regular volume with the company for the foreseeable future? In that case, our ranking of these two customers would be reversed, and we would consider B to be worth more than A. However, if what actually happened was that a competitor derailed A's merger, while B went bankrupt and ceased all operations the following month, then our assessment would still be wrong.

By definition, a customer's value to an enterprise, as a financial asset, is a future-oriented variable. Therefore, it is a quantity that can truly be ascertained only from the customer's actual behavior *in the future*. We mortals can analyze data points from past behavior, we can interview a customer to try to understand the customer's future intent, and we can even conclude contractual agreements with customers to guarantee performance, but the plain truth is that without clairvoyant powers, we can't *know* what the customer's true value is until the future actually happens.

On the other hand, until that future does happen, we can affect its outcome by our own actions. Suppose we were to find a revenue stream for Customer B that allowed it to continue in business, rather than going bankrupt. By our own deliberate action, in this case, we would have changed B's value, as a financial asset.

[1]Don Peppers and Martha Rogers, PhD, *The One to One Future* (New York: Doubleday, 1993).

To think about customer valuation, therefore, we need to use two concepts: **Actual value** is the customer's value as an asset to the enterprise, given what we currently know or predict about the customer's future behavior, assuming there are no major changes in the competitive environment. **Potential value** is all the value that this customer could represent if we were to apply a conscious strategy to improve it, by changing the customer's future behavior in some way.

CUSTOMER LIFETIME VALUE

The actual value of a customer is equivalent to a quantity that is frequently called the customer **lifetime value (LTV),** or the net present value of the stream of expected future financial contributions from the customer.[2] Every customer of an enterprise today will be responsible for some specific series of events in the future, each of which will have a financial impact on the enterprise—the purchase of a product, payment for a service, remittance of a subscription fee, a product exchange or upgrade, a warranty claim, a help-line telephone call, the referral of another customer, and so forth. Each such event will take place at a particular time in the future and will have a financial impact that can be calculated at that time. The net present value, today, of each of these future events can be derived by applying a discount rate to it to factor in the time value of money. LTV is, in essence, the sum of the net present values of all such future events attributed to a particular customer's actions.

One useful way to think about the different types of events and activities that different customers will be involved in is to visualize each customer as having a "trajectory," which carries the customer through time in a financial relationship with the enterprise. For example, a customer could begin his relationship at a particular starting point and at a particular spending level. At some point, he increases his spending, taking another product line from the company; later, he also begins

---

[2] It should be noted that a vigorous body of research and literature is emerging in this important field. A sampling would include:

Peter F. Mathias and Noel Capon, "Managing Strategic Customer Relationships as an Asset: Developing Customer Relationship Capital," white paper, 2003 (Outlines their recommended 6-step approach to developing customer relationship capital); David Bell, John Deighton, Werner Reinartz, Roland Rust, and Gordon Swartz, "Seven Barriers to Customer Equity Management," *Journal of Services Research,* March 2002; Neil Gross, "Commentary: Valuing 'Intangibles' Is a Tough Job, but It Has to Be Done," *Business Week Online,* August 6, 2001 (Makes the point that brand can be a huge part of a company's "intangible" asset (i.e., Apple Computer = 80%, Gross says), but that this intangible can be impaired, say, if your primary brand suffered a "massive safety recall." Worried that FASB will never buy it, because any whiff of subjectivity leads to a label of "voodoo accounting."). Also see important, more recent work by Roland T. Rust, Katherine N. Lemon, and Valarie A. Zeithaml, "Return on Marketing: Using Customer Equity to Focus Marketing Strategy," *Journal of Marketing* (January 2004), as well as work by Sunil Gupta, Donald R. Lehmann, and Jennifer Ames Stuart.

There is no attempt here to exhaust that current overview, as it is developing faster than a textbook or reference book can keep up with. This exposition serves as an introduction and basis for understanding and evaluating the ongoing work by others.

paying more for some added service. Still later he has a complaint and it costs the company some expense to resolve it. He refers another customer to the company, and that customer then begins his own trajectory. Eventually, perhaps several years or decades later, the original customer "leaves the franchise," because his children grow up, or he decides to switch to another product altogether, or he gets divorced, or retires, or dies. At this point, his relationship with the enterprise comes to an end. (The same can be true for a business customer, too. Although a "business" may have an indefinite future potential as a customer, each of the individual potential end users, purchasing agents, influencers, and so forth will eventually either quit, get promoted or transferred or fired, retire, or die.)

Different customers will have different trajectories. In a way, the lifetime value of each customer amounts to the net present value of the financial contribution represented by that customer's trajectory through the customer base. From a customer's stream of positive contributions, including product and service purchases, an enterprise must deduct the expenses associated with that customer, including the cost of maintaining a relationship. For instance, relationships usually require some amount of individual communication, via phone, fax, Web, mail, e-mail, or face-to-face meetings. These costs, along with any others that apply to a specific individual customer, will reduce the customer's LTV. It sometimes happens that the costs associated with a customer actually outweigh the customer's positive contributions altogether, in which case the customer's LTV is **below zero (BZ)**.

We are using the term *contribution*, as opposed to *profit*, deliberately, because the value of a particular customer is equivalent to the marginal contribution of that customer, when he is added to the business in which the enterprise is already engaged. Suppose we add up all the positive and negative cash flows an enterprise will generate over the next few years, and the total is $X. But then Customer A's trajectory of financial transactions is removed from the enterprise, and the positive and negative cash flows will only amount to a lesser total of $Y. The customer's marginal contribution is equal to $X - Y$. The net present value of those various contributions by Customer A is the customer's lifetime value.

In practice, of course, it is not possible for an enterprise to know what any particular customer's future contributions will actually be, and if we want to be able to make current decisions based on this future-oriented number, then we will have to estimate it in some way. Traditionally, the most reliable predictor of a customer's future behavior has been thought to be that customer's past behavior, and so we are usually quite justified in making the common-sense assumption that a customer who has generated $1,000 of profit each month for the last two years will continue to generate that profit level for some period of time in the future, even though we simultaneously acknowledge that any number of forces can appear that will change this simplistic trend at any moment. Various computational techniques can be used to model the trajectories of particular types of customers more precisely, and to project these expected trajectories into the future. Some companies have customer databases that allow highly sophisticated modeling and analysis. Such analysis can sometimes be used to give an enterprise advance warning when a credit card customer, or a cell phone customer, or a Web site subscriber, is about to defect to a competitor.

According to CRM consultant Frederick Newell, LTV models have a number of uses. They can help an enterprise determine how much it can afford to spend to acquire a new customer, or perhaps a certain type of new customer. They can help a firm decide just how much it would be worth to retain an existing customer. With a model that predicts higher values for certain types of customers, an enterprise can target its customer acquisition efforts in order to concentrate on attracting mostly higher-value customers. The LTV measurement can be a more productive way to justify marketing investments than just looking at immediate sales.[3]

Although sophisticated modeling methods help to quantify LTV, many variables will not be easily quantified, such as the assistance a customer might give an enterprise in designing a new product, or the value derived from the customer's referral of another customer. Any model that attempts to calculate individual customer LTVs should employ some or all of the following data, quantified and weighted appropriately:

- Repeat customer purchases
- Greater profit and/or lower cost (per sale) from repeat customers than from initial customers (converting prospects)
- Indirect benefits from customers, such as referrals
- Customer's stated willingness to do business in the future rather than switch suppliers
- Customer records
- Transaction records (summary and detail)
- Products and product costs
- Cost to serve/support
- Marketing and transaction costs (including acquisition costs)
- Response rates to marketing/advertising efforts.[4]

The objective with LTV modeling is to use these data points to create an historically quantifiable representation of the customer and to compare that customer's history with other customers. Then the enterprise can begin to build a statistical model of the customer's trajectory with the enterprise, and project the customer's *future* trajectory—including how much he will spend and over what period.

For our purposes, it is sufficient to know that:

- The actual value of a customer is the value of the customer as a financial asset, which is equivalent to the customer's lifetime value—the net present value of future cash flows associated with that customer. (This is the current value, assuming business as usual.)

---

[3]Frederick Newell, *The New Rules of Marketing* (New York: McGraw-Hill Companies, 1997).
[4]Jack Schmid and Alan Webber, *Desktop Database Marketing* (Chicago: NTC/Contemporary Publishing Group, 1998).

- LTV is a quantity that no enterprise can ever calculate precisely, no matter how sophisticated its models are.
- Nevertheless, every enterprise has an interest in understanding and positively affecting its customers' LTVs to the extent possible.

GROWING SHARE OF CUSTOMER

With respect to its relationship with a customer, the goal of any customer-strategy enterprise should be to positively alter the customer's financial trajectory, increasing the customer's overall value to the enterprise. The challenge, however, is to know how much the enterprise can really alter that trajectory—how much increase in the customer's value can an enterprise actually generate.

Unrealized potential value is a term used to denote the amount by which the enterprise could increase the value of a particular customer if it applied a strategy for doing so. It represents the potential *additional* business a customer is capable of doing with the enterprise, much of which will probably never materialize. As an enterprise realizes more and more of a customer's potential value, however, it can be said to have a greater and greater share of that customer's business.

Increasing share of customer (SOC)[5] is an important goal for a customer-strategy enterprise, and can be accomplished by increasing the amount of business a customer does, over and above what was otherwise expected—that is, by applying a strategy to favorably affect the customer's trajectory. For example, a bank might have a relationship with a customer who has a checking account, an auto loan, and a certificate of deposit. The customer provides a regular profit to the bank each month, generated by his transaction fees and the investment spread between the bank's own investment and borrowing rates, compared to the lending and savings rates it offers the customer. The net present value of this income stream over the customer's likely future tenure is the customer's LTV. This LTV amount is equivalent to the present value of the financial benefits the bank would lose in the future, if the customer were to defect to another financial services organization today.

But suppose that, in addition to the accounts the customer now maintains at the bank, he also has a home mortgage at a competitive institution. This loan represents unrealized potential value for the bank, while it represents actual value to the bank's competitor. The expected profit from that loan is one aspect of the customer's potential value to the bank, which may devise a strategy to win the customer's mortgage loan business away from its competitor.

---

[5]*Share of customer* (SOC) refers to the percentage of total business conducted by a customer with a particular enterprise, in the product and service arena offered by that enterprise. For example, if a voter contributes $1,000 in the 2008 presidential primaries, the candidate that gets a $400 contribution would have a 40 percent SOC with that voter. If a Christmas shopper buys most of his presents at Toys R Us, generating December purchases there of $800, as compared to a combined total of all other shopping of $400, then FAO Schwartz would have an SOC of $800 of a total $1,200 in holiday shopping, or SOC = 67 percent. See Chapter 1 for a complete discussion of share of customer.

Or suppose this customer owns a home computer and modem but doesn't participate in the bank's online banking service. If he were to do more of his banking online, however, the cost of handling his transactions would decline, his likelihood of defection would decline, and his value to the bank would increase. Thus, the increased profit the bank could realize if the customer banked online represents another aspect of the customer's potential value to the bank.

Or suppose the customer is a night student attempting to qualify for a more financially rewarding career. If the bank could help him achieve this objective, he would earn more money and do more banking, and his value to the bank would increase.

As this example shows, there are at least three types of strategies an enterprise could employ to increase a customer's actual value. That is, there are at least three distinct aspects of a customer's unrealized potential value to an enterprise:

1. *Competitive business.* Any business a customer does with a competitor represents potential value. Simply winning that business away from the competitor will increase the customer's actual value to the enterprise.
2. *Behavior change.* Sometimes a customer can be encouraged to change his behavior in such a way that the enterprise's costs will decline, or the loyalty of the customer will increase.
3. *Customer growth.* When a customer becomes bigger, or more profitable, or more capable, one result will often be that an enterprise will end up doing more business with the customer.

DIFFERENT CUSTOMERS HAVE DIFFERENT VALUES

Increasing a customer's value encompasses the central mission of an enterprise: to *get, keep,* and *grow* its customers. When it understands the value of individual customers, relative to other customers, an enterprise can allocate its resources more effectively, because it is quite likely that a small proportion of its **most valuable customers (MVC)** will account for a large proportion of the enterprise's profitability. This is an important principle of customer differentiation, and at its core is what is known as the Pareto Principle, which states that 80 percent of any enterprise's business comes from just 20 percent of its customers.[6] The Pareto Principle implies that a mail-order company arraying its customers into deciles by value is likely to find that the top two deciles of customers account for 80 percent of the business the company is doing. Obviously, the percentages can vary widely among different businesses, and one company might find that the top 20 percent of its customers do 95 percent of its business, while another company finds that the top 20 percent of its customers only do 40 percent of its business. But in virtually every business, some customers are worth more than

---

[6]Philip Kotler, *Marketing Management:Analysis, Planning Implementation, and Control,* 9th ed. (Upper Saddle River, NJ: Prentice Hall, 1997).

> The goal of value differen-
> tiation is not a *historical*
> understanding, but a *predic-*
> *tive* plan of action.

others. When the distribution of customer values is highly concentrated within just a small portion of the customer base, we say that the *value skew* of the customer base is steep.

While LTV is the variable an enterprise wants to know, it is often the case that a financial or statistical model is too difficult or costly to create. Instead, the enterprise may find some *proxy variable* to be nearly as useful. A proxy variable is a number, other than LTV, that can be used to rank customers in rough order of LTV, or as close to that order as possible. A proxy variable should be easy to measure, but it obviously will not provide the same degree of accuracy when it comes to quantifying a customer's actual value.

For instance, many direct marketers use a proxy variable called *recency, frequency, monetary* (RFM) value to rank-order their customers in terms of their value. The RFM model is based on individual customer purchase histories, and incorporates three separate but quantified components:

- *Recency.* Date of this customer's most recent transaction
- *Frequency.* How often this customer buys
- *Monetary value.* How much this customer has spent in the most recent specified period

An airline, in contrast, might use a customer's frequent-flier mileage as a proxy variable to differentiate one customer's value from another's. The mileage total will be a good indicator of the customer's value, but it won't be entirely accurate. For instance, it won't tell the airline whether the customer usually flies in first class or in coach, and it won't tell whether the customer always purchases the least expensive seat, frequently choosing to stay over on Saturdays, and taking advantage of various other pricing complexities and loopholes in order to guarantee always obtaining the lowest fare.

A proxy variable is, in effect, a representation of a customer's value to the enterprise, rather than a quantification of it. Nevertheless, proxy variables can be important tools for helping an enterprise rank its customers based on value, and with this ranking the company can still apply different strategies to different customers, based on their *relative* worth. Sophisticated LTV models can be expensive and time-consuming to create. If an enterprise is to explore and benefit from

---

SIDEBAR 5.1

A Gap in GAAP

A task force appointed by the Securities and Exchange Commission is urging the SEC to find a way to encourage enterprises to provide more information about their intangible assets, such as their brand names, trademarks, patents, and customer lists. This kind of information is often needed by investors but it is not provided by the traditional accounting methods, such as on a corporate balance sheet. Many call it a "gap" in generally accepted accounting principles (GAAP). The task force wants the SEC to encourage the disclosure of additional information about intangible assets, which it hopes will then become standardized within industries.

SIDEBAR 5.1 *(continued)*

··

As an example of possible new disclosures, companies could provide estimates on the lifetime value, in terms of revenue and profit, of the customer base by totaling the sum of individual customer values, as well as of the cost of acquiring new customers. The chairman of the Financial Accounting Standards Board, Edmund L. Jenkins, has said he agreed that voluntary disclosures were needed, but he is unsure about trying to include many such disclosures in financial statements.[a]

[a]Floyd Norris, "Seeking Ways to Value Intangible Assets," *New York Times,* May 22, 2001.

---

customer valuation principles, proxy variables that allow initial rank-ordering of customers by value are a good starting point.

The goal of value differentiation is not a *historical* understanding, but a *predictive* plan of action. RFM and other, similar, proxy-variable methods show that while differentiating among customers can be mathematically complex, it is still fundamentally a simple principle.

CUSTOMER VALUE CATEGORIES

In the quest to tell which customers are more valuable than others, companies may have several motivations. In addition to making better decisions about resource allocation, a firm also has to report the value of its "intangible assets," and the proclivity of customers to buy in the future is an important intangible asset to the firm (see Sidebar 5.1).

It is frequently the case that an enterprise will want to categorize its customers by their different types of value—high value, low value, high growth potential, and so forth. Customers could easily be assigned to four different categories:

1. *Most valuable customers (MVCs).* Those customers with the highest actual value to the enterprise—the ones who do the most business, yield the highest margins, are most willing to collaborate, and tend to be the most loyal. MVCs are those with whom the company probably has the greatest share of customer. These may or may not be the traditional "heavy users" of a product; the MVC may, for example fly a lot less often, but always pays full fare for first-class tickets. The objective of an enterprise with respect to its MVCs is *retention,* because these are the customers keeping the enterprise in business in the first place.

2. *Most growable customers (MGCs).* These are the customers who have the most growth potential; growth that can be realized through cross-selling, through keeping the customer for a longer period, or perhaps by changing customers' behavior and getting them to operate in a way that costs the enterprise less money. MGCs, in effect, are those customers with the highest unrealized potential values. There is likely to be a large gap between the customers' actual value and their potential value. Your

MGCs could actually be your competitor's best customers—just as big as a firm's own MVCs, and often with similar needs. Therefore, these customers are the ones to *grow*. (Of course, the reverse is also true; your own MVCs are your competitors' MGCs.)

3. *Below-zeros (BZs)*. These are customers who, no matter what effort a company makes, will generate less revenue than cost-to-serve. That means that not only is their actual value below zero, but their potential value is also less than zero. No matter what the firm does, no matter what strategy it follows, a BZ customer is highly unlikely ever to show a positive net value to the enterprise. Nearly every company has at least a few of these customers— the telecommunications customer who moves often and leaves the last month or two unpaid at each address, the high-maintenance customer who buys little but needs lots of service, the giant business customer who bullies prices down so low that the vendor's margin is repeatedly demolished. Some companies have many such customers. The enterprise's strategy for a BZ should be to create incentives either to convert the customer's trajectory into a breakeven or profitable one (for instance, by imposing service charges for services previously given away for free) or to encourage the BZ to become someone else's unprofitable customer.

4. *Migrators*. These customers linger on the brink between being not profitable and having some growth potential. The enterprise needs to decide whether they can be nurtured to grow or are not capable of being highly valuable. The enterprise's goal should be to migrate these customers to the MGC group, or at least to get them to show their "true colors" regarding their likely profit for the enterprise over the long term.

One large B2B company performed a value analysis of its customer base and was able to array its customers into these four customer value categories, creating Exhibit 5.1, which portrayed the categories in a way that made it clearer what

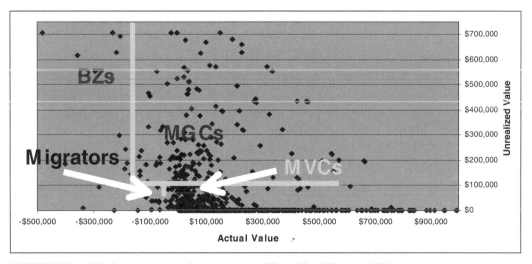

EXHIBIT 5.1   **National Accounts' Actual versus Unrealized Potential Value**

the company's overall customer strategy ought to be. Each of the dots in this exhibit represents a business customer, located by cross-tabbing the customer's actual value and its unrealized potential value, or growth potential. (Note, however, that this particular enterprise has categorized as BZs all customers that have less than zero actual value, even when their potential value might make it possible for the customer to become profitable!)

SIDEBAR 5.2
Is It Fair to "Fire" Unprofitable Customers?

Nothing about customer differentiation means treating anybody badly, ever.

As a company gets better at predicting actual and strategic value, it will become clear that just as 20 percent or so of its customers will likely account for the lion's share of the firm's profitability, another relatively small group of customers is likely to account for the lion's share of service cost and transaction losses. Some retail banks report that they actually lose money consistently on more than a third of their customers. It is not uncommon for a retail bank to do a customer valuation analysis and suddenly learn that 110 percent of its profit comes from just the top 30 percent or so of its customers! Other businesses have similar problems, although retail banking is probably one of the most extreme examples.

Because of traditional marketing's heavy emphasis on customer acquisition, for many companies, it would be anathema even to suggest it, but the plain truth is that in many cases a company will simply be more profitable if it were to *get rid* of some customers—provided, of course, that the customers it rids itself of are the ones who create losses without profit.

Before leaping to the conclusion that this is unfair to customers, consider that it is the profitable customers who are, in effect, subsidizing the unprofitable ones. So "firing" unprofitable customers is not at all a hostile activity, but one designed to make the overall value proposition fairer to all. Nevertheless, there are some important ground rules to follow, when reducing the number of below-zero customers at a company:

- However a company defines the value of a customer, the analysis must apply the same way to everyone. The company engaging in careful customer value differentiation does not care about skin color or gender. It only cares about actual and potential value, and it acts accordingly. This may disadvantage some customers who have long ago abandoned loyalty in favor of coupon clipping or other price shopping, but will appropriately reward the customers who are keeping the business in business.

- Some companies that have enjoyed monopoly or near-monopoly status in the past, such as utilities or telecommunications (or banks, in some countries), have universal service mandates as incumbents. Those companies may choose to define value or customer profitability in a more sophisticated way than simple revenue-minus-cost-of-service. The telephone company that provides basic service to Aunt Matilda in a rural area cannot hope to make a "profit" on her, in the strictest financial sense, but will likely view her not as a BZ but as part of the company's mission to serve the community. Moreover, accomplishing this

MANAGING THE MIX OF CUSTOMERS

One way to think about the process of managing customer relationships is that the enterprise is attempting to improve its situation not just by adding as many new customers as possible to the customer base, but by managing the **mix of customers** it deals with. It wants to create more profitability among its MGCs, while it retains its MVCs for a longer period. It wants to convert BZs to profitability or else expunge them from the franchise. The migrators need to be moved up on the value scale, to become more profitable over time.

Imagine if an enterprise were to plot the distribution of its customer values on a chart, as in Exhibit 5.2, with the value of the customer shown on the bottom

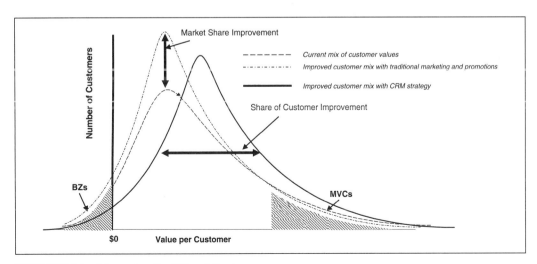

EXHIBIT 5.2 **Managing the Mix of Customers**

axis and the number of customers it serves who have that value shown along the vertical axis. The likely distribution would resemble a bell curve not unlike that shown in this illustration.

In Exhibit 5.2, the dashed-line curve represents a company's customer value distribution—its mix of customers—at present. It can either apply a general, customer-acquisition marketing strategy now—a traditional marketing strategy—or it could initiate a relationship management strategy. If it employs traditional marketing, and it is successful, it will end up acquiring more and more customers, but these customers are likely to show the same mix of valuations as its current customer base, as shown by the dotted line. A successful traditional marketing strategy will end up adding customers to the base and increasing the company's market share.

If, instead, the enterprise employs a CRM strategy, it will not be trying to acquire just *any* customers; it will be focusing its customer acquisition efforts on acquiring higher-value customers. Moreover, it will focus a lot of its effort on improving the value of its existing customers, and moving them up in value individually. The result is shown in the solid-line curve. An enterprise that launches a successful CRM effort will end up shifting the customer mix itself, moving the entire customer base into a higher set of values.

Creating a valuable customer portfolio requires understanding the distribution of customer relationship values and investing in acquisition, development, and retention accordingly.[7] By taking the time to understand the value of a customer, relative to other customers, enterprises can begin to allocate resources intentionally to ensure that the most valuable customers remain loyal. The future of an enterprise, therefore, depends on how effectively it acquires profitable new customers, develops the profitability of existing customers, and retains existing profitable relationships.[8] Customers will want to spend money with the businesses that serve them best, and that is nearly always the companies that know them best and use that knowledge to build relationships in which the customer perceives great value and benefit.[9]

Certainly, one of the most important benefits of ranking customers by value is that the enterprise can more rationally allocate its resources and marketing efforts, focusing more on high-value and high-growth customers, and less on low-value customers. Moreover, the enterprise will likely find it less attractive, as a marketing tactic, to acquire strangers as "customers"—some of whom will never be worth anything to the company. In the next section, Jill Collins outlines the building blocks of customer value and walks the reader through an excellent real-world example of valuation, demonstrating clearly how a more accurate read on actual and potential value at a B2B company changed the company's resource allocation and contributed directly to increased revenue.

[7]Paul Cole and Robert E. Wayland, *Customer Connections* (Cambridge, MA: Harvard Business School Press, 1997).

[8]Katherine N. Lemon, Roland T. Rust, and Valarie Zeithaml, *Driving Customer Equity* (New York: The Free Press, 2000).

[9]Bob Evans, "A Question of Customer Loyalty," *InformationWeek Online* (July 3, 2000).

CONVERGYS: A CASE STUDY IN USING PROXY VARIABLES TO RANK CUSTOMERS BY THEIR VALUE

Jill Collins

Customer value can be categorized as actual and potential. Understanding both types of value allows enterprises to grow through established customer relationships. Defining the specifics around the equation can be a daunting task. It requires a detailed analysis of a company's customer data. This presents challenges for many, as data can be decentralized or lacking. However, in most cases an equation to value customers can be created.

Customer valuation can be viewed as a spectrum:

x	x	x
Proxy-Based	Financial	Statistical

As one moves to the right, the analysis becomes much more quantitatively challenging and results in a *lifetime value model*, which incorporates statistical estimation.

- *Proxy-based analysis*. Analysis based on a group of simple variables, such as the RFM model often used by database and direct marketers. In B2B examples, simple revenue proxies are often found as a predecessor to more sophisticated value analysis.
- *Financial analysis*. A quantitative analysis based on revenue, and if possible, cost information at the individual level. Discounted cash flow or other spreadsheet models are often used. Likely to be used for hospitality (hotels), automotive, some B2B, and others.
- *Statistical analysis*. Builds on proxy-based analysis and financial analysis. In calculating discounted cash flows, assumptions are made as to the length of a customer's relationship and future growth. Statistical analysis incorporates a more rigorous analysis behind these assumptions, such as estimating the probability to purchase. Variables used in this estimation could be those adopted in the early stages of customer valuation with proxy-based analysis. Most likely found in a company with tens of millions of data points, such as credit card companies or telecommunications firms.

Where an enterprise falls on the spectrum is dependent on its current and future business need, the application of the output (which customer action will take place) and accessibility to data.

CONVERGYS: USING PROXY VARIABLES OBJECTIVELY

Convergys is a leading provider of outsourced customer care services. It faces intense competition against established players such as Electronic Data Systems Corporation, a systems consulting company. Convergys must make sure it is closer to the cutting edge with its technology and services. Against newer players in the actual outsourcing market, such as SITEL Corporation and ALLTEL Corporation, Convergys must rely on its advantage with its established client base.

Convergys emerged from Cincinnati Bell as a public company in 1998, after more than a decade of rapid growth. Revenues increased a dramatic 47 percent in 1998, to $1.4 billion from $988 million. But much of that growth, as in past years, had come from acquisitions of other firms. It was not "organic" growth, but financial.

Any customer-focused enterprise must be able to plan and execute different strategies for different customers. By this criterion, Convergys has taken some giant steps since becoming a public company. The enterprise's goal was simply to deal with what it saw as a persistent and significant decline in the productivity of its client-acquisition sales approach. By focusing instead on individual client development, Convergys hoped to produce more reliable and effective business growth.

Account development strategies such as those pursued by Convergys are expensive, labor-intensive, and time-consuming. Any B2B enterprise pursuing an account development strategy has to know which of its accounts are worth penetrating. A B2B that tries to penetrate all of its accounts equally is simply setting itself up for failure. When Convergys shifted its attention from market penetration to customer development, it first had to devise a system for ranking clients according to their true value to the firm, *including their growth potential.* Without such a system, Convergys would have been flying blind. It would have been unable to prioritize its efforts and been incapable of focusing its resources on those clients that would yield the highest ROI on its sales and marketing expenditure.

Once it had prioritized its customers by their actual and potential values, Convergys planned to reconfigure its own service offerings to align itself with the different needs of its different types of clients. And it had to offer its services within a context of providing integrated, well-developed business solutions for its clients' various problems. This, in turn, required the company to improve the technical and business competence of its sales force, and to align its sales compensation structure with the new measure of customer valuation it had devised.

The Convergys team visualized the value of a customer as a function not only of the customer's "inertia" (i.e., what the customer is currently spending and intends to continue spending), but also of whatever changes in the customer's future purchasing behavior could be brought about through the marketer's own initiative. The customer's inertia is its *actual value,* which consists of the value the enterprise will realize on a customer based on that customer's currently expected behavior. Any additional financial benefit the enterprise might be able to obtain by applying a proactive strategy to change a customer's future behavior (such as capturing business the customer was giving to a competitor) represents *unrealized potential.* Convergys needed a reliable system for prioritizing accounts, not just by their actual, current value, but by their unrealized potential, too.

The company's strategy, once it had a better fix on how its different business clients compared in their actual and potential value, would be to organize its sales and marketing efforts around the needs of its most important clients—the ones with not only the most "inertia," but the most growth potential, as well.

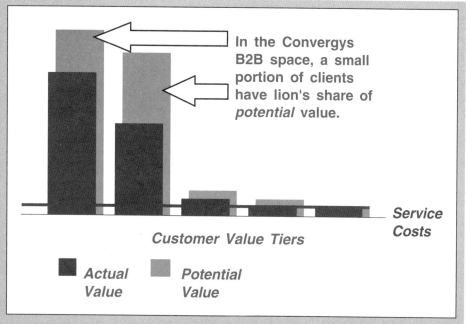

In the Convergys B2B space, a small portion of clients have lion's share of *potential* value.

Customer Value Tiers

Service Costs

■ *Actual Value*   ■ *Potential Value*

EXHIBIT 5.3 **Actual and Partial Value Yields Resource Prioritization and Strategy**

Convergys wanted to develop relationships with them, grow their value, and retain them for as long as possible (see Exhibit 5.3).

Before implementing its strategy, Convergys had one sales force for its Customer Management Group (CMG), and one for its Information Management Group (IMG). Now there is one sales force for the entire company. The functional areas that support the sales force were also consolidated, as well as the marketing departments. None of these changes occurred overnight. They were steps in a process of change that took place over many months. But they began with a single idea: to grow the company by concentrating on account development instead of market penetration.

CALCULATING CUSTOMER VALUE

Ever since its inception, Convergys had calculated the value of its clients the old-fashioned way: by eyeballing last year's revenue and guessing at the "intangible" aspects of customer value. Convergys needed a system of metrics, a reliable tool that could be applied scientifically to clients across the board, despite the company's complex B2B environment.

So the company created a customer valuation model using a system of proxy variables to rank each client by relative importance. The model was based on six weighted indices, ranging from highly objective to highly subjective. More weight was given to the objective indices because the data behind them was considered more reliable and it seemed sensible for the team to hedge its bets. The model was flexible, because the team assumed that the relative weights would change as soon as it was possible to measure the more subjective criteria, such as share of client or partnership, more objectively. The goal of the first model was to break away from the traditional method of ranking clients purely in terms of tangible, historical revenue and create a system that would include less tangible, nonrevenue measures. These would be metrics designed to capture the client's true potential to grow—its strategic value to Convergys, as well as its actual, current value.

A brief glance at the index system in Exhibit 5.4 reveals that annual revenue remains a critical basic measure of value, worth 45 percent when the average revenue score and the change score are combined. Yet each of the six indices plays its part in helping Convergys incorporate different factors in ranking its clients, rationally and objectively, in order to better prioritize its account development efforts.

Average revenue score is determined by averaging a client's actual revenue this year and its projected revenue for next year. A large current client with high projected revenue would rate a higher index than a large client with lower projected revenue. The large client with low projected revenue might even rate a lower index than a medium-size client with higher potential.

Revenue change score is based on the difference between what the client spent with Convergys last year and what the client is spending with Convergys this year. This index gives the team a clear indication of how fast the account is growing or declining.

Technology entanglement was seen as an especially important element in the company's customer development efforts. Let's take a moment to explore how technology entanglement works. Let's say the PC you purchased a few months ago for your home office crashes moments before you need to e-mail an important report to a big client. You call the 800-number provided by the PC manufacturer but the manufacturer has outsourced its technical support service to

INDEX	MEASURES	WEIGHT
Average Revenue Score	➢ Current spending and projected spending	20 percent
Revenue Change Score	➢ Year-to-year change in actual spending	25 percent
Current Relationship	➢ Signed contract length ➢ Total years as client	15 percent
Technology Entanglement	➢ System integration	20 percent
	➢ Reporting	
	➢ Tele-Web	
	➢ Email	
Share of Client	➢ Outsource potential	10 percent
Partnership	➢ Level of contact ➢ Referenceable ➢ Future value	10 percent

EXHIBIT 5.4 **Sample Customer Valuation Model**

Convergys, so your call is actually answered by a Convergys customer support representative (CSR). Because the PC manufacturer and Convergys have integrated portions of their information systems, the Convergys CSR can access your customer data and guide you precisely through the appropriate restart procedure.

As the PC company's end-user customer, you don't know that your call was answered by a Convergys employee, and you don't care. The entire process was seamless and invisible to you because the PC manufacturer had invested the time and the money necessary to integrate its systems with the systems of its technical support service outsourcer. Now, if the PC manufacturer decides to change outsourcers, it must calculate the switching costs. That's what Convergys means by technology entanglement. It's a highly effective barrier against client defection, and a good leading indicator of the growth potential of a client.

Share of client is based on the client's contact center budget and the percentage of that budget that is outsourced. The team acknowledged that its data in this area was sketchy, so it gave the index a relatively low weight.

Partnership produced a similar situation for the team. The numerical value of this variable is based on highly subjective criteria. Basically, the team had to rely on the judgments of the sales force to answer key questions such as: Does the client buy on price only? Are your contacts at a high level or a low level? Would the client serve as a good reference? Does the client regard Convergys as the supplier of a commodity? Does it regard Convergys as a future strategic partner?

With the customer valuation model in place, however, Convergys made some startling discoveries. Some of its clients raised their ranking quite dramatically, while others fell just as precipitously (see Exhibit 5.5).

TOP 20 CLIENTS	NEW RANK BY PROXY VARIABLE	ORIGINAL RANK BY REVENUE	CHANGE IN RANK
Client A	1	1	0
Client B	2	2	0
Client C	3	62	+59
Client D	4	4	0
Client E	5	40	+35
Client F	6	94	+88
Client G	7	12	+5
Client H	8	20	+12
Client I	9	58	+49
Client J	10	3	-7
Client K	11	47	+36
Client L	12	78	+66
Client M	13	5	-8
Client M	14	72	+58

EXHIBIT 5.5   **Client Change in Value Ranking before and after Value Modeling**

TOP 20 CLIENTS	NEW RANK BY PROXY VARIABLE	ORIGINAL RANK BY REVENUE	CHANGE IN RANK
Client O	15	41	+26
Client P	16	23	+7
Client Q	17	9	-8
Client R	18	25	+7
Client S	19	52	+33
Client T	20	11	-9

EXHIBIT 5.5 *(Continued)*

Client F, a large technology firm, had been relegated to ninety-fourth place in the old ranking system, largely because of its relatively low average annual revenue. In the new valuation model, Client F rose to sixth place because of its high change score and a high partnership index.

Client I, a dot-com, climbed from fifty-eighth place to ninth place, based largely on its technology entanglement and change score indices. Client J, a telecom, fell from third place to tenth place. Its prominent ranking had been based almost entirely on current annual revenue. Under the new valuation model, Client J's spending was offset by low levels of technology entanglement, partnership, and share of client.

Overall, seeing the results in black and white made it easier to begin reallocating resources around Covergys's best clients, with the highest growth potential.

It's easy to understand how refining the firm's understanding of the value of each customer—and the subsequent changes in behaviors and decisions that would drive within a firm—works well for a B2B firm, where the number of customer companies is finite and existing relationships make interaction and data gathering practical. But what happens for a utility whose customers are consumers? See Sidebar 5.3.

SIDEBAR 5.3

Case Scenario: Utility Companies Rank Their MGCs

Deregulation of the energy market forced many gas and electric companies to embrace CRM to retain customers and increase the value of their overall customer base. Customers of a utility company vary widely based on value. One customer of an electric company, for instance, might be a large manufacturing plant that consumes millions of kilowatts each month and provides 20 percent of the utility company's total revenues. Another customer might be a homeowner who does not use

---

SIDEBAR 5.3 *(continued)*

....

much electricity at all. Who might be the most valuable customer (MVC) of a utility company and who might be a below-zero (BZ) customer?

An MVC might be a customer that can be served at the lowest possible cost—he rarely complains about his service and pays his bills early each month. A BZ might be someone who is expensive to serve because he frequently moves or calls about problems with his service, even though the problem lies with his household equipment, not the utility's equipment.

Depending on the value of a customer, utility companies could offer different levels of service that focus on meeting specific needs. These service levels for MVCs, for instance, could include:

- Automatic payment
- Centralized billing/consolidated invoices
- Tips for more efficient consumption
- Single point of contact for all questions
- Technology for the management of a customer's utilities
- Special pricing for nonpeak consumption

Rather than competing on price, utilities that learn enough about their customer's needs and act on those needs will create switching costs that will protect margins and lead to higher customer satisfaction. Northeast Utilities (NU) understands the need to have one complete view of the customer to increase customer share. It has built a data warehouse that combines data from all of its business lines (including gas, electric and its Smart Living lighting catalog) to all customer touchpoints. The richer customer profiles can boost cross-sell and upsell efforts, especially with planned products such as new bill-paying methods. Through mailed surveys and inbound call center interviews, NU learned that many customers felt they had insufficient information to choose between competing energy providers. The company responded to that need by positioning itself as a neutral information source, or portal. For instance, the company produces several publications on deregulation, offers links to energy-related government and citizens' groups on its Web site, and makes a representative trained specifically in deregulation and efficiency accessible by telephone. Being a trusted source encourages customers to stay and grow within NU's franchise area. NU has also reshaped its call center to be more customer-centric. It teaches representatives to be courteous and empathetic toward the needs of customers.

SUMMARY

For an enterprise to engage its customers in relationships, it must be prepared to treat different customers differently, so before designing its relationship-building strategy the firm must understand the nature of its customers' differences, one from another. From the last chapter, we know that the value of a customer is a function of the future business the customer does with the enterprise, and that different customers have different values. Knowing which customers are more valuable allows an enterprise to allocate its relationship building efforts to concentrate first on those customers that will yield the best financial return. However, because the future patronage of any customer is not something that can actually be known in the present, making decisions with respect to customer valuation necessarily involves approximation and subjectivity. Companies with large numbers of customers whose transactions are electronically tracked in a detailed way might be able to use statistical modeling techniques to make reasonably accurate forecasts of the future business that particular types of customers will likely do with the firm, but for the vast majority of enterprises, no such scientific models are readily available. Instead, companies that rank their customers by value usually do so by using a mix of judgment and proxy variables at least at first.

As this chapter has shown, the enterprise that defines, quantifies, and ranks the value of its individual customers takes great strides toward becoming a business truly based on growing customer value. By relying on a taxonomy of customer types based on their value, the enterprise can create a useful facilitation model and attempt to alter the trajectories of individual customers. It can devote the greatest portion of its internal resources to serving its most valuable customers and seek ways to eliminate those customers that will never be profitable.

But ranking customers by their value is only a part of the job. In the next chapter, we will explore how the enterprise can differentiate its customers based not just on their values, but on their needs, as well.

FOOD FOR THOUGHT

1. Why is it not enough to consider average customer value?

2. How often should actual value be calculated? Potential value? Why?

3. What are likely to be the best measures of actual and potential value for each of the following customer bases? How would you confirm that your answer is right? Would the company likely be best served by proxy, financial, or statistical value analysis?
   - Customers for a B2B electronics components distributor?
   - Customers for a dry cleaner?
   - Customers for an automobile manufacturer? For an automobile dealer?
   - Customers for a chemical supply company?
   - Customers for a munitions firm?
   - Customers for a discount department store?
   - Customers for a large regional supermarket chain?
   - Customers for a long-haul trucking company?
   - Customers for Disney World? Six Flags? Club Med?
   - Customers for CBS? For HBO? (Caution: They're different. CBS sells viewers to advertisers; HBO sells programming to viewers.)
   - "Customers" for a political campaign? The American Cancer Society? National Public Radio? Habitat for Humanity?

4. For each of the preceding companies, what's the next step? How does a company use the information about customer value to make managerial decisions?

GLOSSARY

Actual value The net present value of the stream of expected future financial and nonfinancial contributions from a designated customer, discounted back to the present, assuming business as usual.

Below zero (BZ) The below-zero customer will, no matter what strategy or effort is applied toward him, always cost the company more than he contributes.

Lifetime value (LTV) The net present value of the stream of expected future financial contributions from the customer.

Migrator A customer whose present value is modest and whose future value is unknown. The strategy to use toward migrators is either traditional mass marketing or a deliberate effort to solicit feedback in order to learn whether the migrator can become an MGC, MVC, or a BZ.

Mix of customer values For a particular company, the mix refers to the percentage of MVCs versus MGCs versus Migrators versus BZs.

Most growable customer (MGC) These are the customers who have the most growth potential; growth that can be realized through cross-selling, through keeping the customer for a longer period, or perhaps by changing customers' behavior and getting them to operate in a way that costs the enterprise less money.

Most valuable customer (MVC) Those customers with the highest actual value to the enterprise—the ones who do the most business, yield the highest margins, are most willing to collaborate, and tend to be the most loyal.

Potential value All the contributions that the customer could deliver back to the company, if the company applied a conscientious strategy to improve that customer's value by changing its own behavior toward that customer, based on that customer's needs.

Unrealized potential value The difference between a customer's lifetime value and potential value.

Value (customer) The financial asset to a firm represented by the customer.

Differentiating Customers by Their Needs

6

Chapter

Although individual customer valuation is still fairly new, it is already well established as an important stepping-stone for managing the customer-strategy enterprise. Academics and business professionals alike spend much time and energy testing the effectiveness of alternative methods and models. The other part of differentiation, though—the needs differentiation of individual customers—is very new, indeed. It is more widely understood that just as companies measure and act on individual, rather than average, values of customers, so too do companies need to measure and act on individual, rather than just aggregate, needs of customers. But we are only now developing usable methodologies for accomplishing this mission. It's a separate activity from measuring and managing value, and the need differentiation field is still in its infancy. No wonder, then, that it is still often confused with more traditional approaches to consumer behavior, especially benefits analyses. But needs differentiation is all about using the feedback from an identifiable customer to predict that customer's needs better than any competitor can who doesn't have that feedback, and acting on that feedback. Customers will likely be grouped together based on individually expressed very-similar needs, but it is the feedback from a particular customer that determines which needs group she is in, rather than any of the traditional approaches to forming segments of customers who are then treated the same. A contribution from Jennifer Monahan and her colleagues gives us some insight into this developing field.

Many CRM practitioners focus exclusively on differences in customer value. They want to know which customers are the most important to the company's financial future, and should therefore be singled out for special care or targeted with growth initiatives. Although having a good knowledge of customers' value is certainly important, the fact is that you need to know much more about your customers than their value if you hope to use CRM tools to increase value. You want to see the company from the customer's perspective. You want to be able to put yourself in the customer's position, with the realization that there are many different types of customers whose perspective you are seeking to understand. Value differentiation by itself will not give you this perspective. Think about it: Customers don't usually know or care what their value is to you. Customers simply want to have their problem solved, and every customer has a slightly different twist on how they want the process handled. The key to building profitable relationships is developing an understanding of how customers are different in terms of their needs, and how such needs-based differences relate to different customer values, both current and potential. What behavior changes on the customer's part can be accomplished by meeting those needs? What are the triggers that will allow the firm to actualize some of that unrealized potential value?

In this chapter we will consider the different **needs** of different customers and the role that customer needs play in an enterprise's relationship-building effort. In most situations, it makes sense to differentiate customers first by their value and then by their needs.[1] In this way, the relationship-building process, which can be expensive, will begin with the company's higher-value customers, for whom the investment is more likely to be worthwhile. (An important exception to this general rule, however, applies to treating different customers differently on the World Wide Web. On the Web, the incremental costs of automated interaction are near zero, so it makes little difference whether an enterprise differentiates just its top customers by their needs, or all its customers.)

DEFINITIONS

Before going too much further, let's pause to define the important terms relevant to this discussion.

NEEDS

When we refer to customer needs, we are using the term in its most generic sense. That is, what a customer needs from an enterprise is, by our definition, synonymous with what she wants, what she prefers, or what she would like. In this sense, we do not distinguish a customer's needs from her wants. For that matter, we do not distinguish needs from preferences, wishes, desires, or whims. Each of these terms might imply some nuance of need—perhaps the intensity of the need or the permanence of it—but in each case we are still talking, generically, about the customer's needs.

It is what a customer needs from an enterprise that is the driving force behind the customer's behavior. Needs represent the why (and often, the how) behind a

---

[1]In the view of some, differentiating by value first, then needs, may appear to focus first on the company's needs, then those of the customers; but another way to look at this order of strategic imperatives is to think about how a company that used to treat every customer's needs as equally important will now focus more on the needs of those customers who contribute the most to the success of the firm, and therefore will put the needs of some customers ahead of the needs of other customers.

customer's actions. How customers want to buy may be as important as why they want to buy. The presumption has been that frequent purchasers use the product differently from irregular purchasers, but it may be that they alternatively or additionally like the available channel better. For that matter, it may be that they like the communications channel better. The point is that needs are not just about product usage, but about an *expanded need set* (which we will discuss fully in Chapter 10) or the combination of product, cross-buy product and services opportunities, delivery channels, communication style and channels, invoicing methods, and so on.

In a relationship, what the enterprise most wants is to influence the customer's behavior in a way that is financially beneficial to the enterprise; therefore, understanding the customer's basic need is critical. It could be said that while the amount the customer pays the enterprise is a component of the customer's value to the enterprise, the need that the enterprise satisfies is a part of the enterprise's value to the customer. Needs and value represent, essentially, both sides of the value proposition, between enterprise and customer.

CUSTOMERS

Now that we have defined both customer value and customer needs, we should pause for a reminder of the definition of *customer* before continuing with our discussion. Back in Chapter 1, we defined what we mean by "customer." On the surface, the definition should be obvious. A customer is one who "gives his custom" to a store or business; someone who patronizes a business is the business's customer. However, the overwhelming majority of enterprises serve multiple types of customers, and these different types of customers have different characteristics, in terms of their value and their individual needs.

A brand-name clothing manufacturer, for instance, has two sets of customers: the end-user consumers who wear the clothes and the retailers who buy the clothes from the manufacturer and sell them to consumers. As a customer base, clothing consumers do not have as steep a value skew as, say, a hotel's customer base, even though some consumers might buy new clothes every week. (In other words, the discrepancy in value between the very most valuable customers and the average will generally be smaller for clothes merchants.) But all consumers of the clothing manufacturer do want different combinations of sizes, colors, and styles. So even though clothing consumers may not be highly differentiated in terms of their value, they are very different in terms of their needs. The retailers also have very different needs: Some need more help with marketing, or with advertising co-op dollars, or with displays. Different retailers will have very different requirements for invoice format and timing, or for shipping and delivery. They may need different palletization, or precoded price tags. Interestingly, the retailers will also vary widely in their values to the clothing manufacturer. Some large department store chains will sell far more stock than can a local mom-and-pop clothing shop. Thus the retailer customers display high levels of differentiation in terms of both their needs and their value.

For this type of business, if the enterprise expresses an interest in improving its relationships with its customers the question to answer is, which customers? And this is, in fact, the type of structure in which most enterprises operate. They won't all sell products to retailers, but the vast majority of businesses do have distribution partners of some kind—retailers, dealers, brokers, representatives, value-added resellers, and so forth. Moreover, a business that sells to other businesses, whether or not these business customers are a part of a distribution chain, is really selling to the *people* within those businesses, people of varying levels of influence and authority. Putting in place a relationship program involving business customers will necessarily entail dealing with purchasing agents, approvers, influencers, decision makers, and possibly end users within the business customer's organization, and each of these will have quite different motivations in choosing to buy.

The logical first step for any enterprise embarking on a relationship-building program, therefore, is to decide which sets of customers to focus on. A relationship-building strategy aimed at end-user consumers can (and in most cases, should) involve some or all of the intermediaries in the value chain in some way. However, it is a perfectly legitimate goal to seek stronger and deeper relationships with a particular set of intermediaries. The basic objective of relationship building with any set of customers is to increase the value of the customer base; thus, it's important to understand from the beginning exactly which customer base is going to be measured and evaluated. Then, when focusing on that customer base, the enterprise must be able to map out its customers in terms of their different values and needs.

It is easy to confuse a customer's needs with a product's **benefits.** Companies create products and services with benefits that are specifically designed to satisfy customer needs, but the benefits themselves are not equivalent to needs. In traditional marketing discipline, a product's benefits are the advantages that customers get from using the product, based on its features and **attributes.** But features, attributes, and benefits are all based on the product, rather than on the customer. Needs, in contrast, are based on the customer, not the product. Two different customers might actually satisfy different needs by enjoying the same benefit, based on the same features and attributes, from the same product.

When it focuses on the customer's need, the enterprise will find it easier to increase its share of customer, because ultimately it will seek to solve a greater and greater portion of the customer's problem—that is, to meet a larger and larger share of the customer's need. And because the customer's need is not directly related to the product, meeting the need might in fact lead an enterprise to develop or procure other products and services for the customer, which are totally unrelated to the original product but closely related to the customer's need. Focusing on customer needs, rather than on product features, in fact, will often reveal that different customers purchase the same product in order to satisfy very different individual needs.[2]

---

[2]A large body of academic research, as well as trade articles and professional work, has been published on the topics of benefits, attributes, and needs, as well as the findings about the different reasons two customers with the same transaction history are motivated to buy the same products.

DIFFERENTIATING CUSTOMERS BY NEED: AN ILLUSTRATION

Consider a company that manufactures interlocking toy blocks for children, and suppose this firm goes to market with a set of blocks suitable for constructing a spaceship. Three seven-year-old boys playing with this set of blocks might all have different needs for it. One child might use the blocks to play a make-believe role, perhaps assembling a spaceship and then pretending he is an astronaut on a mission to Mars. Another child might enjoy simply following the directions, meticulously assembling the ship in exact detail, according to the instructions. Once the ship is built, however, he would be less interested in it. A third child might use the spaceship block set to build something entirely different, drawn from his own vivid imagination. He simply wouldn't enjoy putting together a toy according to someone else's diagram.

Each of these three children may enjoy playing with the same set of blocks, but each is doing so to satisfy a different set of needs. Moreover, it is the child's need that, *if known to the marketer*, provides the key to increasing the child's value as a customer. If the toy manufacturer actually knew each child's individual needs, and if it had the capability to deal with each child individually, by treating each one differently it could easily increase its share of each child's toy-and-entertainment consumption. For example, for the "actors," it might offer costumes and other props, along with storybooks and videotapes, to assist the children in their imaginative role-playing activities. For the "engineers," it might offer blueprints for additional toys to be assembled using the spaceship set; or it might offer more complex diagrams for multiset connections. And for the more creative types, the "artists," the company might provide pieces in unusual colors or shapes, or perhaps supplemental sets of parts that have not been planned into any diagrams at all.

We can use this example to compare and contrast the different roles of product attributes and benefits, versus customer needs. Exhibit 6.1 shows that each product attribute yields a particular benefit that consumers of the product can enjoy.

It should be easy to see that each product attribute can be easily linked to a particular type of benefit. And the benefits will appeal differently to different customers, but each benefit springs directly from each attribute. If, instead, we were to map out the *types of customers* who buy this product, based on the needs

PRODUCT ATTRIBUTE	PRODUCT BENEFIT
Toys in fantasy configurations	Recognizable make-believe situations
Colorful, unusual shapes that easily interlock	Large variety of interesting combinations
Meticulously preplanned, logically detailed instructions	Complex directions that are nevertheless easy to follow

EXHIBIT 6.1   **Attributes versus Benefits**

CUSTOMER NEED	ADDITIONAL PRODUCTS AND SERVICES
Actor: Role playing, pretending, fantasizing	Costumes, videos, storybooks, toys
Artist: Creating, making stuff up, doing things differently	Colors and paints, unique add-ons, nonsequitur parts
Engineer: Solving problems, completing puzzles	More diagrams, problems, logical extensions

EXHIBIT 6.2   Beyond Benefits: Needs

of these end users as just outlined, we could then list the additional products and services that each type of customer might want, based on what that customer needs from this and other products. If we just looked at our actor, artist, or engineer end-user customers to see which needs they wanted to address, then our table would look like Exhibit 6.2.

This is only a hypothetical example, of course, and we could easily come up with several additional types of customers, based on the needs they are satisfying with these construction blocks. For instance, there might be some girls who want the spaceship set of blocks because they are really interested in rockets, outer space, and other things astronautical. Or there might be some boys who want the set because they are collectors of these kinds of building-block toys, and they want to add this to a large set of other, similar toys. Or there might be others who like to use this kind of toy to invite friends over to work together on the assembly. Any single child might, in fact, have any combination of these needs that she wishes to satisfy, either at different times or in combination.

The point is, by taking the customer's own perspective—by concentrating on understanding each different customer's needs—the enterprise will more easily be able to influence customer behavior, and changing the future behavior of a customer is the key to realizing additional value from that customer.

WHY DOESN'T EVERY COMPANY ALREADY DIFFERENTIATE THEIR CUSTOMERS BY NEEDS?

It is reasonable to ask, if the logic outlined is so compelling, why toy manufacturers and other firms aren't already pursuing this type of strategy. But keep in mind that the hurdles are immense. For one thing, most toy manufacturers sell their products through retailers, and have little or no direct contact with the end users of their products. In order to make contact with consumers, a manufacturer will either have to launch a program in cooperation with its retailing partners or figure out how to go around those retailers altogether—a course of action likely to arouse considerable resentment among the retailers themselves. So at least under current market conditions, the vast majority of a manufacturer's end-user consumers are destined to remain completely unknown to the enterprise. Moreover, even if it had its customers' identities, the manufacturer would still require some means of interacting with the customers individually and of processing their feedback, in order to learn their genuine needs. Then it would have to be able to translate those needs into different actions, requiring a mechanism for actually offering and delivering different products and services to different consumers.

These obstacles make it very difficult for toy manufacturers simply to leap into a relationship-building program with toy consumers at the very end of the value chain. That said, the manufacturer does not have to launch such a program for all consumers at once. Rather, if it could start by identifying its most avid fans, its highest-volume, most valuable consumer customers. Perhaps it could devise a strategy for treating each of those highly valuable customers to individually different products and services, in a way that wouldn't undermine retailer relationships. A Web site designed to attract and entertain such consumers could play a role. While the toy manufacturer would still encourage other shoppers to buy its products in stores, perhaps it could begin to offer more specialized sets and pieces directly to catalog and Web purchasers. If it had a system for doing this, then it would be much simpler to launch a program designed to make different types of offers to different types of end-user consumers—based on their individual needs.

Indeed, the primary reason so many firms are now attempting to engage their customers in relationships is that the new tools of information technology—not just the World Wide Web, but customer databases, sales force automation, marketing and customer analytics applications, and the like—are making this type of activity ever more cost-efficient and practical. But for an enterprise engaged in relationship building, the "hot button," in terms of generating increased patronage from the customer, is the customer's need.

CATEGORIZING CUSTOMERS BY THEIR NEEDS

In the end, behavior change on the part of the customer is what customer-based strategies are all about. To capture any part of a customer's unrealized potential value requires us to induce a change in the customer's behavior—we want the customer to buy from an additional product line, or take the financing package as well as the product, or interact on the less expensive Web site rather than through the call center, and so forth. This is why understanding customer needs is so critical to success. The customer is master of her own behavior, and that behavior will only change if our strategy can appeal persuasively to the customer's needs. Being able to see the situation from the customer's point of view is key to any successful customer-based strategy.

But in order to take action, at some point, different customers must be categorized into different groups, based on their needs. Clearly, it would be too costly for most firms to treat every single customer with a custom-designed set of product features or services. Instead, using information technology, the customer-focused enterprise categorizes customers into finer and finer groups, and then matches each group with an appropriately mass-customized product-and-service offering. (More about mass customization and the actual mechanics of the process in Chapter 10.)

One big problem is the complexity of describing and categorizing customers by their needs. There are as many dimensions and nuances to customer needs as there are analysts to imagine them. For consumers, there are deeply held beliefs, psychological predispositions, life stages, moods, ambitions, and so forth. For business customers, there are business strategy differences, financial reporting horizons, collegial or hierarchical decision-making styles, and other corporate differences—not to mention the individual motivations of the players within the customer organizations, including decision makers, approvers, specifiers, reviewers, and others involved in shaping the company's behavior.

Marketing has always relied on appealing to different customers in different ways. Market segmentation is a highly developed, sophisticated discipline, but it is based primarily on products, and the appeal of product benefits, rather than on customers, and their broader set of needs. To address customers as different types of customers, rather than as recipients of a product's different benefits, the customer-based enterprise must think beyond market segmentation, per se. Rather than grouping customers into *segments* based on the product's appeal, the customer-based enterprise places customers into *portfolios*, based primarily on type of need.

A **market segment** is made up of customers with a similar attribute. A **customer portfolio** is made up of similar customers. The market segmentation approach is based on appealing to the segment's attribute, while the customer portfolio approach is based on meeting each customer's broader need. If segments and portfolios were made up of toys, then red fire trucks might be in a segment of toys that included red checkers sets, red dolly makeup lipsticks, and red blocks. But red fire trucks would be in a *portfolio* of toys that included ambulances, fireboats, police cars, and maybe medical helicopters, along with fire hats and axes, stuffed Dalmatians, and ladders. A market segment might be composed of women, over age 45, with household (HH) incomes in excess of $50,000. A portfolio of customers might be made up of kids who like to pretend, act, and fantasize.

In Chapter 13, we will discuss customer management, including the grouping of customers into portfolios. There will be a continuing role for traditional market segmentation, even in a highly evolved customer-strategy enterprise, because understanding how a product's benefits match up with the attributes of different customers will continue to be an important marketing activity. But as the enterprise gains greater and greater insight into the actual motivations of particular categories of customers, it will find that managing relationships cannot be accomplished in segment categories, because any single customer can easily be found in more than one segment. Instead, when they take the customer's perspective, the managers at a customer-strategy enterprise will learn that they must meet the complex, *multiple needs* of each customer, as an individual. And this will require categorizing customers according to their own, broader needs, rather than according to how they react to the product's attributes and benefits.

UNDERSTANDING NEEDS

Understanding different customers' different needs is critical to any serious relationship-building program. Some of the characteristics of customer needs should be given careful consideration:

- *Customer needs can be situational in nature.* Not only will two different consumers often buy the same product to satisfy different needs, but a customer's needs might change from event to event, and it's important to recognize when this occurs. An airline might think it has two customer types—business travelers and leisure travelers—but in reality this typology refers to events, not customers. Even the most frequent business traveler will occasionally be traveling for leisure, and in that event she will need different services from the airline than she needs when she travels on business.
- *Customer needs are dynamic and can change over time, as well.* People are changeable creatures; our lives evolve from one stage to another, we move from place to place, we change our minds. Moreover, certain types of people change their minds more often than others, tending to be less predictable. That said, the fact that a certain type of customer is not predictable is a customer characteristic itself, which can be used to help guide an enterprise's treatment of *that* customer.
- *Customer needs often correlate with customer value.* While not always true, more often than not a high-value customer is likely to have certain types of needs in common with other high-value customers. Similarly, a below-zero customer's needs are more likely than not to be similar to other below-zero customers' needs. A business that can correlate customer value with customer needs is generally in a good situation, because by satisfying certain types of needs it can do a more efficient job of winning the long-term loyalty of higher-value customers.
- *The most fundamental human needs are psychological.* When dealing with human beings as customers (as opposed to companies or organizations), understanding the psychological differences among people can provide useful guidance for treating different customers differently.
- *There is no single best way to differentiate customers by their needs.* As difficult as it is to predict and quantify a customer's value to the enterprise, at least the final result will be measured in economic terms. Value ranking, in other words, is done in one dimension: the financial dimension. But when an enterprise sets out to differentiate its customers by their needs, it is embarking on a creative expedition, with no fixed dimension of reference. There are as many ways to differentiate customers by their needs as there are creative ways to understand the deepest human motivations. The value of any particular type of needs-based differentiation is to be found solely in its usefulness for affecting the different behaviors of different customers.
- *Even in B2B settings, a firm's customers are not really another "company," with a clearly defined, homogeneous set of needs.* Instead, it is a combination

of purchasing agents, who need low prices; end users, who need benefits and attributes; the managers of the end users, who need those end users to be productive; and so on.

EXAMPLE IN THE PHARMACEUTICAL INDUSTRY

Consider, for example, a pharmaceutical company. Traditionally, the firm has not engaged in much relationship building with its end-user consumers (i.e., the patients for whom its drugs are prescribed). Rather, the firm has always considered its primary customers to be the prescribing physicians, along with pharmacies and healthcare organizations. But now, faced with the cost-efficient, powerfully interactive technology of the World Wide Web, this pharmaceutical company wants to begin to establish genuine, one-to-one relationships with at least some of the more valuable consumers of its products. The company sells medicine for diabetes, which can be kept in check through constant vigilance, but as is the case with many such diseases, *compliance* is a problem. Patients often simply fail to keep up the medical treatment or they fail to monitor their own condition properly. The company knows that patients want help in understanding and dealing with the disease, so it sets up a Web site to serve as a resource for information and support. The benefit for the pharmaceutical company is straightforward: A better-informed and -supported patient is likely to exhibit better compliance, which will both keep the patient healthier and sell more of the pharmaceutical company's drugs.

Knowing that different consumers will need different types of support and assistance, the pharmaceutical enterprise undertakes to design a patient-centric Web site. To do so, it conducts a research survey of patients, and discovers that a patient's attitude toward keeping the disease in check will drive her individual needs for using the Web site. Newly diagnosed patients for the most part simply want any and all information related to their disease. They need to be able to select content relevant to their own problems. However, as patients come to grips with their sickness, their attitudes toward the disease tend to fall into one of three primary categories. For this pharmaceutical company, working with a set of diabetic patients, the needs groupings tend to look like this:

- *Individualists.* This type of patient relies on herself to make educated decisions on how to manage her disease. Individualists could be directed to online clinical support, and they could opt for customized electronic newsletters or for online health-tracking tools.
- *Abdicators.* This patient's attitude toward the disease is one of resignation and detachment. She basically decides that she will "just have to live with the conditions of her disease," so she ends up depending on the help given by a significant other. The site directs abdicators to various caregiver resources and provides planning information related to nutrition and meals.
- *Connectors.* This type of patient welcomes as much information and support as she can get from others to help her make educated decisions about

how to manage her disease. The site directs connectors to online chat rooms and electronic bulletin boards where they can meet and converse with other patients. It has an "e-buddy" feature that pairs her up with a patient similar to herself.

For the pharmaceutical company to design a Web site that is truly customer-focused, it should try to figure out, for each returning visitor, what the particular mind-set of that visitor is, and then serve up the best features and benefits for that particular type of patient. The easier the enterprise can make it for different patients to find the support and assistance they need, individually, the more valuable those patients will become for the enterprise.

At this juncture, however, it is important once again to separate our thinking about the features and benefits of the Web site (i.e., the product, in this case) from the actual psychological needs and predispositions of the Web site visitors themselves. Any one of the visitors might in fact use any of the Web site's many features on any particular visit. That means each of the Web site's benefits will probably overlap several different types of customers, with different types of needs. But the customers themselves do not overlap—they are unique individuals, each with her own unique psychology and motivation. It is only our categorization of these unique and different customers into needs-based groups that might give us the illusion that they are the same. They may be similar in their needs, but at a deeper level, they are still uniquely individual, and this will be true no matter how many additional categories, or portfolios, we create. We simply categorize customers in order to better comprehend their differences by making generalizations about them.

USING NEEDS DIFFERENTIATION TO BUILD CUSTOMER VALUE

The scenarios of the toy manufacturer and the pharmaceutical company show how each had to be aware of its respective individual customer's needs so it could act on them. Once a particular customer's needs are known, the company is better able to put itself in the place of the customer, and can offer the treatment that is best for that customer. Each company gets the information about customer needs primarily by interacting. Therefore, an open dialogue between the customer and the enterprise is critical for needs differentiation. Moreover, customer needs are complex and intricate enough that the more a customer interacts with an enterprise, the more learning an enterprise will gain about the particular preferences, desires, wants, and whims of that customer. Provided that the enterprise has the capability required to act on this more and more detailed customer insight, by treating the customer differently, it will be able to create a rich and enduring Learning Relationship.

A successful Learning Relationship with a customer is founded on changes in the enterprise's behavior toward the customer based on the use of more in-depth knowledge about that particular customer. Knowing the individual customer's needs is essential to nurturing the Learning Relationship. As the firm learns more about a customer, the firm compiles a gold mine of data that should, within the bounds of privacy protection, be made available to all those at the enterprise who interact with the customer. Kraft, for example, empowers its salespeople with the data they need to make intelligent recommendations to a retailer. It has assembled a centralized information system that integrates data from three internal database sources. One database contains information about the individual stores that track purchases of customers by category and price. Another database contains customer demographics and buying-habit information at food stores nationwide. A third database, purchased from an outside vendor, has geodemographic data aligned by zip code.

> Information is the raw material that is transformed into knowledge through its organization, analysis, and understanding. This knowledge must then be applied and managed in ways that best support investment decisions and resource deployment.

But to truly get to know a customer through interactions with her, enterprises must do more than gather and analyze aggregated quantitative information. Accumulating information is only a first step in creating the knowledge needed to pursue a customer-centered strategy successfully. Information is the raw material that is transformed into knowledge through its organization, analysis, and understanding. This knowledge must then be applied and managed in ways that best support investment decisions and resource deployment. Customer knowledge management is the effective leverage of information and experience in the acquisition, development, and retention of a profitable customer. Gathering superior customer knowledge without codifying and leveraging it across the enterprise results in missed opportunities.[3]

In the next section, Jennifer Monahan and others introduce one possible methodological approach for needs differentiation.

DIFFERENTIATING CUSTOMERS BY THEIR NEEDS: A PRACTICAL APPROACH

Jennifer B. Monahan
Peppers and Rogers Group

William C. Pink
Millward Brown

Nichole Clarke
Peppers and Rogers Group

Valerie Popeck
Peppers and Rogers Group

Laura Cococcia
Peppers and Rogers Group

Sophie Vlessing
Peppers and Rogers Group

[3]Paul M. Cole, *Customer Connections* (Cambridge, MA: Harvard Business School Press, 1997).

Traditional marketing has become a semi-science of trying to translate demographics and psychographics into a basic understanding of a target audience. Traditional marketers measure dimensions such as awareness and relevance and assess how they influence customers' choices of a product or service. But awareness and relevance are only two of the many factors that might motivate a particular customer to purchase a product or service, or to buy it repeatedly.

WHAT DO WE MEAN BY CUSTOMER NEEDS?

Customer *needs* refer to *why* the customer buys, not *what* the customer buys.[4] Transactional information should still be captured and tracked, but what is crucial is to understand *why* a customer buys what she buys. Importantly, the motivation to purchase may be different, even for customers who are buying the same product. In effect, we use customer needs to highlight the distinction between purchase motivation and purchase behavior to drive customized treatment.[5]

Given our focus on needs as motivating factors, the question becomes, what framework should be applied to understand needs? A framework for understanding customer needs can best be understood as a continuum. At the very beginning of the continuum customer needs are not understood and a company ignores differences among its customers.[6] At the other end of the continuum is true customer-focused treatment, in which the needs of each customer are known. It is in the large area in between these extremes that the learning about customer needs occurs, in an ongoing process.

SIDEBAR 6.1

Scenario: Financial Services

....

A large B2B financial services organization faced both increasing competition and product commoditization. The customers of this firm are *channel* members—the brokers and financial advisers (FAs) who sell stocks and bonds and other financial instruments to consumer clients from their own business. The enterprise sought to increase loyalty and reduce the effects of cost cutting among these channel-member customers by meeting their individual needs, one customer at a time. Research, based on interviews with the enterprise's sales staff and customers, uncovered several key customer needs.

Five needs-based portfolios were identified and given nicknames—High-Potential Newbies, Marketing Machines, Active Growers, Transitional Players, and Cruise Controls—in a research project that combined customer needs information with cus-

---

[4]Don Peppers and Martha Rogers,PhD, *Enterprise One to One: Tools for Competing in the Interactive Age* (New York: Doubleday, 1997).

[5]John Berrigan and Carl Finkbeiner, *Segmentation Marketing: New Methods for Capturing Business Markets* (Philadelphia: National Analysts, Inc., 1992).

[6]Ibid.

SIDEBAR 6.1 *(continued)*

tomer valuation. As a result, the enterprise determined its customers' needs, while at the same time uncovering which high-value customers posed the greatest defection risk. This led to the development of a *defection reduction* strategy to retain those customers. For customers not at risk of defection, the organization developed interaction strategies to begin meeting their needs immediately.

As it builds relationships with these customers over time, the financial services enterprise will seek to increase customer knowledge and to act on the individual needs of its customers. In the process, both the enterprise and its customers will benefit. For the enterprise, an interaction strategy for each FA, based on the individual FA's needs and value, will provide clear direction and focus for the sales force. As more needs are uncovered, the firm will be able to offer more products and services. Ultimately, defection will be reduced, which should substantially reduce marketing and sales costs.

For the customers themselves, the relationship-building program should improve the relevance and usefulness of incoming information from the enterprise. This will enable individual FAs to run their own businesses faster, more efficiently, and in a way that is likely to please their own clients more.

To begin to recognize customer differences, an enterprise must understand how its customers can be grouped by similar needs. In other words, what are the motivating factors that different customers might have in common? Commonalities allow the enterprise to put customers into groups, or portfolios, to be managed by the organization. The portfolios become the basis for a company's decisions to customize treatment. It is the categorization and grouping of customers into portfolios of customers with roughly similar needs that permits an enterprise to cost-efficiently design different strategies and treatments for different customers.

One good place to start in a search for the different types of customers who have needs in common with one another is with traditional consumer research. Most firms—particularly consumer-marketing firms—have access to studies that are based on past research that they have either conducted themselves or contracted for. In many cases, one of the primary outputs of this kind of research includes some conclusions regarding the different demographic or psychological types of consumers who buy the firm's product or service. These types often fall out of the research study in the form of "clusters" or "segments," but the research itself will usually classify the different groups based on their needs and/or their value.

CUSTOMER DEMOGRAPHIC DATA AND CUSTOMER NEEDS

Demographic information often correlates with customer needs, and can be an effective tool to begin an analysis, but this kind of information should be viewed as a building block, not as the end goal. Needs are not defined by demographics,

Needs are not defined by demographics

although people with similar demographic profiles are generally more likely to have at least some needs in common. The problem is that this is not always the case, and there are many situations in which needs extend beyond traditional demographic boundaries. Consider the financial services needs of two 30-year-old women, both of whom have high-income jobs, are married, and have no children. Given their similar demographic profiles, a financial services firm can infer certain needs that these two women are likely to share, such as the need for information regarding taxation laws for married couples. However, the financial services firm would not know the internal conditions that drive each of the women to become and remain customers of the firm. For example, perhaps one of the women needs the firm to act as a trusted advisor, and expects the company to maintain a high level of contact with her, providing recommendations on how she and her husband can best save for their future. Perhaps the other woman, in contrast, prefers to make her own financial decisions; she needs the firm simply to expedite her requests in the most efficient and cost-effective manner. Clearly, these financial services needs cannot be differentiated based on demographic information alone—they can only be learned through dialogue.

The key is to be able to distinguish customers based on needs and overlay this information with the demographic information at hand. This combination can be extremely powerful.

KEEPING AND GROWING CUSTOMERS

To retain its most valuable customers, an enterprise must know those customers' needs and act on them. Consider the banking industry. Typically, banks spend between $200 and $250 to replace each customer that defects. So, if a bank has a clientele of 50,000 customers, and loses 5 percent of those customers each year, then it would need to spend $500,000 or more each year simply to maintain its customer base.[7]

One way for banks to approach this problem is to build customer needs into their retention strategies. Because banks track the typical behavior patterns of individual customers, they can quickly understand the normal level of interactions a customer requires from a bank. If a customer's behavior changes from this norm, it is often a signal that either the customer is dissatisfied or her needs have changed. Banks can build business rules into their customer interaction strategies that mandate contacting the customer at the first sign of trouble. Armed with this information, a bank can intervene early whenever a possibility of customer defection exists, and increase the probability of retention with relevant incentives and offerings.[8]

[7]John Kish, "Before Your Customers Leave; Banks Fight Attrition," *Bank Marketing* (December 1, 2000).

[8]Ibid.

But retaining customers is only part of the challenge. The customer-focused enterprise also attempts to maximize a customer's profitability by increasing its share of customer. By recognizing a customer's needs, the organization is in the unique position to create customized products and services to meet those needs. The result is increased loyalty and sales from the customer.

Consider the highly commoditized business of beauty products. Most beauty products are sold through department or drug stores. Some are offered through home shows or direct mail. A variety of colors and scents are available but don't allow the consumer to create a product that is individually suited to her skin type, coloring, and personal preferences—even though every woman has a unique face, with unique coloring, and every woman has her own tastes and preferences. An exception to this "prefab" world of beauty is the online beauty products company at Reflect.com, where the consumer creates her own products by answering questions that relate to skin type, coloring, preferred packaging (e.g., flip-top versus twist-top), and fragrance. The consumer can then name her product and save it to make it easier to reorder. As a result, Reflect.com has developed a one-to-one Learning Relationship with its customers, increasing loyalty and wallet share. The higher prices that Reflect.com charges are not a deterrent to its loyal customer base, because the customers see the value in receiving personalized and customized products.

> The higher prices that Reflect.com charges are not a deterrent to its loyal customer base, because the customers see the value in receiving personalized and customized products.

Enterprises can use needs-based differentiation as part of an overall customer-focused strategy to build customer loyalty and, as a result, customer profitability. Needs-based differentiation is more than a one-time project. The ability to understand and act on each customer's needs improves as the relationship grows with a customer. The key is to have the right kind of relationship—one that is based on a dialogue between the enterprise and the customer, in which all customer information is shared internally and understood, so that the enterprise can customize its offerings to the customer's individual needs. The enterprises that begin to use needs-based differentiation can have a distinct advantage over their competitors: building, understanding, and using individual customer knowledge to increase customer loyalty and profitability, one customer at a time.

SIDEBAR 6.2
Demographics Do Not Reveal Needs[a]

Thirty years ago, a ground-breaking marketing article asked: "Are Grace Slick and Tricia Nixon Cox the same person?" Grace Slick, acid-head lead singer for the rock group Jefferson Starship, and Tricia Nixon Cox, the preppy daughter of Richard Nixon who married Dwight Eisenhower's grandson, were demographically indistinguishable. They were both urban, working women, graduated from college, age 25 to 35, at similar income levels, household of three, including one child.

SIDEBAR 6.2 *(continued)*

What made this question startling in the early 1970s was that it undermined the validity of the traditional demographic tools that marketers had been using for decades to segment consumers into distinct, identifiable groups. With demographic statistics, mass marketers thought they could distinguish a quiz show's audience from, say, a news program's. Then marketers could compare these audiences with the demographics of soap buyers, tire purchasers, or beer drinkers. The more effectively a marketer could define her own customers and target prospects, differentiating this group from all the other consumers who were not her target, the more efficiently she could put her message across. She could buy media that would reach a higher proportion of her own target audience.

But demographics could not explain the distinctly nondemographic differences between Grace Slick and Tricia Nixon Cox. So, as computer capabilities and speeds grew, marketers began to collect additional information to distinguish consumers, not by their age and gender, but by their attitudes toward themselves, their families and society, their beliefs, their values, and their lifestyles.

[a]Excerpted from Don Peppers and Martha Rogers, PhD, *The One to One Future* (1993), in reference to John O'Toole, "Are Grace Slick and Tricia Nixon Cox the Same Person?" *Journal of Advertising* 2 (1973), 32–34.

COMMUNITY KNOWLEDGE

In the competition for a customer, the successful enterprise is the one with the most knowledge about an individual customer's needs. In a successful Learning Relationship, the enterprise acts in the customer's own individual interest. What if the customer were to maintain her own list of specifications and purchases? If the record of a customer's consumption of groceries were maintained on her own computer rather than on a supermarket's computer, this would undercut the competitive advantage that customization gives to an enterprise. Each week a whole cadre of supermarkets could simply "bid" on the customer's list of grocery needs, reducing the level of competition once again to the lowest price. The customer-strategy enterprise can avoid this vulnerability, as it has devised a way to treat an individual customer based on the knowledge of that customer's transactions as well as on the transactions of many other customers who have similarities to her. This is known as *community knowledge*.

Community knowledge comes from the accumulation of information about a whole community of customer tastes and preferences. It is the body of knowledge that an enterprise acquires with respect to customers who have similar tastes and needs, enabling the firm actually to *anticipate* what an individual customer needs, even before the customer knows she needs it. Also called *collaborative filtering* on the Web, this is, essentially, a matching engine. It allows a company to serve up products or services to a particular customer based on what other customers with similar tastes or preferences have preferred in this particular product or service. For example, Amazon.com uses collaborative filtering to recommend books to you that were read by people with similar interests.

Technology has accelerated the rate at which enterprises can apply community knowledge to better understand individual customers. This tool can help not just the individual consumers of a company like Amazon.com, but also business-to-business customers. The idea of community knowledge has a direct lineage from one of the most important values any B2B business can bring its own business customers: education about what other customers with similar needs are doing—in the aggregate, of course, never individually. Firms know that they must teach their customers as well as be taught by them. An enterprise brings insight to a customer based on the firm's dealings with a large number of that customer's own competitors. Community knowledge can yield immense benefits to many businesses, but especially to those businesses that have:

- *Cost-efficient, interactive connections with customers as a matter of routine*, such as online services, banks and financial institutions, retail stores, and business-to-business marketers, all of which communicate and interact with their customers directly and on a regular basis.
- *Customers that are highly differentiated by their needs*, including businesses that sell news and information, movies and other entertainment, books, fashion, automobiles, computers, groceries, hotel stays, and healthcare, among other things.

Marketing expert Fred Wiersema[9] has said that there are three types of customer coaching: bringing out the product's full benefits, improving the customer's usage process, and breaking completely new ground with the customer. Any one of these types of customer education can come from the knowledge an enterprise acquires by serving other customers. An enterprise with a large number of customers can use community knowledge to *lead* a customer to a product or service that the enterprise knows the customer is likely to need, even though the customer may be totally unaware of this need. It might be as simple as choosing a hotel in a city the customer has never visited, but it could also apply to pursuing an appropriate investment and savings strategy, even though the customer may not have thought of it yet.

SIDEBAR 6.3

Scenario: Universities Differentiate Students' Needs

Like more enterprises around the world, universities are building Learning Relationships with individual students, as well as the corporate concerns that are already providing much of the funding for tuition and research. For many schools, the primary competition now comes from a mix of online coursework vendors and corporate centers of learning and education, rather than from traditional universities. Motorola University, for instance, began in 1981 as an internal quality training

---

[9]Fred Wiersema, *Customer Intimacy: Pick Your Partners, Shape Your Culture, Win Together* (Middleborough, MA: The Country Press, 1996).

SIDEBAR 6.3 *(continued)*

center and it has grown to provide services to other companies to help them become more effective within their businesses, offering courses in meeting planning, cycle-time reduction, and other subjects. Motorola requires its employees to complete 40 or more hours a year of job-relevant training through its university. The fastest-growing sector of higher education is the "corporate university" that provides training for middle and upper management.[a]

Higher education has a variety of different customers. Students, parents, employers, government, states, and donors are just some examples. Instead of measuring the success of a university by the number of students it enrolls, or even the cutoff point for admission, a customer-focused university gauges its success by the projected increase or decrease in a particular student's expected future value. The university no longer focuses just on acquiring more students, but on retaining existing learners and growing the business each gives the institution.

Like for-profit businesses, academic universities want to attract and retain the MVCs and MGCs (i.e., highly qualified, tuition-paying students), and to reap the most benefit from them, not just over their four years of study, but over their many years as alumni as well. As more universities consider their options for achieving those goals, attention often turns to alumni as the answer. Institutions of higher learning have understood that prolonging relationships with alumni can improve the accuracy of the fund-raising list, which in turn improves fund-raising response rates and donor lifetime value. The number of schools that are implementing strategies for those purposes is increasing.

Because it is now possible to keep track of relationships with individual students, the size of a university is becoming a less potent competitive advantage. A university of any size has the opportunity to use information about each student to secure more of that individual's participation. Notwithstanding the "brand" or status value of a handful of high-status Ivy League and top-ranked higher education institutions, securing and keeping the participation of more students will likely depend on who has and uses the most information about a specific student, not on who has the most students.

To compete, the customer-focused university has to integrate its entire range of business functions around satisfying the individual needs of each individual student. The school's organizational structure itself will have to be altered, and it must embrace significant change, affecting virtually every department, division, administrator, and employee. Once it has migrated to a customer-strategy model, the university will be able to generate unprecedented levels of participant loyalty by offering an unprecedented level of customization and relationship building.

Student-customer valuation will require measures of success based on individual student results, not just product or program measures. Rather than seeing whether enough students enrolled in a particular course to justify its existence, for instance, the institution will also predict whether a particular student is valuable enough to justify a certain level of expenditure. The customer-focused university will be able to calculate share of student on an individual, participant-by-participant basis, with the goal of capturing a greater share of dollars, time, and other investment in learning.

The customer-focused university builds a Learning Relationship with each student by interacting over time and continuing to increase its level of relevance to each student by understanding her motivation. Although participation in the university should be motivation enough, the customer-focused university will understand whether a student is, for example, taking a course because of interest in the material, admiration for the professor, a need to be respected, a desire to make business

SIDEBAR 6.3 *(continued)*

....

contacts, as part of a degree program, career participation, or some other reason. Remembering what each student wants and finding ways to make the collaboration effort valuable to the participant leads to mass-customizing the offering, the response, the dialogue process, the level of recognition, the opportunity for active participation, and so on.

The implications of more cost-efficient electronic interaction for higher education are immense. Many universities are pioneers in adopting a customer strategy to develop Learning Relationships with each of their students. Western Governor's University in Salt Lake City, Utah, is creating independent measurements of "output"— their graduates. In addition to traditional assessment of learning outcomes, such as those required by the Association to Advance Collegiate Schools of Business (AACSB)—measuring the university's quality by the number of PhDs on the faculty or books in the library—the school also is rating the academic performance of its students against an objective measure of the student's overall accomplishment.

Franklin University, an independent nonprofit institution serving 5,000 students in Columbus, Ohio, created a new position, Student Services Associate (SSA), designed to be the "customer manager" for its students. Each of the University's 12 SSAs is evaluated and paid based on how many of his or her students make it to graduation. Every SSA interaction with a student is captured on the computer so that anyone interacting with the student can view his or her complete profile and history. In addition, to better meet the needs of busy students, the university became part of a Community College Alliance and started offering courses online. For Franklin, led by university president Paul Otte, customer-focused strategies have translated directly into revenue increases and greater share of student. In the mid-1990s, 60 percent of students were freshmen and sophomores; now, 60 percent are juniors and seniors, another 10 to 12 percent are continuing on to graduate school, and surveys indicate higher levels of student satisfaction.

Students at the University of Phoenix (UP), Arizona, are often underwhelmed at its physical facilities, but they enthusiastically participate in the school's accredited programs in business, nursing, and education because they can get the learning they want and need on their own terms, according to their own schedules. Only one-sixth of America's college enrollees fit the stereotype of full-time students living on campus; UP's students want "the kind of relationship they had with their bank," said Arthur Levine, president of Teachers College at Columbia University, in an article about UP.[b] The university is one of the few institutions where students can get a degree without ever physically meeting their professors or fellow students. This means UP's market is, literally, global.

To draw alumni in and keep the relationships going, academic institutions are building peer-to-peer communities on their Web sites that foster involvement and camaraderie. Free services include a lifelong university-branded e-mail address, searchable alumni directories, and customizable Web pages. For some institutions, the central focus of their Web community is the alumni database, while others take a portal approach, using diverse content as the core property. Most universities hope that alumni will set the school's Web portal as their default Web browser home page.

[a] James Traub. "Drive-Thru U: Higher Education for People Who Mean Business," *New Yorker* (October 27, 1997), p. 116.

[b] Ibid.

SIDEBAR 6.4

Healthcare Firms Care for and about Patient Needs

As much as any industry, healthcare could benefit from applying principles that address individual patients' needs and values. In addition, relationships with donors and volunteers, medical staff, and suppliers would benefit from one-to-one Learning Relationships. But there are special challenges in this field.

Similar to any manufacturing enterprise, a healthcare maintenance organization (HMO) can rank its patients by their value to the HMO. Interestingly for an HMO, its most valuable patients are those it never hears from—those in good health. However, the HMO does not want this group of customers to switch to another healthcare provider; it wants this set of valuable customers to use preventative healthcare procedures and to engage in a dialogue with its representatives so that they can understand each of its customers personal medical-related needs. The goal of a healthcare provider, therefore, could be to create an ongoing, interactive relationship with the customer-patient, a relationship that does not revolve around what happens between admission to the institution and discharge, but rather, between discharge and admission. That's why many HMOs are engaged in building relationships by establishing contact with patients *before* an illness sets in, by inviting them to participate in reduced rates on exercise equipment, classes on smoking cessation, nutrition, and so on. These programs are win-win: They can contribute to the health and well-being of the patient or HMO member, and help the HMO reduce costs through improved health of its patients.

Gary Adamson, who served as president of Medimetrix/Unison Marketing in Denver, Colorado, said the power of healthcare integration lies in creating the ability to do things differently for each customer, not to do more of the same for all customers.[a] One of Adamson's clients, Community Hospitals in Indianapolis, Indiana, for example, implemented "Patient-Focused Medicine," a CRM initiative aimed at four constituent groups: patients, physicians, employees, and payers. The hospital has found that most medical practitioners customize the "care *for* you" component of healthcare by individually diagnosing and treating medical disorders. But Community also individualizes the "care *about* you" component—the part that makes most patients at most hospitals feel like one in a herd of cattle.

The hospital encourages thoughtful, high-level "service" by its doctors and nursing staff because it wants to show patients that they are being cared for; but the hospital also recognizes that random acts of kindness by a dedicated staff are not the same as customizing healthcare, which only works if the patient's special needs are remembered and continued at the next shift and between visits.

The opportunity—and the challenge—for customization lies in caring *about* an individual patient's needs. That means treating different patients differently in a cost-efficient and well-planned way. Healthcare, by its very nature, is among the most personal of any industry. Personal information provided to a doctor, hospital, pharmacy, or insurance company can be valuable to the organization, but is highly private to the customer-patient. Healthcare personalization, of course, has existed for a long time, and certainly since the time when doctors made house calls and local druggists remembered each of their customers' medical histories. Today, so-called telemedicine service providers contact, for example, diabetes patients by phone to remind them to take their insulin shots. But the vast majority of healthcare services could benefit from a shift in focus from event treatment to patient relationships, for the good of the healthcare organization as well as the patient—perhaps starting with an integrated billing system that makes sense to the patient and her caregivers.

SIDEBAR 6.4 *(continued)*

....

Some companies in the healthcare industry already see personalization as a strategic advantage in a crowded marketplace. By adding Web-based services for its customers, Oxford Healthcare, which offers health insurance in New York, New Jersey, and Connecticut, has provided the same level of personalized service a customer would get from a telephone call. The My Oxford program, a subsection of its Web site, reaches individual members, providing the information they need to access their coverage plans and process claims. While reducing its cost to service "customers," Oxford serves each customer better. But personalized online services go far beyond customized content or a listing of available healthcare products or services. The real opportunity lies in building a Learning Relationship between the healthcare provider and the customer. A drug store, for example, might know a customer buys the same over-the-counter remedy every month. But if the same drug store detects the customer is suddenly buying the product every week, it could personalize its service by asking her whether she is having a health problem and how it could assist her with personal information or other types of medication. Already, the pharmacy is the last resort for many patients to help spot possible drug interactions for prescription and over-the-counter drugs prescribed and recommended by a variety of different physicians. Using information to serve the customer better helps the drugstore create a long-lasting bond with this customer.

For instance, Merck-Medco, a pharmacy benefits management subsidiary of Merck & Co., has created a sophisticated information system that links patients, pharmacists, and physicians, helping to ensure the appropriate use of medication for each individual based on her health profile. Merck-Medco customers are issued a pharmacy card that enables the company to identify customers when they fill and refill a prescription. But the company goes the extra step and shows that it not only cares for its customers but cares about them, too. When a customer suddenly stops refilling a prescription, a Merck-Medco representative will likely call or write the customer to see if she has forgotten to refill the prescription or if her health status has changed.

Personalization also lets healthcare providers focus their sales efforts on their most valuable customers. For example, an expectant mother with gestational diabetes could be given week-by-week information-tracking progress that will lead to the delivery of a healthy baby. The goal is to be a resource to patients and help them live more healthy lives and become more knowledgeable partners in a treatment.[b]

[a]Don Peppers, Martha Rogers, PhD, and Bob Dorf, *The One to One Fieldbook* (New York: Doubleday, 1999).

[b]Excerpted from "Healthcare: A Market Ripe for Personalization?" by Gerald Lazar, from *1to1 Personalization* (March 1, 2001).

SUMMARY

We have now discussed the necessity of knowing who the customer is (identifying) and knowing how the customer is different individually (valuation and needs). Obtaining this information implies that the enterprise will need to interact with each customer to understand her better. Once the enterprise has ranked customers by their value to the enterprise, and differentiated them based on their needs, it conducts an ongoing, collaborative dialogue with each customer. This interaction helps the enterprise to learn more about the customer, as the customer provides feedback about her needs. The enterprise can then use the customer's feedback to modify its service and products to meet her needs. Interacting with customers is another critical step of the IDIC taxonomy and is our next point of discussion.

FOOD FOR THOUGHT

1. Why has more progress been made on customer value differentiation than on customer needs differentiation?

2. Is it possible to meet individual needs? Is it feasible? Can you describe three examples where it has been profitable?

3. For each of the following product categories, name a branded example, then hypothesize about how you might categorize customers by their different needs, in the same way our sample toy company and pharmaceutical company did. Unless noted for you, you can specify whether the brand is B2C or B2B:
   - Automobiles (consumer)
   - Automobiles (B2B, i.e. fleet usage)
   - Air transportation
   - Cosmetics
   - Computer software (B2B)
   - Pet food
   - Refrigerators
   - Pneumatic valves
   - Hotel rooms

GLOSSARY

Attributes   Physical features of the product.

Benefits   Advantages that customers get from using the product. Not to be confused with *needs,* as different customers will get different advantages from the same product.

Customer portfolios   Groups of similar customers. The customer-focused enterprise will design different treatments for different portfolios of customers.

Market segments   Groups of customers who share a common attribute. Product benefits are targeted to the market segments thought most likely to desire the benefit.

Needs   What a customer needs from an enterprise is, by our definition, synonymous with what she wants, prefers, or would like. In this sense, we do not distinguish a customer's needs from her wants. For that matter, we do not distinguish needs from preferences, wishes, desires, or whims. Each of these terms might imply some nuance of need—perhaps the intensity of the need or the permanence of it—but in each case we are still talking, generically, about the customer's needs.

Interacting with Customers: Customer Collaboration Strategy

7

Chapter

So far, we have discussed the ways an enterprise can identify and differentiate customers. Both of these efforts help the enterprise to prepare to treat different customers differently. But, essentially, both identify and differentiate are analytical tasks. They are at the heart of the efforts, working behind the scenes to gather information about a customer, to rank him by his value to the company and to differentiate his needs accordingly. These tasks aren't really visible to a customer. In this chapter we introduce a part of the IDIC implementation methodology that gets the customer directly involved: interaction. *We will see different viewpoints on the broad and growing emphasis on interaction with customers. But even as the discussion touches on the general and the particular, the main reason for interaction remains the same—to get more information directly from a customer in order to serve him in a way no competitor can who doesn't have the information.*

Managing individual customer relationships is a difficult, ongoing process that evolves as the customer and the enterprise deepen their awareness of and involvement with each other. To reach this new plateau of intimacy, the enterprise must get as close to the customer as it can. It must be able to understand the customer in ways that no competitor does. The only viable method of getting to know an individual, to understand him, and to get information about him is to interact with him—one to one.

In Chapter 2, we began to define a relationship, and provided a foundation for relationship theory. We listed several important characteristics in our definition of the term *relationship*; but one of the most fundamental of these characteristics is interaction. A relationship, by its very definition, is characterized by two-way communication between the two parties to the relationship.

Interacting with customers acquires a new importance for a customer-strategy enterprise—an enterprise aimed at creating and cultivating relationships with individual customers. The enterprise is no longer merely talking *to* a customer during a transaction and then waiting (or hoping) the customer will return again to buy. For the customer-strategy enterprise, interacting *with* individual customers becomes a mutually beneficial experience. The enterprise learns about the

For traditional marketers, the goal was to generate messages. For the one-to-one enterprise, the goal is to generate feedback,

customer so it can understand his value to the enterprise and his individual needs. But in a relationship the customer learns, too—about becoming a more proficient consumer or purchasing agent for a business. The interaction, in essence, is now a *collaboration* in which the enterprise and the customer work together to make this transaction, and each successive one, more beneficial for both. The focus shifts from a one-way message or a one-time sale to a continuous, iterative process, which *de facto* moves both customer and enterprise from a transactional approach to a relationship approach. The goal of the process is to be more and more satisfying for the customer, as the enterprise's Learning Relationship with that customer improves. The result of this collaboration, if it is to be successful, is that both the customer and the enterprise will benefit and want to continue to work together. For traditional marketers, the goal was to *generate messages*. For the one-to-one enterprise, the goal is to *generate feedback,* creating a collaborative feedback loop with each customer by treating him in a way that the customer himself has specified, during the interaction.

Interacting with an individual customer enables an enterprise to become both an expert on its business and an expert on each of its customers. It comes to know more and more about a customer so that it can eventually predict what the customer will need next and where and how he will want it, and, like a good servant of a previous century, becomes indispensable.

Customer-strategy enterprises ensure that each customer gets exactly what he needs, no matter what. Home Depot, for instance, trains its store clerks to spend as much time as necessary with a customer to determine which product will solve his problem. Their goal is to ensure that the customer gets the right product, no matter how much or how little it might cost. Home Depot's strategy is not just to sell one home-improvement product to any customer who happens to show up, but to sell this customer all of the home improvement products he ever buys. So rather than merely sell home repair items, Home Depot tries to gather information about what a customer needs, remember it, and help the customer by satisfying that need—individually.[1]

In this chapter we will show how a customer-strategy enterprise interacts with its customers in order to generate and use individual feedback from each customer to strengthen and deepen its relationship with that customer. This two-way communication can best be referred to as a dialogue, which serves to inform the relationship.

DIALOGUE REQUIREMENTS

There are six criteria that an enterprise should meet before it can be considered engaged in a genuine dialogue with an individual customer:

[1]Michael Treacy and Fred Wiersema, "Customer Intimacy and Other Value Disciplines," *Harvard Business Review* (January–February 1993), pp. 84–93.

1. *Parties at both ends have been clearly identified.* The enterprise knows who the customer is, if he has shopped there before, what he has bought, and other characteristics about him. The customer, too, knows the enterprise.
2. *All parties in the dialogue must be able to participate in it.* Each party should have the means to communicate with the other. Until the arrival of cost-efficient interactive technologies, and especially the World Wide Web, most marketing-oriented interactions with customers were prohibitively costly.
3. *All parties to a dialogue must want to participate in it.* The subject of a dialogue must be of interest to the customer, as well as to the enterprise.
4. *Dialogues can be controlled by anyone in the exchange.* A dialogue involves mutuality, and as a mutual exchange of information and points of view, it might go in any direction that either party chooses for it. This is in contrast to, say, advertising, which is under the complete control of the advertiser. Companies that engage their customers in dialogues, in other words, must be prepared for many different outcomes.
5. *A dialogue with an individual customer will change an enterprise's behavior toward that individual, and change that individual's behavior toward the enterprise.* An enterprise should begin to engage in a dialogue with a customer only if it can alter its future course of action in some way as a result of the dialogue.
6. *A dialogue should pick up where it last left off.* This is what gives a relationship its "context" and what can cement the customer's loyalty. If prior communication between the enterprise and the customer has occurred, it should continue seamlessly, as if it had never ended.[2]

SIDEBAR 7.1
Clipping Digital Coupons[a]

Catalina Marketing and Respond TV developed a program that allows consumers to receive electronic coupons for consumer packaged goods (CPGs) via their television sets. During select commercials, a viewer is asked if he would like a coupon for the featured item and, if so, he's prompted to enter his supermarket's loyalty card number (using his remote control device) so the coupon can be automatically credited to his account when he comes in to purchase the item. (The consumer only has to enter his number once; Catalina remembers it from then on.) To consumers, the result is a paperless, time-saving way to collect coupons, while CPG manufacturers and retailers build loyalty and gain access to valuable consumer preference data.

The problem interactive television has experienced since its inception was that allowing consumers to purchase products directly from their television screens was not enough to drive the technology, according to Eric Williams, vice president of research and development at Catalina. But Catalina, a $400-million marketing company that maintains a database on the purchase patterns of 55 million people in the

---

[2]Don Peppers and Martha Rogers, PhD, *Enterprise One to One* (New York: Doubleday Books, 1997).

SIDEBAR 7.1 *(continued)*

....

United States, saw an opportunity to extend its marketing reach through the relatively new medium.

"Long term, what we're interested in doing is tailoring the value of the offer, or the type of offer, unique to the consumer. But our starting point is to allow a consumer to build loyalty to a specific store," says Williams. In other words, the interactive television coupons are not personalized as of yet but will be in the future. For now, Catalina is using them to build loyalty to retailers. For instance, when a consumer sees a cola commercial and enters his loyalty card number for a coupon, he has just been given purchase incentive. "What I've now done is tie the cola manufacturer and, obviously, the retailer into a triad with the consumer," says Williams. "Now I can begin to tailor other offers that come onto the system in their home based on the loyalty purchases at the store."

[a]Excerpted from "Clipping Digital Coupons," by Tyson Brown, *Inside 1to1* (May 28, 2001); available at *www.1to1.com.*

IMPLICIT AND EXPLICIT BARGAINS

Conducting a dialogue with a customer is having an exchange of thoughts; it's a form of mental collaboration. It might mean handling a customer inquiry or gathering background information on the customer. But that is only the beginning. Many customers are simply not willing to converse with enterprises. And rare is the customer who admits that he enjoys receiving an unsolicited sales pitch or telemarketing phone call. For an enterprise to engage a customer in a productive, mutually beneficial dialogue, it must conduct interesting conversations with an individual customer, on his terms, learning a little at a time, instead of trying to sell more products every time it converses with him.

If the customer-strategy enterprise is to remain a dependable collaborator with its customers, then it must not adopt a *self-oriented* attitude (see Chapter 2, "Thinking about Relationship Theory"(Edell and Rose), and "CRM: The Customer's View" (Barnes), both of which emphasize the importance to the enterprise of *not* being self-oriented in its approach to customer relationships). Instead of sales-oriented commercials and interruptive, product-oriented marketing messages, the customer-strategy enterprise will use interactive technologies to provide something of value to the customer. By providing this value, the enterprise is inviting the customer to begin and sustain a dialogue. The resulting feedback increases the scope of the customer relationship, which is critical to increasing the enterprise's share of that customer's business.

To understand how radical this idea is, think about television. When advertisers sponsor a television program, they are in effect making an **implicit bargain** with viewers: "Watch our ad and see the show for free." During television's early decades, these implicit bargains made a lot of sense, because viewers had only a few other channels to choose from and no remote control to make it easy to access those other options. In the early days, everybody watched commercials.

But today's television viewer lives in a vastly different environment. Not only are there hundreds of channels from which to choose, but people are also watching television more selectively, with instant—and constant—control. Audiences have the power to tune out commercials at their will. New technologies, such as digital television recording devices, enable consumers to block out the advertisements altogether.[3] The problem for marketers, therefore, is that, because the medium used is *nonaddressable* and *noninteractive*, there is no real way to tie the particular consumer who watches the television show back to the ad, or to know whether he saw it in the first place. There is also no real incentive, usually, for the consumer even to watch the ad.

But with interactive communications technologies, firms are capable of making **explicit bargains** rather than implicit ones. They can interact, one to one, directly with their individual customers, either directly or through various interactive media vehicles. An explicit bargain is, in effect, a "deal" that an enterprise makes with an individual to secure the individual's time, attention, or feedback. Dialogue and interaction have such important roles to play, in terms of improving and enhancing a relationship, that it is often useful for an enterprise actually to "compensate" a customer, in the form of discounts, rebates, or free services, in exchange for the customer participating in a dialogue.

The interactive world is chock full of examples of explicit bargains. Hundreds of Web site operators around the globe, from Hotmail to Yahoo, offer free e-mail to customers who are agreeable to receiving advertising messages or facilitating the delivery of ad messages to others. It is standard practice for a Web site operator to require a visitor to register, providing personal identifying data and preferences, in return for gaining access to the site's more detailed information or automated tools. And this kind of business deal is not confined to the Web. One voicemail services company asks users for personal information that it passes to advertisers, which will transmit highly targeted advertisements when a customer calls in for voicemail. While advertisers will have access to the customer's preferences, as stated in his profile, they will not have access to the customer, outside of the voicemail system. They will be told his general location, but not his identity, his name, or address.

In an interactive medium, an advertiser can secure a consumer's actual permission and agreement, individually. By making personal preference information a part of this bargain, the service can also ensure that the ads or promotions delivered to a particular subscriber are more personally relevant, in effect increasing the value of the interaction to the marketer by increasing its relevance to the consumer. Explicit bargains like this are good examples of what Seth Godin calls "permission marketing" (a concept we will discuss in more detail in

---

[3]Customers who are individually addressable can be sent individually different messages. Mass media are characterized by nonaddressability, since mass media send the same message to everyone simultaneously.

Chapter 9) in which a customer has agreed, or given his permission, to receive personalized messages.

Technology has helped enterprises to consummate the explicit bargain with individuals by enabling them to interact with each customer on a personal level. Many enterprises have used *two-way, addressable media* as individualized customer communication channels.

SIDEBAR 7.2

Two-Way, Addressable Media: A Sampling

- *World Wide Web.* The Web has become one of the most effective media to engage a customer in an individual interaction. An enterprise's Web site is a highly customizable platform for collaborating with a customer and learning about his individual needs effectively and inexpensively. (We'll talk more about the Web as a venue for customization in Chapter 10).

- *Voicemail.* Enterprises have established voicemail systems for their customers that enable them to phone in a question or comment and leave a message. Voicemail has many different potential dialogue applications.

- *Wireless.* Enterprises can push customized information directly to the cell phones, pagers, and personal digital assistants (PDAs) of their customers if their customers choose. The customer also can respond to the enterprise or make an inquiry about an order or product through this channel.

- *E-mail.* Enterprises are using e-mail to write personalized messages to customers about their latest product offerings, sales promotions, customer inquiries, and many other important topics (we will discuss more about e-mail later in this chapter).

- *Fax.* Fax machines are a highly interactive medium. The customer can fax an order to the enterprise. Or the enterprise can use a fax-on-demand service to enable customers to request product or service information via their fax machine. The enterprise also can fax customized catalogs, product information sheets, newsletters, and other documents to the customer upon request. Fax also makes it easy to reach those who do not have online capability.

- *Interactive television.* Interactive television was long an experiment; it is now a reality in a number of markets around the world. Viewers no longer passively watch their favorite programs but have become a part of the action via this technology. Whether it is a live sports event or a highly rated drama show, viewers can use a special remote control to obtain more information about products featured on the program or in the commercial—and then purchase them if they want to. Some shows have begun mixing television with the Web by enabling viewers to go online during the show to participate in interactive surveys or to learn more about what they are watching.

SIDEBAR 7.2 *(continued)*

....

- *Personal video recorders (PVRs)*. The digital recording device, such as TiVo and others like it, has revolutionized television by enabling audiences to create highly personalized TV-viewing experiences. TiVo is also changing television advertising. Instead of bombarding viewers with commercials that are not relevant, advertisers now have the opportunity to personalize their messages. Knowing the viewers' demographics and viewing preferences, advertisers will be better able to match their ads to the right people (see Sidebar 7.3 on PVRs, by Ravi Dhar and Dick Wittink).

SIDEBAR 7.3
Case Scenario: Personal Video Recorders and Interruption Marketing

....

Ravi Dhar, Professor
Yale University School of Management

Dick R. Wittink
George Rogers Clark Professor of Management and Marketing, Yale University School of Management

Personal video recorder (PVR) devices have changed the way people watch television and record programs. The PVRs use a hard disk drive designed to record television shows just like a videocassette recorder (VCR). However, unlike VCRs, the interfaces used to facilitate recording (such as an on-screen program guide) are regularly downloaded to the PVR. Furthermore, once recorded, shows are displayed together on a single screen, and can be played simply by selecting one. PVRs also search out and record specific types of programs—movies starring Paul Newman, for instance—even if those movies are shown on obscure channels or broadcast in the middle of the night.

PVRs can automatically record whatever live program happens to be playing into a data buffer of 30 minutes or more, making it possible for sports fans to run their own instant replays or for harried parents to pause a show when their children demand attention. An added attraction for consumers—but a potential nightmare for advertisers— is the capability to fast-forward through commercials while watching recorded or even live shows that have been paused previously for a few minutes. Some PVRs can record one show while consumers watch another one.[a]

Thus, the PVR has the potential to change the industry far beyond changing consumers' television viewing habits. If consumers record their favorite programs for viewing at a more convenient time later, advertising effectively becomes "unbundled" from the program. Traditional advertising on television is based on the measurement of audience characteristics that serve as a proxy for consumer preferences. Advertisers use audience characteristics such as age and gender to determine which products to advertise during specific shows. This is, at best, an approximate and, at

SIDEBAR 7.3 *(continued)*

worst, a highly inaccurate measure of consumer preferences because such audience characteristics generally do a mediocre job of predicting preferences.

Consequently, in a world of PVRs, there is both an opportunity and a threat for advertising. The threat is obvious: If consumers decide to record the shows to watch at a later time, they are likely to skip the ads so as to minimize exposure to interruption marketing. Given that the program content on commercial television and radio stations is subsidized by the advertisers, a different business approach will be required. One alternative is for consumers to pay for viewing and to exclude advertisers. An example is a new radio-digital network, RealAudio. Consumers can purchase a special radio and pay a subscription fee for access to about 100 channels, all without commercials. Some car manufacturers will have Web-radio devices included. For example, General Motors owns a part of XM Satellite Radio, a startup company that beams radio programs via satellites.

Another alternative is for the ads to become embedded in the programs. Indeed, the television industry is already moving in the direction of having brands included and incorporated more frequently within the programs themselves. If consumer interest in specific shows is related to consumers' product preferences, it may be possible to continue the current arrangement (advertisers paying for the programs) in a similar form. For example, commercials would be shown separately, or products would be featured through product placements in the content itself. Even old reruns could be affected. For example, Logan's coffee cup could be shown as a red Coke can in a showing for one *Law and Order* viewer, but changed to Diet Sprite for another viewer. The primary difference is that there could be a closer match between consumer needs and the ads shown via targeted advertising.

An important issue is who pays for the television shows. In one way or another, consumers pay for the privilege of watching. On one end of the spectrum is the business model for movies, for which audiences tend to pay directly. Thus, the more movies one sees in the theaters, the more one pays. On the other end of the spectrum are the television shows on the commercial networks. Advertisers primarily finance the programs. Consumers do not pay directly for watching television shows.[b]

Besides the "nuisance factor," interruption marketing has a high cost in terms of delivery accuracy. It is difficult to relate the characteristics of audiences for specific shows with the characteristics of the consumers likely to have an interest in viewing particular ads. The question is whether PVRs can improve the targeting of commercials. There is a certain set of commercials that a consumer would be interested in seeing. The issue is how to customize the set of commercials to each individual consumer and how to provide the commercials at the right time. Some commercials have entertainment value. For example, many ads shown during the Super Bowl are of interest to many viewers; in fact, some people tune in to the Super Bowl because they want to see the latest entertaining commercials. Shoe manufacturer Nike produced a number of commercials that mesmerized viewers by showing basketball players dribbling the ball in time to a hip-hop music beat. But the entertainment value created by commercials cannot sustain the production of programs in general. The more important task is to send commercials to specific consumers because of their relevance to individual purchase behavior. Consumers will have to provide additional information to facilitate this.

Privacy is a relevant factor because PVRs record the viewing behavior of consumers, and protecting privacy will require a completely new advertising business

---

SIDEBAR 7.3 *(continued)*

··

model in the future. At present, the consumer's viewing data can be sold to advertisers, which may be able to link the viewing behavior to purchases and other data. This is one way by which advertisers can improve the targeting of commercials. But consumers may not know which company owns the data or how the data will be used. And though the targeting may be improved relative to the traditional television environment, it will still be highly inaccurate.

With an "opt-in" arrangement, however—in effect, a permission-based explicit bargain—the management of the PVR manufacturer would explain to consumers the benefits of data use and how these benefits could be enhanced with additional data. Subject perhaps to some minimum number of commercials, each consumer might identify the product categories of interest to them. Separately, the PVR manufacturer would have to agree *not* to sell the data, unless explicitly agreed to by each consumer. Full transparency is critical. Consumers must understand what the PVR manufacturer does and why the activities are beneficial to them, because many potential data uses are not obvious to most consumers. For example, a consumer's risk-seeking tendencies, inferred from viewing behavior, might be used by insurance companies to set policy premiums.

[a]David P. Hamilton. "TiVo, Replay TV Fail to Take Off Despite Big Fans," *Wall Street Journal* (February 7, 2001), p. 247.

[b]Nevertheless, programming does come at a cost to someone, and one simple and incomplete interpretation is that the firm's cost of advertising is reflected in the prices consumers pay. Largely because of advertising, a branded product can command a higher price at the store than a generic product, but that higher price is partly used to pay for the cost of the advertising. So, while interruption marketing increases with watching, the actual "cost" of the advertising, to any one consumer, is not proportional to the amount of watching, but to the number of products purchased.

SUCCEEDING AT INTERACTION STRATEGY MEANS INTEGRATING ACROSS TOUCHPOINTS

> Today, what most enterprises fail at is not the mechanics of interacting, but the *strategy* of it–the substance and direction of customer interaction itself.

Providing any kind of dialogue tool to customers enables the enterprise to secure deeper, more profitable, and less competitively vulnerable relationships with each of them. The deeper each relationship becomes, and the more it is based on dialogue, the less regimented that relationship will be. The customer may want to expand the dialogue on his own volition because he knows that each time he speaks to the enterprise, it will listen. Today, what most enterprises fail at is not the mechanics of interacting, but the *strategy* of it—the substance and direction of customer interaction itself.

In the early days of the Web, many companies created "bulletin boards" and "brochureware" that directed one-way information *at* customers. In a first stage of interactivity on the Web, electronic yellow pages enabled customers to find the address and phone number of an enterprise, and sometimes linked them to a Web page with a map, list of products, and other information. In a parallel to the realization 50 years earlier that the television was far more than merely "radio with pictures," companies quickly expanded their Web functionality to create sophisticated, highly personalized venues for customer interaction. The result is that the Web now has become one of the most powerful vehicles for sustaining interactive, personalized Learning Relationships (Chapter 8 discusses in greater detail how the Web can be used to build relationships).

Customer-strategy enterprises concentrate not just on the *efficiency* of the communication channel used with the customer, but also on the *effectiveness* of the customer dialogue itself. Measuring efficiency might include keeping track of how long customers stay on hold with the customer service department before they disconnect, while measuring effectiveness might include tracking the ratio of complaints handled or problems resolved on the first call. Critical to the success of the dialogue is that each successive interaction with the individual customer be seen as part of a seamless, flowing stream of discussion. Whether the conversation yesterday took place via mail, phone, the Web, or any other communication channel, the next conversation with the customer must pick up where the last one left off. The enterprise has to integrate all of its customer-directed communication channels so that it can accurately identify a customer no matter how it contacts the enterprise. If a customer called two weeks ago to order a product and then sent an e-mail yesterday to inquire about his order status, the enterprise should be able to provide an accurate response for the customer quickly and efficiently. The company should remember more about the customer with each successive interaction. More importantly, it should never have to ask a customer the same question more than once, because it has a 360-degree view of the customer, and "remembers" the customer's feedback across the organization. The more the enterprise remembers about a customer, the more unrewarding it becomes for the customer to defect. The customer-strategy enterprise ensures that its broadcast and print messages are not just *laterally* coordinated across various media, such as television, print, sales promotion and direct mail, but that its communications with every customer are *longitudinally* coordinated, over the life of that individual customer's relationship with the firm.

Companies that employ such integration of customer data and coordination of customer interaction develop reputations as highly competent, service-oriented firms with excellent customer loyalty. For example, Dell Computer Corporation has developed a customer strategy that uses direct mail, e-mail, personal contact by sales representatives, and special access to what amounts to intranet Web sites for large Dell accounts to stay connected with those customers. The business impact of Dell's customer strategy has been measured by loyal customers, consistent revenue gains, and increased profits.[4]

---

[4]John Wheeler and Mark Krueger, "E-lectrifying Customer Relationships," *Customer Relationship Management* (September 1999).

Over time, a customer will come to feel that he is "known" by the enterprise. When he makes contact with the enterprise, that part of the organization—whether it is a call rep or a service counter or any other part of the firm—should have immediate access to his customer information, such as previous shipment dates, status of returns or credits, payment information, and details about the last discussion. A customer does not necessarily want to receive *more* information from the enterprise; rather he wants to receive better, more focused information—information that is relevant to him, individually.

Sophisticated interactive technologies enable enterprises to ensure that their customer-contact personnel can remember an individual customer and his preferences. A company can use software that creates an "ecosystem" of data about its customers, and cull information from all of the touchpoints where it interacts with customers—call centers, Web sites, e-mail, and other places. If the enterprise can better understand its customers, it can better serve them by providing individually tailored offers or promotions and more insightful customer service.[5]

Because interactive technologies such as the Web and the call center enable a company to interact with customers in a much more cost-efficient way than ever before, in many cases, it is a firm's effort to do a better job at integrating these interactions into its business that first leads the company to begin thinking through the issues involved in customer relationships. One of the very first relationship-building efforts undertaken at many B2C companies involves the consumer-accessible Web site, and coordinating the interactions that take place on the Web site with the interactions that take place at the call center or at the point of sale. For B2B companies, the first relationship-building effort often involves automating the sales force, to ensure that customer interactions are better coordinated within particular accounts, and that the records of these interactions are captured electronically. The point is that the arrival of cost-efficient interactive technologies has pretty much forced companies in all industries, all over the world, to take a step back and reconsider their business processes. To deal with interactivity, they must create new processes that are oriented around the coordination of all these newly possible customer interactions. And they must ensure that the interactions themselves not only run efficiently, but are effective at building more solid, profitable relationships with customers.

In 1993, Don Schultz, Stanley Tannenbaum, and Robert Lauterborn first published a book on **Integrated Marketing Communications (IMC)**.[6] Many companies had for years sent different messages from different parts of the organization, and a single customer would end up seeing a mishmash of uncoordinated advertising commercials, direct-mail campaigns, invoices, and policy documents, and the list goes on. The idea behind IMC was that these efforts needed to be coordinated, that branding strategy needed to be consistent across

[5]Kim Cross, "Captain Connected," *Business 2.0* (April 17, 2001), p. 31.

[6]Don E. Schultz, Stanley I. Tannenbaum, and Robert F. Lauterborn, *The New Marketing Paradigm Integrated Marketing Communications* (New York: McGraw-Hill Trade, 1996).

the enterprise, for example, and that the firm's "story" needed to remain coherent for the customer exposed to many messages. In the following section, Schultz explores the relationship between the original IMC thinking and the current approach to managing profitable customer relationships.

INTEGRATED MARKETING COMMUNICATIONS AND CRM: FRIENDS OR FOES?

Don E. Schultz
Professor emeritus-in-service, Northwestern University

The concepts and practices of Integrated Marketing Communication (IMC) and CRM have been widely debated. Some argue they are complementary; others say in conflict. Still others have tried to set the two camps against each other, with one or the other claiming superiority.

While IMC and CRM developed as academic and professional disciplines in the same time frame, they came from separate geographic areas: IMC in the United States and CRM in Scandinavia.[7] Yet the two are totally compatible. To understand why, a bit of background is needed.

In this section, we describe the history of IMC and the transition it is making to **Integrated Brand Communication (IBC)**. We also identify some of the key elements of the IMC/IBC approaches and demonstrate how they are not only compatible with CRM but actually provide much of the base for a true, customer-focused CRM strategy and implementation. Finally, we speculate on the future of IMC/IBC and what it holds for the customer-focused enterprise.

WHAT IMC IS AND WHAT IMC IS BECOMING

IMC sprang originally from a desire by advertising agencies to protect their client budgets and ultimately their bottom lines. In the late 1970s and early 1980s, three new promotional and communication disciplines grew very rapidly in the United States and began to dominate the marketing scene: (1) sales promotion, driven by a need to find ways and means to dispose of excess product capacity in autos, consumer package goods, consumer durables, and the like; (2) public relations, which moved from a corporate to product focus, and (3) direct marketing, which was fueled by the technology revolution of computers, databases, data analysis, and manipulation.

---

[7]Our references to CRM are more along the lines of the Scandinavian School of Relationship Management as it has been developed by Professors Christian Gronroos at Hanken Business School, Helsinki, and Evert Gummeson, Stockholm School of Business, Stockholm, more than the technology-driven CRM initiatives found in the United States. While the two approaches may ultimately achieve the same goals, our focus on the customer and customer understanding, rather than the technology as the enabler, is the major distinction in the two approaches.

As these new marketing approaches developed, they took funds away from traditional advertising—the lifeblood of advertising agencies. To protect their client budget base, agencies began to purchase, acquire, or affiliate with the three new disciplines. The intent was not to develop a better marketing or communication system for their clients; it was, simply, to stem the loss of billings that were going into these new areas, where they had little if any representation. Thus, advertising agencies developed the concept of "one-stop shopping for marketing communication needs" and coined the phrase "one sight, one sound," which they believed they could deliver if they owned or controlled the other communication elements and activities. Thus, IMC began as an advertising agency strategy to protect income flows.

The problem was, clients did not buy the idea. Major consumer goods client companies saw no evidence that advertising agencies could or would be better at integrating communication programs than they were themselves. So, the IMC of the early 1980s, which was primarily tactical and focused on integrating and aligning the various existing communication approaches, languished until it was revived, not by the agencies, but by the clients a few years later. Driven by globalization, consolidation and concentration in the channels, exploding media options, and an increased focus on and availability of customer data as a result of technology, clients began to drive the development of IMC in the late 1980s.

IMC grew rapidly in both practice and practicality in client organizations in the early 1990s. Advertising agencies, bereft of customer or consumer data, were replaced by direct and database consultants and other strategy-focused organizations that could truly identify and bring some insights and understanding to the marketing process.

Since the early 1990s, IMC has undergone another evolution. Leaders in the field began to recognize that IMC, as it had developed earlier, was essentially an "inside-out" approach to marketing and communication. That is, IMC was focused primarily on how to improve the marketing and communication programs of the selling firm—that is, develop a common platform, have similar offers and programs, create graphic continuity among and between media and promotional efforts, and so on. In other words, IMC was an attempt to improve marketing and marketing communication for the communicator, not for those for whom the communication was being developed.

In the mid-1990s, IMC began to evolve into what I now call Integrated Brand Communication (IBC). The premise of IBC was that customers and consumers have *relationships* with brands and companies, not with marketing programs, advertising, sales promotion, public relations, or other marketer-initiated activities. Thus, IMC is being transitioned into IBC, where relationships can be built with customers and consumers on an ongoing basis. There are really two views of IMC, or IBC, today. One is the original concept used by marketing firms to organize, coordinate, consolidate, and focus their marketing and communication efforts against groups or sets of identified customers or prospects. This usually involves integration and alignment of the various types and forms of marketing and marketing communication. This approach to IMC occurs primarily internally, within the marketing organization, and is developed and delivered to customers and prospects through outbound systems controlled by the marketing firm.

Alternatively, there is a need to integrate all the elements of the brand into one coherent whole. IBC is generally much broader than IMC, for it encompasses all the brand touchpoints—that is, whenever and however the brand "touches" its users, or however they come in contact with the brand. In short, IBC is an *interactive* and networked approach to marketing and communication. Thus, brand touchpoints might include the product, the sales force, the distribution channel, and even the pricing and customer service. In other words, IBC is similar to the concept of CRM but relies more heavily on the communication aspects of the relationship in all its forms and varieties. With this brief background on IMC and the current transition to IBC, we can now describe the principles and processes of both these new disciplines.

RELATIONSHIPS AND CUSTOMER VALUES ARE KEY ELEMENTS

Like CRM, IBC focuses on building long-term relationships with customers, consumers and other stakeholders. The key element in the development and emergence of IBC is a financial focus on communication—understanding the true value of marketing communication.

Historically, communication has been a most imprecise science—if it can even be called a science. The focus of most communication, particularly marketing communication, has been on creating communication effects, or changes in awareness, recall, comprehension, intent to buy, and the like, all having to do with consumer or customer attitudes or attitude changes. IBC, in contrast, is a behavioral and financial model. It is based on the simple concept that the goal of the organization is to serve customers, profitably. Thus, the objective of IBC is to create customer income flows, and from those ongoing income flows to derive an acceptable profit for the firm and its shareholders. From this view, communication then becomes an investment in customers, not an investment in the tools or tactics or techniques used to communicate with those customers. Put simply, organizations spend money for only four reasons:

1. To gain new customers and their income flows.
2. To retain present customers and their income flows.
3. To grow present customers and their income flows.
4. To migrate customers through a product or service portfolio either to provide them with better value and more profitable income flows or to prevent their defection.

Marketing communication is one of the key ways organizations attempt to influence customers and prospects to achieve one of the preceding goals. Thus, in an IBC approach, the goal of communication is to invest finite corporate resources in various communication tools and techniques to achieve one or more of the goals. Communication, therefore, becomes a corporate resource that is used to attempt to create additional corporate resources. As a result, IBC quickly moves beyond the realm of tactical activities and the purchase of marketing and communication "stuff" to becoming one of the key strategic tools senior management has available to influence the direction and return on business investments.

While the previous discussion may sound a bit basic, it is based on very sound business principles. To make an investment, an organization must know the value of the item or area or element in which the investment is being made. Thus, the flow of income from a customer over time determines the value of the activity in which an IBC investment is made. Customer valuations are becoming fairly commonplace in sophisticated marketing organizations today. Using either activity-based costing (ABC) or other forms of data and database analysis, many organizations, such as those cited in this book, are able to determine the short- and even long-term value of their customers and prospects.

Knowing the value of a customer or prospect enables the marketer or marketing organization to estimate or calculate the amount the firm would be willing to invest in a customer or prospect to either gain his business, retain his business, grow that customer's value, or migrate that customer through the firm's product or service portfolio. Exhibit 7.1 illustrates the concept.

Each group of customers has a different value. Indeed, it is possible to take this approach to the individual level. But, whatever the level of granularity, the basic premise is the marketer is investing in the customer in the hope of some future return.

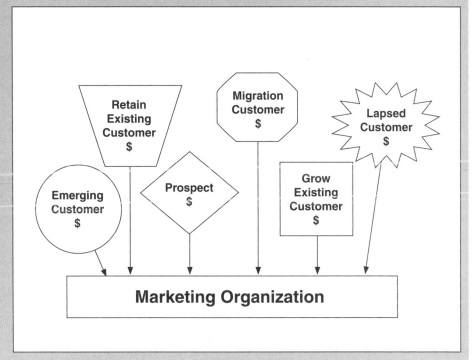

EXHIBIT 7.1   **Customer Value Chart**

There are any number of ways of valuing customers and prospects. This book includes several examples (see Chapter 5). Thus, once the value of a customer is known, an IBC investment strategy can be developed. This provides the base for the determination of the brand communication effort. In other words, customer valuation or potential sets the base for the marketing or marketing communication investment that can or should be made in that customer or prospect or customer group or prospect group. Once this is known, the actual communication program can then be developed.

This determination of investment is one of the key elements in both IMC and IBC, for it moves the focus from selecting some type of communication delivery program to an organizational investment strategy. The IMC or IBC planner focuses on the customer investment that is to be made and the expected returns. Thus, the starting point in IMC or IBC is the answer to the question, what is the behavioral objective to be achieved (i.e., acquire a new customer, retain a present customer, and so on)? By knowing what financial returns the desired behavior will achieve, the enterprise can develop a relevant investment plan. From that, communication activities can be organized or selected. This is a different approach from starting with questions such as: Should we buy advertising or public relations or sales promotion programs with the funds management has allocated? The other advantage of this customer-as-investment-approach is that it allows us to create a closed-loop marketing and communication system as described next.

CREATING CLOSED-LOOP COMMUNICATION SYSTEMS

Increasingly, accountability or marketing and communication metrics are being demanded of senior management. Because communication has traditionally been treated as an expense by the organization (i.e., no one ever made a profit on an expense), marketing and communication budgeting have been generally ignored as a measurable discipline. With the IMC and IBC approach just described, budget determination and measurement are key ingredients. Thus, accountability is part and parcel of the IMC and IBC process.

Because we are building financial models (dollars out and dollars back in), it is incumbent on the IMC or IBC planner to include various forms of return-on-investment—or better said, return-on-*customer*-investment—measures as a basic part of the process (see Chapter 11). IMC and IBC are both based on the idea of a closed-loop system. That simply means that, because the planner knows the value of a customer, he can determine the investment value of changing customer behaviors and can then measure the results of those activities through changes in customer value or customer income flows. Exhibit 7.2 illustrates the process.

As previously described, by knowing the current value of a customer, informed investment decisions can be made about that customer through various marketing or communication programs. Returns on those investments can be made by measuring changes in customer or consumer behaviors (i.e., closing the loop).

The value of a closed-loop marketing and communication system is that it is continuously self-renewing and self-adjusting. By measuring returns on

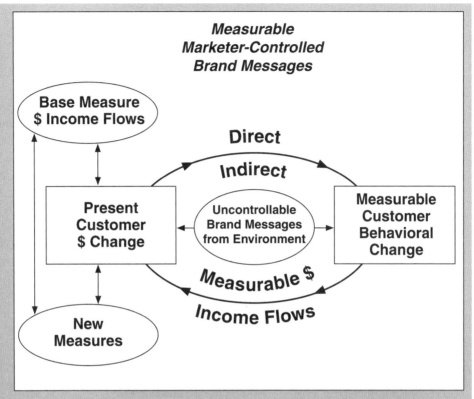

EXHIBIT 7.2   Closed Loop Systems

marketing and communication programs, when one program is completed and the results are known, the next program uses those results as a base of knowledge from which the next program can be developed. Thus, the organization immediately recognizes programs that fail and those that succeed. It is this recycling of results and developing new and improved plans that truly differentiates IMC and IBC from traditional marketing and communication programs.

While the IMC and IBC approach is a major step forward in the development and management of marketing and communication programs, it is still essentially a work-in-progress. That simply means that, as the marketplace shifts and changes, particularly as customers and consumers gain more power or control in the marketplace, IMC and IBC must continuously be adapted, adjusted, and improved. One of the major changes needed is to develop a totally integrated firm, not just an integrated marketing or communication function.

THE GOAL IS TOTAL INTEGRATION

There are two areas of concern in integration. The short-term goal must be the integration of attitudinal and behavioral data. In practice, most organizations focus either on understanding what customers and consumers do, or on how they feel. Traditionally, these two types of customer information, behavioral and attitudinal, have been seldom combined. Thus, the marketing organization may know how customers *feel* but not what they *do*. Alternatively, they may know what customers *do* but not *why* they do those things. Therefore, one of the requirements to become a customer-strategy enterprise must be to combine these two types of data.

Great strides are being made in this area in IMC and IBC research and development. The focus is on *shared values* between the customer and the marketing firm. Marketers value customers in terms of their current financial value and potential. By the same token, customers and prospects value brands in terms of what they know and believe the brand might deliver in terms of both physical and perceptual value. Both these values can be measured and both can be related to some type of financial return to each party. The second challenge is more an internal requirement that is becoming absolutely necessary in any IMC, IBC, or CRM program: the alignment or integration of the entire organization, not just the marketing or communication functional areas. To truly serve customers, marketers must develop customer-centric firms. That means the entire organization must be focused on the customer, not just various pieces and parts. Exhibit 7.3 illustrates what we believe must be accomplished.

As shown, the entire firm must be integrated and aligned to serve customers and prospects. That includes operations, external suppliers, channels and distribution systems, the sales force, marketing, communication, customer service—in short, all the functions and activities of the firm must be focused on the customer and in serving that customer. That is the major challenge facing all types of organizations around the world. To achieve this total integration will require changes in organizational structure, in employee and partner compensation, service

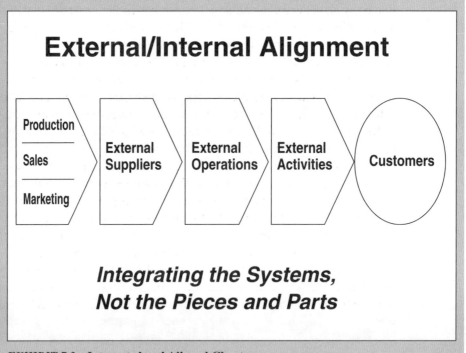

EXHIBIT 7.3   **Integrated and Aligned Chart**

delivery, planning, and implementation. (You'll read more about these organizational changes in Chapter 13.) For many organizations, it will require substantial makeovers of the "marketing" organizations as they exist today. That is why we call this "total integration" a long-term goal; but it is one that must be achieved if IMC, IBC and CRM are to achieve the lofty objectives—and the payoff—that have been promised.

CUSTOMER INTERACTION AND DIALOGUE MANAGEMENT

Whether you think of dialogue management as IMC, IBC, or something that combines message coordination with generating feedback, it's clear that interaction requires the customer's active participation and has a direct impact on the customer, whose awareness of the interaction is an indispensable part of the process. Since interaction is visible, the interacting customer gains an impression of an enterprise interested in his feedback. The overarching objective is to establish a dialogue with a customer that will lead to information and learning. In turn, information and learning lead to knowledge about the customer— knowledge the enterprise can turn into a valuable business asset, because no other enterprise will have that knowledge.

Different customers are different, and they want and need different things. That means we should expect different customers to prefer different *interaction methods*. One customer prefers mail to phone; another likes a combination of e-mail and regular mail. The level of personalization that the Web affords to a customer should also be available in more traditional "customer-facing" venues. Retail sales executives in the store, for instance, should have access to the same knowledgebase of customer information and previous interactions and transactions with the enterprise as a customer service representative at corporate headquarters or customer interaction centers. Enterprises must be able to identify which channels their customers prefer and then decide how they will support seamless interactions. Those enterprises that fail to provide these interaction capabilities can lose sales.[8]

Ideally, the firm will be able to learn from each customer what his own **Preferred Media Package (PMP)** will be. Different customers will have different PMPs, so for each customer, the company will want to set up business rules that reconcile the customer's PMP with that customer's value to the enterprise and the efficiency of using that combination of communication channels. (One customer may prefer telephone calls for all inbound and outbound interactions; but if he's a very low-value customer, he may get a combination of routine selling and service via the Web, with certain sales and support by phone.)

The goal is not understanding a *market* through a *sample*, rather understanding each *individual* in the population through *dialogue*. Each interaction is not only a chance to build a deeper Learning Relationship with each customer, but

---

[8]Todd Wagner, "Multichannel Customer Interaction," Accenture white paper, available at: *www.accenture.com.*

> The goal is not under–standing a *market* through a *sample*, rather understanding each *individual* in the population through *dialogue*.

also a chance to gain important information from a customer that is unavailable to competitors. Such information falls into two general categories:

- *Customer needs.* The best method for discovering what a customer wants is to interact with him directly. Each time he buys, the enterprise discovers more and more about how he likes to shop and what he prefers to buy. Interactions are important not only because the customer is investing in the relationship with the enterprise, but also because the enterprise learns substantive information about the customer that a competitor may not know. Interaction gives the enterprise valuable information about a customer that a competitor cannot act on.
- *Potential value.* With every customer interaction, a customer helps the enterprise predict more accurately his trajectory and potential value with the enterprise. The customer might have specific plans regarding how much he will spend with the enterprise and how long he will use its products and services, and the enterprise might learn of these plans directly from the customer. Insight into a customer's potential valuation would include, among other things, advance word of an upcoming project or pending purchase; or information with respect to the competitors a customer also deals with; or referrals to other customers that could be profitably solicited by the enterprise. This type of information can usually be obtained *only* through direct interaction with the customer, and it is vital to the firm's capability to prioritize its marketing and selling efforts—that is, its capability to allocate the firm's customer investment efficiently.

Because most customers will not sit still for extensive questioning at any given touchpoint, the successful customer-oriented enterprise will learn to use *each* interaction, whether initiated by the customer or the firm, to learn one more, incremental thing that will help in growing share of customer, or SOC (see also, Chapter 1), with *that* customer. This is the concept of what we call drip irrigation dialogue. USAA Insurance in San Antonio, Texas, calls this "smart dialogue." As the basis for intelligent interaction, USAA uses business rules within its customer data management effort to a make a customer's immediate history available to its **customer service representatives (CSRs)** as soon as each customer calls. The CSRs also see a box on their computer screens in which is spelled out the next question USAA needs to have answered about this customer in order to serve him better. This is not a question USAA is asking every customer who calls this month; it is the next question for *this customer*.

In many cases, an enterprise will use *Golden Questions* to understand its customers, and thus achieve needs and value differentiation (see Chapters 5, 6, and 7) quickly and effectively. Golden Questions are designed to reveal important information about a customer, while requiring the least possible effort from the customer. Designing a Golden Question almost always requires a good deal of imagination and creative judgment, but the question's effectiveness is predetermined by statistically correlating the answers to it with actual customer characteristics or behavior,

> Golden Questions are designed to reveal important information about a customer, while requiring the least possible effort from the customer.

using predictive modeling. In general, an enterprise should avoid most product-focused questions, except in situations in which the customer is trying to specify a product or service, prior to purchase. Instead, the most productive type of customer interaction is that which reveals information about an individual customer's underlying need or potential value. To better understand how product-focused questions differ from Golden Questions, examine the hypothetical chart in Exhibit 7.4.

ORGANIZATION GOAL	PRODUCT-FOCUSED QUESTIONS	UNDERLYING NEED OR MOTIVATION OF HIGH-GROWTH CUSTOMERS	GOLDEN QUESTION
My company produces premium pet food. I want to get my message to consumers likely to buy a lot of expensive dog food. I am looking for MVCs.	"Did you buy a lot of dog food last year?" "Do you spend more than $20 a week on dog supplies?"	*I'm a customer, and I really love my pet. I'd do almost anything for him.*	"Do you buy your pet a holiday gift?"
My retail chain sells women's clothing, and I want to find out who is likely to shop at my store and spend a lot of money.	"Did you spend more than $1,000 last year on women's clothing?" "Do you shop for clothes at least once a month?"	*I'm a woman, and my personal appearance is very important to me.*	"Is it okay to wear jeans when you go to the movies or do you prefer something dressier?"
My brokerage firm offers many products. We want to find the existing clients most likely to consolidate their assets with us, to increase total assets under management.	"Do you have more than two investment accounts?" "Do you have more than $500,000 in liquid assets?"	*Retirement is important to me, but I have other interests as well–such as investing for my son's college education and using some "fun money" to play the market.*	"Have you ever used your savings to play a hot stock?"
Our telecommunications firm faces a high churn rate among our wireless subscribers. How can we identify customers most likely to switch to a competitor, without "buying" loyalty via discounts?	"Do you plan to shop around for wireless service?" "Are you in the market for a new cell phone?"	*Technology is important to me, and it's a lot of fun. I need to be wired. I want the latest gadget that networks me to the world.*	"Do you check your e-mail on Saturdays?"

EXHIBIT 7.4 **Development of Golden Questions**

Examples of Customer-Initiated Interactions:
- • Orders and payments for products and services
- • Product or service specifications
- • Inquiries and requests
- • Complaints or disputes
- • Fan letters

Examples of Company-Initiated Interactions:
- • Order fulfillment and product delivery
- • Invoicing, billing
- • Selling, persuading, promoting
- • Informing, educating, benefiting

EXHIBIT 7.5   Examples of Substantive Content

An enterprise has many different mechanisms for interacting with customers, and many reasons to interact. Because it is so difficult to identify all the touch-points a company has with its customers, the best first step is simply to take an inventory of all of the current and potential interaction events between the enterprise and the customer. Customer interaction analysis helps enterprises understand how their customers deal with the organization. It is important to determine a customer's key interaction points and other customer-related activities that occur at each of these points. Once the enterprise has determined these key interaction points, it must ensure that interactions always create value, never confusion, either for the enterprise or for the customer.

It is possible to map how each customer group interacts with the enterprise and which parts of the enterprise perform specific activities for different customers. The company can use this information to improve how it serves the customer.[9]

One way to understand customer interaction is to inventory all possible "interaction events" according to two criteria: the *communication channel* through which the event occurs, and the *substance*, or content, of the event itself.

- • *Communication channel.* Every event takes place in or through a medium. The medium is the *mechanism* for interacting, whether it is over the phone, a face-to-face conversation, or the mail. Enterprises must understand all the current and potential communication channels for interacting with customers, along with the strengths and limitations of each.
- • *Substance.* In addition to a channel, every event also involves some kind of substantive content. That is, we should assume that every interaction between an enterprise and a customer that is worth paying attention to occurs for some purpose—perhaps it is the customer initiating a complaint or the enterprise sending an invoice. Enterprises must understand what the range of content is for interacting with its customers, whether the interaction is initiated by the customer or by the enterprise (see Exhibit 7.5).

---

[9]Brett J. Pinegar, "Getting to Know Them," *Direct* (April 2000), p. 64.

Managing interactivity requires effort. An enterprise can easily outsource the management of a particular communication channel, but it is much more difficult to outsource the management of customer dialogue, across all media.

If an enterprise wants to succeed in managing dialogues with its customers individually, it must manage the *content* of these dialogues, from interaction event to event, across all different communication channels. Dialogue management has to be a core competency of all customer-strategy enterprises. Managing interactivity requires effort. An enterprise can easily outsource the management of a particular communication channel, but it is much more difficult to outsource the management of customer dialogue, across all media.

Enterprises must build intelligent interaction capabilities that link all customer touchpoints. Many are developing Customer Interaction Centers (CICs), with superior communication capabilities. The new centers present a 360-degree view of the customer by consolidating phone, e-mail, the Web, and other channels of customer communication, integrating them with enterprise's business processes.[10]

By creating consistently extraordinary experiences at the customer interface, an enterprise can easily distinguish itself from other enterprises. Indeed, the customer interface is a highly leveraged place to invest, because the systems and people dealing directly with customers create expectations, get feedback on products, and services, and solve problems.[11] But every interaction with a customer costs something, and some interactions are more expensive than others. Ranking customers by their value allows a company to manage the customer interaction process more cost-efficiently. A highly valuable customer is more apt to be worth a personal phone call from a manager, while a not-so-valuable customer's interaction might be more efficiently handled on the Web site. An enterprise requires a manageable and cost-efficient way to solicit, receive, and process the interactions with its customers. It will need to categorize customer inquiries and responses in some effective way so it can customize its interactions for each customer.

By creating consistently extraordinary experiences at the customer interface, an enterprise can easily distinguish itself from other enterprises.

Reducing the cost of customer interaction is partly about reducing and eliminating the interactions that the customer does not want. (Think of all of the catalogs or direct-mail pieces you receive that you never need or respond to—that end up in the trash! These are unnecessary costs that an enterprise could save if it knew for certain that you would never place an order or if it knew that your favorite method of communicating with a company is not by the mail, say, but only online.)

Technology has reduced the expense of interacting with a wide range of customers. Enterprises can streamline and automate what was once a highly manual process of customer interaction. For example, Cisco Systems, which manufactures

[10]Edward Forrest and Richard Mizerski, *Interactive Marketing: The Future Present* (American Marketing Association; NTC Business Books, 1996).

[11]Richard Whiteley and Diane Hessan, *Customer Centered Growth* (New York: Perseus Publishing, 1997).

computer routers and switches, has improved its often-complicated sales process through its Web site, Cisco Connection Online. The site enables customers to configure and reconfigure their own systems and instantly access Cisco's product and system information. Cisco makes it easy for customers to register their system configurations for later upgrades, which saves them time, reduces transaction costs, and ensures that the customer never has to reenter the information again.

Different interactive mechanisms can yield widely different information-exchange capabilities (see Exhibit 7.6). Interacting regularly with a customer via a Web site is usually highly cost-efficient, and can be customer-driven, yielding a rich amount of information. Regular mail, however, is not as practical for dialogue, because it involves a lengthy cycle time, although it can prove effective for delivering more detailed information to the customer, who can keep the hard copy to read later. Telephone interaction has the advantages of real-time conversation, faxing, e-mail, and voicemail. The biggest limitation for both phone and face-to-face interactions, however, is that the enterprise cannot track these as well as it can track electronic exchanges. To be able to improve its relationship over time with any given customer, the enterprise must be sure that the employee responsible for the voice interaction with that customer is actually capturing its key elements for the company's database.

One tool that can help an enterprise reveal redundant and conflicting communications with its customers is a *touchmap*. The touchmap visually depicts how a customer experiences the enterprise's interactions, identifying the points of contact (or "touches") throughout the customer life cycle. Touchmaps expose data silos and other infrastructure gaps that make a customer experience less than ideal, and that waste resources. The enterprise uses the touchmap as a tool to enhance service for each customer by making it seamless; to reduce costs, by

	COST	SPEED	TANGIBILITY*	TRACKABILITY	PRACTICAL OPPORTUNITY FOR PERSONALIZATION
WEB	Low	Instant	Medium	High	High
MAIL	Medium	Slow	High	Medium-Low	Low-High
EMAIL	Low	Instant	Medium	High	High
TELEPHONE	High	Moderately-Slow	Low	Medium-Low**	Medium-High
PERSONAL SALES	Very High	Moderately-Slow	Varied	Medium-Low**	High

* Customer has ability to hold the message in hand or refer back to it easily.
** Depends on capture and recording by CSR or sales representative.

EXHIBIT 7.6 **Information Exchange Capabilities of Different Communication Channels**

removing interaction redundancies; to create more effective customer messages; to bridge gaps in information flow between the enterprise and the customer; and to better integrate its use of individual customer information. For a customer, the touchmap can eliminate the hassle of irrelevant messages or repetitive requests for the same information.

COMPLAINING CUSTOMER AS COLLABORATORS

Customers generally contact an enterprise of their own volition for only three reasons: to get information, to get a product or service, or to make a suggestion or a complaint. Technical Assistance Research Program (TARP) found that 50 percent of individual consumers and 25 percent of business customers who have a problem never complain to anyone at the company.[12] Sometimes, however, a dialogue begins when a customer contacts the enterprise with a complaint.

Thus, one way to view a complainer is to see him as a customer with a current "negative" value that can be turned into positive value. In other words, a complainer has extremely high potential value. If the complaint is not resolved, there is a high likelihood that the complaining customer will cease buying, and will probably talk to a number of other people about their dissatisfaction, causing the loss of additional business. The one-to-one enterprise, focused on increasing the value of its customer base, will see a customer complaint as an opportunity to convert the customer's immense potential value into actual value, for three reasons:

1. *Complaints are a "relationship adjustment opportunity."* The customer who calls with a complaint enables the enterprise to understand why their relationship is troubled. The enterprise then can determine ways to fix the relationship.
2. *Complaints enable the enterprise to expand its scope of knowledge about the customer.* By hearing a customer's complaint, the enterprise can learn more about the customer's needs and strive to increase the value of the customer.
3. *Complaints provide data points about the enterprise's products and services.* By listening to a customer's complaint, the enterprise can better understand how to modify and correct its generalized offerings, based on the feedback.

To a one-to-one enterprise, complaining customers have a collaborative upside, represented by a high potential value. Research from TARP has shown that if a contact center can resolve a customer's problem in a way that works for

[12]John Goodman, Pat O'Brien, and Eden Segal, "Turning CFOs into Quality Champions," *Quality Progress* (March 2000).

> To a one-to-one enterprise, complaining customers have a collaborative upside, represented by a high potential value.

the customer, thus changing a dissatisfied customer to a satisfied one, the enterprise can increase loyalty by 50 percentage points. In general, if the enterprise calls the customer back or the customer has to call a second time, satisfaction and loyalty are decreased by 10 percentage points and the enterprise's costs are doubled because of the "telephone tag." TARP's research has shown that customers who are satisfied with the solution to a problem often exhibit even greater loyalty than do customers who did not experience a problem at all.

Because the handling of complaints has so much potential upside, a one-to-one enterprise will not avoid complaints, but instead will seek them out. An effort to "discover complaints"—to seek out as many opportunities for customer dialogue as possible—becomes part of dialogue management. Complaint discovery contacts typically ask two questions:

> Customers who are satisfied with the solution to a problem often exhibit even greater loyalty than do customers who did not experience a problem at all.

1. Is there anything more we can do for you?
2. Is there anything we can do better?

At one European book club, for example, customer service representatives call new members during their first month and ask one simple question: "Is there anything we can do better?" No sales pitch or special promotion is ever discussed. The results of this customer satisfaction initiative speak volumes to it effectiveness in retaining customers: nearly an 8 percent increase in sales per member, and 6 percent fewer drop-offs after the first year of membership, among those contacted.

By complaining, a customer is initiating a dialogue with an enterprise and making himself available for collaboration. The enterprise focused on building customer value will view complaining customers as an asset—a business opportunity—to turn the complainers into loyal customers. That is why enterprises need to make it easy for a customer to complain when he needs to.

I-Sky (formerly Sky Alland Marketing) is a telephone and Internet service firm that specializes in dialogue management for enterprise customers that want to do more than simply feed messages to their clients. Complaint discovery is a key activity I-Sky performs for its customers. An automobile dealer might retain I-Sky to telephone its new car owners a week after they purchase their vehicles. The I-Sky representative would ask the customer if he is happy with his new car, then send any newly discovered complaints to the automobile dealer for handling.

I-Sky also attempts to uncover any unspoken concerns the customer might have but was reluctant to tell directly to the enterprise. In essence, the company attempts to initiate a dialogue with the customer to gather information about his needs, using his complaint as an opportunity to enhance his relationship with the enterprise (I-Sky's client) and to make him a satisfied and loyal customer.

Moreover, customers usually see complaint discovery as a highly friendly and service-oriented action on the part of a firm. In a survey of 6,500 auto-

---

SIDEBAR 7.4

Using the Web to Customize the Communication

....

Tom Spitale
Principal, Peppers and Rogers Group

"Nice product. Bad price. Let me go check the competition online." Every CEO in the world has felt the double-edged sword of the Web. On one hand, the Internet boosts performance as the enterprise interacts with customers, suppliers, or channels at low costs. On the other hand, it has lowered the cost of entry for every competitor in the world. The Internet is often seen as the weapon of competitive choice.

Executives at one healthcare insurer found a unique approach for using the Web to block competition. The standard question in their industry is, "How do we retain healthy customers who care very little about the features and benefits of our insurance policies?" Your best customer, in this case, may be a 24-year-old man who runs three miles a day—and this dude is not likely to care much about insurance. If you run a health insurance company, you desperately want to hold on to such healthy customers, because the profit you derive from them will enable you to pay medical expenses for other insurance members who fall ill.

Lose enough healthy consumers and your entire company gets sick. A competitor with a lower price—even if it has a lousy offering—is likely to steal healthy customers away.

The executive team at this insurer decided to use the Web to wrap a new layer of value around its core product—health insurance. The company realized this was the best way to become relevant to its desired audience of fit consumers: add communications and services that appealed to their healthy lifestyle, and customize the offers so they were relevant. The Web was the perfect vehicle, because while the firm couldn't hire an army of customer relationship experts to offer personal communications to members, it could use dynamic content generation online to mass-customize the message.

To understand which services would be most appealing, the company catalogued wide-ranging content, including media publications tangentially related to health, and came up with innovative ideas. Fitness runners and weight lifters got unique information; cosmetics and baseball game information was added to the mix—all "expanding the need set"[a] of healthy consumers who previously didn't care. This approach gave healthy customers reason to remain loyal ("my health insurer understands my preferences and provides personally relevant advice") *and* reduced benefit costs by providing information that helped those with problems get better.

The lesson: The Web can block competitors by surrounding your core offering with a layer of personalized information and value.

[a]Read more about the "expanded needs set" in Chapter 10.

---

mobile owners conducted for a car dealer, I-Sky discovered that the very act of asking customers for their opinions made them into happier and more loyal (i.e., more valuable) customers. Customers who received a phone call about their opinion grew more satisfied with the automobile dealer than those who did not receive a call.

SUMMARY

We have shown with this chapter the importance of customer interaction in the Learning Relationship. The enterprise that creates a sustaining dialogue with each customer can learn more about that customer and begin to develop ways to add value that springs from learning about that customer, and consequently to create a product/service bundle that he is most interested in owning or using. And, like drip irrigation, which never overwhelms or parches, a sustained dialogue helps a company get smarter and serve the customer better than sporadic surveys. The customer-based enterprise engages in a collaborative dialogue with each customer in that customer's preferred channel of communication—whether it be the customer interaction center, e-mail, the phone, wireless, the Web, or "snail-mail." We have touched on how different communication channels can help facilitate customer interaction, and relationships with customers in general. But the customer-strategy enterprise realizes that CRM is a process and a strategy and cannot be solved or implemented with technology alone.

In the next chapter, we will address some of the potent tools enterprises use to interact with customers individually, including the Customer Interaction Center, which is often the focal point of the customer interface.

FOOD FOR THOUGHT

1. TiVo collects very specific data about household television viewing. It knows which programs are recorded and watched (and when and how many times), which programs are recorded and never watched, and which programs are downloaded to tape or DVD. It also knows when a particular part of a program is watched more than once (a sports play, or a favorite cartoon, or movie scene, or commercial). What are the implications of that knowledge for dialogue? For privacy? For TiVo's business model? How might TiVo use this information to increase the value it offers to advertisers and marketers? What would a marketer have to do differently to make the most of this information?

2. What's the difference between having a helpful salesperson at Home Depot and having a relationship with Home Depot? If Sam at the Contractor's Desk in Home Depot knows and remembers you, does that mean you have a relationship with Home Depot? Does Home Depot know what Sam knows? What would have to happen for Home Depot to get as smart about you as Sam is?

3. What are some of the explicit bargains companies have made with you in your role as a customer to get some of your time, attention, or information?

4. How does the European book club mentioned near the end of this chapter know that it's the calling program that led to 6 percent fewer drop-offs and 8 percent more sales per member? Might it not have been the book selection that year? Or the economy?

GLOSSARY

Customer service representative (CSR)   A person who answers or makes calls in a call center (also called a customer interaction center, or CIC)

Explicit bargain   One-to-one organizations give something of value to a customer in exchange for that customer's time and attention, and perhaps for information about that customer as well.

Implicit bargain   Advertisers have in the past bought ads that pay for the cost of producing the media that consumers want—television programming, newspaper copy, magazine stories, music on the radio, and so on. The implied "deal" was that consumers would listen to the ads in exchange for getting the media content free.

Integrated Brand Communications (IBC)   Communication discipline driven by the idea that customers and consumers have relationships with *brands* and *companies,* not with marketing programs, advertising, sales promotions, public relations, or other marketer-initiated activities. This is a different approach to "relationships" than that presented by the authors in Chapter 2.

Integrated Marketing Communications (IMC)   Communication discipline driven by the idea that a firm's efforts to communicate to a single customer should be coordinated in order to implement a consistent branding strategy.

Personal video recorder (PVR)   A digital recording device (such as TiVo) that uses a hard disk drive to record television shows just like a videocassette recorder (VCR), but with interfaces (such as an on-screen program guide) that are regularly downloaded to the device.

Preferred Media Package (PMP)   Using the communication channels for which a customer has expressed a preference to reach that customer (sometimes also called PMOC, or Preferred Method of Communication).

Using the Tools of Interactivity to Build Learning Relationships

8
Chapter

Although the strategy *of customer relationships must precede the successful implementation of customer-relationship* technology, *it was the technology that mandated that enterprises map out their path down the road we've been following in the preceding chapters. Customers have always been able to interact with a company, but mainly on the company's terms—through mail, if a customer could get the name of a person to send a letter to; through phone, if a customer could get the right phone number; and maybe through salespeople, if the customer were important enough to warrant a personal sales call and if the salesperson were authorized to provide service to the customer's satisfaction. That was pretty much it. Today, the customer rules. The company that doesn't accept e-mail or feedback through its Web site is a dinosaur. The operators at a company's call center have individual customer records at their fingertips. Customers expect their mail to be relevant—maybe even personalized—or it's chucked out instantly. Think of it this way: Communication has always been an important part of selling stuff. But interaction is key to building Learning Relationships with one customer at a time, and the burgeoning tools and capabilities for interactivity are helping to drive a push toward customer value building. In this chapter, we will look at some of the tools of interactivity, and hear from experts in interactive media.*

Enterprise spending on CRM software continues to increase. In terms of CRM functionality, executives want three primary outcomes from a CRM system:

1. *Improved customer service*, made possible through real-time data availability.
2. *Organization of information*, achieved by combining multiple data sources into a single location.
3. *Better efficiency*—that is, getting more done with fewer resources.[1]

[1]Microsoft Great Plains survey, 2001.

Relationship-enabling technologies help enterprises to understand their key customer groups and customize their products and services for customers. They measure customer activity relative to customer-related projects, such as marketing campaigns and new product introductions. Companies deploy customer-focused technologies, such as call center software and self-service Web sites, to orchestrate and streamline the processes associated with a customer-value business model. When customer-management strategies are executed properly and backed by appropriate and cost-efficient CRM technologies, a company can avoid the confusion and waste generated when a customer receives multiple, uncoordinated messages from various company representatives.

> Although CRM has become the fastest-growing software applications market in the United States, experts agree that a large proportion of CRM technology implementations–probably a majority–have failed badly in achieving their sponsors' objectives.

Although CRM has become the fastest-growing software applications market in the United States, experts agree that a large proportion of CRM technology implementations—probably a majority—have failed badly in achieving their sponsors' objectives. Some of the problems with CRM implementations are, in fact, technological, but the vast majority of failures stem from other factors, including a lack of supporting vision, the absence of an overarching customer strategy, failure to align new technological capabilities with management practices and business processes, inadequate education and training of personnel, and insufficient attention to the kinds of success metrics that are more appropriate for a customer-focused strategy.

While companies once looked primarily for point solutions to address specific front-office needs, the focus soon shifted to more integrated, front- and back-office systems. More and more, companies seek solutions that can tackle both customer-facing and financial functions, because they recognize that, to a truly customer-oriented company—to a one-to-one enterprise— *customers and finances are one and the same*.

Individual point solutions, such as call center software, sales force automation (SFA) applications, or Web-based customer care solutions, add intelligence to the customer relationship process, but one appeal of focusing on customer equity, as a business discipline, is that it integrates all the disparate systems and departments within an enterprise that are responsible for customer interaction. Some enterprises find it most effective to build a CRM software solution and maintain it in-house. Others say it makes more sense to purchase a "best of breed" solution and outsource some of the integration.

CUSTOMER-BASED SOFTWARE SAMPLER

Clearly, a complete customer-based solution requires many components, and there are many ways to categorize the different applications that would go into such a solution. In the following subsections, we will examine a few of these software categories in a little more detail.

SALES FORCE AUTOMATION TECHNOLOGY

At most firms, the sales process can be "automated" by using computer technology to track leads, prospects, and customers, recording all the enterprise's various interactions as they occur.

A robust sales force automation (SFA) tool will generate routine reports (relieving the overworked sales staff of some of the drudgery), and even prompt a salesperson to take some action in the future. This is a particularly strong technology for enabling a mobile sales force to be more productive and coordinated.

CAMPAIGN MANAGEMENT SOFTWARE

Campaign management software is used to get new customers and ensure the loyalty of established customers by providing continuous, permission-based, promotional communications, according to the customer's interests.[2]

The database management tool is used to design and execute single-channel or multichannel campaigns and to track the effects of those campaigns over time. An add-on to campaign management software can be an e-mail delivery engine, which can send high volumes of e-mail promotions, notifications, and other targeted messages to an opt-in base of customers. This outbound messaging platform should be able to integrate with inbound e-mail platforms to deliver automated or personalized responses when necessary.

PERSONALIZATION ENGINES

Personalized engines are another key element of CRM tools. With personalization technology, an enterprise can leverage profiles in a data warehouse to display various content or products to a specified group of Web site visitors and e-mail-specific offers to various customers. It could also enable the enterprise to treat distinct callers differently in the call center.

Personalization systems build profiles of Web visitors based on voluntarily supplied information. They can target products to specific customers based on their preferences and previous purchases. The personalization engine should lend itself to interaction with various customer touchpoints and common business rules that apply across all of them. (We'll talk more about business rules in Chapter 10.) A real-time personalization engine can help the enterprise tailor all of its interactions with individual customers according to the preestablished business rules. Personalization technology, in essence, is responsible for creating business rules and decision support for the various customer contact channels.[3]

---

[2]Rochelle Shaw and Kathleen Taggart, "Campaign Management Software: Perspective," Gartner Group (November 10, 2000).

[3]Dana Serman and Charles Lozner, "Technology: Internet Infrastructure," Lazard Freres & Co. LLC–Equity Research (October 3, 2000), p. 43.

CUSTOMER SERVICE AND SUPPORT SOLUTIONS

Customer service and support (CSS) solutions combine assisted service and self-service capabilities to help the enterprise manage customer service calls. Enterprises might invest in CSS solutions to reduce the amount of time it takes to handle a service call. CSS suites can include field service automation (FSA) systems, which can manage the service delivery chain and provide contract management, warranties, service parts planning and management, and defect tracking.

The Internet is driving the demand for Web-based customer service solutions, which enable customers to resolve inquiries, check an order status, view product and account information, and perform other tasks without the involvement of a customer service representative.

MATCHING ENGINES

Matching engines are decision-support tools for matching customer needs with product or service offerings. They can work from the perspective of the product (i.e., which customer is a likely prospect for buying this product) or from the perspective of the customer (which product or service offering is the most likely to be successful with this particular customer).

Collaborative filtering—which uses a group-based approach to predictions—is the best known of the recommendation engines, but others exist that use purchase patterns and behavior analysis to make their recommendations. Decision-support tools are often used to reveal basic purchasing trends and uncover hidden data insights. Results are then translated into strategies that are executed using campaign management, e-mail management, Web-site personalization and other interaction methods.

REPORTING AND ANALYTICS TOOLS

Also known as *marketing automation tools*, reporting and analytics tools were made possible by the Web. These tools, at their best, can pull up the answers to any number of queries from marketers—often campaign managers; for example: How many minivan drivers east of the Mississippi have their nails done once a week or more? If a company has the data, marketing automation can pull it out. A small handful of companies have the capability to help companies market directly to individuals—in volume.

CONTACT CENTER MANAGEMENT

Contact center management tools have fundamentally changed the function and process of the traditional call center from being a passive group of operators answering calls and handling complaints case by case to a centralized intelligence hub that remembers things for and about customers. The same technologies also help the contact center coordinate with Web feedback, and connect data about a customer in real time.

ONLINE ANALYTICAL PROCESSING TOOLS

Online analytical processing (OLAP) tools let users analyze the data using their own queries. Other decision-support tools run sophisticated models that reveal patterns and hidden relationships that might otherwise remain undiscovered. Using an OLAP tool, a marketing executive in the music industry, for instance, would be able to query customer data to compare purchasing patterns. She could look at the purchasing habits of "male versus female customers over 55 on the West Coast who purchased CDs," and then view that data by type of music purchased. She might use insights from the query she created to design a special promotion for a subset of individual customers, by name.

SOFTWARE SUMMARY

Residing on top of all these core technologies should be an intuitive interface for a company's managers and customer-facing employees.

Most enterprises require outside help in implementing solutions and integrating new capabilities, legacy systems, and other tools. Outsourcing various elements of the customer-facing function itself can offer some immediate advantages, including access to database expertise in the enterprise's own industry, access to value-added services (e.g., customer relationship analytics), and monthly invoices in place of an up-front capital investment. That said, outsourcing may incur a higher long-term cost; and a company might have less direct control and less flexibility on hardware, and would have to decide whether the enterprise trusts the outsider with its customer data. Most large companies implementing a customer-based solution end up hiring an outside systems integrator consultant to install the applications and integrate them with the firm's own legacy systems. The integrator might also train employees on how to use the applications, and help the firm manage its transition to the new system. The trick is to find an integrator with the company's best interests at heart—as opposed to the integrator's goal of keeping a lot of programmers busy for as long as possible.

Clearly, every company, sooner or later, will be engaged in proactive interactivity with customers, seeking feedback as the basis for a profitable Learning Relationships. Not the least of these opportunities for interactivity is e-mail.

USING E-MAIL TO INTERACT WITH CUSTOMERS

Whether wired or wireless, electronic mail has redesigned the way people communicate. For the first time, in 1995, the number of e-mails outnumbered written postal letters, establishing that year as the beginning of the electronic age. Derek Scruggs, an authority on using e-mail to exchange information with customers individually, offers his thoughts on using e-mail to build customer value.

USING E-MAIL TO BUILD CUSTOMER VALUE

Derek Scruggs
Founder and CEO, ESCALAN, LLC

E-mail communication has become a critical component of customer service—and of customer interaction designed to learn about individual customer needs and to deliver customized messages that foster relationships and enhance loyalty. As with any other marketing or service vehicle, e-mail must be planned and managed, with both the customer and the enterprise in mind. Enterprises can enjoy the distinct benefits of e-mail: It is inexpensive and efficient, gets relatively high response rates, and its results can be highly measurable. Meanwhile, customers like e-mail because it is fast and efficient—provided that it is relevant to them as individuals.

Businesses and consumers alike have staked out their uses for e-mail, turning e-mail into both a personal productivity tool and a marketing tool. International Data Corporation predicted in 2000 that the number of combined business and consumer e-mail accounts in the United States would grow from approximately 157 million to 280 million in 2005. The same report projected more than 1 billion e-mail accounts worldwide in 2005.

Many companies find that e-mail offers an effective way to communicate with customers because it is such a personalized, readily available, reliable medium. When customers have questions that cannot be addressed by the content on a Web site, e-mail has become a common form of online inquiry. And outbound e-mail campaigns have proven highly effective in generating responses. IMT Strategies estimates that the conversion cost of a retention e-mail campaign is just $1.13, nearly 96 percent cheaper than the estimated $26.66 for direct (postal) mail. Response rates for e-mail marketing range from 2% to 15%, with 5% being common. This compares very favorably with sub-1 percent response rates for banner ads and 1 to 3 percent response rates for direct mail.

As with direct mail, of course, the response rate generated by an e-mail campaign is a function of many factors, including the offer conveyed, the particular addressees who receive the offer (i.e., the "list"), and the creativity or originality of the message itself. It is likely that as the novelty of e-mail wears off, response rates in general will fall. However, even after this happens, there will still be fundamental differences between e-mail marketing and direct mail that will tend to favor e-mail. For one, the level of permission that has already been given to the marketer by the addressee is almost always higher for the e-mail campaign. Moreover, the ease with which the recipient, who is simply a click away from the marketer, can fire off a response will continue to favor e-mail.

E-mail is indeed a powerful communications medium, but it can be a double-edged sword. Improper use, perceived arrogance, or ignorance of e-mail "netiquette" can backfire, with serious consequences, ranging from loss of a single customer to loss of e-mail communication privileges with all customers. Even when used properly, e-mail is not a panacea. The e-mail inbox has become a very crowded place, where the best efforts of legitimate marketers are often degraded by the side effects of **unsolicited commercial e-mail (UCE)**, widely known as *spam*, the proliferation of which continues at a staggering pace. The longer a customer has been online, the higher the average number of messages she receives every day. Inbox overload naturally leads to lower response rates in the aggregate, but that does not necessarily have to be the case for any particular program. Successful e-mail marketing is possible; but like most direct marketing, success flows directly from the daily grind of implementation, measurement, testing, and improvement.[4]

UNSOLICITED COMMERCIAL E-MAIL IS UNWELCOME

From its debut on Usenet in 1994 as the infamous "Green Card spam"[5] through the rise and fall of Stanford "Spamford" Wallace's CyberPromotions, UCE has grown like kudzu—in spite of the many antispam activists and organizations trying to counter it and the numerous successful lawsuits against spammers filed by America Online, Earthlink, and others.

Many compare UCE to direct mail, and especially to telemarketing, the cyberspace equivalent to annoying but occasionally effective promotional techniques. That said, a few characteristics of UCE render the analogies moot and suggest that it may be as big a threat as the antispam advocates suggest. At a minimum, these characteristics should give pause to any marketer who may be considering UCE.

- *The economics of UCE lead to a "tragedy of the commons."* Unlike direct mail, telemarketing, and other media, the incremental cost of sending an e-mail is practically zero. A traditional direct mailer has two costs associ-

[4]James Sterne, Anthony Priore, and Jerry I. Reitman, *Email Marketing: Using Email to Reach Your Target Audience and Build Customer Relationships* (New York: John Wiley & Sons, Inc., 2000).

[5]Go to *www.eff.org/Legal/Cases/Canter_Siegel/c-and-s_summary.article* for a colorful history of this event.

ated with each piece it sends to a customer: the printing of the correspondence and the postage. It behooves the direct mailer to be vigilant about continuously updating its mailing list so it will not waste money on erroneous mailings. In other media, financial constraints serve as negative incentives for marketers to continually improve their targeting capabilities, which means they are less likely to send mail to or call someone who does not respond. A sender of UCE, however, suffers no added cost for sending a message to an unlikely prospect. Indeed, the cost would occur only if the spammer spent resources weeding out nonresponding names. Thus, an electronic spammer has no financial incentive to measure, test, and refine her list. While this may not be problematic if only one marketer did this, it would be catastrophic if even a small percentage of marketers elected to send UCE. The inbox would quickly become useless. This is why antispam advocates are so vigilant; and it's clear that, for all the UCE on the Internet today, there would be much more if not for their activities.

- *UCE is often associated with fraudulent and offensive offers such as pyramid schemes, pornography, stock scams, and the like.* The perception that you are part of this crowd—the Skid Row of the Internet—could inflict serious brand damage and will, at a minimum, suppress response below what it otherwise might be.
- *The mere presence of UCE in the inbox damages the likelihood that other, legitimate messages will be opened and responded to.* Given this fact, customer-based businesses should be as antispam as most consumers.
- Most Internet service providers (ISPs) have acceptable use policies (AUPs) that expressly forbid the sending of UCE. If you violate the AUP, you will lose your connectivity from the provider and effectively be kicked off the Internet.

OPT-IN VERSUS OPT-OUT

Many marketing organizations collect e-mail addresses on an opt-in basis. That means they give the end user a choice at the time of sign-up (or site registration or during a purchase) as to whether she wants to provide her e-mail address, and whether she wants to receive future communications. Since she voluntarily gave her name and address and asked to receive promotional messages (or at least didn't say *not* to send promotional messages), you are not sending UCE, right?

Maybe. An unfortunate by-product of the so-called spam wars is that legitimate marketers sometimes get caught in the crossfire. If you haven't communicated with a customer for several months, she may forget that she signed up for your list and complain when she receives your message.[6] And sometimes it's hard to know how to opt out at all.

[6]Hans Peter Brondmo and Geoffrey Moore, *The Engaged Customer: The New Rules of Internet Direct Marketing* (New York: HarperBusiness, 2000).

Worse, users sometimes enter an incorrect e-mail address accidentally. At other times, consumers want to avoid UCE. Many end users make little distinction between responsible e-mail marketers and spammers; they assume that all marketers are alike and often believe that Web sites buy and sell e-mail addresses regularly. Sometimes the address is added with malicious intent—someone has decided to play a prank on a friend or, worse, tweak an antispam activist.

These would only be minor problems except that the Internet gives customers much more power than other media, so they complain not just to the enterprise, but also to their ISP and the enterprise's ISP, asking them to block the enterprise's e-mail. In these cases, the "frontier mentality" often applies: ISPs often believe the enterprise is guilty until proven innocent, not the other way around. The onus is on the enterprise to prove otherwise. In the grand scheme of things, complaints like this are rare, often fewer than one in 50,000 addresses. But they become more likely at the e-mail interaction programs' scale—at 1 million addresses, it is statistically likely that even the most responsible marketers will receive complaints, so enterprises need to be prepared for them when they do arrive.

SIDEBAR 8.1

Understanding E-Mail Etiquette

Before undertaking an e-mail marketing program, the customer-focused enterprise would be well advised to learn a few lessons in e-mail etiquette. The Internet has its own set of social customs and rules, which are not necessarily the same as in the offline world—in fact, they may be the exact opposite. To set the stage for success, while dramatically lowering the chances of backlash, follow the nine guidelines presented here:

1. *Send e-mail only to those who have requested it.* Ideally, the enterprise should use *confirmed opt-in*, in which a confirmation message is sent to the recipient, who in turn must reply to the message for the opt-in to take effect. It should avoid *opt-out*, which forces the recipient to receive messages until she says no. (Opt-out is the approach enshrined in some state legislation, which most antispam advocates and ISPs strenuously oppose and do not honor.)

2. *Always honor user requests to opt out.* The enterprise makes opt-out a simple process and includes a Web site URL in every message that allows the user to opt out. (A simple "reply to unsubscribe" does not always work if the user has multiple e-mail accounts, which can be extremely frustrating for the end user.) For some companies, it might make sense to "downsell" the end user. For example, a news site that provides daily deliveries may have success in offering the user an opportunity to downgrade to weekly digests. After all, many opt-outs are a natural reaction to too much e-mail in general; a reduced burden is often welcome.

3. *Confirm everything by e-mail.* This includes the initial opt-in, orders, shipping notification, and changes in the customer profile. Following this guideline blunts the problem of false information. If a fake e-mail address has been

SIDEBAR 8.1 *(continued)*

....

entered, the confirmation will either bounce or be delivered to someone who possibly has never heard of you, in which case she will contact you and let you know your database needs to be updated. Always include an opt-out mechanism in these messages. As an added bonus, use these messages as an upsell opportunity. For example, an airline could offer the user a reduced rate for renting a car from a particular sponsoring vendor in the same e-mail used to confirm a booking.

4. *Enable customers to specify their preferences.* What kind of information do they want to receive? How often? Encourage the customer to give as much information as necessary to allow the enterprise to effectively target her in its e-mail promotions and other e-commerce activities. But the enterprise should avoid asking too much about the customer all at once. Instead, it should structures its interactions so that it gains more information over time—with her permission.

5. *Give and you shall receive.* Customers rarely give out their e-mail addresses and other personal information of their own volition. They do it in exchange for something of value. It could be information (on your Web site, via e-mail or through some other media), a free gift, a coupon, or a chance to win a sweepstakes. The enterprise can be creative, but it should also follow through by delivering real value to the recipient with every message.

6. *Recognize that the e-mail list is an asset that only the enterprise can use.* The enterprise can realize incremental revenue beyond its own offerings by allowing the customers to opt in to receive offers from its partners. That said, the enterprise must ensure that it controls the mailings and that its brand "introduces" other brands. For example: "Because you opted to receive promotional offers of our valued partners, we at United Airlines are pleased to give you a special offer from National Car Rental." If the sponsoring company gets an exclusive from the partner company, it means that only the customers who opt in get a chance to participate.

7. *Do not use rented lists.* The only exception is vendors that work through partners and share offers with the partners' customers who have opted in (see guideline 6).

8. *Respond to customer e-mail inquiries promptly.* A quick response reinforces how valuable the customer is to the enterprise and reminds her that there is a real, live person behind the scenes of the Web site.

9. *Always remember the network effect—bad news travels much faster than good on the Internet.* An angry online customer can broadcast her ire to millions by creating an "I hate [your company]" Web site, e-mailing the experience to friends, posting it on message boards, and other ways.

DEVELOPING AN E-MAIL STRATEGY

Because of the opt-in nature of legitimate e-mail marketing, enterprises require e-mail programs that provide a compelling reason for customers to provide them with their e-mail addresses. The most successful programs do this by adding value in the relationship. Instead of asking a customer or potential customer for an e-mail address, the enterprise might develop and articulate the benefits of signing up to receive e-mail. Benefits can be simple—for example, a clothing retailer might e-mail early notice of next season's fashions—but the enterprise should be wary of relying too much on incentives, which will attract a disproportionate share of "bottom feeders." A good example of adding value can be found in Amazon.com's search results pages. When a customer searches for a book or other product, the search results page includes a sign-up form that invites the user to be notified when new releases arrive that match the search results.

Regardless of how value is added, it is generally a good idea to make the request for someone's e-mail address as conspicuous and ubiquitous as possible. BabyCenter.com, for example, puts the request front and center on its home page. News.com and many other online publications have an opt-in field on almost every page of their Web sites. Many sites invite people to opt in via pop-up windows, which activate when someone first visits a site or leaves it for another site. While most subscribers will likely come from online sources, the enterprise might also have success with offline media. Media such as point-of-purchase displays, direct mail, trade shows, and radio have been demonstrated to be effective for growing an e-mail list.

A common mistake made by many customer-focused Web sites is asking for too much information too soon. Many of us have had personal experience in confronting a long, seemingly pointless form on a Web site. Many customers dislike such requests for information and decide either to leave the site altogether or, worse, provide false data. Bad data is a common problem, and given continuing concerns about privacy, it is likely to remain a problem. In this environment, a good tactic for enterprises is to ask for the least amount of information necessary to fulfill a request (or at least make additional information optional), and then learn more about users over time. Often the enterprise need only ask one or two questions to understand a customer. BabyCenter.com provides a good example of this approach. On the site's home page, BabyCenter invites the expectant mother to enter her e-mail address and the due date for her child. Other data such as name and zip code can be entered optionally, but BabyCenter.com is able to add value just with the e-mail address and due date. When you think about it, this is very powerful data: BabyCenter.com can now send highly relevant newsletters and offers for the next 17 or 18 *years*! Why? Because it now knows a very special date in the registrant's life and what stage of parenthood the mother is going through at any particular moment.

E-mail marketing is an evolving discipline. New technologies, notably rich media, are emerging that make e-mail as pervasive as the Web. The changing environment makes prediction difficult, but there are a few prognostications that can be made with some degree of certainty.

- *Value-add will become more critical.* As the average inbox increasingly overflows with both opt-in e-mail and UCE, response rates will erode. In this context, customers will have to make choices about which messages to open (let alone respond to), which means the messages that deliver the most perceived value will rise to the top of their inboxes.

- *Personalization will be important.* As more companies experiment with e-mail marketing, only the most relevant messages will stand out. Personalization, of course, goes well beyond simple mail-merge capabilities, encompassing deeper profiles of individual customer tastes and needs. World-class e-mail marketers will use these profiles to deliver dynamically generated messages that are customer-centric, not marketer-centric.

- *E-mail will weave its way into the everyday fabric of customer relationships.* In addition to publishing and marketing, companies will increasingly use e-mail for the more routine communications. For example, phone and utility companies will turn to e-mail for billing, surveys, service notifications, even scheduling of service calls. It's important to note the significance of electronic bill presentment and invoicing as a very real, and real-time, form of interaction.

SIDEBAR 8.2

E-Mail Get-Smart Resources

....

Use these resources to learn more about e-mail and telecommunications.

- *Multimedia Telecommunications Association (www.mmta.org).* MMTA is a full-service trade association devoted to expanding markets in the converging computer and telecommunications industries.

- *Total Telecom (www.totaltele.com).* Total Telecom is an online information source for telecommunications professionals. It gives access to current and past articles from *Communications Week International* and *Communications International* and hosts a range of information services, including interactive service applications.

- *Virtual Institute of Information (www.vii.org).* VII is a research tool accessible through the World Wide Web by anyone interested in finding information on the economic, business, policy, and social aspects of telecommunications, cybercommunications, and mass media.

- *International Telecommunications Union (www.itu.int).* The ITU, headquartered in Geneva, Switzerland, is an international organization within which governments and the private sector coordinate global telecom networks and services.

- *Business Communications Review (www.bcr.com).* BCR Enterprises, Inc. is a communications publishing and training firm founded in 1971 to help communications information systems professionals perform their jobs better and advance in their careers.

- *Call Center University (www.callcenteru.com/default.html).* CCU is dedicated to providing professional education and certification for call center personnel.

- *Telecommunications Magazine Online (www.telecoms-mag.com/tcs.html).* This publication contains information and communications industry articles for professional technology managers.

SIDEBAR 8.2 *(continued)*

- *CallCenter Magazine (www.callcentermagazine.com/index.html).* This magazine publishes articles about call center products and services, helping its readers choose, buy, implement, and manage hardware, software, and services.
- *The TeleM@rket (www.telemkt.com).* The TeleM@rket is an online exchange of information on telemarketing and call center issues.
- *Help Desk Institute (www.helpdeskinst.com).* HDI provides targeted information about the technologies, tools, and trends of the help desk and customer support industry, and offers a variety of services to meet the evolving needs of the customer support professional.

While e-mail has made casual interaction a reality, **customer interaction centers (CICs)**—once referred to as *call centers*—are becoming the hub of real-time customer relationships, by providing information about a single customer linked across communication channels. The following discussion by Elizabeth Rech helps us understand what this implies for the way these centers are managed. After that, Fred Newell and Kay Lemon share insights about e-CRM.

EVOLUTION OF THE CUSTOMER INTERACTION CENTER IN THE CONTEXT OF IDIC

Elizabeth Rech
Business Strategy and CRM Consultant

The customer interaction center (CIC) is traditionally at the heart of an enterprise's customer interaction activities. But as enterprises strive to develop individual relationships with each customer, the CIC's functionality has expanded considerably. This section discusses how enterprises need to plan customer interaction strategies carefully and empower contact center representatives with the appropriate customer information—in real time. As we have said earlier, the objective is to integrate channels of customer communication so that a 360-degree view of the customer can be created and used to maximize customer value and customer satisfaction. Let's take a closer look at what it means to be "360."

The typical customer is not concerned with the way the enterprise is organized or how the product travels down the distribution channel. The customer does not care about enterprise systems and procedures. She just wants what she wants, when and how she wants it. The problem is that the typical enterprise is not designed to accommodate the customer's own perspective. Companies, for the most part, are organized by product line, brand, service offering, and department.

The most effective way a company can satisfy the customer's need for straight-forward service is to create one centralized view of each customer across all business units, departments, divisions, sales vehicles, and interaction channels.

This would be a 360-degree view of the customer—one in which every employee who interacts with the customer, regardless of the channel, has real-time access to accurate and actionable data about that individual customer. Certainly, creating a 360-degree view is easier said than done, although many firms find it is a process that improves over time.

EVOLUTION OF THE CIC

The CIC is not a new concept to most enterprises. However, it has acquired new and more important roles. Traditionally housed in remote locations, where labor and operating costs were significantly lower, the CIC was staffed by employees clad with headphones. The CIC either served as a place for customers to telephone and purchase items they had seen in catalogs, newspapers, direct-mail pieces, television, and the Web, or as a troubleshooter/repair center where one could log a problem for dispatch or return. The process seemed simple: The CIC employee answered the phone and took an order or dispatched a technician.

But as products and services sold through direct marketing became more complex, customers began phoning the CIC for reasons other than sales transactions. They now had questions or needed more information about the products they had already purchased. Moreover, some customers might call to complain that something was not right. How would the CIC representatives (customer service representatives, or CSRs) react now? This was further complicated by the need to blend media, if, for example, the CSR needed to interact using e-mail, and even to share Web-browsing chores with a customer.

Not surprisingly, to respond to these new customer needs, contact center representatives required new skills, training, and business knowledge. Moreover, satisfying these new demands often required additional "talk time" (or additional costs to the enterprise) to listen to customers and provide solutions, as well as "after call" time to deal with follow-up and problem resolution.

The CIC, therefore, has evolved into a more complex and costly endeavor for the enterprise than the old call center. Management has sought ways to decrease costs by limiting customer service hours, reducing the number of representatives on duty, and by providing special incentives for representatives who keep their phone calls as short as possible. Some enterprises reduced their contact center costs by deploying a Web site with self-service functionality.

It has taken a while for some companies to realize that a good, interactive Web site may reduce the cost of some of the most routine interactions; but no doubt they will, if interactivity with customers is enhanced through better Learning Relationships, with the result being an *increase* in total calls to the CIC. So it's not surprising for a firm to see a dramatic increase in CIC activity, which in many cases provides better relationship and measurement opportunities. For example, one can imagine that complex products, such as financial investments or insurance, might require more interaction between the customer and the enterprise, to answer questions and comply with regulations. One can also imagine that with round-the-clock access to Web sites, some of the busiest transaction times might well be at 10:00 P.M., not 10:00 A.M. Enterprises need to be available to a customer wherever she wants to interact.

Some companies rely solely on their CICs for the conduct of business, maintaining no storefronts or other physical points of purchase. For them, the efficiency and effectiveness of the CIC is paramount to overall success and profitability. The effective use of the contact center channel is more than an opportunity to sell the first product; it is an opportunity to sell the second, third, and the fourth products, all at higher profit margins. Over time, interactions with each customer enhance loyalty. This dialogue can also be an inexpensive way to conduct customer research, if tracked and documented.

SIDEBAR 8.3

Scenario: USAA

United States Automobile Association (USAA) was formed in 1922 by and for military officers, who could not purchase automotive insurance from traditional insurers because they frequently moved from state to state. The founders of USAA recognized this difference in the needs of military officers and built the company so that no matter where an officer lived or moved, she could be covered.

USAA illustrates the importance of organizing a company around satisfaction of specific customer needs while enabling longer-term growth of its customer relationships with the right technology and quality service. Simply, USAA evolved into one big contact center, in which all member data (USAA calls its customers "members") resided and was shared among all service representatives. For example, when a member called and identified herself with her unique member number, any representative who answered the phone could look up her record or history, transactions, and so on, and provide service for her on the spot. This centralized customer service operation demonstrated its capability to serve members—wherever they were and whenever they called—very efficiently from one location, rather than from multiple locations across the country.

From these humble beginnings, USAA now has 4.5 million members, with assets of $62.5 billion, and ranks as one of the best companies in America for quality customer service.[a] It has some 16,000 customer services agents in approximately 100 automated contact distribution groups, mostly located in San Antonio, Texas. The company handles 147 million inbound and outbound calls per year (average of 403,000 per day), yet it placed first as the most reputable financial services company in America![b]

Of course, enterprises that serve customers via multiple channels have greater challenges, most of which relate to the sharing of customer information with all such channels and identifying each individual customer accurately at each interaction. In fact, USAA, which now serves its members on the Web as well, has learned that further integration and sharing of that information will be critical in keeping the ever-changing member satisfied.

[a]As of mid-2001.

[b]Financial Service Reputation Quotient study, conducted by Harris Interactive. *American Banker*. Thompson Financial Media, "Call It the Contact Center," October 24, 2001.

SIDEBAR 8.4

Case Scenario: Circuit City

....

Circuit City, a leading U.S. consumer electronics retailer, has more than 550 retail stores and has attempted to integrate its traditional sales channel with its Web-based store. Customers can browse the Web site, make price and feature comparisons, check availability at local stores, and then choose to pick up the merchandise immediately at the nearest retail site ("Express Pick-up") or have it delivered to their homes. Customers who register on the Web site can have all of their billing and shipping information and other preferences stored for future use. Customized e-mails keep them apprised of the latest information in products they are most interested in purchasing and of special sales events. If products bought online and delivered to the home need to be returned, they can be taken to the nearest retail store for credit. Of course, for those not comfortable with online shopping, the Circuit City contact center is ready to assist in the sales transaction. To make this kind of multichannel retailer successful, Circuit City followed some basic relationship-building steps:

1. Identify and track the customer.
2. Remember information about her and for her throughout the enterprise.
3. Be available to help.
4. Make the shopping process easy and convenient.
5. Work toward building the relationship with relevant value to the customer.

CICs are much more than just sales transaction points, because enterprises are using them for many different types of communications and a variety of functions. For example, contact centers are now responsible for handling a number of different customer interaction vehicles, starting with the phone, but including fax, Web, mail, point-of-purchase, and other electronic communications. The multiplicity of interaction vehicles, of course, calls for tools and technology that enable contact center representatives to access the right information when they need it—usually in real time. Operationally, this means that customer information must be integrated and shared across all departments, divisions, and channels. And professionally, this means that contact center representatives must have the knowledge and skills to handle all of the above.

CONTACT CENTER TECHNOLOGY AND TRAINING

Contact center representatives must be able to answer simple queries and requests for support, as well as have a broader supply of information at their fingertips, such as product availability, shipment status, and estimated arrival date. They also must be able to offer product recommendations and helpful hints and to provide product maintenance reminders. Contact center reps need the ability to remember and fulfill preferences of individual customers.

To accomplish these tasks, enterprises need to deploy sophisticated contact center technology, equipped with accurate information about customers and the products and services they offer. There are many software applications that integrate information about the products and services with customer database information in real time, regardless of the location or status within the enterprise. Boise Cascade, in late 2000, introduced the Boise Service Standard, a new level of personalized, proactive customer service as part of an ongoing initiative focused on enhancing the level of customer service through advancements in technology and training. (In late 2001, Gartner Group named Boise Cascade the number-one CRM company.[7]) With these advancements, Boise could better anticipate customer needs, provide faster service, and help customers streamline their procurement processes and save money. The tools that make the Boise Service Standard possible include customer interaction software; program management tools; online customer service support; centralized, integrated systems; and a personal identification number (PIN) for each individual customer. With the Boise Service Standard, every customer can benefit from Boise's new technologies, which include the following:

- *PIN*. Assigned to every individual customer within a company, the PIN makes it possible to greet every customer by name, minimizes the need for customers to remember other codes, and provides instant access to order information.
- *Customer interaction software*. Provides detailed information on customers' past interactions with Boise. Eliminates the need for customers to repeat information, provides easy access to previous order information, and increases "done in one interaction" resolution to questions and requests.
- *Program management tools*. Provides purchasing professionals with tools to better manage their procurement processes. These tools include participation and compliance reports, reviews of requisitioner activity, proactive communications with requisitioners, and industry benchmarking reports.
- *Online customer service support*. Enables real-time, online interaction with customer service through instant messaging, live log-on assistance, Web collaboration/screen sharing, and callback request. Assists customers with online product comparisons to help minimize time-consuming searches.
- *Centralized, integrated systems*. Gives customers seamless access to Boise's full range of products, including office furniture, paper, and technology products. Provides customers with up-to-date account information from any Boise contact on point, such as customer service.

With this preponderance of available information and sophisticated technology and tools, the role of the customer service representative can become more significant in terms of *effective*, (not just efficient) interaction with the customer and its impact customer loyalty and profitability.

At Boise, the CSR has matured from a mere order-taker to a *manager of the customers* with whom she is in contact, as well as a *manager of the information*

---

[7]Peppers and Rogers Group client.

about those customers. For example, when a customer calls the CIC, the CSR might be able to identify that customer with caller ID, even before answering the phone. Next, that customer's record, including such data as recent purchases, dates of delivery, pending shipments, delivery instructions, and even past problems, might appear on the CSR's computer screen. The CSR is armed with information that offers answers to some likely questions that might arise. But this rep is also provided with questions that will help Boise learn more about that customer. For example, is that customer interested in some related or ancillary products to those previously purchased? Was that problem shipment corrected to the customer's satisfaction? Is this customer likely to defect, or make referrals?

The significance of the role of CSRs in obtaining customer information and feedback cannot be underestimated. Listening, learning, and changing the enterprise's behavior based on that learning is part of developing a Learning Relationship with a customer. Thus, it's inevitable that CSR training and compensation will be affected. If CSRs are measured by limitations in "talk time," they will keep their conversations short, period. The customer-focused CIC will reward CSRs for the percentage of inquiries and problems handled on the first call, how satisfied a customer is, and how profitable she is, how much share-of-customer data is collected, and—ideally—how much more a customer is worth at the end of a call than at the beginning.

It's undeniable that interactive capabilities have already had a profound effect on the way organizations and customers do business with each other. What we don't know yet is how much effect any one group of technologies will have. Case in point: the lowly cell phone. Not available 20 years ago, wireless communications are now a pervasive part of daily life, even in countries that don't yet have wired infrastructure. The primary change? When you dial a landline number, you are calling a place; when you call a cell phone, you are calling a person.

WIRELESS RULES: HOW NEW MOBILE TECHNOLOGIES WILL TRANSFORM CRM

Fred B. Newell
Chairman and CEO, Seklemian/Newell

Katherine N. Lemon, PhD
Associate professor of marketing, Wallace E. Carroll School of Management, Boston College

Understanding the new rules of mobile CRM (m-CRM) will be critical to any enterprise's long-term success. How will wireless impact the organization? At the highest level—CEO, CIO, CMO—enterprises must develop strategies for wireless. Within the enterprise, wireless solutions will offer new levels of efficiencies for back-end system integration, and will bring significant new challenges. And most important—on the front lines—wireless technologies will transform customer interaction and customer relationships. The best and brightest organizations will work to understand how the new wireless juggernaut is changing the rules of marketing.

As of 2001, there were almost a half-billion wireless devices in use throughout the world, and that number seems to be growing exponentially. In the United States alone (far behind much of Europe and Asia), there were more than 200 million wireless devices in use by the end of 2001. At least 40 percent of business transactions outside North America in the near future will be initiated from mobile devices. And by 2010, experts expect that, throughout the developed world, more than 40 percent of adults and 75 percent of teenagers will be using always-on wireless devices.

Understanding m-commerce and m-communication, and the new challenges and opportunities they bring, will be imperative. Enterprises need to come to grips with the *A-cubed* (A^3) customer, a customer who expects to engage with the organization *anytime, anywhere,* on *any* wireless device.[8] Note that we use the term *customer* (not *consumer*) because we firmly believe that the implications of wireless will impact both B2B and B2C enterprises (obviously, with some subtle differences).

For example, if the purchasing supervisor of a firm's best customer can check on, and do trades in, her modest ($100,000 to $250,000) personal stock portfolio, anytime, anywhere, on her personal wireless device (e.g., the Fidelity Investments Palm program), why should that person expect anything less from the supplier with whom she does several million dollars of business annually?

Wireless technology has put the power to dictate the terms of the business relationship in the hands of the customer. The customer will want to be reached *here and now*, not almost here and almost now, and be able to use whatever wireless device she chooses. From banks in Argentina to ad agencies in Australia, from communications companies in Portugal to big-box retailers in Los Angeles, the question is the same: How will wireless technologies change marketing and the practice of managing customer relationships?

Wireless technology creates a new conduit through which a firm can establish customer relationships—and it is bidirectional. We now have the capability (and burden) to have direct communications with individual customers anytime, anywhere. We now have to think about how we get our customer to first turn on her wireless device, and then (once it is on) to be willing to listen to us.

The fundamental imperative for marketers arising from wireless is that they must become customer-centric. We have seen the beginnings of this with database marketing, and later with one-to-one marketing concepts. Wireless technologies mandate a rapid evolution. While database marketing and one-to-one Learning Relationships will continue to play a significant role in business

---

[8]Frederick Newell and Katherine N. Lemon, *Wireless Rules: New Marketing Strategies for Customer Relationship Management Anytime, Anywhere* (New York: McGraw-Hill, 2001).

strategies (so companies should hang on to their customer systems and programs) the focus of *marketing* efforts must fundamentally shift. Marketers must find new ways to move from their earlier company-centric "tell and sell" (push) efforts to customer-centric "listen and learn" (pull). The communications options have changed, and businesses that fail to capture this new moment will fail in the marketplace of the have-it-now culture of wireless communications.

Wireless opens some amazing new opportunities. Time-sensitive, individual customer alerts/notices will be possible (e.g., real-time price quotes in the field, a realtor instantly notifying a client when the perfect house comes on the market, or a materials supplier notifying the company's best client when the shipment arrives or the price changes). Location-based services could be a very powerful tool (e.g., directions to facilities, offerings based on customer's current location, coupons offered when the customer is at a competitor's location).

There is a critical need for marketing executives to stay ahead of the curve in terms of understanding (and managing) customer interaction as enhanced by wireless capabilities. By engaging customers in ways that are meaningful to and create value for their customers, firms can truly begin to build customer equity.

Enterprises developing a CRM implementation strategy should, at a minimum, address the following challenges posed by emerging wireless technologies.[9]

How will it:

- Address the customers' expectation to be able to engage a firm outside of its normal time of operations and base of operations?
- Ensure accessibility for firm personnel needing access to wireless capabilities in order to deal effectively with the A^3 customer—sales force, customer service, management?
- Gain the customers' permission to market to them wirelessly (i.e., opt in) and to signal their interest for further communication and interaction?
- Determine where the customer's information will reside and who will own it?
- Leverage existing systems and programs (inventory, production, and customer databases, CRM, and advertising)?
- Integrate wireless technologies with legacy systems?
- Determine the payment systems/business models needed to reap financial rewards from wireless CRM solutions?
- Take advantage of the new opportunities for firm/customer interaction available via wireless technologies?
- Get the necessary firmwide multidisciplinary buy-in to address wireless?
- Address vexing issues such as security, privacy, and wireless technological problems (incompatibility, multiple platforms, etc.) in a wireless solution?

[9]Claudia Flisi, "Mobile's New Floating World: As Voice and Data Move to the Mobile Phone, Will Commerce Be Far Behind?" *International Herald Tribune* (December 6, 2000), p. 10-B; Gartner Group: *www.gartnergroup.com*; Don Tapscott, "It's Beginning to Look a Lot Like a Wireless World," *Computerworld* (October 23, 2000), *www.computerworld.com*; The Yankee Group: *www.yankeegroup.com*.

- Determine and assess possible partners (carriers, device manufactures, and wireless application service providers (WASPs)) as a firm develops its m-CRM solutions?
- Manage the timing of the implementation of wireless solution?
- Create a wireless solution that is viable—that creates value for a firm and its customers but won't put you in the tank?

Each new interactive technology will offer consumers new ways to interact with one another and with the companies that provide them with the things and services they want. And each new technology will offer the enterprise with new opportunities to hear from customers and to continue to learn more in order to build greater and greater value.

SUMMARY

We have shown how, for the individual customer, interacting with an enterprise should be a fluid, multidimensional experience. The customer provides feedback to the enterprise about her preferences, her challenges, her red flags, and her hot buttons. The customer, by telling the enterprise her needs, makes it easier to buy there. The enterprise, by interacting with the customer, gets the opportunity to learn more about the customer. Together, the customer and the enterprise nurture an ongoing Learning Relationship that is unique. No competitor knows the information the enterprise gathers from the individual customer. The enterprise is in a prime position to increase its share of customer with this individual so long as it continues to learn from her, and act on that learning.

Enterprises, however, cannot simply interact with individual customers and expect them to remain loyal. The Learning Relationship must mature even further. The enterprise needs to address another task in IDIC by *customizing* the relationship with the customer—by modifying how it behaves with her, how it communicates with her, and how it manufactures products or provides services for her. A relationship can't exist without customization; without a change in behavior that results from feedback, the best a company can do is give the appearance of a relationship. But how can customization be done effectively and efficiently? We will take a closer look at that issue in Chapter 10, after we consider the privacy issue that inevitably arises when we address customer interaction and data.

FOOD FOR THOUGHT

1. You've been appointed as the new CMO for a large packaged goods company. Your CEO has decided that your company will be the premiere "relationship" company in your industry.
   - What could that mean?

- How will you execute that?
- What will you use as data collection tools?
- What role will interactivity play in your plans?
- Is there a role for e-mail? For wireless?
  Be as specific as you can.

2. Now imagine you work for a large automotive company and answer all the questions in number 1. Are your answers different? Why?

3. Now answer the questions in number 1 for:
   - A natural gas company
   - A retail shoe chain
   - A company that makes pneumatic valves for construction
   - The U.S. Navy
   - Other kinds of organizations (you decide)

GLOSSARY

Customer Interaction Center (CIC)   Once the lowly call center, the CIC is now pulling together data from Web and e-mail interactions for a smarter and smarter breed of customer service representatives (CSRs).

Online analytical processing (OLAP)   OLAP tools enable users to analyze data using their own queries.

Unsolicited commercial e-mail (UCE)   Often referred to as spam.

Privacy and Customer Feedback

9
Chapter

Getting customer information is easy. You can buy it from the government, from list brokers, from competitors, even. But getting customer information from customers is not easy, as we saw in the last chapter. Yet it's absolutely necessary, as the only real competitive advantage an enterprise can have derives from the information it gathers from a customer, which enables it to do something for him that no one else can. Competitors without a customer's personal information are at a disadvantage. That is the one compelling reason an enterprise must interact with its customers and reward them for revealing their personal information. It is also the main reason why an enterprise should never misuse the information it owns about a customer, or violate a customer's trust—because a customer is the most valuable asset the firm has, and the ability to get a customer to share information depends so much on the comfort level a customer has with giving that information to an enterprise.

Interestingly, for the first time since we all became aware of privacy as an issue, enterprises and customers share a common interest: protecting and securing the customer's information. At least that's true of customers who are thinking about the implications of their far-flung data, and of enterprises that are building their value through strategies designed to build the value of the customer base.

In this chapter, we will first look at some general privacy issues and how they are being addressed, and will look to experts Larry Ponemon, Seth Godin, Josh Stailey, and Stacey Scruggs for help in understanding some of these complexities. We will next examine the distinct issues raised by data held and exchanged online, and will hear from Esther Dyson about specific online privacy issues.

Every day, millions of people provide personally identifiable information about themselves to data collection experts. As a result, an average U.S. consumer is buffeted by roughly a million marketing messages a year across all communications media, or about 2,750 a day.[1] Consumers sometimes unknowingly

---

[1] John Hagel and Marc Singer, "Private Lives," *The McKinsey Quarterly*, no. 1 (2000), p. 6.

divulge their personal data during commercial transactions, financial arrangements, and survey responses. The Web has escalated the privacy debate to new heights. Never before has technology enabled companies to acquire information about customers so easily. Watchdog privacy advocates and government regulators are mobilizing against the threat to a consumer's right to privacy.

Consider the following:

- Polls are showing privacy concerns at an all-time high.
- The United States and Europe are in the midst of a serious trade disagreement over how personal data is to be collected and managed.
- Privacy policies of individual companies vary tremendously, as does compliance with these policies (largely self-generated and self-enforced).
- Privacy preferences vary tremendously among individuals.
- Courts around the world are awarding significant damages to consumers and Internet users over claims of privacy violation.
- More than 100 new privacy laws were introduced in the 105th (1997–1998) U.S. Congress, nearly four times the number introduced in the 1993–1994 session.
- New technologies of data collection, Internet monitoring, online surveillance, data mining, automatic mailing, personal searching, and identity spoofing are rolling out into the electronic marketplace every month.
- Personalized, customized products and services over the Internet—most of which require users to provide more personal information than they have ever given to companies before—are growing.[2]

> In the twenty-first century, customer data are the most valuable investments of an enterprise, and information about a particular customer that no other competitor has is the most valuable enterprise asset. For a customer-based enterprise to be successful in this century, it needs to protect that information—to hold it sacred.

And yet, in the twenty-first century, customer data are the most valuable investments of an enterprise, and information about a particular customer that no other competitor has is the most valuable enterprise asset. For a customer-based enterprise to be successful in this century, it needs to protect that information—to hold it sacred. Privacy and personalization are inextricably interwoven. Customers who feel like they could lose control over their own information are not likely to become willing participants in a dialogue. Privacy should not be taken lightly by the customer-based enterprise.

Ironically, Americans seem to think privacy is fairly important, but a lot of U.S. popular culture has been inspired by snooping: So-called reality television programs such as *Survivor, Temptation Island,* and *Big Brother* have enabled viewers to peer into the private lives of ordinary *other* people. It has become a cultural norm to be "flies on the walls" of a stranger's personal conversations when his cell phone rings while riding a bus or a plane. Overall, voyeurism is in vogue—so long as no one is snooping on *me.*

---

[2]Charles Jennings and Lori Fena, *The Hundredth Window* (New York: The Free Press, 2000).

For the enterprise interested in increasing its share of each customer's business, there has to be a balance between getting enough information from customers to help them do business with the firm while respecting their right to lead a private life. The dilemma for the customer-strategy firm is how to remain sensitive to privacy while improving the business to suit each customer's individual needs. This is in stark contrast to a product-selling company, which likely views privacy as simply a roadblock on the road to profitability.

The privacy debate continues as the interactive era matures. Despite the ongoing controversy of a person's right to privacy, customers find it difficult to quantify the damage they incur when their privacy has been violated. It is difficult to place a monetary value on the abuse of personal information, unlike other crimes, such as a car theft. For that matter, what does it cost when someone's credit card number is exposed to a third party, who does not use it?

Our society subscribes to two antithetical beliefs simultaneously: that people should have the right to remain inconspicuous to others, but also have the right to learn the identity of someone else when we need to. For instance, a consumer might want anonymity when shopping, especially online. But the same person might support a system that reveals the identity of computer hackers or those who plant e-viruses. To ponder further, our society requires the display of license plate numbers, for public revelation of each automobile owner. Should we also have "license plates" for Internet users so it would be easy to track them down when they commit an offense such as identity theft or launching a virus maliciously?

Have we changed our opinion of privacy since security has become a greater priority as of September 11, 2001?

Besides the Web, privacy concerns have long existed in traditional shopping methods. Walk into a supermarket or department store and the customer is often asked to hand over a loyalty card in exchange for a purchase coupon. But what if he buys something in a retail store, and simply uses a standard bank credit card? In such a case, the store has very little way of tracing the information about that shopping transaction, and may have difficulty linking it to a customer, unless the customer is having the merchandise delivered. (It should be noted that the credit card company will have a complete record of that transactional information, for that customer, store to store.) Nordstrom Inc. has found a way to gather information from nearly all in-store purchases, regardless of payment type. Its store personnel ask customers for permission to affix a bar code to the back of a customer's own (non-Nordstrom) credit card, giving the store the capability to track purchases made with other credit cards.

Profiling of a customer's personal data is standard protocol in the direct-mail industry and has been for nearly a century. Traditionally, this has meant that catalog retailers and credit card companies have collected names and addresses for their own use, and have sold or rented those lists to other direct marketers. Phone a catalog merchant and the buying process involves divulging an address and phone number. For that matter, call L.L. Bean or many other catalog companies and the customer service representative might even be able to identify the customer before he states his name, thanks to the caller ID technology integrated into the company's call center. In an informal customer survey, some shoppers said they did not find this an invasion of privacy and that it even made them feel as if they were getting more personalized treatment.[3]

Remembering a customer and his logistical information makes it easier for him to order and also leads him to believe he is important to the enterprise. The Internet offers the greatest opportunity to date for gathering personal customer information, as long as a mutually valuable relationship between provider and consumer is honored. Over time, data collected about Web site visitors empower companies with a keen ability to identify their most valuable customers and deploy relevant marketing campaigns (we talk more about customer relationships on the Web in other chapters).[4]

> Managing customer relationships in the interactive age requires enterprises to collect information about customers in a "virtuous cycle" in which they can deliver additional value to individual customers.

Enterprises gather information about their customers and create loyalty programs to build lasting relationships. But some customers are sophisticated and enjoy comparing and contrasting products to find the best price and most efficient service. The products themselves have grown increasingly complex and often require more research before purchasing (i.e., a new computer or DVD player). The goal, therefore, is for the enterprise to find out as much information *about* a customer and use it *for* that customer to make his buying experience more valuable to him in various ways. Managing customer relationships in the interactive age requires enterprises to collect information about customers in a "virtuous cycle" in which they can deliver additional value to individual customers. Once the customer begins receiving personalized attention and customized products, he is motivated to divulge more information about himself.

Trust, as we discussed in Chapter 2, is always critical. Customers are dubious of unfamiliar enterprises that have not been recommended to them. A study conducted in 2000 by The Institute for the Future and Peppers and Rogers Group found that 85 percent of adults and 73 percent of teens are concerned about threats to their privacy.[5] While both teens and adults have shown that they want customized offerings and the advantages companies can give them by tracking their data, it is essential to guarantee that the customized benefits provided will not jeopardize their privacy. Customers must know that the company will use that data in a limited way for services agreed on in advance. Without such trust, customization is not a benefit. Once earned, trust in an enterprise enhances customer loyalty. But enterprises need to address customer concerns about privacy, offer guarantees, and stick to them. Those that gain the customer's trust first often will have the first-mover advantage. (We'll be talking more about privacy pledges later in this chapter.)

[3]"Do You Know Who's Watching You? Do You Care?" *New York Times* (November 11, 1999).

[4]"Capturing Visitor Feedback," CyberDialogue, March 1997.

[5]Peppers and Rogers Group/Institute for the Future, "The Future of Consumer Direct: Shopping Behavior in the Age of Interactivity" (1999), p. 74.

Some believe that a customer might be more trusting of an enterprise and would provide the personal information that can foster a mutually beneficial relationship if the enterprise simply first asks the customer his permission to do so. The relationship in which a customer has agreed to receive personalized messages and customized products forms the basis of *permission marketing*, an ideology Seth Godin discusses next.

PERMISSION MARKETING[6]

Seth Godin
Author

Two hundred years ago, natural resources and raw materials were scarce. People needed land to grow food, metal to turn into pots, and silicates and other natural elements to make windows for houses. Tycoons who cornered the market in these and other resources made a fortune. By making a market in a scarce resource, you can make a profit.

With the birth of the Industrial Revolution, and the growth of our consumer economy, the resource scarcity shifted from raw materials to finished goods. Factories were at capacity. The great industrialists, like Carnegie and Ford, earned their millions by providing what the economy demanded. Marketers could call the shots, because other options were scarce.

Once factories caught up with demand, marketers developed brands that consumers would desire and pay a premium to own. People were willing to walk a mile for a Camel, and knew things go better with Coke. When brands were new and impressive, owning the right brand was vital.

But in today's free market there are plenty of factories, plenty of brands, and way too many choices. With just a little effort and a little savings we can get almost anything we want. You can find a TV set in every house in this country. People throw away their broken microwave ovens instead of having them repaired.

This surplus situation, or abundance of goods, is especially clear when it comes to information and services. Making another copy of a software program or printing another CD costs almost nothing. Bookstores compete to offer 50,000, 100,000, or even 1 million different books—each for less than $25. There's a huge surplus of intellectual property and services out there.

Imagine a tropical island populated by people with simple needs and plenty of resources. You won't find a bustling economy there. That's because you need

---

[6]Excerpted from the book *Permission Marketing* by Seth Godin (New York: Simon & Schuster, 1999).

two things in order to have an economy: people who want things, and a scarcity of things they want. Without scarcity, there's no basis for an economy.

When there's an abundance of any commodity, the value of that commodity plummets. If a commodity can be produced at will and costs little or nothing to create, it's not likely to be scarce, either. That's the situation with information and services today. They're abundant and cheap. Information on the Web, for example, is plentiful and free.

Software provides another example. The most popular Web server is not made by Microsoft or Netscape. And it doesn't cost $1,000 or $10,000. It's called Apache, and it's created by a loosely knit consortium of programmers, and it's totally free. Free to download, free to use. As resources go, information is not scarce.

There is one critical resource, though, that is in chronically short supply. Bill Gates has no more than you do. And even Warren Buffet can't buy more. That scarce resource is *time*. And in light of today's information glut, that means there's a vast shortage of *attention*.

> Consumers are now willing to pay handsomely to save time, while marketers are eager to pay bundles to get attention.

The combined shortage of time and attention is unique in today's information age. Consumers are now willing to pay handsomely to save time, while marketers are eager to pay bundles to get attention.

Interruption Marketing is the enemy of anyone trying to save time. By constantly interrupting what we are doing at any given moment, the marketer who interrupts us not only tends to fail at selling his product, but wastes our most coveted commodity, time. In the long run, therefore, Interruption Marketing is doomed as a mass marketing tool. The cost to the consumer is just too high.

The alternative is Permission Marketing, which offers the consumer an opportunity to *volunteer* to be marketed to. By talking only to volunteers, Permission Marketing guarantees that consumers pay more attention to the marketing message. It allows marketers to tell their story calmly and succinctly, without fear of being interrupted by competitors or Interruption Marketers. It serves both consumers and marketers in a symbiotic exchange.

Permission Marketing encourages consumers to participate in a long-term, interactive marketing campaign in which they are rewarded in some way for paying attention to increasingly relevant messages. Imagine your marketing message being read by 70 percent of the prospects you send it to (not 5 percent or even 1 percent). Then imagine that more than 35 percent responded. That's what happens when you interact with your prospects one at a time, with individual messages, exchanged with their permission over time.

Permission marketing is anticipated, personal, relevant:
- *Anticipated*. People look forward to hearing from you.
- *Personal*. The messages are directly related to the individual.
- *Relevant*. The marketing is about something the prospect is interested in.

I know what you're thinking. There's a catch. If you have to personalize every customer message, that's prohibitive. If you're still thinking within the framework of traditional marketing, you're right. But in today's information age, working with customers individually is not as difficult as it sounds. Permission Marketing takes the cost of interrupting the consumer and spreads it out, over not one message, but dozens of messages. And this leverage leads to substantial competitive advantages and profits. While your competition continues to interrupt strangers with mediocre results, your Permission Marketing campaign is turning strangers into friends and friends into customers.

The easiest way to contrast the Interruption Marketer with the Permission Marketer is with an analogy about getting married. It also serves to exemplify how sending multiple individualized messages over time works better than a single message, no matter how impressive that single message is.

TWO WAYS TO GET MARRIED

The Interruption Marketer buys an extremely expensive suit. New shoes. Fashionable accessories. Then, working with the best database and marketing strategies, selects the demographically ideal singles bar.

Walking into the singles bar, the Interruption Marketer marches up to the nearest person and proposes marriage. If turned down, the Interruption Marketer repeats the process on every person in the bar.

If the Interruption Marketer comes up empty-handed after spending the entire evening proposing, it is obvious that the blame should be placed on the suit and the shoes. The tailor is fired. The strategy expert who picked the bar is fired. And the Interruption Marketer tries again at a different singles bar.

If this sounds familiar, it should. It's the way most large marketers look at the world. They hire an agency. They build fancy ads. They "research" the ideal place to run the ads. They interrupt people and hope that one in a hundred will go ahead and buy something. Then, when they fail, they fire their agency!

The other way to get married is a lot more fun, a lot more rational, and a lot more successful. It's called dating.

A Permission Marketer goes on a date. If it goes well, the two of them go on another date. And then another. Until, after 10 or 12 dates, both sides can really communicate with each other about their needs and desires. After 20 dates they meet each other's families. Finally, after three or four months of dating, the Permission Marketer proposes marriage.

Permission Marketing is just like dating. It turns strangers into friends and friends into lifetime customers. Many of the rules of dating apply, and so do many of the benefits.

FIVE STEPS TO DATING YOUR CUSTOMER

Every interaction must offer the prospective customer an incentive for volunteering. In the vernacular of dating, that means you have to offer something that makes it interesting enough to go out on a first date. A first date, after all, represents a big investment in time, money, and ego. So there had better be reason enough to volunteer.

Without a selfish reason to continue dating, your new potential customer (and your new potential date) will refuse you a second chance. If you don't provide a benefit to the consumer for paying attention, your offer will suffer the same fate as every other ad campaign that's vying for their attention. It will be ignored.

The incentive you offer to the customer can range from information, to entertainment, to a sweepstakes, to outright payment for the prospect's attention. But the incentive must be overt, obvious, and clearly delivered.

This is the most obvious difference between Permission Marketing and Interruption Marketing. Interruption Marketers spend all their time interrupting strangers, in an almost pitiful attempt to bolster popularity and capture attention. Permission Marketers spend as little time and money talking to strangers as they can. Instead they move as quickly as they can to turn strangers into prospects who choose to "opt in" to a series of communication.

Second, using the attention offered by the consumer, the marketer offers a curriculum over time, teaching the consumer about the product or service he has to offer. The Permission Marketer knows that the first date is an opportunity to sell the other person on a second date. Every step along the way has to be interesting, useful, and relevant.

Since the prospect has agreed to pay attention, it's much easier to teach him about your product. Instead of filling each ensuing message with entertainment designed to attract attention or with sizzle designed to attract the attention of strangers, the Permission Marketer is able to focus on product benefits—specific, focused ways this product will help that prospect. Without question, this ability to talk freely over time is the most powerful element of this marketing approach.

> The goal is to motivate the consumer to give more and more permission over time. Permission to gather more data about the customer's personal life, or hobbies, or interests. Permission to offer a new category of product for the customer's consideration. Permission to provide a product sample. The range of permission you can obtain from a customer is very wide and limited only by its relevance to the customer.

The third step involves reinforcing the incentive. Over time, an incentive wears out. Just as your date may tire of even the finest restaurant, the prospective customer may show fatigue with the same repeated incentive. The Permission Marketer must work to reinforce the incentive, to be sure that the attention continues. This is surprisingly easy. Because this is a two-way dialogue, not a narcissistic monologue, the marketer can adjust the incentives being offered and fine-tune them for *each* prospect.

Along with reinforcing the incentive, the fourth step is to increase the level of permission the marketer receives from the potential customer. Now I won't go into detail on what step of the dating process this corresponds to, but in marketing terms, the goal is to motivate the consumer to give more and more permission over time. Permission to gather more data about the customer's personal life, or hobbies, or interests. Permission to offer a new category of product for the customer's consideration. Permission to provide a product sample. The range of permission you can obtain from a customer is very wide and limited only by its relevance to the customer.

Over time, the marketer uses the permission he's obtained to change consumer behavior—that is, get them to say "I do." That's how you turn permission into profits. After permission is granted, that's how it becomes a truly significant asset for the marketer. Now you can live happily ever after by repeating the aforementioned process while selling your customer more and more products. In other words, the fifth and final step is to leverage your permission into a profitable situation for both of you. Remember, you have access to the most valuable thing a customer can offer—attention.

PERMISSION IS AN INVESTMENT

Nothing good is free, and that goes double for permission. Acquiring solid, deep permission from targeted customers is an investment.

What is one permission worth? According to their annual report, America Online has paid as much as $300 to get one new customer. American Express invests nearly $150 to get a new cardholder. Does American Express earn enough in fees to justify this expense? Not at all. But the other benefits associated with acquiring the permission to market to a card member outweigh the high cost. Amex sells its customers a wide range of products, not just an American Express card. They also use sophisticated database management tools to track customer behavior so they can tailor offers to individuals. They leverage their permission to increase revenue.

One of the leading brokerage houses on Wall Street is currently paying $15 in media acquisition costs just for permission to call a potential customer on the phone! Yes, it's that expensive, and yes, it's worth even more than that. They've discovered that the yield from an anticipated, welcomed, personal phone call is so much higher than a cold call during dinner that they're willing to pay handsomely for the privilege.

While these (and other) marketers have discovered the power of permission, many Interruption Marketers have found, to their chagrin, that the cost of generating one new customer is rapidly approaching the net present value of that consumer. In other words, they're close to losing money on every customer (and the joke is they try to make it up in volume).

Permission Marketing cuts through the clutter and allows a marketer to speak to prospects as friends, not strangers. This personalized, anticipated, frequent, and relevant communication has infinitely more impact than a random message displayed in a random place at a random moment.

Think about choosing a nice restaurant for dinner. If you learn about a restaurant from a cold-calling telemarketer or from an unsolicited direct-mail piece, you're likely to ignore the recommendation. But if a trusted friend offers a restaurant recommendation, you're likely to try it out.

Permission Marketing lets you turn strangers, folks who might otherwise ignore your unsolicited offer, into people willing to pay attention when your message arrives in an expected, appreciated way.

An Interruption Marketer looks for a job by sending a resume to one thousand strangers. A Permission Marketer gets a job by focusing on one company and networking with it, consulting for it, and working with it until the company trusts him enough to offer him a full-time position.

A book publisher that uses Interruption Marketing sells children's books by shipping them to bookstores, hoping that the right audience will stumble across them. A Permission Marketer builds book clubs at every school in the country.

An Interruption Marketer sells a new product by introducing it on national TV. A Permission Marketer sells a new product by informing all his existing customers about a way to get a free sample.

PERMISSION MARKETING IS AN OLD CONCEPT WITH NEW RELEVANCE

Permission Marketing isn't as glamorous as hiring Steven Spielberg to direct a commercial starring a bevy of supermodels. It isn't as easy as running an ad a few more times. It isn't as cheap as building a Web site and hoping that people find it on a search engine. In fact, it's hard work.

Worst of all, Permission Marketing requires patience. Permission Marketing campaigns grow over time—the opposite of what most marketers look for these days. And Permission Marketing requires a leap of faith. Even a bad interruption campaign gets some results right away, while a permission campaign requires infrastructure and a belief in the durability of the permission concept before it blossoms with success.

But unlike Interruption Marketing, Permission Marketing is a measurable process. It evolves over time for every company that uses it. It becomes an increasingly valuable asset. The more you commit to Permission Marketing campaigns, the better they work over time. And these fast-moving, leveragable processes are the key to success in our cluttered age.

So if Permission Marketing is so effective, and the ideas behind it are not really new, why was the concept not used with effectiveness years ago?

Permission Marketing has been around forever (or at least as long as dating), but it takes advantage of new technology better than any other forms of marketing. The Internet is the greatest direct mail medium of all time, and the low cost of frequent interaction makes it ideal for Permission Marketing.

Originally, the Internet captured the attention of Interruption Marketers. They rushed in, spent billions of dollars applying their Interruption Marketing techniques, and discovered almost total failure. Permission Marketing is the tool that unlocks the power of the Internet. The leverage it brings to this new medium, combined with the pervasive clutter that infects the Internet and virtually every other medium, makes Permission Marketing the most powerful trend in marketing for the next decade.

As new forms of media develop and clutter becomes ever more intense, it's the asset of permission that will generate profits for marketers.

Although we talk about privacy as though it were a single topic, it is really an umbrella term, and if you ask customers what bothers them about privacy, you will get several answers.

- The most common is a concern about criminal activity—misuse of stolen credit card numbers, usurpation of identity. This nearly always comes back to the issue of data security.
- Distinct from the first point is a concern about others knowing things about them they would rather not have "out there" as common knowledge.
- The idea that they would rather not be bothered if they don't want to be— the spam is driving them crazy and the marketing calls at dinner are a nuisance.

Josh Stailey and Stacey Scruggs present a few additional issues to consider in a discussion about privacy.

PRIVACY ISSUES FOR THE INFORMATION AGE

Josh W. Stailey
President, Memegraphics, Inc.

Stacey Scruggs
Development Associate, United Visiting Nurse Association

Privacy is a highly charged issue because of the difficulty society—individuals, organizations, government—has in keeping up with the pace of technology. A technology may mature in a few years, but it could take decades for society to become fully comfortable with the changes wrought.[7] Over the past 15 years, an enterprise's capability to gather, manage, analyze, and use data on an individual's preferences, habits, and choices has improved dramatically (though the enterprise's capability to deal with this data in a single, manageable way is still an issue). Further, it is commonly accepted that information has value and, if appropriate, customer information in particular has a value that can be exchanged in a complex "marketplace."

But it took the advent of the "e-world"—e-commerce, e-CRM, e-business, and so on—in the late 1990s to expose the gap between capability and comfort as a chasm. The e-world brought the issue of privacy to the front as no other

---

[7]Each time there has been renewed interest in protecting privacy, it has been in reaction to new technology. First, in the years before 1890, came cameras, telephones, and high-speed publishing; second, around 1970, came the development of personal computers; and third, in the late 1990s, the advent of personal computers and the World Wide Web. Robert Ellis Smith, "Ben Franklin's Web Site: Privacy and Curiosity From Plymouth Rock to the Internet," *Privacy Journal* (2000).

innovation had been able to do. Now there are sides, as well as regulations, laws, proposals, challenges, hearings, lobbyists, and advocates. Privacy has become an industry, centered on the issue of customer information.[8]

There are three generally accepted layers of customer information: (1) vital statistics, (2) transactional data, and (3) individual data. The debate over consumer privacy spills into the latter two, which generate the most conflict and rhetoric.

VITAL STATISTICS

Vital statistics include life-stage events: for individuals—birth, baptism, marriage, divorce, death, and major legal circumstances; for businesses—corporate ownership, bankruptcy, justice system interventions; and government-required personal information—voter registration, census, personal and property licensing or registration. Most citizens accept that the public has a need for information about these events and are comfortable with the fact that some of this data lies in the public domain.

Businesses cover most of these issues in their contractual negotiations. In addition, most industrialized nations have in place legal safeguards on nonessential data (e.g., secondary census data, vehicle ownership records, etc.) A privacy debate here becomes a conflict between individual privacy and "public good."

TRANSACTIONAL DATA

In today's world, most transactions are so simple as to become invisible, yet records are kept on everyone. A wired, well-to-do American has many transaction "partners." Visa processes more than $1 trillion in transactions every year. Credit-reporting agencies track and rate almost every individual or household in North America. The privacy debate here is one of ownership rights. What can a business do with transactional information?

INDIVIDUAL DATA

Any nontransactional data fits here, and it is often organized from the standpoint of the industry. The total data about any one customer is formidable, but it is scattered among dozens (if not hundreds) of suppliers. Further, some of this data

---

[8]"Politicians can't talk enough about privacy, and are rushing to pass laws to protect it. Increasingly, business and technology are seen as the culprits. . . . Billions of dollars are at stake. A new sector of the economy seems to be coming into being. Among entrepreneurs and venture capitalists it already has a name. It's known as the privacy space." Toby Lester, "The Reinvention of Privacy," *The Atlantic Monthly* (March 2001), pp. 27–39.

is anonymous because the "customer" is a PC-based cookie. In a business-to-business environment, the landscape is more complex, involving multiple individuals, as well as corporate practices and policies.

One unique form of individual data—medical and health information—incorporates all three types of data. In general, medical privacy issues are not only more complex, but far more emotional.

The sum is a complex matrix of data about an individual, collected and stored by dozens of online and offline organizations. Some of the critical characteristics of this matrix are:

- *The data is "owned" by the collector.* Some countries impose restrictions on the collector's ability to sell, distribute, or trade existing customer data—and to collect new data—but they still own what they have collected.[9]
- *The data matrix is vast, interlinked, and fluid.* New data are being added continually, and most new data are exchanged widely. Any individual who wanted to "repossess" his data would find the task impossible, especially if he wanted to remain a functioning member of society.[10]
- *Today, individual and business-level customer information has value to those who "own" it.* Catalog merchandisers regularly sell customer names to one another. Data aggregation is a large and profitable industry. But the individual cannot realize any value for his information, or in most cases prevent the process from happening. And the industry has failed to make a case or show value to the customer for access and use of that data.
- *Channels—chains of enterprises that make, distribute, and add value to products and services—add layers of complexity to the privacy issue.* Now a company can be held responsible for privacy violations committed by partners, suppliers, and resellers.

[9]"The privacy debate is, essentially, a debate about the control of personal information. . . . What is unsettling to a lot of people is the idea that personal data—in this case, one's very life signs—might be converted into information that could be exchanged, bought, or sold for secondary use without one's knowledge or consent." Ibid.

[10]People give away vast amounts of valuable information about themselves, wittingly or unwittingly, by using credit cards, signing up for supermarket discount programs, joining frequent-flyer clubs, sending e-mail, browsing on the Internet, using electronic tollbooth passes, mailing in rebate forms, entering sweepstakes, and calling toll-free numbers. Such behaviors are essentially voluntary (although a somewhat abstract case can be made that they are the product of what has been called "the tyranny of convenience"), but many other ways of participating in everyday life basically require the divulging of information about oneself. A person can't function in American society without regularly using a Social Security number, which has become a de facto national ID number—and which, as such, is the key to all sorts of private information. If one needs a mortgage, as almost everybody buying a home does, one has to turn over pages of detailed background data, some of which banks can then sell to whomever they like. People who buy prescription drugs now leave a trail of highly sensitive (and therefore valuable) personal information that is often gathered up and sold. The proliferation of surveillance cameras in public places means that one's comings and goings are increasingly a matter of public record. Ibid.

- *A case can be made for sharing data with companies and marketers.* While maintaining reasonable levels of privacy, marketers can utilize customer data to simplify and enrich individual customers, saving them time and money.
- *With a few exceptions, law and regulation are applied to specific privacy issues.* The world of commerce is becoming a minefield of "spot" regulation, with more on the way.

A broader resolution of privacy issues will happen only when several key questions are surfaced and resolved.

WHO OWNS CUSTOMER INFORMATION, AND WHO SHOULD PROFIT FROM IT?

The winners will be enterprises that can retain specific, personal information—and use it profitably—while delivering clearly perceived value to that customer. They must agree with the customer on the value of that information and provide an explicit bargain for the use of it. The swift alternative is regulation that forces the marketplace to divest information back to the individual customer, which an enterprise earns back again via explicit bargains. The likely approach will be market-based, but it will eventually reach the same goal: customers who are willing to divulge information in return for convenience, knowledge, money, time—something they consider to be valuable.[11]

IS ANONYMITY AN ACCEPTABLE, WORKABLE SOLUTION TO PRIVACY?

If the market-driven process (just described) fails to work—or to move quickly enough—customers may end the debate by becoming invisible to marketers. The weapon of choice is the *privacy intermediary*, most commonly available online through software called *anonymizers*. The same approach can work offline: specialist intermediaries—trusted agents—can negotiate and purchase on behalf of individuals without ever divulging names. The bonus would be lower prices gained from aggregating multiple customers under a single intermediary.

---

[11]"We believe that consumers are going to take ownership of information about themselves and demand value in exchange for it. . . . Consumers probably will not bargain with vendors on their own, however. We anticipate that companies we call infomediaries will seize the opportunity to act as custodians, agents, and brokers of customer information, marketing it to businesses on consumers' behalf while protecting their privacy at the same time." John Hagel and Jeffrey F. Rayport, "The Coming Battle for Customer Information," *Harvard Business Review* (January 1997).

IS THE CURE WORSE THAN THE DISEASE?

Can robust privacy make life more difficult and costly for the average consumer? For the average consumer, privacy means increased complexity in a world that is already too busy. Further, businesses trying to extend their relationships with customers of any type are facing difficult systems and business policy changes to ensure compliance with the myriad rules and regulations currently in place or expected shortly. To comply with existing laws and conventions, companies bombard customers with boilerplate messages designed to relieve the corporation of liability. To ensure some level of interaction, enterprises are asking for multiple levels of permission—as many as a dozen checkboxes for different types of messages. Yet no one has a sense of when the consumer will say "enough" and simply walk away from the relationship.

Simple solutions are not the answer either. Today, Americans can opt out of direct mail through an association's "do not send" list. But we have to opt out of everything, including the handful of catalogs we shop regularly. Choose to accept even one, and they must opt in for anything a marketer wants to mail to them. Too much of these issues and the "value" offered by most marketers will disappear.[12]

Is compliance impossible? How can an organization "privatize" its data resources in an open and complex business environment? Robust privacy requires data security measures that are difficult in today's light-speed business environment. Often, customer information is integrated real time from multiple databases, some of which may not belong to the marketer. Ensuring that business partners and channels adhere to the letter and spirit of a company's privacy policy may be currently impossible. And in a permission-driven country, simply getting the okay to integrate the data may be more trouble than it's worth.

PATH TO PRIVACY

How can privacy managers plot a path between the lawyers and the marketers? It will not be easy, and it will change constantly, but there are a few signposts:

1. The goal of becoming a trusted agent is a worthy one. But it has to start and end with the customer(s): Companies will find and serve the customer's definition of trust, not their own. The enterprise will know how they are working, because the test for trusted agents is simple: Either they help relieve the issues and anxieties around privacy and begin to propagate, or they don't and begin to die out.

---

[12]Patricia Odell discusses how the Gramm-Leach-Bliley Act has prompted some financial institutions to halt data sharing with third parties altogether for a variety of reasons, including the costs of building opt-out systems, a reassessment of nonaffiliates and reputation risk management. See Patricia Odell, "Time's Up for Banks," *Direct* (May 1, 2001), pp. 1–29.

2. Enterprises must develop a strong business rule-making capability. In most companies, the data capture and management capabilities far outstrip the organization's capability to manage customer interaction processes around that data. Every new customer interaction requires a new rule for data management and use. Most enterprises cannot manage the complexity after the first few interactions.

3. Permissions:
   - An enterprise will need to get a customer's permission first or risk losing any chance for trusted interaction.
   - Honor them always. Mess up once and the enterprise is back to square one.
   - Change them rarely. The customer wants simplicity.

As each organization moves to globalize its operations, its leaders will need to be aware of and comply with the many legal requirements of the nations in which they serve customers, and they will need to respect the individual cultures of these countries. Moreover, enterprises need to protect the accuracy, transmission, and accessibility of their customer records. In the next few sections, we examine how enterprises protect the precious customer data they collect. We also peer into the many differences between privacy rules in the United States and Europe.

INDIVIDUAL PRIVACY AND DATA PROTECTION

Larry A. Ponemon, PhD
Chairman, The Ponemon Institute
Partner, Peppers and Rogers Group

Businesses and governments have a responsibility to maintain the security and integrity of personal data that they process. The competitive pressure to profit from data collected about a customer by analyzing it for the purposes of personalization and customization collides with privacy concerns. Advocates believe it can help customers save time and effort, supply them with better targeted offers and improved customer service. When users provide personally identifiable information during a transaction, they are looking for assurance that their personal data will not be misused. The competitive pressure to profit from data is, however, running up against increased privacy concerns. While it can be traced to a computer, most data collected are anonymous. It is when a user provides personally identifiable information by filling out a form or volunteering personal information during a transaction that the concerns of potential abuse grow stronger. Other areas of particular concern include linking personally identifiable profiles with more extensive demographic or credit card information, or connecting and reselling information from disparate data sources.

SIDEBAR 9.1

Chief Privacy Officers Emerge to Protect Customer Privacy

Some enterprises, recognizing the new importance of the spectrum of privacy issues, particularly if their business faces global trading issues, have created the full-time position of Chief Privacy Officer instead of assigning this responsibility to existing positions, such as the Chief Information Officer or the Chief Technology Officer. Corporate icons like American Express, Citigroup, Prudential Insurance, and AT&T have all hired privacy officers who in many cases report directly to the chairman or the CEO. At the Internet Advertising Bureau's Privacy Forum, Rich LeFurgy, IAB chairman and general partner, Walden VC, explained, "At the center of all business models is consumers. Protecting their PII (personally identifiable information) is the key to the future."

The responsibilities of the CPO (often undertaken by the Chief Information Officer) include addressing the following:

- How does the company ensure that consumers will be notified about what information is collected?
- How can the company protect personal data from unauthorized use?
- How does a company provide consumers access to their personal information and the ability to change it?
- How does a company have guidelines for the use of personal information?
- Does it have a complete data-flow map showing the flow of information?
- What procedures ensure consumers are notified of changes in privacy policies?
- What procedures exist to ensure business partners use personal information according to policy?
- How often does the company train employees on fair information and privacy practices?

While most privacy discussions focus on business-to-consumer (B2C) interactions, new business models in the business-to-business (B2B) community have also raised concerns. B2B exchanges are joint efforts by companies to buy and sell goods. Designed to save millions of dollars in back-office costs, the sites compile huge amounts of data and are often jointly owned by corporate rivals. Beyond the issues relating to the sharing of corporate confidential information, the types of data to be exchanged require close examination. For example, data that B2B exchanges wish to share reveal demographic trends in sales and may contain personally identifiable information that may require data cleaning or masking so that it can be shared without raising concerns.

Ultimately, the business concerns about issues surrounding privacy fall into two categories:

1. *Individual privacy.* On an international level, the United Nations Declaration of Human Rights and the European Convention on Human Rights recognize privacy as a fundamental human right. Many nations have constitutional provisions, legislation, or court decisions that define the individual's right to privacy as the right to be left alone—to be free from unwarranted intrusion.
2. *Data protection.* Businesses and governments have a responsibility to maintain the security and integrity of the data that they process. For businesses, this primarily means information gathered about individual customers and employees that is collected in the course of completing business transactions.

Privacy, often narrowly associated with computer security, comprises a number of core elements, including:

- The right to see and correct one's data
- The right to limit the collection, use, and disclosure of personal information
- The right to establish enforcement mechanisms and remedies to ensure compliance

As enterprises continue to globalize their operations, they need to be sensitive to, and in compliance with, the legal requirements and cultural sensitivities of the individuals with whom they do business. In addition, they need to protect adequately the accuracy, integrity, transmission, and accessibility of their electronic records and, in some nations, paper records. Regulatory compliance is not achieved without cost to the organization; and where regulation exists, it must be complied with. However, beyond reducing the risk of regulatory noncompliance, the benefits of good privacy practice include:

- *Reduction of cost* by eliminating the collection and management of unnecessary information.
- *Reduction of the risks* associated with inaccurate or out-of-date information.
- *Improvement in consumer and employee trust* and confidence in the use and security of personal data.

Today, consumer privacy concerns have been heightened by the technological changes surrounding the Internet. Technological improvements also put new pressures on businesses. Online companies that are under intense pressure to differentiate themselves are motivated to enhance value by personalizing their sites with increased personalization, requiring more granular customer data. Consumers express concern that inaccurate information can be used against them or affect them into the future, that personal information will be disclosed to third parties without their knowledge and consent, and that the security that surrounds their data is lacking. Identity theft provides just one example of how real these concerns are.

SIDEBAR 9.2
Sun Switches Gears on Security

In a surprise move, Sun Microsystems backed a security specification for Web services created by Microsoft, IBM, and VeriSign. Its WS-Security specification is a technology that encrypts information and ensures that data passed between companies remains confidential. Sun had been devising its own rival Web services security specification, though the now royalty-free licensing of WS-Security specifications allayed Sun's concerns, according to a source familiar with the negotiations. The companies recently submitted the specification to the Organization for the Advancement of Structured Information Standards (OASIS).

Sun's support of WS-Security has diffused worries regarding a possible standards war over Web services security. Such services, which allow companies to interact and conduct business via the Internet, will not work unless the entire tech industry coalesces around a single set of standards. Bill Smith, Sun's director of Liberty Alliance technology, says that Sun would now focus all its development work on WS-Security and work with its rivals to improve the specification through the OASIS group.

Lack of security is the biggest obstacle to the adoption of Web services, say analysts, and WS-Security takes a big step in addressing the issue. IBM, Microsoft, and VeriSign also plan to build five more security specifications in the next 18 months to provide additional security measures that businesses may need for Web services.

The challenge faced by many enterprises that wish to take full advantage of data-rich relationships with their customers, partners, and employees is to make sense of the myriad privacy-related regulatory and self-regulatory frameworks that exist. To determine which of these are applicable, and proactively address the requirements to support strategic business objectives, necessitates an ongoing commitment to compliance—resources, policies, and procedures.

A comprehensive approach to data protection and privacy compliance identifies and resolves the issues while noncompliance creates unnecessary risks. By identifying the elements of current regulatory and self-regulatory approaches to privacy, it is possible to derive a set of common elements that can serve as a starting point for an organization's global privacy compliance initiatives. Such a framework should include the following key elements:[a]

- *Notice.* The enterprise provides data subjects with clear and prominent notice of who is collecting their personal information, the intended use of the information, and its intended disclosure.

- *Choice.* The enterprise offers data subjects choices as to how their personal identifying information will be used beyond the use for which it was provided; choices would encompass both internal secondary uses such as marketing back to data subjects, and external secondary uses such as disclosing data to other entities.

- *Access.* The company enables data subjects to obtain appropriate access to information that it holds and to correct or amend that information where necessary.

- *Data security.* The enterprise takes reasonable precautions to protect data from loss, misuse, alteration, or destruction and ensure that those to whom data is transferred have adequate privacy protection.

> **SIDEBAR 9.2** *(continued)*
> ....
>
> - *Data integrity.* The firm keeps only personal data relevant for the purpose for which it has been gathered, consistent with the elements of notice and choice.
> - *Onward transfer.* The firm transfers data only as consistent with the elements of notice, choice, and security.
> - *Enforcement.* The company ensures compliance with key privacy elements and provides recourse for individuals, such as complaint and dispute procedures, verification of ongoing compliance, and obligation to remedy problems arising from noncompliance.
>
> [a]Wylie Wong "Sun Switches Gears on Security," CNET News (July 25, 2002).

PRIVACY IN EUROPE IS A DIFFERENT WORLD

The privacy debate in Europe is just as fierce as in the United States, although the rules about privacy are starkly different in Europe. In the United States, an individual's habits and behavior may be examined by an employer, a retail merchant, and by companies on the Web. This information is then used to target the customer for marketing purposes or is resold to other companies. By contrast, in most European countries it is illegal to monitor an individual under any of these circumstances and use the information to target the customer. The ground rules for privacy for members of the European Union (EU) are laid down in the European Union Data Protection Directive, which applies to electronic and paper filing systems, including financial services. In October 1995, the EU adopted the directive, which requires EU member states to amend national legislation to guarantee individuals certain rights to protect their privacy and to control the contents of electronic databases that contain personal information. The data covered by the directive is information about an individual that somehow identifies the individual by name or otherwise. Each European nation's government implements the directive in its own way.

Under the directive, information about consumers must be collected for specific, legitimate purposes and stored in individually identifiable form. Those collecting the data must tell the consumer, who will ultimately have access to the information. The rules are stricter for companies that want to use data in direct marketing or to transfer the data for other companies to use in direct marketing. The consumer must be explicitly informed of these plans and given the chance to object. U.S. and European principles on privacy share a key similarity. The Data Protection Directive and U.S. privacy laws attempt to protect human rights. However, both do little to check the growth of government databases or information collection powers. In his white paper, "Privacy and Human Rights: Comparing the United States to Europe," Solveig Singleton writes:

The view that uses of information for marketing in the private sector themselves violate human rights is a peculiar one. Why should a business not be free to record and use facts about transactions, about real people and real events, to develop products and to identify people who might have an interest in its products? Once a consumer enters into a transaction with another entity, this entity has as much of a right to use the information about the transaction as the consumer. Why would it violate someone's rights to use information about him to sell him something? This is a far cry from torturing him or seizing his home.[13]

Europeans do not allow the sharing of personal information between enterprises, whereas this is not yet regulated by the U.S. government. In contrast to the United States, where more of a free market approach is taken to many things, including customer privacy protection, the European Privacy Directive prohibits enterprises from transferring electronic records of personal information—including names, addresses and personal profiles—across borders. It is at least partly intended to reduce trade barriers within the EU by standardizing how various companies treat individual information in different countries. If European nations must follow the same standards about privacy protection, then trade between nations can occur more freely. Personal data on EU citizens may be transferred only to countries outside the 15-nation block that are deemed to provide "adequate protection" for the data.

SIDEBAR 9.3

European Organization for Economic Cooperation and Development Privacy Guidelines

1. Data must be collected using lawful and fair means and, where possible, with the consent of the subject.
2. Data must be accurate, complete, and up to date to ensure quality is adequate for use.
3. Purposes of data usage should be specified prior to collection and should not be subsequently extended.
4. Personal data should not be disclosed without legal cause or the consent of the data subject.
5. Data should be protected by reasonable security safeguards.
6. The existence and nature of personal data should be discoverable.
7. Data should be available to the subject to enable the correction of inaccurate information.[a]

[a]Excerpted from the OECD Web site, *www.oecd.org.*

---

[13]Solveig Singleton, "Privacy and Human Rights: Comparing the United States to Europe," CATO (December 1, 1999), available at *www.cato.org/pubs/wtpapers/991201paper.html.*

Most European countries have very strict privacy guidelines. In Europe, the general attitude of the regulators is that the consumer, not the companies, owns and controls his own personal information. In the United Kingdom, the Telecommunications Regulations of 1999 state that no databases may exist that contain personal data (other than a name and telephone number) related to a telecom subscriber unless the subscriber has given consent. In the Netherlands, a bill passed in late 1999 states that personal data may only be collected for specific, explicitly defined, legitimate purposes, and may only be processed when the data subject has given consent.

Data protection negotiations between the United States and the EU reached a pivotal point in July 2000, when the European Commission declared that the Safe Harbor arrangement put in place by the U.S. government to protect personal data transmitted in the course of Internet commerce must meet EU standards. The Safe Harbor agreement states that if U.S. enterprises agree to a certain set of minimal privacy standards when doing business in Europe, they will be free from litigation. It was aimed at heading off the possibility that data transfers to the United States might be blocked following the enactment of the EU's Data Protection Directive. Under Safe Harbor, U.S. companies can voluntarily adhere to a set of data protection principles recognized by the commission as providing adequate protection, and thus meeting the requirements of the directive regarding transfer of data out of the EU.

The Safe Harbor standards, however, are not as rigorous as what Europeans have set for themselves. As part of the agreement, the U.S. Federal Trade Commission (FTC) and U.S. judicial system will be authorized to impose sanctions on companies that violate data privacy rules. The U.S. Commerce Department will keep tabs on self-regulating companies, which will have to apply annually for membership in the department's register. Although participation in the U.S. Safe Harbor scheme is optional, its rules are binding on U.S. companies that decide to join, and are enforced by the FTC.

While trans-Atlantic e-commerce will likely progress as a result of the agreement, U.S.-based enterprises and their customers continue to tussle over domestic privacy and data-protection issues. Because the Web does not recognize international borders, personal information collected online is not tied to borders. The Privacy Directive serves an important purpose within Europe, by synchronizing these various government policies, to make it easier for any company to do business across the continent. However, some U.S. enterprises are criticizing it as little more than a nontariff trade barrier, designed primarily to ensure that any new, pan-European customer service infrastructures are staffed by employees working within the boundaries of the EU itself.

IMPLICATIONS OF THE EU PRIVACY DIRECTIVE

A regulatory approach such as the Privacy Directive may or may not be effective at curbing the abuse of individual consumer privacy, where it exists. But it could potentially curb Europe's economic growth prospects and threaten consumers' own interests, as well. Managing relationships in the interactive age depends on the collection and use of individual customer information and, as enterprises become increasingly global, it is vital that this information be accessible to sales, marketing, and customer care professionals worldwide. It is the only way to provide seamless, personal service—based on a unified view of the customer—across borders. Call centers or Web sites in Ireland might serve consumers in the United States or Argentina, as well as in France or Italy.

The potential impact of the directive, if enforced as written, is extreme. Sweden's privacy agency told American Airlines in 1999 that it could not transmit information about Swedish passengers to its U.S.-based Sabre system. This, in effect, prevents the airline from individualizing its service offering to its Swedish customers. Under the directive, it is even conceivable that a person could be arrested for saving business card data to his laptop and trying to cross the border with it.

No matter where in the world it conducts business, the customer-strategy enterprise tries to remain sensitive to how privacy rules are enforced and respected. Critical, too, is that the enterprise show to the world that it respects each customer's right to privacy through a written privacy pledge.

PRIVACY PLEDGES BUILD ENTERPRISE TRUST

If the enterprise is to establish a long-term relationship with a customer based on individual information, it will recognize that customer data is its most valuable asset, will secure and protect that data, and will share the policy for that protection in writing with its customers, partners, and vendors, in the form of a privacy pledge. The privacy pledge will spell out:

- The kind of information generally needed from customers
- Any benefits customers will enjoy from the enterprise's use of this individual information
- An individual's options for directing the enterprise not to use or disclose certain kinds of information
- Any events that might precipitate a notification to the customer by the enterprise

Enterprises jeopardize their relationships with customers by engaging in unethical moves that compromise customer privacy for short-term marketing gain. Enforcing a privacy policy is reassuring to many customers. Apparel manufacturer Land's End believes that its customer loyalty depends on trust, and it strictly enforces its online privacy policy. The company does not send e-mail promotions to its customers, except by request, and never sells or trades online customer data.[14]

[14]Judy Kincaid, "Devise a Customer Privacy Policy . . . and Stick to It," *Target Marketing* (March 2001).

But being careful with customer data is not enough for the enterprise. Such a company must also get agreements in writing with all its vendors and partners that confirm they too will comply with enterprise privacy standards. A Midwestern bank committed to protecting its customers' information learned that a printing company that produced checks for the bank's customers had been copying the names and addresses of customers, routinely printed in the upper left corner of the checks, and reselling that information to list brokers. These list sellers in turn were selling the information to insurance agencies, garden supply companies, other financial services institutions, and others.

What greater assets does any company, online or off, have to dangle in front of other companies than the private data of thousands, or even millions, of customers? Do the rules change when a company is bought out or goes bankrupt? What happens to a company's privacy pledge when there no longer is a company? And what guarantee is there that the new owner of your data will honor the same privacy standards as the former owner?

There is a simple, universal solution: The global business community needs to prevent such abuses, and preferably without government intervention. In this information age, technologies are cropping up to help the process. Software enables online users to control how sites collect, control, use, and share their personal information. With privacy pledges under scrutiny, more enterprises are adopting and publicizing them. Nonetheless, there are still many enterprises that do not state their policies or share user data with third parties.

What constitutes a good privacy protection policy? For starters, it should explain to customers what kinds of information the company needs from them, how the information will be used, and how it will *not* be used. It should also explain the benefits a customer would gain by sharing personal information. Enterprises need to promote their privacy policies beyond the Web site and corporate promotional collateral, including it in direct-mail pieces, invoices, and other company mailings. A privacy policy will reinforce the foundation on which each customer relationship is built. Trust is an essential part of any Learning Relationship, and a privacy policy helps build that trust.

Building a trusted relationship goes far beyond simply writing a privacy policy and posting it on the Web site. Unless the enterprise is careful as to how it uses sensitive customer information, the opportunity for forming Learning Relationships may disappear. It is important to recognize, however, that there are individuals who do not want companies to know which Web sites they visit or anything about their personal information. In the headlong rush of enterprises to use the latest databases, data-mining techniques, neural nets, and Internet-based information collection systems, some have neglected or overlooked this important issue. Moreover, a customer's willingness to collaborate with an enterprise by interacting with the firm could be an important measure of the customer's value to the enterprise.

It is important to explain the motives for wanting to create a relationship with a customer. Enterprises need to describe to customers how they will benefit by exchanging personal information with them. Once customers have read the

---

SIDEBAR 9.4

Ten Points to Consider in Developing a Company's Privacy Pledge[a]

....

Every enterprise that maintains a Web site or collects personal information about its customers needs to establish an explicit privacy protection policy. The enterprise might call it a Privacy Pledge or a Privacy Bill of Rights, but it needs to consider covering the following key points:

1. Itemize the kind of information it collects about individual customers.

2. Specify how personal information will be used by the company. If its policy is to use this kind of information only within the company on a need-to-know basis, and not to make it accessible to unauthorized employees at any time, the enterprise needs to explain this policy explicitly.

3. Make whatever commitments it can make with respect to how individual customer information will *never* be used (e.g., personal information is never sold or rented to others, or never used to change prices or insurance premiums, etc.).

4. State the benefits an individual customer can expect as a result of its use of his information (faster or preferential service, reduced costs, etc.).

5. List a customer's options for directing the enterprise not to use or disclose certain kinds of information.

6. State how a customer can change or update personal information it has collected. For example, can the consumer access his profile or account information online or modify it?

7. Identify events that might precipitate a notification to the customer by the enterprise. If, for instance, a court subpoenas your customer records, will you notify any customers whose information was subpoenaed?

8. Assign a corporate executive as the "data steward," charged with overall responsibility for assuring the adherence to company information and privacy policies.

9. Specify the situations in which it accepts or denies liability for damages incurred through the collection and use of customer data, such as through credit card fraud or misuse.

10. Provide specific procedures allowing a customer to order the company to stop collecting data about him, or to purge his information files at the company.

[a]Don Peppers, Martha Rogers,PhD, and Bob Dorf, *The One to One Fieldbook* (New York: Doubleday, 1999).

Privacy Pledge and understand that their personal information will not be sold or shared irresponsibly, they simply want to know how providing their personal data will affect customer service. Beyond the security or convenience of the actual transaction, what assurance does a customer have that his personal information will not be misused or abused? After all, most customers have experienced the irritation of "getting on a list" and, as a consequence, received unsolicited direct mail and outbound telemarketing calls. Ironically, if a customer does not provide information to an enterprise about what he likes to buy, the likelihood is that he will receive more junk mail or direct-mail pieces that promote products and services of little interest to him and his needs. Clearly, this question has yet to be definitively resolved.[15]

These and many other privacy-related questions may never be fully settled. But the customer-based enterprise has to monitor changing privacy issues closely. Intensifying the privacy debate is the way customer information is being collected and used on the Internet. The Web has created a powerful new medium to collect and analyze customer data. But how can enterprises afford customers the same privacy protection online as they do in the "real world?" And how sensitive are customers to divulging personal information on the Web?

SUBMITTING DATA ONLINE

The World Wide Web has become a viable shopping medium for enterprises and consumers alike. For many who buy online, the protection of their personal information is a valid concern. To the selling enterprise, however, information is like currency—it enables them to identify customers and customize their offerings based on that information.

By personalizing their products and services for online customers, enterprises stand to enhance their revenue. More than half of frequent online shoppers are more likely to make a purchase on a Web site that offers personalization features.[16] Still, online users believe that Web sites should be accountable for explaining to them how their information will be used. Consumers who participated in a survey by PricewaterhouseCoopers[17] overwhelmingly said that online shopping sites should ask them first before they share any private information with other companies. Other survey results indicate a fervent consumer attitude toward individual privacy protection[18] (see Exhibit 9.1).

Web site personalization requires consumers to submit information about themselves, such as their names, zip codes, interests, and even credit card numbers. Consumers personalize the online sites they visit to enhance their online experiences, but many do not want to have their information shared among Web sites without their knowledge. Internet users do not seem highly concerned about giving up personal information in exchange for improved online service, such as live interactive chat via the Web. Only 15 percent of users polled by the Personalization Consortium (established in April 2000 to promote responsible

---

[15] Dan Seligman, "Too Much of a Good Thing?" *Forbes* (February 23, 1998), pp. 64–65; James W. Peltier and John A. Schribrowsky, "The Use of Need-based Segmentation for Developing Segment-specific Direct Marketing Strategies," *Journal of Direct Marketing* (Autumn 1997), pp. 53–62; Rob Yoegel, "Fulfillment on the Net," *Target Marketing* (July 1996), pp. 30–31.

[16] According to a survey of online shoppers conducted by CyberDialogue, 2001.

[17] PricewaterhouseCoopers, 2001.

[18] Claudine Thompson. "The ePrivacy & Security Report," eMarketer, Inc. (January, 2001), p. 12.

	PERCENT WHO AGREE
Online shopping sites are responsible for asking me before sharing any of my personal information with other companies.	97%
Online shopping sites are responsible for asking me before using my personal information.	95%
It concerns me that online shopping sites store my credit card information for future use.	65%
I make most of my purchases from a few online shopping sites to limit how many companies have access to my personal information.	48%
I prefer to pay for my online purchases by calling a 1-800 number instead of entering my credit card number online.	28%

Source: PricewaterhouseCoopers, 2001.

EXHIBIT 9.1 **Internet User Attitudes toward Online Privacy**

and beneficial use of technology for personalizing consumer and business relationships) stated their unwillingness to do so. More than twice as many had no opinion on the subject, while a slim majority of 51 percent said they would be willing to trade information for service (see Exhibit 9.2).

Personalization online helps the customer to access the specific content and products he is looking for while giving the enterprise access to his browsing habits. For many enterprises, the objective of personalization on the Web is to increase customer loyalty through return visits. Privacy advocates claim that the instances of abuse of consumer data are a sign of how Internet marketers are overstepping their boundaries. The marketers, in turn, argue that data gathering is merely a nonthreatening way of fine-tuning marketing for the convenience of consumers. As discussed in the last chapter, a firm will have to accomplish two things to break down the mistrust barrier between the customer and the online merchant:

1. *Offer assurances of confidentiality.* Customers want to know whether or not their personal data will be sold or used beyond simply information gathering.

	PERCENT
Will provide for better service	51%
No opinion	33%
Will not provide even for better service	15%

Does not total 100% due to rounding

Source: Personalization Consortium, 2000.

EXHIBIT 9.2 **Willingness to Provide Personal Information**

2. *Build Learning Relationships on trust.* Enterprises will need to develop individual, personalized relationships with their customers to promote trust and enhance loyalty.

As privacy-protection advocates in Australia, the United States, and Europe continue to fuel the debate that it is wrong for companies to abuse personal information about their customers on the Web, enterprises will need to take a balanced view, not second-guess what their customers "really" want. The customer-strategy enterprise will strive to protect an individual's privacy online but also weigh the real benefits of personalization against its real costs.

SIDEBAR 9.5

Should Customers Have Options Other Than "In" or "Out"?

As the privacy debate rages, customers are, more and more, aware of whether they are given a chance to *opt in*—proactively elect to receive future communications from the enterprise, or *opt out*—tacitly choose to receive them by inaction, unless they actively opt out. Consumer groups tend to favor opt-in as a better protection for consumers, whereas industry groups point to very low participation levels and, ironically, fewer targeted messaging efforts, and therefore tend to favor opt-out.

But why is the choice all or nothing? Off or on? Why can't an enterprise, in true one-to-one fashion, offer the customer a volume dial? Is it really good for the customer to make him choose between taking any and all communications an enterprise may choose to send him, through any channel, from itself or any partners, as often as it likes, *or* to never learn anything else about this enterprise and never hear from it again? We anticipate more and more companies offering customers the ability to self-design their own opt-in—then he could let a company know he'd like to hear from it again—say, twice a year, and only through regular mail or e-mail; and if e-mail, never on weekends; and never, never by telephone.

So much changed about the United States national attitude toward privacy on September 11, 2001. With the terrorist attacks on New York and Washington, DC, U.S. national security was threatened as it had never been before. But on a more personal level, U.S. citizens felt that their individual safety was in jeopardy. The threat of additional terrorist attacks led to a heightened state of security at many public places, including airports, sporting events, and bridges and tunnels.

In the immediate aftermath of September 11, 2001, the civil rights of private citizens became a public issue. How much could the government encroach on a person's right to privacy in the shadow of terrorism? How much was okay if it made us all safer? What if it only made us *feel* safer? Could the government begin to check the backgrounds and personal information of anyone it deemed to be a suspicious terrorist?

As you read Esther Dyson's contribution, think about what the world will be like in a few years. What would happen if enterprises and the government became adept at combining personal information about individuals from different sources? What would it mean for people who participate in society and those who do not (such as the Amish)?

SIDEBAR 9.6

Universal I.D.

....

One solution offered after September 11, 2001, was the creation of a Universal ID card for each citizen to carry. The card would contain an electronic thumbprint of the cardholder so the person could be easily identified if questioned. This concept is akin to automobile license plates, which automatically expose the owner of the vehicle to the police, who simply need to check the plate number against their database. Would citizens be opposed to carrying a card that revealed personal information to anyone who swipes their card?

PRIVACY ON THE NET

Esther Dyson
Chairman, EDVenture Holdings

The following is excerpted from Release 2.0: A Design for Living in the Digital Age, *by Esther Dyson, published by Bantam Doubleday Dell Broadway Books, New York, 1997.*

By 1997, consumer privacy had become a big issue in the United States. A number of trends had been combined. More data was being collected, online and off. Direct marketers, telemarketers, and assorted shady people were invading people's privacy, and press coverage highlighted this issue. The Federal Trade Commission held hearings on consumer privacy, saying in effect: "Tell us the problems and propose some solutions, or we'll have to regulate."

There were also several bills pending in Congress, likely to change form over time: the Consumer Internet Privacy Protection Act of 1997 (Rep. Bruce Vento, D-MN); the Children's Privacy Protection and Parental Empowerment Act (Rep. Bob Franks, R-NJ); and the Communications Privacy and Consumer Empowerment Act (Rep. Ed Markey, D-MA).

With some justification, many people, both potential users and potential government regulators, perceived the Net as a scary, unregulated place. The Net makes it even easier for lots of people, not just well-capitalized mass marketers or obsessive creeps, to get at information and use it for undesirable and even dangerous ends.

BEYOND WEB SITES, BEYOND LABELS

These issues of privacy didn't begin with the Internet, and they can't be resolved by controlling what happens on any, or even all, individual Web sites. The problem arises when information travels among Web sites—or away from them to places where people and companies assemble databases of information gleaned from many Web sites and from non-Web mailing lists, directories, news reports, listings . . . and other databases. A lot of this information has traditionally been available to people willing to go to a lot of trouble, visiting county document vaults, calling companies posing as a prospective employer or old boyfriend, or spending several hundred dollars to get an investigator's license. It has also been available on a random basis to criminals in jail doing data-entry work, bored clerks at the IRS, and various other untrustworthy people in trusted positions.

Many companies, notably TRW, Equifax, Metromail, and some credit card providers, manage huge amounts of such data and trade it among themselves. Yes, it makes the economy more efficient and keeps revenues up and costs down. But not all of the companies who manage the information are especially honorable—nor are all of their employees.

> Often, facts are innocuous until they're combined with other facts.

The growing presence of the Web increases the ease of both collecting such data and assembling it. The interconnectedness of the Net makes safeguarding privacy an increasing challenge. People are rightly concerned about the *combination* of data from different sources: Web behavior, buying habits, travel history, income data. Often, facts are innocuous until they're combined with other facts.

The user wants a seamless experience as he explores the Web, but he wants to appear as a discrete entity to each place he visits, with a legitimate identity revealed as appropriate—a credit rating, an employment record, a bank account, or a medical history. Indeed, a person's identity gets splashed all over the Net in little fragments—no problem. But then someone in particular—anyone from a benign marketer only after the customer's business, to an employer, a stalker, or a blackmailer—can start collecting those fragments. One version of the problem is when the data are incorrect (and the user is the last to know); another version is when they are true.

In response, the marketplace and the government are setting up systems to foster privacy. As a society, we can't totally guarantee everyone's privacy. But we can create a situation where people can choose the level of privacy they want according to trade-offs they determine for themselves, and provide them with a means of recourse when promises are breached. When that happens, I believe, people will feel more comfortable on the Net overall and no longer fear the visibility it fosters.

TWO KINDS OF INFORMATION

There are two broad classes of information about yourself that you create on the Net: one kind that you generate when you engage in a one-to-one transaction with someone, and another kind that you generate when you do something in "public"—post an opinion, send out a message to several people, or supply information on your own Web site. (You may also appear in someone else's comment; we'll deal with that kind of situation later.)

The "one-to-one" data is created by a variety of individual exchanges and transactions—anything from visiting a Web site to buying a racy book, revealing personal data in order to win a prize, or stating your income on Barron's site for investors. In principle such information is private—but not in practice. Here's one tale of woe from Russell Smith, a privacy activist who testified at the Federal Trade Commission hearings:

> . . . my every move on the Internet could potentially be tracked. For instance, I recently did a search of newsgroups via the DejaNews service. In my search I was searching on my username 'russ-smith.' The search turned up an entry in some type of an adult newsgroup. When I clicked on the message it turns out it had nothing to do with me. However, the banner ad I received was for an adult site from a widely used banner network called The Link Exchange. Does my profile now include this information? Is my search criterion ('russ-smith') also associated with this information? Do they have my name and address since I have purchased products (and entered personal information) at other sites with these banner ads? Is it being sold? How can I find out? Can I expunge it?

COOKIES

Aside from data supplied knowingly by users, there are other means of collecting information—most notably "cookies." Cookies is the innocent name for data about a user's visit to a Web site that is, ironically, placed remotely on the user's computer by a Web site computer. That explains a couple of things you might wonder about: First, when you visit a Web site, your hard drive may keep gurgling long after you've downloaded the page you're looking at. That's your computer and the Web site talking in the background.

Second, if you return to that Web site, it may seem to know more than you might expect. For example, specific pages that you've already looked at are marked in some way (the type is in green instead of gray, for example), or the site refers to something you did last time. (For example, my favorite cities—San Jose, Moscow, Warsaw—are already marked whenever I visit the USA Today weather pages.)

The frustrating thing about cookies is that even though they reside on your PC, they are unintelligible to any normal person. (Clever crackers understand them all too well and can create fictitious cookies to log on and impersonate another user.) Real cookies can also be passed from site to site, so that one site, for example, can see where you came from and what you were doing there. Recently, some "good" hackers have developed tools that allow users to erase cookies or send back a "wafer"—a sort of anticookie with a user's complaint on it. Both Netscape and Microsoft now offer users an option to turn cookies off in the latest version of their browsers—but the default is to keep them.

Cookies, in some cases, *can* be useful—in saving your password, say, as long as it is not passed on elsewhere. A cookie can also contain the information needed to offer you customized news items or your favorite weather. The issue is simply that this kind of information should be under *your* control. Even if you're willing to give that Thai tie company your information, do you want them selling it to the Bangkok Bamboo Shack?

WHAT DO "THEY" KNOW?

Merchants' growing excitement about the Net mainly stems from the fact that it's so much easier to track a Web user's activities than to correlate, say, what a television viewer watches with his subsequent purchases. Web sites can keep track of what a person looks at, how long he stays, which ads provide the best response, whom he communicates with, what he says (in public discussion groups), how his behavior changes over the course of a day. Do drinkers buy more stuff in the evening, when they've had a few? Are customers of Web catalogs more price-sensitive than customers of paper catalogs? Are people who book airline seats through the Web more likely to be no-shows? Are customers getting so sophisticated that middle seats will have to be priced lower to sell? Alternatively, would you be willing to pay extra for an aisle seat? The possibilities for one-to-one everything are endless.

In principle, a merchant could compare a person's musical tastes to her reading preferences, or the political Web sites she visits to the magazines she reads. It could scour the newsgroups and send e-mail to all people whose comments appeared on a particular site or matched a particular profile (as measured by statistical sampling of words). Using the new directory services, a merchant can match up e-mail, name, and address, and all the other data linked to any of these. Try it on yourself. Thought your comments on libertarianism went only to people on that newsgroup? Think again! How did they get your name for that spam about a Caribbean island with a friendly government?

Some of this information is just statistical, but a lot of it marketers want in order to track you individually. Merchants would also like to know how ads affect your subsequent behavior: Do you see something online and then go buy it in a store with a credit card? Of course, the marketers don't really care who you are; they just care what you (can be induced to) buy. They want to be able to predict behavior. The problem is that the information they gather has a way of spreading further, and further.

Much of this information is in fact unnecessary, because much of what defines a person is the communities he is part of. Advertisers should be happy (or at least reconciled) to support those communities without knowing the "true" identities of each of their members. A company can place its advertising where the right customers show up; it's why you have bottled water ads in health clubs and resort ads on airport television. Likewise, community members want to know one another because of shared interests, not because of personal information.

Nonetheless, we have a friction-free market where consumer data is freely traded by giant corporations careless of people's identities—or worse, by small sleazy organizations with no reputations to protect. The companies out there collecting data on you may be small or large; these front-line data collectors get information from forms people fill out, from transaction records, and from various kinds of filings—many of them from government organizations. But the major companies buying, aggregating, and reselling data—Equifax, Metromail, TRW, and the like—are large and powerful, and are well represented by the Direct Marketing Association.

Marketers glibly say that the consumer is king, but in practice he's not. In the real world, experienced marketing and consumer-affairs hands will tell you, consumers aren't very good at protecting their own interests. They're too busy consuming, or working, or just living regular lives. The groups that claim to protect their interests often end up with their own agendas, which may have more to do with Washington power battles and fund-raising than with genuine consumer interests.

A customer can't easily express his privacy preferences: He may have one preference for a site dealing with computer-industry issues, and another for his neighborhood after-school chat. We present different faces at work, at school, at church or temple, at the doctor's office. The difficulty is that personal information changes character as it travels, in a way that packaged "content" does not. Besides, your concerns for security may depend on the kind of interaction you are having: Are you simply giving your name, or are you transferring cash or revealing deep dark secrets? Of course, you can refuse to supply any data, but greater granularity would be beneficial to both customers and marketers.

FLAWED SOLUTIONS

The solutions most often presented in response to this situation generally miss the point. We don't need new government regulation that stops the free flow of information voluntarily given, outlaws cookies, and makes customization difficult (except perhaps where children and coercion are concerned).

Nor do we need a Direct Marketed Association—a force equal in power to the Direct Marketing Association but aligned with someone's vision of consumers' interests. After all, consumers don't all have the same interests; what they really need is choice.

Instead, we need the kinds of policies that the Liberty Alliance is fostering, which would allow users more control over the kind of data that gets passed from vendor to vendor. An even more user-focused initiative is PingID, based in Denver.

Personally, I like both initiatives because they are not moralistic, evangelistic, or dependent on government—other than for enforcement on the basis of fraud. They are examples of the kind of efforts at decentralized regulation and customer control that I hope to see proliferate on the Net.

TOOLS FOR CUSTOMER EMPOWERMENT

Much as I hate the term, what I'm talking about here is customer "empowerment," not "self-regulation"—transforming passive customers into active customers who can monitor vendor practices for themselves. That implies some kind of broad movement to give customers the tools to do so, but the actual enforcement and use of the tools should be decentralized into users' hands.

The reason to avoid government regulation is not that government oversight is always bad; government courts and other enforcement mechanisms are a necessary backup to systems such as TRUSTe and Liberty Alliance. It's simply that front-line customer enforcement is likely to be more flexible and more responsive to actual conditions than government regulation. A decentralized system scales up nicely and crosses borders with ease. Customer enforcement will give users greater choice, while at the same time giving them confidence that they can trust the medium. People can pick data-control practices that suit them, rather than be forced to operate in a one-rule-fits-all environment. The overriding rule should be that providers must disclose—label—themselves clearly and honestly. And then they must do what they promise.

The goal is not to regulate cyberspace, nor to solve all problems concerning privacy (or content) online, but rather to carve out enough clean, well-lighted territory so that the dark parts of the Net lose their power to scare people away. In the end, most people will prefer to live in safe neighborhoods, while potential predators will find few victims other than their own kind.

PRIVACY IN PRACTICE

In practice, privacy protection is more than data or technology. How can we achieve it without making the world into a sterile place where everyone is anonymous? Most customers actually like to be treated as known individuals by marketers that they in turn know and trust. The rhetoric promises a global village, not a global city. Real privacy—which is respect for people rather than mere absence of data—depends on human judgment and common sense.

Take Four11, a leading Web "white pages" company. Its basic service is collecting and maintaining a database of individuals' names, e-mail addresses, phone numbers, and other data. The telephone data is licensed from Metromail; the e-mail addresses come primarily from user registrations, public-domain directories on the Net, and Usenet. While visitors are encouraged to register with their own data, you can also ask to be stricken (even if your data shows up again from another source).

All this data is available to anyone who visits Four11's Web site—but only a bit at a time. Aside from its acceptable-use policies (restricting wholesale reuse and general abuse), Four11 avoids hard and fast rules in order to be flexible enough to address new problems as they arise. For example, the company makes it difficult for users to collect names for mass e-mailing on or for building any kind of secondary database. It supplies information only one e-mail address at a time, and it monitors user activity for unusual behavior, such as downloading one address after another. It doesn't care who you are; it just cares what you do.

Also, you can't find a name from a phone number or from an e-mail address, or so-called "reverse look-up"; you need to know a person's name before you can get anywhere. However, that wasn't always true. The company licensed its database to Yahoo!. Yahoo! did allow reverse searching, using the Four11 data—quickly creating the Net's most visible, most-used reverse look-up for phone numbers at the time. Four11 CEO Mike Santullo says he felt uncomfortable about the reverse look-up service, but both parties note that it was tremendously popular and did not actually lead to many problems.

Both companies were punctilious about de-listing people who asked for their names to be removed. Meanwhile, police departments, suicide prevention centers, and other "good guys" made good use of the service. "Bad guys" didn't seem to be more prevalent than the sometimes annoying people who use caller ID to call you back. But a few months later, in response to perceived pressure, the companies dropped the service. Similar information is still available, but sometimes from companies that may be less careful than Yahoo! and Four11.

It's a pity that such a potentially valuable service should be abandoned and relegated to nonmainstream providers. The moral of this story—which is not yet over—is that a little self-regulation or fine-grained control over personal data may actually yield a situation where information is more readily available than would no control at all.

That's the long-term question: How can you make information available selectively? Four11 is addressing that in part, although not with reverse look-up for now. People willing to register with the service can get selected additional information about others; presumably, being registered themselves makes them less likely to abuse the information. For example, they are allowed to search the database for people by affiliation, such as Princeton High School or violinist. This information comes from individuals and from the groups themselves; they can specify which information can be made available, and to whom. For example, some groups let only group members query on group-oriented data, so only PHS alumni (as verified by PHS) could find out which other people are PHS alumni.

Yes, it sounds cumbersome and awkward and somewhat arbitrary, but isn't that the way it is in real life? The folks at Four11 have thought about all this a lot, and will refine their approach as they encounter new problems over time, says CEO Mike Santullo. Call it a continuing arms race between the data-providers and the data-snatchers.

JUNO: FREE E-MAIL IN EXCHANGE FOR YOUR INFORMATION

Some sites and services make explicit bargains. Juno, for example, has offered customers (including my stepmother) free e-mail in exchange for exposing the user to specific advertising based on the user's characteristics. The service has been a success with end-users: About 2.5 million people have signed up for it, filling in a detailed profile in exchange for free e-mail. They do not have to have Internet access, since Juno offers its own local dial-up throughout the United States, and they do not *get* Internet access, but they can send and receive e-mail across the Internet. They can also view graphics-filled ads from Juno's advertisers and from Juno itself. The site looks something like a Web site and its ads look like Web banner ads, but the only people who can use it are registered Juno customers.

Although the service is free, it's not quite "the people's e-mail." It still skews Internet-wards, said former Juno president Charles Ardai: Mostly male (two-thirds) and higher income. You may not need to pay for Internet access, but you still do need a computer with a modem.

The users' identity is not revealed to the advertisers, who simply get a report such as "5,482 men between 18 to 49 who have expressed interest in a new car saw your ad last month; please pay $2,741 within 30 days." Juno may also tell them, for example, that 25 percent of the people who clicked on their ad were female. Note that this is people who actually saw the ad when they logged on to check e-mail; it's more targeted and more intense than a page you might have passed in a magazine.

But how is an advertiser to know this is true? Juno's financials and other numbers, including claims to advertisers, are audited by Coopers & Lybrand. "Unlike a Web site, we're pretty simple to audit," notes Ardai. The only people who visit are its own registered and profiled customers, using Juno's proprietary software.

Juno has discovered that it can also sell products itself to its customers—a cookbook to someone who's indicated an interest in cooking, for example. She can send back a purchase order with ease, he notes, and her credit card never goes over the Internet. (That may not be a real issue, but it makes some customers feel more secure.) People who respond to an advertiser's direct offer, of course, lose their anonymity.

TRANSPARENCY AND TRUST

Mechanisms such as TRUSTe and P3 that give individuals control over use of personal data collected in a formal way by marketers, and companies such as Four11 and Juno who promote their privacy practices, should help to give people an overall sense of security on the Net and clarify the distinction between private and public transactions. When you engage in an explicit transaction, it should be private—with the treatment of the data under your control. When you do anything else, it's public. This sense of boundaries and control is likely to be important both in getting people onto the Net and in making them feel more secure when they get there. In the long run, it's likely that this control will ultimately spread from the Internet back to other transactions: Consumers will demand the same control over data from transactions generated *off* the Net. Or people will prefer to do business on the Net, where they know that they *can* negotiate.

Indeed, I believe that even as people's concern about privacy on the Net lessens, they will become more comfortable about their visibility in the public parts of cyberspace.

WHAT WOULD DEEP BLUE BE LIKE WITH HORMONES?

Let's try a thought experiment. Imagine that you have lived your entire life on the Net, isolated from the physical world. You know a lot of people intimately: You've heard their ideas; you've argued with them; you've watched them mature, get angry, trade jokes, do business, make and lose friends. You have made and lost friends yourself. These people are real to you; you want their respect; you ask them for advice. And you are real to them. You and they take your Net presence for granted—all the things you have ever posted, all the data about you, all the Net chatter about you. But you have never seen them.

Now suppose you meet these people in real, physical, terrestrial life. They're fat or thin; blond or dark; young or old; white or African American or Asian; male or female. There's more! Each person has these little peculiarities—a scar, asymmetrical eyebrows, a particular style of dress or pattern of speech, and so on. None of them is any big deal; they're merely expressions of each person's identity. (Yes, some people do hate their nose, undergo cosmetic surgery, or have an obsession with their own hair, but few people wear a mask.)

None of these features is any big secret, and most are familiar (if not explicitly so) to that person's friends and even acquaintances. Others—for example, presidents and movie stars—are known to the world. Some are genetically determined; some are shaped by the person; some are an artifact of culture (such as a woman's shaved legs).

But how about you? You would probably at first be very sensitive about your *own* physical being. You would feel vulnerable and exposed as you joined the physical world. All these people can see how you look, judge your hairstyle, criticize your weight or your taste in shirts . . . . Should you shave? Should you wear your trousers rolled?

But after a while you would probably relax, just as you have already in the real world since being an awkward teenager. People know how you dress and how you look, and most of them now are accustomed to it. Meanwhile, you're accustomed to the face you present to the world. You may be taken aback to see your profile or, worse, the back of your head in a mirror. But on the whole, you're probably relaxed about your physical existence because it has come to seem normal.

That same thing is likely to happen with your Net persona.

THE NEW PRIVACY

As people feel more secure in general on the Net, they will become accustomed to seeing their words recorded and replayed. They will no longer feel uncomfortable being on display, since everyone around them is on display too. In the same way, feelings of physical exposure tend to depend on fashion and custom as well as innate sensibility. Thirty years ago the sight of a woman's navel was shocking except by the pool; now it's routine. One hundred years ago, a nanny told my grandmother she was a "shameless hussy" for taking off her shoes at the beach.

Everyone has personal preferences for privacy, but they are influenced by the surrounding culture and by the surrounding economy. It's hard to fulfill a desire for privacy if you're living in a one-room apartment with the rest of your eight-person extended family. If you travel or mingle with people from other cultures, you will notice that Americans expect a lot more "personal space" than most people.

Nowadays, people reveal much more about themselves—for better or worse—than they used to. It's inevitable that people will simply become more comfortable with the fact that more information is known about them on the Net. The challenge is not to keep everything secret, but to limit misuse of such information. That implies trust, and more information about how the information is used. At the same time, we may all become more tolerant if everyone's flaws are more visible.

WHAT WILL BE KNOWN?

Indeed, much of the Net will become more private than it is now. In addition to the [1-to-1] privacy protections I described earlier, people will have the ability to close themselves off with filtering tools, community boundaries, intranets, and the like. Ultimately, people will spend much of their time within relatively closed spaces, much as they do now in real life. They can stay within a corporate intranet, and venture forth only to find commercial information. But I hope they don't; they'll miss a lot if they do.

VISIBILITY AS A DESIRABLE NORM

Within communities, most people will become accustomed to seeing reflections of themselves. There will be rules about what is recorded and what is erased after, say, ten days, but more and more will end up being archived. Perhaps we're too narcissistic as a species, but human nature is to save everything. There will be records *somewhere* of almost everything you've posted, e-mails you've sent, and of course things other people have said about you. Most communities will have registered members but they will be open—to new members, and often to data searches from outside.

Conversely, members will be able to wander outside to anywhere on the Net for public information, send e-mail to anyone (although not everyone will be willing to receive it), and keep in touch with and do business with others worldwide. The challenge is to make sure that something is left outside, in those open spaces. I hope to encourage people to make mainstream of cyberspace nice enough that people *will* want to live their social lives there. To gain trust, people need to be visible—as they expect others to be. The Net will not have a single culture, but the default needs to be healthy, with people online working actively to maintain clean, well-lighted places.

THAT IS, VOLUNTARILY VISIBLE

There are commercial, social, and political reasons for us to be voluntarily visible in the potentially murky world online. Disclosure is a foundation for open markets. It's also a foundation for clean politics, whether on the Net or off. And finally, it's a foundation for trust.

People with communities may want to shield themselves from the outside, but they will mostly want transparency and visibility inside. On a much larger scale, so do governments. They want records that are complete and open—except perhaps their own. Although the Electronic Frontier Foundation and many other groups and individuals are fighting vigorously to keep governments and businesses from prying into our private lives without our consent, that urge on the part of governments won't go away. The difference is that communities do it *with* our consent.

Governments all over the world are cooking up schemes to listen to our conversations and tap our lines. Some governments insist that they will require a court order to do so; others are less punctilious and their promises meaningless.

What can we do in response? In some countries, we have hope of keeping our privacy; in others, it will be more of a challenge. And the more a government feels threatened, usually because it is not liked by those it rules, the more likely it is to spy on its own citizens (and certainly on foreigners, too) in order to retain power.

FAIR PLAY

Our best defense is offense: Spy back!

We need the ability to follow more closely what our governments are doing. So while the Electronic Frontier Foundation, the Center for Democracy and Technology, and other organizations defend our privacy, they are also fighting for more open government. What are governments doing with all the information they collect? Who is looking at it? Who are they talking to? Why aren't they talking to us? Where do government officials receive their outside income? Who pays their bills? How is it biasing their judgment? How are they spending their—our—money? (Could we spend it better ourselves?)

This kind of information will help reverse the imbalance of power. Governments are legitimately concerned about large-scale organized crime rings and terrorists operating in shadows. But I am also concerned about large-scale *governments* operating in shadows. Government rule is based on the legitimate concept that we have to decide collectively on some rules and on the allocation of some of our social resources. But we also have a right to oversee how the rules are followed by those in charge and how the resources are used. Surely, even more than investors have a right to disclosure about their investments, we, as involuntary "investors," deserve a right to disclosure from our government.

This applies to online communities, too. Even though they are voluntary, there's a risk that community managements will become large and bureaucratic just like terrestrial governments and established businesses.

In general, I don't want too many restrictions on what people can say or do, but I do want strong expectations of disclosure from those who hold or want positions of public trust. Ideally, we would not even need laws (but laws wouldn't hurt). There would be no law requiring Steve Forbes or Ross Perot, for example, to disclose their tax returns, but few people would vote for them if they didn't.

There's no easy, immediate answer. The capabilities to get and share data about individuals becomes cheaper and easier daily. Smart-card manufacturer Schlumberger already has the smart card that can carry your retinal scan and fingerprints with you everywhere. And Intellicheck already enables bars to swipe your driver's license to ascertain your legal age (and then, in many states, to also suddenly "know" your Social Security number, gender, weight, address, and so on).

The real commercial questions are these:

- What do we need to "know" to serve a customer better and make him more valuable to us?
- What information do we really need to "know" that?
- Once we get that information, how do we balance distribution at the front lines with the need to protect a customer's privacy?
- What are the limits in how we will share or distribute data?
- How will we protect and secure the data?

SUMMARY

The fluid collaboration between enterprise and customer is ceaseless throughout the life of the relationship. But for the relationship to flourish, the customer sometimes will have to reveal personal information about herself to the enterprise. The enterprise, in turn, will have to promise to keep this private information private. Indeed, privacy—the customer's right to it, and the enterprise's protection of it—has become an important, and controversial, subject of the information age. That's why we devoted Chapter 9 to it.

FOOD FOR THOUGHT

1. Who owns a customer's information?
   - Who should profit from it?
   - How would that work?

2. Is anonymity the best solution to privacy?

3. What is the difference between *privacy* and *data security*, and how should that difference affect the way we use customer data?

4. Compare the situation of Big Business versus Big Brother having detailed information about you.

GLOSSARY

TRUSTe An organization that endorses each customer's control of his own information, and offers a publishable mark to organizations that meet TRUSTe's requirements for privacy protection.

Using Mass Customization
to Build Learning Relationships

10

Chapter

On average, each American household has about 300 branded products—food items, cleaning goods, over-the-counter-remedies, grooming products. Yet there are 30,000 stock-keeping units (SKUs) in the average supermarket. That means that each shopper sifts through 100 times as many products she doesn't want as she does finding the ones she buys. No wonder we've come to confuse "choice" with getting things our way. But try on this idea: Choice is not *the same as **customization**, and most of the time, for routine purchases,* people don't want more choice. They just want what they want. *Getting just that, within reason, is the payoff of the Learning Relationship—to the customer and to the company. This chapter shows how the customer-based enterprise should use what it learns about each customer to customize and/or personalize some aspect of its business with that customer, in order to increase its share of that customer's business. The whole point is to know more about a customer than the competition does, and then to deliver something in a way the competition cannot.*

Treating different customers differently could be prohibitively expensive, if every interaction and transaction had to be individually crafted as a tailored offering for a single customer. Fortunately, information technology can be used to improve and streamline the manufacturing and service delivery processes, so that an enterprise can deliver individually different products or services to different individual customers cost-efficiently. This technique is called **mass customization**.

For the past 100 years, enterprises have standardized their products and services to take advantage of economies of scale. They have standardized the product and their messages about the product, and they have standardized its distribution. In the process, they have also standardized the customer. Even sophisticated segmentation strategies aggregate customers into groups a marketer defines as being alike, so the communication and the offer made to all customers in a segment can be standardized. By contrast, the customer-strategy enterprise, spurred by the rising power and declining cost of information processing, interactivity, and customization technologies, identifies its most

> For the past 100 years, enterprises have standardized their products and services to take advantage of economies of scale. They have standardized the product and their messages about the product, and they have standardized its distribution. In the process, they also have standardized the customer.

valuable customers, remembers everything it learns about each one, and acts on that learning in all its dealings with that customer.

Mass customization can be defined as the mass production of goods and services in lot sizes of one. Stan Davis, who first coined the term in his groundbreaking book *Future Perfect*, says the term implies delivering "customized goods on a mass basis."[1] The principles of mass customization are not limited to physically produced goods; they can also be applied to the customization of services and communication. For some customers, being treated individually with personalized services and communication may be an even more important dimension than being treated to uniquely tailored products made possible by individualized production.[2]

HOW CAN CUSTOMIZATION BE PROFITABLE?

The mechanics of mass customization are simple in theory. A mass customizer does not really *customize* anything at all—at least not from scratch. What a mass customizer actually does is not customization, but *configuration*. The mass customizer preproduces dozens, or hundreds, of "modules" for a product, and/or its related services, delivery options, payment plans, and the like. Then, based on an individual customer's needs, the company puts different modules together to yield thousands, or even millions, of possible product configurations.[3] When an enterprise embraces mass customization and determines how to modularize its offerings, it must thoroughly understand all of the component elements its products or services can be combined with, connected to, reduced from, or built onto. By determining the related products or services it could offer to customers, either by producing them itself or by forming alliances with other firms, the enterprise takes a critical step in the mass customization process (see Exhibit 10.1).

Consider how a credit card company might go about mass-customizing its credit card. Perhaps the company is capable of offering 10 different interest rates, 5 different annual fee schedules, and 4 different physical card designs. Altogether, in other words, the credit card company can make 19 different modules of the product. But these modules fit together to make a total of 200 different credit card configurations. This is the basic principle of mass customization, and it applies to manufacturing in the same way. A window manufacturer, for instance, could offer 5 different sash types, 10 windowpane styles, 3 grades of

---

[1]M. Davis Stanley, *Future Perfect* (New York: Addison Wesley, 1987).

[2]Ian Gordon, *Relationship Marketing* (New York: John Wiley & Sons, Inc., 1998).

[3]Don Peppers, Martha Rogers, PhD, and Bob Dorf, *The One to One Fieldbook* (New York: Doubleday Broadway Books, 1999).

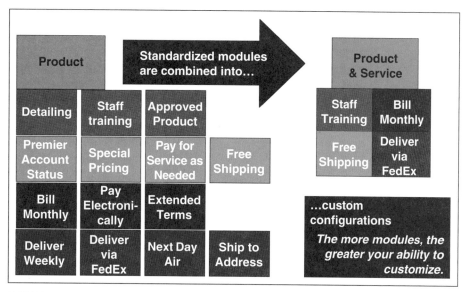

EXHIBIT 10.1   How Mass Customization Works: Example

insulation, and 12 frames. That would be 30 modules that could configure a total of 1,800 different windows.

The biggest obstacle to mass-customizing a manufactured product, as opposed to a delivered service, is simply ensuring that different parts actually work with one another and can be fit together easily. But if a product's components can be put together in a standardized way, or *modularized*, then the process of mass customization can actually reduce a company's all-in costs, when compared to traditional mass production. Using modularization, building to order is inherently more efficient than building to forecast, because the enterprise need not take ownership of the parts any earlier than it needs them, and often the final product itself isn't even built until it has already been paid for by a customer. Mass customization can significantly reduce speculative manufacturing as well as inventory costs, and these two benefits are often enough to more than offset the cost of producing digitally combinable components. Indeed, cost reduction is one of the principle reasons manufacturing companies consider mass-customization technologies in the first place. [4]

Analogous cost reductions are possible when mass customizing a delivered service. By giving a customer exactly what she wants—and especially if the enterprise remembers this preference for the next interaction—the entire transaction can be streamlined, made not only more convenient for the customer, but more

---

[4]Mass-customized products: Mila D'Antonio, "Profiles in Leadership," *1to1 Magazine* (January 3, 2003), p.34. Mass-customized clothing: Martha Rogers, "Custom Clothing Sets One to One Retail Examples," *Inside 1to1* (June 16, 2003); Martha Rogers, "Custom Apparel Can Be a Profitable Fit," *Inside 1to1* (March 8, 2003); Mila D'Antonio, "Is Custom Apparel Finally Taking Off?," *1to1 Magazine* (March 1, 2003), p.24; "Another Retailer Turns to Online Mass Customization," *Inside 1to1* (November 9, 2002).

cost-efficient for the firm. In Australia, the St. George's Bank automated teller machines will remember your "usual" ATM transaction, if you have one. When you put your card into its ATM, the first menu item will offer you your usual cash withdrawal amount and receipt preference. Not only does this provide faster and highly convenient service for the bank customer, but it is also a more efficient use of the ATM, because the line of customers can move through it faster.

NOT ALL CUSTOMIZATION IS EQUAL

Management advisor Joe Pine literally wrote the book on mass customization.[5] He and his partner James H. Gilmore have chronicled a business evolution— from creating standardized value through mass production to creating customer-unique value through mass customization. Pine and Gilmore have hypothesized four distinct approaches to mass customization:

1. *Adaptive customizers* offer a standard, but customizable, product that is designed so that customers can alter it themselves. One lingerie company makes a slip that a customer can cut off in a finished way to make the slip the length she wants.
2. *Cosmetic customizers* present a standard product differently to different customers. Lillian Vernon encourages buyers to personalize backpacks and sleeping bags with a child's name.
3. *Collaborative customizers* conduct a dialogue with individual customers to help them articulate their needs, identify the offering that fulfills those needs, and then make customized products for them. This is how Ross Controls operates (see the section on "A Few Exemplars" in the Pine contribution, later in this chapter), with an integrator to assist the customer in collaborating directly with the mass customizer.
4. *Transparent customizers* provide each customer with a customized product or service without necessarily telling her about the customization itself. This is what the Ritz-Carlton does, when it configures a guest's stay based on the preferences the guest expressed during previous visits to the hotel chain. The guest who gets a hypoallergenic pillow in her room may not even be aware that this is customized service—she may think this is how all guests are treated.[6]

Notice that *adaptive* and *cosmetic* customizers offer customers a better way to get what they want, compared to a mere standardizer; but also notice that these customizers *have no memory* of the **personalization** they do or offer, thereby requiring the customer to begin the specification process again with the

[5]B. Joseph Pine II, *Mass Customization* (Cambridge, MA: Harvard Business Press, 1993).

[6]For more on the four faces of mass customization, see James H. Gilmore and B. Joseph Pine II, "The Four Faces of Mass Customization," *Harvard Business Review* (January–February 1997).

next order. And that next transaction will depend entirely on the customer for its initiation. Therefore, adaptive and cosmetic customization offer no real sustainable competitive advantage against a competitor offering the same thing.

In contrast, notice that *collaborative* and *transparent* customizers maintain a distinct competitive advantage because they *remember* what a customer wants and predict what she will want next time. In many instances, the company takes a proactive role in offering to the customer what she's most likely to want next. The customer is able to get from a collaborative or a transparent customizer something she can't get elsewhere—even from a competitor that offers the exact same thing—unless she goes to the trouble (and risk) of starting all over in a new Learning Relationship.

> The customer is able to get from a collaborative or a transparent customizer something she can't get elsewhere–even from a competitor that offers the exact same thing–unless she goes to the trouble (and risk) of starting all over in a new Learning Relationship.

Gilmore and Pine say that many companies resist mass-customizing their offerings and instead "manage the supply chain" by placing more and more variety into their distribution channels and leaving it to buyers to fend for themselves. Manufacturers maintain large inventories of finished goods, and service providers maintain excess personnel and provisions to meet potential demands. These practices add costs and complexity to operations. Customers then must sort through numerous alternatives to find the one that most closely approximates what they want. In many situations, a majority of buyers never do find an exact match for their own personal tastes, instead settling for the one that seems to be the best fit overall, considering both the positives and the negatives. Producing greater variety in anticipation of potential, yet uncertain, demand often represents a last-ditch attempt to preserve the mass production mind-set in the face of rapidly fragmenting markets, say Gilmore and Pine.[7]

An enterprise focused on building customer value, by contrast, brings information about an individual customer's needs directly into its operations in order to achieve efficient, on-demand production or provisioning. This effectively turns the old supply chain into the back end of a *demand chain*. In this process, the firm diminishes the importance of product *price* in favor of *relationship value* (see Exhibit 10.2).

---

[7]James H. Gilmore and B. Joseph Pine II, *The Experience Economy* (Cambridge, MA: Harvard Business School Press, 1999); B. Joseph Pine, *Mass Customization* (Cambridge, MA: Harvard Business School Press, 1993).

MASS PRODUCTION	MASS CUSTOMIZATION
Supply chain Management	Demand chain management
Economies of scale	Economies of scope
Make to forecast	Make to order
Speculative shipping costs	Goods presold before shipping
Inventory carrying costs	Just-in-time inventory

EXHIBIT 10.2   **Supply Chain versus Demand Chain**

SPAR is the brand name for a chain of more than 16,000 grocery stores and outlets, operating in 30 countries and generating some $26 billion in worldwide sales annually. The company refers to itself as a kind of "soft" franchise operation, because most of its stores carrying its brand name are owned and operated independently, while SPAR is the wholesaler for the stores in the chain, providing most—but not all—of the products sold by the member stores. SPAR's customers are the store operators themselves, and the company performs many services for them, in addition to wholesaling. For some storeowners, SPAR does the books and minds the payroll, for instance.

One of SPAR's innovations worth a closer look has been implemented in Austria, a relatively strong market for the firm, where it has a 30 percent share. In 2003, SPAR Austria implemented a system that preconfigures its wholesale deliveries to a store in the same order in which the items are shelved in that store. So, as the stock clerk rolls the trolley down the aisle at her store she can effortlessly find the next items for the store's shelves, simplifying the process and saving considerable time and cost for the storeowner. Importantly, the ease with which SPAR Austria's products can be placed on a store's shelves provides an incentive for the storeowner to rely as much as possible on SPAR, rather than going to the trouble of dealing with an additional supplier. Even if for a few items the other supplier might offer a more advantageous price, getting goods onto shelves costs less with SPAR.

Of course, each store's configuration is different, so SPAR's preconfiguration requires the firm to maintain an up-to-date record of each store's individual configuration. But it must also *act* on that information cost-efficiently, by changing the actual product delivery configuration for each store. Until this program was launched, the configuration of grocery products as they leave SPAR's own warehouses was not actually something that would have been considered a "customer-facing" activity. Mass-customizing those configurations, however, so as to treat different customers differently, is very definitely a customer-facing action, and perfectly illustrates how difficult CRM makes it to draw a line between supply chain and demand chain activities.

The instant application of information at various points along an enterprise's value chain allows it to respond quickly to changes in demand and market conditions. In addition, whole new classes of mass-customized products and services are made possible by such technologies as computerized databases, which can respond instantly to individual requests for information, and telephone and entertainment services, which can be delivered to individual homes through fiber-optic wires.[8]

Mass customizers can easily adjust to changes in markets and technology, as they can rapidly shift their production, creating new products to accommodate changing environments. Fewer customer orders will be lost because mass customization can always, within overall capacity limits, build the products in demand. This contrasts again with mass production factories, each of which has its own capacity limitations—limitations that cannot usually be offset by excess

---

[8]B. Joseph Pine II and James H. Gilmore, *Mass Customization* (Cambridge, MA: Harvard Business School Press, 1993).

capacity elsewhere in the company. Distribution based on less inventory from a build-to-order factory can prevent shortages caused in distribution channels. The result is fewer opportunity losses.[9]

Because customized products can be ordered with only the options customers want, they will not be forced to buy a "bundled" option package to get the one option they really want. Even at a premium price, customers may still save money by avoiding unwanted options.

The mass-customizing enterprise is driven by observing and remembering individual customer requests and by comparing them to what other customers have requested. The success of mass customization as a relationship-building tool stems from the fact that a customer can participate in the actual design and development of her own product. As a result of her own collaborative effort, the customer is much more likely to be satisfied with the overall performance of the product and to find it costly to start over with a competitor, even when that competitor can do the same thing the same way.

SIDEBAR 10.1
Dell Computer[a]

Problem/Objective

In the competitive world of computer hardware, Dell was looking for a way to differentiate itself and simultaneously create barriers to switching for customers who were accustomed to making a purchase choice based on price.

Solution/Action Taken

Dell created custom corporate sites called Premier Pages, which provide information customized for each of its business customers, including the customer's own contract prices, purchase history, corporate-approved SKU numbers and order status. Premier Pages provide controlled multiuser access levels, links to corporate intranets and paperless purchase orders, plus customized IT asset management advice. Dell grouped its customers into 10 basic value categories, including global accounts with 18,000-plus employees worldwide; large corporate accounts with 3,500 to 18,000 employees; and education, healthcare, and consumer accounts. Each group of customers is assigned an administrator who is responsible for the creation, maintenance, and updates of Dell's Premier Page program. Each site is really mass-customized for each user company.

Result

Dell is now the computer industry's fastest-growing and most profitable company. With 28,000 Premier Pages in 14 languages currently in use, Dell is employing fewer sales reps and has reduced processing costs. Mass customization also allows the company to provide the same services to small firms that it has always provided its largest customers.

[a]From Don Peppers and Martha Rogers, PhD, *One to One B2B* (New York: Doubleday Broadway Books), 2001.

---

[9]David M. Anderson, *Agile Product Development For Mass Customization* (New York: McGraw-Hill Professional Book Group, 1997).

SIDEBAR 10.2

Mass Customization: Some Examples

Examples of mass customization abound in business today, both in business-to-consumer and in business-to-business settings:

- Select Comfort of Minneapolis, Minnesota, designs and manufactures mattresses with air chamber systems that automatically contour to the bodies of those who lie on them. Customers can select the level of firmness they desire, and couples can select different levels on each side of the bed.

- Lenscrafters can mass-customize eyeglass lenses in about an hour, while the customer waits. (Customers don't just buy lenses off the rack!) The Miki Corporation, a Japanese eyewear firm, has taken eyeglasses a step further. At Paris Miki, a prototype store in Paris, a person not only specifies the lens prescription, but can also design the actual frame, and tailor its shape and lenses to any one of thousands of configurations.

- Mattel Inc. has used the Internet to allow children to create the doll of their dreams by selecting the hair, skin color, and clothing of their choice. The My Twinn doll company goes a step further. Customers input the doll's desired features, which are then assembled from a fixed assortment of parts. Once the customer receives her customized doll, My Twinn continues to sell clothing and accessories to fit the growing-girl customer as the doll "grows up" with its human twin.[a]

- Land's End and Brooks Brothers teamed with North Carolina–based Image Twin Inc., to use a new body-scanning technology that measures a person's body dimensions in 12 seconds. The data are stored on password-protected Web sites to be used by consumers to make purchases. Image Twin's plan is to develop 50 body-scanning kiosks in malls and at other retailers. Brooks Brothers plans to use the computer-generated patterns to mass customize suits and shirts.

- Mercury Asset Management has taken mass customization in the print arena to a whole new level. To better serve its customers, Mercury, owned by the Merrill Lynch Group, released its first mass-customized magazine, *The Mercury Investor's Guide*. The 46-page, twice-yearly magazine mixes common pages with personalized pages in 7,700 versions.

- Shoe manufacturer Nike, Inc., has enabled customers to customize their own sneakers, including style, colors, and a personal ID tag, at its Web site, Nike.com. Nike delivers the customized shoes directly to the customer. The site remembers information about individual customers so it can recommend products to them when they return.[b]

[a]Laurie J. Flynn. "Built to Order," *Knowledge Management* (January 1999).

[b]For additional examples, see Mila D'Antonio, "Blockbuster," *1to1 Magazine* (January–February 2003); Jane Zarem, "Sun, Sand, and Customer Strategies Mix Well at Sandals," *Inside 1to1* (June 23, 2003); Eric Yoder, "Fairway & Greene Scores a Birdie in Relationship Management" (April 28, 2003).

YOU'RE ONLY AS AGILE AS YOUR CUSTOMERS THINK[10]

B. Joseph Pine II
Co-founder, Strategic Horizons LLP

Like it or not, customers (whether consumers or businesses) are becoming more demanding about getting exactly what they need, while increasing competitive intensity—arising in particular from the globalization and convergence of industries—dictates that costs keep decreasing as well. Where companies used to pursue either a low-cost or a high-differentiation strategy, today companies find they must adopt strategies embracing both efficiency *and* customization. Instead of mass-producing standardized goods or incurring high costs to produce great variety, companies are in fact discovering that they can combine the best of both strategies to mass-customize their offerings. They must, in short, *mass*-produce individually *customized* goods.

A FEW EXEMPLARS

Many companies are already effectively meeting this challenge. Consider the Healthcare Support Services division of the managed services company ARAMARK. It created a program called INTERSERV that provides customized, integrated, nonclinical support services to hospitals. The company collaborates with its clients to design the specific process modules desired in the areas of food service (catering, menu distribution, etc.) and environmental (discharge and cleaning, hose-down, etc.). Together, company representatives and clients redesign the overspecialized, functional-silo methods hospitals have traditionally used to create a customized, integrated, modular architecture that provides customer-unique value. Finally, Healthcare Support and the hospital develop a multiskilled, comprehensively trained workforce (which may include the hospital's personnel, ARAMARK's personnel, or, as often occurs, a combination) that operates as a team.

For each implementation, a local ARAMARK Resource Center maintains, in a database, descriptions of all team members, all process modules contracted by the hospital, and a list of which team members can execute which modules. It further classifies process modules as scheduled or unscheduled and interruptable or uninterruptable. This allows hospital personnel to schedule many tasks ahead of time yet still arrange for some tasks—such as "move this patient to X ray, stat"—to be requested and dispatched at any time. Whenever needed, the Resource Center software (INTERSERV's linkage system) immediately

---

[10]This section draws upon material from the book, *Agile Product Development for Mass Customization: How to Develop and Deliver Products for Mass Customization, Niche Markets, JIT, Build-to-Order, and Flexible Manufacturing*, by David M. Anderson, with an introduction by B. Joseph Pine II (New York: McGraw-Hill, 1997).

determines which team members have the right skills, are performing an inter-ruptible task, and are closest to the point of need. This person then receives a message via an on-premise pager system to perform the more pressing task. In this way, ARAMARK adjusts in real time to the facility's constantly changing needs, helping the hospital stage decidedly better patient experiences.

But that level of customization is nothing compared to what some other com-panies are doing. Consider window manufacturer Andersen Corporation, of Bayport, Minnesota, which has millions, and very possibly billions, of possible window configurations, and saw the number of unique end items actually shipped explode from 10,000 in 1980 to more than 200,000 in 1996. To handle this rapidly increasing level of customization, Andersen developed a multimedia system called the Window of Knowledge.™ The system features an icon struc-ture of more than 50,000 possible window components to let distributors col-laborate with end customers in designing their own windows and interactively see exactly how potential designs would look—with such added touches as videos of beautiful, cloud-swept vistas viewed through the online windows. This rather sophisticated design tool automatically generates error-free quota-tions and manufacturing specifications and transmits completed orders directly to Andersen's factory.

While the goods created by Andersen are sold to consumers, mass customiza-tion has made just as much of an inroad—if not more so—in industrial applica-tions. For example, ChemStation, of Dayton, Ohio, mass-customizes industrial soap for factory floors, car washes, restaurants, and other commercial outlets. It independently analyzes each customer's needs and then uses its patented H7 technology and exclusive process to customize the concentration strength, PH-level, enzyme concentration, foaminess, color, odor, and so forth, for that cus-tomer. These unique formulations are delivered in bulk into ChemStation's own plastic storage tanks—with the ChemStation logo emblazoned on the front for all to see—that are provided to customer sites to completely eliminate the need for drums. The company further enhances its overall service simply by ensuring that customers never run out of their particular formulation. By constantly monitor-ing its tanks at customer sites, and thereby learning each customer's usage pat-tern, the company presciently replenishes inventory before a customer ever has to ask—eliminating any need for the customer to create or even review orders.

As just one more example of the many manufacturers that have embraced mass customization, consider the case of Ross Controls, a 70-year-old Troy, Michigan-based manufacturer of pneumatic valves and other air control systems used in heavy industrial processes in such industries as automobile, aluminum, steel, and forestry. Through its ROSS/FLEX process, Ross learns about its cus-tomers' business needs so it can collaborate with them on precisely tailored designs. It then quickly and efficiently produces customized valve systems that meet each customer's needs, often starting with a series of prototypes before finding the one design that can be replicated across the customer's various pro-duction lines. By integrating its efficient customization capabilities with the ability to learn about each customer's needs over time, Ross develops a connec-tion to them that grows with every successive interaction.

To make this happen, the company instituted an integrator position that productively combines marketing, engineering, and manufacturing functions into one person. The integrator's primary task is to "mine the knowledge" of her assigned customers to resolve their own manufacturing process problems. Interestingly, because the integrator's responsibilities are so antithetical to the normal engineer's way of working—one person must talk with customers, engineer the valve designs, and then determine the manufacturing specifications (including the tool paths for the machines)—Ross found that it had to hire new engineers from college who had not yet learned that engineers were supposed to do engineering only, not all that marketing and manufacturing "stuff" as well.

TO WHAT END AGILE MANUFACTURING?

What these companies are doing is, of course, very different from traditional mass production. Surprisingly, it is also quite different from how many companies that have abandoned mass-production processes leverage agile manufacturing. Rather than embrace the full promise of agile manufacturing, some organizations merely use it to introduce and produce an ever-increasing number of stock-keeping units (SKUs) in the markets they serve. For some, it has become a way of forestalling true customization, trying desperately to maintain the mind-set of mass production in the face of rapidly fragmenting markets.

This is unfortunate, for *variety is not the same as customization*. Variety is still producing a product and putting it in finished goods inventory in the hope that some customer will come along and desire it. In contrast, it is only customization when it is produced in response to a particular customer's desires. Variety is about giving more customers more choices in the hope that each can find something close to what she needs, individually. But, often, companies overwhelm customers with so much proliferation that customers throw up their hands at having to go through a lengthy decision-making process with little or no support, and simply walk away.

It is important to realize that, fundamentally, customers do not want choice; they just want exactly what they want. Being agile may help manufacturers become more cost-efficient in introducing more and more variety, but unless agility is directed at mass-customizing in response to actual demand, customers will not think you're agile—only bursting with options. Complexity and costs on the shop floor will only be replaced by confusion and chagrin on the shopping floor.

Instead, customizers figure out exactly what individual customers need (often through direct collaboration) and then produce it, generally using design tools (like Andersen's Window of Knowledge) that eliminate the problem of too much choice. And *mass* customizers do so efficiently, at a price customers are willing to pay and at a cost that allows for profitable margins. Mass customization is not being

> It is important to realize that, fundamentally, customers do not want choice; they just want exactly what they want. Being agile may help manufacturers become more cost-efficient in introducing more and more variety, but unless agility is directed at mass-customizing in response to actual demand, customers will not think you're agile–only bursting with options.

everything to everybody; rather, it is doing *only and exactly* what each customer wants, when she wants it. Indeed, most mass customizers find that—although there may be a significant up-front investment in developing the products, processes, and technologies required—mass-customized products can cost nearly the same as mass-produced ones. And for some, they actually cost less, particularly when markets become fragmented enough that mass-production techniques can no longer effectively predict what customers need.

> Mass customization is not being everything to everybody; rather, it is doing *only and exactly* what each customer wants, when she wants it.

Further, most customers are willing to pay a premium (often 10 to 50 percent) simply because customized products *have greater value* than standardized ones—they more closely match each individual's needs. In fact, much of the added value comes from the customer's investment in collaborating with the firm to create a product or service that the customer cannot get elsewhere. Margins, therefore, often increase greatly, especially once a company realizes the gains from the elimination of the carrying costs of finished goods inventory, the reduction in the number of customers walking away because they can't get what they want, and the alleviation of having to put some product on sale because no one wanted it. Think of the financial gains in a company that could be realized through the elimination of finished goods inventory alone.

MASS CUSTOMIZATION: THE NEW IMPERATIVE

Because of these tremendous advantages, mass customization is moving from being at the frontier to fast becoming an imperative in industry after industry. It is, in fact, the next logical step in the evolution of business competition.

This can be seen clearly through the framework given in Exhibit 10.3.[11] To understand the model, first recognize that product change (meaning the degree to which a good or service changes over time, or for individual customers) can be

[11]The origins of this framework were developed by Bart Victor and Andy Boynton of the University of North Carolina (visiting the International Institute for Management Development in Switzerland at the time of this writing) and extended in collaboration with Joe Pine. It evolved considerably over time to become a very robust way of looking at the world of business competition. To trace that evolution, see Andrew C. Boynton and Bart Victor, "Beyond Flexibility: Building and Managing the Dynamically Stable Organization," *California Management Review* (Fall 1991), pp. 53–66; B. Joseph Pine II, *Mass Customization: The New Frontier in Business Competition* (Boston: Harvard Business School Press, 1993); A. C. Boynton, B. Victor, and B. Joseph Pine II, "New Competitive Strategies: Challenges to Organizations and Information Technology," *IBM Systems Journal* 32, no. 1 (1993), pp. 40–64; B. Joseph Pine II, Bart Victor, and Andrew C. Boynton, "Making Mass Customization Work," *Harvard Business Review* 71, no. 5 (September–October 1993), pp. 108–119; B. Joseph Pine II, Bart Victor, and Andrew C. Boynton, "Aligning IT with New Competitive Strategies," in Jerry N. Luftman, ed., *Competing in the Information Age: Strategic Alignment in Practice* (New York: Oxford University Press, 1996); Bart Victor and Andrew C. Boynton, *Invented Here: Maximizing Your Organization's Internal Growth and Profitability* (Boston: Harvard Business School Press, 1998); and, finally, B. Joseph Pine II and James H. Gilmore, *The Experience Economy: Work Is Theatre and Every Business a Stage* (Boston: Harvard Business School Press, 1999), pp. 7–24.

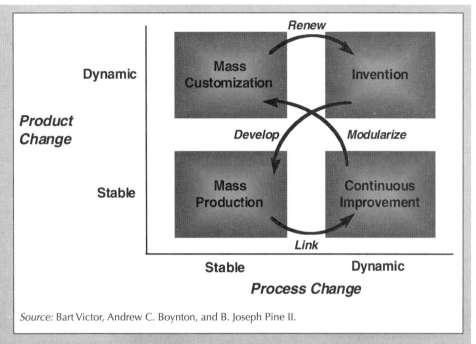

Product Change

Dynamic

Stable

Process Change

Stable   Dynamic

Source: Bart Victor, Andrew C. Boynton, and B. Joseph Pine II.

EXHIBIT 10.3   **Evolution of Business Competition**

either stable—slow, evolutionary, predictable—or dynamic—much more erratic, unpredictable, or revolutionary, and, at its limit, resulting in a different product every time one is produced. Similarly, process change—how an organization goes about producing the good or delivering the service—can be either stable or dynamic (at its limit a different process is executed every time). This, then, defines the four generic *business models* that companies choose—consciously or otherwise—based on their particular configuration of products and processes.

The Invention model includes craft producers, entrepreneurs, R&D units of large companies, and others that compete on high differentiation. These organizations constantly create new products as well as the processes by which they are produced; both product and process change is very dynamic. For centuries, all businesses were craft producers (often craftspeople) that basically followed the Invention model—if a customer wanted something an artisan didn't know how to make (either a new product or customized version of a current one), she might still offer to make it and then figure out how. Should the craft producer try to make the same thing twice, it would always come out at least slightly different because the production process had never been stabilized. By its very nature, the Invention model has constantly changing products and processes, and its practitioners—true inventors—often tinker and experiment, tweak, and then start over, just to see what new output emerges.

With the advent of the Industrial Revolution, and in particular Henry Ford's development of the assembly line, came the capability for the Mass Production model—the exact opposite of the Invention model. Here, everything is stable: These organizations find the one best way to produce a given product and then move down the learning curve as fast as possible to do it. Both product and process change come only very slowly to ensure fixed costs are recouped. Every once in a while (typically four to five years or longer) mass producers would have to depend on some other invention organization (usually its own R&D labs) for a new product idea that would be brought down to the mass-production organization to be mass-produced. In their heart of hearts, mass producers want to stabilize everything—establish the *one best way* to do everything—and then duplicate that one path over and over again. If they had their way, most manufacturing managers would produce a single standard item via one setup, and then run the production line until the cash cows came home.

Mass producers were thus very dependent on invention organizations to create new products, and invention organizations were often dependent on mass producers to provide a ready market for their highly differentiated creations.[12] This synergy between mass production and invention organizations worked very well for a very long time. It was at the heart of America's economic success during the twentieth century. In fact, it became a basic "law" of business that companies had to choose between either low costs or high differentiation—that one organization could never do both, because each required such different business models.

What Japanese companies (in particular, but not exclusively) discovered was that if they continually improved their processes, they could achieve both lower costs and higher quality than the typical mass producer. By embracing dynamic process change, they moved to a new business model and gained a significant advantage over their competitors. This was so different from the old way of doing things that it took American companies a long time to uncover the business model's true nature. Now, most companies subscribe—at least in principle, if not fully in practice—to the Continuous Improvement (or "lean production") model and incorporate such innovations as statistical process control, total quality management, just-in-time inventory, cross-functional teams, and customer satisfaction measurements, to name just a few. At its ideal, organizations following this model have a process life cycle of one execution; every execution is different from—and better than—the last. Yet the output change remains relatively stable; Japanese producers in particular had less variety than their American counterparts when they first invaded the latter's domestic markets. This tends to change over time as cross-functional process teams—the basic structure of continuous improvement organizations—set their sights on setup and change over time, improving the organization's capabilities for greater variety.

---

[12]The idea that mass production and invention organizations were dependent on each other was first articulated by MIT Professor Michael Piore of the Sloan School of Management. He noticed that mass producers were utterly dependent on specialized machine makers to provide them with the customized machinery required to make an assembly-line efficient. It was applying this insight to the framework that led to discovering the figure-8 path that leads from Invention, through mass production and continuous improvement, to mass customization, and back again to invention. For discussions on the concept of "industrial dualism," see Michael J. Piore, "Dualism as a Response to Flux and Uncertainty" and "The Technological Foundations of Dualism and Discontinuity," in Suzanne Berger and Michael J. Piore, eds., *Dualism and Discontinuity in Industrial Societies* (Cambridge, England: Cambridge University Press, 1980).

While companies everywhere seem to be making great strides in quality by embracing continuous improvement, many firms are already moving beyond mere variety to the Mass Customization business model.[13] Here, stable but very flexible and responsive processes provide a dynamic flow of products, enabling companies to achieve both low costs and individual customization. In this business model, the organization's primary thrust is to identify and fulfill the individual wants and needs of each and every customer. Ideally, the product life cycle is one unit: Every product is different from the last—and exactly suited to that particular customer's needs.

Organizations can move between business models, and their products and processes may be scattered across multiple approaches, but there is a definite order to the sequence that must take place to reach mass customization. The first such movement, from invention to mass production, is the well-known activity of development. It requires articulating and stabilizing the product and process, making each definable and repeatable for high-volume, low-cost production.

The resulting mass-production organization has historically been very hierarchical and bureaucratic, with very little information flow between functions. To equip the organization for continuous improvement, these vertically separated functions must be linked (the second move) through cross-functional teams, information sharing, and a horizontal process focus. The islands of automation that grew up within each function must come together to provide one common base of data from which each views the process. Further, the organization must link with its suppliers (value chain integration, versus the old vertical integration) so they have the same information about what is going on in the marketplace and can respond just in time with the components necessary to satisfy market needs. The result is a set of tightly coupled, high-quality processes capable of being continuously improved,[14] yielding a high degree of customer satisfaction—the key measurement of continuous improvers.

The third move, to mass customization, requires that goods and services be modularized to provide individual combinations for each customer. This lets companies deliver individual modules of customer value efficiently—whether it be a particular jean fit, a specific pitch of window, a certain PH factor in industrial soap, or an exacting pneumatic valve connection—within the structure of a modular architecture. The architecture determines what universe of benefits the company intends to provide customers and, within that universe, what specific

[13]For a fuller description of the differences between the Continuous Improvement and Mass Customization models, and of the difficulty in making this transformation, see B. Joseph Pine II, "Challenges to Total Quality Management in Manufacturing," in James W. Cortada and John A. Woods, *The Quality Yearbook*, 1995 ed. (New York: McGraw-Hill, Inc., 1995).

[14]In fact, process improvement is rarely if ever constant; rather, it is episodic. As explained by Marcie J. Tyre and Wanda J. Orlikowski in "Exploiting Opportunities for Technological Improvement in Organizations," *Sloan Management Review* 35, no. 1 (Fall 1993), pp. 13–26, a burst of activity is followed by a time of gradual stability, followed by another burst once new challenges surface (or unresolved problems become too great to ignore). In essence, those organizations that have mastered continuous improvement really "bounce" between that model and more stable mass production on an episodic basis.

permutations of functionality will be provided at this time, to this particular customer. These permutations are, in turn, defined by a modular schema that specifies which types of modules can be used and which linkage system will connect them together to create specific products for specific customers.

To understand modularity, think of Lego® building blocks. What can you build with Lego's? The answer, of course, is anything you want—because of the variety (although a finite variety) of sizes, shapes, and colors of different kinds of blocks, and a simple, elegant system of tabs and holes that enables them to be easily snapped together. Every mass-customization architecture needs to standardize these two basic elements: a set of modules and a linkage system to dynamically connect them together. Without standardization here, no company can hope to efficiently customize anywhere. Modularity, once again, is the key to mass-customizing any good or service.[15]

In addition to customizing the actual product itself, the most robust mass-customization implementations, as demonstrated with the examples described, break apart and modularize the tightly coupled processes created by continuous improvement. Specific, stabilized process modules are then free to dynamically link with other process modules as required to create the end-to-end value chain that will best satisfy each customer. The result is a dynamic—rather than static—network of linkages between people and processes loosely coupled to deliver mass customized goods.

THE CYCLE THAT TRULY COUNTS

Mass-customization organizations must also be able to renew themselves, to realize when they cannot satisfy a particular customer or cannot go after a particular market opportunity with their current universe of customization. This, the fourth and final move in the exhibit, causes them to "go back" and invent a new product module, a new process, or link to an organization inside or outside of the firm to provide the new capability required. And at times, firms may have to overthrow their entire product or process architecture—before their competitors do—and invent one that will once again provide a distinct competitive advantage.

Although the organization will never again want to "live" in mass production, it does have to go through the activities outlined—the figure-8 pattern through

---

[15]There are at least six different ways of modularizing and myriad ways of doing each, depending on a company's particular circumstances; see B. Joseph Pine, *Mass Customization*. Other good resources on this are Karl T. Ulrich and Steven D. Eppinger, *Product Design and Development* (New York: McGraw-Hill, 1995); G.D. Galsworth, *Smart, Simple Design: Using Variety Effectiveness to Reduce Total Cost and Maximize Customer Selection* (Essex Junction, VT: Omneo, 1994); Toshio Suzue and Akira Kohdate, *Variety Reduction Program: A Production Strategy for Product Diversification* (Cambridge, MA: Productivity Press, 1990); Ron Sanchez and Joseph T. Mahoney, "Modularity, Flexibility, and Knowledge Management in Product and Organization Design," *Strategic Management* 17 (December 1996); and Carliss Y. Baldwin and Kim B. Clark, "Managing in an Age of Modularity," *Harvard Business Review* (September–October 1997), pp. 84–93. The six types of modularity discussed in *Mass Customization* are based on earlier work by Ulrich and one of his students.

the framework—for each new product, process, or organization module created in invention. Each one still has to be developed and stabilized, linked to the rest of the organization and made of high quality, and finally made to fit the modular architecture. The organization is *mass-customizing*, not just pursuing an end-state of mass customization or "living" in any one business model; the figure-8 cycle of developing-linking-modularizing-renewing never ends. The result? Customers experience the constant enhancement of capabilities over time.

Mass customization, then, is not the ultimate. Rather, organizations must manage the ongoing cycle of successive transitions between each business model—rather than making a one-time selection of any particular model. Consider, for example, one of the early pioneers of mass customization, the Motorola Paging Products Group in Boynton Beach, Florida. During the 1980s, Motorola moved beyond the traditional mass production of electronic products to embrace a continuous improvement mind-set. It implemented many quality and cycle-time improvement programs, with the company's vaunted Six Sigma program (which strived to reduce defects to 3.4 parts per million) becoming the most well-known. But when Japanese competition significantly stepped up the competitive requirements with their own continuous improvement activities, the Paging Group went beyond the competition to mass customization at an organizational level.

Motorola put together a project that, in just 18 months, created an (almost) fully automated manufacturing system that could produce any one of 29 million different combinations of pagers in Boynton Beach within an hour and a half of the order being taken via a sales representative's laptop computer anywhere in the country. This drastically changed the nature of competition in the industry. Motorola became the sole surviving American producer of pagers, and commanded a worldwide market share of more than 40 percent. And it didn't stop there.

Since that original project—code-named Bandit to encourage its members to "steal" from any source inside or outside of the company to create the best possible manufacturing system—the Paging Group moved far beyond its original capabilities. It created what it calls the Fusion Manufacturing System because it unifies and integrates engineering, manufacturing, and marketing into one enterprise system that, at an operations level, enables it to accomplish all of the transitions shown in Exhibit 10.3.[16] With this information technology infrastructure in place, the Paging Group engineers can invent new module designs on a computer-aided design (CAD) system (renewal), simulate the performance of that "virtual" design using various electronic tools (development), ensure that the manufacturing processes exist with sufficient raw materials inventory and capacity to physically create the module in concert with the rest of the manufacturing processes (linking), build the

[16]For a complete description of Motorola's Fusion Factory, see Russ Strobel and Andy Johnson, "Pocket pagers in lots of one," *IEEE Spectrum* 30, no. 9 (September 1993), pp. 29–32. Since this article was written, it appears that Motorola went too far with the automation of its current architecture of pagers and has had trouble responding to demand for features outside of that modular architecture. As good as its Paging Products Group is—and it is among the best of mass customizers—its current experience is a testament to the need discussed earlier to renew not just capabilities but architectures as well (what can be called macro-renewal).

complete product specifications and dynamic manufacturing instructions online (modularization), and, finally, send them to the Fusion Factory for production. As a testament to how far Motorola has come: One of the company's customers (a vice president of a paging services firm) told us how his people collaborated with the Paging Group to design a new feature peculiar to their consumers' needs. The Motorola engineers left on Friday afternoon with an agreed-to description of the feature and came back Monday morning with working pagers! And there were no yellow wires in the back; these pagers were produced on the same assembly line as the company's production pagers. Although Motorola's engineers may not realize it, the system they put together enables them to go through the figure-8 pattern to renew over a weekend.

Unfortunately, the figure-8 pattern cannot be effectively shortcut. Invention organizations cannot go directly to continuous improvement precisely because they have not yet stabilized their processes. As all those intimately familiar with Total Quality Management techniques know, unless a process is definable and repeatable, it cannot be continuously improved because it can never be determined whether the results of the next execution derive from the improvements or from the natural variability of a process that has not been locked down via the activities of development. Similarly, one cannot go directly from mass production to mass customization. While both use stable processes, the mass-production organization is so hierarchical and compartmentalized, its focus so inward, and its processes so rigid and ossified, that it cannot possibly be modularized without first linking the organization together to focus (sometimes for the first time in decades) outward on the marketplace and begin incorporating flexibility and responsiveness into the processes through continuous improvement.

One clear result of the success of Japanese competitors and others that embraced the Continuous Improvement model was the tremendous force for change it became. Not just at particular companies like Motorola, but company after company in industry after industry had to increase quality and reduce costs in order to compete in the face of a clearly superior business model. A second result, perhaps less clear but of equal importance, is that all of this improvement taught customers to become more demanding. Once they discovered they could get both low costs and high quality from one company, they stopped putting up with poor service from others and began demanding that companies provide goods and services exactly as promised. Indeed, these two effects were reinforcing, driving each other to greater and greater levels, until today in most industries, continuous improvement only gets companies into the game;[17] quality is no longer a differentiator.

---

[17]Note that this is the same thing that happened in the movement from craft to mass production. Once customers got used to having low costs in automobiles and textiles, they began demanding it across other industries (including service industries, for which back offices became the equivalent of assembly lines). As a result, thousands upon thousands of craft producers went out of business, and millions of craftspeople became assembly-line workers, just as many people have been reengineered and downsized out of their jobs in the past two decades because of the inability of their companies to provide what their customers wanted at a price they were willing to pay.

We are nowhere near that point yet with customization, but companies in the next decade will be faced with the same precise predicament. Once customers—again, whether consumers or businesses—begin to see that they can get products made just for them that almost exactly match their needs at a price they are willing to pay, you can believe that they are going to ask for it elsewhere. And that's precisely why mass customization is becoming an imperative.

ULTIMATE ADVANTAGE OF MASS CUSTOMIZING

Implementing mass customization not only offers better products to customers, but opportunities for stronger relationships as well. By interacting with each customer on a personal basis *for the purpose of customizing products just for her*, companies can better learn the wants, needs, and preferences of each. The more the customer teaches the company about her *unique* needs, the better it can provide exactly what she wants—when, where, and how she wants it—and the more difficult it will be for her to be enticed away by a competitor. Company and customer thus enter into a Learning Relationship that grows and deepens over time—and thereby create a singularly powerful competitive advantage.

The beauty of mass customization is that modular architecture enables a company to do this incrementally, one module at a time, at very low costs. Instead of massive development efforts—which often end up with a large share of the time spent reinventing what someone else somewhere has already done—new modules can be created and dynamically linked into an existing architecture with a fraction of the effort. This is exactly what Motorola does so well with its Fusion Factory, and it's what Ross does every time it works with a customer to determine how its pneumatic valves can enable that customer to realize more value. These companies don't completely reinvent a new pager or a new valve; they work from existing designs to reuse 80 to 90 percent (or even 95 or 99 percent!) of what they've used before, and then spend their truly creative effort only on what has to be innovated to meet that particular customer's needs.

> By interacting with each customer on a personal basis *for the purpose of customizing products just for her*, companies can better learn the wants, needs, and preferences of each. The more the customer teaches the company about her *unique* needs, the better it can provide exactly what she wants–when, where, and how she wants it–and the more difficult it will be for her to be enticed away by a competitor. Company and customer thus enter into a Learning Relationship that grows and deepens over time–and thereby create a singularly powerful competitive advantage.

CONTINUOUS INVENTION

The ability to mass-customize will be crucial to where business competition will go in the future. Reconsider Exhibit 10.3, and note that it takes us from craft to mass production with the Industrial Revolution, from mass production to continuous improvement with the quality revolution of the past few decades, and then on to mass customization in recent years of increasing market fragmentation and customer demands. But it doesn't stop there: Business competition will not cease its evolution once this new business model is mastered. Rather, as one can surmise from the exhibit, it will go back to invention. The next logical step in business competition is a markedly higher degree of inventive capability, one that builds on mass-customization techniques to enable the rapid, constant, efficient creation of new, innovative products—not just customized versions of existing products—or what my partner at Strategic Horizons LLP, Jim Gilmore, has termed "continuous invention."

For mass-customized variations within a given product architecture, virtually instantaneous development cycles with efficient production are already a reality.[18] However, it may be science fiction to think of instantaneously creating the architectures themselves, inventing new product categories, or even developing major innovations for well-established products. But there are a number of promising lines of research and practice that will, now and in the future, yield marked improvements in this direction. Three possibilities stand out: modular design, invention databases and expert systems, and collaborative technologies.

Modular Design

Component modularity, based on physical elements, is already being widely used to develop architectures for mass-customizing products. Taking it up a level, Susan Walsh Sanderson of Rensselaer Polytechnic Institute has demonstrated how design modularity—what she calls "virtual" design—can modularize functional elements to reuse them across product families.[19] Higher and higher levels of modularity will yield greater and greater degrees of innovativeness. One can envision certain classes of "functionalities" being reused across very different products, with tools in place to make their reuse quick, efficient, and effective.

Essential to design modularity is incorporating more and more of the product essence inside of information technology, as Motorola has made great strides in doing with its Fusion Factory. A key tenet of mass customization is anything that can be digitized can be customized. Once any product, service, or communication resides in the realm of bits—ones and zeroes—it can be instantly changed on demand to a different, but still meaningful, set of ones and zeroes. In some cases,

[18]See Christoph-Friedrich von Braun, "The Acceleration Trap," *Sloan Management Review* (Fall 1990), pp. 49–58, and "The Acceleration Trap in the Real World," *Sloan Management Review* (Summer 1991), pp. 43–52, for a rather interesting and thought-provoking argument that decreasing the life cycles of new products can be very detrimental for a company's health. While his argument is inherently sound, it assumes that there is always a natural limit to how quickly new products can be developed, and therefore to how low life cycles can go. I believe that this assumption is false, thanks to such techniques as are discussed here. However, it is clear through von Braun's work that such an environment will become increasingly turbulent, with potentially large ups and downs in revenue and profits (as new products attract customers to buy before they might otherwise, reducing revenue in the future).

[19]Susan Walsh Sanderson, "Cost models for evaluating virtual design strategies in multicycle product families," *Journal of Engineering and Technology Management* 8 (1991), pp. 339–358.

the product itself can be digitized, such as with greeting cards, sheet music, and other information-based goods (not to mention telecommunications, insurance, and financial services that are all fundamentally information-based). In other cases, as with Motorola pagers, the specifications for the product design and its manufacture can be digitized for almost instant realization in a physical, customized product. In the future, as information technology continues to advance, greater and greater functionality will be digitizable, yielding virtual design and something that could easily deserve the label of continuous invention.

Invention Databases and Expert Systems

Many functions, however, cannot be digitized or even modularized, and may never be. Many stubborn development problems, for example, require resolving fundamental engineering contradictions for which there are no easy solutions. But what if you could attack it from every possible angle, quickly apply various inventive principles and physical effects to the problem at hand, have an expert system suggest alternatives, and learn by analogy from thousands of innovative creations?

That is exactly what one software product, called Invention Machine Lab from Invention Machine Corporation of Cambridge, Massachusetts, is already on the market to do.[20] It has three modules. The first, IM:Principles, helps developers find solutions to engineering contradictions by presenting inventive principles gleaned from analyzing more than 2.5 million patents. The second module, IM:Effects, contains a knowledge base of more than 1,350 physical, geometric, and science-engineering effects to assist users in understanding the ramifications of alternative approaches. And the third, IM:Prediction, helps developers predict the possible technological evolution of their invention to lead them down the path of creating entirely new products. Motorola, for example, has licensed more than 1,000 copies of Invention Machine Lab to speed the creation of new, innovative products from its various R&D labs.

> Anything that can be digitized can be customized.

Collaborative Technologies

Technologies such as groupware, liveboards, argumentation spreadsheets, and rapid prototyping—to name a few—are but a shadow of what will come as these technologies merge into collaborative environments. The new generation of collaborative technologies will have two effects on product development processes: They will enable many activities to be done that could never have

---

[20]Bryan Mattimore,"The Amazing Invention Machine: Software for Creative Geniuses," *Success* (October 1993), p. 34, and Audrey Choi, "Invention Machine's Software Wins Orders for Picking Brains of Inventors," *The Wall Street Journal* (February 12, 1996), p. B10a. According to the latter, the Invention Machine Lab "codifies the invention principles behind some two million international patents and the inventive techniques of some of the world's greatest inventors."

been done before, and they will allow activities that could be done to be completed much faster, more efficiently, and more effectively.[21]

Included in this latter group will be the ability, through virtual reality and other simulation technologies, to rapidly examine and test new product concepts without having to build the physical components. Combined with design modularity, the potential time savings in the testing phase of new product development are enormous. As just one example of the possibilities that are fast becoming achievable, professors at the University of Illinois at Chicago have created a virtual reality system called Cave Automatic Virtual Environment (CAVE, a reference to Plato's cave) that enables researchers to walk around—without bulky headsets—three-dimensional representations of products.[22] General Motors, Caterpillar, and other companies are already using CAVE in their new product development activities.

FUTURE LANDSCAPE

Of course, technology will not solve all invention or collaboration issues, and not all innovations are amenable to digitization or modular design. And no matter which technologies or techniques are developed in the future, many development projects—and certainly the most important and the most inventive among them—will still take significant amounts of time to complete. While development times for most anything can be greatly lowered from where they are today, they often cannot be rushed without detrimental consequences.[23] There is more than wine that cannot be sold before its time.

Nevertheless, there is still a tremendous amount of progress that can be made in the direction of continuous invention. With new systems, technologies, and techniques, one can indeed envision the day not too far in the future—some time in the twenty-first century—when the development and life-cycle times of major new platforms such as automobiles and computers are measured in months, consumer electronics products in weeks, and many products in days or hours. Like many mass-customized products today, custom variations created in minutes will be commonplace. And if there is any problem with achieving these numbers, it will come—as it should—from customer acceptance issues, not from the inability of producers to do it.

For those agile manufacturers that wish to become continuous inventors, the path is clear. It begins by embracing the principles of mass customization.

---

[21]Of course, the time it takes to do new activities will detract from the time savings of doing old activities faster. Whether it's supposedly leisure time at home, working time at the office, or either/both on the road, we continually find new things to do as technology frees up time on the more mundane tasks.

[22]See Carolina Cruz-Neira et al, "The Cave: Audio Visual Experience Automatic Virtual Environment," *Communications of the ACM* 35, no. 6, (June 1992), pp. 64–72; and Gene Bylinsky, "The Digital Factory," *Fortune* (November 14, 1994), pp. 92–110.

[23]See J. Utterback, M. Meyer, T. Tuff, and L. Richardson, "When Speeding Concepts to Market Can be a Mistake," *TIMS Interfaces* 22, no. 4 (July–August 1992), pp. 7–13.

TECHNOLOGY ACCELERATES MASS CUSTOMIZATION

In the previous section, Pine pointed out an important truth: No matter how much value an enterprise adds, it is the value a customer adds for herself that makes a product or service worth a higher price. As the demand for personalized and customized products grows, more enterprises are offering build-to-order services to enable customers to configure products to their own needs—and improvements in technology have made it possible. Technology is enabling enterprises to meet their customers' demands through mass production, but in ways that offer people their own choice of products that are personalized and made to measure.[24] The Web, for

> It is the value a customer adds for herself that makes a product or service worth a higher price.

instance, has become an ideal tool for mass customization, precisely because anything that can be digitized can be customized. The Web permits consumers to submit their specifications online directly to the manufacturer or sales executive. Cabletron Systems, a billion-dollar networking hardware manufacturer, lets customers configure products on its Web site and then choose whether to order those products directly from Cabletron or from one of its resellers. Customers can create more than 5,000 possible products on the site by combining interoperable components. Although 5,000 combinations are possible, many of the products will never actually be produced. A configuration engine guides customers through the process. If they opt to buy from Cabletron, the engine submits orders to Cabletron's sales software from Siebel Systems Inc. for billing and credit, which then passes the order to an ERP system from SAP that manages the manufacturing and shipping process.[25] If customers opt to buy from a reseller, they can click a button that sends a price quote for the configured product to a reseller's e-commerce system, and the reseller will contact the customers to close the sale. Cabletron estimates that taking configured orders online has saved the company more than $12 million a year on returned materials.

Capital One Financial Corp developed a successful mass customization model that changed the credit card industry.[26] The company is best known for gathering and analyzing consumer and customer data. Technology enables Capital One to observe and evaluate customer preferences and behavior, and to do so dynamically, by market segment. The company can forecast trends and strategically shift its focus away from commoditized products, such as balance transfer cards, before the market is saturated with offers from competitors. Cap-

[24]Richard Worsley and Michael Moynagh. "This Century Was Off-the-Peg: The Next Will Be Tailor-made," *Brand Strategy* (November 1999), pp. 16–17.

[25]Justin Hibbard, "Assembly Online—The Web Is Changing Mass Production into Mass Customization," *Information Week* (April 12, 1999) p. 85.

[26]Capital One, of course, mass-customizes products that take the form of digitized information, and in that sense, has an easier challenge than, say, an industrial manufacturer. But the same principles apply to both: modularization, closing the feedback loop, improvement through increased service levels at decreased cost to serve, and so forth.

ital One planned for the obsolescence of balance transfer cards and plotted a course to move the credit card company into mass customization. This strategy enabled the firm to leverage its information resources to identify customers with low-limit, high-fee potential and to send these customers the marketing materials about products that would likely interest them, such as secured cards for people with poor credit. Using a database that contains the histories of all consumer interactions with Capital One has enabled the firm to customize its credit card offerings. (See Sidebar 10.3. We'll also discuss Capital One's restructuring around customers in Chapter 13).[27]

Customizing products and services can yield a competitive advantage if the enterprise deploys the correct design interface and remembers its customers' unique specifications and interactions. By linking an individual customer's interactions with previous knowledge of that customer, and then using that learning to drive the production process, the enterprise takes an integrative approach to competition—one customer at a time.

SIDEBAR 10.3
Capital One

Problem/Objective

Competition in the credit card market is fierce. With low introductory teaser rates and balance transfer offers, customers are opening and closing accounts in record numbers. Capital One, one of the top credit card issuers in the United States, wanted to increase cardholder loyalty and retention so its customers would think twice before moving their accounts elsewhere.

In order to increase customer loyalty, optimize the customer experience, and reduce operational costs, Capital One sought to reduce the time card members spend on the phone with call center reps. In addition, because outbound telemarketing is becoming less and less effective, Capital One wanted to take advantage of inbound calls to sell additional products and services.

Solution/Action Taken

Capital One analyzed data from 7 million consumer households, as well as data from its current customers. Using this information, the company is able to anticipate a cardholder's needs based on past calls and transaction records, and to prepare a customized offer for each customer before the call center rep even picks up the phone.

Result

Customers are getting answers faster. A cardholder who calls in monthly for an account balance is presented with that option first on the IVR menu. Customers are also getting personalized offers; for example, a frequent traveler may be offered a special rate for a rental car, whereas a power shopper may be offered discounts at

---

[27]Judith Trotsky, "FutureBankers of the Year: Capital One Financial Corp.'s Richard Fairbank & Nigel Morris," *FutureBanker* (December 1998), p. 106.

> **SIDEBAR 10.3** *(continued)*
>
> retail outlets. The best service representatives are now selling new products and services to 15 percent of incoming callers with problems. If a customer calls wanting to close an account, the rep is empowered to say, "I could lower your rate," and then be rewarded with a bonus for saving the business.
>
> **Next Steps**
>
> With its capability to customize offers based on customer needs and values, Capital One has begun cross-selling additional products and services, such as cellular phone service, to its customers.

CUSTOMIZATION OF STANDARDIZED PRODUCTS AND SERVICES

When the executives of a company believe they can sell only standardized products, sometimes those executives bemoan their inability to participate fully in the strategic payback of the customer relationship revolution. It's important to realize that even companies that cannot customize a product *per se* can still customize what they offer to individual customers, and thus build Learning Relationships. A company may, for example, be able to change the product, add features, or combine it with other products. It may be able to sell standardized products, but provide various services that enable a customer to receive personalized attention before and after she buys the product, and make it possible for her collaboration with the firm to benefit her. The company that truly cannot mass-customize its products can look for service and communication opportunities to build in mass customization that makes the customer's investment in the relationship pay off—for both the customer and the company.

> It's important to realize that even companies that cannot customize a product *per se* can still customize what they offer to individual customers, and thus build Learning Relationships.

There are many customization options beyond the physical product itself, and many ways an enterprise can modify how it behaves toward an individual customer, other than customizing a physical product. These include:

- Configuration of the product or services surrounding it
- Bundling of multiple products or services
- Packaging
- Delivery and logistics
- Ancillary services (repair, calibration, finance, and so forth)
- Training
- Service enhancements
- Invoicing

- Payment terms
- Preauthorization

The key, for any enterprise trying to plan ways to tailor its products and services for individual customers, is to visualize the "product" in its broadest possible sense—not simply as a product, but as an object that provides a service, solves a problem, or meets a need. This is where a strict adherence to the discipline of differentiating customers by their *needs* will pay off. What a customer needs and what she buys are often two different things. But if an enterprise has a full understanding of the customer's own need, then that enterprise can often devise a customized set of services or products that will meet that need. Meeting the customer's need is the service being performed by the enterprise, and the product itself is the means for delivering that service.

This "product-as-service" idea can be thought of in terms of three successively complex levels in the **enhanced need set** or expanded need set (see Exhibit 10.4):

1. The *core product* itself includes its physical nature, if it is an actual product, or its component services and executional elements, if the core product is actually a service. Customizing the core product could include:
   - Product configuration
   - Features or capabilities
   - Fit and size
   - Color, design, style
   - Timing or frequency
2. The *product-service bundle* includes the services and features that surround the core product. Customization of the product-service bundle could include:
   - Invoicing, billing, and cost control (from the customer's standpoint)

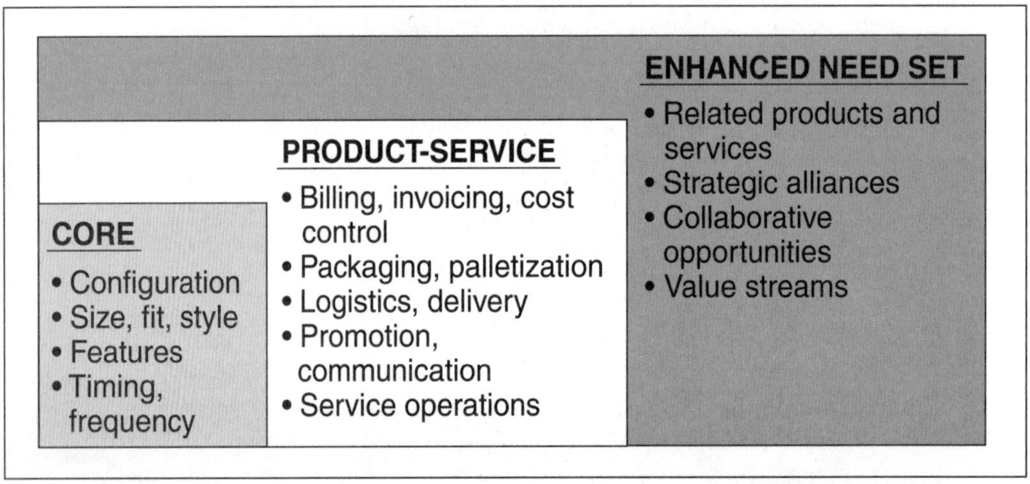

ENHANCED NEED SET
- Related products and services
- Strategic alliances
- Collaborative opportunities
- Value streams

PRODUCT-SERVICE
- Billing, invoicing, cost control
- Packaging, palletization
- Logistics, delivery
- Promotion, communication
- Service operations

CORE
- Configuration
- Size, fit, style
- Features
- Timing, frequency

EXHIBIT 10.4   **Enhanced Need Set**

- Additional services
- Packaging and palletization of the products
- Promotion and marketing communication
- Help lines and product support

3. The *enhanced needs set* includes product or service features that could meet related customer needs, enhancing or expanding the customer's original set of needs. Activities undertaken to customize an enhanced need set could include:
   - Offering related products or services.
   - Forming strategic alliances with other firms serving the interests of the same customers.
   - Providing the customer with opportunities to collaborate in product or service design.
   - Offering *value streams* of services or benefits following the actual sale of a product or service (more on value streams later in the chapter).[28]

As the definition of the customer's need is broadened, and as the need set is expanded, the definition of the product itself will become more complex. With a more complex product the enterprise can make customization more beneficial. At each successive level of product complexity, the enterprise has another opportunity to remember *something* that will later make a difference to a specific individual customer. As discussed in Chapter 7, in the "Needs-Based Differentiation" section, when a customer base is characterized by customers with dramatically different needs, remembering an individual customer's own personal needs or preferences will be highly beneficial to the customer. The more different the customers are in terms of their needs, the more benefit each customer will see in engaging in a Learning Relationship.

Thus, when customers have more uniform needs, as is particularly true of companies selling commodity-like products and services, then the customer-strategy enterprise should try to expand the need set. Customers then will be seen as more diverse in the way they individually define their needs. The enterprise should assess which products and services it now offers that can cement the loyalty and improve the margin on its customers, even if the firm's competitors offer the same products and services at the same price, customized in the same way. Simply improving the quality of a product or service, while advantageous in the short term, will not necessarily yield a competitive benefit over the long term. A customer-strategy enterprise instead tries to improve a product's quality by customizing some aspect of it to suit the different needs of an individual customer, in order to build a collaborative Learning Relationship with that customer. If the firm is selling a commodity-like product, then what it actually customizes might not be the core product, but the bundle of services surrounding the product, or a configuration of additional products and services designed to meet an expanded definition of the customer's need.

[28]Don Peppers and Martha Rogers, PhD, *Enterprise One to One* (New York: Doubleday Broadway Books, 1996).

One of the easiest ways for a B2B enterprise to customize its product-service bundle, for example, is to remember how and when *each customer* wants to be invoiced. A credit card company with corporate cards, a phone company, or any other firm that sells a high-transaction product or service to other businesses, might consider offering some customers the opportunity to tailor the invoices to weekly totals, rather than monthly. Or a firm could provide the invoices on a quarterly summary basis, or even offer to allow the customer itself to specify which time periods to invoice at one time. Some banks are already offering some personalization capabilities for formatting of monthly statement options. Enterprises that offer products already customized can benefit by customizing these ancillary services even further.

In addition to the services and operations that naturally accompany a core product, most products and services can easily be associated with other, related needs on the part of a customer. When a customer buys a car from a car dealer, for instance, she will likely need automobile insurance, loan financing, a good mechanic, and, possibly, a car-wash subscription. Catering to an enhanced need set means providing extra services to meet the customer's broadest possible set of needs.

Hotel La Fontana, in Bogotá, Colombia, caters to the international business traveler. If a guest has a trip to Bogotá planned the hotel will set up her appointments in advance for her. All the guest need do is tell the hotel the names and phone numbers of the people she will meet. The deeper an enterprise can penetrate a particular customer's needs, the more likely that enterprise will be able to cement a Learning Relationship with the customer, earning the customer's loyalty, not simply out of gratitude, but because it is more convenient for the customer to remain loyal. As long as she is certain her own interests are being protected, the customer will trust the enterprise with a greater and greater share of her business.

VALUE STREAMS

Some enterprises believe they have nothing to offer their end-user customers to entice them to want relationships. A firm that produces a single product, infrequently purchased, is in this kind of situation. One strategy for a one-product company would be to create a "stream of value" behind the actual product sale. Here's the choice: Find another customer for the product you sell, and then another and another, to generate more and more transactions. Or find a related stream of products and services you could offer, in order to get a greater share of customer from each of the customers you've already acquired.

> Here's the choice: Find another customer for the product you sell, and then another and another, to generate more and more transactions. Or find a related stream of products and services you could offer, in order to get a greater share of customer from each of the customers you've already acquired.

Usually a value stream relies on some type of follow-on service, after the product sale, but it could also be an interaction designed to generate income later from customer referrals. The home builder who, in order to satisfy customers and generate more referrals, calls her customer the week before the one-year warranty expires and offers to inspect the home for any persisting problems, is creating a value stream behind the sale of the home. The simple fact is that most people who build a home won't build another any time soon. But having received this kind of service, they will likely tell their friends about their positive experience, and the builder could generate a much higher level of referral service.

There are other examples we could cite. A furniture retailer could create a different kind of value stream behind its infrequently sold products, selling a sofa with a free upholstery cleaning, to be scheduled by the customer one year after the initial purchase. That way, when it comes time to schedule the cleaning appointment, the retailer would be reestablishing contact with the customer, to the customer's own benefit. At that point, the retailer could generate more revenue from the customer in any number of ways—selling a longer-term subscription to furniture cleaning, or selling items of furniture to go with the original purchase, and so forth. A clothing store could offer a dry cleaning or repair service for the clothing it sells. Customers who buy their suits from the store and pay an extra fee could have all of their dry cleaning, pressing, laundering, tailoring, and sewing done for the first two or three years, perhaps.

Note that in each of these hypothetical cases, the enterprise increases the revenue generated from each customer by expanding the needs set, building an interactive Learning Relationship at the same time. The value stream approach has been used to encourage warranty card registration, particularly by software vendors whose products are bundled into the original equipment manufacturer's personal computer hardware. Those who mail in the registration (or who connect to register online) could receive 90 days' free advice and help in putting the software to work. Value streams eventually lead to supplemental revenue streams for the enterprise. A customer is willing to pay for the ancillary product or service because it is valuable to *her*. But, meanwhile, the enterprise will be strengthening its ongoing relationship by exchanging information with the customer, as the value stream is delivered.

> Value streams eventually lead to supplemental revenue streams for the enterprise. A customer is willing to pay for the ancillary product or service because it is valuable to *her*. But, meanwhile, the enterprise will be strengthening its ongoing relationship by exchanging information with the customer, as the value stream is delivered.

SIDEBAR 10.4

Bentley Systems Creates Value Streams[a]

What is the best way for an organization to remain actively involved with each of its customers—even when those customers may be years away from making another purchase? This is a key question for companies in some types of business, and it is a question likely to be faced especially by B2B organizations.

SIDEBAR 10.4 *(continued)*

Bentley Systems faced just such a dilemma: It already owned a huge share of its market, so a strategy focused primarily on market development would not deliver the kind of results sought by the company's management. Instead, Bentley turned to a strategy that emphasized account development, launching an entirely new, subscription-based service to meet the needs of its clients.

Most B2B organizations don't have a strategy or system in place to take advantage of the quiet intervals between sales. It's not that they're unaware of these intervals. More likely they've been trained or acculturated to see them as lost time, as dead zones in the purchase cycle. Sometimes these quiet times represent opportunities simply to deploy their customer acquisition resources elsewhere.

Or perhaps they're looking at the problem backward. Most enterprises believe it's important to know the purchase cycles of their customers: If you know the moment when your customer is ready to buy, you will be in a better position to sell your customer something—at that moment.

This type of reasoning works if you're in a business where you get to see your customers relatively often. Some B2C businesses—such as supermarkets, drug stores and other retailers—can count on seeing their customers at least once or twice a week. But organizations that sell products such as boats, cars, refrigerators, manufacturing tools, real estate property, or high-end business equipment have customers who purchase much less frequently. If you have customers who buy from you only every few years, how can you establish and cultivate customer relationships?

Bentley Systems Incorporated is one of the world's leading providers of software for the engineering, construction, and operation (E/C/O) market. With annual revenues topping $200 million, Bentley's primary products consist of architectural and engineering design software applications that it sells for a workstation environment. The typical Bentley customer buys a three-year software solutions contract worth $1 million, and might take as long as 18 months to close the deal. At any given moment, Bentley might have dozens of such deals in the works, all in various stages of development. Once a deal has been inked, it might be four or five years before the customer is ready for another purchase of similar magnitude. If nothing else, this makes it exceptionally difficult to project revenue very far into the future, as all of next year's revenue has to come from new customer sales or winbacks.

There are two basic ways to address this type of challenge: You could sell or give away a range of additional services related to your product—cleaning, adjusting, calibrating, refilling, repairing it under a warranty's terms, configuring other products and services to go with your product, and so forth; or you could alter your business model to "subscribe" customers to your product, rather than selling it to them. In either case, you're talking about trying to create a value stream to supplement or replace a sales pattern marked by infrequent spurts of purchasing activity, enabling you to maintain and strengthen relationships with your clients over a longer period of time.

Greg Bentley is the one who spearheaded the company's evolution beyond product sales. His choice was to wrap a wide array of ancillary services and perks into a single, all-encompassing subscription plan called SELECT.

SELECT provides subscribing customers with literally dozens of benefits, such as 24/7 technical support, discounts on Bentley products, free platform swaps, and free software upgrades. SELECT customers are allowed concurrent licensing of their Bentley software, which essentially means the licenses are transferable from moment to moment within the company. This benefits the customers by giving them greater

SIDEBAR 10.4 *(continued)*

flexibility to redeploy expensive software applications among their users. And it benefits Bentley by expanding usage and creating demand for more software products.

The beauty of SELECT is that it functions as both a dependable income stream and a robust customer retention tool. When a customer signs up for the subscription plan, Bentley can bank on that customer's loyalty. For the duration, Bentley has a window of opportunity to sell more products to a customer who already has declared her allegiance.

For example, a large architectural firm with an installed base of 200 MicroStation users might be a good prospect for an upgrade to TriForma, Bentley's 3D modeling application. Or an electric utility with 100 seats of MicroStation might be a prime candidate for other Bentley products, such as GeoOutlook, which can be interfaced with truck-mounted global positioning system (GPS) equipment.

The important idea here is that it is not only possible but also essential to create a practical system for bridging the gap between infrequent sales, if you plan to build your business success around customer relationships. SELECT is an example of a system designed to bridge this gap. It helps Bentley stay involved with its customers; it makes it easier for Bentley to cross-sell a variety of its products; and it allows Bentley to focus on growing the firm's share of customers instead of just its share of market.

In the final analysis, the most enduring legacy of SELECT may be how it fundamentally changed the way Bentley Systems measures success and allocates resources for the future. Under the old model, Bentley set annual goals for increasing its sales revenue, and it measured its own performance against these goals. This essentially kept the company locked into a customer acquisition mode, no matter how many innovative programs or initiatives it designed to break free. The launch of SELECT, and its rapid acceptance by customers, liberated Bentley to measure its performance with a refreshingly simple set of metrics tied to customer development.

Bentley has found it advantageous to move "up the food chain" to deliver more comprehensive service packages to its clients. For now, SELECT can be used to provide seamless document management, including filing, archiving, and transmittal to involved third parties. And the right way for Bentley to gain the most leverage out of SELECT is for the company to reorient its thinking about the nature of its customer base to begin with. With SELECT, rather than selling products to customers, Bentley is *subscribing* customers to an ongoing stream of products and services. Running a subscription business is very different from running a product transaction business.

In addition, many of Bentley's customers almost certainly want to develop their own value streams of services to transcend the periodic projects they do for their own clients. SELECT provides Bentley with an ideal opportunity to begin helping them in this task.

SELECT is a program that should be configured in such a way as to allow an architectural firm to go into not just the "project" business of designing and constructing a building, but into the "long-term management" business of taking care of the building, maintaining it, and upgrading it even after it has been built. Because Bentley's program can provide continual, updated documentation of a project's design, it can also help the architectural firm do a lot more than just creative work. A building is a complex system of pipes, wires, ducts, heating and cooling elements, and lighting treatments, not to mention the surrounding landscaping, lawn maintenance, irrigation and gardening care, as well as driveway and parking lot construction and maintenance. The more of this comprehensive system that SELECT can accommodate, the more Bentley's clients will rely on it to drive their own profitability.

SIDEBAR 10.4 *(continued)*

....

When Bentley looks for additional ways to strengthen its relationships with its customers, the company might want to consider services that aren't tied directly to SELECT. It's not hard to imagine Bentley helping its customer firms with the preparation and financing of the bid they render for a project. Or instituting training classes for a client's engineers or architects—not just in the use of Bentley's software, but in the nuances of design. Or hosting Web sites and other IT infrastructure for a client, allowing the client to manage its own far-flung collection of independent architects and engineers more efficiently. See Exhibit A for a comparison between Bentley's old "product" business model and the new "relationship" business model.

- ■ **High market share**
- ■ **Infrequent sales spikes**
- ■ **Next year's sales goal: Find new customers to meet sales quotes.**

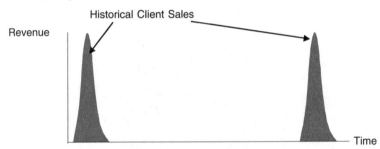

- ■ **Broaden product line to meet more client needs over time.**
- ■ **Focus on end-user needs instead of market development.**
- ■ **Next year's sales goal: Re-up the SELECT subscribers, sell $500 of product to each licensed seat, get a few new customers.**

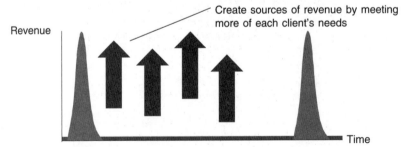

EXHIBIT A   **Infrequent Sales versus Continuing Value Streams**

One of the greatest challenges within an organization is deciding who will be accountable for building the value of a particular customer—and another and another. This is the issue of "managing customer relationships," and it will be discussed more completely in Chapter 11. But in the context of our discussion on tailoring as a way of keeping customers longer and growing them bigger, we need to consider: Who within the organization will be responsible for making the customization happen?

WHO WILL WRITE THE NEW BUSINESS RULES FOR PERSONALIZATION?

Bruce Kasanoff
President, Now Possible

Business rules are the instructions that tell software—or people—how to operate. They are a reusable set of instructions that enable an organization to operate in a consistent yet flexible way. Ronald Ross, co-founder of the consulting firm Business Rule Solutions, LLC, says, "Business rules are literally the encoded knowledge of your business operations." "Upgrade platinum flyers to first class before gold flyers" is a business rule. So is "Most valuable customers are those who order at least $1,500 of merchandise in a year."[29]

> "Personalization is the killer app for business rules,"

"Personalization is the killer app for business rules," says Ross. He argues that because business rules drive most of the leading personalization and e-commerce applications, companies now have a compelling reason to invest the time and effort in documenting the way they want to do business.

INSTRUCTIONS THAT LIVE OUTSIDE OF PROGRAMMING LANGUAGES

Business rules are not new; what is new is that today many rules are being created and changed via interfaces accessible to nontechnical business managers. Rules used to live deep within programming that was difficult and time-consuming to change. The resulting inflexibility of systems resulted in equally inflexible companies. By "externalizing" some business rules, enterprises are seeking to be more adaptable and efficient as they get closer to their customers, to deliver personalized and customized service. Not every rule should be accessible to business managers, who lack the technical training—

[29]Ronald Ross, quoted in Bruce Kasanoff, *Making it Personal* (New York: Perseus Publishing, 2001).

or the inclination—to manage systems reliability and security, but far more should be accessible than is generally the case. "Almost every one of our clients is pursuing a strategy of having business ownership of basic rules," says Alan Crowther, an executive with Adjoined Consulting. "They want to allow business units to specify and make changes to rules quickly, without heavy IT involvement or coding."

Dealing with inflexible companies can be maddening for customers. Take a bank, for example, that requires a loan application for every customer, regardless of the customer's net assets or history with the bank. You can almost hear the assistant manager saying, "The system won't let me process your application without a completed application." She's right; that requirement is probably buried deep within the bank's programming, where it would take years to change.

The business rules approach makes it possible for such requirements to be contained in a far more accessible location. Thus, the bank could create a rule that would accommodate special circumstances. The rule might say: "If the customer has a clean credit report, the loan is secured, and the customer agrees to keep at least 20 percent of the loan's value in cash in her account, then waive the application requirement."

TRANSFERRING KNOWLEDGE FROM YOUR HEAD

It is difficult to transfer the knowledge of each employee—and of the organization as a whole—into a set of effective rules, and the very fact that it is so difficult is one reason business rules are so valuable. Think about the best salesperson you have ever met. Wouldn't you like to be able to capture what makes her so talented, and imbue an automated system with those qualities? That is one promise of business rules, but the challenge is to translate her approach into a manageable number of repeatable principles. In this example, you might start with rules such as these:

- Listen to the customer's needs before you present any products, services or offers.
- Present offers specific to the customer's stated needs before you show her other special offers.
- Show the blue items first, because this customer has shown a preference for blue, then yellow, then gray.

Stew Leonard's is a Connecticut-based "dairy store" that is world-renowned for staying close to its customers and generating immense sales. In a largely nonautomated setting, the store has captured its principles in a set of rules that produce extraordinary service and a highly effective merchandising system.

One of those rules is that if an item is not properly marked for price, the customer gets it for free. I experienced this firsthand while buying an eight-pound piece of filet mignon for a holiday celebration. When a price didn't come up on the register, the cashier gave it to me for free. I began to protest—the meat was worth at least $50—but she explained that because the company did so much volume it was cheaper to give the meat away than to hold up the checkout line. And, besides, Stew Leonard's has "The customer is always right" carved in stone at the front of the store.

Ken Molay, director of product marketing at Blaze Software (now part of Brokat), explained that business rules can also be used to balance the needs of a customer with those of the enterprise: "The goal of personalization is not just to give a customer whatever he needs, but rather to keep him happy while also ensuring that the company profits from delivering the service."[30]

NEW RULES, NEW SKILLS

It is not hard to create a simple business rule, such as, "Send a thank-you e-mail to every customer who places an order." It is difficult, however, to create and manage a full complement of rules; yet this is exactly what is required when the goal is to treat different customers differently.[31] As rules multiply, the odds increase that they will cancel each other out or cause unexpected results. This is especially problematic when multiple business units target the same customers. What if 10 units create rules that specify what happens when a new prospect visits the firm's Web site? Does the prospect get 10 different offers, all seemingly oblivious to each other, or does one take precedence?

> "The goal of personalization is not just to give a customer whatever he needs, but rather to keep him happy while also ensuring that the company profits from delivering the service."

Rules have the potential to produce outcomes that are undesirable or even illegal. Alan Crowther warns, "Enterprises have to be careful that rules do not result in certain content that is accessible only to certain people based on inappropriate data. For example, a financial services site that uses location to determine which people see loan officers might generate outcomes that could be considered redlining. While no one may pursue this explicitly, algorithms that augment business rules can make this happen inadvertently." Colleen McClintock, product manager at iLog Software, admits that there is a political aspect to the creation of business rules. "Rules can support the interests of the organization writing the policies," she said.

> It is not hard to create a simple business rule, such as, "Send a thank-you e-mail to every customer who places an order." It is difficult, however, to create and manage a full complement of rules; yet this is exactly what is required when the goal is to treat different customers differently.

But many think this is a good thing. Business managers already have profit-and-loss responsibility, and giving them direct access to the instructions that

[30]Ken Molay, quoted in ibid.

[31]Alan Crowther, quoted in ibid.

control customer interactions should result in far more behaviors designed to build customer value. Responsibility for rules gives the business manager more control over her fate.

The reality is that businesses have incredible new tools, and they have barely begun to build the skills necessary to exploit them. Few business managers have the training, expertise, or demeanor necessary to create and manage business rules, even when those rules are written in plain English. Ryan Martens, director of product management at BEA Systems, believes that critical jobs, such as Web channel manager tactician, which would have responsibility for writing the rules, haven't yet been identified on the business side. "Programmers are used to the thought process necessary to create and manage business rules, but until recently business managers never had to think in similar terms," he says. Truth is, the language and detail involved in managing rules can make business managers' eyes glaze over.

Here's an excerpt from "Creating and Managing Rules," posted at BEA Systems' Web site:

> Content selector rules construct queries on the fly and return content based on the user profile. This type of rule adds time and content components to the basic classifier rule and may use references to classifier rules to define it. It also produces dynamic queries at run-time to select content from a document collection.[32]

This kind of language and approach works for programmers, not business managers. But business managers increasingly are responsible for defining how the enterprise will interact with individual customers.

DOCUMENT WHAT?

When enterprises use business rules to automate existing practices, the first step is obvious: Document the way the business operates. Members of an IT or consulting team will typically interview the business manager and document current practices. This makes life manageable: IT possesses the project management and programming skills; the business manager understands the business and the needs of its customers. But what happens when companies want to invent new business models, or personalize the way they serve individual customers? When it comes to achieving this kind of business transformation, many of the existing business practices may no longer be considered valid, or even helpful. Suddenly, the process becomes unwieldy, and it's no longer easy to separate tasks into neat little packages.

Business rules expert Ross suggests a three-step process to deal with such a situation:

[32]Accessed at *www.bea.com.*

1. Record and manage the current rules of engagement with customers.
2. Make new or modified rules of engagement operational quickly.
3. Manage the rules of engagement on the business side, not the IT side. In other words, reempower the business users to manage the rules directly.

It is the second step that confounds most enterprises. Established companies are successful because they have learned to perform the same tasks repeatedly; that is what makes them scalable. But creating new rules of engagement means inventing new approaches and services, and business rules experts are not natural inventors. They tend to come from a data or project management background, and out of necessity learn to focus on semantics, process, and precision.

The result is a wide-open field for professionals with initiative who are willing to stretch their boundaries and develop a hybrid skill set. In practical terms, the experts on using business rules are those who roll up their sleeves and test new approaches that leverage CRM and personalization applications.

Rich Lloyd, senior manager of online relationship marketing for Dell Home Systems, notes that theory is often much different from practice, and personalization rules are no different. "Rules get written through trial and error, by testing and retesting. We start with some sort of hypothesis, and then we work hard to isolate the confusing noise from what's really working." For example, Lloyd's team might try an approach in which the division sends an e-mail promoting printers to everyone who purchased a laptop but not a printer in the past 10 months. But they don't look at the result of that promotion in isolation; they track results over three months to determine whether the e-mail reduces the response to other promotional messages sent to the same group of customers. The question to ask, says Lloyd, is, "Am I better off with this additional rule in place or not?"

One of the first challenges for these pioneers is to develop rules for interacting with individual customers. While personalization and customization[33] have become hot topics in recent years, many enterprises have only recently identified their customers, or begun efforts to do so. Until the rise of the Web, any firm that sold through a distribution channel had long been disconnected from its end users. Even enterprises that deal directly with customers have often engaged in monologues ("buy this; it works") rather than true dialogues.

WHO IS THE CUSTOMER?

The first challenge in creating customer interaction rules is to agree on the definition of a customer. Author and consultant Terry Moriarty told me that many companies define customers in too limited a manner. "Most information

---

[33] Authors' note about the difference between personalization and customization: Many companies and writers in this field use these terms interchangeably, and that's probably okay. But generally, when there is a distinction, it's usually as given here in the Glossary. Perhaps it's helpful to think of personalization as Pine and Gilmore's "adaptive" and "cosmetic" customization, whereas what we refer to as customization is more along the lines of "collaborative" and "transparent" customization.

systems today have a billing view of the customer," she said. They know only the one responsible for paying the bill, but that isn't necessarily the one to whom you market the product." This is not just a B2B problem; even in a consumer setting, children or roommates can influence when and from whom a person buys. But there's no information about those parties. "The ultimate business rule says: here's what a customer is," Moriarty continues. She believes that systems should have fields such as "involved party" and "role" (i.e., decision maker). Building such flexibility into its database enables a business to capture real-world data about how purchasing decisions are made.

In a household with teenagers, the odds are good that the teenagers have more influence than the parents over which ISP the family chooses or which computer they buy for the family room. In a business, there are always experts whose influence isn't acknowledged on the organizational chart or by the vendors' systems. But these influencers tend to be active participants on Web sites that contain facts and opinions about these services, thus companies have the capability to identify them and build relationships. "If the database provides separate building blocks, a firm can derive any relationship they will ever need," Moriarty says. "Each business unit can manage its line of business; the enterprise can manage the total relationship."

WHO "OWNS" THE CUSTOMER RELATIONSHIP?

In a typical company, Product Manager A wants the Web site to send an offer for her product to every new site visitor. But Product Manager B wants to send an offer for her product. No one can document the correct processes, because no one agrees on them. Thus, the increasing use of business rules to drive the automation of customer interactions will accelerate the pressure on enterprises to shift from product management to customer management organizational structures. If one division "owns" a certain group of customers, then it is clear who is responsible for managing the rules that apply to those individuals. The process of creating and managing rules highlights the limitations of product management structures. These organizations were logical when the toughest challenge an enterprise faced was creating and selling high-quality products. But today the toughest challenge is managing relationships, often in real time. If divisions are competing internally, they make decisions that aren't in the customer's interest.

Alan Crowther observes, "Organizational barriers mean that personalization objectives are often compromised to individual business objectives. Even though it may make sense to personalize a site so that certain products or services are not highlighted, a business unit may have the clout to demand it." Of course, the real loser is the company that remains burdened by an organizational structure that is illogical in today's era of real-time interactions. Most customers are starved for time and increasingly unwilling to tolerate treatment that doesn't make sense to them. The bottom line: Creating rules for e-commerce and personalization is much easier when one person or business unit has clear ownership of a portfolio of customers.

Even with such clarity, large enterprises are still, well, large. So business rules need to be created using a common vocabulary. Ron Ross explains: "You must be able to trace who is using what terms in what context; you need to be able to trace the impact across the business environment." While business rules can theoretically be created using everyday language, each term must be used with more precision and consistency than we use in normal conversation.

Another issue in large businesses is traceability: being able to follow the impact of certain rules across the entire business environment. "You need to know what task each rule relates to," says Ross, "and you also want to be able to trace rules to the parties that have a stake in a particular rule. When it comes time to change the rule, you must know whom to call."

WHAT TO EXPECT

The more you study the use of business rules to drive personalization, the more obvious it becomes that the approach has tremendous potential but is still in its infancy. While there are no tried-and-true best practices, it is possible to offer some conclusions about what will likely work best.

- *Minimize the number of enterprisewide rules.* Only about 2 to 3 percent of all business rules are "core rules" that impact the entire enterprise and specify qualities that give the firm its identity and differentiating qualities, Ross says. These rules usually existed long before the advent of automated systems. Here is an example that used to apply at Domino's Pizza: All pizzas are delivered within 30 minutes or the pizza is free. This rule drove the company and its marketing messages, but it eventually was changed after communities began to question whether the pressure on drivers to deliver so quickly was resulting in serious traffic accidents. Note that rules such as this need to include two portions: the rule itself and what happens if the rule is violated.
- *Use the simplest approach possible.* The more complex an approach, the more likely it is to fail. The question is to ask, "What are the simplest changes that will have the most powerful positive impacts on customer relationships?" One practice to consider is that all databases containing customer information have at least one field with a common, firmwide format, enabling the firm to link individual customer data, from one unit to the next, when necessary. This can sometimes be a simpler approach than building a data warehouse or requiring all business units to conform to more restrictive data conventions.
- *Combine business rules with other approaches.* Matching business rules with specialized data mining, domain-specific algorithms and other applications will generate better results, Crowther says. Black Pearl, a personalization software company that specializes in the financial services industry, is a good example of this multipronged approach. Its Knowledge Broker system combines business rules with a recommendation system that is

powered by data-mining technology and an ontology that enables communication between multiple computer systems. Ontologies provide a consistent, logical model for accommodating multiple data sources and goals. Done right, they provide a flexible system for understanding and managing interactions with individual customers.

- *Maintain a separate rule base.* A rule base is essentially a database for rules. By separating business logic from specific applications, rules can be shared by numerous applications. This approach speeds development and increases flexibility. As the number of rules grows, it becomes increasingly important to be able to test in advance what impact the addition of new rules will have. This task is easier when all the rules are stored in a common location and format.

The payoff for enterprises that engage in customization is twofold. In most cases, by employing automation and business rules to mass-customize its products or the delivery of its services, the enterprise can actually reduce its unit production costs, on an all-in basis, essentially because it will only make those goods that customers will have already bought. More important, however, customization will enable the enterprise to engage in a *collaborative* Learning Relationship with each customer.

SIDEBAR 10.5
Customization in the Context of Branding

Eric Petitt
Consultant

Ann M. Diver
Consultant, Peppers and Rogers Group

Two hundred years ago when you needed a new pair of shoes, you could sit down with your local cobbler and he would carefully take enough measurements of your feet to create a realistic wooden model of them, around which he would craft your shoes. He easily dealt with that embarrassing issue of one foot being slightly larger than the other. And you could talk to him face to face about any special desires for the design of your shoes, or their composition, or their quality. The cobbler, understanding your preferences, would create a pair of shoes to meet your needs. In the process, the local cobbler would also be building a relationship with you and your family over time, giving you faith that your feet were in good hands.

> In place of trusted localized relationships we now have brand names; and in place of true personalization, we now have abundant choice.

Fast-forward 150 years. Twentieth-century technology has enabled the modern-day shoe merchant to mass-produce hundreds of different kinds of shoes of every size, quality and shape imaginable. In place of trusted localized relationships we now have brand names; and in place of true personalization, we now have abundant choice.

SIDEBAR 10.5 *(continued)*

Today's "cobbler" is much more than just a cobbler, and she sells more than just shoes. Today's shoe manufacturer sells not only a whole array of complementary products, but also a way of life for wearers, a sense of status and cultural cache. Furthermore, branding has enabled shoemakers (and similarly most manufacturers) to garner a higher price for their products than they would otherwise have achieved.

Enter personalization—back from a 150-year or so hibernation thanks in part to a whole new set of enabling technologies. Today, on its Web site, international shoe cobbler Nike invites customers to "express yourself" and "Build Your Own Shoes" online, by choosing shoe size, color, and style, and printing up to 10 letters on the back of its shoe of the customer's choice. While most customers choose to personalize their shoe by inscribing their names, one MIT student recently caused a PR uproar by adding the word "sweatshop" to his shoe design. Nike vetoed the student's request, obviously not happy with the student's implication that Nike runs Asian sweatshops. (The student's contention was that he was only exercising his right to express himself, as Nike had encouraged.[a] But personalization, in the service of a company's commercial gain, had found a limit.)

Personalization transfers control over product design characteristics from the manufacturer to the customer. As companies allow customers to influence their own products, the entrenched qualities that define their brand could also be affected. How far will companies let their customers express themselves through personalization? Will Nike allow a customer to manufacture a shoe as "uncool" as a pair of Zips from the discount chain store? Will J. Crew ever allow its customers to design clothing emblazoned with its logo but looking more like Gap-wear?

It remains to be seen to what extent companies will relinquish the voice of their "brands" to their customers' individual preferences.

[a]Anya Schiffrin. "Nike 'Sweatshop' Story Has Legs," *The Industry Standard* (February 28, 2001).

SUMMARY

Instead of expecting a customer to use what she knows about a company to figure out what she should buy, the one-to-one enterprise uses what it knows about the customer to figure out what she needs. In the process, such an enterprise increases the number of transactions it gets from a customer, makes it progressively easier for that customer to come back to that enterprise for purchases and service, and increases the profit per transaction.

Our story of managing customer relationships in the interactive era now takes a turning point. We have laid the foundation of relationship theory and provided a comprehensive examination of each of the four tasks of the IDIC methodology. We have shown the importance Learning Relationships and the sensitive issues related to privacy protection. We have peeked at the technical tools and software that help to accelerate the relationship management process and reinforced how technology does not, nor should not, do the CRM job alone.

With Part Three (beginning with Chapter 11) we begin to look at what it means to manage the CRM process. We discuss the challenges an enterprise faces in measuring and maintaining a customer-based initiative and look at the quantifiable metrics associated with CRM. We delve into the science of CRM analytics as a method to predict each customer's behavior and anticipate his needs so he will be treated the way he wants and remain a customer. Finally, we show how transforming to an enterprise that grows through building customer value requires a number of different infrastructure changes that will need to be addressed by managers who fully understand and support the underlying concepts we have been discussing so far—and so much more that we have yet to discuss.

FOOD FOR THOUGHT

1. How will M&M Mars practice mass customization? Will it put my initials on the M&M candies? Let me choose the colors to match my kitchen or wedding theme? (Hint: No—at least not in the foreseeable future.) To think about mass customization for M&M, consider:
   - Who are the customer types for M&M Mars? (Think B2B.) Who are the MVCs? The MGCs? The BZs? (See Chapter 5.)
   - What are customers buying when they buy M&Ms? (It's not "sweet treats.")
   - If they buy packages of M&Ms to resell, what else do they need? What is their expanded need set?
   - What is the opportunity to lock customers into a Learning Relationship and build share of customer for M&M Mars?
   - Is there any opportunity, ever, at all, to build Learning Relationships with any end user? How and why?

2. If customization is such a good idea, why don't we see more of it in the marketplace right this minute?

3. Name half a dozen examples of mass customization or expanded needs sets in the enterprises where you do business.

GLOSSARY

Customization   Most often, customization and mass customization refer to the modularized building of an offering to a customer based on that customer's individual feedback, thus serving as the basis of a Learning Relationship.[31]

Enhanced needs set   The capability of a company to think of a product it sells as a suite of product plus service plus communication, as well as the next product and service the need for the original product implies. The sale of a faucet implies the need for the installation of that faucet, and maybe an entire bathroom upgrade and strong nesting instinct.

Mass customization   See Customization.

Personalization   Refers to a superficial ability to put a customer's name on something—to insert a name into a message, for example, or to monogram a set of sheets.

PART Three

Measuring and Managing to Build Customer Value

Customer relationships cannot be installed; they must be adopted. And building customer value requires process, organization, technology, and culture management. It's a shift in strategy after 100 years dominated by mass marketing, so it can't happen overnight. The management of customer relationships to build the value of the customer base is a journey, not a destination.

Measuring the Success of Customer–Based Initiatives

11

Chapter

Traditional marketing measures such as response rates, cost per thousand, gross ratings points, and awareness levels may help a company understand how successful a campaign has been or how successful or efficient a message is, on average, in reaching a target market. But in a discussion about growing customer value, the importance of measuring the success of a campaign pales next to our need to measure the growth of the value of the customer base. In this chapter, we will look at several different approaches to understanding how much a customer is worth. The ability to measure customer value is directly related to our ability to manage it—that is, to make intelligent managerial decisions all day every day about strategy and resource allocation, to reward employees for doing the right thing, to report in a useful way, to anticipate problems. Katherine Lemon, Roland Rust, and Valarie Zeithaml help us consider three alternative ways of thinking about "equity," and James Goodnight offers a view on the maturation of CRM metrics.

Any proposal for funding an initiative to build customer relationships must clearly demonstrate how the initiative will affect key measures that are important to the company financially. Moreover, the benefits that together provide the total return on a relationship-building project are likely to become an ongoing scorecard for the project, and for the enterprise, well beyond the project's initial implementation.[1]

Customer-focused projects can easily cost several million dollars, not counting the time, human resources, and organizational "angst" involved in the process itself. Quantifying the right things for the enterprise's senior management will not only increase the chances of getting a project approved but also pave the way to improving the enterprise's customer performance in terms of customer value. Determining the appropriate measurements to be used in quantifying a financial return on investment, however, is a particularly elusive task, since the very culture at many firms is intertwined with traditional measures of

---

[1]D. Hagemeyer, "Quantifying the Impact of a CRM Project," GartnerGroup (March 26, 2001).

success—or what we might call *legacy metrics*—quarterly product sales, cost of goods sold, number of new customers acquired, earnings before interest, taxes, depreciation, and amortization (EBITDA)—the tried and true. These companies may find it challenging to supplement these legacy metrics with metrics that will drive management decisions focused on increasing the value of the company by increasing the value of the customer base.

In the era of mass marketing, enterprises typically sampled consumer attitudes to understand how their products were being perceived and how they could be positioned relative to their competition. They examined ways to differentiate their products and services to achieve the greatest awareness among a desired audience. Before embarking on a mass-marketing campaign, an enterprise took careful consideration of a set of metrics to monitor what would determine the success or failure of its efforts. For example, it needed to gauge the relative market size it was penetrating and its potential market share. To determine marketing's impact on its bottom line, the enterprise would measure marketing expenditures as a percentage of sales. **Brand equity** was a term often used to describe or measure the total value of a brand in a particular target market (although, truthfully, very few companies ever made any attempt to quantify this term).

BRAND EQUITY VERSUS CUSTOMER EQUITY

Although there have been a number of academic papers written on how to measure brand equity, there is no commonly accepted method to quantify it. Brand equity is, simply, built through image and meaning. According to Rust, Zeithaml, and Lemon, the brand serves three vital roles. First, the brand acts as a "magnet" that can attract new customers to the enterprise. Second, the brand can serve as a reminder to customers about the enterprise's products and services. Finally, the brand can become the customer's emotional tie to the enterprise. Brand equity has often been defined very broadly to include an extensive set of attributes that influence consumer choice. But it can be defined more narrowly as "the customer's subjective and intangible assessment of the brand, above and beyond its objectively perceived value."[2]

Brand equity has never really been calculated as a monetary amount in any satisfactory way. This is unlike *customer equity*, which, though challenging, is more straightforward. In many ways, customer equity is easier to quantify, model, and visualize in monetary terms. The firm's customer equity, as discussed in Chapters 5 and 11, can be thought of as the sum of the lifetime values (LTVs) of all the customers in the customer base. Brand equity, in contrast, is often used to describe the *tendency* of a consumer to prefer one brand over another, or to describe a product's advantage over the competition in a given market.

[2]Roland T. Rust, Valarie A. Zeithaml, and Katherine N. Lemon, *Driving Customer Equity: How Customer Lifetime Value Is Reshaping Corporate Strategy* (New York: The Free Press, 2000.)

While the metrics associated with product-centric marketing are still useful, enterprises of the interactive era engage in a customer-value-building strategy that requires additional, more quantifiable metrics. Customer equity can describe the effectiveness of customer strategies and implementation because it is primarily determined by the total value of the enterprise's customer relationships. Robert Blattberg and John Deighton define customer equity as follows: [3]

> An enterprise's customer equity is the total of the discounted lifetime values of all of its customers. The enterprise views the value of a customer in terms of his current profitability and also with respect to the net discounted contribution stream that the enterprise could realize from the customer over time. Adding these up provides the total value of the customers of the enterprise.

Customer equity is an important component of the value of the enterprise. But brand equity and customer equity are synergistic. In many cases, the more an enterprise tries to build its brand equity, the more customer equity it adds, too—although the strategies and tactics required can be completely different, and the way the two quantities are measured is different as well. It can never be known precisely what an individual customer will do in the future, but technology does enable a company to compare individual customers in highly quantitative ways, in order to arrive at an LTV figure for one customer relative to a particular statistically similar group.

There are many who consider customer loyalty to be one of the biggest single benefits of relationship management, and there is no question that a customer's loyalty is likely to grow when the customer is, in fact, engaged in a relationship with an enterprise. The real issue is: What is loyalty worth? Ultimately, it is worth whatever it yields in terms of an increased customer LTV.

But before going further, we should first reprise what we really mean when we say that a customer is "loyal" to an enterprise.

NATURE OF CUSTOMER LOYALTY: ATTITUDE OR BEHAVIOR?

Consider a customer's relationship with his bank. Perhaps he has kept a savings account with a local branch for 15 years because it is near his home, even though he does not particularly enjoy doing his banking there for one reason or another. He doesn't even like this bank, but continues as a customer there because it is too difficult to switch to a different bank. Is he or is he not a loyal customer of the bank? Haven't we demonstrated, not only here, but since Chapter 2, that "duration" and "loyalty" are not necessarily the same thing?

The fact is, when we discuss loyalty we are sometimes talking about specific customer behaviors and sometimes about attitudes. Although both the

---

[3] Robert C. Blattberg and John Deighton, "Manage Marketing by the Customer Equity Test," *Harvard Business Review* 74 (July–August 1996), pp. 136–144.

behavioral definition and the attitudinal definition are valid, they have different implications and lead to very different prescriptions for businesses.

As we have seen, the attitudinal definition of loyalty is about preference and liking. The behavioral definition of loyalty, in contrast, is a description of a customer's actual conduct. By this definition, a customer is loyal to a company if he buys from it and then continues to buy from it.[4]

The behavioral definition of loyalty—based on a proclivity to buy or a preference for a company or brand, is clearly what *we've* been talking about when we discuss Learning Relationships and customer collaboration. It's usually the case that a customer treated to more personalized service based on past preferences will tend to like the company and be more satisfied with it; but when we say the customer is loyal, must we mean that he *prefers* a brand? Or are we saying only that he is a repeat purchaser—whether or not he is satisfied or happy. In other words, are we still saying that if he repeats, he is loyal, and if he does not repeat, then he is not loyal?

Although we agree that customers who are loyal because they prefer a brand are actually more loyal than those who buy repeatedly because no alternative is readily available, we still prefer using the behavioral definition of loyalty, largely because defining loyalty in attitudinal terms leads to a number of conceptual ambiguities, while providing less real guidance in terms of what the enterprise should actually do to increase the value of its customer base. For instance, consider the fact that **attitudinal loyalty** and brand preference may be completely interchangeable concepts. A customer's willingness to pay a higher price for Brand X, relative to Brand Y, is not only the definition of attitudinal loyalty, but also of brand preference, as we discussed in Chapter 2. So these terms could be viewed as redundant.

ECONOMICS OF LOYALTY

In Chapter 2, we introduced the idea that "loyalty" should be related to the economics of the enterprise. In this chapter, we can now see that if we are talking about the *measurement* of the financial and operational results that can be obtained by focusing on individual customer relationships, then customer loyalty must surely drive some economic effect. Yet if loyalty is an attitude, then by itself it has no measurable economic effect. Internally held attitudes have no intrinsic value to a firm, because there is no financial result to measure until and unless these attitudes are somehow translated into actual customer behaviors. And the financial benefit of increased customer patronage could easily accrue to a firm despite the fact that its customer is no more (or less) attitudinally loyal than before. Suppose, for instance, that a consumer packaged goods manufac-

---

[4]Views and definitions of loyalty are myriad and controversial, and no attempt is made here to exhaust these discussions, but they are fairly easy to locate.

turer selling laundry detergent, tracking the buying patterns of its most valuable consumers (MVCs), finds that one customer of five years has begun to purchase three boxes of detergent each month instead of the one box he had been buying previously. Does this change in the customer's detergent-buying pattern mean that the customer has become more loyal; or did his wife just have a baby, or maybe twins? Or did he find a new source of coupons? How does the enterprise measure and quantify such a change and then interpret the results?

It is still the behavioral definition of loyalty that will be the more useful for anyone trying to understand the actual mechanics and techniques of managing customer relationships, because the implied benefit of managing a customer relationship is that the customer's future actions (i.e., the customer's behavior) can be influenced in a way that benefits the enterprise.

There are, of course, situations in which it would be useful to define customer loyalty in somewhat more attitudinal terms—particularly, for instance, when trying to analyze the process of converting *known prospective customers* to actual customers. Two prospective customers who have never purchased a particular brand could still have entirely different attitudes toward it, and these attitudes could easily be affected by various nonpurchase interactions with the brand. For example, a man might wear a Harley-Davidson leather jacket because he aspires to own a Harley-Davidson motorcycle someday, even though he has never purchased one in his life, and almost certainly never will, because he simply cannot afford one. He is loyal to the Harley-Davidson brand (attitudinal loyalty) but he is highly unlikely ever to buy the product (**behavioral loyalty**). Harley-Davidson has high brand equity with this customer because he so clearly prefers its product line to all the other motorcycles. But for this man, Harley-Davidson has low customer equity because he's unlikely ever to buy one of its motorcycles. When we describe the value of a customer, we generally talk about the profit the enterprise will make on the customer, in the future. The enterprise, of course, makes no profit at all on this customer's "attitude" of loyalty, but it is still useful for us to try to manage the attitude, not just because of the possibility that the customer's actual behavior may change, but also because the customer's good feelings about Harley-Davidson might influence other customers who do have buying power.

In this chapter, we are focused primarily on the behavioral aspects of loyalty, because this is the definition of loyalty that is most closely related to a customer's true economic value to the enterprise. Elsewhere, in Chapter 13, we will discuss the specific issues involved in managing relationships with identified prospects who have not yet become customers of an enterprise.

Customer equity is not the sole metric to determine the value of the entire enterprise. But understanding how to grow and manage customer equity is crucial to long-term success. It is difficult to determine how to increase customer equity to yield the highest return on investment. Lemon, Rust, and Zeithaml suggest that in addition to brand equity, the enterprise should pay attention to two other drivers of customer equity: **value equity** and **relationship equity**. According to Lemon and her colleagues, within each of these drivers are actions the enterprise can take to increase its overall customer equity.

SIDEBAR 11.1
What Drives Customer Equity?[a]

Katherine N. Lemon
Associate professor of marketing, Wallace E. Carroll School of Management, Boston College

Roland T. Rust
David Bruce Smith Chair in Marketing, Robert H. Smith School of Business, University of Maryland

Valarie A. Zeithaml
Professor, University of North Carolina

Consider the questions a typical brand manager, product manager, or marketing-oriented CEO might ask himself: How do I manage the brand? How will my customers react to changes in the product or service offering? Should I raise price? What is the best way to enhance the relationships with my current customers? Where should I focus my efforts?

Strategy based on customer equity can help a business executive answer these questions. This makes it possible for the enterprise to make trade-offs between customer value, brand equity, and customer relationship management. A new strategic framework reveals that the key drivers that increase the enterprise's customer equity are what we call value equity, brand equity, and relationship equity (which can also be thought of as retention equity). The Customer Equity Diagnostic in this section enables managers to determine what is most important to the customer—and to begin to identify the enterprise's critical strengths and hidden vulnerabilities. Customer equity is a new approach to marketing and corporate strategy that finally puts the customer—and, more importantly, strategies that grow the *value* of the customer—at the heart of the organization.

For most firms, customer equity is certain to be the most important determinant of the long-term value of the enterprise. While customer equity will not be responsible for the entire value of the enterprise (consider, for example, the physical assets, intellectual property, research and development capabilities, etc.), the enterprise's current customers provide the most reliable source of future revenues and profits—and provide a focal point for management strategy.

Although it may seem obvious that customer equity is key to long-term success, understanding how to grow and manage customer equity is much more complex. How to grow customer equity is of utmost importance, and doing it well can lead to significant competitive advantage. Brand equity was discussed briefly elsewhere; here we identify the other drivers of customer equity—value equity and relationship equity—and explain how these drivers work, independently and together, to grow customer equity. Within each of these drivers are specific, incisive actions ("levers") the enterprise can take to enhance the enterprise's overall customer equity.

Role of Value Equity
Value equity is basically the amount of value a customer perceives in the company's product or service; it serves as the keystone of the customer's relationship

SIDEBAR 11.1 *(continued)*

with the enterprise. If the enterprise's products and services do not meet the customer's needs and expectations, the best brand strategy and the strongest retention and relationship marketing strategies will be insufficient. Value equity is defined as the customer's objective assessment of the utility of a brand, based on perceptions of what is given up for what is received.[b] There are three key levers that influence value equity: quality, price, and convenience. Quality can be thought of as encompassing the objective physical and nonphysical aspects of the product and service offering under the enterprise's control. Think of the power FedEx holds in the marketplace, thanks, in no small part, to its maintenance of high-quality standards. Price represents what is given up by the customer that the enterprise can influence. New e-world entrants that enable customers to find the best price such as *www.mysimon.com* have revolutionized the power of price as a marketing tool. Convenience encompasses those actions the enterprise can take to reduce the time costs, search costs, and efforts of the customer in doing business with the enterprise. Consider Fidelity Investments' new strategy of providing Palm devices to its best customers to enable anytime, anywhere trading and updates—clearly capitalizing on the importance of convenience to busy consumers. Together, quality, price and convenience represent three levers available to the enterprise to grow value equity.

Role of Relationship Equity

Think about a firm with a great brand and a great product. The company may be able to attract new customers to its product with its strong brand, and keep customers by meeting their expectations consistently. But, is this enough? Given the significant shifts in the new economy—from goods to services, from transactions to relationships—the answer is no. Great brand equity and value equity may not be enough to hold the customer. What's needed is a way to "glue" the customers to the enterprise, enhancing the "stickiness" of the relationship. Relationship equity represents this glue. Specifically, relationship equity is defined as "the tendency of the customer to stick with the brand, above and beyond the customer's objective and subjective assessments of the brand."[c]

The key levers, under the enterprise's control, that may enhance relationship equity are loyalty programs, special recognition and treatment, affinity programs, community-building programs, and knowledge-building programs:

- *Loyalty programs* encompass the set of actions that enterprises may take to reward customers for specific behaviors with tangible benefits. From airlines to liquor stores, from Citigroup to Diet Coke, the loyalty program has become a staple of many enterprises' marketing strategy.

- *Special recognition and treatment* refers to actions undertaken by the enterprise to recognize customers for specific behavior with intangible benefits. For example, US Airways' Chairman Preferred status customers receive complimentary membership in the US Airways Club.

- *Affinity programs* seek to create strong emotional connections with customers, linking the customer's relationship with the enterprise to other important aspects of the customer's life. Consider the wide array of affinity Visa and MasterCard choices offered by FirstUSA (in the thousands at last count)—designed to encourage increased use and higher retention.

SIDEBAR 11.1 *(continued)*

....

- *Community-building programs* seek to increase the stickiness of the customer's relationship with the enterprise by linking the customer to a larger community of like customers. In the United Kingdom, for example, soft drink manufacturer Tango has created a Web site—*www.tango.com*—that has built a virtual community with its key segment, the nation's youth.

- *Knowledge-building programs* increase relationship equity by creating structural bonds between the customer and the enterprise, making the customer less willing to re-create the customer-enterprise relationship with an alternative provider. The most often cited example of this is Amazon.com, but Learning Relationships are not limited to cyberspace. Enterprises such as British Airways have developed programs to track customer food and drink preferences, thereby creating bonds with the customer while simultaneously reducing costs.

Taken together, these levers—loyalty programs, special benefits, affinity programs, community, and Learning Relationships—will maximize the likelihood of customer repurchase, maximize the value of a customer's future purchases, and minimize the likelihood of the customer switching to a competitor.

Customer Equity: A Strategic Approach

We have now seen how it is possible to gain insight into the key drivers of customer equity for an individual industry or for an individual enterprise within an industry. Once a firm understands the critical drivers of customer equity for its industry and for its key customers, the enterprise can respond to its customers and the marketplace with strategies that maximize its performance on elements that matter. To maximize marketing performance using customer equity, marketing executives might spend their next marketing dollar where it will have the greatest impact on the lifetime values of their customers.

Taken down to its most fundamental level, customers choose to do business with an enterprise because they perceive that: (1) it offers better value, or (2) switching away from it is too costly. Customer equity provides the diagnostic tools to enable the marketing executive to understand which of these three motivators is most critical to the enterprise's customers—which of these will be most effective in getting the customer to stay with the enterprise, and to buy more. Based on this understanding, the enterprise can identify key opportunities for growth and illuminate unforeseen vulnerabilities. In short, customer equity offers a powerful approach to marketing strategy, replacing a product-based strategy with a competitive strategy approach based on growing the long-term value of the enterprise.

[a] Reprinted with permission from *Marketing Management,* published by the American Marketing Association.

[b] Roland T. Rust, Valarie A. Zeithaml, and Katherine N. Lemon, *Driving Customer Equity: How Customer Lifetime Value Is Reshaping Corporate Strategy* (New York: Simon & Schuster/Free Press, 2000).

[c] Ibid.

The single biggest benefit of managing individual customer relationships is that the loyalty, patronage, and *value* of an individual customer engaged in a relationship will increase. But the improvement in any customer's overall value to the enterprise will only be realized during future financial periods, as the customer remains loyal for a longer period and buys more things.

The practical problem with this should be obvious. Companies measure their financial success in terms of current sales revenues, not customer lifetime values. The values of customers are inherently future-based. But at most enterprises, what is reported to shareholders, and what therefore drives activity, is not the increasing (or decreasing) lifetime values of the customers being served, but income-generating customer activity in the current period. So, to build the business case in favor of managing customer relationships, and to measure the enterprise's success at doing it, a manager must adopt a different set of metrics and standards of performance. Ultimately, the manager will need to align performance measurement, compensation, and budgeting policies with these new standards.

CUSTOMER PROFITABILITY METRICS

Enterprises seek to balance the long-term benefits of migrating to a customer-value-building architecture with the short-term operational expenses they might incur during the transition. The most fundamental long-term benefit derived from an initiative to build Learning Relationships is that it will increase the overall value of the enterprise's customer base. In the short term, a few of the metrics by which an enterprise can judge the progress of its transition to a customer-strategy enterprise include:[5]

> The most fundamental long-term benefit derived from an initiative to build Learning Relationships is that it will increase the overall value of the enterprise's customer base.

- *Increased cross-selling*. If the enterprise can track some of the transactions coming through its business, it can compare the amount of added benefit it receives from cross-selling and upselling. This could result in higher unit margins, as long as it tracks the metric on a per-customer basis. The store that sells the grill to a customer may also be able to sell him charcoal briquettes and lighter fluid again and again over time.
- *Reduced process or transaction costs*. The customer-strategy enterprise ultimately tries to make it more convenient for a customer to interact and buy from it. The enterprise can track the extent to which this reduced friction translates to increased revenues or lower processing or interaction costs. Every bank customer who moves to Web banking not only becomes

[5]Don Peppers, Martha Rogers, PhD, and Bob Dorf, *The One to One Fieldbook* (New York: Doubleday, 1999).

more entangled with the bank, making a move to a competitor less likely, but also costs less for the bank to serve.

- *Reduced customer attrition.* Customer loyalty will likely increase as a result of efforts designed to increase customer relationship building. The enterprise can measure its customer defection or churn rate accurately and determine how to reduce it. When measuring retention rates, the enterprise needs to think of its customers in terms of *vintages* or *cohort groups*.

- *Faster cycle times for processing purchases and other transactions.* Increased convenience for the customer typically shortens the time between order transactions. Some companies measure the changes in *duration* (how long a customer stays a customer) and *trajectory* (the pattern of purchases; e.g., one customer stockpiles infrequently, while another buys small amounts frequently but returns about 20 percent of purchases for credit).

- *Higher customer satisfaction.* Enterprises have tracked customer satisfaction through customer surveys. (But customer satisfaction remains a controversial measure of customer value; see discussions in Chapter 12 and elsewhere.)

These few metrics can help the enterprise begin to gauge its progress during the first initiatives and the transition to a customer-strategy company. The first three items on the list have an immediately measurable cash impact on the enterprise. The last two items are noncash benefits. Faster cycle times can sometimes be converted to a profit-and-loss equivalent, but customer satisfaction scores are not converted so easily.

The good news about measuring the economic results of the relationship-building process is that, for the most part, managing customer relationships is a customer-specific activity. This means that the enterprise can set up field experiments using control groups to validate most metrics reliably. By comparing results between a test group and a control group, the enterprise can track the effect of different treatments on retention rates, cross-selling rates, and other customer-specific metrics. Using a control group is more practical in some situations than others, however.

An enterprise typically measures the success of its different divisions based on the profit and loss of the products they sell. The data are frequently linked by function, from shipment to billing, for instance, but there is little incentive to link data on a customer-by-customer basis. This is exactly the type of data integration that the customer-strategy enterprise requires, however: it needs to link its customer data across functional and divisional boundaries.[6] Data warehousing and other business intelligence systems empower enterprises with the capability to link customer data, among other benefits. Managers can then serve individual customers more effectively by accessing data more efficiently. Assume for a moment that a company can measure the all-in profitability of each customer. Would it be okay to have unprofitable products if every customer were profitable?

> Would it be okay to have unprofitable products if every customer were profitable?

[6]Don Peppers and Martha Rogers, PhD, *Enterprise One to One* (New York: Doubleday, 1996).

One dilemma facing enterprises setting up the kind of metrics needed to become a customer-value-building business is handling the fossilization of established systems of sales commissions, quotas, and bonuses that are focused exclusively on sales of products and services. In addition to tracking customer value, either in the form of an LTV model or a series of proxy variables, the customer-strategy enterprise will measure a new range of intermediate metrics that are related to the successful cultivation of customer relationships and rising customer equity.

It is critical to create the right metric of success for each customer-based effort as early as possible. The enterprise could measure the customer service department, for instance, on customer satisfaction scores among its most valuable customers (MVCs) and most growable customers (MGCs), instead of simply measuring satisfaction across the board. It could recognize salespeople for increased contact frequency with MGCs. It could count the number of MVCs identified for the first time. It could calculate the cost savings from a reduction in headcount of below-zero (BZ) customer services, or the profit that results from serving fewer BZs. Or it could sum the increased percentage of accurate and updated customer records in its database.

LONGITUDINAL METRICS AND SHORT-TERM GAIN

Enterprises traditionally have measured success in *lateral* terms, using figures such as quarterly product sales. But the value of a customer is a *longitudinal* asset, because the customer's relationship goes on through time, reflecting tomorrow's sales, not just today's.

To illustrate the principle, consider the highly simplistic example of a magazine publisher that wants to build its subscriber base. To evaluate the economics of its effort, the publisher must estimate the LTV of the new subscribers it will be recruiting. Making this estimate will be done in a probabilistic calculation, aimed at predicting the long-term spending pattern of a "typical" subscriber, beginning with the first dollar received from him. The publisher, in essence, wants to model the likely trajectory of its average new customer.

Perhaps the publisher plans to offer new customers a one-year subscription at an introductory price of less than half the regular rate, in the hope that a portion of the new subscribers who accept this offer will go on to renew their subscriptions for several years. With experience, what the publisher has found is that, at the end of the first year, only about 60 percent of its first-year customers usually elect to renew their subscriptions at the regular price. This figure—60 percent—is not a hard-and-fast number, by any means; but after reviewing its records of previous years, the publisher's best judgment is that a 60 percent first-year renewal rate is about what it can expect. At the end of the second year, moreover, it is the publisher's experience that 65 percent of those who are still subscribing elect to resubscribe, 70 percent the year after that, and so on (see Exhibit 11.1).

What the publisher has found is that the longer any particular population of customers remains, the lower the annual customer attrition rate becomes. This is

YEAR	TOTAL SUBSCRIBERS	RENEWAL RATE	SUBSCRIBER REVENUE	VARIABLE COSTS	NET PROFIT	NPV AT 15%	10-YEAR LTV
1	1,000	60%	$35,900	$30,000	$5,900	$5,900	$66.94
2	600	65%	$45,540	$18,000	$27,540	$23,948	$118.12
3	390	70%	$29,601	$11,700	$17,901	$13,536	$129.15
4	273	75%	$20,721	$8,190	$12,531	$8,239	$138.35
5	205	78%	$15,541	$6,143	$9,398	$5,373	$143.45
6	160	79%	$12,122	$4,791	$7,330	$3,645	$145.55
7	126	80%	$9,576	$3,785	$5,791	$2,504	$146.81
8	101	80%	$7,661	$3,028	$4,633	$1,742	$146.81
9	81	80%	$6,129	$2,422	$3,706	$1,212	$146.81
10	65	80%	$4,903	$1,938	$2,965	$843	$146.81
					nearly	approx.	
					$100,000	$67,000	

*This hypothetical table could also be thought of as a survival table.

EXHIBIT 11.1   **Estimated Stream of Future Profit of 1000 New Customers Over a 10-Year Period***

an important characteristic of customer attrition, and it is true in virtually every type of business—and in our simplistic example we can make it quite clear. The fact is, within any statistically uniform population of customers, there is always some probability that a random customer will choose to defect during some period of time. We cannot predict the future, so we cannot know when a particular customer will defect, but we can track the statistical population and map the defection rate over time. What we will find, *in every case,* is that as time goes on, the overall defection rate within the population will tend to decrease. The reason is that the customers who are most likely to leave at any given time are more likely to be the first ones out the door, and so as time goes on the remaining population tends to be made up of customers who have a lower and lower average probability of leaving.

But now let's put the magazine publisher's problem on paper and try to evaluate the economics of adding new subscribers to its customer base. The publisher's introductory subscription costs $35.90, compared to the regular rate (after the first year) of $67. Variable costs (mailing, printing, and other costs, net of advertising revenues, which for reasons of simplicity we'll simply treat as a negative cost) total $30 per year. Given the renewal rates that the publisher expects, over a 10-year period, if the publisher recruits a thousand new customers in year 1, by year 10 only 65 of those original subscribers will remain; and over this 10-year period, they will have contributed profit to the publisher every year. To assess the financial economics of this pattern, the publisher discounts future revenues and costs at a rate of 15 percent annually, in order to derive today's net present value of this estimated stream of future profit, as shown in Exhibit 11.1.

Year 10 is the last year modeled by the publisher in doing the assessment, because by year 10 the net present value of annual profit from the original population of customers has been reduced to a very small proportion of the overall value to be realized from the population. It has been reduced not just by the compounding effect of the financial discount rate, but also by the ever-shrinking population of customers, as more and more of them finally attrite. In this case, the spreadsheet shows the net present value of year 10 profits at less than $1,000 in today's dollars, making up less than 2 percent of the total NPV for this customer population of some $67,000. The $67,000, however, represents the present value of the entire 10-year stream of future profit, derived from a population of 1,000 new customers recruited today. This amounts to an average lifetime value, for each of these 1,000 new customers, of about $67.

Note that the publisher is not trying to determine the exact value of any particular customer; instead, the company is simply estimating the average revenue it would get from a population of customers. But you can imagine that an actual magazine publisher, with the comprehensive past records of perhaps more than a million current subscribers, could divide up its customer base into many different statistical populations in order to make more and more accurate predictions.

It is this LTV of $67 that the publisher has to consider when budgeting for the marketing campaign designed to recruit new subscribers. The new subscribers are unlikely to appear out of thin air. The publisher will have to launch a television ad campaign, a direct-mail effort, or some other proactive marketing program in order to recruit the new subscribers. If the cost of the entire campaign were, say, $500,000, and a total of 10,000 new subscribers were recruited, then the average acquisition cost, per customer, would be $50; subtracting that from the average customer LTV would yield a true "profit," over and above acquisition costs, of $17 per customer.

Using this LTV model, if the publisher increases its renewal rate by only 2 percent a year, from 60 percent to 62 percent in the first year, and 67 percent in the second year, and so on, then the average new customer's LTV would increase 7.5 percent. If the cost to acquire these customers remained at $50 per customer, then this 2 percent increase in the annual retention rate would increase the actual value of each new customer by more than 25 percent—from $17 to $22.[7] In this simplistic example, customer LTV is a straightforward function of the cost to acquire the customer and the probability of the customer's attrition.

But most businesses are much more complex than this. The publisher's subscription model was chosen for its simplicity to illustrate our point. In most businesses, quantifying customer retention is much more complex, and even defining the concept might be problematic. Think of an automobile manufacturer, for instance. If a customer owns three models of its cars, but finances them through a bank and not through the manufacturer's lending company, is the customer being "retained" or has he defected?

Even in the simplistic magazine subscription model, it is easy to get tripped up in measuring customer retention. Return for a moment to the declining customer attrition rates that characterize all customer populations—the principle

[7]Example excerpted from ibid.

that the retention rate, from year to year, of any given population of customers will always increase. This factor must always be considered carefully, when measuring customer retention, because it means that the retention rate among any particular population of customers is partly a function of the length of time that the population of customers has already been with the enterprise. This simple statistical fact will confound most efforts to describe a firm's average retention rate across its whole base of customers, because a customer base is composed of customers who have joined the franchise at many different times in the past. Instead, it would be more accurate and useful for the enterprise to visualize its customer base as consisting of several different customer populations, each of which first became a part of the customer base at a particular point in the enterprise's past—in a particular year, or with a particular marketing campaign, for instance. We can call these populations *vintages*, or *cohort groups*.

To see just how this affects the measurement of retention, let's suppose that our publisher, having gone into business in year 1, begins tracking the average customer retention from year to year, with an eye toward improving long-term customer loyalty. Let's also assume that the publisher successfully manages to recruit another 1,000 customers every year for the first five years, at which time the customer acquisition effort is terminated (an unlikely scenario, to be sure!). We'll assume that each batch of new customers has exactly the same trajectory, so that the first year after acquisition, 60 percent are retained, 65 percent of the remaining ones in the second year, and so forth. We call these batches of customers vintages, and we label them with the year in which they were first recruited. We could just as well have different vintages for different marketing campaigns. In direct marketing, it might be said that the customers of one vintage all have the same *source code*.

As Exhibit 11.2 shows, our publisher could easily conclude, by measuring simply the average customer retention rate, year over year, that its customer loyalty programs must be working very well indeed. Over the first five years of doing business, the retention rate steadily increased, from the initial rate of 60 percent to 66 percent in the sixth year. This is because, as time goes on, the proportion of longer-tenure customers in the publisher's customer base will continue to increase; and the longer tenure any group of customers has, the less likely any one of them is to defect.

Moreover, when the publisher stops recruiting new customers altogether after the fifth year, we can see that the annual retention rate over the entire customer base begins rising even more dramatically.[8] What this all goes to show is that, because all customer populations tend to become more loyal with longevity, the average annual customer retention at a firm is more likely to be a function of the mix of newer and older customers, rather than a reliable indicator of the success of any relationship-building effort or customer loyalty program. Instead, reten-

---

[8]A manager rewarded solely for "increased retention rate across the customer base" might realize that the best way to accomplish that retention increase would be to stop getting new customers! This ironic and impractical example demonstrates the importance of choosing the correct metrics to drive managerial decisions.

YEAR	VINTAGE 1	VINTAGE 2	VINTAGE 3	VINTAGE 4	VINTAGE 5	TOTAL CUSTOMERS	AVERAGE ANNUAL RETENTION
1	1000					1000	
2	600	1000				1600	60.0%
3	390	600	1000			1990	61.9%
4	273	390	600	1000		2263	63.5%
5	205	273	390	600	1000	2468	64.9%
6	160	205	273	390	600	1628	66.0%
7	126	160	205	273	390	1154	70.9%
8	101	126	160	205	273	865	75.0%
9	81	101	126	160	205	673	77.8%
10	65	81	101	126	160	533	79.2%

EXHIBIT 11.2   **Tracking Customer Retention by Vintage**

tion has to be measured at precise points along the customer trajectory. Rather than measuring the average retention across the entire customer base every year, a better measure would be to pick a point in the typical customer trajectory, and measure retention at that point for successive vintages of customers. For instance, it would make sense to measure the retention rate from year 2 to 3, for vintage 3 customers, compared to what the rate was for vintage 2 or vintage 1 customers.

Ultimately, while an enterprise may recognize that measuring the effects of relationship management might require a longitudinal set of figures, tracked over a long period of time, it is also helpful to have *real-time metrics* that can warn the enterprise of threatened decreases in customer equity and/or potential increases in the value of the customer base. These *leading indicators* can help the enterprise to increase long-term customer value. As a tactic to detect possible defectors among its customers, an enterprise might create a set of leading indicators that monitor positive and negative trends in each customer's behavior. Some indicator metrics might include:

- Days since last sale
- Sales acceleration or deceleration (sales in last quarter/average quarterly sales for previous four quarters for a particular customer)
- Share of wallet increase or reduction
- Increase or reduction in number of categories purchased in last year
- Increasing or decreasing price sensitivity
- Increase or decrease in canceled orders, returns/exchange
- Increase or reduction in enhanced services or entanglement
- More or less frequent orders
- Same-time previous-year orders (seasonality adjustments)
- Increase or decrease in number of complaints

- Referrals (change in advocacy levels)
- Change in communication patterns (more or less frequent)
- Multichannel shopping ratios, comparison to a norm, or an index

Other leading indicators of customer value can be obtained by careful screening of the customer database. As we've learned, one credit card company calculated from its data that when the husband and wife in a household each carried and used a card on the same account, the customer defection rates were much lower, compared to nonjoint cards. So this credit card company can tell a good deal about likely future customer retention simply by tracking the number of active joint spousal accounts. Moreover, if it wants to change its customers' behavior, making them more loyal, it might consider ways to induce those husband-wife households that do *not* own jointly used cards to acquire them.

SIDEBAR 11.2

Profitability Metrics to Consider[a]

Customer profitability metrics can enhance the enterprise's understanding of its long-term success in managing customer relationships effectively and increasing the value of its overall customer base. Some additional metrics include:

- *Share of customer.* Perhaps the most useful way of visualizing how much effort should be allocated to grow the customer into a bigger, more valuable customer is to know how much share the enterprise has of a customer's business. Financially, share of customer (SOC) can be defined as an enterprise's level of penetration of a customer's total expenditures. But philosophically, SOC represents the degree to which the enterprise is succeeding in meeting its customer's need, in the broadest possible sense. (Note: different "share of . . ." measures are appropriate in different situations, and must be considered carefully. For example, if an automaker or dealer measures "share of garage," then the goal is obviously to sell a customer all the cars in his garage, and refers to automobile sales. Or the same auto seller may want to measure share of customer instead, and try to get not only auto sales, but also maintenance, repairs, upgrades, and financing and credit cards as well.) Few enterprises use SOC as a metric because of the challenges associated with acquiring customer-level information about how much business a customer gives competitors, yet it is a highly relevant and strategically beneficial metric to track. At a minimum, it helps direct the firm to "keep" or "grow" strategies for a particular customer. In many cases, most growable customers have potential value because of the opportunity to win share of customer away from competitors.

- *Customer response rate (CRR).* A customer's historic rate of response is the ratio of customer-initiated interactions or responses relative to all attempted contacts initiated by the enterprise. CRR serves as a proxy for the strength of relationship between a customer and an enterprise. An analysis of CRR can indicate customer preferences with respect to interaction channels and customer touchpoints, and a willingness to collaborate on the part of the customer.

- *Revenue per dollar (or euro or yen) spent on customer initiatives.* This metric is calculated by dividing total revenue by total expenditures on managing

---

SIDEBAR 11.2 *(continued)*

....

customer relationships. Use of this measure can mislead the enterprise, however, as reductions in spending can increase the ratio in the near term. But when used together with customer life-cycle metrics, revenue per investment enhances the enterprise's understanding of the overall effectiveness of relationship-building expenditures.

Although the enterprise can establish customer-specific profitability metrics to gauge the longer-term benefits of a customer-based initiative, such as improved customer loyalty and increased profitability, these metrics will produce few benefits for the business as long as short-term metrics still drive its compensation structure. Sales commissions remain a powerful motivation tool, but the compensation structure built around commissions and bonuses for selling products and meeting monthly quotas is often highly resistant to the change needed during the transition to customer management. Commissions typically spawn rivalries among the sales team or different divisions, as one tries to outdo the other. The odds are that the conflicts arise not because the enterprise is measuring the wrong things, but because it is not correctly applying the metrics it already has. By changing some established compensation systems, the enterprise can alleviate such conflicts. (We'll talk more about compensation structures in Chapters 12 and 13).

No matter how the enterprise handles profitability metrics, the metrics themselves have to be carefully defined to achieve accurate results. Management should never forget that the purpose of setting up a metric in the first place is to track success and failure, to navigate the marketing landscape, and to justify financial investments. Thus, sooner or later, even leading indicator metrics must still be translated into financial terms in some way. This is not always easy, and intuitive judgments can easily be wrong. As an example, let's look at the problem of measuring customer satisfaction and converting it to a useful type of profitability metric.

[a]Summarized from Michael Maoz, "The Changing Nature of Marketing Metrics," Gartner Group, March 21, 2001.

MEASURING CUSTOMER SATISFACTION

Earlier, we discussed two perspectives on customer loyalty: attitudinal loyalty and behavioral loyalty. Many enterprises equate customer satisfaction with customer loyalty, so even though we have addressed the topic of "customer satisfaction" elsewhere, we will think here about the *measure* of customer satisfaction. Enterprises want to increase both the loyalty and satisfaction of their customers, but require an accurate method for measuring each independently. The fact is, not all satisfied customers are loyal customers, in the behavioral sense of the word. As we will see, it frequently happens that one who has been measured as a "satisfied" customer will nevertheless leave the franchise to patronize a competitor, perhaps because he feels he will be just as satisfied with the competitor, or perhaps because there are other benefits offered by

> Enterprises want to increase both the loyalty and satisfaction of their customers, but require an accurate method for measuring each independently.

the competitor (price, for instance) that offset the customer's own desire to be completely satisfied.

The simple fact is that an enterprise does not make a customer loyal in order to satisfy him, nor will simply satisfying the customer be sufficient to make him loyal. There are several points of view on how to define customer satisfaction and relate it to loyalty. For instance, Gartner Group maintains that an enterprise can have satisfaction without loyalty but not loyalty without satisfaction. According to Gartner, four separate components go into the measurement of customer satisfaction and loyalty; and though the firm is not specific with regard to behavioral or attitudinal loyalty, from the list of components, one can deduce that Gartner has likely not made the distinction. Nevertheless, these factors are worth considering, insofar as they can be said to be contributors to both satisfaction and customer loyalty: [9]

- *Brand.* The enterprise image, values, and consistency of the proposition
- *Quality.* The perceived quality/professionalism of the enterprise, its service and products
- *Interrelationship.* The degree to which customer needs are met, amount of use, dependence, and convenience—all in the context of competitors
- *Performance.* Service delivery, product reliability, and response times

Some other experts say customer satisfaction is the degree to which a customer feels his needs are met by the enterprise. It is the relative value to him of what is supplied compared with the satisfaction of purchases from other enterprises.

As a general premise, customer satisfaction is clearly a worthwhile and useful goal for any company to try to achieve. But it is not synonymous with customer loyalty. There are many examples of companies that have satisfied customers who are not behaviorally loyal, while other companies have dissatisfied customers who remain behaviorally loyal. From the customer's standpoint, this should not be difficult to see. The customer, calculating his own economic self-interest, will ask: What are my alternatives? How much trouble will it be for me to switch to another company? Especially if I don't think anyone else will do a better job, I may choose to continue doing business for the time being even though I'm not really thrilled with the current situation.

> Customer satisfaction is a helpful, but not a sufficient condition for maintaining customer loyalty.

What all this means is that customer satisfaction is a helpful, but not a sufficient condition for maintaining customer loyalty. Moreover, in many industries, a high level of customer satisfaction has become virtually a competitive requirement, becoming a *parity* offering in the category, rather than a competitive advantage, despite the fact that satisfaction by itself does not guarantee loyalty. In any business in which high product and service quality standards have become the norm, it requires a relatively major effort for a firm to differentiate itself with an even higher-quality offering; and, in

[9]Scott Nelson, "If They're Satisfied, Why Are They Leaving?" Gartner Group (March 23, 2001).

any case, from the customer's standpoint, the amount of perceived benefit is likely to be less and less persuasive.

Research cited in Frederick Reichheld's book, *Loyalty Rules! How Today's Leaders Build Lasting Relationships,*[10] suggests that only 30 to 70 percent of satisfied customers are usually loyal. Indeed, customer loyalty is the highest standard, as it implies that the perceived value of a relationship with an enterprise outweighs the apparent benefits or incentives of competitive offerings. Ray Kordupleski, who served as AT&T's director of customer satisfaction in the 1990s, has conducted extensive research on the customer satisfaction level of the telecommunications enterprise. In one study he conducted with Roland Rust and Anthony Zahorik, he discovered that while AT&T was measuring many variables to calculate share of market and to find out cost efficiencies, AT&T's customer satisfaction scores apparently had *no* correlation to market share, growth, or profit.[11]

In one case, for example, while customer satisfaction for one of AT&T's products was reported at 97 percent in the Pennsylvania market, the index for the same product in New York was only 78 percent. Yet the Pennsylvania business was actually losing market share while New York was gaining share. Moreover, among all markets in the United States, Pennsylvania reported the most satisfied customers, while New York customers were the least satisfied. It seemed that AT&T was losing customers in spite of satisfying them. This is a common problem among many enterprises—the inability to link increases or decreases in customer satisfaction to market results has led many to question whether customer satisfaction programs pay off financially.

Kordupleski concluded three things in his research. First, the only kind of satisfaction that matters is the top box, the one marked "very satisfied." Second, while price contributes to the overall value proposition, many other factors, from service quality to responsiveness, also matter when determining a customer's satisfaction. It is realistic to satisfy a customer with a quality product even if it is sold at a higher price. Third, customer satisfaction is useful for explaining competitive business results only when it is measured relative to the competition's satisfaction scores. Kordupleski showed that when *relative* customer satisfaction is measured, the correlation with business performance is remarkable. In the case of AT&T's business phone "install" rate, for example, a small increase in relative satisfaction was a four-month leading indicator of share growth. New Yorkers, it seemed, rate *everyone* lower than the more tolerant people who live in Pennsylvania, apparently because New Yorkers are simply more predisposed to be highly demanding of their vendors and less forgiving as customers. Thus, even though customer satisfaction scores in New York were lower than those in Pennsylvania, what mattered in the end was the satisfaction score *relative to the competition in*

[10]Frederick Reichheld, *Loyalty Rules! How Today's Leaders Build Lasting Relationships* (Cambridge, MA: Harvard Business School Press, 2001).

[11]Raymond Kordupleski, Roland T. Rust, and Anthony J. Zahorik, "Why Improving Quality Doesn't Improve Quality," *California Management Review* 35 (Spring), pp. 82–95.

each market. If New Yorkers rate AT&T's competitors even lower than they rate AT&T, then market share growth will likely still happen.

In the long run, an enterprise that carefully defines the metrics it uses to gauge profitability will be able to assess whether it is headed down a path to prosperity or a dead end of red ink. Metrics provide powerful ways to measure success, but they are of no use if they are not meaningful or if they have an incorrect or inaccurate meaning.

In addition to purely financial measurements of ROI and profit, an enterprise will want to measure its progress in becoming more customer-oriented. The transition from a product-centric to a customer-strategy enterprise is an ongoing process. As we have said previously, becoming a customer-based firm is not really a destination, but a journey. It is a continuously improving set of business practices. Success does not occur overnight, and everyone in the enterprise will be involved. Moreover, many of the business processes at the enterprise will need to be completely rethought, as the organization begins to deal with new information, new technologies, and a revised organizational structure.

Benchmarking the transition from a product-centric to a customer-strategy enterprise is time-consuming and expensive; it requires a substantial commitment across the enterprise. The enterprise may apply these metrics on an ongoing basis to ensure continued funding of its customer-based initiatives. Managers involved in the transition are often faced with the task of justifying

---

SIDEBAR 11.3

Process Implementation Metrics

Process metrics are used to track the success of each phase of the IDIC (identify, differentiate, interact, and customize) taxonomy outlined in Chapters 3 to 10. The enterprise measures how well it is managing customer feedback and serving the customer on a customized level. The following are some of the key process metrics a customer-value-building enterprise can measure to assess its effectiveness at each level:

Identify
- Percent of customer base with unique customer identifier (UIC)
- Percent of customers identifiable at all major touchpoint channels
- Ability to identify relocating/lapsed customers upon reacquisition (yes or no)
- Percent of customers with captured e-mail addresses

Differentiate (Value)
- LTV model in place (yes or no)
- Proxies used to build the LTV model
- Ability to rank order customers by value
- Percent of customers assigned to value tiers (MGCs, MVCs, BZs)
- Percent of customers with measured LTV
- Percent of customers still measured by number of sales

SIDEBAR 11.3 *(continued)*

....

Differentiate (Needs)

- Individual needs-related customer data elements defined (yes or no)
- Needs-based "gateways" identified for major touchpoints
- Golden Questions used to identify different needs
- Percent of customers assigned to needs clusters

Interact

- Percent of customers with more than half of needs data collected
- Percent of customers providing customer service feedback within last year
- Golden Questions defined (yes or no)
- Average cost per interaction
- Critical customer data available in each communication channel (yes or no)
- Last customer interaction available in each communication channel (yes or no)
- Touchmap analysis data
- Business rules in place to guide subsequent interactions (yes or no)
- Percent of customer inquiries with first contact resolutions

Customize

- Percent of customers purchasing customized products within the last year
- Percent of product line that is mass-customizable
- Cost per customer of mass customization
- Savings per customer of mass customization and make-to-order
- Percent of customers receiving customized communication
- Percent of customers with personalized Web pages
- Percent of customers with add-on services

---

expenditures to their superiors. By effectively measuring the success of the customer management transition, a manager can prove ROI and justify the cost of its continued implementation.

Sometimes the various divisions within the enterprise have different methods of measuring and reporting on the success of their customer-related campaigns. The result can be consistent confusion between the departments and senior management about the measures of success for these initiatives.[12] It is imperative to establish universal metrics around customer dynamics.

To measure its progress in developing the capability to build profitable relationships with customers, the enterprise should also monitor how well it is adjusting internally to this transition. The migration from a product-centric to

---

[12]Melinda Nykamp and Carla McEachern, "Measuring CRM Success," *DM Review* 10, no. 1 (January 2000), pp. 36, 78. ISSN: 1521-291.

customer-value-building business model involves many delicate changes within the organization, and will likely include changes in many fundamental business processes. Effective operations management is critical to the internal success of the enterprise. This will be a trying time for management and other leaders and role models within the enterprise. They will need to work closely with one another and their subordinates to ensure a smooth transition with little disruption in the flow of business. By tracking the alignment of the organization with its processes and information systems, the enterprise can move forward in its migration. As Exhibit 11.3 shows, with each stage in the transition come many different efforts on the part of leaders and those who communicate those efforts to employees.

While the transition is often arduous and sometimes unsuccessful, the enterprise might ease the burden on itself by focusing on some key areas of change. In a nutshell, four primary enterprise issues are affected by the transition, and change metrics should be developed to measure them. These include:

1. *Organization.* The enterprise should track how well its people, culture, and organizational structure are adjusting.
2. *Process.* The new customer focus of treating different customers differently will require new and unique business processes that the enterprise has to adopt, likely in stepwise fashion.
3. *Information.* The enterprise is more information-focused than ever before. It strives to turn its customer data into knowledge that it can use to make it easier for the customer to buy from it. This will require new ways

CAPABILITY	Strategy Implementation Level			
	IDENTIFY	DIFFERENTIATE	INTERACT	CUSTOMIZE
ORGANIZATION	Consistent recognition of one customer	Understanding of customer differentiation	Customer skills, training and metrics	Accountability for each customer
PROCESS	Privacy policy, backed up by privacy pledge and commitment	Models for value and research method for needs	Enterprise-wide memory of customer at all touchpoints	Cross-functional flow of systems
INFORMATION	Common coding system for customer IDs	Ease in defining the right proxies	Framework for capture of value and needs	Adequate information to allow customization
TECHNOLOGY	Shared customer database	Strong data analysis tools	Able to capture data at all points of interaction	Integration between front, back-office systems

EXHIBIT 11.3 **Implementing Customer Strategy**

of storing the data, analyzing the information, and ultimately disseminating the information throughout the enterprise.

4. *Technology.* Investments in new technology are likely a result of the migration. The enterprise will need to monitor how employees are adapting to new software and whether the software is helping customer-strategy projects.

By focusing on these core issues, the enterprise can look to fill gaps in its capabilities and take the necessary action steps to improve how it performs internally.

In the next section, James Goodnight, whose company, SAS Institute, is a world leader in data analysis, addresses the elements and journey of customer-strategy metrics.

MANAGING CUSTOMER RELATIONSHIPS: METRICS CASE STUDY

James Goodnight
CEO, SAS Institute

Measuring customer relationships is a critical success factor in implementing customer-based initiatives, which begin by delivering value to individual customers. The circle is closed by measuring how personalized value creation results in profits for the enterprise—and how the value creation process can be improved. Measurements are required to differentiate customers, personalize products and interactions, provide employee incentives, make management decisions, and quantify the effectiveness of programs.

> The circle is closed by measuring how personalized value creation results in profits for the enterprise–and how the value creation process can be improved.

But there is more than one path to developing customer-centered measurements. Moreover, customer-based metrics can vary widely based on the industry, number of customers, and channel strategy of an organization. This section provides a composite view of the customer-based measurements used by three companies:

- *Eddie Bauer* is a Seattle-based apparel retailer building one-to-one relationships with 15 million customers across retail, catalog, and Internet channels.
- *Travelocity* is ranked as the largest online travel site worldwide with more than 38 million registered members.
- *Newport News* is a catalog and Internet division of the Spiegel Group selling quality women's clothing.

These companies give us a glimpse of how CRM metrics are developed and used today. We will examine how these companies have approached:

- The three categories of CRM metrics
- Providing access to these metrics and getting them accepted by their organization
- The bottom-line impact these measures have had
- How CRM metrics have evolved from mass-marketing metrics and what distinguishes the two categories from each other
- Next steps that progressive customer-value-building enterprises are taking to develop and use customer-centered measurements

TYPES OF MEASURES

Harold Egler, Eddie Bauer's former vice president of customer relationship management, defines the enterprise's use of CRM metrics: "We measure the connection between profitability, revenue, and customer satisfaction. Optimizing these three areas is our CRM business strategy." Customer-centered measures provide a scale that balances organizational profitability and individual customer value (see Exhibit 11.4).[13] If the enterprise places too much emphasis on profitability, it will fail to serve customers and will begin to lose customers—damaging the brand in the process. If the enterprise places too much emphasis on retaining and serving customers, it may soon begin to lose profitability and will subsequently lose customers when it begins to raise prices, reduce incentives, or cut back service levels.

Within that definition, CRM metrics might fall into three fairly distinct categories: (1) cost justification, (2) value assessment, and (3) preferences. As will be explained shortly, these three types of metrics are used to measure individual customer performance, marketing campaign performance, employee performance, and the overall performance of a CRM initiative.

COST JUSTIFICATION

"One of our toughest challenges has been to avoid being distracted by vendors selling something that they call 'CRM' but that really isn't a good match for our business model," notes Paul Briggs, Travelocity's customer management director. But numerous companies have not been as cautious, and have spent millions of dollars on solutions that were destined to fail. If anything has slowed down the adoption of CRM in the marketplace, it has been stories of these failures.

Factors that lead to significant CRM costs often include additional business personnel, technology support personnel, time spent integrating different CRM systems, computer hardware, and software licenses. Costs can also include specialized equipment for mass customization of products, services, and customer

---

[13]"Customer Connect helps companies develop balanced relationships with their customers." See *www.cust-connect.com*, April 2001.

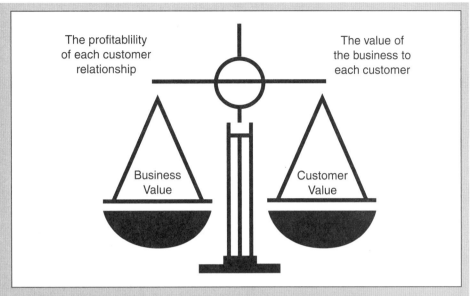

EXHIBIT 11.4 Balancing Organizational Profitability and Individual Customer Value

interactions. To gain acceptance of new CRM initiatives, companies have found that they must first build a solid business case for justifying these costs.

Typical methods for justifying the cost of capital expenses associated with CRM include return on investment (ROI), net present value (NPV) or internal rate of return (IRR). Although this book cannot serve as a primer on financial analysis, an excellent quick study on this can be found in a white paper published by Quaero: "The Return on Investment: Justifying CRM Investments." Specific areas that should be estimated when calculating a potential return on CRM investment include:[14]

Costs	Revenues
Personnel to support new function	Increased sales from additional marketing
Personnel to support technology	Increased sales through improved conversion rates
Consulting	Increased revenue through improved retention
Hardware costs	Increased margins
Software licensing	Decreased costs through more targeted marketing
Systems integration	Decreased business planning cycles
User training	Decreased staffing growth through marketing and sales automation

[14]Steve Schultz, "Return on Investment: Justifying CRM Investments," Quaero, LLC (Charlotte, NC, 2001), pp. 3, 4.

Although CRM makes intuitive sense in many cases, enterprises that follow disciplined cost-justification processes will always demand an estimated return for their investment before approving the required funds. Approaches typically used for cost justification include:

- Showing cost savings through improved customer selection
- Demonstrating a break-even or cost savings on technology investments
- Forecasting clear revenue gains and a process for measuring these after implementation
- Reducing the time to market for execution

When Travelocity observed the power of e-mail marketing for revenue generation, it quickly realized an enterprise marketing automation tool would be required to attain its e-mail marketing goals. Travelocity's Briggs remarks, "We knew these tools would yield an exponential increase in our ability to provide relevant, timely communications to our customers, while freeing up our CRM specialists for more strategic work than pulling lists." But Travelocity management wanted real numbers to justify the expense of the new technology. "We observed conversion rates from past e-mail campaigns," continues Briggs, "and we estimated the changes in these rates that would result from more frequent, timely, personalized, and relevant contacts with our customers to justify the cost of the technology."

Understanding history with other initiatives, similar to the enterprise's CRM initiatives, is critical to forecasting the return on a CRM investment. However, other methods are available. "Whenever possible, revenue impacts should be based on past experiences. For enterprises with no or limited CRM experience, this may not be possible. Published information, consultant expertise, and competitive intelligence may fill this void satisfactorily."[15]

For enterprises investing in CRM, there are many benefits that are either intangible or difficult to forecast. Because it is difficult to quantify these benefits, many companies approach the cost justification process by demonstrating a cost savings rather than increased revenues. Dick Lee, author of *The Customer Relationship Management Survival Guide,* responded to an online inquiry, "I view all the ROI formulas I've seen to be sleight of hand. Fundamentally, the ROI from CRM comes from changes in customer behavior, which has to be measured over considerable time."[16]

Van Rhodes, marketing analyst and data warehouse administrator with Newport News, agrees, "We decided to migrate our multiple mainframe decision support systems to a single client/server warehouse. Cost justification was difficult because we couldn't reach clear agreement on what kind of improvements to forecast. We knew we would get orders of magnitude improvement—but we couldn't quantify it." Newport News was able to justify the expense of a new

[15]Ibid.

[16]Dick Lee, "Return on Investment," *CRM.Talk*, Digest No. 062 (April 11, 2000), at *www.crmguru.com.*

CRM decision support system by coupling it with another mandatory technology change and showing a break-even scenario. "Because we had to bring our mainframe decision support systems into Year 2000 compliance, we were able to convince management to integrate these systems onto the client/server solution for the same cost," Rhodes concluded.[17]

Eddie Bauer's Egler found that although the cost justification couldn't be precise, even conservative projections showed a strong return. "We didn't have enough data to prove that we would get cost savings or revenues, but we could hypothesize, 'if we could do this, here's how much we think it would be worth.' We came up with some pretty huge numbers and actually scaled those back to be a little safer." Egler is quick to add that crunching numbers to forecast ROI is not enough, ". . . you *must* have a visionary sponsor at an executive level who intuitively knows it will work and gets behind it *regardless* of what you're predicting for ROI."

VALUE ASSESSMENT

Understanding the value of customers affects every aspect of the way a business interacts with customers. At an individual level, sales and service approaches can be tuned to manage the growth of customer relationships. At a segment level, direct marketing, sales and Web information can be tailored to a retention or growth strategy. At a management and operational level, a business can make more informed strategic decisions that impact all customers.

Business management strategies have typically been measured by product, business line, or channel. A revenue management strategy has been utilized with product or business lines, while a cost management strategy was utilized with channel or other business cost centers. It was assumed that by using this strategy, the intersection of cost and revenue management would automatically provide the right balance of business and customer value. This approach is illustrated in Exhibit 11.5. The problem with this approach is that a business unit can make a seemingly good business decision that has a negative impact on the overall customer relationship. To truly understand the relationship a business has with a customer, the *intersection* of all products and all channels must be understood for *each customer*.

Insurance and pharmaceutical benefits companies have stumbled across this imbalance as they have struggled to manage their call centers. These call centers are often managed as cost centers. The directors of call centers receive no incentive to generate new revenue or to grow wallet share. Instead, they are incentivized to run an efficient call center and are measured based on average call duration, hold time, and, perhaps, customer satisfaction. Because they can be "punished" for doing the best thing for the customer, few call center managers are willing to extend calls by 15 to 60 seconds in order to gather information

---

[17]The Year 2000 issue involved the revision of billions of lines of code within computers and software to enable them to read and interpret dates after 1999 as 2000, not 1900.

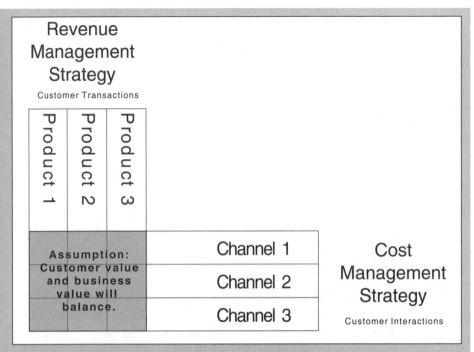

EXHIBIT 11.5 Customer Relationship Must Be Understood at the Intersection of Products and Channels

about customers that could be used later to add value to that relationship. (You'll find more about the changes in customer interaction centers (CICs) in Chapter 8.)

Enterprises that understand the value of individual customer relationships find that they come to some new conclusions about how to provide value.

Eddie Bauer found some startling trends when it began to measure complete customer relationships. "We found a very valuable subsegment within returns customers," comments Harold Egler. "Customers who return a lot are buying a lot—in fact, they're among our most valuable customers. They are a self-identifying audience that we want to treat differently." Until 1998, Eddie Bauer didn't have a single source for customer information for all channels—making this type of observation impossible.

In general, most enterprises use a similar approach to calculate customer value. Newport News creates its most "granular" level of data so that it can satisfy the reporting needs of each business area. Maureen Fagan, divisional vice president of marketing, outlines the company's process: "We begin with customer transactions and interactions. Using calculations made at that level, we aggregate this data to the customer level, and further aggregate this information to the segment level." This approach (see Exhibit 11.6) is becoming widely accepted as a methodology for calculating customer value.

But calculating the precise financial value of customers can be a tricky process. Companies have found that going directly from mass-marketing measures to actual customer value is too large of a chasm to cross all at once. The time and expense required to understand the revenue, fixed and variable costs,

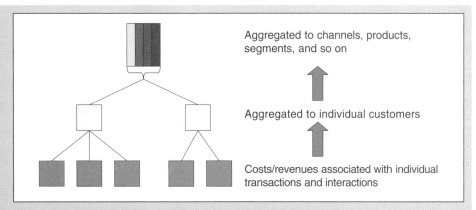

EXHIBIT 11.6   **Granular-to-Aggregate Reporting**

and margins associated with every interaction can be overwhelming. A series of steps is often taken prior to developing an actual customer value calculation.

As a cataloger, Newport News has always used direct marketing metrics. But when it expanded to the Internet, added a private label credit card, and launched a discount club, it found that direct marketing metrics alone were no longer enough. "We have been measuring recency, frequency, and monetary value (RFM) for over 20 years now and we're still using it," Van Rhodes says. "But we have also found that our best customers shop on both the Web and through our catalog, and even better customers belong to our discount club or own our private label credit card." As a result, Newport News captures all of this information into its data warehouse and measures customers using RFM, channel, card ownership/activation, and discount club membership type. Profitability is a next step that Newport News is beginning to experiment with.

While an estimated customer value such as RFM can be a good start, an actual value, calculated by customer, is desirable. Egler notes, "Subtle differences between estimated and actual profitability can cause you to make different decisions."

When banks and insurance companies begin to examine customer profitability, they often find that their sales force can actually create unprofitable churn among their customer base. Sales numbers can be going up, while earnings are going down. What they find is an increase in sales incentives that exceeds revenues from new sales. The reason? Salespeople are given a commission every time they close a sale. But many of the sales really just move existing customer business into a new product every three to six months. Promoting churn is bad for the enterprise and bad for the customer.

The problem is easier to identify than it is to solve. Salespeople need to be motivated to grow wallet share—not just to sell products. However, until an enterprise can measure the actual value of a customer relationship, it cannot attach an incentive to it. When these incentives are changed, it changes the way salespeople think about customers. Many companies find that salespeople who didn't really want to spend much time talking about customer profitability suddenly start asking for the numbers before the reports can be produced.

A common observation among all the organizations interviewed was that changing customer behavior involves modifying the way that the organization makes decisions about customers—from executive management out to the front lines. In fact, achieving a sustained change in customer behavior involves a five-step cause-and-effect process (see Exhibit 11.7), beginning with improving the way customer behavior is measured. Capturing and reporting customer value plays a foundational role in this process.

Understanding the value of each customer is critical to balancing the value between a business and its customers. The process of understanding this value begins by creating a consolidated source of customer information such as a data warehouse. As an enterprise's metrics mature, it typically moves from simply measuring sales to measuring profitability, and even measuring potential profitability. The holy grail is to model the actual lifetime value of each customer, as well as the customer's potential value (see Chapter 5). The more mature an enterprise is with CRM measures, the better its position to optimize the value exchange between enterprise and customer.

PREFERENCES

Preference measures are not necessarily CRM metrics. Nevertheless, preference information is what must be gathered and managed in order to develop and improve customer relationships over time. These are the granular data elements that are used to build CRM metrics. Preference data are also required to differentiate between customers.

Observing, listening to, understanding, and predicting customer preferences covers a broad scope of measures that vary widely from one organization to another. The common thread, however, is the purpose for these measures: to make doing business easier, smarter, safer, faster, and more relevant for the customer—simply put, to make the enterprise more valuable to the customer.

Broadly speaking, this process of gathering data from customers can be thought of as a dialogue with customers. During the course of doing business, an enterprise learns a customer's buying patterns, likes, and dislikes. By observing this information, it can answer questions about customers such as:

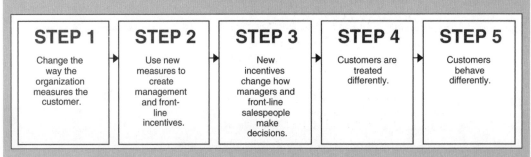

EXHIBIT 11.7   **Process for Achieving a Sustained Change in Customer Behavior**

- At what times of the day or year do they prefer to make certain decisions?
- What are their seating, color, size, and other preferences?
- What are they planning for the future?
- What do they care about?

The enterprise uses this information to engage the customer in interactions that are increasingly timely, individually relevant, and valuable.

Preference data gathered through this dialogue process can be broken down into five distinct categories: (1) actual behavior, (2) scores, (3) segmentation, (4) explicit dialog, and (5) overlay data.

Actual Behavior

Actual behavior is the observed behavior of the customer as it relates to the enterprise. This can include: Web behavior, purchases, returns, complaints, response to marketing promotions, channel usage, and other actual interactions and transactions. It can include average transaction amounts, color and size selections, seating preference, product categories, and product cross-sell ratios. These data are composed of all the current facts and figures that the enterprise has about its customers, and they are usually gathered invisibly, as the customer interacts with the business.

Actual behavior data are the most important data that an organization can remember about its customers. In fact, what customers do is more informative than what they say they are going to do (although it's sometimes still a poor predictor, as it's historical). But past behavior can be indicative of future behavior.[18] Actual customer behavior provides richer, deeper, more accurate, and more actionable information than any other information source.

Eddie Bauer had always done a good job of capturing customer behavior data. But until recently, these data were held in "stovepipe" systems for each of their three channels (catalog, retail, and Web). These systems could not link the behavioral data into a single picture of the customer. Egler provides an example of the power of making this connection: "A customer could shop at the store on a regular basis. But he might use the catalogs to decide what he wants to purchase before he goes to the store. In the past, we might have looked at this customer and concluded that he isn't a good catalog customer because he's not buying anything from the catalog. Now we'll say, 'I'm going to invest catalog dollars in this customer to help him make his purchasing decision and increase the profitability of the retail channel.'" Egler uses SAS software to measure that hypothesis by comparing a control group of customers to a group that receives a catalog and sees how their behavior varies in the store.

Since the introduction of its data warehouse, Eddie Bauer has started making this connection and has unearthed some valuable new knowledge. Specifically,

[18]Geoffrey Ables, "Predictive Modeling for Non-Statisticians: Usage of Predictive Modeling in Direct Marketing," *Target Marketing Magazine* (April 1997), p. 114.

it has found that customers who shop in two channels are more profitable than customers who shop in only one channel. Customers who shop in three channels are even more profitable—as much as five times more than single-channel customers. Using this information, Eddie Bauer can hone in on the channel that customers prefer, fine-tuning the experience to match the preferences of the customer.

Travelocity uses information about customer behavior on the Web site to make sure it consistently provides timely, targeted, and relevant information to customers. For instance, states Briggs, "If you live in New York, and you do a search on Honolulu, we can get a 50 percent lift in our e-mail campaigns by targeting you with New York-to-Honolulu deals." Experimenting with the timeliness of the offers has also yielded increased profits (and customer satisfaction). When targeting the same customers within two weeks of the time they last performed a search, Travelocity can achieve an additional 100 percent lift in response.

Travelocity has also found that its Web data are valuable for making strategic operational changes that impact all customers. Through path analysis (understanding the path that a customer takes through the site prior to making a purchase) and bailout analysis (understanding how many customers "bail out" of the site on a specific page) Travelocity can rapidly test changes to its infrastructure. As an example, Briggs cites, "We changed a page on our Web site last week; this week we can see if more customers got all the way through the process or not, and adjust accordingly." Other companies have found that their Web, call center, point-of-sale (POS), and other channel data can be used in a similar manner to optimize their operations; but the most powerful analysis comes from combining actual behavior data from all channels.

Newport News will soon populate its data warehouse with Web usage data. Fagan says, "We are beginning the process of linking up Web usage data, such as page views and product views, with actual purchasing behavior." This information can be used to better customize the Newport News site to customer's needs. Actual behavior data is not only valuable for personalization, it is also a key element utilized to derive customer profitability, segmentation, share of wallet and predictive modeling scores.

Scores

Scores are a critical element in balancing customer value and business value. These are weighted predictions that a customer has a certain preference, will take a certain course of action, is worthy of a certain risk level, or will attain a certain profitability level. Scores are usually numeric values based on statistical data-mining techniques (known as *predictive models*) that can be used to profile customers who have clearly demonstrated a specific preference and find other customers who are likely to have the same preference. Using predictive modeling with data-mining software, a company with 5 million customers might predict which 100,000 of them are most likely to buy something—anything—and target a mailing for them. If each customer spends an average of only $2 more, that's $200,000 in new revenue.[19]

"To describe this in simple terms: Predictive modeling is to 'database marketing' what a fish finder is to fishing. It may not guarantee success every time—but it makes the odds of success much greater than what they would have otherwise been."[20]

Travelocity has been successful in having customers make airline reservations online, but it has not had the same level of success with cross-selling hotel and rental car reservations. Ned Cullen, former database marketing manager for Travelocity states, "We know that the hotel and rental car preferences of leisure and business travelers are substantially different. But until recently, we could not easily distinguish between business and leisure bookings to personalize our cross-sell efforts." Travelocity decided to use predictive modeling and scoring to define the difference between the two groups of travelers. "By using the scores associated with each customer, we are in a better position to build mutually beneficial relationships with our customers because our marketing will be more tuned to the hotel and rental car choices they prefer," says Cullen.

Segmentation

Segmentation metrics are used to categorize customers into groups that display similar needs and preferences. Some organizations use a single segmentation system, while others overlay multiple segmented views of each customer. This information is valuable for management reporting, targeted marketing, and to prompt point of sale/service personnel with suggestions for managing customers.

Like many catalogs, Newport News has been a practitioner of segmentation for over 20 years, beginning with RFM segmentation. It continues to evaluate and examine new segmentation strategies in order to better understand its customer groups and personalize its service. "RFM is still important for us," comments Maureen Fagan, "but we're starting to layer in other ways of segmenting our customers." This includes segmentation by private label credit card usage, discount club membership, and product category purchasing. Fagan continues, "We don't stick to specified segments; we will run P&Ls on dynamic customer segments."

Types of segmentation used by firms include: profitability segmentation, demographic segmentation, channel usage segmentation, RFM segmentation, attitudinal segmentation, preference segmentation, and behavioral segmentation.

[19]"Using SAS to Tailor Customer Relationships"(April 2001), at *www.sas.com/news/success/eddiebauer.html*.

[20]Geoffrey Ables, "Predictive Modeling for Non-Statisticians," *Target Marketing Magazine* (April 1997), p. 114.

Explicit Dialogue

Explicit dialogue occurs when a customer intentionally provides feedback to the organization by indicating preferences, answering questions, or making a service request. Gathering this data requires an intentional process on the part of the enterprise, one that involves requesting, recording, and remembering the information.

Exclusive hotels gather explicit dialogue information in a free-form manner. Rather than asking customers to fill out a questionnaire, they record a customer's stated preference. For example, a customer may call and ask for a hypoallergenic pillow. When housekeeping delivers the pillow, they will make a note of this on a clipboard, along with the customer's room number and the date. This information is keyed into a database nightly so that the next time the customer stays at the hotel, the hotel will automatically provide the correct pillow. Direct sales organizations often capture similar free-form information directly into sales force automation (SFA) tools.

Other organizations capture information on customers that can be used to customize their experience on a massive basis. This may include remembering the color preferences, sizes, seating preferences, birthdays, anniversaries, and other information that is captured at the time of a transaction. It may also mean proactively collaborating with customers to determine what their likely needs will be in the near future, and then catering to these needs.

By using this type of information to provide greater value to the customer, organizations in turn earn customer trust and loyalty. The customer is then willing to provide more information to the organization because he realizes it creates value. The significance of this value exchange should not be underestimated, as Eddie Bauer's Egler notes: "This power of dialoging is going to become tremendously important to the future of CRM—the ability to change how we react based on what a customer overtly tells us he wants/doesn't want." In other words, our ability to *remember* and *use* information we get from customers.

Overlay Information

Overlay information can be purchased from third parties. This is not always considered "customer dialogue" because the customer does not necessarily know that the organization has access to this information. This information is, however, coming under increased scrutiny by privacy organizations; nevertheless, it can be valuable in determining customer preferences.

Although overlay data comes at a cost, it can be far simpler to gather than actual behavior information. The time and expense associated with creating a data warehouse that merges data from legacy systems across the organization can be prohibitive for organizations that are testing the waters of CRM. Overlay data can be purchased relatively inexpensively and readily be stored on PC databases for reporting, analysis, and targeted marketing projects.

Specific types of overlay information include: age, income, number of children, marital status, home ownership status, creditworthiness, inferred segments, and lifestyle/hobbies. For business-to-business organizations, this can include credit rating, SIC code, number of employees, and years in business.

These five categories of preferences metrics are suited to different CRM business tasks, summarized in Exhibit 11.8. As enterprises evolve in their CRM capabilities, they often find that starting with overlay data is a low-risk first step. These overlay data are then enriched over time with basic scores and segmentation. Integrating actual behavior data not only provides tremendous value for marketing and personalization, but also for strengthening and expanding upon scores, segmentation, and value assessment metrics. In general, explicit dialogue information is one of the last (but potentially most powerful) categories of data collected and applied to managing customer relationships.

EMBRACING CRM METRICS

Developing CRM metrics represents only the first phase of getting a business to adopt a customer-centered mentality. Next, the enterprise must make it easy for decision makers, from the front line to the executive suite, to be able to access and understand these metrics. But even with a distribution system in place, no one is likely to use new information unless he is given appropriate incentives. An internal sales, marketing, and education process can help raise awareness and usage of these new numbers. Only when the metrics are a part of the infrastructure and sales incentive process of the enterprise has the focus truly shifted toward CRM.

For CRM metrics to be embraced internally, they must be easily accessible throughout the enterprise. Pushing measurements out from the customer data

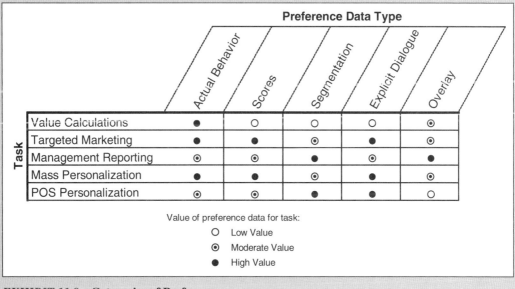

Preference Data Type

Task	Actual Behavior	Scores	Segmentation	Explicit Dialogue	Overlay
Value Calculations	●	○	○	○	◉
Targeted Marketing	●	●	◉	●	◉
Management Reporting	◉	◉	●	◉	●
Mass Personalization	●	●	◉	●	◉
POS Personalization	◉	◉	●	●	○

Value of preference data for task:

○ Low Value
◉ Moderate Value
● High Value

EXHIBIT 11.8 **Categories of Preferences**

warehouse generally involves two core processes: (1) integration of automated online analytical processing (OLAP) reporting tools and advanced data-mining tools with the warehouse and, (2) linking information from the warehouse to other systems, such as sales force automation, Web site, call centers, and ATM networks.

"We have been using OLAP reporting tools to distribute basic customer information around our organization," reports Briggs of Travelocity. These tools allowed users all over the organization to review reports and customer trends. "But we're finding that these reports create questions that require drilling even deeper into the warehouse," continues Briggs. "So we need to provide our business analysts with powerful CRM analytics tools. Using these tools, not only can our analysts perform advanced data mining, they can also create new metrics and reports that other end users can access via the OLAP tool."

Eddie Bauer is planning to take this one step further. Now that it understands that customers who have a high level of returns can be their most valuable customers, it wants to take action. Communicating this type of "self-defined segment" behavior to the retail channel is a starting point. Retail managers can watch for this behavior and automatically know that they need to treat these customers differently. These kinds of insights actually change the way the individual customer is treated at the point of sale. The process of making CRM metrics from the warehouse available throughout the enterprise is shown in Exhibit 11.9.

Once the metrics can be accessed, an internal strategy for generating awareness and acceptance must be developed. CRM managers have often found that their internal sales and marketing process is at least as important to the adoption of CRM as is the analytical process of developing and using the metrics.

Briggs has moved Travelocity toward this acceptance through internal partnerships. "Every two weeks we have prioritization meetings with product development," he says. "We have direct input into that process, so we have a voice in keeping it customer-centered. Using CRM metrics, we can find out if something we have designed is really working—often within minutes of launch."

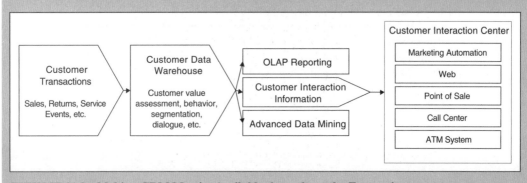

EXHIBIT 11.9   **Making CRM Metrics Available throughout the Enterprise**

Taking an incremental approach to having the organization adopt CRM measures is a common strategy. Eddie Bauer links the measures that individual business units are accustomed to seeing to CRM measures. Egler reports that, "Now when we share results, we share broader results. When we show the results, we also show the ripple effect."

Newport News found that the quality and productivity it gained by using CRM measures created the organizational momentum it needed. Maureen Fagan comments, "When we consolidated everything to a data warehouse, the accuracy of our forecasting system far exceeded the accuracy of the old system. This information is used every week to staff the call center, report to management, plan marketing activity, and make financial projections." In addition, the new method for calculating and reporting these new measures resulted in tremendous efficiency gains, freeing Fagan's team and internal partners to spend more time planning and executing projects that contribute directly to the company's bottom line. "It gave CRM importance and credibility across the enterprise," concludes Fagan.

IMPACT

Clearly, CRM can enable an enterprise to serve customers in a more timely, relevant, and personalized way. But at the end of the day, companies need to know that their investments are producing a payoff or they will not continue to invest in CRM. Research has shown that understanding the impact of CRM is critical for practitioners. Most companies with formal CRM programs (82 percent) are tracking the benefits of their efforts.[21]

"When we added new services, we went way beyond the ability of our old data-mining package to keep up. We cost-justified the tool by showing we could implement it and reduce the cost of maintaining multiple reporting systems on different mainframes," says Van Rhodes. But after the system was implemented, results were what mattered. And once Newport News began to see results, it became much easier to discuss allocating additional resources to expanding its capabilities. "Corporate acceptance is pretty much accomplished now," reports Rhodes, "Our CFO uses our performance report frequently, and both the president and the CFO have the tool right on their desktops to view important CRM metrics."

Briggs points to Travelocity's impressive conversion rates as evidence of the success of CRM within the organization. "We've always been customer-driven; our CEO calls us a database-marketing organization," declares Briggs. "Our sole focus is getting timely and relevant communication to the customer."

Eddie Bauer has made steady progress evangelizing and integrating CRM across technology, merchandising, marketing, and channel groups. "Our Retail Operations Group is investigating new POS systems. They have invited us to work with them, make presentations, and analyze customer behavior so they can

[21]Julien Beresford, "Add it Up," *1to1 Magazine* (September 2000), pp. 35–40.

better understand the scope of their project," says Egler. But he also cautions that getting cooperation because you are showing results is just the beginning. "When we talk about managing relationships better at the point of sale, they see the scope move from an inch to a yard. Changing the way the entire organization thinks about customers can cause scope creep—it's a factor we have to learn to deal with."

While few enterprises are willing to share the specific accomplishments of their CRM programs, all three of the companies interviewed shared a common pattern. After an initially modest investment in CRM, they have continued to reinvest. Now considered to be among the more mature practitioners of CRM, their budgets and infrastructure have continued to increase over five or more years.

MATURATION OF CRM METRICS

Measuring customer behavior has evolved from mass marketing to direct marketing and now to CRM, as illustrated in Exhibit 11.10. There are gray areas

Companies Mature into CRM Metrics →

Focus	METRIC TYPE		
	MASS MARKETING (MARKET)	DIRECT MARKETING (CAMPAIGN)	CRM (CUSTOMER)
Objectives	Grow share of market. Control costs.	Improve campaign profitability. Control costs.	Grow share of customer. Control costs.
Strategy	Improve advertising. Improve service process.	Improve marketing process.	Improve customer interactions. Customize/personalize.
Sample Metrics	Unaided awareness Customer satisfaction (estimated) Market penetration	Response rate Revenue per catalog RFM Campaign NPV	Behavior Halo effect Cross-sell ratio Share of wallet Customer satisfaction Potential NPV Lifetime value

← CRM Metrics Improve Market and Campaign Metrics

EXHIBIT 11.10   **Evolution of Customer Metrics**

between these different types of metrics, but there are also important distinctions. As CRM measures become more mainstream, they are changing some of the old mass-marketing metrics, and displacing others.

One important distinction between CRM and mass-marketing metrics is that CRM metrics begin by measuring *each individual customer*. This is an important distinction because the heart of CRM is enabling the business to better manage *each* customer relationship. Traditional market metrics merely allow the enterprise to make operational decisions that affect all customers—but not individual customers.

Mass marketing and campaign measures are improving because of CRM. CRM measures can often be aggregated to a campaign or market level to create more accurate and comprehensive measures than had previously been available. For instance, Newport News ran a double-discount promotion for customers who used their private credit card to make a purchase. According to Fagan, "We generated a better response, but lost money on the campaign." In the past, that would have been the end of the story. But now Newport News measures more than just the campaign; it can measure the "halo effect" of a campaign for at least 12 months to see whether the goodwill generated results in long-term customer profitability. "What at first appeared to be an unprofitable campaign can actually create more profitable relationships in the long term," notes Fagan. This type of information was not available in the past using one-off campaign metrics.

Similarly, many companies have long discussed retention campaigns, but few actually implement sustained retention projects. The simple reason is that it is too difficult to understand the long-term value of saying, "thank you" or "we apologize." It is nearly impossible to show a return on a single thank-you card campaign. But if the impact of this communication is measured across the next 12 months of customer relationships, versus a control group, a true impact can be quantified.

Individualized customer metrics are not completely displacing traditional market and campaign metrics. Businesses continue to find that many of these measures are still important for understanding growth and customer acquisition strategies.

Mass marketing, or market metrics, measure trends to facilitate operational changes. Direct marketing, or campaign metrics, measure projects to facilitate marketing process improvement. CRM, or customer metrics, measure each customer relationship and can be aggregated to the campaign, segment, or market level to help an enterprise with decision making in these areas. Interestingly, aggregated CRM metrics can produce more accurate and actionable numbers than the generalized numbers used in the past.

WHAT'S NEXT?

Lifetime Profitability and Point-in-Time Profitability measures are a focus at Newport News. Lifetime Profitability will be the actual financial value of the customer since the day he first became a customer. Point-in-Time Profitability will measure the "halo effect" of promotions by watching how individual promotions affect customer behavior over the long term. "Because of a special promotion, we may lose money on an order. But we want to know if that loss leader paid off in the long term," says Rhodes.

Travelocity's Paul Briggs knows that their needs will continue to change and has built flexibility into their warehouse as a result. "We don't know what the measures will always be, so we err to the side of remembering more detail about our customers rather than less." Travelocity also has a focus on using more trigger- and event-based campaigns to improve the timeliness and relevancy of everything the company says.

But Briggs also must continue to educate internally. "It's getting difficult for the entire company to understand all the metrics that we're using now," Briggs says. "We need to educate our internal users of customer information on exactly which measures they're looking at and how to use them."

Recognized as an advanced CRM enterprise, Eddie Bauer still struggles to integrate customer strategies across all organizational divisions. "If I manage a channel and am asked to make decisions about my channel in the best interest of the customer, rather than my channel, it takes more time and might require me to make a personal sacrifice," observes Egler. "That's a tough battle to fight: to get people to do something for the greater good."

Paul Briggs offers this advice to those still struggling with the basics, "It's not always about sales and marketing. Sometimes it's just adding value by educating customers, or making them aware of options and risks, or proactively servicing them before they ask."

The tension between customer value and business value constantly presents new issues and opportunities to CRM practitioners. Striking the right balance is an ongoing process to which there is no one-size-fits-all answer. Maureen Fagan advises, "It is a constant issue. There is no magic, no silver bullet. It takes constant monitoring, watching to be sure the product you are offering is the product the customer really wants to purchase."

Measuring both the opportunities for growth and the actual financial effects of managing customer relationships is critical to CRM business practices. Companies that pursue other components of CRM without a disciplined approach to measuring customers are almost certain to stumble. CRM metrics are the flashlight in the practitioner's toolbox; without them, there's no basis for prioritizing projects, treating different customers differently, measuring your efforts, strategically abandoning unprofitable activities, and centering your organization on the customer.[22]

In the first wave of the interactive era, enterprises learned to build data warehouses that could store as many bytes of customer information as they might care to collect. In the next wave, enterprises are figuring out how to turn this data into useful intelligence and bottom-line results.

[22]According to Nelle Schantz, Director of CRM for SAS Institute.

SUMMARY

The metrics associated with managing customer relationships can provide an invaluable insight to the profitability potential of the enterprise's customer base and the viability of the enterprise's new customer-strategy business processes. The customer-based enterprise does, however, have to concern itself with other measurements and analyzing other pieces of information that are more specific to growing the overall value of each customer. Treating different customers differently can entail a detailed analysis of each customer to determine how the enterprise can alter his trajectory with the enterprise. Often, this analysis can help turn customer information into knowledge the enterprise can use to help the customer meet his needs.

The triggers, or predictors, of individual customer action and opportunity cannot usually be seen without detailed analysis. This is the increasingly complex and far-from-intuitive science of *customer-based analytics*, and having this discipline well represented on an enterprisewide cross-functional team is critical. Sophisticated statistical models powered by technology can uncover some remarkable and highly predictive patterns. The ability to "mine data" is so valuable that its precise manifestations can be proprietary within certain companies. In the next chapter, we'll uncover some of these scientific applications of analytics within the customer-strategy enterprise.

FOOD FOR THOUGHT

1. But seriously: Would it be possible for a company to be profitable if each of its customers were profitable—even if some products were unprofitable? What would have to happen for a company to measure its profit by customer, rather than product?

2. Which measurements would you want to have to help you make the management decisions that will grow the company by growing the value of the customer base:
   - If your company makes blue jeans, which you have traditionally sold to retailers under three different brands?
   - If you run a high-end department store chain with its own credit card and delivery fleet?
   - If you own a company that makes shopping bags for stores and store chains?

GLOSSARY

Attitudinal loyalty   A preference, proclivity, or affinity for a product or company.

Behavioral loyalty   Repeatedly purchasing from a particular company.

Brand equity   The difference between what a customer is willing to pay for a product that does versus doesn't have a brand, or the tendency of a customer to prefer a product of a certain brand (Lemon et al.).

Relationship equity   According to Lemon et al., "the tendency of the customer to stick with the brand, above and beyond the customer's objective and subjective assessments of the brand."

Value equity   The bankable component of a customer's perception that a particular brand, company, or product delivers value (Lemon et al.).

Customer Analytics and the Customer–Strategy Enterprise

12
Chapter

To the customer-value-building enterprise, data about individual customers are like gold nuggets that, if collected and used effectively, can increase the value of the customer base significantly. **Data mining** *is a frequently used term for the process of extracting useful nuggets of information from a vast database of customer information; but as the relationship revolution has taken hold, the data-mining process itself has also undergone an important transformation. In the preinteractive age, data-mining techniques were used to uncover information about the types of customers to whom particular offers should be made, answering the question: Who is the next most likely customer to buy this product? Today, the question asked by companies engaged in managing ongoing, interactive relationships with individual customers, is: What is the next most likely product that this particular customer will want to buy?*

In truth, each of these questions has a role to play in any competitive enterprise's efforts to get, keep, and grow customers. But in the interactive age, much more so than in the past, individual customer information drives the central engine of competition. Without reliable insights into the value and needs of individual customers, the customer-based enterprise will be completely rudderless.

In this chapter we will look at **customer analytics**—*the way we think of data mining now—and we will hear from Judy Bayer and Ron Swift about the fundamental issues facing customer-strategy companies when they are working with and using large amounts of customer data.*

Experts define data mining largely in terms of its usefulness in uncovering hidden trends or yielding previously unknown insight about the nature of a firm's customers. SAS Institute defines data mining as "the process of selecting, exploring, and modeling large amounts of data to uncover previously unknown patterns for business advantage."[1] Michael J. A. Berry and Gordon S. Linoff, who have written several books on the subject, define data mining as "the process of exploration and analysis, by automatic or semiautomatic means, of

---

[1] www.SAS.com.

large quantities of data in order to discover meaningful patterns and rules."[2] And Ronald Swift, Teradata vice president of strategic customer relationships, says data mining is "the process of extracting and presenting new knowledge, previously undetectable, selected from databases for actionable decisions."[3]

Rather than limit ourselves to the term *data mining*, however, we prefer the term *customer analytics*. Although data mining and customer analytics are not really different things, the analogy to mining itself implies a batch process, with the enterprise searching out nuggets of information and then putting them to use. The reality, however, in the interactive age, is that businesses need to have continuously developing, real-time insights into the nature of their individual customers, not only so that the right marketing campaign can be created and launched, but also so the customer can be given the appropriate offer in real time **(real-time analytics)**, while she is on the phone, shopping at the Web site, or standing at the checkout counter.

> Customer analytics enables the enterprise to classify, estimate, predict, cluster, and more accurately describe data about customers, using mathematical models and algorithms that ultimately simplify how it views its customer base and how it behaves toward individual customers.

Customer analytics, therefore, offers the missing link to understanding customers: prediction.[4] Prediction helps enterprises use the value of customer information to optimize each interaction with each customer. Today, leading companies integrate the most relevant elements of their data-mining algorithms into their actual touchpoint applications. If a customer behaves a certain way, then the mathematical algorithm can analyze that behavior and instantly access the most relevant offer for that customer, taking into account everything the enterprise knows or is able to predict about each customer, in *real time*. Customer analytics enables the enterprise to classify, estimate, predict, cluster, and more accurately describe data about customers, using mathematical models and algorithms that ultimately simplify how it views its customer base and how it behaves toward individual customers.

The dilemma facing many companies that amass huge customer databases today is simply how to make sense of the data. Analytical software has become a critical component of the customer-strategy enterprise, and those who can operate such software are in great demand. The mathematical data models that analytical software can produce are inherently simplifications of the "real world"—they represent how customers have behaved before and will likely behave again. They enable a company to view correlations within large sets of customer data and within and among various parts of its business. By analyzing historic information and applying it to current customer data, these mathematical models and algo-

---

[2]Michael J.A. Berry and Gordon S. Linoff, *Mastering Data Mining* (New York: John Wiley & Sons, Inc., 2000). See also Jill Dyché, *e-Data: Turning Data into Information with Data Warehousing* (Reading, MA: Addison-Wesley, 2000).

[3]Ronald S. Swift, *Accelerating Customer Relationships* (Upper Saddle River, NJ: Prentice Hall, 2001).

[4]Sue Phelan, "Increasing Customer Value: Harness the Power of Predictive CRM," Customer-Centric Solutions white paper, date; available at: *www.spss.com/customercentric*.

rithms can predict future events, with varying degrees of accuracy, based not just on the amount of data collected, but also on the power of the analysis applied to the data. Using customer analytics, an enterprise can sometimes predict whether a customer will buy a certain product or will defect to a competitor.

Companies produce large amounts of data through a wide array of customer-related business processes, including order entry, billing, reservations, complaint handling, product specification, Web interactions, sales calls, and so forth. The data are often fed into a data warehouse, where much of it lies hidden in "data tombs," and can be forgotten about for years. Often the result is that, even when a firm has the customer analytics resources necessary to unleash the value of its data, it soon discovers that much of its information is "dirty" (expired, irrelevant, nonsequential, or nonsensible) and needs to be "cleaned" (eliminated, updated, correlated, and refined). As customer analytics tools and technology become more affordable and easier to use, however, enterprises are starting to feel competitive pressure to improve their capabilities in this area.[5] The various activities involved in readying customer data for analysis, and the **analysis process** itself, include:

- *Classification*, or assigning instances to a group, then using the data to learn the pattern of traits that identify the group to which each instance belongs.
- *Estimation*, for determining a value for some unknown continuous variable, such as credit card balance or income.
- *Regression*, which uses existing values to forecast what continuous values are likely to be.
- *Prediction*, or using historical data to build a model to forecast future behavior.
- *Clustering*, which maps customers within the database into groups based on their similarities. (See more about clustering in the following section.)

Although customer analytics is a powerful idea supported by an increasing array of software tools, surprisingly it is used by only about half of CRM implementers, according to META Group. Often, companies are discouraged by the failure of their previous analytical efforts, including failed data warehousing projects or databases full of dirty data.

Customer analytics is especially useful for consumer marketing companies that collect transactional data through call centers, Web sites, or electronic points of sale. Banks, credit card companies, telecommunications firms, retailers, and even airlines have adopted customer analytics as a vital part of their business operations earlier than other companies. These kinds of companies tend to generate large volumes of customer-specific information in the natural

---

[5]See also Hugh J. Watson, Dale L. Goodhue, and Barbara H. Wixom, "The Benefits of Data Warehousing: Why Some Organizations Realize Exceptional Payoffs," *Information and Management* 39 (2002): 491–502; and Hugh J. Watson, David A. Annino, Barbara H. Wixom, K. Liddell Avery, and Mathew Rutherford, "Current Practices in Data Warehousing," *Information Systems Management* (Winter 2001): 47–55.

SIDEBAR 12.1
Grouping Customers Using Cluster Analysis

Judy Bayer
CRM Practice Partner, NCR Teradata

Ronald E. Swift
Vice President, Strategic Marketing and Customer Relationships, NCR Teradata

Peter Heffring
President, Southeastern Mortgage

The idea behind *cluster analysis* is that objects (customers) can be clustered together into groups such that each group is both homogeneous within the group and substantively different from all other groups. The marketing rationale behind this idea is compelling. Clustering allows the marketer to speak to a group with such strong similarities that it is the next best thing to speaking to an individual customer—knowing all that customer's relevant characteristics. This has important implications as companies move rapidly toward one-to-one relationship management.

In cluster analysis, there are four major categories of technical issues that must be addressed in order to segment customers:

1. *Variable selection issues.* How to select the set of variables to be used.

2. *Data transformation issues.* Standardizing variables and selecting a measure of similarity or dissimilarity.

3. *Solution issues.* Selecting a clustering algorithm, deciding on the number of clusters, and identifying outliers.

4. *Validity issues.* Making an initial selection of a preferred solution, assessing the reliability and stability of the cluster solution, and assessing the usefulness of the solution for solving the specific marketing problem of interest.

Variable Selection Issues

There are several considerations when selecting variables. Important variables, which are associated with the usefulness of the cluster solution, must be incorporated. It is possible to obtain a cluster solution that is technically valid but has no usefulness in solving an organization's business problem. It is crucial, therefore, to incorporate variables based on an understanding of the relationships between possible variables and the business problem being solved. Variables that do not help discriminate among clusters must be eliminated. Including irrelevant variables may distort a cluster solution. Variables that are highly correlated will create interdependencies, giving disproportionate weight to certain dimensions among which clustering will be carried out.

All variables chosen in a final solution must be available for any customer, who will eventually have to be scored into the clustering solution. Some clustering solutions are developed for both customers and noncustomers, so that the model will be useful not only for customer marketing, but also for customer prospecting. In this case, a prospect scoring model must be developed that can assign prospects to clusters based solely on the subset of information available related to prospects.

SIDEBAR 12.1 *(continued)*

For models geared toward known customers, rather than unidentified prospects, the analysis should include value-based variables—such as transactions, revenue, and profit. For a *channel migration analysis*, we would also include channel usage information. For solutions involving prospects, in addition to standard demographics/product usage variables, variables such as cable television, Internet usage, and mail-order sensitivity might be important to include.

Variables identified from the other market research could be used to help assure that the cluster solution incorporates key variables. Additionally, analysis is done of variables to assess heterogeneity among customers with respect to the variables, relationship to sale behavior, and correlation between variables. Based on these procedures, an appropriate set of variables is selected.

Data Transformation Issues

Standardization of numeric variables is often undertaken when using clustering methods to avoid overweighting variables due to scaling issues. For example, without scaling, income would tend to overwhelm age. A measure of similarity or dissimilarity must also be selected. Generally, use of a particular similarity or dissimilarity measure will not determine the final cluster solution. That said, some measures are better able to correct for interdependencies among the variables. Use of a specific measure will depend on the analysis and selection of variables.

Solution Issues

Next, the clustering solution is created. To do this, decisions must be made about which clustering algorithm to use, how many clusters to create, and whether to include outliers. The decision as to method is important, because different clustering methods may generate different solutions to the same data set. A discussion of the many alternative clustering methods is beyond the scope of this book; but the primary method selected for many analysts is K-means clustering, so that is the method described here. With this method, the analyst makes a determination as to the number of clusters in the solution. An initial center point of each cluster, a *centroid*, is also estimated. Customers are assigned and reassigned to clusters with the nearest centroid, and centroids are updated, until a solution is reached. The K-means procedure shown in Exhibits A, B, and C is a two-dimensional representation of the steps involved:

1. Determines the number of clusters and the initial cluster centroids (see Exhibit A).

2. Assigns each customer to clusters (see Exhibit B). A customer is assigned to the cluster with the smallest distance between the customer and the center of the

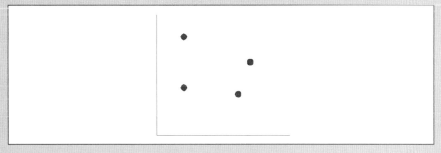

EXHIBIT A   **K-means Clustering: Step 1**

SIDEBAR 12.1 *(continued)*

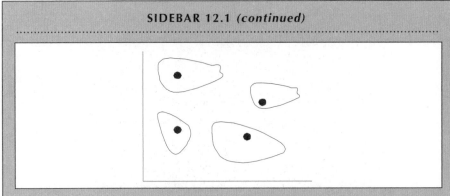

EXHIBIT B   **K-means Clustering: Step 2**

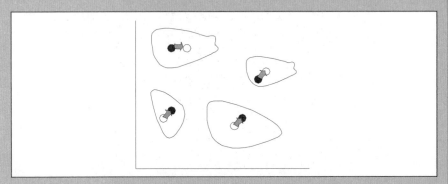

EXHIBIT C   **K-means Clustering : Step 3**

cluster. This results in customers more or less grouped around the centroids, as shown in the exhibit.

3. Adjusts the centroids based on the attributes of the customers in each cluster (see Exhibit C).

This process of allocating each customer to a cluster and computing the new centroid of the clusters iterates until either there is no change in clusters or some other limit is met. Note that we drew these diagrams in just two dimensions for illustration purposes, but the overwhelming majority of K-means clustering analyses are done in multiple dimensions. The mathematical principles, however, are exactly the same; only the equations are more complex.

K-means clustering is often selected as a primary clustering method because it is robust with respect to the presence of outliers and choice of distance measure. It is also less affected by the presence of irrelevant attributes in the data than are many other clustering methods. With this method, however, the number of clusters and initial centroid values must be determined. A multistage clustering procedure can be used to obtain a high-quality solution, as follows:

1. Initial solution approximations are obtained using hierarchical clustering. This method is suitable only for small sample clustering and is not as robust as K-means. Several small sample hierarchical solutions are usually generated.

2. The results of these preliminary analyses are examined and used to determine candidates for numbers of clusters and starting points. Outliers are also analyzed during this stage.

SIDEBAR 12.1 *(continued)*

....

3. K-means clustering is done using the number of clusters and cluster centroids from preliminary analysis. Alternative solutions will be generated based on alternative initial solutions.

4. Cluster solutions are evaluated against each other and in terms of overall validity.

5. The process iterates until an appropriate solution is obtained.

Validity Issues

Alternative solutions have to be evaluated against each other. The preferred solution must also be assessed in terms of **reliability** and **validity**.

Individual cluster solutions are compared. The customer data in better solutions have greater between-cluster differences and smaller within-cluster differences. A small number of candidate solutions are then tested for reliability.

Reliability is the extent to which a solution is stable and reproducible. Reliability testing is crucial for methods such as clustering where group membership is unknown and subject to nonobjective criteria. Two methods will be used to assess reliability: The first is cross-validating based on a split sample; the second is *cross-validating based on a different clustering method*.

For the split sample approach, the cluster analysis is done on only part of the sample of customers. Customers in the holdout sample are then assigned to one of the identified clusters based on the smallest Euclidian distance to a cluster centroid. The stability of the solution is assessed by the degree of agreement between the nearest centroid assignments of the holdout sample and the results of a cluster analysis of the holdout sample. A coefficient of agreement is used as an objective measure of stability. If the results are stable, the holdout sample can be combined with the rest of the data to obtain a final clustering solution.

Depending on the results of this process, a sample of the company's customers can also be clustered using a neural network approach to clustering. A Kohonen network, also known as a self-organizing network, can be estimated on a sample of customers. Results can be compared to the K-means clustering outcome to assess reliability.

Validating cluster results must also be done. This involves showing the usefulness of the solution for the business problem being solved.

---

course of operating their businesses, often resulting in vast data warehouses, containing terabytes of data.

National Australia Bank (NAB) was an early adopter of a customer-value-building strategy. Over the past several years, exploiting a data warehouse structured to provide a single source for information about customers across its entire enterprise, the bank has developed highly sophisticated analytical software and modeling techniques for generating hundreds of thousands of sales leads and communicating customer opportunities to thousands of its bankers. The "relationship optimization" CRM LEADS System gives NAB the capability to maximize customer lifetime value and coordinate all customer access channels. NAB provides enabling information to cross-sell relevant products and services to individual customers, providing a single, consistent view of each customer throughout the entire enterprise. As a result, not only can NAB serve its individual customers better, but it has also been able to reduce its marketing expenses significantly, targeting only those customers who have a high propensity to make a purchase.[6]

Customer analytics contributes to better sales productivity and lower marketing costs in many different ways, including:

- By making it possible to send more relevant information and offers, analytics helps to improve shopper-to-buyer conversion rates.
- Instead of offering one product to a lot of customers, analytics makes it possible to offer specific and more targeted cross-sell and upsell opportunities, which can result in measurably increased sales.
- By taking steps to keep customers longer, analytics can help increase customer profitability.
- Companies use analytics to improved operational effectiveness, through smarter, more relevant (and therefore, usually, faster and less costly) customer service.
- Analytics can be used to reduce the interaction time and effort, making information exchange or transactions easier, faster and, therefore, more likely.
- Analytics improves the customer's perception of the level of service as a result of relevant messaging during an interaction.
- Analytics makes improved service levels for best customers possible.[7]

Department store Nordstrom uses human-based knowledge combined with data-mining techniques from its Personal Touch program to build long-term customer relationships. The Personal Touch shoppers that Nordstrom hires are fashion consultants who are trained in color, current fashions, and how to match their store's products to a customer's appearance, taste, and lifestyle. Supported by technology, Personal Touch shoppers try to sell customers ensembles, instead of individual clothing items, using two systems that capture customer information and knowledge. The first is a database of personal profiles in which they record a customer's tastes, dislikes, lifestyle, and apparel needs learned from interacting with the customer. The second database stores customer purchase history, in order to assist the shopper by suggesting items that might complement a previous purchase.[8]

Those who use customer analytics, therefore, are trying to create an unobstructed view of the customer, allowing the enterprise, essentially, to see things from the customer's own perspective. By delving into a customer's history, analytical programs can help the enterprise customize the way it serves a customer or manufactures a product for a customer to suit that customer's individual

---

[6]Ronald S. Swift,"The New Economic Opportunity of Business—Creating Increased Profitability through CRM," Montgomery Research white paper, July 2002; available at: *www.mriadmin.com.*

[7]Kevin Cavanaugh, "Achieving Intelligent Interactions with Analytical CRM," *DM Review* 11, no. 5 (May 2001), pp. 44–47.

[8]Jeanne Harris, "Crouching Customer, Hidden Insight," Montgomery Research white paper, June 2002; available at: *www.mriadmin.com.*

needs, in essence helping the enterprise to transform its customer data into critical business decisions about individual customers. Customer analytics software can reveal hidden trends about a customer and compare her behavior to other customers' behavior.[9] In addition, customer analytics can play an important role in customer acquisition, by helping the enterprise decide how to handle different prospects differently, and by predicting which ones are more likely to become the most valuable customers.[10]

In 2001, Tesco, the U.K. retailer with the highly successful Clubcard frequent shopper program, bought a 53 percent stake in Dunn Humby, its data-mining partner. Tesco knows that its customer data is its most valuable asset. Dunn Humby and Tesco became partners in 1995, when Tesco was launching its Clubcard initiative, and since then the firm has helped Tesco evaluate and act on what it learns from its Clubcard customers, managing massive data sets and enabling Tesco to increase the value of its customer base.[11]

Tesco and other astute customer-strategy enterprises have learned that customer data have a dollar value associated with them, and the more accurate the information, the better the enterprise can compete. Customer analytics can provide *metadata*—information about information—spotting characteristics and trends that enhance customer retention and profitability. Furthermore, customer analytics can be a technique for examining the profitability of specific products that individual customers purchase. As Fred Newell points out in *Loyalty.com*, analytics helps profile customers so that characteristics of loyal customers can be identified to predict which prospects will become new customers. Data mining can manage customer relationships by determining characteristics of customers who have left for a competitor so that the enterprise can act to retain customers who are at risk of leaving. Moreover, analytics helps an enterprise learn the mix of products to which a group of customers is attracted so it can learn what the customers value. "With this knowledge," Newell writes, "we can mine the customer file for similar customers to offer suggestions they are likely to value. Without data and its being analyzed to develop information and knowledge about the way things are happening in the real world, all we have are opinions. Every expert we have talked to gives the same answer: "Data mining is knowledge discovery."[12] Customer analytics is not a technology—it is a *business process*.

> Customer analytics is not a technology–it is a *business process*.

The next level of analytics might be applying financial characteristics to the data analysis, in order to yield a more accurate view of the actual economic con-

[9]Angela Karr, "Analytics: The Next Wave of CRM," *Customer Interface* 14, no. 5 (May 2001), p. 44.

[10]Thomas J. Siragusa, "Implementing Data Mining for Better CRM," *Customer Interaction Solutions* 19, no. 11 (May 2001), p. 38.

[11]Martha Rogers, PhD, "It's Aces High for Tesco and Dunn Humby," *Inside 1to1* (August 6, 2001), available at: *www.1to1.com*.

[12]Frederick Newell, *Loyalty.com* (New York: McGraw-Hill Professional Book Group, 2000).

sequences of particular customer actions. For instance, an enterprise might know that a promotion should go to customers fitting a certain profile, but will probably have more difficulty correlating the cost of the promotion with its likely outcome, at least on a customer-specific basis. In the next epoch of customer analytics, the mathematical algorithms will look across a range of promotions and associated costs to determine which tactics will generate the most profit. Ultimately, customer analytics will generate a revolution in how marketing decisions are made, driving companies increasingly toward solutions based on highly detailed marketing simulations.

In the end, however, the reason for analyzing all of this data is simply to develop a deeper relationship with each customer, in an effort to increase the overall value of the customer base—or, as Judy Bayer and Ron Swift of NCR Teradata point out in the next section of this chapter, to "optimize" the enterprise's customer relationships.

OPTIMIZING CUSTOMER RELATIONSHIPS WITH ADVANCED ANALYTICS

Judy Bayer
CRM Practice Partner, NCR Teradata

Ronald S. Swift
Vice President, Strategic Marketing and Customer Relationships, NCR Teradata

Customer interaction and transaction data enter a company's database system from thousands of customer contact touchpoints, through many selling and service channels—in continuous waves. A critical challenge any business faces is that of leveraging this dynamic tidal wave of customer information to gain the vital insight that can help optimize a customer relationship. It has been said that the market value of a company is a direct reflection of the value of its customer relationships. This is certainly true in a time when information—or intelligence—is the primary source of economic value. When analytical intelligence is systematically applied to optimize customer relationships, enterprises can expect improved customer equity and enhanced business performance. This section will serve as an introduction to the subject of advanced customer analytics, which refers to the methodologies that experts use to exploit knowledge of a company's current and future customers to create intelligence for better business decisions and optimal customer relationships.

Advanced customer analytics involves tracking and evaluating data, and examining highly complex patterns and trends. It builds and expands on traditional data mining by applying statistical and reporting techniques and tools to information culled from customer contacts. And, with the help of advanced CRM technology tools, analytical intelligence can be created and applied within days, minutes, or even seconds of a customer interaction. Referred to as *real-*

time analytics and enabled by advanced analytical CRM software applications, these powerful applications systematically accelerate analytic processes to incredible speeds.

SIDEBAR 12.2

Customer Analytics

....

Managers and business analysts use customer analytics to:

- Rank customers by business value.
- Model customer behavior to predict an individual's migration into a spectrum of value groups.
- Simulate and predict customer buying behavior based on a variety of promotion strategies.
- Perform a marketing influencers analysis to identify which customers can be influenced in their value migration, then communicate to them in ways that move them in the right direction.
- Learn what proportion of customers purchase goods or services through single and multiple channels—and know how valuable they are.
- Learn which products or services sell best through certain channels.
- Learn what impact new channels will have on current business.
- Determine which channels would be most effective for specific customer groups.
- Predict which customers will switch or begin sharing business across channels.
- Make assessments of each customer's affinity to a message, product, or service.
- Learn how frequently to contact each customer—and which channel is best for specific messages.
- Perform detailed market-basket analysis, product-structure analysis, cross-product correlation analysis, multiple campaign response models, customer growth models, churn and attrition models, and customer lifetime value models to spot revenue and profit opportunities.

Armed with reports generated by advanced customer analytics, enterprises can more accurately predict customer behavior, forecast buying trends, identify opportunities, and ferret out the reasons for their marketing failures and successes. Customer analytics include segmentation studies, customer migration analysis, LTV modeling, cross-sell/upsell analysis, new customer models, customer **contact optimization**, merchandising analysis, customer attrition and churn models, credit risk scoring—and more.

Just for example, one of the practical problems facing marketers is that customer values are typically changing; they are rarely constant. Most marketers promote to customers based on their current value to the business, but with advanced customer analytics, a company will be able to predict whether a particular customer's value to the enterprise is moving up or down, and how quickly the movement is occurring. A company could then take action to affect this customer movement positively. Customer migration analysis can help a firm better communicate and market to its customers in ways that move them up the value chain.

Contact optimization is another problem that must be addressed with customer analytics. Given that different customers have different needs for information and different sensitivities to various offers, how can the enterprise optimize its contact strategy so as to yield the highest possible increase in value for each particular customer?

Contact optimization is actually the polar opposite of today's typical marketing practices, apparently focused on "contact bombardment"—showering the largest possible number of prospects or customers with messages, even when those messages are often irrelevant or ill-timed. For instance, is a zero-percent financing offer on a new car always relevant to every consumer? What if a person had just bought a new car a few days prior to receiving the offer? Would she be thrilled that other customers were now able to take advantage of the financing benefit? Not likely. Does technology make it possible for the company to know who has recently purchased a car and thus should not be the target of such an offer? Yes, it does. Advanced customer analytics can leverage database intelligence so that the enterprise can plan and develop communications with more relevance and timeliness, satisfying customers rather than driving them away. Some of the questions to be answered in a comprehensive analysis of customer data might include:

- What does it mean for individual messages and sales offers to be "relevant?"
- How many contacts should each of your customers receive from you—taking into account both inbound (customer-initiated) and outbound (company-initiated)?
- What should be the timing of your communications with your customer?
- How should the budget be allocated across customers to make optimum use of corporate resources?
- Which products or services, which messages through which channel, are most effective in driving customer value?

Yet another practical problem, and the one that we will consider in detail for the remainder of this section, has to do with the way different customers use different buying-and-interaction channels in their dealings with the enterprise. The problem of channel management affects many marketers in a variety of industries. Consumer marketers, particularly, often find themselves in possession of a wealth of data points that capture all the various channel interactions and transactions of their customers; but making sense of these data points can be very difficult.

USING CUSTOMER ANALYTICS TO UNDERSTAND CHANNEL MANAGEMENT

You may not think you're ready to take out your next home mortgage from an ATM machine. But your bank would like you to reconsider. Recent studies suggest that customers who purchase through multiple channels tend to be more valuable than single-channel customers—the multichannel lift has been found to be as much as 20 to 40 percent. There may be a number of reasons for this finding. One possible reason is that the experience of using multiple channels deepens the customer's relationship with the company, driving additional purchasing. An alternative and equally plausible explanation, however, is that customers who are already predisposed to a better relationship with a firm are simply more likely to avail themselves of multiple channels. In reality, both of these dynamics are probably at work in most business situations. But if, by analyzing different customers' channel usage patterns over time, the enterprise could separate out the cause-and-effect involved in multichannel relationships, then it should be able to influence customer behavior in such a way as to increase the value of its customers. Developing single-channel customers into multichannel customers might indeed help a company achieve its revenue, customer retention, and profitability goals. Knowing the actual mechanics of the relationship between channel usage and customer value will allow the enterprise to monitor its CRM investment and quantify its success.

To do such a multichannel analysis requires longitudinal data. Understanding the true impact of customers migrating to multiple purchasing channels, therefore, requires enough customer purchasing history to measure "before and after." A group of single-channel customers is identified at a specific point in time, and their data are analyzed over a time interval that is meaningful based on the company's business—usually six months or a year. All purchasing information is collected and analyzed for that time frame, including such things as revenue, transaction frequency, transaction characteristics, types of products purchased, profit margin, and returns per customer. Another analysis is then performed on these same customers' data during a later time period of equal duration and with similar seasonality. In this later analysis, however, the customers are split up based on the number of channels in which they now shop. The average customer value and characteristics of the "still single-channel" customer are compared to that of the "now multichannel" customer. A comparison is also made to the value of these customers in the past. Additional analysis can be initiated to learn how the single-channel customers who became multichannel customers were similar to or different from those customers who remained single-channel customers.

As more companies expand their opportunities into various sales channels, it is important to remember that customers themselves do not treat the multiple channels of a company as separate entities. From the customer's own perspective, the channels all lead to the same place: the company they are doing business with. Organizations should be thinking exactly the same way: They should have a single, integrated view of each customer regardless of the sales channel. Successful companies recognize customers regardless of where they shop and leverage customer information across multiple channels to drive marketing strategies and strengthen customer relationships.

A channel management solution provides many measurable business benefits, but from an analytics standpoint, it allows the marketer to:

- Identify the proportion of customers who purchase goods or services through multiple channels and show how this changes over time.
- Determine the relative value of multichannel versus single-channel customers.
- Analyze the patterns of product and service sales through the different channels.
- Assess the impact new channel initiatives will have on the business.
- Predict which customers will switch or begin sharing business across multiple channels and quantify the impact of the predicted changes in channel behavior.

A channel management solution addresses these issues through channel analysis and predictive modeling.

CHANNEL MIGRATION MODELING

Channel migration modeling is a way to predict which customers will begin purchasing from more than one channel. By identifying customers most likely to begin to purchase from multiple channels, companies may be able to migrate a portion (if not all) of a customer's business to a more profitable mix of sales channels.

There are several types of analytical methods used for this type of modeling. The channel migration models are estimated at the level of the customer; that is, each customer (or account or household) has a value calculated based on the predictive model estimated based on historical data. The classes of analytical methods that can be used include logistic regression modeling, decision trees, and neural networks. Each customer is scored based on the model. Scores range between zero and one and represent the probability that the customer will migrate to multiple channels.[13] Scored customers could then be profiled to identify descriptive characteristics of single versus multichannel customers. If logit regression is used as the modeling technique, key drivers of multichannel behavior can also be assessed.

SEGMENTATION MODELING

Statistical segmentation of customers can be a valuable tool for CRM. Within the context of channel management, segmentation involves grouping like customers based on various channel-related factors such as:

---

[13]Alternatively, models could be developed that would predict whether the customer would be a single-channel customer, two-channel, three-channel, and so on. In this case, methods such as multinomial logit could be used to develop the model. The disadvantage to doing this would be that the model might not be as robust as one in which the prediction was that the customer would be single- or multichannel.

- Proportion of purchases by channel
- Frequency of purchases by channel
- Types of products purchased by channel
- Average value of purchase by channel

Customer interaction channels can also serve as the basis for customer groupings. For example, criteria could include prior response to particular types of direct-mail campaigns. Group-scoring models are also developed as part of this solution. These models can be used to automatically assign customers (new and existing) to their appropriate strategic segment on a continuing basis.

The idea behind creating statistical segments is that customers within a segment are homogeneous with respect to the segmentation variables. Across segments, they are heterogeneous. This allows the marketer to create customer strategies for communicating with customers that are both appropriate and efficient, thus profitable.

Methodologies used for statistical segmentation, also known as clustering, fall under a class of analytical methods known as *unsupervised learning*. This means that the cluster model is created without knowing what the "correct" answer is. The methods discussed previously, used for channel migration modeling, require historical data where the correct answer—that is whether or not a customer was a multichannel customer—is known and included within the data set used for modeling. With clustering methods, the objective is to group customers based on how similar they are to each other. There is no predetermined correct answer for the clustering solution.

Specific clustering techniques used by companies often include K-means clustering, hierarchical clustering, and Kohonen networks. Hierarchical clustering methods are often used in the early stages of developing a clustering solution, on small samples of data. This is done to help define the number of clusters (segments) in the solution. With many other methods, the analyst predefines the number of clusters in the final solution.

CHANNEL VALUE FORECASTING

What is the value of the various sales channels in the short term? What about in the long term? Channel value forecasting involves developing predictive models to forecast the revenue contribution of each channel. Possible seasonal fluctuations by channel could be uncovered and leveraged in the revenue forecast. The objective of this is to develop revenue predictions for each channel, taking into consideration seasonal and cyclical effects. This can help the company match resource allocations to customer demand for the different sales channels.

Traditional time-series forecasting methods can be used to develop channel sales models. These methods use historical data of whatever metric we are trying to predict. In this case, the metric could be channel revenue. Observations over multiple time periods are used to develop a forecast. The advantages to time-series forecasting methods are that these methods require a minimal amount of data and are fairly accurate when used at an aggregated level, such as for a segment of customers. The disadvantage is that no information comes out of the model about the key drivers behind the channel forecast; other analysis is required to provide this information.

SIDEBAR 12.3
Applying Channel Management to a Retail Business

In a real-world situation, an advanced customer analytics team recently focused on the impact of multichannel expansion in these key areas of a major retail company: changes in the value of the customer to the business, customer attrition/retention rates, spending increases or decreases, and changes in the type and amount of products purchased.

The analysis began with a group of customers who bought "in the store only" in Year One. A call center and Internet channel were added, going into Year Two. The analysis showed that, at the end of Year Two: 40 percent of customers still shopped only in the store; 20 percent were no longer store customers; 10 percent still shopped in the stores but also shopped on the retailer's Internet site; 25 percent still shopped in the store but also used the call center; 5 percent of customers used all three channels.

To perform the analysis, the team used a combination of analytical CRM software tools. Based on this analysis, the team helped the retailer make these discoveries around the business impact of going multichannel:

- Customer value tended to stay the same for the 40 percent of customers who remained single-channel, store-only shoppers.

- For the segment that migrated to two channels, individual customer value increased by 20 to 60 percent.

- For the segment that migrated to all three channels, customer value increased by 60 to 125 percent.

- The attrition rate was lower for customers who began using two or more channels.

- The types of products purchased by customers who shopped in more than one channel increased in breadth and variety.

Yet there was more to learn. What exactly caused customers to change shopping behavior? The analytics team could not pinpoint the causality. They only knew that many customers increased their interaction with the retailer and thus became more valuable. Was it because they sought a deeper relationship with the retailer? Or was it because the retailer simply made it easier and more convenient to shop more frequently?

In any case, the team observed that when store-only customers became multichannel customers, they were more likely to continue or increase their shopping activity. Attrition rates decreased. Customers increased the type and quantity of products they bought and, thus, customer value increased.

There are many fascinating areas still to be explored by this retailer. These include learning how the business can create synergies between channels—to grow customer value, retention, revenue, and customer satisfaction further.

Channel management is a useful issue to examine because it represents a common CRM problem and requires a fairly wide range of advanced customer analytics techniques. Many other CRM-related analytical problems require the same types of analytical methods. (For example, contact optimization addresses the psychology of language as well as context. It helps with decisions about timing, budget, relevance of messages, selection of product and message to offer a particular customer, and so on. It can be viewed as the polar opposite of typical twentieth-century marketing practices that seem to be focused on contact bombardment.) What is important to realize here is that advanced customer analytics is primarily focused on the business problem, rather than on an analytical technique. In all cases, the objective is not to create a model, but to generate a solution.

SUMMARY

We have now covered two critical parts of customer-based enterprise "measurement." We have examined some of the ways an enterprise can measure the success of its customer-value-building initiatives and we have explored how advanced customer analytics can help predict how a customer will behave in a relationship, how a firm can positively influence that relationship behavior, and how much it's worth to the enterprise to do so. If we can measure it, we can manage it, and that's why the next chapters are specifically about how to manage an organization to build the value of the customer base.

> If we can measure it, we can manage it

Making the transition to a customer-strategy enterprise requires a careful examination of the way the company is structured and a rethinking of many business processes. The next chapter will focus on two key themes: What does a relationship-building enterprise, based strategically on growing customer equity, look like? What are the organizational and transitional requirements to become a customer-based enterprise? Let's take a closer look.

FOOD FOR THOUGHT

1. From the customer's perspective, which is better: to buy through one channel or several channels? The obvious answer is to have multiple channels available—order from the Web, make returns at the store, check on delivery by phone—and have all of those contact points able to pick up where the last left off. But is there any advantage—to the customer—of using only one channel? Why does research show that customers who use more than one channel are more likely to be more valuable than those who use only one?

2. The challenge with predictive models is a widespread misunderstanding of the nature of cause and effect. What is more important: to understand *what* will happen next or *why* it will happen?

3. Customer analytics can be used for improving retention rates. How?

GLOSSARY

Analysis process   Includes classification, estimation, regression, prediction, and clustering.

Contact optimization   The capability of a company to send and request information for each customer in the way that is preferred by each customer. Contact optimization is similar to the Preferred Media Package (PMP) referred to in Chapter 7. When contacts are optimized, a customer hears from and responds to a company on her timetable, about topics that are most relevant to her.

Customer analytics   Enables the enterprise to classify, estimate, predict, cluster, and more accurately describe data about customers, using mathematical models and algorithms that ultimately simplify how it views its customer base and how it behaves toward individual customers.

Data mining   The process of exploration and analysis, by automatic or semi-automatic means, of large quantities of data in order to discover meaningful patterns and rules, according to Berry and Linoff.

Real-time analytics   Instant updates to the customer database that allow services in multiple geographies, communication channels, or product lines to respond to customer needs without waiting for customary weekly or overnight updates.

Reliability   The extent to which a finding is stable and reproducible. A study with high reliability can be run again with nearly the same results.

Validity   The extent to which research measures what it says it measures and does so in a way that yields answers to the actual research question. Do the operationalizations make sense?

Organizing and Managing the Profitable Customer–Strategy Enterprise

13

Chapter

Throughout this book we have described the customer-strategy enterprise by defining the principles of creating a customer-strategy business. In this chapter we will focus on how a firm establishes itself as an enterprise focused on building the value of the customer base and how it can make the transition from product management to managing for customer equity (MCE). What does a customer-value-building enterprise look like? How does a company develop the organization, skills, and capabilities needed to execute customer-oriented programs? How does the enterprise create the culture that supports these principles? How will it integrate the pieces of the organization that have traditionally been managed as separate silos (or "chimneys" or "smokestacks")? George Day and Miriam Kendall offer some structure to our thinking about the way the customer-strategy enterprise is different from the traditional organization. Fred Reichheld shares his important perspective on loyalty-based management. And Marijo Puleo, Miriam Kendall, and Elizabeth Rech give us insights into the ways organizations change to build customer value.

If we can measure it, we can manage it. Now that we have become better at the metrics of customer valuation and equity, can we hold somebody responsible for increasing the value of customers and keeping them longer? Most companies have brand managers, product managers, store managers, plant managers, finance managers, customer interaction center (CIC) managers, Web masters, regional sales managers, branch managers, or merchandise managers. But with the exception of high-end personal and business services, few companies have customer relationship managers. Now that technology drives a dimension of competition based on keeping and growing *customers,* the questions to ask are:

- Who will be responsible for the enterprise's relationship with each customer? For keeping and growing each customer?

- What authority will that customer manager have to change how the enterprise treats "his" customers, individually?
- By what criteria and metrics will success be measured?

Now that technology drives a dimension of competition based on keeping and growing *customers*, the questions to ask are:
- Who will be responsible for the enterprise's relationship with each customer? For keeping and growing each customer?
- What authority will that customer manager have to change how the enterprise treats "his" customers, individually?
- By what criteria and metrics will success be measured?

In this chapter, we ask the questions: How will executives at the enterprise develop management skills to increase the value of the customer base? How will our information about customers—and our goal to build the value of the customer base—inform every business decision we make all day, every day?

We have shown that in the customer-strategy enterprise, the goal is to maximize the value of the customer base by retaining profitable customers and growing them into bigger customers, by eliminating unprofitable customers or converting them into profitable relationships, and by acquiring new customers selectively, based on their likelihood of developing into high-value customers. The overriding strategy for achieving this set of objectives is to develop Learning Relationships with individual customers, in the process customizing the mix of products, prices, services, and/or communications for each individual customer.

It should be apparent that the new enterprise must be organized around its customers, rather than just its products. Success requires that the entire organization reengineer its processes to focus on the customer.[1] In this chapter, we will examine the basics of management at a customer-strategy enterprise. Our goal will be to understand the capabilities necessary to create and manage a successful customer-strategy company. We will draw a picture of what the organizational chart will look like and explain how to make the transition, overcome obstacles, and build momentum. We'll also have a look at the role of employees in the customer-strategy enterprise.

SIDEBAR 13.1
Becoming a Customer-Strategy Organization

....

Marijo Puleo
Director, Peppers and Rogers Group

To become fluent in managing to build customer equity, the enterprise needs to adopt an infrastructure that can support all of the business-related processes and functions that characterize a customer-focused model. Large financial investments can be made in information technology, employee training and hiring, communica-

---

[1]Gary E. Hawkins, *Building the Customer Specific Retail Enterprise* (New York: Breezy Heights Publishing, 1999).

SIDEBAR 13.1 *(continued)*

tion systems, and other areas related to the transformation, but one major challenge often has nothing to do with the purchasing or installation of the required tools and technologies; rather, it is all about adapting the enterprise and its employees to using them. The majority of customer-strategy "failures" didn't crash and burn because of software integration problems or employee software training. Most customer efforts fail because the company never learns to *manage* the enterprise in the light of new company capabilities, or to *align* those capabilities with customer management.

> The majority of customer–strategy "failures" didn't crash and burn because of software integration problems or employee software training. Most customer efforts fail because the company never learns to *manage* the enterprise in the light of new company capabilities, or to *align* those capabilities with customer management.

Once an enterprise commits to adopting a customer-centric model, it needs to rethink the product-centric customs and processes it has relied on for years. Traditionally, enterprises develop their technologies, support, and infrastructure to manufacture products or services, and deliver those products and services to the customer in the most cost-efficient way. In turn, the technology and information captured in the systems drive business processes that influence employee behavior and how these employees interact with customers.

This may not appear too much of a change—just put the customer in the middle instead of products (see Exhibit A). Most enterprises, in fact, will say that this shift is not a big departure from the way they do business today, because they have already designed their products or services for particular customer segments. However, the internal processes and metrics are designed to increase share of market around defined customer segments. For example, metrics around cost of delivery, cost to manufacture, commissions, and so forth, abound in a typical enterprise. Many enterprises understand the cost to process and pay an invoice, but they do not understand the value of a customer beyond a total revenue measure. Some enterprises have a "sense" of which customers are valuable, but they lack the facts and figures to justify a particular level of service, and continue to engage in product-centric business, as shown in Exhibit B.

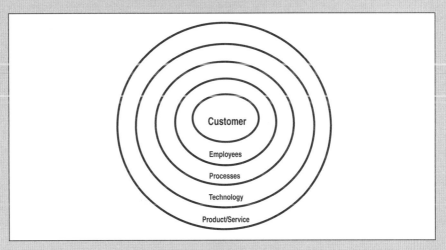

EXHIBIT A   **Customer-Centric Business**

SIDEBAR 13.1 *(continued)*

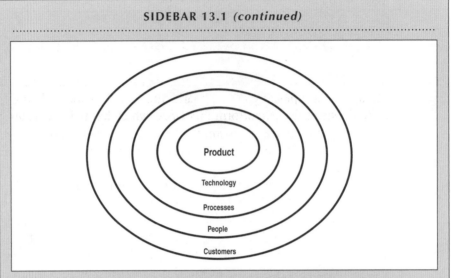

EXHIBIT B   **Product-Centric Business**

Change management requires a firm to view all of the interrelated elements of the business and its components. According to author and marketing expert Harvey Thompson, "A holistic, balanced view includes both the company and the customer. These two views must be successfully integrated, and when they are in conflict, they must be reconciled. Designing the new round (customer-driven) processes to replace old square ones does not end the journey; the challenge is how to maintain an alignment with customers while changing the processes, the support infrastructure, and the behavior of the people who implement the processes."[a]

It is difficult for employees in an enterprise to make this transition because truly adopting a customer-focused strategy can challenge many of their deeply held values and beliefs about how business is done and how they define success. One of the most challenging aspects of this new strategy is the amount of coordination and trust that needs to be developed between departments and functions. Managing customer relationships can be an unorthodox way of doing business for them, and it requires many unique skills, such as negotiation and understanding a broader view of the enterprise.

Frequently, the enterprise must also encourage its customers to change how they operate, a critical step that is often ignored in the process. Everything begins and ends with the customer. The customer-centric enterprise depends on customer participation, even when the customer is unaware of his involvement. The customer's input defines how employees will interact with customers, in turn creating processes, developing new roles, and effecting change in the basic "how" of new product and service creation. The entire organization changes, and the voice of the customer is present in every area, department, division, and all throughout the business.

[a]Harvey Thompson. *The Customer-Centered Enterprise* (New York: McGraw-Hill Professional Book Group), 2000.

CAPABILITIES FOR FORGING CUSTOMER RELATIONSHIPS

George S. Day
Geoffrey T. Boise professor, The Wharton School, University of Pennsylvania

Does scale still matter in the credit card industry, where soaring customer acquisition costs are pushing annual marketing budgets over $1 billion? How does Capital One easily outperform FirstUSA, which has twice as many customers? By leveraging a superior capability to attract and retain customers, Capital One gets 40 percent more interest income from each customer and has twice the profit margin.

The differences between the two firms begin—and end—with their strategies. FirstUSA's priority is rapid growth in the "prime market": It targets relatively low-risk consumers, who have established credit histories, with low-interest cards. Because many other card issues are chasing the same people, these customers are neither loyal nor especially profitable. FirstUSA was more successful selling "affinity" cards, through organizations like universities that offer the cards to their members. Otherwise, they gave little consideration to differences among customers as to credit risk or potential profitability. The real thrust of FirstUSA's strategy, according to Richard Vague, the former chairman, was "to be laser-focused on operating efficiency and pass those savings on to consumers."

Capital One follows a different strategy because it has a superior customer-relating capability. The essence of its strategy is captured in its mission to "deliver the right product, at the right price, to the right customer at the right time." Capital One consciously avoided the low-profit and high-churn prime market, in favor of the **superprime** and **subprime** segments. Its capability to treat different customers differently means it can profitably meet the needs of these disparate groups. In the superprime segment, its laser is focused on finding the "high chargers" who generate high merchant fees in place of interest charges from revolving balances. In the less appealing, but underserved subprime market, Capital One targets people with limited credit histories, such as college students. Risks are contained with cards that have low credit limits and are partially secured. Capital One wants to begin a relationship with these people while they are early in their credit life cycle, so they stay loyal when they become more affluent. Because Capital One knows this market so well, it can hold down its risk, and have the lowest loss rate in the industry.

FirstUSA would like to be able to do what Capital One can do. As the credit environment worsens, FirstUSA has to deal with a customer attrition rate that climbed from 12 to 19 percent and contributed to a 23-percent decline in revenue in 2000, and its first loss. Its efforts were severely constrained by not having the right orientation, information, or configuration in place to become customer-responsive.

The efficiency bias of the FirstUSA strategy is the cause and consequence of a self-centered orientation that doesn't see customers as individuals. Its insensitivity has led to some notably wrong-footed decisions. In mid-1999, FirstUSA eliminated the grace period for late payments while raising late fees. Not surprisingly, customers departed in droves, and the bank was forced to rescind the move. But this move reveals a deeper problem. The policy was applied across the board, paying no attention to differences between valuable and less valuable customers. The company mind-set evidently did not appreciate the lifetime value of customers.

FirstUSA grew by acquiring **customer portfolios** from other credit card companies, or using third parties such as Affinity Partners to source potential partnerships with associations. This placed greater distance between FirstUSA and its customers, and prevented the company from building data warehouses to hold the rich customer information that is the raw material of the customer-relating capability. And without this information, FirstUSA has moved away from customer-based profitability models to simply treating customers as part of aggregated portfolios.

The configuration of FirstUSA also impedes its struggle to hold onto its best customers. It has historically been hierarchically organized around products or functions such as operations, collections, and systems. Within the Brand Marketing division, which manages all cards under the FirstUSA name, there are separate groups for acquisitions, portfolios, and e-business—but no one has responsibility for customer retention.

Incentives are also misaligned. Because its information system cannot tease out individual customer profitability, the front-line contact employees cannot be rewarded for keeping valuable customers. Instead, FirstUSA tries to retain everyone—whether good, bad, or indifferent long-run prospects. Profit responsibility resides at the top of FirstUSA, completing the picture of an organization where decision and directives are top-down.

By contrast, customer responsiveness is in all the pores and capillaries of Capital One. Its orientation is fundamentally shaped by the belief that microsegmentation of its customers is the only way to identify and keep the most valuable ones. One result is that employees at all levels have implicit permission to act as customer advocates and take initiative to solve customer problems. They work within a collaborative context, where, for example, the IT department cooperates with the customer interaction center to make sure technology is not adopted for its own sake, but supports the goal of nurturing customer loyalty. Customer representatives are measured not just on their performance, but on how supportive they are to colleagues as well. The sense of shared values and collaboration contributes to a low turnover rate—5 percent per year among customer contact people versus an industry average of 30 percent—which further improves service and helps keep costs down.

Capital One's capability to handle customer information is unsurpassed in the industry. Whenever a customer calls, computers instantly access the full history of the account and cross-reference it with data about how millions of other customers behave. Some customers judged to be poor prospects are routed to a voice response unit and allowed to close their account. Those warranting human interaction are routed to a representative, along with two-dozen pieces of information about the caller and his likely reason for calling. This prepares the customer service representative to anticipate problems and rehearse the best way to maintain the relationship.

Suppose a customer calls to cancel his credit card. Capital One's Intelligent Call Routing system immediately displays three counteroffers, from a 12.9 percent annual interest rate down to 9.9 percent. This arms the customer service representative with the information he needs to negotiate with the customer; and the customer-centered culture gives him the freedom to take action to keep the customer. If the customer accepts the 12.9 percent proposal, the retention specialist is rewarded for keeping the customer with a bonus that acknowledges the preservation of extra profitability over the 9.9 percent final offer.

Few enterprises invest more in learning about their customers to stay ahead of their changing requirements. Each year Capital One conducts more tests; in 2000, it ran 45,000 tests on product variants, procedural changes, and customer interactions. All results are recorded in a database, which in turn tracks the behavior of current and potential customers. It can test an idea for a new product on a small sample of customers, tweak it, and then launch fast. With more than 6,000 product variants, Capital One is approaching mass customization.

The alignment of the entire Capital One organization with its customer-focused strategy is further reinforced by its organizational configuration. Within Capital One, the US card business is structured by market segment groups such as: Prime, Medium-Response, High-Response, Partnership, Affinity, and Small Business. Each of these segments is further divided down to the Individual Business Manager level, where profit responsibility resides. For example, the manager of lifestyle cards, within the Prime segment, has the autonomy and the team to run a small business. In essence, the functional roles of marketing research, pricing, and program execution are replicated within each business team. Instead of a cumbersome top-down organization, Capital One is adroit at sensing opportunities from the bottom-up, and is motivated to pursue them fast. It is the epitome of a customer-responsive organization.[2]

These differences in customer-relating capabilities are found in every market. There will be some enterprises that excel at forging close relationships, and are rewarded with high rates of loyalty, while others have a "conquest mentality" that emphasizes customer acquisition. Like FirstUSA, most realize sooner or later that this is a counterproductive approach, and at that point they may try to catch up to the leaders. However, investments in CRM software, good intentions, and the emulation of best practices will not suffice. The differences are too deep-seated to be overcome with incremental programs. In the next section, we will show how a superior capability leads to improved performance, and then diagnose the elements of this capability.

GAINING A RELATIONSHIP ADVANTAGE

Understanding the role and functioning of the customer-relating capability requires an enterprise to distinguish between the resources that are the source of

[2]More evidence of customer responsiveness: Capital One promises *no* telemarketing to its customers.

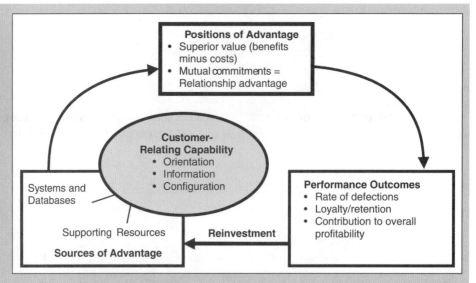

EXHIBIT 13.1   **Achieving a Relationship Advantage**

its competitive advantage, and the consequent positional advantages and performance outcomes, as shown in Exhibit 13.1. This is a cyclical process that relies on consistency and alignment of the elements to achieve advantage, and continuous reinvestment and learning to sustain the advantage.

Sources of Advantage

These are the resources the firm deploys, comprising the assets such as databases and systems that are firm-specific, factors of production that are readily available, and the capabilities that enable these resources to be deployed advantageously.

The diagnosis of an individual capability—such as the customer-relating capability—requires that the scope be disaggregated down to a level where the skills and execution of the capability are competitively superior. Broad generalizations such as consumer marketing skills will not suffice, when the distinctive capability may lie only in demand stimulation through image-based advertising, and the other ingredients such as pricing or channel linking may be merely average.

Disaggregation is necessary, but it may also be misleading if it doesn't consider two factors: first, that each capability is nested within a complex network with many direct and indirect links to other resources; second, there are strategic themes that prioritize, orchestrate, and direct the collective resources toward the delivery of superior customer value. Sometimes the valuable resource is an adroit combination of capabilities, none of which is superior alone, but when combined, makes a better package. Then competitive superiority is due to either (1) the weighted average effect—the business does not rank first on any asset or capability but is better on average than any of the rivals, (2) the firm's system-integration capability, so the capabilities are mutually reinforcing, or (3) the superior clarity and focus of the strategic thrust that mobilizes the resources.

Positions of Advantage

What we see in the market—from the vantage point of the customer or competitor—is positional superiority achieved with superior capability. This requires the reliable provision of superior value to customers on the attributes they judge important when they make a choice. Whether there is a relational advantage per se depends first on the customer's judgment that having a close relationship with a supplier confers benefits that exceed the costs. Typical benefits include time savings, technical assistance, assurance of performance, access to latest developments (in software and technology, for example), superior responsiveness to service requests or problems, and a superior fit to the customer's needs because of personalized solutions. Of course, the customer must feel these benefits outweigh any costs due to loss of flexibility and the restricted ability to play one supplier against another.

The strongest positional advantages are gained when customers are willing to make mutual commitments. These can range from information exchanges to cross-firm coordination of interdependent activities such as new product development to multiple social linkages that engender trust and facilitate sharing of information, and possibly to relation-specific investments such as online Electronic Data Interchange (EDI) connections or the adoption of common interface standards. A firm that is better able to forge such close relations with the high-value customers in a market has secured a strong positional advantage.

Performance Outcomes

We would expect a relationship advantage to be rewarded with lower rates of defection (churn), greater loyalty and retention, and higher profit margins than the competitors. But the linkage from positional advantage to performance outcome has proven troublesome to understand because of confounding effects, and a relationship advantage is no exception. First, customers buy a complete package of benefits, so it may be difficult to untangle the contribution made by the relationship itself. Then the construct of loyalty is itself difficult to study. Much of the attention has focused on proxy measures such as satisfaction, which have a complex, asymmetric relationship to loyalty. Whereas loyal customers are likely to be satisfied, all satisfied customers will not be loyal (see Chapter 2). Loyalty is gained with a combination of performance superiority that ensures high satisfaction, plus trust and mutual commitments.

DIAGNOSING THE CUSTOMER RELATING CAPABILITIES

A superior customer relating capability results from a clear focus on and deft orchestration of three organizational components: (1) organizational *orientation* toward relationships, comprising the relevant values, behaviors, and mindsets; (2) *information*, reflecting the availability, quality, and depth of information about customer relationships and usage of CRM technology; and

(3) *configuration* that ensures clear accountability for relationships, the process for personalizing the offering, and the incentives for retaining the best customers.

Orientation toward Relationships

A relationship orientation is embedded within the overall culture, and establishes what is appropriate and inappropriate behavior for the enterprise. It signals the importance of customer relationships and the willingness of the organization to treat different customers differently. As part of the culture, it includes relevant *values* that are often deeply embedded as tacit assumptions. The more accessible outcroppings of the culture are behavioral *norms*, the shared *mental models* used to make sense out of complex realities, and the *behaviors* that people exhibit as they make choices about how to spend their time.

To understand better how a relationship orientation was likely to be manifested we undertook extensive interviews with knowledgeable managers and consultants, perused the voluminous professional literature, and abstracted from detailed case studies. From these we derived the following indicators of a superior orientation:

* Customer retention is a priority shared throughout the organization.
* There is a willingness to treat different customers differently, and a commitment to act quickly on information from these customers (complaints, queries, and changes in requirements).
* All employees exhibit an appreciation of customer lifetime value.
* Employees have considerable freedom to take action to satisfy customers without having to take time to get approval. Their judgment on what action to take is shaped not just by business rules (an important function), but also by simple observation of what other employees have done, stories about initiatives that have been recognized, and basic training programs that provide role-playing opportunities.

Information about Relationships

Provided that an organization has a suitable relationship orientation, tracking and using customer information will become a critical success factor. Success depends on how well the firm can elicit and manage the sharing of customer information, and then converting it into knowledge to be used to change how the organization collectively behaves toward the customer. Competitive advantage in the use of customer information means outperforming rivals on each of the following steps:

1. *Capturing customer information.* Capacity of customer databases to reveal individual customer histories, connections, requirements, expectations and purchasing activity, as well as the overall rate of customer defections.

2. *Collating.* Having information from all customer touchpoints in one place.
3. *Retrieving.* Remembering customer information and obtaining it when needed.
4. *Utilizing.* Ability to differentiate among customers as to their importance, long-run potential, and anticipated needs.
5. *Sharing.* Mechanisms for learning and sharing the resulting lessons throughout the organization.

Managing customer data effectively is extremely difficult, for three reasons. First, the sheer scale of most customer databases, and the rapid rate at which information about customers goes out of date and degrades the quality of the database. Even so, most databases are inherently incomplete because they contain only the record of the customer interactions with one company, hence can't provide a full picture of all customer buying activity. Second, these databases are usually part of larger customer support systems that provide information to customers in response to their queries, complaints, and service requests. Front-line staff need accurate and immediate answers to increasingly complex questions, while varying their response in light of previous interactions. The potential for conflicts between these two requirements is considerable.

> The deeply held knowledge of customer contact and service people, acquired through problem solving and trial-and-error learning, is especially difficult for the rest of the organization to access. This makes it all the more critical for the organization to begin with a strong relationship orientation.

But, third, at the point at which the information must actually be put to use effectively throughout the organization it will have become knowledge that is partly tacit, highly contextual, and goes beyond the surface-level, explicit contents of the database. This makes it difficult to communicate and share the knowledge with others. The deeply held knowledge of customer contact and service people, acquired through problem solving and trial-and-error learning, is especially difficult for the rest of the organization to access. This makes it all the more critical for the organization to begin with a strong relationship orientation.

Configuration

For an enterprise with a relationship-oriented culture and a reasonably robust information-sharing-and-utilization system, success will depend on the degree to which the organization can be configured, as follows:

- There is a general consensus about goals and means for achieving a relationship advantage.
- The organization is designed around customers, rather than products or functions. This design could include structural variants such as customer teams and customer managers to oversee the customer portfolio.
- The performance measures, incentives, and coordinating mechanisms emphasize retention.

- The aspects of the configuration are aligned with a compelling customer value proposition that recognizes customer differences and puts customer retention at the center of strategy.
- There are enabling processes within the resource base so the organization is able to personalize or mass-customize communications, products, and services.
- Resources are allocated to initiatives that give a high priority to database development and other activities that support the overall strategic thrust.

RELATIONSHIP GOVERNANCE

One of the biggest single difficulties in making the transition to an enterprise that pays attention to its relationships with individual customers, one customer at a time, is the issue of relationship governance. By that we mean: Who will be "in charge" at the enterprise, when it comes to making different decisions for different customers?

The challenge most companies face when they make a serious commitment to managing customer relationships becomes obvious once the firm pulls out its current organizational charts, which are usually set up to manage brands, products, channels, and programs. Most companies will have organized themselves in such a way as to ensure that they can achieve their objectives in terms of product sales or brand awareness, across the entire population of customers they serve.

But in the age of interactivity, managing customer relationships individually will require an enterprise to treat different customers differently within that customer population. Inherent in this idea is the notion that different customers will be subject to different objectives and strategies, and that the enterprise will undertake different actions with respect to different customers. So, we ask again: With respect to any particular customer, who will be put in charge, within the enterprise, to make sure this actually happens? And when that person is put in charge of an individual customer relationship, what levers will he control, in order to execute the strategy being applied to "his" customer? How will his performance be measured and evaluated by the enterprise?

This is the problem of relationship governance. It's one thing for us to maintain, safe between the covers of this book, that in the interactive age a company should manage its dialogues and relationships with different customers differently, making sure to analyze the values and needs of various individual customers, adapting its behavior for each individual customer to what is appropriate for that particular customer. It's another thing to carry this out within a corporate organization when, at least for many companies at present, no one is actually in charge of making it happen.

Exhibit 13.2 is an oversimplified example of a "typical" Industrial Age organization chart. In such an organization, each product or brand is the direct-line responsibility of one individual within the organization. In this way the enterprise can hold particular managers and organizations responsible for achieving various objectives related to product and brand sales. The brand or product manager is, in fact, the "protector" of the brand or product, watching out to make sure that it does well and that sales goals or awareness goals are achieved. The manager controls advertising and promotion levers to ensure that the best and most persuasive message will be conveyed to the right segments and niches of customers or potential customers. This is all in keeping with the most basic goal of an Industrial Age company: to sell more products.

The most basic goal of the customer-strategy enterprise, however, is to increase the long-term value of its customer base, by applying different objectives and strategies to different customers. Yes, in the process it is likely that more products will be sold in the short term, also. But in order for the primary task to be accomplished, someone within the organization has to be put in charge of making decisions and carrying out actions, with respect to each individual customer.

In Exhibit 13.3 a different organization chart is drawn for the customer-value-building company, one that emphasizes *customer management* rather than product management. In an enterprise organized for customer management, ideally every customer will be the direct-line responsibility of a single customer manager (even though the customer may not be aware that the manager is in charge, working in the background to determine the enterprise's most appropriate strategy for that customer, and then to make sure it is carried out). Because there are likely many more customers than there are management employees, it is only logical that a customer manager should be made responsible for a whole group of customers. We will refer to such a group as a customer *portfolio,* avoiding for the present the word "segment," in order to clarify the concept. A customer portfolio is made up of unduplicated, unique (and identified) customers. No customer should ever be placed into more than one portfolio at a time, because it is the portfolio manager who will be in charge of the enterprise's

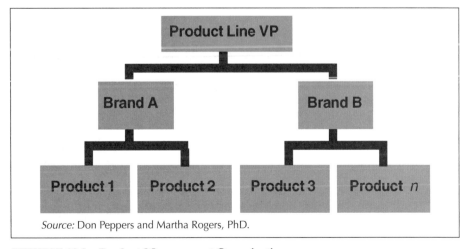

Source: Don Peppers and Martha Rogers, PhD.

EXHIBIT 13.2   **Product Management Organization**

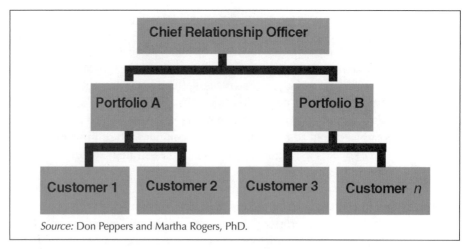

Source: Don Peppers and Martha Rogers, PhD.

EXHIBIT 13.3   Customer Management Organization

relationship with the customers in his portfolio and the resulting value of that relationship. If we allow a customer to inhabit two different portfolios, then we are just creating another relationship governance problem—which portfolio manager will actually call the shots, when it comes to the enterprise's strategies for *that* customer? How will we calculate that customer's value accurately? And who gets credit or blame if the customer's value rises or falls?

The customer manager's primary objective is to maximize the long-term value of his own **portfolio of customers**—that is, to keep and grow the customers in his portfolio—and the enterprise should reward him based on a set of metrics that indicate the degree to which he has accomplished his mission. In the ideal state, the enterprise's entire customer base might be parsed into several different portfolios, each of which is overseen by the customer manager, like a subdivided business.[3]

SIDEBAR 13.2

Customer Management[a] at Credito Emiliano

In Italy, the regional bank Credito Emiliano offers another instructive example of a customer management program being put into practice. Credito Emiliano is based in Reggio Emilia, where it has 260 branches serving roughly 360,000 customers. Credito ranked its customers into three tiers based on their value, and differentiated the customers further into 30 portfolios, based on such customer needs as investment goals, aversion to risk, and so forth. The information the bank needed for this differentiation came from a combination of questionnaires, brief interviews with customers, and third-party data.[b]

Each portfolio is now the responsibility of a "segment manager" at Credito's headquarters, who sets the objectives and strategy for dealing with the customers in his

---

[3] At Peppers and Rogers Group, we have called this managing portfolios of customers, or MPC.

> **SIDEBAR 13.2** *(continued)*
>
> portfolio. The branch managers are the primary sales channel for interacting with the bank's customers, but their job is to follow the strategy and achieve the objectives set by the segment managers. So when a customer comes in to a branch to discuss a banking matter, the branch manager calls up on his screen not only the customer's name, address, and account information, but also the tier and portfolio to which this particular customer belongs, along with the objectives set for the customer and some suggested strategies to achieve these objectives, including products or services to be offered.
>
> [a]Don Peppers, Martha Rogers PhD, and Bob Dorf. *The One to One Fieldbook: The Complete Toolkit for Implementing a 1to1 Marketing Program* (New York: Currency/Doubleday) 1997.
> [b]Ibid. Confirmed by phone interview with Iones Montepietra at Credito Emiliano on June 1, 1998.

Clearly, if we plan to hold a customer manager accountable for growing the value of a portfolio of customers, then we'll also have to give him some authority to take actions with respect to the customers in the portfolio. The levers that a customer manager ought to be able to pull, in order to encourage his customers to attain a higher and higher long-term value to the enterprise, should include, literally, every type of action or communication that the enterprise is capable of rendering on an individual-customer basis. In communication, this would mean that the customer manager would control the enterprise's addressable forms of communication and interaction—direct mail, as well as interactions at the call center, on the Web site, and even (to the extent possible) in face-to-face encounters at the store or the cash register. In effect, the customer manager would be responsible for overseeing the enterprise's continuing dialogue with a customer. In terms of the actual product or service offering, ideally the customer manager would be responsible for setting the pricing for his customers, extending any discounts or collecting premiums, and so forth. The customer manager should own the offer,[4] and the communication of the offer, with respect to the customers in the manager's portfolio.

> The customer manager should own the offer,[4] and the communication of the offer, with respect to the customers in the manager's portfolio.

The enterprise will still be creating and marketing various programs and products, but the customer manager will be the "traffic cop," with respect to his own portfolio of customers. He will allow some offers to go through as conceived, he will adapt other offers to meet the needs of his own customers, and he will likely block some offers altogether, choosing not to expose his own customers to them.

In a high-end business or personal services firm, such as a private bank, the role of customer manager is played by the firm's *relationship manager* for each

---

[4]The phrase "owns the relationship" disturbs some people; after all, a relationship can't be "owned." Within the context of this book, "owning" a relationship means "is accountable for," in the sense of "owns up to."

client. The relationship manager owns the relationship, and is free to set the policies and communications for his own individual clients, within the boundaries set by the enterprise. The enterprise holds him accountable for keeping the client satisfied, loyal, and profitable. The company probably does not formally estimate an individual client's actual LTV, in strict financial terms; more than likely it has a fairly formal process for ranking these clients by their long-term value or importance to the firm. A relationship manager who manages to dramatically improve the value of his client's relationship to the enterprise will be rewarded.

However, most businesses have many more customers than a private bank, or a law firm, or an advertising agency. For most businesses, it would simply be uneconomic for a relationship manager to pay individual, personal attention to a single customer relationship, to the exclusion of all other responsibilities. Realistically, then, the way most of the addressable communications will be rendered to individual customers, at the vast majority of companies, will be through the application of business rules. Just as business rules are used to mass-customize a product or a service (see Chapter 10), they can be applied to mass-customize the offer extended to different customers, as well as the communication of that offer. Thus, one of the customer manager's primary jobs will be to oversee the business rules that govern the enterprise's mass-customized relationship with the individual customers in his own portfolio.

In addition to customer relationship managers, the one-to-one enterprise will need *capabilities managers* as well (see Exhibit 13.4).[5] Their role is to deliver the capabilities of the enterprise to the customer managers, in essence figuring out whether the firm should build, buy, or partner to render any new products or services that might be required by customers. We could think of capabilities managers as being something like "product managers at large." The products and capabilities they bring to bear, on behalf of the enterprise, will actually be marketed, not directly to customers, but to the customer managers in charge of the enterprise's relationships with customers.

None of this is to say that companies can afford to forget about product quality, or innovation, or efficient production and cost reduction. These tasks will be just as important as they always have been, for the simple reason that few customers would choose to continue relationships involving subpar products or service. However, as we've already discussed, product and service quality by themselves do not necessarily lead to competitive success, because no matter how stellar a company's service is, nothing can stop a competitor from also offering great service. In the final analysis, the most important single benefit of engaging a customer in an ongoing relationship is that the rich context of a Learning Relationship creates an impregnable competitive barrier, with respect to that customer, making it literally impossible for a competitor to duplicate the highly personalized service the customer is now receiving.

[5]From B. Joseph Pine II, *Mass Customization* (Cambridge, MA: Harvard Business School Press, 1993).

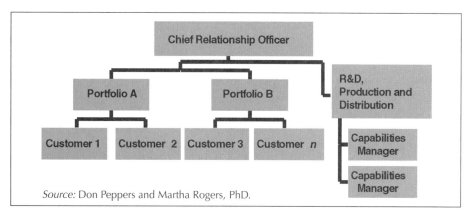

Source: Don Peppers and Martha Rogers, PhD.

***EXHIBIT 13.4*   Product Managers Become Capabilities Managers**

HOW TO GET THERE FROM HERE: TRANSITIONS TO CUSTOMER MANAGEMENT

It should go without saying that an enterprise will not simply be able to paste a customer-management organizational structure atop its existing organization. Moreover, the change, in terms of success metrics, management roles, and responsibilities, and the required capabilities of the enterprise, are profound. In truth, the transition never actually ends, because there will always be additional steps the enterprise can take to improve its relationships with its customers. Nevertheless, when starting as a well-oiled, product-marketing organization, taking the first tentative steps toward customer management requires a good deal of planning. During the transition to a customer-centric model, enterprises frequently underestimate the degree to which all facets of the business will be affected by the changes, as well as the ongoing efforts that will be required to achieve full business benefits.

The organizational and cultural transition to customer management represents a genuine *revolution* for the enterprise, but it is more likely to be successful when it can be treated as an *evolution* within the organization. In this section, we'll discuss three ways to speed this evolution process, any or all of which can be adopted by an enterprise:

> The organizational and cultural transition to customer management represents a genuine *revolution* for the enterprise, but it is more likely to be successful when it can be treated as an *evolution* within the organization.

1. Pilot projects and incremental change
2. **Picket fence** strategy
3. Segment management

PILOT PROJECTS AND INCREMENTAL CHANGE

Most companies launch their customer initiatives in a series of pilot projects. There are so many things to do, if a customer-specific perspective is to be adopted, that it is usually a relatively simple process for a company to "cut and paste" various self-contained customer initiatives into the enterprise's current method of operating. The objective, over the longer term, is to accumulate a large number of small improvements.

It is not necessary to resolve the customer-governance problem, in order to launch a pilot project or to make an incremental change. Instead, the IDIC (identify, differentiate, interact, customize—see Chapters 3 to 10) implementation process itself is an ideal vehicle for conceiving and executing incremental changes. A small change might involve, for instance, obtaining, linking, and cataloguing more customer identities, using a sweep of existing databases containing customer information. Or it could involve setting up a prioritized service level for customers now identified as having higher long-term value to the enterprise, or higher growth potential. Many incremental change initiatives are also likely to involve streamlining the customer interaction processes, so as to cut duplicative efforts or resolve conflicting communications.

Particularly for large and complex organizations, it is often the case that the most direct and immediate route to a broad transition for the overall enterprise is to implement a series of incremental changes, one small step at a time. Hewlett-Packard (HP), for instance, began trying to wean its corporate culture away from the simple worship of products several years ago, launching an effort to create a better balance for the enterprise, in which both customer growth and product excellence would be prized.

According to Lane Michel, at that time a consulting relationship manager at HP (and more recently a partner at Peppers and Rogers Group), staying focused on incremental gains helped Hewlett-Packard win acceptance for its overall program. "We try to avoid boiling the ocean," says Michel. "Then again, it's important to show immediate results. Those early successes earn you the right to take bigger steps."[6]

One example of such an incremental step was the customer-interaction program engineered by the Barcelona Division of HP's Consumer Products Group, which produced, among other things, the DesignJet high-end printer. In order to make it possible to have a continuing dialogue with its customers, the division developed a Web site, HP DesignJet Online, to serve as a user-friendly channel for interactive customer communication. The password-protected site offers self-diagnostic tools to DesignJet customers, as well as a quarterly newsletter, a user feedback section, new product notifications, and an upgrade program. The division is counting on the site to increase market share, reinforce customer loyalty, and provide a steady stream of timely market knowledge.[7]

Another incremental but important step taken by HP was the development of an electronic customer registration system, along with a master set of questions and a database to store the information. The initiative was born from ideas and feedback generated across several of the company's groups and divisions. The new system replaced paper registration, which had proved a poor method for collecting usable customer data.

[6]Don Peppers, Martha Rogers, PhD, and Bob Dorf, *The One to One Fieldbook: The Complete Toolkit for Implementing a 1to1 Marketing Program* (New York: Currency/Doubleday, 1997).

[7]Ibid.

Over time, baby steps like these can add up to great strides. By 1999, Hewlett-Packard had roughly 100 such incremental initiatives under way at various locations around the world, which they called "one-to-one campfires." Each was being tracked and monitored centrally, with information made available throughout the HP enterprise on the firm's intranet at a special relationship marketing section. Nearly every one of these initiatives, also, could easily be categorized in terms of which aspect of the IDIC implementation process it represented. Keeping the process going requires champions and leaders of change. At HP, these leaders have titles such as relationship marketing manager, customer advocacy manager, and installed base loyalty manager.[8]

A large number of incremental changes can add up to big change. In addition, an incremental change project could itself serve as a pilot for rolling out a particular idea or strategy across an entire division or enterprise. Pilot projects are a common method many companies use to make the kinds of changes required in the transition to a customer-strategy enterprise. But a pilot project differs, slightly anyway, from other forms of incremental change. A pilot project is, in essence, a feasibility study. It usually represents a test bed for trying out a new policy or strategy that, if successful, will be rolled out in a broader application. Therefore, the success metrics of the individual pilot project will have less to do with the actual profitability or business success of the pilot itself, and more to do with an assessment of whether the idea represented by the pilot project would be beneficial, if it were rolled out to the broader organization. And pilots have a built-in advantage when it comes to metrics. Because, by their nature, they usually involve only a selected portion of the enterprise, it is easier to measure the pilot's performance against a "control group"—meaning, in essence, the rest of the enterprise, doing business as usual.

Incremental change projects are rarely undertaken to resolve the problem of relationship governance for the enterprise. One of the key benefits, in fact, of concentrating on the IDIC process implementation methodology is the fact that significant progress can still be made without having to come to grips with this very thorny problem. At some point, however, any enterprise that wants to begin engaging customers in actual relationships, individually, will have to deal with the issue of relationship governance, and there are at least two methods for dealing with it on an incremental or transitional basis.

PICKET FENCE STRATEGY

The right way to transform a company gradually into a customer management organization is not to do it product by product or division by division, but customer by customer. And one way to begin such a transition is by placing just a few customers "under management," then adding a few more, and a few more (see Exhibits 13.5 and 13.6). In order to make this type of transition successful, it must be recognized that the enterprise will be operating under different rules with respect to the customers under management than it will be with respect to

---

[8]Ibid.

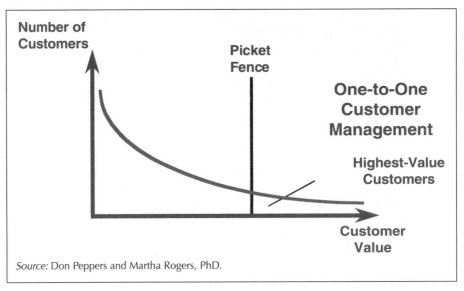

Source: Don Peppers and Martha Rogers, PhD.

EXHIBIT 13.5   Set Up a Picket Fence

all other customers. In essence, the customers under management will be fenced off and treated differently from the remainder of the customer base. As the transition progresses, the number of customers behind this "picket fence" will increase. As the portion of the customer base behind the picket fence continues to grow larger, the enterprise will be effecting a gradual transition to a customer management organization.

If an enterprise has ranked its customers by value, it can prioritize its transition in such a way as to place the more valuable customers behind the picket

■ Link individual data over time.

■ Calculate individual SOC and LTV.

■ Establish and maintain dialogue—get them off the mailing lists.

■ Mass-customize to meet individually-expressed needs.

■ Allocate resources to this customer relative to this customer's value.

■ Find products for customers.

One to One Picket Fence

EXHIBIT 13.6   How to Treat Customers behind the Picket Fence

fence first. When customers go under management, the implication is that a customer manager in the enterprise will be setting objectives and strategies for each of them, individually. The objective and strategy set for any particular customer should reflect the entire enterprise's relationship with that customer so, at least with respect to the customers behind the picket fence, the customer managers must have not only an integrated view of the enterprise's offering to, and interactions with those customers, but they must also have authority to make policy and implement programs, on behalf of the enterprise.

The picket fence transition strategy is especially compelling for companies that already identify their customers individually, during the natural course of their business. This would include banks and financial services firms, telecommunications companies, personal services businesses, some retailers, and most B2B companies with internal sales organizations. The highest-value customers at many companies like these are already being singled out for attention. If a retailer, for instance, has identified any customers at all who merit special treatment, it is likely they are the store's very high-volume, repeat spenders; the "special treatment" might easily include assigning personal shoppers or relationship managers to watch over the individual interests of such customers. Because at such a firm the picket fence strategy is already in place, the enterprise's goal should be to extend the idea and automate it, by codifying the business rules that are being applied, and ensuring that proper metrics are in place.

Remember that the customer manager should own the business rules for determining all of the communications that his customers receive. This means that the enterprise's direct-mail pieces would not go to customers behind the picket fence without the initiation or approval of the customer manager responsible for that customer. For each customer behind the picket fence, there should be a particular objective and a strategy for achieving that objective, set by the customer manager. In fact, the customer manager will himself be rewarded and compensated based on his ability to meet the objectives set for each of his customers, one customer at a time. Over time, as technology makes it better and more cost-efficient to process customer information, and the enterprise gains more knowledge and confidence in the process, it can expand the picket fence and put more people behind it.

Although the transition involves expanding the area behind the picket fence—that is, placing more and more customers under management—the enterprise most likely will never actually place all of its customers behind the fence. Some customers, for instance, just may not be willing to participate in a relationship of any kind. Moreover, no matter how cost-efficiently the enterprise has automated the process, there will always be customers who are not worth engaging in relationships.

SEGMENT MANAGEMENT

Another way to begin the transition to a customer management organization is with segment managers. While the picket fence transition is a customer-specific process that places an increasing number of individual customers under management, the segment management transition is a function-specific process that gives segment managers an increasing number of roles and capabilities with respect to their segments.

Remember that we chose the term *portfolio* rather than *segment* with deliberation, when we introduced the concept of customer management. The primary reason for this was to convey the thought that, in a customer portfolio, the customers themselves are uniquely identified and unduplicated—no customer would be in more than one portfolio at a time.

But even if an enterprise has not identified its customers uniquely, it can still differentiate them approximately, using survey-based consumer research and other tools. Even though the enterprise might not be able to classify any specific customer into a particular segment with certainty, nevertheless the segments themselves represent different types of customers who have needs and values that are different from the customers populating other segments.

Segment management is particularly appropriate for the types of businesses that have greater difficulty identifying and tracking customers individually. The picket fence transition works best for companies that either identify customers in the natural course of their business or can easily do so, whereas the segment manager transition works for all other companies. A consumer packaged goods company, for instance, might have a highly developed customer management organization already in place to ensure that its relationships with its retailer customers are profitably managed, but the company is unlikely even to have the identities of more than a microscopic fraction of its consumer customers. Such a firm might establish an organization of consumer segment managers who are responsible for shaping the firm's advertising and promotion efforts with respect to particular segments of consumers, across a variety of different products and brands.

A *segment management* organization, therefore, can be thought of as a transition state somewhere between product management and customer management. The most critical missing ingredient in a segment management operation is likely to be the capability to identify individual customers and track their interactions with the enterprise over time. Until the enterprise is able to add this capability, it will not be able to move from segment management to true **management of portfolios of customers (MPC)**. But even in the absence of customer-specific capabilities, a segment management organization can still be a useful tool for an enterprise to begin treating different customers differently, and for creating the value proposition for the relationships that could eventually come.

THE MANAGER OF PORTFOLIOS OF CUSTOMERS

At the heart of the customer management idea is the concept of placing customer managers in charge of portfolios of separate and individually identifiable customers who have been differentiated by their value to the enterprise and grouped by their needs. It is these customer managers who are charged with managing customer profitability. This is the core structure of the customer management organization, one in which each individual customer's value and retention is the direct responsibility of one individual in the enterprise. Managers may each be in charge of a large number of customers or portfolios, but the responsibility for any single customer is assigned to one customer manager (or, in a B2B setting, often, a customer management team). That manager is responsible for building the enterprise's share of customer (SOC) for each of the customers in his portfolio, increasing each customer's LTV and potential value to the enterprise (see Chapter 5).

The responsibility for customer management may spring from the marketing department, or sales management, or product development, or even, occasionally, from the IT department, where the customer data is housed. Wherever the organization resides, however, it must have a clear voice in the enterprise and have enough power to make decisions and influence other areas of the enterprise. One difficulty for this group is that the enterprise might try to hold them accountable for increasing the value of customers, but without giving them the authority to take the appropriate actions with respect to those customers. In the customer-value-building enterprise, the customer strategies should become the unifying theme for the organization; other areas of the enterprise should be made to understand how their own departmental goals relate to the customer strategies developed by the customer management group, and these other departments should be held accountable for executing the strategies.

STAGES OF CHANGE TO BECOME A CUSTOMER-STRATEGY ENTERPRISE

Miriam Washington Kendall
President, Ratio Consulting, Inc.

An organization that decides to focus on building customer profitability should execute all of the stages described here. While these activities are listed roughly in chronological order, many can be conducted in tandem (see Exhibit 13.7 for a graphic representation). To gain traction and build momentum, enterprises should execute these activities through a series of customer development cycles—distinct groups of implementation activities targeted to produce measurable results in no more than three months.

This cyclical approach can produce some quick and early successes that can convince some skeptical employees (and maybe some managers!) that the customer-value-building effort is worthwhile. Moreover, it can assist in securing both corporate funding and employee commitment.

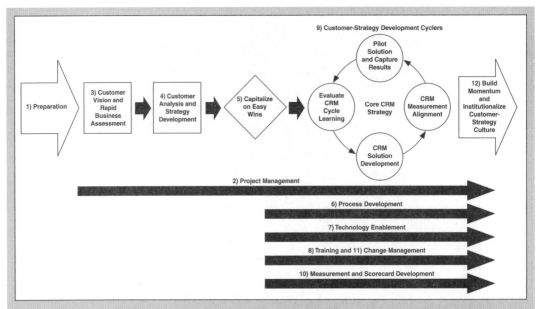

EXHIBIT 13.7   **Stages in Becoming a Customer-Strategy Enterprise**

PREPARATION

Before an enterprise begins the transformation, senior management must have a clear understanding of why the change is needed so that they may "buy into" the customer initiative. The organizational changes that occur when an enterprise shifts to a customer focus will undoubtedly cross numerous departmental lines. Therefore, it is imperative that senior-level executives support the migration every step of the way. Without the assurance of the CEO, CFO, and CIO in particular, and all of senior management in general, the transition could fail. The sooner this support is secured and communicated, the higher the chances of success. Once the enterprise has a good idea about why it is taking this journey, realistic expectations need to be set regarding the process and anticipated results.

PROJECT MANAGEMENT

The most effective way to coordinate the many tasks required to embed customer focus into an organization's culture is to treat the transition as a project.

The enterprise must assemble a stellar, multidiscipline implementation team that is led by a qualified project manager—ideally, a senior-level and respected executive within the organization. This team should then set up the governance structure of sponsors, team leaders, subject matter experts, and so on, within the organization to support and guide the project.

The project management office (PMO) should develop a project plan with timelines, milestones, and metrics. In all likelihood, there will be multiple projects running concurrently; therefore, an overall roadmap with a long-term vision for the enterprise and short-term goals for each project will be needed. The timing and criteria for success must be measurable and support business results. Finally, the PMO is responsible for project communications.

CUSTOMER VISION AND RAPID BUSINESS ASSESSMENT

The enterprise must also define—or redefine—its customer vision. Specifically, the organization needs to identify what it can provide its customers that meets their needs and therefore fosters loyal and profitable relationships. This vision must be aligned with the overall business philosophy and objectives. To support this vision, organizational resources will need to be reallocated to match each customer's value and needs.

CUSTOMER ANALYSIS AND STRATEGY DEVELOPMENT

An enterprise must understand its customer base and target segments in order to develop the most effective customer strategies. Once developed, these strategies should be validated with relevant constituent groups, starting with the enterprise's customer-facing employees. Then these strategies should be tested with customers and channel partners and revised as necessary.

EASY WINS

A prime opportunity for quick and visible progress occurs after specific customer strategies have been developed. These "easy wins" must be quantifiable and not subject to interpretation; otherwise, the project critics will offer alternative interpretations for the results or label them "soft results." There are two major ways to accomplish this: First, act on quick implementation ideas that are sure to have surfaced during project preparation, visioning, customer analysis, and strategy definition. Ideas such as "stop sending expensive catalogs to dormant customers" will provide an enterprise with an immediate improvement in the bottom line. Second, leverage the enterprise's current strengths and best practices by replicating and/or integrating them into all relevant parts of the organization. Focusing on the positive will help build momentum within an enterprise.

PROCESS DEVELOPMENT

To be truly customer-centric and to leverage the power of a customer-value-building business model, processes must be designed around the customer experience. First, the enterprise needs to understand the range of customer experiences before it can identify those that are positive and those that cause confusion or pain. Processes that are working well can be automated, but processes that harm the customer's experience will need to be reevaluated and redesigned (including channel processes).

When the customer project is technology-focused, the team ends up building functional requirements for a customer-strategy implementation without considering their impact on external customers or internal workflows. In the end, "the company ends up automating—rather than eliminating—bad processes, and as a result, helps the business run more inefficiently more quickly."[9]

TECHNOLOGY ENABLEMENT

With more than 500 vendors that sell customer relationship management products, selecting the best customer-strategy technology and vendor can be a challenge.[10] The enterprise can improve its decision in several ways:

- Understand fully the business and functional requirements.
- Base the technology selection on how closely candidates meet both the enterprise and end-users' needs.
- Use a methodical Request for Proposal (RFP) process, which allows different vendors to bid on providing defined specifications and results.

Once the technology is deployed, the enterprise can assess the gaps between its current technological capacity and the new technology's full capacity. Enterprises should focus on three primary areas for technology improvement:

1. Full integration with all other enterprise systems that contain customer data.
2. Customization of the technology so it works the way employees work, starting with those features the sales organization feels are a priority.[11]
3. Alignment with the customer vision and strategies and the revised processes and business rules.

TRAINING

A firm will likely spend 5 percent of its total customer-strategy investment on training.[12] Required training typically includes job-level and executive training

[9]Howard Berg, "Avoiding the Stresses after CRM Installations." *ComputerWorld* (January 15, 2001), available at: *www.computerworld.com.*

[10]Chiranjeev Bordoloi, "CRM Projects: A Framework for Success," an IQ4hire, Inc. white paper (2000), available at: *www.iq4hire.com.*

[11]Glen S. Petersen, *Customer Relationship Management Systems* (Downers Grove, IL: Strategic Sales Performance Inc., 1999).

[12]Howard Berg, "Avoiding the Stresses after CRM Installations," *ComputerWorld* (January 15, 2001), available at: *www.computerworld.com.*

in new customer-value-building business models, cultural shifts, processes, and systems use. Ensuring adequate training will also minimize the risk of having unqualified or uncooperative users jeopardize the initiative's success.

CUSTOMER-STRATEGY DEVELOPMENT CYCLES

Once an enterprise has properly planned and prepared for the transformation, it should begin to implement through customer-strategy development cycles. These cycles allow it to start small, with a controlled test or pilot group, then learn from the pilots, and refine the subsequent implementation cycle. Take note: It can be paralyzing to wait until everything is perfectly in place to begin the pilot, or the rollout. A firm should not wait for perfection; 80 percent readiness is sufficient to begin an organizationwide rollout of the customer-strategy processes. Implementation should be packaged in 10- to 12-week cycles, and adjustments should be made throughout the journey.

MEASUREMENT AND SCORECARD DEVELOPMENT

Few customer-strategy projects emphasize the importance that all stakeholders agree on how success will be measured.[13] Many projects cannot even measure their results (as discussed in Chapter 11). But for a customer strategy to be successful, metrics must be aligned to new approaches and goals, and clear measures and targets must be established at all levels: individual, work unit, development cycles, and the corporate trans-formation. One of the best ways to measure the transition to a customer-value-building strategy is with a "balanced" ROI scorecard. This scorecard incorporates both lag and lead indicators. Lag indicators could include revenue, market share, and other classic financials. Lead indicators could include share of customer, revenue mix, and customer satisfaction.[14] The most important criterion for a customer-strategy scorecard is that it incorporate metrics into the enterprise's priorities.

CHANGE MANAGEMENT

Many executives who have watched customer implementations fail know the importance of change management. Gartner Group reports that 65 percent of executives who state they are implementing a customer initiative will lack the alignment among customers, associates, and the executive leadership team on goals, strategies, and action plans.[15]

---

[13]Ibid.

[14]David Sims, "A New ROI for New Economy CRM? And Just Why Doesn't High-Tech Get It?" CRMGuru.com (April 4, 2000), available at: *www.crmguru.com/content/*.

[15]Jeff Golterman, "CRM Business Transformation: Key Business Decisions to Make before the Technology Is Deployed," Gartner Group CRM Summit 2001 (March 19, 2001).

Change management helps enterprises not only to reorient the leadership of the company, but also to change the behaviors of employees and front-line resources. If done properly, change management helps to:

- Surface the risk factors and key issues that hinder success.
- Preempt much of the likely employee resistance.
- Drive leaders to lead—rather than just sponsor—the change.
- Foster awareness, understanding, consensus, and acceptance of the customer initiative.
- Recognize—and plan for—the required changes in mind-set, skill sets, and behaviors.
- Drive people to work effectively together across the silos, which is not something that comes naturally to the employees of most companies.
- Ensure that the right people are in the right jobs, prepared and motivated to perform in the customer-strategy environment.

Pockets of resistance will be encountered throughout the project and throughout the enterprise. (We will discuss how managers can deal with resistance later in the chapter.) It should be noted that a change in culture and practices must shadow the entire customer-strategy project. This requires a complete alignment of vision, strategy, business objectives, organizational structure, operating procedures, compensation plans, and metrics.

BUILD MOMENTUM AND INSTITUTIONALIZE CUSTOMER-STRATEGY CULTURE

The last component of a successful transformation to a customer-strategy culture is not necessarily the final step, but rather a continuing process. Building momentum and institutionalizing a customer-strategy culture should be performed throughout the project and continued on a permanent basis. Just as customer-strategy principles should be incorporated into the natural practices of an enterprise, enterprises should embed momentum building into the workplace by continually learning, communicating, improving, and celebrating successes.

TRANSITION ACROSS THE ENTERPRISE

Many companies believe the biggest hurdle to becoming a successful customer-strategy enterprise is choosing and installing the right software. This unfortunate outlook has led to poor results on customer initiatives. Many organizations learn the hard way that management of portfolios of customers (MPC) cannot be installed; it must be *adopted*. The biggest hurdles to successful customer

> Many organizations learn the hard way that management of portfolios of customers (MPC) cannot be installed; it must be *adopted*.

management have little to do with technology. The greatest obstacles are a firm's traditional organization, culture, processes, metrics, and methods of compensation. The transition needed will affect not just the whole enterprise, but each of the parts as well. Let's take a look at the changes that will face the enterprise.

TRANSITION PROCESS FOR THE SALES DEPARTMENT

The sales force plays a critical role in the customer-strategy enterprise. As the "eyes and ears" of the organization, salespeople often interact with the customer at the customer's place of business. It is during these visits that salespeople develop an information-rich point of view of the customer. Using sales force automation (SFA) software, sales reps now easily share customer learning with their firms.

Some of the sales force is focused on driving transactions for lower-volume customers, and the skill sets of these salespeople are well suited for these activities. Other salespeople have different skills, and work with customers across all levels of the customer organization and focus on maximizing share of customer. Once considered the "lone wolf" of the organization, these salespeople effectively divide their time between sales calls, analysis of customer information, and participation in internal customer strategy development. Regardless of position, however, the salesperson understands how to develop customer insights and to provide customer information to the enterprise in an actionable way. Some information is entered into the SFA tool, and other information is shared during customer review meetings or via communications with the R&D department, customer service, or other departments.

The transition to a customer-strategy enterprise will be easy for some salespeople, whereas it will challenge the skill sets of some of the top sales performers. These principles will make a great deal of sense for the salespeople who have already been practicing visionary selling, consultative selling, or strategic selling, and they will probably readily embrace these ideals. But the salesperson who relies on retailers to "buy forward" in order to make quarterly product sales quotas may find the transition more difficult. Applying customer management principles requires taking a long-term view of the customer, which conflicts directly with the short-term focus that often prevails in many sales organizations.

The sales team can help confirm that those selected as MVCs are indeed the best customers. The sales team can also find MGCs that have been missed. It will be important to provide the sales team with information across other touchpoints in the organization, such as the Web and the customer service center. Real-time information is required to coordinate all interactions with a customer, and this can be a significant change for many salespeople. The trade-off is that the enterprise can handle a lot of the most tedious record-keeping and servicing very efficiently, thereby freeing up the salesperson for real relationship building and customer growth.

One of the most significant changes for a newly automated sales force is that the daily life of salespeople will wind up "on-screen" for all to see. In addition, fewer salespeople will have greater responsibility,[16] putting pressure on all sales personnel to conform and adopt new policies and procedures. During this process, therefore, it is important to negotiate some key agreements when implementing new policies and programs:

- Prioritize key information that is needed about customers. Salespeople should not be spending their time typing. They should be interacting with customers and learning more about customer needs.
- The firm will always score points if it can address ways that salespeople can save time and earn higher commissions.
- Integrate customer information wherever possible—some salespeople spend significant amounts of time typing the same information into applications that have different purposes (order entry system, billing system, forecasting reports, etc.).
- Negotiate which information is for enterprise use and which information is "for-their-eyes-only." It is important for the salesperson to remember key customer information such as family-member names, spouse's birthday, and so on, to create a personal bond; but this may be interesting only to others in the enterprise if someone has to substitute for the sales rep in a personal meeting.

Multidivision Customers

Knowledge-based selling traditionally has occurred in B2B scenarios, but has not always been applied across divisions of a company. One reason a customer-centered approach to doing business is so compelling is precisely because it enables an enterprise to leverage a single customer relationship into a variety of additional profit streams, cross-selling many different products and services to a customer in a coordinated way. The sales function plays a critical role in this relationship, but is not alone in executing it.

Customer-strategy enterprises rarely isolate their customer initiatives within a single division. In a multidivisional enterprise, the divisions sell to overlapping customer bases, doing business with a single customer in several different divisions. Enterprisewide cross-selling is not possible if the pilot project is limited to a single division and if the division databases are not integrated to facilitate a "one customer" view.

In many cases, a B2B enterprise that sets out to transform itself into a more customer-oriented firm will end up restructuring the sales force entirely, in order to ensure that the sales of different products to the same customers will be better coordinated, and appear more rational to the customer.

---

[16]Richard A. Lee, *The Customer Relationship Management Survival Guide* (St. Paul, MN: HYM Press, 2000).

SIDEBAR 13.3

A Multidivision Success Story at 3M Corporation

....

3M Corporation, which offers its customers more than 60,000 products from more than 50 divisions, formerly encouraged division-focused selling and product-focused commission structures. Although each unit had a plan to coordinate sales and reach its targets, the enterprise's customers were exposed to different plans from different divisions. Customers perceived its selling effort as uncoordinated. 3M later launched an initiative known as Customer-Focused Marketing (CFM) to encourage cross-selling between its divisions and reduce the number of contacts a customer would need in order to do business with the enterprise. A salesperson in one 3M division would get a commission even if the products in his division were sold by somebody else to his customer. In addition, the salesperson would be rewarded if he sold products from other divisions to his customers. The customer program encouraged formalized agreements between and among divisions at 3M, which could then bring the products of multiple divisions to a customer in one effort.

   The initial results of the CFM initiative proved highly successful. Profits in CFM divisions were twice as great, and their sales teams were twice as productive as those of the product-focused divisions. CFM divisions have grown at three times the rate of the non-CFM domestic average, and companies doing business with CFM divisions rate 3M a much friendlier company with which to do business.[a]

[a]Don Peppers and Martha Rogers, PhD. *Enterprise One to One* (New York: Doubleday Books), 1997.

Compensating the Sales Force

Sales force compensation is often one of the most important drivers of change, partly because the salesperson's salary and bonus usually depend on product sales results. One challenge facing the enterprise is deciding how to compensate salespeople and others for encouraging and ensuring customer loyalty and growing the long-term value of a customer, even when there may be no short-term product sale involved. The fact is that many salespeople are compensated in ways that make them indifferent to customer loyalty. In some cases, new-customer incentive programs actually *benefit* the salesperson when customer churn increases, enabling them to resell a product or service to a relatively educated customer. If customer loyalty and profitability are the objectives, then the enterprise needs to explore compensation systems that reward sales reps on the basis of each individual customer's long-term profitability (or LTV). There are two basic ways an enterprise can accomplish this:

1. *Value-based commissions derived from customer, rather than product, profitability.* The enterprise identifies certain types of customers who tend to be worth more than others and pays a higher up-front commission for acquiring or selling to this preferred type of customer. It considers lower commissions for "price" buyers or returning former customers, as well as other variable commission plans that emphasize acquisition and

retention of customers whose value is greatest to the enterprise overall, not just to the salesperson.

2. *Retention commissions*. The enterprise pays a lower commission on the acquisition of a customer. Instead, it links compensation to the profitability of a customer over time. For example, instead of paying a $1,000 commission just for landing a customer, the company pays $700 for a new account and $200 per year for every year the customer continues to do business with the enterprise.

TRANSITION PROCESS FOR MARKETING

The marketing group is responsible for traditional marketing activities, including creating brand image and awareness, communicating with the customer, utilizing the Internet and other old and new channels, and often, creating communications within the enterprise (e.g., an intranet, company newsletters, and project communications).

In the customer-strategy enterprise, the marketing department will perform these traditional roles for customers who remain outside of the picket fence, and may help prepare communication messages or even business rules for customer managers who are building relationships for customers under management. In addition to deploying the traditional instruments of marketing, such as advertising and promotion, there are a number of other functions for the marketing department to perform that are unique to a customer-specific approach, including:

- Customer analytics (see Chapter 12), a specialized skill set that involves building customer LTV models, gathering and manipulating data, and programming. The customer analytics group may also be responsible for tracking and reporting the internal metrics needed to measure the effectiveness of customer programs.
- Establishment of test cells and control groups.
- Campaign development and management, including dialogue planning.
- Offer specification, designed to appeal especially to higher-value customers and prospects.
- Customer management, as a line-management function, which has been described previously.

TRANSITION PROCESS FOR CUSTOMER SERVICE

A service organization might be the appliance repair personnel, the hotel staff, operators answering the 800-telephone number, or the delivery crew. Every product that is created has a service organization associated with it in some way, whether the product is sold by the enterprise or by a channel organization. In the customer-strategy enterprise, the service organization has access to more customer information than other traditional enterprises, and uses this information to deliver a valuable experience or to collect information (or both). For example, in a customer-strategy enterprise, the delivery driver might be asked to survey a customer's warehouse informally and take note of the number of competitors' cartons that are stacked within view of the delivery door. This information can help an enterprise begin to understand share of customer.

Ironically, as pressures mount for enterprises to cut costs and improve efficiency, the customer service area may be squeezed in the process. In the customer-strategy enterprise, the customer service area plays a key role in executing customer strategies while servicing the customer. Customer calls are routed based on value and need, and the most appropriate customer service representative is assigned the call based on the skills of the rep. During the call, customer-defined business rules are applied to maximize the impact of the interaction with the customer, and the reps have been trained in how to interact most effectively with various customers. Also, the individual needs, talent, and experience of the rep are considered in the routing decisions. The rep is encouraged to enhance the skills needed to serve the customer efficiently and effectively. As customer needs change, the skills of the reps also must evolve.

Increasingly, customer transactions are moving to an e-commerce model, and transactions normally handled with a phone call are now being done electronically, via the Web site. In many customer service areas, this has changed the mix of calls that are handled by the customer service rep. "Easy" transaction (order-taking) calls are now being replaced with more difficult customer situation calls (complaints, inquiries, billing and invoicing questions, etc.). This can increase the level of stress experienced by the customer service representatives.

Traditional measures for customer interaction centers (CICs) have focused on "talk time" and "one and done" measures. (See a more complete discussion about the CIC in Chapter 8.) As we dig deeper into customer metrics, we start measuring average talk time for valuable customers versus customers who call into the customer interaction center frequently and yet do not generate enough revenue to warrant high levels of service. We begin to understand which customers are buying a wide range of products and services offered by an enterprise and which customers should be but aren't. Many CIC managers are left to fight a battle to increase talk time for the customers who warrant more attention, but they lack the analytics and resulting insights ("the facts") to be able to justify that decision. This is where partnering with the customer manager is key—the justification for these measures should be in the customer strategies.

The fact is, however, that a customer-strategy company can often keep its costs down by centering on customer needs. Calls are more often resolved in one session and in less total time. Customer service reps do not "chase down" information or transfer customers from department to department. Voice response unit (VRU) options are reordered to present the most likely option desired by *that* customer as soon as the customer is identified. This process can significantly decrease phone costs for an enterprise maintaining a toll-free phone line. This requires that people within the enterprise start thinking like customers, or learning about the customer's point of view during key interactions (such as a sales call or customer care call) and combine this point of view with the customer strategy and business rules that have been identified for this customer.

Change often demands new skill sets. As the enterprise begins to define specific roles and responsibilities (or job descriptions) for various customer care representatives, it will also need to develop training and development plans and recruitment and staffing plans. These descriptions include competencies and behaviors that will be required of all employees—things like customer empathy— and skills associated with different roles. Employees might determine how they "touch" the customer directly or indirectly by supporting another department.

An often-neglected step in this process is planning around the way customer care representatives are supported, measured, and compensated to reinforce the new behaviors, which should incorporate the customer-centered metrics described earlier. Unfortunately, the reporting capabilities in many enterprises are not up to the task, and some great customer-oriented efforts have gone awry because this last step was not implemented. Employees often want to "do the right thing" but are not supported or measured adequately or correctly. More important, many companies equate CRM with customer service, when in fact customer service— important as it is—is *not* the same as relationships. The heart of a Learning Relationship is a memory of a customer's expressed needs so that this customer can be treated in a way that works for him without his having to be asked again. Customer service, in contrast, is often more like *random acts of CRM*.

SIDEBAR 13.4

Customer Service at an Online Financial Services Firm

In one instance, an online financial services firm was reengineering the customer interaction center to implement many of the aforementioned principles. The firm separated its customer base into four groups based on key customer characteristics (assets and use of the services). Once it identified its customer groups, it was easy for the firm to identify the knowledge, skills, and abilities that were required to support them. The firm implemented routing technology to redirect customer calls based on the customer grouping and the skill set of the available representatives. The firm created automated business rules that could utilize the best available personnel to handle the needs of each individual customer in the call queue. Prior to this change, any customer could be routed to any customer service representative (CSR). It was not unusual, for example, to have a most valuable customer (MVC) routed to a newly hired and ill-informed rep, or a rep who lacked the required skills to execute particular transactions. This required a customer hanging up and (if the firm was lucky) calling again; or perhaps the customer would be transferred to another CSR. The changes resolved these problems. A key benefit for the rep was the ability to work through a learning curve—he was directed to the types of calls that he could handle and this significantly decreased stress levels.

High-quality customer service is one of the beneficial outcomes of adopting customer strategies. Enterprises must keep in mind the cost of *not* providing sufficient service, thereby risking the loss of customers and the expensive task of acquiring new ones. General wisdom places the estimate for customer defections due to a poor sales or service interaction between the customer and the enterprise at about 70 percent.

Moreover, an enterprise must balance the cost of providing customer service with the needs and desires of the customer in such a way that the customer will find sufficient value in the enterprise to remain a customer. At a minimum, certain standards of accuracy, timeliness, and convenience must be in place to placate most customers. The right technology and processes must first be deployed, followed by the training and adoption of service practices by customer-facing representatives.

But what is the "right amount" of customer service? What is the least expensive amount for the enterprise that is still acceptable for the customer? Which channel should they be encouraged to use? And should different levels of service be offered to different kinds of customers? Might customer service mean different things to different customers? When is self-service appropriate? Certainly these and other questions should be addressed if an enterprise is to find the balance of service that serves both the customer and the budget. According to CRM experts Seth Shulman and Stanley Brown, "It is. . . essential to ensure that the balance between unassisted/self-serve (including e-mail), agent-assisted and wholly voice calls (where the customer can dictate instructions) is carefully planned to provide self-serve maximum value to the customer, and not just to reduce costs."[17]

Is "good" customer service in the eyes of the beholder? Some criteria an enterprise could consider from the customer's perspective include:

- Saving time or money
- Convenience
- Accuracy of a transaction
- Speed of service
- Ease of doing business
- Providing better (not just more) information
- Recording and remembering relevant data
- Allowing a choice of ways to do business
- Treating customers as individuals
- Acknowledging and remembering the relationship
- Fixing problems quickly
- Thanking the customer

Not all of these elements are equally important to all customers. Any one of these criteria could be a deal breaker to one customer and of no consequence to another. Adding or upgrading customer services uniformly for everyone is an expensive way to raise the bar. Better to know what's important to an individual customer, and then to make sure that customer gets the services most important to him.

---

[17]Seth Shulman and Stanley A. Brown, *Customer Relationship Management* (New York: John Wiley & Sons, Inc., 2000).

Adding or upgrading cus-
tomer services uniformly
for everyone is an expensive
way to raise the bar. Better to
know what's important to an
individual customer, and
then to make sure that customer gets the services most
important to him.

Many enterprises have learned that the integration of the contact center with all other communication vehicles is the first step toward successful completion of the customer's mission. For example, live online customer service, text-based chat, and Web callbacks are some of the vehicles that can elevate good, basic customer service to excellent and highly satisfactory service, the latter of which translates into customer retention, growth, loyalty, and profitability.

SIDEBAR 13.5
Customer Service Case Study: Liz Claiborne

....

Elizabeth Rech
Business Strategy and CRM Consultant

Named for the founder of the clothing company based in New York, Elisabeth is a division of Liz Claiborne that offers women's accessories and clothing in plus sizes (14 through 24), as well as clothing for petite women. Like its parent, the division has its own stores and makes its line of clothing available to department stores and specialty shops.

Unlike its parent, Elisabeth offers live online customer service. The division introduced this option when it launched its Web site in November 2000. Customers, especially frequent Web site visitors, can easily look up previous purchases and create "wish lists" of clothing and accessories at Elisabeth.com. When customers request live assistance, either by calling or sending live text messages from the Web site, they reach an agent from PeopleSupport, a service bureau based in Los Angeles. This group of agents, located at PeopleSupport's office in St. Louis, Missouri, are available round the clock, 24/7.

The agents conduct live online chat sessions and consolidate information they collect while communicating with customers by phone or online. Elisabeth started offering live service from its Web site based on findings from the market research firm Forrester Research, which indicated that women who wore clothing in plus sizes could not easily find what they wanted in stores and preferred to shop from their homes. In offering live chat, Elisabeth faced two challenges: It presented a new means of communication to customers who were inexperienced with shopping online, and it was depending on a third-party service bureau to do it.

Online visitors use text chat to request help with navigating Elisabeth.com, especially with locating specific items of clothing, and they do not have to provide any information to identify themselves during text chat sessions. Customers typically call the phone number on Elisabeth's Web site to place orders, ask about shipping options, or update their contact information. They send e-mail messages when they have questions that require long answers, such as when they request lists of local stores that sell the Elisabeth line. Liz Claiborne has Web access to transcripts of online correspondence, and tracks the number of calls, e-mail messages and chat sessions the customer service agents handle.[a]

[a]Joe Fleischer. "Changing the Fabric of Customer Service: How Five Companies Put the Concept of eCRM into Practice by Meshing Live Service over the Phone and over the Internet." *Call Center Magazine*, (May 7, 2001).

TRANSITION PROCESS FOR OTHER KEY ENTERPRISE AREAS

Finance, human resources (HR), research and development (R&D), and information technology/information services (IT/IS) also need to make the transition to a customer-strategy organization, but these changes are not as readily apparent as the changes required by the marketing, sales, and customer service organizations. All four areas are directly responsible for *capabilities building*—or how well the organization is able to adapt and change to the new processes. For now, let's look at how the transition affects these other areas of the enterprise in more detail.

Finance

The finance function takes on new roles within the enterprise, and these are required to help implement a smooth transition:

- Many accounting systems are not set up to measure customer profitability and LTV easily, and the enterprise will need the support of the financial area to help define these metrics.
- Having defined and learned to report these metrics, the finance leadership will work with line and staff managers and HR to develop appropriate customer-based compensation and reward systems for employees whose responsibility is to build customer equity and manager customer relationships and retention.
- Building a strong customer-based organization requires financial support to implement new programs and technology. The financial area can play a role in developing the business case for implementing initiatives designed to increase the value of the customer base and in demonstrating ROI.

Human Resources

The customer-strategy enterprise requires knowledge workers—people who will recognize and act on relevant customer information. There are several ways that HR can directly influence the changes:

- *Redefining the organization.* By taking an active role in defining the new roles and responsibilities, the HR function can map out the transition plans for many key areas of the enterprise. Part of this requires that it help the business define the changes, and understand how employees will be affected by these changes.
- *Evaluating whether the company has the capability to change as required by the newly developed customer strategies.* There may be some important limiting factors that arise, such as the qualifications of the labor pool available and local salary expectations.
- *During the transition plan, addressing all of the key training and ongoing support issues.* Is there adequate funding to help employees migrate to these

new responsibilities? Often, these are "line items" in a project plan, but are not incorporated into annual training and development budgets or plans.

- *Creating career path opportunities that did not exist before.* For the customer interaction center rep or the salesperson, their responsibilities can grow over time as their skill sets can mature. For the more senior-level executives, a well-rounded employee who has worked directly with customers will become more valued in a customer-value-building organization.

The HR function has the opportunity to take a proactive approach and directly deal with cultural issues and issues of resistance (this topic will be addressed later in the chapter). Employees view many HR functions unfavorably: HR "polices" the rules and procedures, or it is viewed as a purely administrative function. The transition to customer management can serve as an opportunity for HR to address proactively the many issues that arise in the transition, because the changes are wide and deep.

Research and Development

Research and development is another key area in many customer-strategy enterprises. R&D is responsible for creating innovative customer solutions and, therefore, works closely with marketing or sales (as it has traditionally done in the past). However, in the customer-strategy enterprise, it is the depth and quality of customer information that makes the difference. The customer manager group works within its own department to understand common customer needs, and these common needs drive some of the R&D group's work. For some customers, there are needs driving the R&D efforts that will not be seen by other customers for a long time because the most valuable or most growable customers are intimately involved in the R&D work. This work will give these customers a competitive advantage in the marketplace. For example, an MGC might be a service organization working with a technology supplier to create a wireless network for the sales force and service workers that will enable them to react to their customer needs instantaneously. This capability to respond dynamically will have a competitive advantage.

Information Technology/Information Services

Often, there is a centralized technology function (IT) within large enterprises that is responsible for the technology infrastructure (networks, mainframes, routers, etc.). There may be groups (IS) that are dedicated to functions within the company and that work with the departments to implement applications that help conduct business (HR applications that manage payroll and employee records, other applications that run the order-entry system, logistics and planning, customer interaction center systems, etc.). Both of these functions are directly responsible for enabling the execution of customer strategies.[18]

[18]Barbara H. Wixom and Hugh J. Watson, "An Empirical Investigation of the Factors Affecting Data Warehousing Success," *MIS Quarterly* 25, no. 1 (March 2001): 17–41.

> If the IT organization can-
> not align the technology
> implementation and the
> business strategy, the cus-
> tomer management effort
> and the entire PMO should
> be governed by the business
> end of the enterprise.

Many IT/IS organizations go awry when they sponsor the CRM projects. Sometimes IT specialists overestimate their own skills in business strategy, but more often than not, the IT/IS organization runs the project management office (PMO) of the CRM project. This can work when IT/IS actually understands the importance of aligning technology implementation with the business strategy. If the IT organization cannot align the technology implementation and the business strategy, the customer management effort and the entire PMO should be governed by the business end of the enterprise. That said, business units often lack the project management skills to implement large-scale projects—and this expertise is often in the IT/IS area.

MANAGING EMPLOYEES IN THE CUSTOMER-STRATEGY ENTERPRISE

The road to becoming a customer-value-building enterprise is fraught with speed bumps. We have shown so far how the transition requires a new organizational infrastructure—one that is populated by customer managers and capabilities managers who fully support the migration from day one. The enterprise moving to a customer-strategy business model will likely require new capabilities for relating to customers individually. It will need to assess where the gaps lie in its established capabilities so it can improve its focus on customers, not just products, and build profitable, long-term customer relationships.

Change is important, but never easy. Many believe that change can revitalize the enterprise to compete in ways that it never could have before. Resistance to change, however, is imminent, as many employees who oppose or resist the new infrastructure will step forward. How does an enterprise cope with these changes? How does an executive manage employees in this new business environment?

OVERCOMING EMPLOYEE RESISTANCE

Marijo Puleo, PhD
Director, Peppers and Rogers Group

One of the most difficult issues in change management is how to handle employee resistance to change. Veteran employees have grown accustomed to a particular "culture" at the enterprise, representing the basic pattern of shared assumptions, values, and beliefs considered to be the correct way of thinking about and acting on problems and opportunities facing the organization.[19] The

---

[19]Steven L. McShane and Mary Ann Von Glinow, *Organizational Behavior* (New York: McGraw-Hill Companies, 2000).

enterprise will have an established culture, but so will many of the operating units and individual departments within the enterprise. Breaking through these established patterns can be difficult, especially if the post-transformation future of the enterprise cannot be clearly spelled out. A survey of executives from large U.S. enterprises found that the most important feature of successful change efforts was a clear strategic vision of the proposed change.[20] This helps to minimize employee fear of the unknown and provides a better understanding about the behaviors employees must learn.[21]

Adopting a customer-strategy-friendly infrastructure will change some aspects of the company that many employees might not readily accept. Just a few of the cultural barriers might include:

- A senior manager who refuses to commit to organizational changes and prefers a "wait and see" approach.
- Deep-rooted corporate policies that require all customers be treated the same no matter their value to the enterprise.
- A social atmosphere that reinforces product-oriented behaviors
- A tradition of reward and compensation that encourages transactional rather than relationship-oriented efforts.

Customer-strategy initiatives require as much ownership as possible throughout the organization and a process of proactive communication—sharing information throughout the enterprise— about every success achieved and each missed opportunity. In his book *Loyalty.com*, Frederick Newell writes:

> To succeed at CRM, the company must get everyone onboard, and they must teach all the players to see CRM as a benefit to them and to their customers . . . .
> It is important to understand that CRM and the CRM dialogue become tools to help you understand the power of your brand and the image it creates in the customer's mind. The height of these hurdles is raised in the selling of CRM to management. A company's dedication to CRM as a way of doing business will require fundamental changes within the organization. Understanding the value of CRM requires a significant shift in mind-set—learning to value qualitative rather than just quantitative benefits. Managers new to CRM must understand that tapping its real power requires a new way of doing business . . . .

Some employees are concerned about the consequences of change, such as how the new conditions will affect their status within the enterprise. Others might labor over how the changes will be implemented and how they will handle breaking old habits and learning new skills. People resist change because they are concerned they will not be able to adapt to the new behaviors, or perhaps because

[20]B. McDermott and G. Sexton, "Sowing the Seeds of Corporate Innovation," *Journal for Quality and Participation* 21 (November–December 1998), pp. 18–23.

[21]D.A. Nadler, "Implementing Organizational Changes," in *Managing Organizations: Readings and Cases* (Boston: Little, Brown, 1982).

they fear that their own economic interests or their status within the organization will be harmed. Once the enterprise has envisioned the ideal customer experience and how it will do business, it will need to make that vision a reality throughout the workforce. The goal is to define it in some detail, but the different functions need to define it and adopt it themselves. This is one of the most difficult steps to get through because there can be a lot of politicking and infighting. In some cases, different people in the organization are rewarded for achieving the *exact opposite* goals. To be blunt, some people "win" in the new scenario, and some "lose." For

> Once the enterprise has envisioned the ideal customer experience and how it will do business, it will need to make that vision a reality throughout the workforce.

example, the production function moves more efficiently if new products are introduced infrequently, but the customer management function needs a variety of modular offerings to be able to build the value of MVCs. Some people are astounded when they *really* begin to understand the scope and nature of the change at hand. Some may resign. However, many vie to reestablish a new power base in the new organization. Others will resist, and outright sabotage, any effort at change. And, yes, there will be some that say, "It's about *time!*" These employees are the change advocates and change agents and they should be encouraged and supported whenever possible.

One of the most challenging aspects of this new strategy is the amount of coordination and trust that needs to be developed between departments and functions, especially if the political environment is a volatile one.

ROLE OF EMPLOYEES IN BUILDING THE CUSTOMER-STRATEGY ENTERPRISE

Building a compelling work environment that nurtures individual employee relationships is a strategic imperative. Employees are an integral part of any customer-based strategy, especially for service organizations. Moreover, as any company shifts to an increasingly make-to-order type of business, it will inherently become more of a service organization. CEOs must ensure that each of their employees' needs is fulfilled.

Success will ultimately depend on how well employees are trained and educated to understand the new customer-strategy infrastructure and all of its related processes. Employees will need to achieve a comfort level high enough to ensure sustained cooperation and loyalty to the enterprise. In *The Experience Economy*, B. Joseph Pine II and James H. Gilmore wrote: "The success of any business obviously relies on picking the right people to play various parts. The notion that employee turnover stems from hiring under- or overqualified candidates for jobs often obscures a more fundamental source of employee dissatisfaction and defection: casting *mis*qualified people in roles ill-suited to their capabilities in the name of getting the best and the brightest."[22]

---

[22]B. Joseph Pine II and James H. Gilmore, *The Experience Economy* (Cambridge, MA: Harvard Business School Press, 1999).

Hiring the most effective employees is crucial when it comes to delivering customer-value-building services and products. Customer-strategy change management emphasizes the need to embed the customer at the center of the company strategy first, then align the people and the organization, then the processes and technology. In the interactive era, where knowledge, not equipment, drives profit, employees are the source of competitive advantage.

As the customer strategy focuses on the changing needs of the customer, a change management strategy must also focus on core individual employee needs. An employee is hard-pressed to "treat different customers differently" if the employee feels like a number to the organization. A salesperson needs good information to service the customer's needs. That salesperson, and the call center person and other front-line personnel need the support of the organization to enable them to do their jobs effectively. Employees need to feel that they are given an opportunity to do what they do best every day. Meanwhile, effective managers must instill feelings of accomplishment in their employees. People need reinforcement that their opinions count, that their colleagues are committed to quality, and that they have made a direct, personal connection between their work and the company's mission.

Although building one-to-one Learning Relationships with employees is beyond the scope of this book, the principles for building valuable relationships with customers provides a great foundation for applying *employee relationship management* (ERM). Managers will continue to play a critical role in the newly formed customer-strategy enterprise. Their leadership qualities will be tested as they guide their employees through the difficult transition (we'll talk more about leadership in the appendix). Just as the customer-strategy enterprise strives to keep and grow its customers, so too must it seek to keep and grow its best employees. Loyalty, as management consultant Fred Reichheld explains in the next section, is a term that aptly applies to employees, not only to customers. Developing a loyalty-based management philosophy is important, but not always easy, for the enterprise to execute.

LOYALTY-BASED MANAGEMENT[23]

Frederick F. Reichheld
Fellow, Bain & Company

Many companies diminish their economic potential through human resource policies that ensure high employee turnover, in part because they can't quantify the economics of retaining employees. Executives might say they want to keep employees, but if doing so means raising salaries, their conviction soon fades.

[23]Shortened and adapted from "Loyalty-Based Management" by Frederick F. Reichheld, *Harvard Business Review*, March–April 1993, © Harvard Business School Publishing, with permission. The complete article is available at *www.hbr.org*.

They question the wisdom of increasing pay by, say, 25 percent in order to decrease employee turnover by 5 percent. Yet the fact is that employee retention is key to customer retention, and customer retention can quickly offset higher salaries and other incentives designed to keep employees from leaving. The longer employees stay with the company, the more familiar they become with the business, the more they learn, and the more valuable they can be. Those employees who deal directly with customers day after day have a powerful effect on customer loyalty. Long-term employees can serve customers better than newcomers can; after all, a customer's contact with a company is through employees, not through the top executives. It is with employees that the customer builds a bond of trust and expectations, and when those people leave, the bond is broken.

Companies wanting to increase customer loyalty often fail in their effort because they don't grasp the importance of this point. While conducting customer focus programs, they may be terminating or rotating the people who have the most influence on the customer's experience. While they are reengineering their business processes, they are failing to reengineer career paths, job content, and compensation so that employees will stay with the company long enough to learn the new processes. Just as it is important to select the right kinds of customers before trying to keep them, a company must find the right kinds of employees before enticing them to stay. That raises the issue of hiring. The goal is not only to fill desks but also to find and hold onto workers who will continue to learn, to become more productive, and to create trusting relationships with customers. State Farm, the loyalty leader among auto insurance companies that sell through agents, has a distinctive agent-appointment strategy. Prospective agents may spend a year or more in a recruiting and selection process. During this time, they are in competition with several other well-qualified candidates. The lengthy process enables the company's field managers to select the best-qualified person. State Farm often looks for candidates with roots in the community who are already likely to have long-term relationships with prospective customers.

One way for any company to find new hires who will likely stay is to look at the patterns of their own employees who defected early. Had they found the job at your company through newspaper ads, college recruiting, or personal referrals? Equally important, how long had they stayed with employers before coming to you? In a loyalty-based system, skills and education are important, but not as important as how long a prospective worker is expected to stay and grow with the business. Although longevity deepens familiarity, some company policies render familiarity useless. Banks, for instance, are notorious for offering branch managers career paths that rotate them through a series of branch offices. Each time managers move, they take with them the knowledge learned at the branch where they put in their time. They have to start over again in each branch, building a network with the customers and the other employees. Their incentives to acquire the right customers and employees are reduced, as it is their replacements who will reap the benefits. In a major bank with several hundred branches, branch managers who had been in the system an average of 12 years stayed at a given branch for only 2 years. Only one branch manager had remained in place and, not surprisingly, his office had the highest customer-retention rate in the entire system. It's worth noting that most banks have 50 to 100-percent-a-year teller turnover, which is also costly. Because most bankers cannot quantify the systems costs of these policies, they cannot justify the investments required to fix the situation. But not all businesses follow those practices. The highly successful Olive Garden restaurant chain goes against the industry norm of moving successful managers to open new restaurants or to run bigger ones every few years and letting assistants take over. The chain hires local managers whose major asset is that they are known and trusted in the community. These managers are then kept in place so their asset appreciates in value. Learning accumulates as people stay on the job. By becoming intelligent about the business, getting to know customers, and providing the advantages knowledge gives, long-time hires add value to the company.

Leo Burnett Company's strong position in the advertising industry is largely attributable to its slavish devotion to employee retention. Most advertising firms experience high turnover of their creative people, and they make a point of rotating people through various accounts. They also experience constant client churn, accompanied by massive layoffs and severe downturns in revenues and profits. At Leo Burnett, in contrast, new staffers are assigned to their first account "for life," in the words of one executive. Layoffs are rare, and customer retention is high.

Even businesses that don't rely on direct relationships between customers and employees can benefit from boosting employee retention. USAA has an information system that lets any employee pull up a customer's records instantly, so customers don't have to speak with the same employee every time. But USAA's employee turnover of around 7 percent—one-third the industry average—is one of the most important reasons its productivity is the best in the business. The learning unleashed by employee retention helps in other ways. When the marketing department wants to know more about customer needs or reactions to a new product, it can hold a focus group meeting of employees whose daily customer contact provides powerful insight.

Of course, employees won't stay and apply their knowledge unless they have an incentive to do so. All other things being equal, the best people will stay with the company that pays them the most. Loyalty leaders share their "loyalty surplus" with employees as well as stockholders. They view their best employees as they do their best customers: Once they've got them, they do everything possible to keep them. And they provide incentives in the form of higher salaries or bonuses and commissions that align the employees' self-interest with the interests of the company. Bonuses can be based on aggregate customer retention rates, and commissions can be designed to be small initially but grow the longer the customer stays with the company. There are many ways reward programs can be structured to recognize loyalty. Olive Garden found that its experienced waiters and waitresses resented the fact that new hires were receiving the same base wage as they did, so management established a slightly higher base wage for employees who had served $25,000 of meals.

> Loyalty leaders share their "loyalty surplus" with employees as well as stockholders. They view their best employees as they do their best customers: Once they've got them, they do everything possible to keep them.

If employees are expected to be long-termers, companies can justify investing more in them. It becomes worthwhile to teach employees to do the right thing for the customer, which in turn leads to happier customers and, ultimately, increased profits, which can be put toward the higher salaries of long-term employees. And the commitment to creating a loyalty-based system has spillover effects. Employees take pride in delivering value to a customer time and again. Their satisfaction in contributing to a positive goal is another thing that induces their loyalty to the company.

MEASURES OF LOYALTY

Even the best-designed loyalty-based system will deteriorate unless an effective measurement system is established. Competitors, customer preferences, technologies, and employee capabilities are constantly changing. Measures establish the feedback loops that are the foundation of organizational learning. Only through effective learning can an organization consistently deliver value in an ever-changing world.

Unfortunately, most accounting systems do not measure what drives customer value. They can show the benefits of the one-year "magic cure" but not of programs and practices that take three to five years or longer to affect profits. Managers who have a year to earn a bonus, or two years to turn a business around are forced to think of the usual shortcuts to higher profits: raising prices and cutting costs. Those actions alone rarely create value for customers; and although customers don't all leave at once, if they are not getting the best value, they will eventually turn to a competitor. To make matters worse, the best customers are often the first ones to go. The first step in developing effective measures is to understand the cause-and-effect relationships in the system. The primary mission of a loyalty-based company is to deliver superior value to customers. Success or failure in this mission can be clearly

> Managers who have a year to earn a bonus, or two years to turn a business around are forced to think of the usual shortcuts to higher profits: raising prices and cutting costs.

measured by customer loyalty (best quantified by retention rate or share of purchases or both). Customer loyalty has three second-order effects:

1. Revenue grows as a result of repeat purchases and referrals.
2. Costs decline as a result of lower acquisition expenses and from the efficiencies of serving experienced customers.
3. Employee retention increases because job pride and satisfaction increase, in turn creating a loop that reinforces customer loyalty and further reduces costs as hiring and training costs shrink and productivity rises.

As costs go down and revenues go up, profits (the third-order effect) increase. Unless managers measure and monitor all of these economic relationships, they will default to their short-term, profit-oriented accounting systems, which tend to focus on only the second- and third-order effects. Focusing on these symptoms—instead of on the primary mission of delivering superior value to customers—often leads to decisions that will eventually reduce value and loyalty. In the life insurance business, for instance, a five-percentage point increase in customer retention lowers costs per policy by 18 percent. However, very few companies have quantified this relationship, and as a result, they focus their cost-reduction efforts on process reengineering and layoffs, which appear to lower costs but in fact lower employee motivation and retention, leading to lower customer retention, which increases costs!

When life insurers want to grow, they hire more agents, raise commissions, drop prices (to new customers only, if possible) and/or add new products. The result: more inexperienced salespeople (low productivity and high cost) bringing in the wrong kind of customer (disloyal price shoppers) with escalating costs of product-line complexity. The only way to avoid these mistakes in insurance, or any business, is to develop systems that allow employees to track and understand the cash-flow consequences of changing customer loyalty. It is only the true defection of the target customer that should be of concern because that means something may have gone wrong, and if it has, it's worth a considerable amount of effort to find out what. It could mean that another company has done something innovative that gives customers a better value. It is important to define customer retention carefully and what it means in a particular industry. In the auto business, for instance, a manufacturer should worry about a customer who switches to another brand—but not about a customer who sells his car and takes public transportation. In an industrial setting, customers might shift a percentage of their purchases to competitors, so changes in purchase patterns and share of customer should be watched as carefully as customer defections.

Customer satisfaction is not a surrogate for customer retention. While it may seem intuitive that increasing customer satisfaction will increase retention and, therefore, profits, the facts are contrary. Between 65 and 85 percent of customers who defect say they were satisfied or very satisfied with their former supplier. In the auto industry, satisfaction scores average 85 to 95 percent, while repurchase rates average only 40 percent. Current satisfaction measurement systems are simply not designed to provide insight into how many customers stay loyal to the company and for how long.

STATE FARM'S LOYALTY-BASED SYSTEM

State Farm insures more than 20 percent of the nation's households. It has the lowest sales and distribution costs among insurance companies of its type, yet its agents' incomes are generally higher than agents working for the competition. Its focus on customer service has resulted in faster growth than most other multiple-line insurers; but rather than being consumed by growth, its capital has mushroomed (all through internally generated surplus) to more than $18 billion, representing the largest capital base of any financial services company in North

America. Because of careful customer selection and retention, State Farm is able to price below the competition and still build the capital necessary to protect its policyholders in years such as 1992 when it incurred $4.7 billion in catastrophe losses. These impressive achievements can be traced to State Farm's well-designed employee loyalty-based system. State Farm began by choosing the right customers. The company was founded more than 70 years ago to serve better-than-average drivers, first in farming communities and now throughout suburban and urban markets across the United States and in three Canadian provinces. State Farm agents work from neighborhood offices, which enables them to build long-lasting relationships with their customers and provide the personal service that is the basis of the corporate philosophy.

This kind of personal service can start at an early age. Teenagers in State Farm households are usually written while still under the umbrella of their parents' policies. Many State Farm agents routinely sit new drivers down in their offices for a "Dutch uncle" speech about the responsibilities of driving and the impact an accident or ticket—particularly for drunken driving—would have on their rates. Also, in an effort to educate all teens on safe driving, agents have available company-produced safe-driving materials for high schools. All these efforts tend to make the young drivers that State Farm insures more careful, and their parents grateful for the interest and help.

When agents are rooted in the community, they often know whom the best customers will be. For example, they can scan the local newspaper for the high school honor roll and recognize their young customers' good grades with premium discounts. Agents make it their business to get to know the people they insure. The most powerful computer and the brightest underwriter at headquarters simply can't compete with that level of customer insight. Pricing policies work as a magnet to retain good customers. At the end of three years, accident-free customers get a 5 percent discount, followed by another 5 percent decrease three years later. The discounts make customers feel they've earned special status and value, and they create a disincentive to jump to another company, where they might have to start all over again.

State Farm agents not only want to attract and keep good customers, they also have the incentive to do so. Commissions are structured to encourage long-term thinking. Agents receive the same compensation rate on renewal auto and fire policies as for new policies, thus rewarding agents for serving existing customers, not just for drawing in new business. Unlike organizations that say retention is important while pushing salespeople to find new customers, State Farm consistently conveys the message that both are important. Remaining focused on its target customers, State Farm provides a full life-cycle product line. Rather than bringing in lots of new customers, the company's marketing efforts encourage existing customers to buy additional products, such as home and life insurance. The homogeneity of their market means that one agent can sell and service everything. The full product line preserves the agent's relationship with the customer and allows the agent to learn more about the customer's needs. In addition to benefiting the policyholder and company, this approach serves the agent well, as multiple-line customers are less expensive for the agent to service than are single-line customers. Multiple-line customers have also proven to stay with the agent longer.

State Farm agents themselves are loyal. According to industry studies, more than 80 percent of newly appointed agents remain through their fourth year, compared with 20 to 40 percent for the rest of the industry. And the average agent at State Farm has 13 years of tenure, compared with 6 to 9 years for the industry. This retention advantage can be attributed both to the lengthy recruiting and selection process before appointment and to the fact that State Farm agents are independent contractors who sell and service State Farm products exclusively. Because agents have built and invested in their own businesses, they are more likely to remain with State Farm than their counterparts representing other companies.

In return, State Farm is loyal to its agents, and distributes its products only through them. The company has built a marketing partnership with its agents and involves them in key decisions that affect them or their customers. Agent retention and customer retention reinforce one another. The agent who is committed to a long-term relationship with the company, and, indeed, to his own business, is more likely to build lasting relationships with customers. In addition, loyal customers make life easier for the agents, who spend more time working with people they know and like and far less time chasing new customers. Finally, agents like being part of a system that consistently delivers superior value to customers. Agents' experience, plus the fact that they spend more time servicing and selling to proven customers, raises agents' productivity to 50 percent above industry norms. State Farm's business systems support its focus on loyalty. Measures of customer retention and defections are distributed throughout the organization. Agents and employees at all levels know whether the system is working and can adjust their activities. Agents find a list of their nonrenewing customers each morning when they switch on their computers, which they can use to prompt telephone follow-ups to try to retain the account. And management can use the same kind of information as a check against policyholders' satisfaction with the service, product, and price they receive.

> Agents' experience, plus the fact that they spend more time servicing and selling to proven customers, raises agents' productivity to 50 percent above industry norms.

State Farm's success in building customer loyalty is reflected in retention rates that exceed 90 percent, consistently the best performance of all the national insurers that sell through agents. State Farm agents make more money by operating in a business system engineered for superior loyalty. And they are more productive, which makes it possible for them to earn superior compensation (after adjusting for the fact that State Farm agents pay their own expenses) while the company actually pays lower average commission rates. The result is a 10 percent cost advantage. The company also keeps its costs relatively low because it avoids excessive administrative and claims costs associated with acquiring and servicing a large percentage of new customers. State Farm's system provides outstanding value to its customers and benefits for its agents, hence has created a company that is a financial powerhouse.

MANAGING FOR LOYALTY

The success of State Farm and other loyalty leaders shows the direct linkages between providing value for customers and a superior financial and competitive position. Doing the right thing for customers does not conflict with generating substantial margins. On the contrary, it is the only way to ensure profitability beyond the short term. Creating a loyalty-based system in any company requires a radical departure from traditional business thinking. It puts creating customer value—not just maximizing profits and shareholder value— at the center of business strategy, and it demands significant changes in business practice: redefining target customers, revising employment policies, and redesigning incentives.

> Creating a loyalty-based system in any company requires a radical departure from traditional business thinking. It puts creating customer value–not just maximizing profits and shareholder value–at the center of business strategy, and it demands significant changes in business practice: redefining target customers, revising employment policies, and redesigning incentives.

Most important, if companies are really serious about delivering value and earning customer loyalty, they must measure it. And while senior executives may be daunted by the time and investment required to engineer an entire business system for high retention, they may have no alternative. Customer loyalty appears to be the only way to achieve sustainably superior profits. Managing for loyalty serves the best interests of customers, employees, and investors. The only losers are the competitors who get the leftovers: an increasingly poor mix of customers and employees and an increasingly less tenable financial and market position. As loyalty leaders refine their ability to deliver value by more effectively harnessing the economics of loyalty, their advantages will multiply. Competitors must respond, or they will find it increasingly difficult to survive on the leftovers of the marketplace.

MOMENTUM BUILDING IN THE CUSTOMER-BASED ENTERPRISE

We have been reinforcing the idea that a customer-based initiative is not an off-the-shelf solution, but rather a business strategy that will imbue an enterprise with an ever-improving capability to know and respond to its customer's individual needs. Executed through a cyclical process, customer-strategy principles can provide an enterprise with a powerful source of competitive advantage. But it requires organizational commitment, careful planning, and, ultimately, a well-orchestrated array of people, culture, processes, metrics, and technology. Successful implementation comes only with an understanding of the nature of this comprehensive business model. Organizational questions include:

- If a customer's value is measured across more than one division, is one person placed in charge of that customer relationship?
- Should the enterprise establish a key account-selling system?

- Should the enterprise underwrite a more comprehensive information system, standardizing customer data across each division?
- Should the sales force be better automated? Who should set the strategy for how a sales rep interacts with a particular customer?
- Is it possible for the various Web sites and call centers operated by the company to work together better?
- Should the company package more services with the products it sells, and if so, how should those services be delivered?[24]

To answer these questions, the transition team will have to encourage a more integrative, collaborative attitude among all employees. It might establish a multidepartment task force that can standardize a way for reporting customer information and other related issues. Ultimately, throughout the entire transition, the team will need to revisit each of the steps and refine and revise how it is executing them. After all, the transition to a customer-strategy architecture never really ends.

SUMMARY

We have reached another pivotal juncture. Our discussion of how to measure and manage customer-based initiatives has set the stage for another important arena that every customer-based enterprise will enter. For once it has realigned itself around customers, the enterprise must begin to do what it set out to accomplish in the first place: manage the demand chain. If you recall, demand chain management is the opposite of supply chain management. Demand chain management implies that the enterprise is interacting with its customers individually, listening to and remembering each of their needs, and then ensuring that its products and services can fulfill those needs. These concepts also imply that the enterprise will somehow extend its products and services to its customers through certain channels of delivery and distribution.

Throughout the book we have been using the term *channel* as a medium of communication. Communication channels provide a platform for the enterprise to interact with the customer (see Chapter 7 for more on interacting). We now turn our discussion to channels of distribution. Whether it sells products to consumers or other businesses, the customer-strategy enterprise encounters some significant challenges with channels. Customer-strategy principles are critical to the enterprise that operates in consumer-directed and business-to-business scenarios, but each channel is fraught with its own set of issues and models. The next chapter of the book uncovers these B2C, B2B, and channel management issues.

---

[24]Don Peppers, Martha Rogers, PhD, and Bob Dorf, *The One to One Fieldbook* (New York: Doubleday Books, 1999).

FOOD FOR THOUGHT

1. Choose an organization and draw its organizational chart. How would that chart have to change in order to facilitate customer management and to make sure people are evaluated, measured, and compensated for building the value of the customer base?

2. For the same organization, consider the current culture. Can you describe it? Would that have to change for the organization to manage the relationship with and value of one customer at a time? If so, how?

3. At the same organization, assume the company rank-orders customers by value and places the MVCs behind a picket fence. What happens to customers and to customer portfolio managers behind that picket fence?

4. In an organization, who should "own" the customer relationship? What does that mean?

GLOSSARY

Management of portfolios of customers (MPC)   The deliberate management of a *portfolio of customers* to optimize the value of each customer portfolio to the firm. By utilizing the feedback from each customer, a portfolio manager analyzes the differing values and needs of each customer, and sets up the best *treatment* for each customer to realize the largest return on each relationship, often in an automated way using *business rules.*

Picket fence   An imaginary boundary around customers selected for management. While customers outside the picket fence will likely be treated as customers have always been treated, using mass marketing and traditional customer care, customers behind the picket fence will each be the management responsibility of a customer portfolio manager, whose primary responsibility will be to keep and grow each of the customers assigned to him.

Portfolio of customers (also, customer portfolios)   Rather than thinking in terms of target markets and *segments,* the customer-strategy enterprise will manage portfolios of individual customers. Whereas segments of customers are treated as lookalikes within the segment (meaning that segment marketing is really mass marketing, only smaller), customers within a portfolio are grouped by value and understood by the needs they have in common, as well as the needs they have individually expressed by their interactions and transactions through various touchpoints over time.

Subprime, superprime   Superprime customers are those with good credit that all enterprises want as customers. Subprime customers are those who have not yet established credit histories, such as college students. (See George Day's discussion of FirstUSA and Capital One.)

Delivery Channel Issues of the Enterprise Focused on Building Customer Value

14

Chapter

Business 101 teaches us that a distribution channel *is the combination of institutions through which a seller markets products to industrial buyers or consumers. Channels perform the task of moving goods from producers to consumers and other businesses. The enterprise's chosen distribution channels directly affect its marketing decisions, including pricing, product placement, and promotion.[1] Manufacturers sometimes distribute and sell their goods to customers through* **intermediaries** *or indirect channels—sets of interdependent organizations involved in the process of making a product or service available for use or consumption. Manufacturers use intermediaries because they can perform marketing functions more efficiently than manufacturers, or because manufacturers lack the financial resources or expertise to market directly to consumers. In other cases, manufacturers sell directly to end users. The increasing role of the World Wide Web in facilitating the sale of products and services directly to end-user consumers is a major trend threatening* disintermediation, *which is just the formal name for the process of cutting out the middleman. The complex dynamics of channel management is a subject best left to other books and courses in marketing and sales. However, for the purposes of a book on managing customer relationships, we will briefly review some* channel management *concepts. In this chapter, we will also address the basics from a customer strategy perspective.*

From a customer relationship point of view, distribution channels are the routes to market used by an enterprise to interact with its ultimate customers. **Distribution channels**—not to be confused with **communication channels**—include orga-nizations such as wholesalers, retailers, and value-added resellers, whereas communication channels include customer touchpoints, such as the sales force, telephone, retail point-of-sale, and the Web. As this chapter will

[1]Louis W. Stern and Adel El-Ansary, *Marketing Channels,* 5th ed. (Upper Saddle River, NJ: Prentice Hall, 1996).

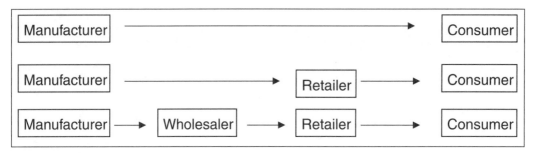

EXHIBIT 14.1   **Marketing Channels for Consumer Goods**

show, enterprises are rapidly moving to establish more collaborative partner relationships with traditional sales and distribution channels. Traditional channels are seeking ways to add greater value to products and services and lessen reliance on manufacturers and product developers. Strategic alliances are a common form of business relationship across all industries. Enterprises compete not only for customers, but for distribution partners as well, and applying customer-relationship principles within a channel community can build partner loyalty in the same way it builds customer loyalty. (See Exhibit 14.1.)

For the manufacturer operating in the interactive era (and therefore focused on growing the value of the customer base), channel partners provide the critical customer relationship link. Channel partners most often are in control of the relationship with the end-user customer. Therefore, deep collaboration with channel members is vital to the success of the manufacturing enterprise.[2] This chapter discusses the importance of learning about channel partner needs, in order to promote more effective relationships with partners and customers. This includes logistics partners, because no matter how many transactions take place directly and electronically, physical shipping will depend on the shippers, and so an important element of the satisfaction of transactions, and, ultimately, of the relationship, will depend on logistics partners.[3] We'll discuss channel conflict and how an enterprise can best manage "channel pain" to get closer to its end-user customers.

DEALING WITH CHANNEL PAIN

How do channels of distribution affect the customer-strategy enterprise? The simple truth is that, often, the most intractable barrier to doing business as a

---

[2]A. Coughlan, E. Anderson, L. Stern, and A. Ansary, *Marketing Channels* (Upper Saddle River, NJ: Prentice Hall, 2001).

[3]An anonymous reviewer of this book points out that freight carriers, warehouses, inventory managers, and the like are all part of the process of building customer value. Companies like L.L. Bean, Amazon.com, and others build their extraordinary loyalty among customers in large part because they get the logistics right—even though good logistics management is transparent to the end user.

Flows	Representative Costs
Physical possession	Storage and delivery
Ownership	Inventory holding
Promotion	Advertising, promotion
Negotiation	Time and legal
Financing	Credit terms
Risking	Repairs, warranties
Ordering	Order processing
Payment	Collections
Information	Customer data

EXHIBIT 14.2   **Channel Flows and Costs**

customer-focused enterprise is the sales channel and distribution system itself. Enterprises need to consider how much value the channel adds or detracts from the process of reaching and interacting with customers. (See Exhibit 14.2.) The customer, after all, is everywhere these days, shopping from multiple channels, whether it be the store, a catalog, or online. The enterprise that is "nearest" to the end customer typically has the competitive advantage, especially in developing a Learning Relationship. The one who can communicate directly with the customer is better positioned to enhance the customer's value to the enterprise and gain a greater share of the customer's business. A customer of a local electronics store who purchases a computer, for instance, interacts with that retailer's own customer service employees when buying the product. But, ultimately, the customer will turn to the telephone help line or online Web site of the product manufacturer when she gets home and needs assistance installing the hardware and software. Customers typically are ambivalent about which distribution channel they deal with, whether it be an authorized distributor, a reseller, an independent dealer, retailer, warehouse, or street vendor. And a customer usually interacts with her preferred communication channel contact.

> Enterprises need to consider how much value the channel adds or detracts from the process of reaching and interacting with customers.

Customers have become more shrewd and sophisticated as shoppers in recent years. They are now comparison-shopping more frequently, looking for the products they need and want at the best price—no matter where they are sold. Customers have come to expect consistent policies, procedures, and relationships with the enterprise that manufacturers the product or provides the customer service. Moreover, customers demand near-instant access to pricing, product, and competitive information. They crave better, faster service and higher-quality products. They ultimately want a consistent experience across all shopping channels.

For their part, companies have been adopting multichannel strategies to reach more customers. The benefits of adding channels sometimes come with consequences, however. New channels may add convenience for the customer, but typically introduce conflict and control problems. The heart of channel conflict is simple: Manufacturers don't care which store you shop in as long as you buy their product, and stores don't care which product you buy as long as you buy it in their store.[4] Channel conflict can occur when two or more company channels end up competing for the same customers. Control problems occur to the extent that new channels are more independent and make cooperation more difficult.[5] Channel conflict endures in many industries. Manufacturers want channel members to conform to their standards for selling, servicing, or repairing their products. Meanwhile, channel members claim they *own* the customer relationship. The channel closest to the end customer typically asserts "ownership" rights:

> The heart of channel conflict is simple: Manufacturers don't care which store you shop in as long as you buy their product, and stores don't care which product you buy as long as you buy it in their store.

- It markets to the customer.
- It is the point of transaction.
- It provides value-added services.

No matter how well channels are designed, there will likely be some conflict, either vertically or horizontally. **Vertical channel conflict** occurs when there is conflict between different levels within the same channel. For example, BarnesandNoble.com sells the same books as its sister store chain, Barnes and Noble Booksellers. Conflict can occur when these two related entities offer different prices, different return policies, or just different customer service philosophies. **Horizontal channel conflict** occurs when there is conflict between members of the same level within the channel. An automobile dealer for a particular automaker, for example, might engage in channel conflict with another dealer for the same manufacturer in the same town, if the second dealer begins to advertise too assertively. In addition, multichannel conflict can occur when the manufacturer has established two or more channels that compete with one another in selling to the same market. For example, discount retailers might become upset when a clothing manufacturer that distributes its apparel through their discount stores also elects to sell through a specialty store channel. A good example of horizontal conflict can be seen in the efforts of electronics manufacturers to price their products differently from one country to another.

Manufacturing enterprises have three important reasons to want a collaborative relationship with the companies that take their products to market:

---

[4]Obviously, this point is oversimplified, as pointed out by an anonymous reviewer for this book. In reality, manufacturers do care which retailers you patronize: They'd rather you go to the retailers that provide the best support for their brand. And retailers would rather you buy the brand that will return them the highest margin. But, generally, the conflict of which store versus which brand makes negotiations challenging and necessary.

[5]Philip Kotler, *Marketing Management: Analysis, Planning, Implementation, and Control*, 9th ed. (Upper Saddle River, NJ: Prentice Hall, 1997).

1. The battle for the customer must be won at the channel level before the end customer can be secured.
2. The intermediary adds value to the product that the manufacturer cannot easily or economically add.
3. The intermediary can be an enduring basis for creating new value with customers and for taking costs out of current systems.[6]

A strong base of channel partners helps relieve so-called channel pain and helps to avoid hurting customers. One enterprise that found a way to alleviate its channel woes is Simpson-Lawrence (USA) Inc., a leading distributor to the marine leisure industry. The Florida-based company faced intense channel conflict because its sales force was pitted against its wholesale distribution channel. As a $12 million company with only six regional salespeople serving all of North America, the company found it impossible to serve all of its small marine dealers properly. Initially, its road warriors would pitch to any marine shop they happened upon, regardless of size. But with sales rep salaries averaging $70,000 each annually, this equation didn't add up. To further fan the flames, distributors were not very happy that Simpson-Lawrence was selling to the distributors' smaller customers. At the same time, Simpson-Lawrence wanted to focus on larger accounts, so it looked for a way to strike a deal with distributors. The enterprise broke its customer base of 1,100 into two groups: those who could be profitably served directly and those who could not and had to be handled by a distributor. A little analysis showed that its top 150 customers generated 90 percent of the company's revenue, so the direct sales force now focuses on them; the remaining customers have been directed to its distribution network. Simpson-Lawrence now sends its salespeople out with distributors on sales calls. By having a salesperson concentrate on helping a distributor manage its own sales, the company immediately unites these once-competing teams, reducing channel conflict at the same time.

SIDEBAR 14.1
How Bendix/King Landed Relationships with Pilots[a]

Bill Millar
Business writer

Bendix/King, an aircraft instrumentation subsidiary of Honeywell International, Inc., wanted closer relationships with its end-user customers, but a distribution network—a channel—stood in its way. Meanwhile, Bendix/King wanted to streamline its business processes, improve services, and reduce costs, while developing an e-business strategy.

Bendix/King designs and builds altimeters, flight management systems, ground proximity warning devices, transceivers, transponders, and all manner of handy,

---

[6]Ian Gordon, *Relationship Marketing* (New York: John Wiley & Sons, Inc., 1998).

SIDEBAR 14.1 *(continued)*

sophisticated electronic devices that not only make flying safer, they're required before the FAA will allow an aircraft to leave the ground. But because FAA regulations also prohibit the direct sale of such equipment to pilots—the rule is these components have to be purchased through and installed by licensed, certified technicians—Bendix/King reaches its end customers through a dealer network. Given this strategic topography, explains Rick Click, executive director of e-business and information technology at BRGA Honeywell, "We went about designing an e-business solution that could meet all of our objectives." The answer became BendixKing.com.

BendixKing.com is a collaboration with e-business software provider, Entigo. According to Entigo's Vice President of Marketing, Mark Demers, "This was a fairly unique concept, because it isn't strictly B2B or B2C." Rather, explains Demers, "our challenge was to create something that could strengthen the channel, not *disintermediate.* Accordingly, BendixKing.com is designed to enable direct relationships with end customers while maintaining the integrity of the dealer network. Pilots love the site, says Click, "because they can search, find the products they want, learn the technical detail around those products—pilots love details because these are critical components—find dealers, then submit an RFQ." Bendix/King routes RFQs to dealers or to a region as indicated by the pilots. Dealers bid, Bendix/King relays the information to the pilots, and the pilots choose their supplier and installer.

All of this "gives us a route for building a direct relationship with the end customer," explains Click. In turn, that information is handed over to the company's data warehouse, where it can be mined for sales, marketing, logistics, and design intelligence.

A relationship with a pilot also gives the company greater control over a given sale. "If a customer walks in and that dealer doesn't carry or have our product in stock, the dealer can push another product." With sales initiated by BendixKing.com, "the dealer knows this business is tied to a Bendix/King product, and if she doesn't have it on the shelf, she knows she needs to use the system to order from us."

Dealers also get a handful of advantages from using the system. "This is a fully functional e-business site," explains Click. "It's tied in to our systems in real time, so they can review our products, review technical specifications, check our inventory, see their pricing, order, and everything is integrated and automated." Moreover, dealers are incentivized to place their orders over BendixKing.com, as dealer rebates today are based exclusively on business conducted through the site. The result, says Click, is that "everyone, from large 'tier one' customers to 'tier three' mom-and-pop shops now deals with us through BendixKing.com."

The site itself features both a significant number of personalization features, as well as controls. Pilots, for example, can customize the site to show "only those components compatible with a Cessna 172"; or for a larger customer, for "whatever might be in their fleet," explains Click. As for dealers, they see their own pricing based on their relationship with Bendix/King—not just standard catalog pricing. "So it customizes and simplifies the relationship." Going forward, the site's goal is to create an even greater sense of community for pilots. For example, there are chat rooms, along with occasional "meet the expert" events, explains Demers.

Of still greater interest to Bendix/King are the opportunities to add services to grow share of customer—outside the existing channel. As Click explains, "The FAA requires pilots to update their flight management systems (FMS) every 28 days." Traditionally, this is a labor-intensive process requiring, for example, the mailing of

---

SIDEBAR 14.1 *(continued)*

....

CD-ROMS or PCMCIA disks and other dirt-world headaches such as payment processing. But at BendixKing.com, "We've turned this into a simple download from their PC," with payment by credit card, explains Click. Today it's FMS updates, but the company is looking to add other services, such as automated flight plan development and submission. "These are improvements in the ownership and operation of airplanes," explains Click. "And to the extent they create new revenue streams for us, it's a win-win."

The site is definitely a "step forward," says Greg Linton, an avionics supervisor at Cessna Aircraft, a Bendix/King dealer near Stewart Airport in Newburgh, New York. In particular, he likes having warranty information available online. "That's very helpful." Nonetheless, there's always room for improvement. For example, he explains, "It would be nice if there were a way to check the status on units that are being repaired. When will the work be done? When will the unit be shipped?"

BendixKing.com isn't finished. As Click explains, "We're learning, and adding improvements all the time." But by the company's standards, the site is already a great success. For example, traffic has grown from 20,000 unique visits per month when first launched to more than 120,000 a month today. "Recognize," says Click, "when we're talking about pilots, we're not talking about a particularly large segment of the population." Even more impressive, the company is projecting sales volume this year will range from $30 to 50 million—representing 23 percent of Bendix/King's total business. Overall, explains Click, "this not only introduces significant e-business efficiencies for our own operations, it's also proving to be a means of building stronger relationships with our end customers and our dealers—and we're doing it at the same time."

[a] Adapted from Martha Rogers, "The Sky's the Limit for Bendix/King," *One to One Magazine,* (December 10, 2001).

DISTRIBUTION SYSTEM MANAGEMENT

If an enterprise sells an information-related or entertainment-related product, it is often not difficult for the enterprise to customize the product to an individual's tastes, nor is it difficult to picture how to use an interactive media company to distribute the product to the customer who wants it. But if an enterprise sells a physical product, such as a car or a packaged good, the distribution system also will be physical and often will represent the single biggest obstacle preventing the enterprise from developing a Learning Relationship with the customer. (See Exhibit 14.3.) Some of the questions that naturally arise are:

- How should an enterprise deal with the barriers that its distribution system might pose—barriers that lie between the enterprise and its end-user customers?
- Under what circumstances should an enterprise risk "going around" its existing distributors?
- What role will logistics play in these considerations about distribution? (See Exhibit 14.4.)

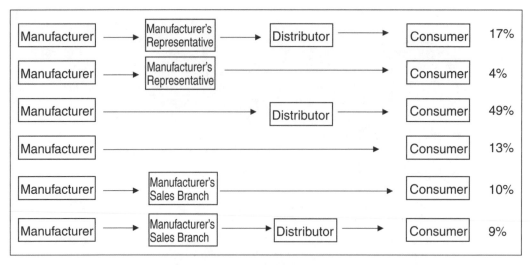

EXHIBIT 14.3   **Marketing Channels for Industrial Goods (Sample Year 1989)**

- When does it make sense for the enterprise to treat the members of the distribution chain themselves as customers? What are the advantages and drawbacks of this strategy?
- If an enterprise is itself engaged in the distribution of products or services for other companies, then which strategy makes the most sense for dealing with these new technological trends, many of which are threatening to "cut out the middleman?"

Even if an enterprise exists close to its customers and lacks any formal channel of distribution, the barriers that inhibit customers from doing business with it can still probably be traced to distributionlike issues. For example, many

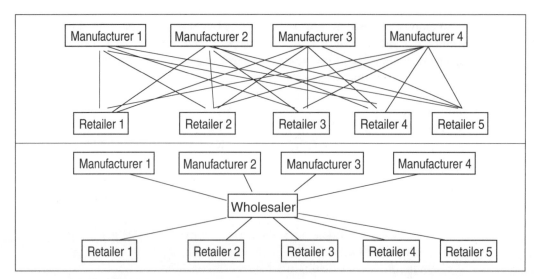

EXHIBIT 14.4   **Contact Points: Role of the Mediator**

automobile manufacturers recommend that owners change their car's engine oil every 3,000 miles. But few car owners claim to do so. Suppose that, for an additional $20 fee on top of the price of the oil change, the car owner could have someone come to her home and change the oil at her convenience. Not every car owner would be willing to pay for this service, but the customer-strategy enterprise is in the business of treating different customers differently anyway. In reality, many oil change centers could make money on the home-service component, separate from the oil change transaction itself. It could generate additional transactions with each of the customers who buy the home service, make more profit per transaction with them, and enhance each customer's loyalty for a longer time.

Notice that the home-service oil change has no system of distribution between the auto mechanic and the end customer; there are no retailers and no warehouses in between. Nonetheless, a home-service engine oil change could be perceived as a form of distribution channel enhancement, as it removes the barrier between the customer and the seller. The customer is more willing to buy the service because the seller has made it more convenient for her to use the service. The oil change service provider has eliminated the barrier of distribution and improved the relationship between itself and the customer. It is often easier for the enterprise to avert the barriers represented by its established system of distribution by creating a new, separate distribution system, instead of changing the old system.

> It is often easier for the enterprise to avert the barriers represented by its established system of distribution by creating a new, separate distribution system, instead of changing the old system.

No matter which industry the enterprise is in, it is most likely not the distributors themselves that are the barriers, but the distribution system, which in most industries evolved from a produce-and-sell world of manufacturing, inventorying, and distributing. In the customer-strategy world of mass customization, a new distribution system is needed. The alternative to circumventing a well-established distribution channel is to bring the channel in on the venture or to treat the channel member as a "customer"—or partner.

Treating the distributor as a customer helps the customer-strategy enterprise to create more loyal distributors and to increase profit margins. That said, it's important to be aware of the differences between the end-user customer and the distributor-as-customer. Unlike the end-user customer, the distributor likely perceives other distributors as its main competitors. The enterprise needs to use caution when treating different distributors differently so that it is not seen as favoring one competitor unfairly over another. Important information about how one distributor likes to be dealt with must be kept within the bounds of the relationship the enterprise has with that distributor. The distributor also will likely work for the enterprise's competitors, too. To be of use to its own customers, a distributor has to carry a variety of products from which to choose. So, although the enterprise might influence a distributor, earning a higher share of its business, it can never convert the

> Unlike the end-user customer, the distributor likely perceives other distributors as its main competitors. The enterprise needs to use caution when treating different distributors differently so that it is not seen as favoring one competitor unfairly over another.

distributor to carrying the enterprise's products alone. To convert it would undermine the distributor's own purpose. Therefore, any transfer of expertise or knowledge from manufacturer to intermediary, from enterprise to distributor, should be assumed to work to the benefit of the enterprise's competitors as well. When an automobile manufacturer teaches its dealerships about how to improve customer service, it must assume that those dealers that handle other brands of cars will use these techniques to benefit the other brand names, too.

GENERAL MOTORS' VAUXHALL DIVISION: MANAGING THE CUSTOMER EXPERIENCE ACROSS CHANNELS AND TOUCHPOINTS

Patricia B. Seybold
CEO, The Patricia Seybold Group

British consumers have been up in arms for several years. Their complaint: unfair pricing. They claim that prices in Britain are artificially higher than they are in other parts of Europe. And they blame this state of affairs on entrenched industry practices and lack of government attention to globally competitive pricing. Consumers are particularly annoyed about the relatively high prices for cars in the United Kingdom. Part of the problem in Britain has to do with the fact that only 20 percent of cars are sold to consumers; the rest are bought for employees by their companies, which negotiate bulk contracts. Consumers pay higher prices, and, of course, believe that they are getting the short end of the stick. And they are—or at least they were. In October 2000, a government commission called for substantial changes in the way cars were priced and sold to consumers in Britain.

At least one company was ready for the changes. Vauxhall (a division of General Motors) had been working for over a year to change its pricing and policies. Vauxhall used the Internet as a medium through which it could give more power to customers. It was the first automobile manufacturer in the world to sell new cars direct over the Internet. To do so, the manufacturer had to come to terms with its car dealerships—its only distribution channel. What happens to the dealer when customers want to buy direct via the Internet, and manufacturers want to sell direct online? Vauxhall has paved the way. Its dealers support the Internet sales and have the opportunity to service the online customers.

Vauxhall's savvy management team also realized how critical it is to build a strong branded relationship with each customer and each household. But how *does* an automobile manufacturer with hundreds of independent and powerful exclusive dealerships build a closer relationship with its customers without taking dealers out of the loop? Vauxhall had the answer. It pioneered a new, closed-loop relationship management approach with the cooperation of *both* its U.K. dealers and of a variety of other business partners. Here's the story of how Vauxhall has met and surmounted its customer relationship challenges.

IMPROVING THE TOTAL CUSTOMER EXPERIENCE

In mid-1998, Paul Confrey, a 31-year-old marketing manager at GM's Vauxhall Motors, was tapped by Nick Reilly, the group's aggressive chairman, and Ian Coomber, its sales and marketing director, to head up a new Relationship Marketing division. Confrey had spent 10 years at Vauxhall in marketing, brand management, and direct sales in the United Kingdom and Germany. The goal of this new division was to build tighter relationships with Vauxhall's customers, while at the same time offering its 450 dealers—which ranged from individual family businesses to large, multidealer groups—services that would increase their profitability. Vauxhall management knew that it was critical to increase customer loyalty in order to build market share and boost long-term profitability. Vauxhall's market share in the United Kingdom was averaging 13 percent; its loyalty rate—repeat purchases by the same individual household—was running at 50 percent per year, average for the U.K. new car market. Reilly, Coomber, and Confrey knew that a good way to increase customer loyalty would be to improve customers' experiences in dealing with the different faces of Vauxhall. "We recognized that selling metal is not a great way to make money. We wanted to wrap the customer in the Vauxhall blanket—insurance, accessories, warranty, used cars, accident repair, and so on with a customer-centric, cross-selling approach that takes as many of the hassles of running a car away as possible."

The Vauxhall management team didn't think of its mandate as saving the customers time; they were focused on improving customers' relationships and increasing customer loyalty. Yet in tackling the issues that mattered most to customers, they wound up saving customers time and aggravation. They redesigned business processes across business partners to give customers a more seamless and streamlined experience. Vauxhall took on the responsibility of coordinating all customer-impacting business processes so that it could better control the quality of the customer experience. In short, Vauxhall took responsibility for the quality of the total customer experience that was being delivered to customers through a variety of partners.

DO CUSTOMERS WANT A RELATIONSHIP WITH THE MANUFACTURER?

Like most manufacturers, Vauxhall was very nervous about supplanting the customers' relationships with its dealers. It was heavily reliant on this channel, as there was no other practical way to sell, service, and maintain customers' cars. But when the company asked customers whether they wanted a relationship with the manufacturer, customers claimed that they already had such a relationship—it just wasn't a very good one. Most dramatically, customers' feelings came through loud and clear: "You don't act as if you care about me. You're just trying to solicit my business. You call me several times about different, seemingly unrelated issues. You're wasting my time!" The moral of the story is that if you sell a branded product, customers will feel they have a relationship with

The moral of the story is that if you sell a branded product, customers will feel they have a relationship with you and your brand. If you don't control the quality of the customer's total experience with your brand, you're missing the boat. Customers will sense that you don't care about their experiences in doing business with you and they'll defect.

you and your brand. If you don't control the quality of the customer's total experience with your brand, you're missing the boat. Customers will sense that you don't care about their experiences in doing business with you and they'll defect.

Vauxhall customers knowingly or unknowingly dealt with at least five different companies—each one providing a part of the Vauxhall experience. But Vauxhall wasn't contacting owners or prospects directly. The dealer was the first point of contact for purchasing and servicing the vehicle, and third parties were involved in warranty extension programs and car insurance; GM's subsidiary, GMAC, handled financing.

Building a Customer Relationship Management Foundation

In order to provide a more seamless customer experience across these partners, Paul Confrey took over responsibility for upgrading Vauxhall's customer marketing database. He focused on delivering a unified customer relationship management system that would improve customers' experience of doing business with Vauxhall and all of its partners. Each of GM's business partners would continue performing its piece of the puzzle, but they would all be working from the same master customer-strategy system and they would coordinate their efforts much more closely.

Although Vauxhall's marketing agency had been collecting basic customer information since the late 1980s, Vauxhall wasn't really taking advantage of that information, except to execute direct-mail campaigns. Vauxhall's customer-focused project had taken years to get off the ground, but now, suddenly, it had a mission—to improve customers' experiences in dealing with Vauxhall—and some hard deadlines.

Within a year, the new Oracle-based CRM database was fully operational, with 5.5 million current customers and hot prospects gleaned and updated from the old marketing database, car ownership records, and the results of recent lead-generation campaigns. All of Vauxhall's marketing partners—GMAC, GM Card, CGU Insurance, GGT (a direct marketing agency), Direct Dialog, and the SureGuard warranty program—were working off the same database and beginning to coordinate marketing efforts based on what customers wanted.

Vauxhall's customer relationship management program wasn't created in a vacuum; it is the strategic beachhead for GM's European operations. The same customer database tools and the appropriate best practices are being adopted by the other GM divisions throughout Europe

Getting the Dealers to Buy In

The real trick, of course, was convincing Vauxhall's independent dealers that the manufacturer wouldn't be inserting itself between these retailers and their customers. To that end, in mid-1998, Confrey met with Vauxhall's dealer council and explained the progress that had already been made. He told them that he could drive even more business their way by contacting customers on their behalf when it was time to bring their cars in for service and/or when their cars' financing programs were up for renegotiation. The dealer council approved Confrey's plan to pilot this proactive customer-focused program for a year in the south of England, involving 12 of Vauxhall's 450 dealers.

Piloting a Life-Cycle Customer Relationship Management Program

For the customers in the 12-dealer pilot area, the Vauxhall customer relationship management team and its partners took a very proactive approach. They developed a set of key initiatives that were tightly coordinated and tracked, some of which include:

- When it's time for the first service on a new car (12,000 miles or 12 months), a telemarketer from Vauxhall's telemarketing agency, Direct Dialog, calls the customer to remind her that it's time for a service tune-up. The customer is asked if she would like to have the dealer call to schedule an appointment and, if so, which days and times would be most convenient. This information is then passed directly to the dealer's service department, along with the customer's preferred contact phone numbers. In that same call, the customer is reminded that her warranty will be expiring soon and asked if she would like to extend the warranty.
- When a customer's financing deal has reached its "trigger point"—that is, the point at which the customer needs to make a decision about payment plans or refinancing (usually at the three-year anniversary), the telemarketing firm calls the customer and offers her a complete "car valet" service, along with a brand-new loaner car. If the customer agrees, the dealer's representative brings the customer the new car of her choice to try out for two days, while her old car is thoroughly cleaned and its value is appraised. When the salesperson returns the spiffed-up old car, she brings along a contract that shows the customer what it would cost to keep driving the brand-new car (e.g., "For only £45 more pounds per month, you can keep driving this wonderful new car.").

The results from the first nine months of the pilot spoke for themselves. In the 12-dealer area, cross-sells of warranties rose to 30 percent of customers from 11 percent. And dealers' service business increased a whopping 60 percent. But the real clincher was that 90 percent of the customers who took advantage of car valet service and free trial at the trigger point for their financing deals bought the new car! By October 2000, the pilot was extended to include 100 dealers. By early 2001, Confrey expected to have the entire United Kingdom covered.

SELLING DIRECT VIA THE INTERNET

Another part of Paul Confrey's mandate included all customer-facing points of contact: all direct marketing programs, all telemarketing programs, and, of course, the Internet and the Web. At the time, Vauxhall already had a Web site; in fact, the division was the first U.K. car manufacturer to do so. Launched in 1996, it provided core information about Vauxhall's new and used cars, including pricing and financing options. During 1997 and 1998, a number of incremental enhancements made the site more "sticky"—encouraging customers to return over and over again. For example, the TrafficMaster section provided road traffic speeds for all the major highways. It was updated once a minute, so drivers could check traffic conditions before embarking on a trip. Another section, co-sponsored by the Ski Club of Great Britain, targeted customers (or prospects) for Vauxhall's four-wheel drive Frontera model.

Another Web application, Vauxhall BuyPower, was launched in the summer of 1999, enabling prospects to preconfigure their cars online, selecting options and pricing. These prequalified customers were then delivered as leads to the dealers. This game plan worked reasonably well—30,000 customers registered and 5,000 of them actually turned into leads for the dealers—but BuyPower made the dealers nervous about Vauxhall's plans for cutting them out of the loop altogether.

But it wasn't until July 1999 that Nick Reilly got serious about selling cars online. "That's when Nick called me into his office for a chat," Confrey recalls. "Nick is very Internet-literate and he's very aggressive in terms of being first." Reilly gave Confrey the opportunity to "set up some way for consumers to buy cars on the Internet from us. He didn't tell me how to do it; he just said, 'Figure it out.' Of course, Nick realized that the dealers would be a big challenge. He said, 'See how you can get the retailers on your side.' "

Project Team Approach

Confrey quickly pulled together a team of about 20 people from a variety of internal and external groups. The team quickly decided that the best way to sell Vauxhall cars online was to launch with specific, Internet-only car models. These so-called dot-com cars would be configured and ordered via the Net but would be delivered and serviced by the closest dealer, and dealers would still receive a commission on the dot-com models.

The team decided on three popular models for the initial launch, based on Vauxhall's current product lines: the Corsa.com, the Vectra.com, and the Astra.com. These were standard Vauxhall models that were available with the most commonly requested options. But these "special editions" were available at lower prices. They could only be ordered via the Internet. And each car had a distinctive chrome dot-com logo on the side. People would know that its driver was a dot-com kind of person.

Seducing the Dealers

At first, the team had hoped to include a few dealers in its planning process, but they quickly realized that such inclusion would make it impossible to keep the project under wraps. It had to be done as a stealth project. Confrey's team didn't want to leak the plan prematurely to the Vauxhall dealers. Confrey, who had once worked as a car salesman in the mid-1990s, played the role of dealer advocate on the team.

The game plan all along was to get the dealers' buy-in. Without it, the project would be dead in the water. But the team had to aim for a November 1, 1999, launch date, knowing full well that the project might be killed at the last minute. "Anything that affects the retailers has to go before the Franchise Board for approval," Confrey explained. "We scheduled ourselves onto the program for October 5. We were planning to announce to the press on October 14, a few days before the big Birmingham International Motor Show on October 19."

At the meeting, Confrey presented a marketing overview of the Internet landscape. His presentation included demographics—how many of Vauxhall's target customers were already online and how many would be going online—and the fact that the most profitable lifetime customers for the company were going to be Internet early adopters. Then he gave examples of what was happening in the United States, where intermediaries such as Autobytel.com and CarsDirect.com were having a major impact on customers' car-buying practices. These "Yankee" practices were clearly about to hit the U.K. market.

The pitch Confrey made was direct. He stated clearly that the customers now had options, and they could control whom they bought from. Thus, the company had to respond to this power. "We can sit back and let these intermediaries own some of the customer experience or we can take control of the total customer experience. We can offer a car that's unique to Vauxhall on the Net. We aren't trying to cut you out of the deal. This isn't an experiment in selling direct and bypassing the retailer. We don't want World War III. We just want to keep this highly profitable customer segment happy. And we can only do it with your support."

The retailer gross margins were reduced by 3 percent on the dot-com models, but the retailers were promised that they would retain at least as much profit as they did through their offline sales. And because the cars were priced at a good value level, and there would be no price haggling involved, the retailers would be getting pretty much the same commissions. They would simply be taking a different role to earn that commission. They would need to take a demo car to the customer's house for a test drive if required. They would still need to value and accept the customer's trade-in car. And they would have to deliver the new car to the customer and take the old one away. The rest of the time-consuming sales process (interacting with customers about features and functions) would be taken care of through the Web site and by the call center specialists, who would be supporting Internet customers.

"What if someone orders a car online and then changes her mind," the dealers asked. "You're not going to lose money on this," Confrey reassured the board. "Whatever goes wrong, we'll make it good. We'll reimburse you for any costs. We'll do whatever it takes to make this initiative a success."

After three hours of active discussion, Confrey's proposal got the green light to pilot the sale of these special-edition dot-com cars on the Web site for a year. The results would then be evaluated.

THE RESULTS

One of the early phone calls that Vauxhall's customer assistance center received as a result of the prelaunch publicity was from a 60-year-old woman who wanted to be the first Internet customer. Mrs. Tavner wasn't particularly computer-savvy, but she loved the idea of being able to buy a car without the bother of going to a dealership, and she especially liked the whole concept of having her new car delivered directly to her door. Always embarrassed about having to drive an unfamiliar car home from the dealership, where strangers may be watching, she wanted to be able to practice first in her driveway before venturing out on the public roads. So Mrs. Tavner became the first dot-com car buyer when the new site went live at noon on November 1.

In nine months, Vauxhall sold 1,000 dot-com cars, 2 percent of its retail sales volume in that period. "That's all we could handle without ramping up our four-person customer support center," Confrey explained. "Each of the four customer support representatives who are dedicated to the dot-com program can handle about 50 customers per month. And since we agreed to a one-year pilot program, we're not going to push more volume through the site until we've reached our one-year anniversary."

CHANGING THE RULES OF THE CAR-BUYING GAME

The automobile industry in the United Kingdom is under tremendous pressure from angry consumers. By fall 2000, the U.K.'s competitive commission was calling for major changes to be made in the way that cars were being priced and sold to consumers in Britain. Thanks to its dot-com initiative, Vauxhall was more ready than most of its competitors to deal with a new set of rules. As of October 2000, the Franchise Board approved opening up online sales to all Vauxhall model cars. "The key to this being able to happen is the spirit of partnership we have with our retailers. We're not cutting them out; we're changing the game together," said Confrey. This has meant a move to a different pricing structure with fewer "hidden costs" (e.g., financing charges bundled into the price) and a whole new ballgame in terms of Internet sales volumes. Vauxhall became the first automobile manufacturer in the world to offer all of its car models for sale on the Net.

TAKEAWAYS

What can we learn from Vauxhall's experience? Vauxhall dealt with channel conflict by soliciting and receiving buy-in from its dealer council. The company piloted direct sales via the Internet for a year. And it delivered results, both through online car sales and through the cross-selling and upselling of services to all GM Vauxhall customers. Notice that customers want to be able to buy cars direct from the manufacturer via the Internet; yet they are happy to have the dealers, as the manufacturer's representatives, deliver and service their cars.

Customers appreciate the convenience of not having to leave home to purchase a car. And customers are willing to pay a single, no-haggle price. Car dealers can make just as much money on commissions by letting manufacturers make the sale, as long as they're willing to provide the pre- and postsales service.

Vauxhall dealers benefit by letting the manufacturer solicit service business and warranty extensions. The customer benefits by having a seamless experience with the branded Vauxhall customer experience. Vauxhall's coordinated customer initiatives should result in increased customer loyalty to the brand and to the dealer that provides the actual service.

Finally, note that GM Vauxhall used customer scenario-based design. Every offer is organized around a trigger event (e.g., warranty expiration or refinancing deadline) with the outcomes that matter to the customer (e.g., "Get my car serviced and my warranty extended quickly and easily," or "Give me a new car for the same price I'm paying for my current car").

SUGGESTIONS FOR VAUXHALL

What's next for Vauxhall? Both the customer-focused initiative and the Internet sales began as pilot programs, the former within a limited geographic territory and the latter with a few car models and offers. The careful groundwork that Confrey and his team have done should pay off. It's unlikely that any of Vauxhall's U.K. competitors will be able to ramp up as quickly to sell cars direct via the Internet. Vauxhall is moving aggressively to cement its lead on the Internet, and began selling all cars in November 2000.

It's also unlikely that competitors will be able to replicate Vauxhall's ambitious, integrated customer efforts quickly. The power of the combined e-commerce initiative and the customer experience initiative will be hard to beat. Now it's time for Vauxhall to push, full steam ahead, on both the Internet and the CRM front.

Based on customer-focused initiatives and Internet pilots, GM's U.S. operation has a lot to learn from the accomplishments of Vauxhall in the smaller U.K. market. We hope that the GM organizations in other countries build on Vauxhall's learning and don't start off in a different direction. Although consumer behavior is very different in GM's various markets around the world, all customers will appreciate being treated better than they are now. And GM, like every car manufacturer, has to figure out how to make cars easy for customers to buy online, while keeping its dealers in the loop. Building on the learnings of the Vauxhall group and coordinating efforts around the globe may be an organizational challenge, but it's one well worth trying for.

There's a lesson here for every company that wants to use the Web as a touchpoint, but that has an entrenched retail base that could be affected by it. It's actually a simple one: There's no reason the two touchpoints can't coexist, if the company and the channels are really willing to work together. And the auto industry is showing the way, which can only be to the good, especially if, as Mark Hogan, president of e-GM unit predicts, one day *all* auto buyers will go to the Internet before making their buying decisions.

DEMAND CHAIN AND DISTRIBUTION

In a traditional economic system, manufacturers have typically controlled the supply chain—the chain of transactions that accounted for all of the components of a final, manufactured product. At the top of the supply chain were the raw materials that composed the manufactured product. Without such materials, there would be no transactions anywhere else along the supply chain, and no products could be manufactured. In the new, mass-customized economic system, in contrast, it may be more important to manage or control the **demand chain**—the chain of transactions and relationships that lead from the customer up through the various distribution channels to the actual product or service specification process (see Exhibit 14.5). The manufacturer is simply one element of this demand chain. At the base of the demand chain is the end-user customer. Each level considers the level below to be its customer base, and every link in the chain can be viewed as a separate customer base. The demand chain is really just the supply chain viewed from the opposite direction (see Exhibit 14.6).

> In the new, mass-customized economic system, in contrast, it may be more important to manage or control the **demand chain**—the chain of transactions and relationships that lead from the customer up through the various distribution channels to the actual product or service specification process

> The demand chain is really just the supply chain viewed from the opposite direction

Competition for share of customer exists at *every level* of this demand chain. The computer manufacturer, for example, competes with other manufacturers; the wholesale distributor competes with other wholesalers; and the reseller

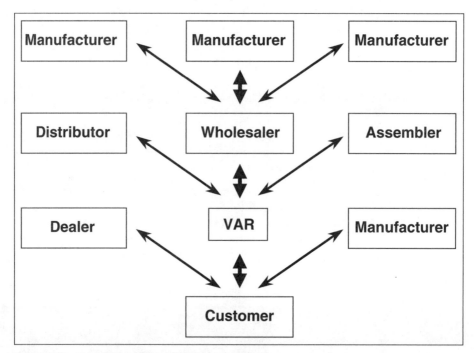

EXHIBIT 14.5   **Demand-Chain Management**

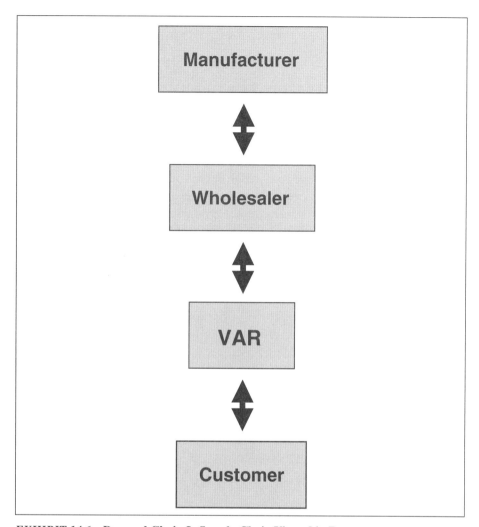

EXHIBIT 14.6 **Demand Chain Is Supply Chain Viewed in Reverse**

competes with other resellers. Each enterprise has its own base of customers and prospects and its own set of competitive issues and business strategies. To create collaborative Learning Relationships with a business customer—which is what each member of the demand chain is—the manufacturing enterprise might find ways to make that business customer more successful or profitable within its own competitive set. Each enterprise in the channel faces the task of generating greater loyalty and protecting unit margins within its own customer base; but it is also part of the customer base of the enterprise it buys from. The manufacturer has to think of such relationships as having two different angles: one between the manufacturer and the channel member, and one between the channel member and its own customer base.

When the manufacturer sells to the wholesaler, this base of "customers" has a wide range of valuations (some very large, while others are niche players), but they have the same basic needs from the manufacturer: For the most part, each wants the entire range of products to be delivered on time and efficiently. The manufacturer's strategy for dealing with wholesale distributors might be a key account sales strategy designed to allocate more time and attention to the very large distributors accounting for the bulk of its product sales, while also attempting to "expand the need set" for all its wholesaler customers, adding services that are more customizable. These services could help serve as a basis for more individualized relationships with individual wholesalers.

From the perspective of most individual wholesalers, the same basic strategies would apply to their own relationships with retailers, because retailers also are a customer base with a high degree of valuation skew, but low differentiation in terms of needs. However, the wholesaler also has to remember that the manufacturer's brand name is on the product, so even though the wholesaler sells the product to a retailer without the direct participation of the product manufacturer, the manufacturer certainly has the potential to create a relationship with the retailer (and with the end-user consumer). If the manufacturer doesn't want to circumvent the wholesaler, then its strategy should be to develop a relationship with the retailer that also respects the wholesaler's own interests. A similar motivation might apply when the manufacturer is considering its relationship with the individual end-user customer. The manufacturer must lock in the loyalty of the individual end user, but it must do so in a way that also respects the interests of the retailer. Each tier of the distribution system represents its own type of customer differentiation.

By managing its supply chain efficiently, an enterprise can reduce its production and distribution costs, boost profit margins, and increase customer satisfaction. Without efficient delivery systems and effective logistics, even the best-designed customer strategies will fall short. Retailers, distributors, and manufacturers alike are focusing on how to incorporate customer-centric principles and customer information into the delivery channel. The next section by Roger Blackwell and Kristina Stephan shows how effective supply chain management meshes with the customer-strategy enterprise.

SUPPLY CHAIN MANAGEMENT AND MANAGING CUSTOMER RELATIONSHIPS

Roger Blackwell
Professor of marketing and logistics, Fisher College of Business, The Ohio State University
Co-author of *Brands That Rock*

Kristina Stephan
Co-author of *Brands That Rock*

Supply chains continue to evolve and become more productive as channel members experience heightened pressures from customers and end users to produce and deliver products they want to buy at the times and places they want to receive them. The need to satisfy customers, coupled with today's hypercompetitive environment, is causing suppliers, manufacturers, wholesalers, and retailers alike to rethink their strategic initiatives with both suppliers and customers. At the forefront of these initiatives is the generation of the service levels and profit margins required for long-term success.

For the most part, supply chains are efficient when it comes to delivering new products to consumers. Thousands of new products are conceived, designed, and produced by the manufacturer; delivered to the marketplace, and made available to consumers. Most move through the supply chain in reasonably efficient and cost-effective ways, due in part to innovative streamlining of the distribution process, improved logistics strategies, and technological advancements.

The glaring shortcoming of a traditional supply chain is the potential of creating and delivering products that end users don't need or don't want to buy. Approximately 80 percent of new products fail in the marketplace, usually because consumers don't buy enough of them to be profitable for supply chain members. Market leaders are beginning to transform the traditional supply chain thinking from the old, left-to-right paradigm into a new paradigm of non-linear, cross-boundary partnering.

SHIFT IN POWER

Throughout history, dominance of the supply chain has shifted among channel members. During the period of American history from the Revolution to the Civil War, the most influential member of the supply chain was the wholesaler, or trader. Traders served as connectors between products from England and U.S. markets. Without these wholesalers, products did not make it to the new colonies for sale to retailers and individuals.

During the period of the Civil War to World War II, manufacturers were usually the most powerful firms in the supply chain. They were in charge of what was produced and ultimately made available for consumers to buy. If they wanted to produce 1 million black cars, they did—regardless of how popular some other colors might potentially be with auto buyers.

During the last half of the century, the era of the megaretailers kicked in. During this time, retailers such as Sears, Circuit City, Toys 'R' Us, and Home Depot began to take more control in the supply chain because they provided a powerful connection between manufacturers and wholesalers to the elusive consumer. When Wal-Mart emerged as the giant among retail giants, it set a new standard for control of what the supply chain would produce and how it would be sold. Although Wal-Mart and its thousands of vendors and partners continue to shape how the world does business, the real power in the supply chain continues to shift to a new and higher power—the consumer.

With myriad products and a morass of distribution alternatives available to them, *consumers* now hold the key to unlocking the future of supply chain management. This type of paradigm shift requires a completely redrawn supply chain—a *demand chain* that caters and responds to customers and is facilitated by a customer-centric model.

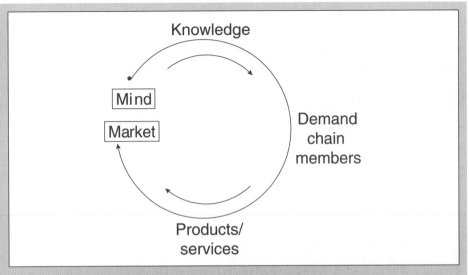

EXHIBIT 14.7   **Product and Information Flow in the Demand Chain**

The key is that *consumer behavior, consumer analyses,* and *customer-focused principles* fuel the direction of the demand chain. Rather than building and operating their supply chain from manufacturer to market, the best firms are creating alliances with channel partners best able to fulfill consumers' needs and wants, solve their problems, and conform to their lifestyles.

The demand chain gets its name from serving the needs of consumers and focusing on the demand, not just the supply, side of the equation. As Exhibit 14.7 shows, a demand chain represents a circular process that encompasses the flow of information, feedback, and ideas from consumers through the various supply chain entities and back again to consumers (collectively defined as the *market*) in the form of consumer-driven products and services.[7] The key is that *consumer behavior, consumer analyses,* and *customer-focused principles* fuel the direction of the demand chain. Rather than building and operating their supply chain from manufacturer to market, the best firms are creating alliances with channel partners best able to fulfill consumers' needs and wants, solve their problems, and conform to their lifestyles. One key is the flexibility of the manufacturer to be proactive in adapting to changing customer requirements,[8] thereby affecting the speed with which the channel can react to consumer wishes.

CHANGING NATURE OF COMPETITION

In the past, retailers fought retailers for dominance in the marketplace, while wholesalers and manufacturers followed suit. Each entity was strong enough to

---

[7]Roger Blackwell, *From Mind to Market* (New York: HarperBusiness, 1997).

[8]Donald J. Bowersox, Patricia J. Daugherty, Cornelia L. Droege, Richard N. Germain, and Dale S. Rogers, *Logistical Excellence* (Burlington, MA: Digital Press, 1992).

take on its own competitors. Whether these companies survived and flourished or languished and folded was largely a result of how they performed in relation to their peers.

Today, the rules of battle are being rewritten. Organizations will still duke it out in the marketplace, but not just against individual competitors in their field. Rather, they are often fortified by supply chain alliances. In essence, *competitive dominance is achieved by an entire supply chain, with battles fought supply chain versus supply chain.*

This change in philosophy has affected marketing strategies for many leading firms in a variety of industries. They realize that effective marketing strategies can no longer be built upon the activities of a single organization. Manufacturers as large as General Motors and Nestle, retailers as large as Wal-Mart and Carrefour, and wholesalers as large as Cardinal Health and Ingram Micro are seeking new partners and new methods of managing the total flow of goods and services to meet the changing needs of *consumers*. Strategy is shifting from the scope of a single organization to partnerships and alliances involving many organizations.

The importance of supply chain partnerships is perhaps most evident in online retailing, or e-tailing. Getting Web sites right (finding just the right combination of glitz, glamour, and functionality) represents the easy part of e-tailing. The key to profitability and loyalty lies, however, in what happens after an online order is placed. Pure-play dot-coms without established supply chain partnerships and no experience[9] in retailing found it next to impossible to solve the logistics and distribution problems that arose with direct-to-consumer distribution. This became particularly evident during the 1999 holiday season, when parents ordered presents and toys online only to have them delivered weeks *after* the holidays ended. Firms like eToys and Pets.com scrambled to find partners with experience in distribution to help them fulfill orders promptly. The $150-plus million needed to build distribution outlets and customer service centers[10] dried up after second-round funding had all but disappeared. It became clear that e-tailers were competing not just with established retailers (and the brands they had built over the years), but with their entrenched and well-tested distribution systems as well.

CUSTOMER-FOCUSED SUPPLY CHAIN

As CRM enhances the relationships between individual buyers and sellers, the demand chain principle is strengthened and, in many instances, can be taken to the next level of customer intimacy. Not only can customers create products

---

[9]Heather Green, Rochelle Sharpe, and Arlene Weintraub, "How to Reach John Q. Public," *BusinessWeek* (March 26, 2001), pp. 132–133.

[10]Michael J. Mandel and Robert D. Hof, "Rethinking the Internet," *BusinessWeek* (March 26, 2001), pp. 117–122.

tailored to their specifications and needs, but they can also create the distribution and transportation functions to meet their needs—dictating where the product is shipped (to the home, office, or a store for pick-up) and when it should arrive. Dell has adopted a demand chain model that builds computers based on the specifications of individual customers; in turn, it has had to create one-to-one supply chains to design, assemble, and fulfill customized orders—often, orders of one.

Today's B2B models are the foundation for tomorrow's B2B2C strategies—those that look further down the supply chain, all the way to the end user. Covisint, the new-breed e-commerce conglomerate founded by General Motors, DaimlerChrysler, Ford, Renault, and Nissan, expects to handle as much as $750 billion in annual purchases by automakers and suppliers. It links the makers of engines, tires, steel, glass, and all the other components needed to make a car via the Internet. Its goals include reducing overall costs by streamlining the procurement processes between buyers and sellers, expanding the reach for suppliers of components, and achieving greater reach for buyers. But this model does not stop with the B2B functions; it deals directly with producing and delivering built-to-order cars to consumers more efficiently and at lower costs.

How far off into the future is the reality of the Covisint model, especially as the success of this business unit is far from assured? From a business standpoint, the reality is here. From a consumer standpoint, it still resides in futuristic fables and dreams of possibilities that lie ahead. Imagine logging on to the Web, selecting interior leather colors and grade, audio equipment, paint color, and wheel treatments; submitting the order and payment; and receiving the car of your dreams a short time later, perhaps in a matter of days.

Will it work? No one really knows at this point. Covisint may or may not succeed, as a business. But the potential rewards are immense, even if this model only replicates and improves speed and transaction costs in the existing supply chain. So whether it's Covisint or a successor, sooner or later the model's success is likely.

CREATING CUSTOMER-DRIVEN DEMAND CHAINS

Supply chain management has evolved over the years to provide strategic and competitive advantages to the enterprises involved in efficient and successful supply chains. Demand chain management adds an emphasis to delivering to the marketplace what consumers will buy. Demand chains unite channel members with the common goal of delighting customers and solving consumer problems by completing traditional supply chain functions and focusing on the following activities:

- Gathering and analyzing knowledge about consumers, their problems, and their unmet needs to form a clear picture of the market (and to promote innovation through free information flow).[11]

---

[11]Lisa C. Troy, David M. Szymanski, and P. Rajan Varadarajan, "Generating New Product Ideas: An Initial Investigation of the Role of Market Information and Organizational Characteristics," *Journal of the Academy of Marketing Science* 29, no. 1 (2001), pp. 89–101.

- Identifying potential supply chain partners to perform the functions needed to create and deliver products/services to end users.
- Developing communication channels between models, including using the Web to transmit shipment, order, and inventory status.[12]
- Sharing knowledge about consumers and customers, technology, and logistics with demand chain members in order to align sales forecasts and improve forecasting accuracy.[13]
- Developing, in conjunction with other firms in the demand chain, products and services that solve customers' problems better than existing solutions.
- Shifting the functions that need to be performed by the channel to the organization that can perform them most effectively and efficiently.
- Developing and executing the best logistics, transportation, and distribution methods to deliver products and services to consumers in the marketplace in the format desired by consumers.
- Developing and implementing CRM programs to build stronger relationships with customers and gather customer-specific information that will help direct future marketing and channel activities to meet customers' needs and wants.
- Managing and interpreting customer data to drive the supply chain in the long run.

As supply chains begin to function as single entities and compete with other partnerships, building and maintaining strong relationships throughout the supply chain becomes a necessity. Sharing of information, benefits, and burdens and collaborative processes among channel members are important in creating a solid supply chain relationship.[14]

Let's refer back to the Covisint example. Today, manufacturers make cars, based on their attempts to predict consumer demand. With Covisint, a more accurate picture of demand and supply will be available to all levels in the supply chain in the form of current available inventories, supplier capacities, accurate customer demand information, and alerts when demand exceeds supply. Shared information throughout the channel fosters better forecasting and supply planning, as well as collaborative production planning and scheduling. Through Internet-based collaboration, supply chain partners will be encouraged to participate in the development of new products and processes—sharing information and ideas freely. This is expected to increase speed-to-market and decrease the risk of creating products that the market doesn't want. The final outcome of this demand chain is expected to be greater customer satisfaction, greater loyalty, and lower prices.

---

[12]Steve Geary and Jan Paul Zonnenberg, "What It Means to Be Best in Class," *Supply Chain Management Review* 4, no. 3 (July 2000), pp. 42–48.

[13]Peter Bradley, "The Certainty of Uncertainty," *Supply Chain Management Review* 5, no. 2 (2001).

[14]Bernard LaLonde, "Building a Supply Chain Relationship," *Supply Chain Management Review* (Fall 1998).

In creating a shift from supply to demand orientation, several misconceptions occur:

- *Consumers buy from retailers.* Consumers buy from supply chains, and their buying choices affect the future success of each partner and the entire supply chain.
- *Business-to-business firms don't need to monitor consumer trends.* All customer/industrial demand for third-party providers is derived from consumer demand. Business-to-business customers will not order more parts or contract for more transportation if consumers are buying fewer of their end products.
- *Small firms will be left out of the most powerful supply chains.* Clout in the channel will no longer be determined just by size; it will be determined by information about, alliances with, and loyalty from consumers. But because size still counts, the smaller, independent firms found in fragmented industries are banding together for collective bargaining power.
- *Marketing strategies and goals should be based only on an individual firm's activities.* Demand chain partners realize that effective marketing strategies must increase their scope beyond just a single organization and consider the activities and goals of the entire supply chain.

EFFECTS OF TECHNOLOGY AND E-COMMERCE ON SUPPLY CHAINS

The Internet and e-commerce have affected supply chain management in many ways. In addition to reconfiguring supply chains to meet individual, direct orders fostered by online sales to consumers, supply chain managers must understand how to capitalize on the efficiencies available to them via the Internet.

Regardless of which business a company may be in, certain marketing functions must be completed in order to move its products from inception to point of consumption. These *universal marketing functions* are inescapable business activities required to get goods from producer to consumer. They include the *exchange functions* (buying and selling), the *physical distribution functions* (transporting, distributing, and storing), and *facilitating functions* (standardizing, financing, risk taking, and securing marketing information). These marketing functions might be completed by any channel member, or shifted from one channel member to another, but they must be completed in any case.

Wal-Mart and The Limited became retail mavericks in the twentieth century by mastering several marketing functions, giving each of them significant advantages over their respective competitors. Wal-Mart attacked department stores where they were most vulnerable: price and value (especially in rural America where department stores believed the demand too small to be worth their attention). The Limited attacked department stores where they were strongest: selling fashion apparel with personal service. But these retailers made real strides over competitors by achieving excellence in distribution and *logistics*—the design, implementation, and control of the physical movement of products from manu-facturing to consumption, including materials management, transportation, warehousing, and distribution. And studies indicate that logistics does influence a firm's overall performance, including its ability to satisfy customers.[15]

And that's where we were by the late 1990s, when e-tailing burst onto the retail scene with more fanfare than any innovation of the past. E-tailers soon dis-covered that unless they could perform all of the universal marketing functions with excellence, they would struggle to remain viable in the market. Paramount among those functions is logistics. On average, marketing costs make up about one-half of the cost of consumer products, and about half of the marketing cost usually involves logistics. Logistics functions are far more expensive for most online retail operations than for location-based retailers. Certainly, digital prod-ucts such as stocks and electronic airline tickets move easily through cyber-space; however, the functions and costs of selling clothing, home products, and other "stuff" electronically mirror those of catalog retailers—which on average are lower in profitability than comparable retail stores.

THE INTERNET: CHANGING THE WAY BUYERS AND SELLERS CONNECT AND INTERACT

Projections for B2B online transactions are staggering. Merrill Lynch projected $2.5 trillion of B2B e-commerce sales, and Gartner Group envisioned $7.8 tril-lion in global sales, both for the early 2000s. Compare these to the forecasts in the mere $100 billion range for B2C, and one can understand the focus on the B2B arena.

The Internet brings buyers and sellers together, whether it's through a firm's own Web site or through portals that may include other firms. When multiple firms are accessed through a third-party portal, they may be called hubs (or e-hubs), hubs and spokes, exchanges, or marketplaces. Portals can be **sell-side, buy-side,** horizontal, vertical, or a combination. Some exchanges are sponsored by suppliers themselves (sell-side) and some are sponsored by groups of buyers (buy-side), as Covisint illustrates. Some are sponsored by trade associations or industry groups, and some are owned and sponsored by commercial organiza-tions in the business of establishing and operating these exchanges and perhaps selling the software, servers, and other "solutions" needed to operate them. Increasingly, they are organized by a combination.

Sell-Side Portals

As sites representing one firm, such as those of Dell or GE, become effective as e-commerce portals, groups of suppliers feel the need to join together to provide

---

[15]Michael Treacy, "The Importance of Logistics Efficiency to Customer Service and Firm Perfor-mance," *The International Journal of Logistics Management* 9, no. 2 (1998), pp. 65–81.

their own portal. The goal is to reach many buyers, including some new customers, for the benefit of the group's members. Often the impetus arises in a trade association, which hopes to perform sales functions at lower costs for its members and perhaps to generate revenues from sales for the association. Some portals are owned by a single firm just hoping to make a lot of money aggregating catalogs from a group of suppliers to attract a larger audience. These catalog hubs work best in fragmented industries where this type of information consolidation is helpful to the customer.

Buy-Side Portals

When buyers in an industry get together to organize an exchange, they are called buy-side, or procurement, portals. They usually are organized by relatively few firms to obtain price advantages and perhaps expand the reach to additional suppliers. Fortified by "strength in numbers," it may be difficult for suppliers to decline participation in this type of buying consolidation program, especially in the *many-to-one* purest form of a buy-side portal or the *many-to-few* portals such as Covisint.

PaperExchange.com is an example of a typical buy-side portal that offers its member-buyers in the pulp and paper industry direct access to broader supply sources on a global basis. This type of model works best with replenishment contracts, something that is typical of the paper industry. PaperExchange.com enables buyers to access sellers directly, thereby dislodging paper distributors from the supply channel and, in theory, reducing costs and transaction fees. PaperSpace does not charge buyers for its services, but receives a 3 percent commission from sellers on transactions conducted through the site.

Market Exchanges

The distinction between sell-side and buy-side portals, although pertinent in understanding how a firm can benefit from involvement in each, is negligible in the long run because it takes lots of both genres to make a portal or hub effective. It is easier simply to group these sites as **market exchanges.**

The significance of market exchanges is that they allow all firms up and down the supply chain to buy most anything they need or want on the Web, thereby creating value in the buyer-seller relationship through reduced costs.[16] Some markets are vertical in nature, with the buying and selling of products of interest to a specific industry, while others are horizontal in nature, cutting across a wide range of industries and products. The most common application in both is maintenance, repair, operating (MRO) products, such as sprockets, paint, and conveyor belts, which tend to be low-value goods with relatively high transaction costs. These products, while used by nearly every business, may not be core products for a company's operations.

[16]Joseph P. Cannon and Christian Homburg, "Buyer-Supplier Relationships and Customer Firm Costs," *Journal of Marketing* 65, no. 1 (2001), pp. 29–43.

The hope for exchanges is disintermediation. If a company is a wholesaler or distributor of peripheral or noncore products, the threat of being eliminated from the channel is higher than in most any other areas of new-era commerce. With commodities, the buyer is willing to buy from anyone with the lowest price. But, if a manufacturer is thinking about selling through exchanges, that firm will do well to remember that its largest distributors may decide to cut its products from their offerings because that manufacturer has, in effect, become a competitor rather than just a supplier.

There are some areas in which exchanges work well, such as those that facilitate buying and selling in markets that fluctuate greatly in capacity of supply and volatility in demand.

After examining the successes and failures in exchanges, one may conclude that:

- Exchanges most likely to be successful are in industries in which *buyers* force sellers to enter the exchange. The more concentrated and powerful the *sellers*, the less motivation they have to enter the exchange.
- Management must understand motivation and human behavior in the industry. If industry members don't like Internet-based exchanges, they won't use them, regardless of how compelling the reasons to join.
- Exchanges that provide proprietary software or other technologies that can add value beyond the existing methods of commerce are most likely to succeed.[17]

MIGRATION OF THE SUPPLY CHAIN TO THE INTERNET

In the 1980s and 1990s, enterprises mostly used Electronic Data Interface (EDI) to buy and sell from each other. Large firms like General Electric, General Motors, and Wal-Mart built systems to increase efficiency and decrease costs through supplier/vendor electronic ordering and communication. These corporate giants pioneered e-commerce with their supply chain partners, achieving fast growth, improved profits, and big payoffs in asset management. The advances possible with EDI required dedicated terminals and lines that were cost-efficient mostly for a few large firms and their trading partners. By developing software and integration processes for basic commerce functions, they paved the way for an Internet-based solution.

Retailers, distributors, manufacturers, and other supply chain members are now banding together to migrate their supply chains to the Internet. Thanks to the Internet, the efficiencies that EDI brought to a few large firms are now possible for millions of medium-sized and smaller firms. The supply chains once composed of elite, large firms able to invest big bucks in the development of EDI systems are now open to small firms with Internet capabilities.

[17]Roger Blackwell and Kristina Stephan, *Customers Rule! Why the E-commerce Honeymoon Is Over and Where Winning Businesses Go from Here* (New York: Crown Business, 2001).

MANAGING THE SUPPLY CHAIN

Successful and efficient supply chains must consist of well-managed companies, working together to create customer-driven products, services, and buying experiences. **Supply chain management** is the process of coordinating the flow of information, goods, and services among members of the distribution channel. Some of the goals of supply chain management are increased innovation, decreased costs, conflict resolution within the channel, and enhanced communication and involvement of channel members.[18] Conflicts within the channel may result when one member engages in behavior that could be destructive to the relationship.[19] For example, when some Home Depot vendors expressed interest in selling directly to consumers online, they received strong letters from Home Depot discouraging such actions. The value of the relationship to Home Depot and distribution in its more than 800 stores was too valuable to risk.

Efficiencies in the channel are gained through economies of scale, when the channel produces, distributes, and transports large quantities of the same product to a few distribution points. Today, channel management is not just about managing customers or predicting customer behavior in order to offer a standardized experience. As more customized products are created, supply chain management will have to focus on decreasing the costs associated with differentiated products and channels, and that means focusing on long-term, mutually beneficial relationships between suppliers and customers.[20]

Effective channel management utilizes knowledge about individual customers to provide the right mix—and levels of services—to distinct customer segments in the most economic manner. Suppliers must manage channels flexibly and creatively. This means using differing formats within the same channels and alternative channels to deliver the desired service and product bundles to the target customer segments. Grouping customers by order behavior allows firms to offer appropriate logistics service arrangements.[21]

WHAT WILL THE SUPPLY CHAIN OF THE FUTURE LOOK LIKE?

The explicit reason for creating many of the market exchanges described here is to bring buyers and sellers together directly, cutting out the wholesalers (or distributors) that currently handle two-thirds of the commercial transactions for physical products. But if disintermediation occurs in the exchange-based B2B

[18]Louis E. Boone and David l. Kurtz, *Contemporary Marketing*, 10th ed. (Harcourt, 2001).

[19]Jonathon D. Hibbard, Nirmalya Kumar, and Louis W. Stern, "Examining the Impact of Destructive Acts in Marketing Channel Relationships," *Journal of Marketing Research* 38 (February 2001), pp. 45–61.

[20]Gwyn Groves and Vassilios Valsamakis, "Supplier-Customer Relationships and Company Performance," *The International Journal of Logistics Management* 9, no. 2 (1998), pp. 51–64.

[21]Danielle J.M. Van der Veeken and Werner G.M.M. Rutten, "Logistics Service Management: Opportunities for Differentiation," *The International Journal of Logistics Management* 9, no. 2 (1998), pp. 91–98.

marketplace, who will perform the required business functions that many wholesalers perform today?

The wholesale industry gained power in the supply chain by performing functions that other companies either couldn't or wouldn't perform as efficiently as the distributor. Today there are more than 150,000 wholesaler-distributors, accounting for more than $4.4 trillion in sales. About 6.5 million people work for distribution firms, handling everything from ball bearings to baseballs, with most (51 percent) in firms with sales below $1 million.

Distributors exist because they increase efficiency of supply channels and reduce the costs of products for other members of the distribution channel by reducing the number of transactions. Without distributors, every seller would have to contact every buyer, and every buyer would have to contact every seller, a very expensive endeavor in terms of labor, packaging, transportation, distribution, and supply chain management.

If "transactions" were just a matter of placing and receiving orders, that function could be easily replaced with an e-portal, but transactions include much more. Wholesalers' functions include gathering information about the needs of the buyer, making a sales contact, picking and storing products for each buyer in the assortment that fits specific buyers' needs, and packing the goods so they arrive unharmed. The transaction also means scheduling deliveries to arrive during the precise "window" of availability at the destination. It also includes assessing the creditworthiness of the buyer, assuming credit risk, providing technical information on products, and standing ready to correct problems or accept returns if something goes wrong with the transaction.

A closer examination of exchanges reveals that they aren't as likely to create disintermediation as they are to create *reintermediation*—the addition of another step in the supply chain. Given that the functions of marketing can be shifted but not eliminated, the addition of Internet-based transactions has the potential for increasing costs when added to the existing portfolio of transaction methods.

Companies will continue to experiment with e-commerce, sorting out which functions can be sourced online and which will be sourced offline. Supply chain managers must monitor trends occurring in the areas of logistics, technology, and customer buying behavior. Their knowledge must address the capability and likelihood of retailers or manufacturers assuming the functions traditionally performed by intermediaries. The most valuable (and costly) functions are the most difficult to shift to direct channels, making distintermediation among bricks-and-mortar distributors and manufacturers less likely. The existing bricks-and-mortar manufacturers and distributors thrive, however, only if they continue to perform with excellence the functions that don't migrate well online, and develop their own Web sites and portals to perform the functions that do.

ROLE OF CRM IN DEVELOPING AND
NURTURING SUPPLY CHAIN RELATIONSHIPS

The strength of the supply chain is determined in part by the strength of the relationships between channel members. Technology enables relationships between data, but the strength of those still rests on the personal relationships between the people in each entity of the supply chain. Managing customer relationships will play an increasingly important role in designing and strengthening relationships between channel partners, ultimately increasing the supply chain's productivity.

Customer-focused principles, when applied throughout the supply chain, may:

- Create a shift from product-centric to customer-strategy planning and forecasting.
- Identify buying preferences of customers for related products across multiple channels.
- Allow sharing of data about customers and buying preferences up and down the supply chain.
- Create collaborative and more accurate forecasts for various partners in the channel based on sales and other data collected with customer management software.
- Introduce analytics that identify causal factors in customer behavior.
- Reduce inventory and markdowns associated with excess production by supply chain partners.

Many developments in the market continue to improve supply chain management and logistics efficiency. Some of the forces converging on channel partners are technology and information exchange, quality, customer service encounters and concerns, distribution systems and costs, and speed-to-market.

Businesses need to look beyond how these forces affect them and their supply chain partners and toward how these forces affect end customers—an added twist to traditional supply chain management. When analyzed from a corporate standpoint, end-use forces will determine how things are done in the supply chain and how best practices of supply chain operations will emerge in the future. The effect is primarily on the process of supply chain management: how firms manage the various functions that need to be completed to produce and deliver goods to end users. But when analyzed from a consumer standpoint, forces such as technology and changing lifestyles will help determine *what* is done. Customer characteristics, many captured with sophisticated customer-focused tools and technology, will ultimately influence the mission and goals of supply chain integration and management.

SIDEBAR 14.2
Online B2B Exchanges

Rapid growth in online exchanges is reshaping supply chain management. Vertical exchanges exist in particular industries; the more obscure and narrowly focused the industry is, the more usefulness can often be obtained from a vertical exchange. Horizontal exchanges link buyers and sellers within a certain discipline, rather than within

SIDEBAR 14.2 *(continued)*

an industry. A B2B exchange is simply a mechanism for ensuring that the supply of a product or service meets demand for that product in an efficient and timely way.

An enterprise can do business at a B2B exchange without suffering any of the "friction" of thumbing through old contact meeting notes, business card files, or address books. Moreover, the pricing model used by an exchange can be altered to fit the type of commodity or product being sold. Not just auctions, but English auctions, Dutch auctions, reverse auctions, private auctions. And not just haggling over individual prices, but sealed bids, call markets, and multiple-attribute auctions.[a] Exchanges add value to the transaction by developing a relationship between the buyer and the seller. Auctions tend to replace relationships with the purest characteristic of business transactions: selling the item for the highest price to the bidder willing to bid the most.

A B2B exchange can also offer a number of additional services. It could describe itself as a marketplace, although a more apt term might be shopping mall. At such an exchange, sellers offer technical data specifications, pictures, diagrams, or maps, but the site might also feature related products and services, order histories, financing options, and so forth. Probably at the top of the food chain of B2B exchanges is the vertical Web portal, sometimes called an *affinity portal, vertiport,* or *vortal.* This is a site not only for consummating e-commerce transactions, but also for acquiring information, education, and other services associated with a particular business issue, process, or problem.

Portals have evolved to meet the needs of the corporate market, offering a central entry point to information from numerous sources. Pure corporate portals provide a single, easy-to-access starting point for an enterprise's own internal constituents to locate information, participate in a business process, or to collaborate with other users. They can be resources for employees, suppliers, partners, or stockholders, serving a variety of roles, from supply chain extranet to employee-focused intranet.

The mission of an online exchange is to create new buyer-seller relationships and opportunities; to streamline, strengthen, and customize existing relationships; and to reduce the cost of doing business in highly competitive, often fragmented markets such as apparel, and particularly in commodity businesses such as oil, steel, plastics, chemicals, and farming. Exchanges offer fully automated systems that reduce suppliers' transaction processing costs, lower buyers' purchasing costs, and shorten order-to-delivery cycle time. For some enterprises doing business this way, profit margins will increase. A META Group study noted that investment priorities will shift to accommodate the trend toward installing and integrating supply chain systems. META projects that marketing will decline as a prime investment focus, from 77 to 41 percent.[b] According to the same study, customer service and support, as a priority, will drop from 69 to 54 percent, and direct sales investments from 65 percent to 44 percent. Conversely, distribution and logistics systems will attract greater investment focus, growing from 39 to 43 percent; inventory management from 32 to 34 percent; and supply chain management from 28 to 34 percent. Of course, this assumes you can draw a line through the blur between demand chain and supply chain!

Online exchanges are born primarily out of frustration over the current limitations of existing business models. The most common complaint is industry fragmentation. The steel industry, for instance, is highly fragmented and has been unprofitable for many years. The steel industry lacks a central marketplace, and there are hundreds of thousands of end users, including mills, service centers, and fabricators. In 1999, an

---

SIDEBAR 14.2 *(continued)*

··

online exchange called e-STEEL was formed with free membership for buyers and sellers of steel. Sellers were not charged for listing products, but paid commissions based on the value of each transaction. Buyers could post a request, negotiate on price, and receive offers tailored to them; or sellers could opt to auction an item. E-STEEL maintains the confidentiality of each bid and individual transaction. The site gives buyers and sellers the power to mirror their existing relationships on the Web. Users can customize their reach to customers and markets based on existing relationships, pricing structures, and distribution arrangements. For example, sellers can offer the same product to different customers under different conditions. Thus, long-term customers might get an offer for a particular item with certain conditions, while others get the same item offered with different conditions. Similarly, buyers may send inquiries to one supplier, several preferred suppliers, or to a universe of potential suppliers.

E-STEEL suppliers can selectively choose who receives permission to view their portion of the site, and buyers can opt out of receiving information from up to 20 companies. Through STEEL DIRECT, buyers and sellers control the online distribution and accessibility of their own often sensitive and highly competitive information. Other features include members' ability to exchange e-mail and to save searches and postings for future use. E-STEEL is also continually tackling systems-integration issues. Some exchanges provide an order-tracking feature—called *auto messaging*— that allows buyers to trace their orders through every step of the production cycle, including components that get outsourced and then returned to be incorporated into the final product. Because the process runs in real time, buyers can make adjustments if problems or delays occur. (Is this "distribution" or "customer service"? Does it matter?)

Once a user is recognized by the exchange, the site becomes highly personalized. One time-saving tool is DATAJET, which enables sellers to upload product inventory information from their systems into a user's private "holding bin" on the e-STEEL exchange. A seller might have a spreadsheet with 60 specifications relating to each product, and manually entering this much data for each steel product would be labor-intensive; thus, it is in a seller's interest to enter each field, as any additional attribute might represent additional value for a buyer. With DATAJET, the supplier can inform the user of these valuable attributes without additional effort, leveraging the information that's already in his system. Second, because e-STEEL automatically updates this inventory information for orders concluded on the site, it is less work for a seller to execute transactions via the site, as opposed to offline.

An exchange needs both buyers and sellers—and to succeed it will need to address the needs of both. Successful exchanges adhere to customer-focused principles and the continual improvement of related functionality. They need to devote time to customer relationship analytics and expand strategic alliance bases quickly, in addition to meeting the basic requirements of a good customer experience. A good exchange should *solve problems* for its visitors. A corporate customer should be able to use a B2B exchange as an access point for increasing its profit or revenue, reducing its costs, improving its sales or production cycle, or improving its own customer relationships. An exchange must be designed not just to connect buyers and sellers, but to develop relationships with them—and sometimes between them.

A B2B exchange should set its long-term goals on generating revenue and customer loyalty by offering a variety of value-added services, including transaction

SIDEBAR 14.2 *(continued)*

history maintenance, operation consulting, automatic replenishment, data storage, and technology entanglement. The more an exchange can help a customer find the products it needs to conduct its business efficiently, the more the customer will return.

Ultimately, the B2B exchange needs to organize everything around individual customer needs. Different customers will need different things, even at an exchange that deals in commodity products. By organizing the entire site around customer needs, rather than around product varieties, or service selection, an exchange can position itself to create relationships with its users, whether they are buyers *or* sellers. If the exchange deals with commodity products, it will need to emphasize value-added services such as the ones mentioned. Even though the customer may buy the same commodity products, different users are still likely to have different inventory issues, different payment processes, different ordering parameters, and perhaps different manufacturing or delivery processes.

[a]Don Peppers and Martha Rogers, PhD. *One to One B2B* (New York: Doubleday Books), 2001.
[b]META Group, "E-Reality Sets In," 2000; available at: *www.metagroup.com.*

SIDEBAR 14.3
Challenge of Channels

Bill Millar
Business writer

Suppose you have been named chief channel manager of a large enterprise, and the CEO wants a report, by close of business tomorrow, on the thinking behind the current performance of, and the future plans for, your company's relevant strategies.

Here is your company profile:

- You are a global brand, but you do not—at least not today—conduct transactions directly with end users. In other words, you do not *own* the end customer, but instead rely on your channel partners (B2B) to sell, install, and service your products (B2C). Nonetheless, your enterprise recognizes the need to focus more on customers and less on products. Your products are becoming increasingly complex, your customers need expert advice, and the concern is that you may need to do a better job of training your channel partners in sales, installation, and service.

- More than a dozen major retailers carry your product lines—and that is just in the United States. The top four retailers worldwide represent more than half of your sales, but only a quarter of your profitability. Each of your channel partners has its own target margins, along with its own unique sets of customer service, return, warranty, and related policies, and capabilities. You have an extranet tied in to your company's ERP systems, and this confers real-time pricing and inventory information to the majority of your partners and, at the same time, helps your company gather valuable data. But this system handles only a minority of your total sales.

SIDEBAR 14.3 *(continued)*

....

- Your three largest channel distributors have their own order/fulfillment systems. Because of their high volume, you are compelled to work through their systems—even though you find these systems inadequate for your more end-customer-focused mission. There is a growing secondary market in your products—last year's production that was overbought by a channel partner (or two or three) then dumped en masse to discounters. This concerns your CEO, as it could be training customers to defer purchases.

What should the CEO expect you to know? What will *you* need to know to competently advise your enterprise? Some potential questions to think about are:

- Are our channel partners adding value? Do they generate sales leads? Do they customize our intermediate goods to meet the eventual needs of the consumer? Do they add some set of essential, customized services based on intimate knowledge of their target end users? Are certain partners more valuable to end customers than others?

- Are our channel partners collecting the right sorts of customer data? Do they have adequate sophistication in mining this information to more accurately anticipate and address the needs of customers? If they do not, should we do it and how can we assist or perhaps intervene? What can we do to promote a higher degree of one-to-one thinking and effectiveness?

- Are our suppliers throwing darts to anticipate demand? Or are they using a relationship-oriented approach to more accurately mate their orders and inventory levels to customers' needs?

- Are our channel partners sharing customer intelligence that could be used to improve manufacturing, product-development, and logistic processes between all appropriate points—your company especially—along the value-chain? Are certain partners more capable than others? What can be done to encourage capable mining of data and the sharing of appropriate intelligence?

- How collaborative are our partners in terms of operations? What early-warning or feedback mechanisms are in place? Are we made aware of possible design issues in a timely manner? Of installation or connectivity problems? Of pricing, demand, or related logistics factors? How effective are our partners in detecting such patterns, and how capably do they enable us to respond to changing end-customer needs and demand?

- How profitable are our relationships with specific channels? Are certain channel partners more valuable to us than others? What concrete measures can we employ to more accurately assess the performance of each relationship? If we have this knowledge, what are we doing with it?

- How profitable is our relationship to our channel partners? Do they sell our products exclusively or are we pitted against competitors? Are we doing everything we can to make it easier for our channel partners to promote our products more aggressively than the competition's?

- What variations in pricing exist for our products? Are the various channels confusing to our end customers? Are we optimizing profitability? Are we contributing needlessly to any degree of channel conflict?

> ### SIDEBAR 14.3 *(continued)*
>
> ···
>
> - What variations are there in service and support for our products? Do certain channel partners support our brand more effectively? Is there a way to encourage comparable best practices among our other channel members?
>
> - What are we doing to better support our channel partners? Do they have access to the latest information relating to design, installation, and service issues? Are they being made aware, in a timely manner, of emerging issues? How would they rate our support? What investment is warranted in more capable support?

SUMMARY

Our discussion of distribution channel issues that affect the customer-strategy enterprise now turns to consumer-specific issues. Businesses traditionally have made their customers come to their products through product placement strategies, mass marketing, and effective stocking of store shelves. Customer-focused business models will rely heavily on an integration of many different consumer sales channels. And enterprise will ensure that the customer who buys a product in its store will be treated just as she likes to be treated when she buys from its Web site.

An increasing number of manufacturers and retailers are bringing their products directly to consumers. The burgeoning consumer-direct channel, which is enabling enterprises to establish more intimate customer relationships, is the subject of the next chapter, in which we consider the "store of the future."

FOOD FOR THOUGHT

1. Imagine the following scenario: You, a parent of a very large family that generates lots of dirty clothes, get the following offer: ABC Corporation wants to get a sample of your water, find out how your kids get dirty, and formulate detergent just for your family, who are clearly MVCs for any detergent seller. The offer continues: Rather than haul home big boxes of detergent frequently, ABC will deliver directly to your door, using adjustable automatic replenishment (meaning it will estimate how much you think you'll use, and then automatically supply you; moreover, you will get a postage-free card in each box so you can easily speed up or slow down the rate of delivery). How much will this cost? The price you usually pay when you clip a coupon, but you won't need to bother with coupons or waiting for red-ribbon days. Now the coup de grace: If you agree to buy all your detergent from ABC for the next five years, at the end of that period, ABC will give you a new washer and dryer. Consider:

   - Does Tide still have "brand awareness" in the household?
   - Does Tide get any more sales?

- What brand *does* your family buy? (Hint: It doesn't matter anymore, but we could easily put your family's name on it!)
- Why does this work economically?
- What percentage of families nationwide would be good customers for this promotion?
- Now for the kicker: Who makes the detergent ABC sells? Why can't Procter & Gamble sell Tide this way?
- What *else* could ABC sell your family, now that it has a relationship with you?

2. How can a company use new technologies and IDIC tasks to build a Learning Relationship not possible before e-commerce? (Think about the total cost of a relationship versus cost of products.)

3. Internet sales to consumers have been growing steadily, but not nearly as fast as some predicted in 2000. Why not?

GLOSSARY

Buy-side portals   When buyers in an industry get together to organize an exchange, they are called buy-side or *procurement* portals. They usually are organized by relatively few firms to obtain price advantages and perhaps expand the reach to additional suppliers. Fortified by "strength in numbers," it may be difficult for suppliers to decline participation in this type of buying consolidation program, especially in the many-to-one purest form of a buy-side portal or the many-to-few portals, such as Covisint.

Communication channels   Customer touchpoints; the route(s) used to get information to and from a customer, such as sales force, Web site, telephone, or retail point-of-sale.

Demand chain   The chain of transactions and relationships that lead from the customer up through the various distribution channels to the actual product or service specification process.

Disintermediate   A business that formerly sold through intermediate channels may decide to sell directly to end users. This is called *disintermediation*.

Distribution channels   Route by which a product gets to market, such as wholesalers, retailers, and value-added resellers.

Horizontal channel conflict   Occurs when there is conflict among members of the same level within the channel.

Intermediaries   Between the entity that makes a product and the end consumer who buys it or uses it, there may be wholesalers, distributors, and retailers that are the intermediaries between the maker and the buyer.

Market exchanges   The distinction between sell-side and buy-side portals, although pertinent in understanding how a firm can benefit from involvement in each, is negligible in the long run because it takes lots of both genres to make a portal or hub effective. It is easier simply to group these sites as market exchanges.

Sell-side portals   As sites representing one firm, such as those of Dell or GE, become effective as e-commerce portals, groups of suppliers feel the need to join together to provide their own portal. The goal is to reach many buyers, including some new customers, for the benefit of the group's members. Often the impetus arises in a trade association, which hopes to perform sales functions at lower costs for its members and perhaps to generate revenues from sales for the association. Some portals are owned by a single firm hoping to make a lot of money aggregating catalogs from a group of suppliers to attract a larger audience. These catalog hubs work best in fragmented industries where this type of information consolidation is helpful to the customer.

Supply chain management   Managerial decision making focused on optimizing the relationships with distribution channels.

Vertical channel conflict   Occurs when there is conflict between different levels within the same channel.

Store of the Future and the Evolution of Retailing

15

Chapter

Stores have become the beacons of consumer shopping, evolving over hundreds of years from shops and street vendors to malls and megastores. Although traditional stores will maintain an important role in delivering goods to end-user consumers and servicing them after the sale, this chapter isn't about traditional **retailing marketing functions**. *(We recommend you have a look at any good retailing text to get the basics of that important field.) Rather, this chapter looks at the future of retailing, and speculates about the most likely scenarios that will play out in the near future. Patricia Seybold illustrates the changing multichannel way of shopping and selling with a case study of Tesco. And Ravi Dhar and Dick Wittink offer a view of online branding. The main point here is not that new technologies will* replace *traditional stores, but that they will* enhance *them in significant ways.*

For hundreds of years, consumers have shopped for goods and services at physical stores. While the products and services have diversified and multiplied throughout time, the rudimentary process of shopping has not changed much. When he wants to make a purchase, a consumer must still engage in several steps, often including:

1. Dress appropriately.
2. Leave home.
3. Walk or drive to a store.
4. Search for the product he wants from among many others he doesn't want.
5. Wait in line.
6. Exchange money for the product with the sales clerk.
7. Carry the product home on his own.

To mass marketers who existed before the age of interactivity, physical stores served as the primary venues at which to display their merchandise. Mass marketers frequently saturated their key target markets with messages that touted their products. Then they stockpiled shelves with those products and hoped that consumers had heard their messages and would go to their local stores to buy them. Because they had to rely solely on one-way and nonaddressable media, yesterday's marketers had to ensure that their products could be found in every logical retail store in a given market. If a mass marketer advertised a new soap on television or in the newspaper, it had to be sure that the soap was made available in every drugstore, supermarket, discount store, and corner grocery store within the geographic region where its message was heard.

To the customer-strategy enterprise, in contrast, the store concept is much less relevant. The store's existence, in fact, can actually serve as a barrier to reaching the customer directly and establishing a Learning Relationship with him. After all, the customer-strategy enterprise is most concerned with interacting with the customer directly, learning about his needs, and making it as convenient as possible for the customer to interact and buy.

But stores have become more and more confusing over time. Many discount chain stores are leased in enormous converted warehouses; their aisles overflow with thousands of different products, each one "screaming" for attention: New! 33 percent more! Lower price! Consumers are challenged to find the products they need quickly. The manufacturer, meanwhile, is challenged with differentiating its products among all of the competition. Historically, a new product is doomed from the start—not because nobody wants it, but because not enough people want to buy it from any one store to justify the store setting aside enough of its precious shelf space to carry it.

As a rule, consumers don't dislike shopping; they dislike the inconveniences of shopping. Most enjoy browsing around a mall when they have the time, but they do not want to be burdened with multiple trips to a store for things they buy every week—groceries, clothes, books, toys, and so on. Consumers not only search for a good price, they also want to acquire a product easily and conveniently and ensure that the product is relevant to the need they want to satisfy. Stores, it turns out, are not necessarily the most convenient form of shopping; they do not make it particularly easy for customers to find the products they need.

Historically, the store has had many important roles to play, including breaking bulk and setting up payment options, but these many roles really boil down to two primary purposes:

1. It provides a location for the physical storage of products.
2. It facilitates the exchange of information. The seller communicates the price and specifications of the item with a label on the product, while the customer communicates intent to purchase by taking the product off the shelf and putting it into his shopping cart.

These two purposes—storage of products and information exchange—are fused together at a store. The age of interactivity, however, has begun to "unbundle" these two functions, challenging the viability of the need for stores themselves. It is becoming impossible for stores to communicate *all* the information about *all* of the products that they sell because so many niche products have cropped up on the market. Physically transporting all products and all interested consumers into the same stores to facilitate information exchange is more difficult when there are tens of thousands of products, rather than just a few hundred. Moreover, largely because of the influence of the Web, the informational role of the store can be performed separately, with no geographic restriction at all. Granted, stores are still the most popular venues for shopping, but their popularity is being challenged. Many enterprises are supplementing their store sales channels with more direct selling channels, including catalogs, direct mail, the Web, and toll-free phone numbers. The **consumer direct (CD)** channel is making it much more convenient for consumers to buy the products they want and need. In the process, it is also enabling today's marketers to establish direct, interactive relationships with each and every customer.

The store of the interactive era does not have walls, aisles, and cash registers. It never closes. It is an interactive information service backed up by a warehouse and, perhaps, home-delivery function. Consider how supermarkets are set up today and what they might look like in the not-too-distant future. Through loyalty card programs and cash register receipts, a supermarket maintains an electronic database about each customer's purchase histories, including the brands they prefer and the total amount of their purchases during each shopping trip. Such data are used for inventory control, accounting, and in-store management. These data on an individual customer also could be used to make it more convenient for the shopper to buy the groceries he needs from week to week—especially because most grocery shoppers buy repetitively. (In any given month, only 15 percent of a shopper's purchases are new; he bought the other 85 percent in the same sizes and flavors last month.) The store could have all of his frequently purchased groceries ready for him in a basket upon his arrival, expediting his shopping trip to the store. Or it could ask him to check off items he wants to buy on a list that he e-mails or faxes to the store an hour before he arrives. All he need do is pay for the items upon picking them up. Many supermarkets, however, are reluctant to offer this kind of value-added service because they can't see the benefit in it. For years, their goal has been to "generate pedestrian traffic," and this type of service would take customers out of the aisles where they might pick up "impulse" items, estimated to account for nearly one-third of grocery-store purchases.

> The store of the interactive era does not have walls, aisles, and cash registers. It never closes. It is an interactive information service backed up by a warehouse and, perhaps, home–delivery function.

The store of the interactive age, in contrast, sees great benefit in increasing its share of each customer's business. Some grocery store chains in the United States and Europe, in fact, have adopted this new business model. In recent years, bricks-and-mortar supermarkets and Web-only grocers have enabled their customers to use the Web to shop and buy groceries, which are delivered to their homes. The goal has been to enable customers to select their orders online and have them ready to pick up at the local store. But the added convenience of home delivery has made some of these businesses very successful in their respective markets (see Patricia Seybold's case study of

Tesco, the British retailer, later in this chapter). As compelling as this idea is in principle, it is nevertheless quite hard to implement correctly. A handful of early Internet start-up grocers have failed, largely because their business models and funding levels failed to make adequate provisions for performing all the *universal marketing functions*, spelled out by Blackwell and Stephan in Chapter 14. To reprise, Blackwell and Stephan's universal marketing functions:

> . . . include the *exchange functions* (buying and selling), the *physical distribution functions* (transporting, distributing, and storing) and *facilitating functions* (standardizing, financing, risk taking, and securing marketing information). These marketing functions might be completed by any channel member, or shifted from one channel member to another, but they must be completed in any case.

The key to success in a home-delivery service such as groceries is to unbundle the two roles of the store mentioned previously—information exchange and product storage. A home grocery delivery store, for instance, captures information about what each customer buys every week and then delivers those goods conveniently to his doorstep. Moreover, as it learns what he likes to buy regularly, the grocer can increase its share of his business by customizing some aspect of the process. It could make recommendations to him about other items he might like to buy based on his preferences. Or it could get him to "subscribe" to the products he purchases regularly so that he never runs out of them (see the section on **automatic replenishment (AR)**).

CONSUMER DIRECT CHANNEL[1]

Shopping is a way of life to the typical consumer. What is changing is how and where people shop. Shopping in the consumer direct channel is growing increasingly popular among U.S. consumers, for good reasons. Direct-to-home delivery of goods and services saves consumers time and is more convenient than shopping "the old fashioned way." In 1999, 83 percent of all U.S.

---

[1]In 1998, Peppers and Rogers Group and Institute for the Future formed a partnership to examine the evolving consumer direct (CD) shopping channel. The goal of the three-year study was to understand the scope and impact of the trend toward increased use of the direct-to-consumer shopping and delivery channel, as well as the roles most likely to be played by retailers, manufacturers, and consumers. The study also uncovered the unique opportunities for consumer direct merchants that lie at the intersection of the CD channel and one-to-one principles. FedEx, General Motors, the Grocery Manufacturers of America, Kraft Foods, Peapod, Procter & Gamble, Ralston Purina, Skymall, Unilever, United Parcel Service, and the United States Postal Service were among the firms that participated in the study and drove its research agenda. Executive directors were Greg Schmidt and Martha Rogers.

TRADITIONAL CHANNELS	1998	1999	PERCENT CHANGE
Mail, etc.*	24%	22%	(8%)
Catalog	70%	67%	(4%)
NEW CD CHANNELS			
Online	5%	12%	140%
Grocery direct	<1%	<1%	—

*Includes purchases made in response to direct-mail ads, television, radio, Yellow Pages, and newspaper/magazine ads.
Source: Peppers and Rogers Group and Institute for the Future (IFTF), 2000.

EXHIBIT 15.1   Shift in Shopping Channels, Early Interactive Age

consumers shopped in at least one CD channel, such as online, catalogs, and direct mail, up from 75 percent in 1998.[2] The largest revenue growth occurred in online shopping, which more than doubled, and direct-to-home grocery delivery (see also Exhibit 15.1).

NEW CHANNELS TAKE A GREATER SHARE OF REVENUE (PERCENT OF CD REVENUES)

The burgeoning consumer direct channel enables enterprises to establish more intimate customer relationships. Consumers are bundling CD and bricks-and-mortar shopping experiences to make their purchasing decisions. A single purchase could involve a trip to the mall, flipping through a catalog, and searching the Web for information as well. Consumers are migrating to the CD shopping channel rapidly. CD shoppers continue to integrate multiple CD channels into their shopping mix, maintaining their use of catalogs, while diving head first into new venues such as online and home grocery. CD shoppers are motivated to try remote shopping because of its inherent lifestyle benefits. Key benefits— including the ability to find unique items, convenience, and time savings—as well as discounts like free shipping or promotions are among the factors leading consumers to try the CD channel for the first time.

   During the age of interactivity, consumers will, more and more, integrate bricks-and-mortar stores and the consumer direct channel seamlessly to make their purchasing decisions. Increasingly, they may find an item in one channel and purchase it in another. In the end, when enterprises are deciding how to market and

[2]Peppers and Rogers Group and Institute for the Future, "Consumer Direct: Shopping in the Age of Interactivity" (August 2000).

interact with consumers, it will not matter very much *where* consumers make their purchases but *how they got there*. The hybrid nature of shopping will make it more important than ever for enterprises to build Learning Relationships with their customers. By engaging in a dialogue with each customer, and learning something about him that no other company knows, the customer-focused CD merchant will grow smarter about that customer over time and reduce the likelihood of losing that customer—ever. CD merchants will treat the customer with the same level of service across all channels, win his trust and truly act on his behalf.

The smarter a merchant becomes about its customer's unique shopping needs, the more it can customize its offerings to suit those needs and the less likely the customer will abandon the merchant to shop elsewhere. The Learning Relationship benefits both the customer and the company: The customer is less likely to shop elsewhere because he is getting customized treatment while the company earns his respect and trust and repeat business.

Despite growing evidence that consumers enjoy the direct channel, merchants still face many barriers, including:

- *Social aspects of shopping*. Direct-to-consumer selling lacks the social requirements many consumers desire when shopping, including the experiences of going to a store, interacting with friends and relatives, or just being physically among other shoppers.
- *Desire to examine products before purchase*. The ability to control product selection and examine the goods before buying is a high priority for shoppers and a primary reason that many consumers avoid the CD channel.
- *Price and delivery costs*. Many CD providers believe that consumers will pay extra for the convenience and time savings of shopping the CD channel. But, in fact, some sophisticated consumers expect products offered in the CD channel to cost less, especially in the absence of customization or other services.
- *"Hassle factor."* Consumers believe that in the CD channel they might find it more difficult to locate the items they want or to return unwanted goods.
- *Need for immediacy*. Shopping in stores enables consumers to get the merchandise right away, whereas shopping in the CD channel often means waiting for delivery.
- *Identity and control*. Consumers often find that some products—and the channels they use to buy them—are central to their identity. A teenager likes to buy jeans with his friends at a particular store in the mall. Your dad liked to kick the tires before he bought a car, just to show he was the man in the family. Overcoming this barrier will require educating consumers to recognize that the CD channel does not eliminate these identity and control issues.
- *Browsing for new products*. Online and grocery delivery services are perceived as difficult to use when browsing for products. CD businesses will need to reassure customers that they have a more complete selection than bricks-and-mortar stores.

- *Quality CD*. Shoppers wonder whether what they see in the picture is what they'll actually get delivered to their doorsteps. CD providers that skimp on quality will suffer losses in customer retention.
- *Trust and security*. Consumers are concerned about security when purchasing things online or from unknown catalogs. Trust in a CD company can lead to high levels of consumer loyalty.
- *Logistics and infrastructure*. One of the greatest barriers to the CD channel's growth is the need to overcome substantial logistics and infrastructure barriers to delivering products to households quickly (see the "Final Mile to Consumers" section, later in the chapter).

To reach their various customer groups most profitably, direct-to-consumer merchants will need to adopt a customer-focused infrastructure. They will need to develop systems to capture what they learn about a single shopper across all delivery channels (stores, catalogs, and online) and personalize their responses to individual customer interactions. Successful CD models often integrate both CD and physical store channels to best meet the needs of individual consumers, thereby improving the overall experience for consumers. Opportunities abound for intermediaries, or "agents," to help busy consumers navigate the CD purchasing process. By removing some of the "pain" associated with shopping in the channel, such agents can eliminate the barriers discussed earlier that prevent CD shoppers from using the channel more often.

One way to bring more consumers into the consumer direct channel on a more regular basis is to persuade them to use it for the regular replenishment of the goods and services they use daily, weekly, or monthly. Enterprises can offer their customers automatic replenishment (AR) services to ensure that they are always in stock of certain products, and that services are always performed regularly.

AUTOMATIC REPLENISHMENT: SUBSCRIBING CUSTOMERS TO PRODUCTS

Consumer-marketing companies in a variety of industries are exploring ways to capitalize on the booming consumer direct channel, which affords them many benefits, including tighter control of inventory, closer relationships with their customers, and simpler distribution systems. In 2000, the number of U.S. adults who made purchases online totaled more than 116 million. To put this number into perspective, consider that the entire population of Mexico is about 100 million people. With the number of users of the CD channel, online and offline, continuing to grow, the channel continues to refine how it delivers and fulfills orders.

Any consumer direct transaction that involves the purchase of a product requires getting that item into the customer's home. Some products and services marketed and sold in the CD channel are more conducive to delivery and, therefore, more logistically efficient. These include less frequently purchased items such as computers or apparel, as well as everyday, repetitively purchased staples such as groceries or health and beauty products.[3]

In the consumer direct channel, the continuous fulfillment of repetitively purchased goods and services is known as automatic replenishment (AR). AR enables a consumer to order from a merchant once and then receive a product or service at set intervals, "subscribing" to the product in nearly the same way as he might subscribe to a weekly magazine or a daily newspaper. AR is a concept as old as the milkman, who would deliver a fresh bottle every morning, or the Book-of-the-Month Club, which would ensure that a new title arrived in the mailbox every 30 days or so.

AR can be applied to many different consumer-marketing situations. Picture this:

- A battery manufacturer installs a storage unit in your home that keeps tabs on your supply of batteries. When you run low on any particular variety, a signal is sent to the distributor, more batteries are delivered, and your daughter's Nintendo Gameboy really does keep going and going and going.
- A rubber tire company installs sensors on your car's tires that determine when it's time to replace them. The sensors signal the tire manufacturer to alert a local dealership to tell you that you need new tires.
- A bank automatically sends a new supply of checkbooks a month prior to your using your last check to ensure that you will not be without checks to make payments.
- A lightbulb manufacturer sends a new supply every month to ensure you're never in the dark.
- A local beauty salon phones every six weeks to remind you that your coif needs attention.
- Your automobile service station puts a sensor in your car's engine to determine when the oil is running low and then notifies you to come in for an oil change.

Why should consumer direct merchants consider adopting AR strategies when they already are faced with improving imperfect delivery mechanisms? AR makes sense for CD firms for the following reasons:

---

[3]As soon as they hear the words, "automatic replenishment," many people automatically think of milk delivery of ages past, or of companies like Schwan's frozen foods, which make their rounds to the same neighborhoods over and over. The fact is that neither of these are very good examples of what is meant today by AR. Milk delivery eventually succumbed to rising labor costs and declining margins on a single small set of products, whereas today's AR firms are delivering a variety of products to the same household, spreading the delivery overhead over a constantly increasing number of products. Likewise, Schwan's is a great example of interactivity and home delivery, but not of automatic replenishment. The last time we checked, you had to choose items from the little booklets distributed by the driver, who would deliver them the next time he was in the neighborhood, *if* he still had the items you most wanted on his truck, and *if* you were home when he came around. Try as you might, you cannot arrange a delivery time unless you are a very large customer, and you can't automatically replenish at all. Every order is a new order, so there is no Learning Relationship at all with Schwan's, even if you're lucky enough to have a driver with a good memory.

- Continuous fulfillment of products and services makes shopping the CD route even more convenient for consumers.
- AR will increase a merchant's share of customer. The CD provider can learn more about the changing needs of each customer, enhance relationships with that customer, and build SOC customer loyalty.
- AR creates more advertising, promotion, and selling opportunities, because personalized recommendations and incentives to purchase other products can be included in the AR deliveries. (Web grocers report that the capability to personalize suggestions results in impulse purchase barely lower than in-store impulse buying.)
- Service providers and product manufacturers increase their awareness of customer consumption levels. Manufacturers can, therefore, better control inventory levels on products they discover are purchased more frequently. Service companies can hire additional help if customers increase their regular use.
- Because merchants will be able to forecast inventory more accurately, they will find it easier to manage their delivery systems, reduce shipping and stockkeeping costs, and anticipate quarterly revenues.
- AR helps to entrench brand positioning. Consumers routinely purchase the same brand, as it will be regularly delivered to their homes.
- AR helps to establish routine payment modalities. CD merchants who deploy an AR component benefit from regular revenue streams and increase the lifetime value of customers who are locked in to their products over time.

Besides the obvious convenience and time savings, AR offers benefits to consumers:

- AR means consumers don't have to run out of the fundamental things they need and use most: medications, pet food, disposable diapers and baby formula, and so on.
- AR enables consumers to set their own delivery schedules instead of working around the schedules of the delivery companies.
- AR enables consumers to retain greater control over household management. The customers can determine how frequently products and services are delivered, and select the brands they like to buy.
- AR enables consumers to sample new products. With each successive delivery, CD merchants can include samples of other products the customer might like, based on what they've learned about that customer's preferences and tastes. This benefits both their CD firm and the consumer.
- Home delivery offers a way for a customer to be remembered individually and to do business with a company that is smarter and smarter about him. The consumer direct firm serves the customer better while closing the gap on missed opportunities through automatic replenishment.

While it is an old idea in business, AR is becoming a more prevalent part of the consumer direct provider's delivery offering. Overall, however, many CD businesses have been slow to adopt AR strategies. One reason is probably the simple fact that retailers have traditionally organized their efforts around taking orders from their customers—and nothing else. Businesses have been so focused on getting customers into their stores and selling their wares and services that they have failed to hear the customer who is saying, "Listen to me and I'll tell you what I really need." Another reason probably involves the psychology of buyer-seller relationships. Consumers are apt to purchase recommended brands and products from trusted sources. Many are reluctant to purchase products regularly from a company if they know little about the business or its products or services.

> The key to AR is to offer routine products and services, not items consumers like to browse for.

Therefore, building meaningful relationships with customers is an essential prerequisite for any AR initiative. The customer must trust the company enough that he will volunteer to place certain items on the AR list. Yet another barrier to the proliferation of AR programs is the fact that most companies lack the appropriate technical infrastructure to run such an initiative effectively. The capability to monitor customer product preferences and delivery schedules, and synchronize them with inventory, requires substantial investment in information systems and logistics and customer-relationship management software.

Automatic replenishment sounds like a logical component to include in every CD offering, particularly for frequently purchased consumables, such as groceries and health and beauty products.[4] Two of every five buyers shop for consumables online, according to ActivMedia, which further estimates that $3.8 billion was spent online in 1999 on those items.[5] In ActivMedia's estimation, the buyers of consumable products online represent 56 percent of online purchasing power. Given the purchasing power and shopping habits of this group, Activ-Media sees strong potential for cross-selling and promotion in this sector. It also puts a premium on developing customer loyalty.

It is obvious why enterprises would want to sign up customers for AR services; but do consumers want such services, and, if so, which ones? Consumer interest in automatic replenishment depends largely on the product. More than 40 percent of CD shoppers would like to use AR for prescription medicine refills, for example, and more than 20 percent are interested in such a service for groceries and household items such as lightbulbs.[6] The key to AR is to offer routine products and services, not items consumers like to browse for.

CD providers are grappling over whether it is more cost-effective to outsource the delivery or build their own delivery infrastructures. On top of that, many consumers still have to be at home to accept the deliveries when they arrive, especially if they include perishable items. But are consumers receptive

[4]"$120 Billion in Consumables by 2005," eMarketer.com (January 26, 2000).

[5]www.activmedia.com

[6]Peppers and Rogers Group and Institute for the Future, "Forecasting the Consumer Direct Channel" (August 2000), p. 82.

enough to automatic replenishment that they will accept the inconvenience of being at home for the delivery? A study of 1,600 consumers by Chilton Research Services showed that while 65 percent reported waiting at home for deliveries, 25 percent refused to do so for very long; 28 percent said they would use a home-delivery service if they had a way to receive their orders in a secure way without having to be there.[7]

Many consumer-direct merchants are exploring ways to deliver the goods and services without the customer being home. Unattended delivery models are gaining popularity, but do not work for every type of product or service. One company, for example, is addressing the need for secure, unattended automatic replenishment centers installed at the point of delivery—the household—and seeks to outsource these portals to CD merchants across vertical markets. Brivo Systems, Inc., an e-commerce infrastructure company, acquired the patent to the Brivo Box, a secure and climate-controlled accordionlike compartment that attaches to the side of a house or garage. In essence, the Brivo Box serves as a delivery center for goods ordered online or through direct mail. It comprises three distinct elements:

1. A physical portal at the home linked to an Internet-based communications device, to permit secure delivery of online orders.
2. An Internet-based agent to control access to the bin and act on the customer's behalf when he orders goods online.
3. A Web site to provide customers, merchants, and transport companies with easy access to order services.

An unattended delivery model can also facilitate shipping return items back to the manufacturer or grocer. The unneeded products are placed in the bin to be picked up as the delivery person arrives to drop off an order.

Enterprises considering adopting an automatic replenishment component might examine the different AR business models and decide which will provide the most efficient fit for their type of product or service. The three models are:

1. *Fully automatic.* The company alone ensures that certain products or services never run out and delivers them without the customer's intervention.
2. *Company-driven reminders.* The service provider or manufacturer monitors consumption levels at the household and alerts the customer when inventories are running low or when a service call is due. If the customer agrees, the service or product is added to his next delivery. (This method turns out to be the most popular, according to a U.S. nationwide survey.[8])
3. *Consumer-driven scheduling.* Customers determine how frequently they want their orders delivered and how much of a product to receive.

[7]Chilton Research Web site: *http://research.chilton.net.*

[8]Peppers and Rogers Group, and Institute for the Future, "Consumer Direct: Shopping in the Age of Interactivity" (August 2000).

For automatic replenishment programs to run efficiently, consumers need to do their part, too. They must manage their delivery schedules to ensure that the goods or services they want to replenish routinely are sent when they need them. Now and then it is expected that some overflow, or *asynchronicity*, will occur when a customer's supply of the continuously replenished goods exceeds his demand for it, or falls short. A plausible solution would be for consumers to have the capability to notify CD merchants about changes in their delivery preferences. Each customer would naturally have different delivery concerns but should be in control of how he wants to notify the merchant about modifications in scheduling—whether it be via the Web, e-mail, postcard, or telephone.

It could work the other way, as well. Service providers and manufacturers that are monitoring delivery and service schedules will need to alert customers that they might be running low on products, or require a service call, via a courtesy e-mail. This would work best for items that carry expiration dates, such as prescription medication or fresh foods, or for services that are routinely performed, such as automobile oil changes, dry cleaning, housecleaning, or pest extermination. Because the merchant would keep copious records of the household's consumption of these products and services, he would be able to predict, with a high degree of accuracy, when the customer is in need of replenishment.

The reminders could themselves upsell other related products. For instance, Eckerd Drugs, a division of JC Penney, sends an e-mail to a customer that reminds him to refill his family's drug prescriptions and personalized vitamins. The reminders carry messages about other special drugstore offers to consider, such as a sale on vitamins. A battery manufacturer could e-mail a customer when it's time to replace the batteries in his smoke detector, and include an electronic coupon for the purchase of a new smoke alarm, fire extinguisher, or other related product. A bank could send reminders when a customer's loan payments are due or certificates of deposits are nearing their maturity. Or an automobile manufacturer could send service reminders to its customers with coupons for oil changes at local dealers. Ford Motor Company offers an Owner Connection service in which car owners can log on to a Web site, register their vehicles, and receive personalized reminders about routine maintenance.

By notifying customers that they need to refresh their supply of products or schedule another service call, companies will do their part to help consumers manage their households and, essentially, to manage their lives. And they'll foster deeper relationships with those customers to boot, through frequent meaningful interactions and deeper understanding of each one's needs.

AR programs have long succeeded in business-to-business. Throughout the business supply chain, AR has demonstrated cost savings without jeopardizing shipment and warehouse service levels. By placing supply chain partner trading relations at the center of the replenishment decision-making process, automatic replenishment programs can give companies a competitive advantage. Hewlett-Packard (HP) has long been successful in B2B direct selling with its HP Shopping.com online store that facilitates shopping in a highly customized environment. The My Printing Supplies Store, for instance, helps users simplify the purchasing process for HP printing supplies, and eliminates time-consuming searches. Customers can select their HP printers from a menu and indicate their printing needs. HP Shopping.com matches the information and does the rest. The next time customers enter the virtual store, they will see those supplies designed to work with their printers, as well as printing projects that apply to their needs.

HP also has succeeded in adopting an AR component to its product fulfillment. It recently enhanced its instant and automated office supplies delivery system, HP Express (formerly HP SupplyStore). HP Express reduces the burden of reordering office supplies by automatically replenishing them when they run low. An online host network manages the system. It enables HP to monitor key information remotely, such as inventory level, product demand, and necessary maintenance. HP Express machines are designed to streamline the supplies selection process with a multimedia interface. Customers can interact with the machine's touch-screen and follow the software interface prompts to determine the correct supplies for their HP printing devices.

A new computing platform provides the capability to incorporate other, non-HP office supply product lines. Office managers are able to produce usage reports to better manage the ordering process. The managers also can learn who is accessing the machine and what is being purchased, and then tailor the e-station accordingly. The station's automated replenishment feature eliminates the need to track inventory levels and reorder supplies manually. In short, HP Express makes office supplies available around the clock, eliminating the need to overstock for emergencies. Additionally, because the system builds a purchase-pattern database at the e-station level, it can be used to cater to specific consumer needs. [9]

More businesses are integrating their office equipment into their computer networks to improve efficiency. Devices that consume something, such as printers, often require human intervention to replenish the supply. How many times, for instance, has your home computer printer run out of toner and you've had no supply in reserve? HP is making it possible to see in real time exactly which devices need resupplying, and when. For companies, this means less personnel time is wasted on the "busy work" of maintaining toner inventory. HP's proprietary communications protocol creates "intelligent" printers that silently signal the cartridge shipper when toner supplies get low, automatically replenishes toner supplies, and ensures there is as little workflow interruption as possible. One HP line of printers has a smart chip memory device to tell the printer when cartridges are low or out of ink and when to replace printheads. The information is displayed on screen so users can check ink levels before printing, minimizing waste.[10]

In the next section, Patricia Seybold and Ronni Marshak describe how U.K.-based supermarket chain Tesco has succeeded in selling directly to its customers—and in building stronger relationships with them along the way.

---

[9]HP Shopping Village Web site: *www.shopping.hp.com.*

[10]"HP Rewrites the Rules for Office Desktop Printers," Work-Group Computing Report (April 27, 1998), p. 19.

USING OPERATIONAL EXCELLENCE AS
A COMPETITIVE ADVANTAGE: TESCO[11]

Patricia B. Seybold
CEO, The Patricia Seybold Group

Ronni T. Marshak

Time-pressed customers have made it clear that they want the convenience of having groceries delivered to their homes, but many of the attempts to develop successful online grocery businesses have failed. How do you win the hearts and minds of consumers? With convenience and seamless integration into their normal lives and routines, and a flawless, cost-efficient logistical execution. Customers who shop for groceries once a week are familiar with their local store. They know which products are on special offer; they know how these are laid out. Unless you can offer them the identical products at the identical prices they're used to receiving, along with the convenience of shopping from home, you'll never gain their loyalty.

Tesco plc. is a U.K.-based global supermarket chain with annual revenues of well over £20 billion. An established presence with a huge bricks-and-mortar infrastructure, Tesco is also the world's most successful and profitable online grocer.

There are three reasons that others have failed in the online grocery business, where Tesco has succeeded:

1. Other companies have had to develop the food distribution infrastructure from scratch; Tesco leverages its existing store-based distribution processes.
2. Other companies have developed pick, pack, and delivery from separate warehouses, adding a layer of cost into the equation. Tesco's in-store pick-and-pack system avoids this duplication and ensures that customers will get exactly the same products with which they're familiar.
3. No other online grocer has seamlessly integrated customers' in-store shopping and their online shopping. With its highly popular frequent shopper program, Tesco keeps track of what each family has bought, not only online but in the store as well. And it doesn't violate customers' privacy by sharing that information with suppliers.

All the large supermarket chains are battling for their share of families' stomachs, and most are competing on price. Tesco is competing on customer loyalty and customer experience, although it keeps its own prices competitive in each local market. Equally important, Tesco knows who its customers are and deepens its relationships with them over time. There are more than 14 million active Tesco cardholders.

Tesco's online business, Tesco.com, uses the Balanced Scorecard[12] "steering wheel" as its in-store counterpart. Tesco measures and monitors what matters to

---

[11]From *The Customer Revolution* by Patricia Seybold and Ronni T. Marshak, © 2001 by The Patricia Seybold Group, Inc. Used by permission of Crown Publishers, a division of Random House, Inc.
[12]Balanced Scorecard is a service of the Balanced Scorecard Collaborative®.

customers, including which items are close to out of stock, how quickly its delivery vans make it through traffic, and how it performs customers' shopping scenarios from different Internet service points across the country.

CUSTOMER LOYALTY AND "SHARE OF STOMACH"

Most enterprises worry about the share of each customer's wallet they have. In the food and grocery sector, this is jokingly described as "share of stomach." But stomach share is no laughing matter to the players who are duking it out in increasingly global markets. According to an annual survey done by retail consultancy Verdict Research, Tesco was the "undisputed leader in the U.K. food and grocery sector." In second place, but hot on Tesco's heels, was invader Wal-Mart, which had acquired the ASDA chain. J. Sainsbury was running third.

In its report, Verdict went on to explain that, "Across the U.K. grocery sector as a whole, loyalty has been eroded over the past 12 months—the inevitable result of a price war, which helps to destabilize shoppers' perceptions and behaviour." The researchers measured a five-point decline in overall customer loyalty, as measured by the number of shoppers who said they would shop elsewhere if they could (from 75 percent in 1998 to 70 percent in 1999). Yet Tesco ranked at the top of the customer loyalty numbers.

By early 1999, Tesco was not only the U.K.'s largest grocer, it had become the world's largest *online* grocer, with £125 million revenues from 250,000 customers doing online shopping with profit margins of 12 percent. In the fall of 1999, when we asked U.S. supermarket executives which business they thought was doing the best job in online shopping—Webvan Group, Peapod, or MyWebGrocer.com—they replied that Tesco had the business model they admired most.

Tesco Direct Experiment

In 1994, Tim Mason, then Tesco's marketing director, pitched the idea of direct shopping to Tesco's board. Mason wanted to set up a call center, mail order, and online operation geared toward increasing the nonfood side of Tesco business. Customers could receive mailers promoting special items, and call, fax, or e-mail in their orders. The orders could be shipped out the next day. This strategy would also enable Tesco to market items not normally sold in its stores—gift items, toys, and other consumer products. The board approved the strategy.

Mason pulled together a small team and they launched Tesco's original call center/mail order/e-commerce operation in Dundee. Then, Mason took a different job, and the small group carried on.

Moving the Experiment into the Real World

At that point, Gary Sargeant was tapped to head up Tesco Direct. Sargeant had risen through the ranks as a store manager. He decided to combine the call center/mail order operation with in-store fulfillment. Local customers could order any item carried in their local stores and receive same-day delivery. He piloted this concept in Osterley. And he expanded the call center operation to accept Internet e-mail orders, as well as phone and fax.

Piloting with a Target Customer Group. Having figured out his game plan, Sargeant went looking for a target set of customers, first looking at homebound old-age pensioners. He approached the local authority responsible for old-age pensioners in the Brimford neighborhood and got its blessing to offer this service to their clientele. "This was an easy market for us. Most of these folks relied on part-time helpers or neighbors who would do their shopping at a local convenience store. The prices and the selection offered were terrible. We could do much better for them," Sargeant explained.

Expanding the Pilot. Once the kinks were out of the system, the Tesco Direct team expanded the home shopping offer beyond the older, housebound customer base. Then they added a second store and a third. Soon Tesco had a customer base between 300 and 400 home-shopping customers per week. Most of these folks would call or fax in their orders; only 6 percent of the orders came via the Internet. Yet Sargeant knew in his bones that online shopping was where the real growth opportunities lay. By 1997, consumer usage of the Internet was increasing exponentially. Dixon's Freeserve—"free Internet" service (users still had to pay for their phone calls)—had captured the hearts and minds of thousands of British customers.

Sargeant decided to target busy, upscale professionals, the kinds of people who would most value the home shopping service and who would be more likely to want to shop online. He added another store, this time in a very affluent neighborhood: Hammersmith. "Our research showed that these households were more than four times as likely to shop online," Sargeant explained. The average income of these families was £55,000. They owned two cars. They were either two-working-parent families, wealthy households, or starter singles. Gary's team did a marketing blitz of the area, and 9,000 people expressed interest in Tesco's online shopping offer. "Yet the day we went live, we received a single online order," Sargeant moaned. Online shopping was obviously going to have a slow ramp-up.

What Sargeant and his team learned from the slow start in Hammersmith was that, just because you offer online grocery shopping, customers won't necessarily use it. In hindsight, he recognized that his team had done very little to prepare fertile ground. "We just did blanket marketing. We dropped leaflets everywhere. We should have realized that there's a distinct group of people we needed to reach: working women and people who had already outsourced a number of household tasks, like ironing, cleaning, and so on." By trial and error, the Tesco Direct team refined its marketing and began to lure customers online.

MOVING FROM PILOT PROJECT TO MAINSTREAM

By late 1997, Tesco Direct was still primarily a call-center-based operation, with a handful of participating stores offering Tesco's full line of groceries to customers in their shopping areas. Others might have given up at this stage, but Sargeant was undaunted. Still convinced that online shopping was about to take off, he turned his attention to streamlining operations and tweaking the business model so that he could offer online shopping profitably to all of Tesco's customers. He was supported by John Browett, a Tesco business strategist.

Many online grocery services presume that it's more cost-effective to handle inventory and fulfillment operations from a distribution warehouse, but Sargeant continued to hone the in-store fulfillment model. He wanted all customers to be purchasing online from the store in which they would normally shop in person. Customers would receive the same price for each item online as the price in the store nearest their home. This would permit regional pricing variations to be maintained, boosting overall profits. (In the supermarket business, certain neighborhoods support higher prices than others.) Yet customers' online prices would always be competitive with the prices charged by local stores. By linking the online shopping application directly to each store's inventory systems, it was unlikely that customers would order a product that was not available, saving considerable time and effort for both customers and for Tesco; moreover, customers are familiar with the selection of products available in their local stores. Finally, the servers in each store could save a history of each customer's favorite products, to ensure that these were always in stock.

Sargeant handpicked a team of logistics experts to help design the optimal in-store pick-and-pack system. The new streamlined system works like this: The pickers use a specially equipped shopping cart with six trays and an online display. The display gives them their routes through the store and a list of the items to be picked as they go down each aisle. The store routes are optimized to avoid the peak in-store traffic areas. Items are scanned as they're dropped into each customer's tray, so they can't be mixed up. And if the item the customer ordered has gone out of stock in the few hours that have elapsed since the order was placed, the picking application proposes an alternate product from a list of items that the customer has previously purchased, either in the store or when shopping online (75 percent of Tesco's online shoppers also shop at the store from time to time). And because most of them use Tesco's loyalty card, Tesco has a complete history of each customer's orders.

Once the shopping cart is filled, the trays are loaded directly into the delivery vans that are ready and waiting behind each store. Again, the routing is optimized so that produce doesn't sit for hours but is delivered immediately after being picked from the store. Deliveries are scheduled based on customers' preferences (within a two-hour delivery window to allow for traffic delays). Any items that have been substituted are carefully placed on the top of each order so they can be reviewed and accepted or rejected when the order is delivered.

Honing a Profitable Business Model

Tesco charges customers £5 (about $7.50) per delivery. This fee covers 60 percent of the operational costs of actually performing the service. The rest of the costs are covered by the fact that online in-home shoppers order more profitable items than in-store-only shoppers.

Grocers measure customer profitability by shopping basket. Sargeant reports that the "basket mix" of Tesco's online shoppers is 2 to 3 percentage points more profitable than the average customer's in-store market basket. Why is that? We would speculate that, when a grocery customer shops online, it's easier to check off a list of items and add to that list than it is to lumber down supermarket aisles picking out each item by hand. And Tesco's online shopping site does a good job of cross-selling and upselling. When you check off an item (like bread), other related items (such as marmalade or butter) pop up on the screen.

The total profit margins for Tesco's online shoppers, including all operational costs, run 10 to 12 percent. This is consistent with Tesco's overall profit margins.

Rolling Out across the United Kingdom

Once the Tesco Direct team had refined the logistics and proved out its business model, they began to roll the operations out in a number of stores. By mid-1998, 11 stores were online. Perhaps more exciting to Sargeant and his team was the fact that 85 percent of the orders being placed were Internet orders. Internet-savvy customers had discovered how convenient it was to do their grocery shopping online.

In July 1998, Sargeant met with Terry Leahy, the company's chief executive, Mason (now chairman), and Browett (now the chief strategist). "We should stop promoting phone and fax ordering," Sargeant explained. "The cost of having customers enter their own orders is so much lower, even with the handholding that's required. Let's focus on doing a really good job with online ordering," Sargeant suggested. They all agreed that Tesco Direct should become an Internet-only operation. Of course, they kept the call center operation. Existing customers who didn't have Internet access could still call in their orders—about 300 of them still do—but all new customers would be Internet-only customers.

One lesson the Tesco Direct team learned was to set customers' expectations. "The first time you do your grocery shopping online, it's going to take you a good 40 minutes to complete your order. We hadn't prepared people for that. Online shoppers were used to the experience of ordering a single book or a compact disc," Sargeant reported. The Tesco team also discovered that it needed to focus a lot of effort on encouraging customers to place their second and third orders after the shock of food shopping online for the first time. "After your third online order, you're hooked," he explained. But getting customers to that point takes handholding and follow-through.

Tesco Direct began life as an orphan. Under Sargeant's stewardship, it grew to become a strategic weapon in Tesco's battle for stomach share. In the spring of 2000, Tesco.com became a separate subsidiary, under the leadership of John Browett, who was made CEO, and Carolyn Bradley, COO. While it's still 100 percent owned by Tesco, the separate governance has allowed the dot-com unit to continue to move at Internet speed. "We were beginning to get bogged down in the corporate business processes," Sargeant reports. "We needed the ability to move faster." Now Browett has a direct line to Tesco's board. And the subsidiary is able to create its own incentive structure that is more competitive. "All Tesco employees will benefit from our success," Sargeant reports, "but with our own stock options and pay structure, we can compete for talent."

MONITORING CUSTOMERS' EXPERIENCES

Tesco has long been a practitioner of the Balanced Scorecard approach to management. At Tesco this is a Balanced Steering Wheel. It has four quadrants: Customers, People, Operations, and Finance. Each quadrant contains a set of objectives. Examples of specific metrics that appear in each quadrant include customer loyalty, employee turnover, percentage out-of-stocks, and profit target. Each store has a large steering wheel posted where every employee sees it, and each one has a traffic light next to it: Green means you're right on target; red means you're not achieving it; yellow means that you're in danger of missing your goal. The metrics are updated weekly. What kind of steering wheel did the Tesco Direct team implement for its operations? They use the same metrics and add a few of their own. For example, they measure the customer's total time online, number of pages viewed, and size of each order, and correlate these to streamline the ordering process. Sargeant and his team understand that customers don't want to hang out online; they want an efficient grocery shopping experience.

The Tesco Direct team takes the customer experience very seriously. They monitor on-time deliveries, accuracy of orders, and customer satisfaction. They also simulate customers' online shopping experiences to proactively monitor the state of the end-to-end customer experience. Sargeant's team runs shopping scenario robots using a variety of different browsers, Internet service providers (ISPs), and dial-in numbers. This constant monitoring of the conditions that customers are facing helps Tesco proactively sort out problems as they occur. For example, Sargeant reports that one well-intentioned ISP was caching the Tesco site (keeping a local copy in memory and serving it up to customers) so as to speed access. The problem was that it had cached the information, including pricing and availability, from one of 200 stores. But because each online customer might be shopping at a different store, this approach aggravated rather than improved customers' experiences.

Sargeant's team uses simple sanity checks as well. By trial and error they discovered that, if any store's orders fall 15 percent below the orders for the same time period on the previous day, there may be a technical problem. The team now has a simple alert set to go off whenever that condition occurs.

SUSTAINING TESCO'S CUSTOMER EXPERIENCE

A big part of Tesco's brand image is to be friendly and helpful. It's no wonder that the folks who deliver groceries to Tesco.com customers are often asked to lend a helping hand. Some of the most popular requests that Tesco's delivery personnel have received during the last year are:

- Borrow the Tesco van to help move.
- Request a ride.
- Help change a tire.
- Hold the ladder.
- Put things in cupboard (for elderly customers).
- Change clock on video or set video to record.
- Help choose wallpaper
- Request fashion opinion ("Does my bum look big in this?").
- Post a letter.
- Change a lightbulb.
- Answer the phone and give messages.
- Unblock a sink.
- Return videos/library books.

Some of the more unusual requests made in the last year were:

- Feed a pet while owners on holiday.
- Join customer for candlelit dinner (after customer was stood up).
- Offer marital advice.
- Take a family photo/video.
- Give a pregnant customer a lift to hospital (false alarm).
- Babysit.
- Witness a will.
- Drive customer to a wedding (car failed to show up).
- Call in sick for customer.
- Drop the kids off at school.

Carolyn Bradley, Tesco.com's chief operations officer, commented: "At Tesco we pride ourselves on looking after our customers, but there are limits. We are advising our drivers to be as helpful as they can, but we have to strike a balance without inconveniencing other customers by being late."

From Groceries to One-Stop Shopping

Once a company is successful in building and sustaining customer loyalty through its customer experience—both in store and online—most companies begin to extend their product offerings. Tesco is no exception. Even before the advent of online grocery shopping, Tesco offered its loyalty card, the Tesco Card. Next the grocer offered a credit card. Soon other personal financial services followed. Today, you can have a Tesco savings account and checking account with online banking. You can invest in an individual retirement account, locate a mortgage, and buy insurance for your house, car, pet, and your next trip.

In addition to selling groceries from its stores, Tesco Direct continued to offer a line of giftware, housewares, and apparel, both online and via catalog. Next it offered a baby store with everything that busy parents might need, including diapers, formula, baby clothes, and strollers. Then came the online bookstore, followed quickly by the online music and entertainment store and the consumer electronics store.

From Commerce to Community

Once it had established itself as the most widely used online shopping site in the United Kingdom, the company found that its customers, many of whom were women, seemed to be looking for a missing ingredient in the Tesco online experience: community. Tesco.com management entered into a joint venture with iVillage, the popular American women's portal site. Together they formed iVillage.co.uk, which will be linked to Tesco.com. iVillage U.K. was set up to function as an independently managed entity to provide women in the United Kingdom and the Republic of Ireland with an interactive community. Tesco and iVillage plan to provide a combined total of approximately $70 million in marketing, branding, cash, intellectual property, and other resources in support of the venture through online and offline activities. Tesco will provide $18 million in cash over the next three years, online and offline promotional considerations, and expert knowledge of the deepest and broadest customer relationships in the United Kingdom. iVillage will provide the i-village women's brand online, intellectual property, content, online community know-how, and deep understanding of what women want on the Web. iVillage.co.uk will also promote Tesco.com's retail business. Revenue will be derived primarily from advertising and sponsorship.

RESULTS

By 2002, Tesco.com had nearly a million registered customers and had blanketed 95 percent of the United Kingdom. In other words, 95 percent of the grocery-shopping customers in Britain could avail themselves of Tesco.com. The run rate had hit 85,000 orders per week, contributing to a 24 percent volume growth between 1998 and 2002. In 2000, Tesco reported record sales and earnings, with an overall increase in U.K. sales of 7.5 percent, and 5.8 percent increase in 2002. Tesco's personal finance business had 3 million customers by fall 2002 (more customers than Egg, the popular U.K. internet bank!).[13]

What accounts for this success? Three principal factors:

1. *Flawless execution.* From the careful design of its in-store pick-and-pack system to the daily monitoring of customers' online experiences, the Tesco Direct team keeps its eye on the ball.

[13]Tesco Annual Report, January 2003; available at: *www.tesco.com.*

2. *Separate operating entity.* Once the e-business group began to gain traction, Tesco management placed it into a separate, unencumbered business unit. Although this gave the team enough independence to ensure the best possible program, it was also important for Tesco.com to remain tightly integrated with the in-store operations.

3. *Completely integrated customer experience.* Customers' order histories are maintained across all touchpoints, including not just the online store but also the physical one, giving Tesco the capability to view its total business from each individual customer's actual perspective, and yielding a much better all-around shopping experience. For instance, if an item is out of stock by the time the picker gets to the shelf, a more intelligent substitution can be made based on the customer's total purchase history.

Some similarities existed between Tesco's home delivery service and the failed internet-based grocers in the United States—most notably, the very high levels of customer satisfaction with the service. There were, of course, huge differences as well, such as sharing overhead costs with existing stores. One of the biggest differences, however, was that all new Web-only retailers have to establish a new *brand*, starting from scratch to win hearts and share of mind. Tesco had a well-established brand and a solid reputation going into the endeavor. Next, Ravi Dhar and Dick R. Wittink offer their perspective on the role of the brand in online shopping.

THE ONLINE STORE AND THE ROLE OF THE BRAND IN ONLINE SHOPPING

Ravi Dhar
Professor, Yale School of Management

Dick R. Wittink
George Rogers Clark Professor of Management and Marketing, Yale School of Management

Although the most successful "store of the future" will utilize multiple channels, the Internet bears special examination. Under what conditions is online consumer commerce especially attractive? How do such conditions relate to the opportunity for mass customization? What are the consequences of online consumer commerce for traditional marketing functions such as brand management? Will the consumer be easily manipulated online, as some people argue is the case for offline commerce?

Let's look at the conditions under which an online consumer direct option is viable and consider the role of branding in an online channel.

THE VALUE PROPOSITION

The overarching objective of an enterprise is to increase the total value of its customer base. A firm creates value by engaging in activities—such as research and development, production, and marketing—targeted to meet the needs of specific customers. Because customers differ in what matters to them, and because what constitutes value is subjective, it is important for managers to understand the determinants of value from the customer perspective. We note that these determinants change over time, and customers must continuously be differentiated by need (see Chapter 6). Online interaction is an attractive medium for firms to gather preference information and to engage in two-way communication with customers so as to adapt supply to heterogeneity in demand.

The value created through an exchange between a firm and its customer (in a narrow sense, payment in exchange for an object purchased) is a function of product attributes and the resulting benefits. Products differ in the nature and amount of value they create via physical and informational attributes. For many products, such as financial services and newspapers, the primary value creation activities are informational. Physical activities, such as record-keeping for stocks or mutual funds and delivery for newspapers, are secondary. For other products, the main value creation activity is physical—as in the manufacturing of airplane engines. However, even for engine manufacturers, there is an opportunity for information attributes to enhance the value of the product in both its composition and its use by customers. Enhanced value is created if the customer specifies needs, the firm responds to the needs, and the two parties continue to interact. CRM systems are designed to formalize this continued interaction, adding value to the transaction (see Chapter 3).

In general, the larger the component of informational attributes in value creation, the greater the suitability of selling direct to the customer. In reality, most products have a combination of physical and informational attributes. Consider the business General Motors is in. Its cars are physical products, but GM's profits also come from financing activities, which are informational. Among more recent developments, Onstar is perhaps a critical component of future growth for General Motors. This feature can create value for automobile owners through information attributes, such as locating a vehicle in the case of a severe accident. Automobile manufacturers increasingly compete on such supplemental benefits. Over time, it is conceivable that physical differences in attributes between products will become modest, while information-based differences will increase. For enterprises to deal successfully with such changes, it is important that managers have a thorough understanding of individual customer preferences (a critical basis for mass customization). Also, managers must create economies of scale in information management.

The Internet may be an appropriate marketing medium even for physical products with limited informational attributes. Product attributes can be categorized into *search* and *experience* attributes. Search attributes are those for which customers can determine which options they prefer prior to buying, while experience attributes require some trial before customers can determine their value to them. If a physical product is composed primarily of search attributes, the online environment provides consumers with an efficient way to look for the best alternative. Consider the purchase of a personal computer: Alternatives may differ on speed, storage, screen size, and other attributes for which the product characteristics can easily be determined prior to purchase.

In contrast, one common barrier to an automobile purchase online is the need for a consumer to test-drive a car before buying. This need for "experience" requires some offline activity; however, it does not necessarily mean that dealers should store a vast inventory of vehicles on their lots. For now, the automobile industry generally expects that only the initial stages of decision processes (information gathering) will migrate online. But one possible remedy to the problems of inventory management and demand forecasting plaguing the automobile industry is for the customer to inspect a prototype, specify his preferences, and receive a mass-customized car, made to order, in a matter of days. By giving the customer visual access to part of the production process, focusing on the purchased car that is customized to the customer's needs, it may be possible to further reduce the customer's traditional expectation to test-drive prior to purchase.

The automobile industry offers high potential for improvements in customer satisfaction and loyalty if the purchase process is modified. Today, the industry aims for an inventory of automobiles roughly equivalent to two months of sales, or 2 to 3 million automobiles in the United States. The investment and storage costs associated with this inventory amount to several billions of dollars every year. But the greatest difficulty the industry faces is forecasting demand for each of the different models. Even for a given make, the large number of product characteristics (such as color, automatic versus manual shift, the presence/absence of a sunroof) makes it impossible for any dealer to have exactly the preferred specification available for a given customer at the right place, at the right time, and at the right price. Consequently, the industry incurs a much larger cost, potentially 10 times as high as the cost of inventory, by providing rebates and other incentives to sell units with insufficient demand and that ultimately compromise the customer's preferences. At the same time, customers who insist on a specific set of features face long waiting periods for delivery at a premium price (this premium tends to be captured by the dealer or other intermediaries). Clearly, a new system in which demand precedes supply offers automobile manufacturers the potential to capture additional value.

Despite the untapped opportunities in many industries to enhance customer value through online activities, products dominated by experience attributes can be less suitable for online commerce—for some people. Consider cashmere sweaters that must be tried on before an initial purchase, or perfumes that need to be applied. The in-store environment is also critical in influencing purchase decisions for luxury goods. The demand for such goods is at least partly created by advertising and sales activities. It is, however, a challenge to create an emotional experience online. Thus, if a customer's preferences and ultimate purchase depend on such outside influences, the online environment presents limitations. There are two caveats worth mentioning here: First, the argument that experience is critical applies only to a first-time purchase, strictly speaking.

A regular buyer of Chanel perfume should feel comfortable going online to replenish her existing supply of the perfume. Also, in the online environment, the data reveal her purchase patterns, therefore her tastes and preferences can be inferred by comparison across customers. Sellers can then recommend additional items that complement existing purchases based on collaborative filtering (see Chapters 7 and 10); Amazon has used this effectively for books. Second, the technology can modify some search attributes into experience attributes. For example, consumers have the opportunity to download a sample of a song or an excerpt of a book to determine its "fit" with their interests.

Customers know that the experience of purchasing in a store environment has both positive and negative aspects. On the positive side, they may appreciate the attention they receive from clerks. On the negative side, they may feel a lack of privacy for some decisions. The active consideration of cosmetics sales staff in a store environment may be reduced if a customer feels the potential for embarrassment or sales pressure, for example. In addition, the salesperson's objective is often not aligned with that of the customer. The salesperson wants to push those items for which she receives the highest commission. The customer, of course, wants to buy the product that makes her most satisfied. It is possible, therefore, that an online venture such as Reflect.com provides compelling value to customers. The benefits offered by this firm include customization of cosmetics, trial by seeing how specific items look on an image of one's face that appears on a computer screen, and the opportunity to try alternative cosmetics on the screen as long as desired without interference. Of course, the online experience can be created in such a way as to duplicate many of the characteristics of the traditional, offline environment. Thus, the seller can still push products in such a way as to impede a full information-based choice by the customer.

The Internet may be ideal for products that already have a wide assortment that cater to heterogeneous tastes or for which the heterogeneity in demand is far greater than what is provided in the traditional supply. Akin to the automobile industry situation discussed earlier, any one stockkeeping unit (SKU) may have limited appeal to all consumers. Yet it is difficult for an outlet to stock all available SKUs. A direct distribution channel can alleviate this problem, in part because it is easier to have a wide variety of products available in a central warehouse. For example, Procter & Gamble allows customers to make online purchases of unusual sizes of its disposable diaper brands.

A parallel challenge in the store environment is the information overload customers face in deciding among available options. Research has shown that customers are likely to postpone a purchase if the choice between alternatives is difficult (for example, when the number of available alternatives is large or when alternatives differ in characteristics but are similar in terms of the customer's value, as when a customer likes blue and yellow equally and the shirt is available in either color). The Internet provides an option for sellers to customize product attributes after the customer specifies needs and desires, so that the characteristics of the supply match those of the demand. If the process of eliciting preferences is efficient, this has the additional advantage of making the consumer's choice task easier, thereby increasing the likelihood of purchase.

Even if production precedes selling, enterprises can still benefit from capturing customer preferences in an online environment. The task then is to estimate the fit between each unit in inventory and the individual customer's preferences to determine which available unit best serves a given customer's needs. Alternatively, the top five or so units can be identified, from which the customer can then make a choice. This process makes the search more efficient, and again, should increase the incidence of category purchase.

A firm's capability to customize an offering is sizable when informational attributes dominate, especially if preferences vary greatly across customers and the offering can be easily customized. Most online brokerage firms, for example, allow customers to follow just the stocks they are interested in, and to monitor prices on a continuing basis, if desired. Contrast this practice with newspapers that publish data on thousands of stocks in tiny fonts, unavailable until the subsequent day. Customization is also feasible for physical attributes if direct customer interaction enhances the fit with customer tastes and, consequently, product development. Volkswagen's decision to offer many of the paint colors for the new Beetle only online might be related to this point.

IMPLICATIONS FOR BRANDS IN AN ONLINE ENVIRONMENT

Traditionally, one of the most important tasks facing a marketing manager is to build successful brands. Although a brand cannot have a relationship with a customer, because a relationship requires interaction and a brand is a one-way icon, the image of a product, service, or store has nevertheless played an important role in relationship building. In that sense, brands are a critical source of customer loyalty. A major question facing marketing managers is whether the online environment changes the role and value of brands, and if so, how. Some observers argue that brands are irrelevant in an online environment. Others suggest that brands matter even more online than offline.

Historically, brands have performed four types of functions for a firm:

1. *Awareness*. Mere awareness of a name can increase the chance that consumers buy a specific brand in two ways: Awareness either allows a brand to be in a consumer's consideration set, along with other alternatives, or it leads directly to purchase.
2. *Risk reduction*. The branding of products guarantees a certain amount of quality and consistency for consumer products. And when individuals make purchases for others, as in industrial markets, they may be held accountable for their choices. IBM® used the slogan: "No one ever got fired for buying IBM®." The economic argument is that advertising is information: Firms will not advertise products that fail to meet common standards of quality.
3. *Information communication*. The Healthy Choice® brand reduces search costs for consumers by communicating characteristics of a relatively healthy entrée (low fat, low sodium, low calories, etc.).

4. *Consumption value.*[14] Consumption value communicates to the consumer, and to others observing the consumer with the product, what type of person one is or aspires to be. If one drives a BMW® rather than a Cadillac®, this communicates something about the car owner.

These functions of a brand are all related to informational aspects of marketing, so it is natural for the Internet to have an impact on the relevance of each function. The main benefit of the Internet for commerce is that it is a medium for inexpensive communication and distribution of informational attributes. The question is, which of these four functions will continue to be performed by the brand? Or, which functions can be performed more effectively or efficiently on the Internet? The answers to these questions also depend on the objectives a firm pursues for the brand name.

Suppose that a product benefits from branding primarily because it belongs to a category in which consumers buy largely as a result of mere awareness (function 1). How important is building awareness online? If consumers tend to use bookmarks or other guides to help them search online, then awareness becomes less important. After all, one can use a bookmark to determine many different sources from which to buy pizza or flowers. But if a person does not use Web bookmarks, and instead relies on memory, then it is just as important online to have the name of a brand or Web site, such as 1-800-FLOWERS®. To the extent that people do not use bookmarks, brand awareness will be even more important on the Internet because available memory will be the only way to find the site from among countless alternatives. Unless a consumer has the opportunity to have characteristics of products and services explicitly considered in a customized or personalized way (in which case he can identify the alternative that is optimal for him), and the specific brand name by itself provides no additional benefits, brand name will continue to influence choice, albeit in a narrow sense.

The role of brands extends to reducing purchase risk (function 2). Consider a large insurance company. Offline, firms may communicate stability and longevity through physical assets displayed in advertising. Thus, insurance companies tend to show large, solid, and old buildings in advertisements to express reliability: "Established in 1852." With only a virtual online existence, one cannot do this effectively. So how does a firm communicate online the stability and reliability consumers value? A brand identity can provide this reassurance. In this case, a brand name will be even more important online than it is offline because there are no bricks-and-mortar assets to deliver this message. What brand name might work, and how quickly can one create the required image? In the banking industry, Bank One chose the name WingSpan for its online business, minimizing the chance of association with its existing brand name. Presumably, management wanted to protect its established name, and probably believed that the risk to the existing business of extending the Bank One name exceeded the benefit to the new business. But if people are searching

---

[14]Author note: We call this *badge value*.

for assurance that their money is in safe and reliable hands, a new name may not be effective or will take excessive resources to communicate. In contrast, Schwab and E*trade built physical branches to reassure consumers with a complementary physical presence.

Brands convey information for a vector of product attributes (function 3). Healthy Choice® communicates the message that it is healthy. Yet it may not be the healthiest entrée in the supermarket. Nevertheless, the brand name communicates to consumers that they will be eating (relatively) healthy foods, and because most consumers do not want to spend a lot of time searching supermarket aisles, they may just decide to buy Healthy Choice®. What happens online? There are other, more powerful and precise ways for a consumer to determine which are the healthiest options available. He can go to a search engine at a grocery Web site and specify that he wants to identify, say, all chicken entrees with fewer than 5 grams of fat, 0 mg of sodium, and so on. The search engine may come up with multiple options, and the consumer may find that Healthy Choice® is neither the only option nor the best option.

Interestingly, the online intermediaries differ in their business models. For some, to be included in the listings of alternative products requires a fee. For others, no fee is required but sellers have the option to pay extra for better placement. Thus, it is possible, as in the offline environment, to pay for better placement. Still, most online intermediaries provide the consumer with the option to arrange the alternatives in a variety of ways, for example according to price (an option typically unavailable offline), but these options are not necessarily highlighted. Similar to the offline environment, the consumer faces the trade-off of having to spend extra time to identify the cheapest or best alternative versus the expected dollar savings or the potential of improved fit with needs.

In the offline world, performing this task is much more cumbersome, hence less likely to be performed except by a small segment of consumers (such as the readers of *Consumer Report*). Thus, brand names are less relevant for the communication of information about search attributes because online devices can facilitate product selection. Similarly, for the selection of mutual funds, brand names offer little promise in the online world. Funds may be selected primarily based on past performance. A firm can advertise that a particular fund or investment manager has created superior past performance, and this may then generate additional business. But if performances are regularly published, and the performance advantages are ephemeral, any brand name advantage is also temporary. Therefore, the availability of comparison data can reduce or eliminate the positive effect a brand name might create. In these scenarios, the role of brands is likely to diminish.

The fourth function that a brand provides is consumption value: the positive feeling created by a brand with a certain prestige (e.g., Rolex® or American Express®). The benefit for consumers comes primarily but not exclusively from usage in the presence of others. For example, a customer might use the Platinum American Express® card to pay for a meal in an expensive restaurant so that others can recognize his ownership of the card. But if he shops online, where other people he cares about will not see this, there is no utility associated with the use of the Platinum or Gold Card—except for that which comes from internal reflection. If the consumption value of a specific brand name is reduced, online consumers may prefer to use a card that provides tangible benefits, such as frequent-flyer miles. However, American Express also provides a concierge service with some cards, with the personalization and quality of the service dependent upon the annual fee. The use of this service provides access to certain restaurants, theater performances, and so on, which is otherwise difficult to arrange. Thus, online services may provide consumers with access to amenities that create the status they seek (which may not be unique to the online environment).

Online shopping (along with catalog shopping) offers consumers a kind of privacy. Whereas mall shopping is visible to others, complete with store-branded shopping bags, consumers can buy from Walmart.com or the Eddie Bauer catalog without being seen by friends or neighbors. In addition, Wal-Mart and other online counterparts to bricks-and-mortar stores now offer online items and services that consumers would rarely see in the physical stores. Often, these are items that are impractical to stock in every store, but tuck neatly into a centralized warehouse. Thus, the online environment can complement offline, both on the consumer side and on the seller side.

It is important to understand how the consumption value of a brand changes from offline to online. If consumption value is a critical component of an offline experience, the online store of the future has to determine how a special experience can be created that matches, say, Tiffany's aqua-colored box, or the walk into a Sephora cosmetics store. The store of the future is also less likely to communicate with the consumer in traditional ways. If the product or the service is being customized, the appeals should also be tailored to specific tastes. Thus, the nature of the appeal, as well as the timing and the manner of the communication, can be personalized. This does not mean that advertising will be replaced by direct marketing. Rather, technology will change the way by which the advertising industry operates (see also the TiVo discussion in Chapter 7).

FINAL MILE TO CONSUMERS

Any purchase made in the consumer direct (CD) channel requires getting that item into the customer's home or office—often referred to as the "final mile" of the purchase process. Such is the dilemma faced every day by catalog and direct-mail companies, online merchants, and other companies involved in CD. Today, the final mile of CD is often a rocky road. Shoppers in the CD channel typically prefer:

- Low or no delivery fees
- Immediacy of delivery
- Control of time and place of delivery

CD enterprises have been challenged to make the delivery of goods as convenient and inexpensive as possible. Few are equipped with the types of logistics and fulfillment systems required to deal with the final mile. Today's logistics infrastructure is still operating in the mid-twentieth-century mode of delivery trucks and airplanes. CD companies are challenged to build effective fulfillment centers and make the final delivery to the home easier for themselves and their customers. Not all CD companies have the capital to invest in such an infrastructure. Many are relying on third-party services for fulfillment and delivery. While such strategies benefit the large delivery companies, such as FedEx, United Parcel Service, and the U.S. Postal Service, it is doing little to combat the perpetual final mile problem that stretches to the consumer's home.

Some argue that the future lies in eliminating the final mile altogether—that is, establishing pick-up points such as day-care centers, large workplace parking lots, and neighborhood gas stations, where consumers can collect deliveries, thereby dramatically reducing costs while still providing much greater overall convenience. The problem is that many consumers prefer to have things delivered to their doors, and don't want to suffer the inconvenience of that final mile of delivery.

To rectify these problems, changes in delivery models are underway. Under these new models, opportunities abound for delivery companies to become agents for the consumer. Indeed, the delivery provider as agent is a critical transformation in the supply chain. Leading-edge retailers already realize that the final mile is just the beginning of a relationship with the consumer that they might be able to nurture into long-term loyalty (see the list of errands, favors, and small tasks that Tesco's customers ask of its delivery drivers earlier in this chapter).

One of the main reasons consumers order through direct channels is to have products delivered and to avoid trips to the store. It is not surprising, then, that almost 90 percent of catalog and online purchases and over 93 percent of all grocery deliveries are made directly to the home.[15] This skew is likely to grow. Consumers say that over the next two years they would like to *increase* the share of packages delivered to their homes over all other locations, such as where they work—if, of course, the delivery schedule, cost, and frequency are on their terms.

Whereas new technologies and business models have facilitated more efficient means of browsing, comparing, selecting, and buying products remotely, very little innovation has occurred in the delivery of goods and the processing of returns. Four issues will need to be addressed: unattended versus attended delivery, flexible delivery times, lower-cost deliveries and returns, and customer-focused delivery people.

---

[15]Peppers and Rogers Group, and Institute for the Future, "Consumer Direct: Business Models for Success" (August 2000).

UNATTENDED VERSUS ATTENDED DELIVERY

Unattended deliveries (when the parcel is left at the door when the customer is not at home) offer greater flexibility and take less time, and are thus more cost-effective. This is especially the case for groceries, as delivery people often help unload orders, rectify mistakes, and process payments, all of which take time. There are downsides, however. According to our research, over half of all shoppers prefer to be home when deliveries arrive. That number approaches 75 to 90 percent for high-ticket items, perishables, and prescription drugs. Unattended delivery models must allay consumer concerns about spoilage, in the case of groceries and other perishables, and, more generally, fears of theft and robberies.

Providers of unattended deliveries must contend with two key problems. First, many locations in dense city neighborhoods—townhouses, apartment buildings, busy streets, for example—do not have reasonable places to leave unattended deliveries. Second, some states mandate that goods be delivered before a payment can be collected; thus, unattended deliveries may delay payments.

FLEXIBLE DELIVERY TIMES

Delivery firms prefer to deliver in off-peak hours when roads are not crowded. Midday deliveries, for example, mean much less time in traffic, fewer labor hours, lower fuel costs, and less idle time for the trucks. Consumers, in contrast, want attended deliveries at times convenient for *them*: either early in the morning before leaving for work, in the early evening, or on weekends. Ultimately, consumers want to pick their own delivery times—in effect, define personalized delivery schedules. In fact, many suggest that if they had more control over the delivery time, they would shop more often online or through catalogs. To complicate matters, different households will have different time requirements for attended delivery. Successful firms will need to develop a flexible system. Efforts are already underway, as in the case of FedEx, which now offers a premium delivery service that allows consumers to schedule deliveries for a certain time, including into the evening hours.

LOWER-COST DELIVERIES AND RETURNS

The cost of shipping and handling is the main reason consumers do not shop from direct channels more often. Today, the cost of delivery is about $6 to $7 for a unique parcel ordered online or through a catalog. Grocery delivery costs range from free for orders over $50 or $75 to a monthly fee of $25 to $30 for unattended delivery. If the **CD** firm can spread its cost over a greater number of items, delivered either to the same house or to nearby houses, then the per-item cost could be reduced. The larger the volume within a given delivery system, the more sophisticated the technology that can be used to make the delivery—automatic picking;

software for tracking; larger, more efficient trucks; trained personnel, who spend more time with consumers. Consolidated orders will drive down costs, but will require a new logistics infrastructure. Consumers also want companies to make returns easier: They rank the hassle of returns second only to delivery fees and inconvenient schedules to explain why they do not shop direct more often.

CUSTOMER-FOCUSED DELIVERY PEOPLE

The delivery provider has the opportunity to build a Learning Relationship with each customer. A delivery person can take orders, provide information on other products, accept payment, take unwanted products back, or resolve complaints. Although these services take time, they take even more time after the fact—in stores, over the phone, or on the Web. Although a delivery person can do these efficiently in a face-to-face encounter, companies must balance the added cost with its ultimate value. A friendly delivery person who builds a trusted relationship with the consumer can give that delivery provider an edge over others. Trust in delivery people is critical for encouraging more orders through the direct channel (again, think about all the tasks/favors that Tesco's delivery drivers were asked to do).

One example of where this issue is a competitive factor is in the rivalry between FedEx and UPS for package-delivery business. FedEx, which began its highly successful overnight delivery operations as Federal Express in the 1970s, built its business on the basis of operational efficiency and cost reduction. The famous Memphis hub, where packages would be shipped at night to be connected to other planes and shipped out for next-day delivery, is only the most obvious symbol of FedEx's dedication to massive automation and efficiency. On the ground, FedEx delivery drivers use portable computers to help them navigate their routes more quickly, and waste less time picking up or dropping off packages, driving the costs of operating the network as low as possible. In contrast, the UPS ground system employs drivers who are less concerned with minimizing the time spent at locations, and more involved with the company's relationships with individual shipping customers. A UPS driver is much more likely to stop at a pick-up location to help a customer fill out a form. Moreover, the UPS driver's portable computer is more likely to have customer-specific data that can help the driver with each pick-up point. As a result, even though UPS's ground operations may not be as efficient as FedEx's, the clerical, secretarial, and mailroom personnel at the customer locations served by UPS often have a much greater loyalty to the UPS firm, and *their* UPS driver, whom they likely know by name.

By understanding the consumer's household characteristics, and building on personal interaction, the delivery person can enable a company to develop Learning Relationships with its customers. Thus, the delivery person is essential, not only for improving the consumer's confidence in the delivery company, but also for improving manufacturers' and retailers' ability to relate to their customers, individually. Given this double duty, a huge challenge will be to develop personnel with a wide range of skills: driving, loading, and relationship-building. Delivery people must be able to answer customers' questions on the one hand and to provide value-added services to the product providers on the other. This means delivery people will require better mobile technology and more expensive training, as they will represent both the delivery company's *and* the product providers' brand images.

LOGISTICS BUSINESS MODELS FOR SUCCESS

To accomplish all this, a relatively inexpensive delivery system with a way of responding to the needs of each consumer will need to be developed. Delivery providers must be able to reduce the cost of delivering, and returning, a package. If delivery providers can offer customer-focused services that are valuable to consumer direct providers, they will be enticed to absorb a good portion of that extra cost to promote even greater use of the channel. By bringing the cost to a level more palatable to consumers, the system will enjoy true scalability, with more packages running through on a regular basis. That will result in an additional drop in the per-item delivery cost, and increase the flexibility of the system in responding to individual households.

Throughout the interactive age, a number of new logistics models will likely emerge to meet these needs:

- *Aggregated delivery solutions.* A consolidated delivery provider for parcels and groceries, leveraging size and scale to lower their cost.
- *Immediate Solutions.* A niche delivery model that fills the gaps left by Aggregated Delivery Solutions. It provides consumers immediate gratification in the form of same-day or even one-hour delivery from both online and bricks-and-mortar retailers.
- *Pick-up locations.* Will offer an alternative to consumers who are uncomfortable with unattended delivery and want the flexibility that comes with never having to abide by a delivery schedule. At pick-up centers, consumers have the option of picking up deliveries on *their* schedule—as well as a chance to socialize.

Of course, traditional models like the U.S. Postal Service, and deliveries by some retailers (e.g., furniture stores, Costco) will still exist, but the bulk of deliveries could be made through new models that improve on what today's players offer.

By the end of the next decade, these three models could account for more than three-quarters of all packages delivered. They will reduce the cost of delivery to the consumer in an absolute sense through efficiencies and scale, and through subsidizations by their B2B retail partners in light of their capability to offer value-added, customer-focused services (see Exhibit 15.2).

	AGGREGATED MODEL	IMMEDIATE DELIVERY	PICK-UP	RETAILER	OTHER (E.G., USPS)
Number of Transactions Delivered (in Billions)	2.5	0.5	0.5	0.7	1.0
Real Cost	$4.00	$6.00	$2.00	$4.50	$3.00
Consumer Cost	$2.00	$5–10.00	$1.00	Free over a certain dollar value	$1–5.00

Source: Peppers and Rogers Group and Institute for the Future (IFTF), 2000.

EXHIBIT 15.2   **Next-Generation Delivery Models: Share of Market and Cost Structure (1999–2000)**

SUMMARY

It's not clear yet just how much consumers will use the new technologies in their shopping. In Japan, teenagers buy soft drinks from vending machines by clicking their cell phones. We have a friend in the United States who recently bought both a house and a car online. Sears Canada has learned that customers who shop through more than one channel—who use a mix of online, catalog, and store shopping—tend to spend more money overall than those who shop through only one channel. That said, huge investments have been lost in failed attempts at direct-to-home Web-based grocery selling. And some shoppers, some of the time, for some products, will always prefer to touch and try before they buy.

What is clear is that just as new technologies have affected everything else about the way customers and businesses relate to each other, these technologies will also affect the way people shop and the way stores sell to them.

Though this is the last chapter of this book, be sure to continue reading, as in the appendix we present the Customer Manager's Briefcase, which contains a number of things to think about for those who will become customer managers, or who will manage those who are.

FOOD FOR THOUGHT

1. Have you ever bought anything from a catalog? Online? How were these experiences different from buying in a traditional store? How were they the same? What was better? What did you miss?

2. What do you think the future of retailing will be?

3. Imagine you own a traditional cycle shop in a medium-small town. One morning you read in the local paper that, in a year, both a Wal-Mart and a large sporting goods store will open in your hometown. It could mean the end of your business. Does it have to? Without going online, how could you use Learning Relationships and customer strategies to beat the giants? (This question was prompted by a true story, by the way.)

4. We've learned from the Webvan experiment that many people are not ready to abandon old shopping methods—even in Silicon Valley, where Webvan was based. However, Safeway is helping to bring home delivery to the United States in a way that parallels the Tesco story. Are there fundamental differences between the United States and the United Kingdom? Perhaps Tesco's English customers live in densely populated urban areas, where driving is a hassle for people who don't own cars. Perhaps Tesco buyers follow the traditional European style of buying small amounts frequently. If those are the elements of success, then how will Safeway be affected in the long run if its customers live in the suburbs and own huge freezers and pantries, and drive home from Safeway stores that provide large parking lots suitable for SUVs?

GLOSSARY

Automatic replenishment (AR) An arrangement whereby products are automatically replaced and billed to the customer, similar to magazine subscriptions. See "Automatic Replenishment" section in this chapter for the three types of AR models.

Consumer direct channel (CD) Also sometimes called *direct to home*, CD refers especially to companies that build direct relationships with consumers, often through direct ordering and delivery of goods and services.

Retail marketing functions These include exchange functions (buying and selling), distribution functions (transporting, distributing, and storing), and facilitating functions (financing, risk taking, securing marketing information, etc.)

Where Do We Go from Here?

As long as this book is, it could easily have been longer. We are learning more every day about how to grow the value of the customer base. For now, however, we will close our discussion of managing customer relationships in the interactive age—but not until we address one more topic: Where do we go from here? That's the topic of most interest to you, based on Martha's work at Duke and Yale Universities and the University of Virginia; and Don's visits to Harvard Business School, and Cranfield in the United Kingdom. We will start by looking at the traits and behaviors that will be needed by a company's first chief marketing officer (CMO) (consider how everything we've talked about in the past 15 chapters makes marketing into a real job, accountable at the chief level with the help of good customer-value and other metrics), chief relationship officer (CRO), or customer-manager-in-chief. Then we'll look to Geoffrey Moore to help us envisage the journey to customer management from the business-adoption perspective.

The most important part of this section has yet to be written: the part you want most. We are already thinking about the second edition of this book. Please get back to us via e-mail at MCRtext@fuqua.duke.edu and let us know how we can improve this book, especially this appendix, which is designed to offer help beyond the basics.

If we've learned anything from clients, research, and academia in the past 10 years, it's this: Building customer value and becoming more customer-oriented is not a destination, it's a journey. And it's very, very difficult to do well. But the payoff can be huge. More and more, the question is not how much will it cost to become a customer-strategy enterprise, but how much will it cost *not* to. We can't fit everything we know today about building customer value, or about how to become a customer-strategy enterprise, into this book, because—as we said at the beginning of this appendix—we are learning more every day. What we've tried to do here is to establish a basic foundation of what customer-management is, how it helps an organization, and how companies are starting to benefit from it, to enable you to understand it.

> Building customer value and becoming more customer-oriented is not a destination, it's a journey.

Suppose you are a newly minted MBA, and have taken a position as a customer relationship manager at a product-centric enterprise: We would expect that many of the ideas and tools you have learned about in this book would help. But what should a manager of customer relationships expect to find in her briefcase? In other words, what are the leadership qualities of an effective manager in a customer-strategy environment?

We'll start the discussion with the answer to a question we are asked all the time: What will be the characteristics of those who first manage customer relationships for a firm?

LEADERSHIP BEHAVIOR OF CUSTOMER RELATIONSHIP MANAGERS

When an enterprise undertakes a customer-focused effort, it requires a great deal of integration in all aspects of the enterprise. The management team has to buy in at the very top; and if they do, we should expect certain types of activity and behavior at the leadership level. The leaders of any enterprise engaging in a transition to a customer-strategy enterprise will accumulate expertise about managing customer relationships, and will become a cheerleader for this new business model. The leader will highlight it in company meetings and in business gatherings; she will openly share her expertise in and around the organization; in sum, she will become an authority on the relationship management business model.

In a leadership role, the manager must be capable of sponsoring a customer-focused project and sheltering the people involved in the pilot project. The easiest way to make progress in a customer-value-building journey is to engage in a series of increasingly comprehensive pilot projects. But a pilot project does not necessarily make money on its own. Most small pilot projects, in fact, never even have the possibility of making money. They are proofs of concept for larger projects that will be rolled out only if they make sense on the smaller level. The pilot project might be an operational test of a customer-strategy program, or a test of the value-building effectiveness of the program, and so forth.

Because the participants in a pilot project are exposed in the business financially—that is, they don't have enough profit underlying their activity to justify their existence—they are supported only by the learning they will gain from the pilot project. It is up to the leader, therefore, to shelter them from any economic downturn that might affect the enterprise from keeping them onboard. Ideally, a pilot project needs to be funded at the beginning, then given some running room—often one or two years—before any future decisions can be made.

A leader will measure the success of herself and her people differently, establishing new types of metrics for the enterprise's activities and accomplishments. But she will also create a new set of rewards structures. We know from previous chapters that the central goal of managing customer relationships is to increase the value of the customer base. This value is nothing more than the sum total of LTVs of all customers; but the problem is that LTV is a future number based on future behaviors of a customer. It's a number that has to be predicted or foretold, and it is impossible to measure exactly. Thus, a leader has to figure out what the leading indicators are of this future customer value that can be measured, and determine how a firm can tie organizational performance and compensation to those metrics.

A leader should be willing and able to cross boundaries to generate enterprisewide results. One thing we know about customer-specific initiatives is that although they are customer-specific, they are not division-specific nor product-specific. Rather, the customer has a relationship with the enterprise that might go across several different divisions and encompass the purchasing of several different products and services. The organization of the enterprise is almost certainly along product and service lines, and that means those divisional structures will have to be crossed to serve a customer across several different divisions. Taking a share-of-customer approach to a business inherently means crossing boundaries. The leader is constantly on the lookout for ways to expand the scope of her customer relationships beyond her own product or division and to reach out and encompass aspects of that relationship that go beyond her particular domain. Crossing boundaries is one of the main reasons to engage the senior leaders at a customer-strategy enterprise, and their involvement is critical because they can cross boundaries more easily and with greater effect.

Finally, good leaders will insist on having direct contact with customers. They will attend the focus groups, do phone interviews, listen in at the CIC, and have meetings with business executives at the customer organization. Leaders *want* to be directly connected to customers in as much detail as possible. Leaders *want* to have a realistic picture of what it is like to be a customer of their enterprise. Seeing their enterprise from the customer's point of view is one of the key tasks of making this kind of transition successfully.

A lot of "real" leadership is needed. As stated repeatedly, whether we call this customer-strategy journey "CRM" or "one-to-one" or "demand-chain management," it can be a real challenge. Everybody claims to know what it is. Every consulting company and ad agency offers expensive advice about it. Every boss thinks she understands how to go about this. It reminds us so much of the principles first described by Geoffrey Moore in his challenge books about "crossing the chasm" and "inside the tornado" that we asked him to think of managing customers in those terms. Here are his insights.

MANAGING CUSTOMER RELATIONSHIPS: THE TECHNOLOGY ADOPTION LIFE CYCLE

Geoffrey A. Moore
Chairman, founder, and managing partner, TCG Advisors LLC; venture partner, Mohr, Davidow Ventures

CRM is both a business concept and a technology infrastructure. In either form it has the potential of being a disruptive innovation, creating opportunities for dramatic increases in competitive advantage, but also creating incompatibilities with existing systems. As such, its adoption can be expected to follow the patterns of the Technology Adoption Life Cycle, a series of twists and turns that can bewilder and confuse an unwary management team.

The purpose of this section is to present a summary view of CRM in interaction with the life-cycle model, with the goal of empowering management teams to leverage it in two ways. First, we will look at CRM as a *source of disruptive innovation* in itself and see, by determining where it is in the adoption life cycle in a particular industry sector, how a firm can best take advantage of its potential to improve a company's performance. Second, we will consider the use of CRM as a *tool for coping with disruptive innovation* coming from some other source, that is, as a set of facilities for managing customers and the company through a difficult technology transition. At the end of this section, the goal is for the management team to be fully versed in the ins and outs of technology adoption forces as they might impact CRM deployments.[1]

CRM AS A SOURCE OF DISRUPTIVE INNOVATION: REENGINEERING FROM A TRANSACTION TO A RELATIONSHIP MODEL

Let's first think of CRM in relatively broad terms, incorporating both a software systems view, in which interactions at multiple touchpoints with the customer are automated, and a management view, in which the relationship with the customer itself becomes something to be managed (or what was called, earlier in this book, *operational CRM* and *analytical CRM*). In this broad sense, companies adopting CRM must not only reengineer their software but their entire business approach, migrating from a transaction-based to a relationship-based model.

Such reengineering is disruptive to established roles and responsibilities, metrics and compensation, organizational structure, business process ownership, planning and reporting, to name just a few. As such, it will win enthusiastic support from early adopters, skeptical wariness from conservative late adopters, and a cautious wait-and-see response from the pragmatist majority. This is the classic self-segregation of any community faced with disruption into a set of "adoption response" postures.

The end result of this self-segregation is that there are four inflection points in the unfolding of any disruptive innovation, each of which rewards a different

[1]Readers may see a parallel between the ideas Moore has expressed here, drawing from his two best-selling books and extensive speaking and consulting work, and that of Everett M. Rogers in his work from the last decades of the twentieth century on adoption of innovations. (See Everett M. Rogers, *Diffusion of Innovations* (New York: Free Press, 1962)). Moore's work, of course, is based on his experience with the disruptive forces of technology, while Rogers's work is based on a more stable paradigm of adoption. Both have helped to inform us about the challenges and methods of how to get from here to there. Also see Don Peppers, Martha Rogers, PhD, and Chris Nadherny, "Anatomy of the Customer-Focused Leader," *Point of View: Perspectives on Leadership* 2 (2002), pp. 16–19.

management approach. It behooves the team implementing CRM to understand this model and to select which of the four points best represents their current situation, and thus which management approach is likely to yield the best outcome. Here's how it plays out.

The Early Market

The early market for adopting disruptive innovations is led by technology enthusiasts and visionaries. The former engage out of sheer love for exploring the properties of any new system. The latter engage whenever they see a chance to exploit a new paradigm to gain a dramatic competitive advantage in their line of business. The two working together create the energy behind early-market adoption.

If one sector or region is late to adopt CRM, then a particular company may have an opportunity to get ahead of the competition and set them back on their heels. In order to bring this outcome to pass, however, a firm *must* have the sponsorship of a visionary line-of-business executive with sufficient seniority and power to drive through rapid adoption despite internal resistance from less enthusiastic colleagues. Without this support an early-market project is doomed.

With this support, typically garnered by the opportunity to create a 10X return, albeit involving substantial risk, the key going forward is to treat the entire effort not as buying a product but rather as implementing a custom project. The focus of the project is the 10X return, and every vendor involved must sign up for that goal. The general contractor for the effort should be a systems integrator, with strong business reengineering skills, someone who has the confidence of the executive sponsor regarding the vision, but who also has the skills to win support from the pragmatic rank and file who must implement the new processes.

The desired end result of this effort is a system unique to the sponsoring customer implemented well in advance of any other company in the competitive set. It is a major undertaking, and there is no guarantee of success—hence the importance of having a genuine opportunity for getting a 10X return. This is not for the faint of heart; it is for those who live by the saying, "Faint heart ne'er won fair lady."

Examples of companies who have successfully leveraged CRM in the past as an industry disrupter include from past decades American Airlines with its SABRE system and United Airlines with its frequent-flyer program, and in the current Internet era, Dell Computers and Amazon. In each case, the sponsoring company was able to leapfrog its competition by using CRM to create a compelling disruption in established business practices.

Crossing the Chasm

Once innovations have been deployed by the first movers, there are no more rewards for early adoption, and the enthusiasts and visionaries move on to greener pastures. The next adoption strategy to come on is that of the *pragmatists*. Their approach is to convert to new technologies as soon as they know other people like them are doing so. It is a bit like dances in junior high: Everybody is willing to go out on the dance floor, just as long as somebody else from their group goes first. This creates a hiatus in adoption that we at The Chasm Group have termed the *chasm*.

To cross the chasm means to get the first herd of pragmatist adopters to switch over to the new technology. Experience has taught us that this first group will make the move only under duress. Specifically, the classic profile is that of a department manager, in charge of a *broken, mission-critical business process,* who has been served notice that she had better fix this process soon or management will find someone who can.

In the case of CRM, this department manager is likely to be in charge of either customer service or customer support. Customer service processes often break, for example, when companies give prospects lots of options when their back-end delivery systems are not capable of handling the complexity reliably. The result is a raft of customer shipments that do not match the customer's order, leading to irate calls and returned merchandise. The advent of self-service order entry over the Web has only driven this problem deeper into many industries.

The other problem area is customer support. Here the challenge derives from the complexity of the final installed system. In the PC industry, for example, the total number of possible combinations of different vendors that might have component subsystems interacting inside a single PC is astronomical. As a result, when something does not work, it is enormously challenging to track down the root cause. In the early 1990s, this led to 40 minute hold times just to speak to a customer support operator who, sadly, often had to refer the problem on to someone else, leading to all kinds of customer unhappiness.

If an industry has seen its early adopters of CRM but has not widely adopted it as a standard way of doing business, these are the kinds of issues that would drive executives to make the leap. In such cases, it is key that they band together, even when they are direct competitors, to make sure that the solution vendors work together to provide what we call the *whole product.* This is a complete, end-to-end solution that addresses a common set of needs specific to a particular segment. Some will end up paying a premium to get this solution because, as it is specific to one segment, vendors cannot amortize their expenses across a large customer base. But it will be well worth it if it fixes the broken, mission-critical process once and for all. The only losing behavior here is to get 90 percent of the total solution on the cheap and never get the last 10 percent put in place.

Inside the Tornado

If a company did not choose to be an early adopter, and if it wasn't forced to be a chasm crosser, then like as not that company is a pragmatist not under duress, waiting to switch to the new systems as soon as everyone else does. Well, guess what—it is! All of a sudden everyone in your sector has a project under way to do CRM, and you get the call from upstairs, "Where's ours?"

This is what defines a tornado: the stampede of the pragmatist herd. That, in turn, creates a vortex of demand that sucks every vendor in the space into a frenzy of activity, trying to create sufficient supply for what has become a sudden, overwhelming escalation in demand. The pressure to get on the bandwagon is intense, and there is little time to do a thorough review of the options. As a result, customers increasingly "ask around" to learn who is the market leader, the vendor nobody ever got fired for choosing. That company's sales go through the roof, even though it becomes increasingly onerous to deal with, simply because it is the *safe buy.*

This safety goes well beyond immediate issues of reliability. As the industry goes forward, experience shows that everyone other than the market leader has an increasingly difficult time keeping partners committed to keeping their side of the interfaces up to date. Moreover, service providers will invest the bulk of their training and development to build a practice around the market-leading system, further weakening the competitors' position. As a result, those companies' customers get a weaker and weaker whole product, regardless of how good the core product might be.

The object lesson here is simple: If a company is buying during a tornado, then it should lean heavily toward the market leader, unless it's in a niche that has special requirements, which the leader is unmotivated to meet. In that case, a strong niche vendor who is willing to make a commitment to a customer firm's vertical is a better choice. Finally, if the technology is open systems, such that there are clones of the market leader that are totally compatible with their technology, a firm can afford to use them to shop price, especially for the less critical installations.

As of this writing, CRM applications are still in the tornado, despite a recent economic downturn. As witness, Morgan Stanley recently released a CIO survey that showed that CRM applications were the least likely to be cancelled of any IT project on their books. In this tornado, Siebel Systems has emerged as the market leader for the enterprise market, especially for sales force automation and customer support. The battle for marketing automation is still more open at present, with E.piphany probably having the inside track. But there are dozens of companies making a living in this market, and as gorilla positions solidify, these other vendors will likely be driven to adopt vertical specializations or else go down market where the gorillas typically do not field a significant offering. The resulting competition, regardless of who wins where, bodes well for CRM customers.

On Main Street

Once technology has passed through the tornado, it can be classified as adopted, and all subsequent purchases are postadoption. That simply means that the technology is assimilated and no longer poses special challenges to any customer rolling out a new system. For pragmatists, this is a time of buying more of whatever they already bought during the tornado or chasm-crossing phase. But for conservatives and laggards who held off, this is now their time to enter the market.

Why would one wait so long? Actually, if business processes can function effectively without investing in new systems, the longer a firm waits, the better the deal to be had once they do buy in. Every year, that is, systems become more reliable, more highly featured, and cheaper. Moreover, if a company has a system that works today, what is the gain in being subjected to a new learning curve? Better to focus that energy on some business process for which you can get an immediate payback.

Eventually, however, the world comes to expect a certain minimum set of technologies, simply to get along, and when that happens, then the conservative must make the change. For example, increasingly, it has become expected that companies maintain a Web site, at minimum to publish the information to put in a corporate brochure, and in most cases to provide some way to make email contact. Companies that are putting up Web sites for the first time this year are gaining no competitive advantage by so doing. They are not fixing a broken, mission-critical process. Nor are they going with the herd, who actually went several years ago. Instead, they are simply dealing with a hygiene requirement. That is classic late-adoption strategy.

> It is not that the software won't work, and not that you cannot learn how to work it. It is the impact on the rest of your business processes that you need to be mindful of.

If a company does choose to adopt late, the key is not to overadopt. Even though the vendors are now touting second- and third-generation capabilities, you probably want to restrict your implementation to first-generation ones. It is not that the software won't work, and not that you cannot learn how to work it. It is the impact on the rest of your business processes that you need to be mindful of.

By contrast, pragmatists who are now rolling out their second or third upgrade will be very interested in these new capabilities. The truth is, as the life cycle moves onto Main Street, most of the productivity gains promised during the tornado have yet to be achieved, in large part because the software wasn't quite there yet at the time. Well, now it is, and now is the time to actively engage the end users in picking and choosing which features would make them more effective in their work. And because the technology is more mature, it should permit greater mass customization, meaning that different groups should be able to customize the system in different ways to make their work-flows more productive.

Overall, then, the Technology Adoption Life Cycle creates four natural buying points during the evolution of a new technology's acceptance into the marketplace. Each point offers a different motive for buying in at that time, which might be summarized as follows:

In the early market: Go ahead of the herd for a dramatic competitive advantage.

Crossing the chasm: Fix a broken, mission-critical business process.

Inside the tornado: Go with the herd to get on the new infrastructure.

On Main Street: Go after the herd to get better values.

Customer relationship management systems are no exception to this pattern. To be sure, depending on where they are in the life cycle in a particular sector, some of these options may now be passed, but the key idea is to align corporate expectations and intentions with what is deliverable during each phase. You can't come late to the party and expect competitive advantage, just as you cannot come early and expect to get better values. By taking some time to think through the various adoption points and their corresponding opportunities, a company can increase the chances that a CRM implementation is a resounding success.

> You can't come late to the party and expect competitive advantage, just as you cannot come early and expect to get better values.

ON MAIN STREET: ONE-TO-ONE RELATIONSHIPS

Technology adoption life cycles are an anomaly in themselves. In high tech, to be sure, they are frequent occurrences, but outside the sector, they are not. There has not been a truly disruptive innovation in the automobile sector in my lifetime, nor is there one on the horizon. Photography has gone 70 years without essential disruption, albeit today, with the rise of digital imagery, it is headed into one. Tried any new salt lately? I'll bet not. And so it is that most markets most of the time live on Main Street. And it is here that one-to-one customer relationships come into their own.

The natural target of Main Street marketing is the *conservative* in the Technology Adoption Life Cycle. This is a customer who is predisposed to keep things as they are. The key to Main Street, then, is that the core offer has become so assimilated into business as usual or life as usual that we no longer register the thing itself as innovative or differentiable. But because choice depends on differentiation from the customer's view, and because margins depend on differentiation from the vendor's view, innovation does not stop: It just relocates.

There are two classic directions innovation takes on Main Street. One is in the direction of ever-increasing operational excellence, up and down the supply chain, seeking to wring out costs so that one can squeeze out a half-point of margin at the point of sale. If this seems like a lot of work for a small outcome, recognize that on Main Street the volume of purchases can be huge, and thus even a small increment of improvement, if it truly scales across the entire market, can have major impact. This is the focus of the operations and finance people for the most part.

The other direction is championed by marketing (and the two are by no means mutually exclusive). And that is toward ever-increasing customer intimacy, improving not the product itself as much as the *experience of the product*. Experience, however, lives halfway between the thing in itself and the mind of the experiencer, thus no two people ever share the exact same experience. So, if companies are to deliver better and better experiences, one of the things they need to do is learn more about each of their customers.

For a long time, this has been the home turf of demographic information.

Because human beings are social animals, and because we take a lot of our values from the community we live in—indeed often work to conform to the community's values when they are in conflict with our own—demographics works. That said, however, contemporary marketing has relied on this tactic for so long that, going forward, it will provide diminishing returns. That is, it will move from the realm of being a key to differentiation to being a market requirement for acceptable performance. Of course a firm will be demographically astute—but what will that firm do that's different or new?

Enter the Internet. The great excitement about the Internet is that it has the potential to set up highly intimate relationships, which at the same time retain anonymity. That is, while customers want what they want, they do not want to bare their secrets in order to get it. How is that possible? Largely through self-service. And that is what the Internet is best at (see Chapters 7 and 9).

Self-service begins with options, and so in the first generation of marketing systems we have seen a proliferation of *offer configuration* systems. But these systems can become so complex they can bewilder the user, and so the next generation focuses on *ease of use*. That is more or less where we are today. The truth is, however, customers don't want ease of use except in the areas they want to express a new preference. Everywhere else they want the system either to *default* to the best choice or to *remember* what they chose last time. And this is the focus of an emerging set of systems.

One of the major challenges here is *privacy*. What are vendors going to do with all this personal, privileged information? In prior eras, they resold it to other merchants, leading to increasingly more demographically targeted mass marketing. But the information was never all that personal. Now it can be, and that is unacceptable to a significant part of the population. To date, there is no generic solution to this problem, but there are a number of promising ideas in play. Until standards congeal, however, progress will be tracked largely as a set of experiments rather than grand successes.

At the end of the day, what we must succeed at is positioning *customer expertise* close to the customer. At the very high end of the market, we can do this with attentive people armed with their own diaries about past interactions with their clientele. Elsewhere, however, we need to apply *data processing skills* and *marketing imagination* to win the day.

One of the best examples to date has been Amazon's system of *collaborative filtering*, which compares an individual's purchase history of, say, books, across the entire database of customer histories, looking for customers who have bought the same books, and then looking for the most commonly found book in their records that has not yet been bought by this individual. The resulting recommendations are typically spot-on, largely because books reflect communal interests. However, even here is the occasional misfire, perhaps by neglecting to mention that one has bought a certain book as a gift, with a resulting inundation of off-target offers. Amazon now allows customers to go in an edit a profile when this happens, which is a start, but most of us have better things to do, and this may *not* be the sort of customer experience we are ultimately looking for.

In sum, CRM on Main Street is becoming an increasingly technology-based discipline. Here, as noted, we are going through a Technology Adoption Life Cycle of our own in marketing, sector by sector, with financial services and retail taking the lead in business-to-consumer, and with manufacturing supply chains taking the lead in business-to-business. In both instances it is easy to overreach, and so we can expect to see plenty of false starts; but because there is such rich opportunity to eliminate waste and to increase customer satisfaction, this will be a rich vein to mine for many, many years to come.

Even as recently as a few years ago, companies didn't know how to hire a CMO or a CRO. In many cases, customer management was turned over to the marketing department, because in the minds of many CEOs, the customer was relegated to the marketing department and the rest of the company "did business." Or to the data management or IT people, as they had custody of the customer information. At Peppers and Rogers Group, we developed a small search function to match up the companies—clients mostly—that were looking for relationship managers, with the individuals who had the experience and know-how to put a program in place designed to build relationships with one customer at a time, shed traditional thinking and tactics, and build the value of the customer base. In 2002, we relinquished that function to the pros; the major search firms now have specialists in CRM or its related areas.

SUMMARY

It's clear from the experiences of traditional companies trying to make the change from the Industrial Age to the information age, and from new companies run by people born and raised in the Industrial Age (that's everybody above first grade), that using information as the heart of competitive advantage is *hard*. Many companies have gone awry. Some firms aren't trying. But payoff is happening, for the companies that redefine their core business opportunity as growing the value of the customer base. We learn more about how to do it every day. And the field is growing into one that offers new career opportunities to those who become fluent in a decision-making approach that puts growing the value of the customer base ahead of other tactics.

There's a lot of work to do. Every company on the planet that succeeds in the next two decades will do so because of their ability to concentrate on getting, keeping, and growing the best customers in their industry.

Index